LETTERS OF
Katherine Anne Porter

LETTERS OF
Katherine Anne Porter

Selected and Edited and with an Introduction by
ISABEL BAYLEY

THE ATLANTIC MONTHLY PRESS
NEW YORK

Published simultaneously in Canada
Printed in the United States of America
FIRST EDITION

Library of Congress Cataloging-in-Publication Data
Porter, Katherine Anne, 1890–1980.
[Correspondence. Selections]
Letters of Katherine Anne Porter/selected and edited and with an
introduction by Isabel Bayley.—1st ed.
ISBN 0-87113-286-9
1. Porter, Katherine Anne, 1890–1980—Correspondence. 2. Authors,
American—20th century—Correspondence. I. Bayley, Isabel.
II. Title.
PS3531.0752Z48 1990   813'.52—dc19   [B]   89-31242

Design by Laura Hough

The Atlantic Monthly Press
19 Union Square West
New York, NY 10003

FIRST PRINTING

For William Hewitt Bayley

Love and kisses to Hew, that mere Gibralter of men! Do you know, my dear, you have said, or written to me, quite the most lovely and loving things about Hew that I ever heard from any woman about her husband, and that so casually, just tossing them off, sparks from the anvil, that I wonder sometimes if you do know what a portrait you have given me of him. No softness, no illusory fog, no sentimentality, of course not! Just something altogether good and human and intelligent—I rely on it completely as real.

Katherine Anne Porter to Isabel Bayley
19 July 1954

ACKNOWLEDGMENTS

The measure of the devotion of Katherine Anne Porter's friends has been the quickness and generosity of their response to my inquiries about her letters. James Stern took his collection from his home in Tisbury to London to have them photocopied by a "reliable and trusted friend" at his publisher's. James Powers didn't even take the time to reread his before he mailed the copies he kindly made for me, for the photocopy place and the post office were close to each other. To these faithful friends I am deeply grateful.

In 1983, Glenway Wescott invited me to spend three wonderful days going over his collection under a good lamp at his work table in Rosemont, New Jersey. He then sent me home through the autumn countryside with six cartons of papers that now, for Katherine Anne Porter's centenary, become a gift to the University of Maryland at College Park Libraries in his name and in his memory. Monroe Wheeler was in Istanbul when I was in Rosemont, but when I next worked in the University of Maryland archives, the obliging staff photocopied letters from the large collection he had presented to the library in 1969, the year after Katherine Anne Porter had made the university a gift of her papers. And Seymour Lawrence, who possessed the valuable records of the years from 1956 to 1962 when Katherine Anne Porter worked on her novel and wrote to him as her editor at the Atlantic Monthly Press, generously presented this correspondence to the library.

The University of Maryland at College Park Libraries acquired special collections: the Katherine Anne Porter letters to Donald Elder, to Paul Porter, to Ann Heintze. The Cyrilly Abels letters added to the great body of her papers. All letters not mentioned specifically below are in the University of Maryland at College Park Libraries.

I am grateful to Dr. Donald Farren, Associate Director of Libraries for Special Collections at the University of Maryland Libraries, and to Dr. Blanche T. Ebeling-Koning, Curator for Rare Books and Literary Manuscripts, for providing the necessary documents with promptness and rare sense of responsibility. And for Dr. Joanne Harrar, Director of Libraries, I feel a special appreciation.

Many to whom Katherine Anne Porter wrote have helped me in a number of ways, and to them go my deep thanks: John Malcolm Brinnin, Eleanor Clark, Albert Russel Erskine (who kindly photo-copied his letters of 1945 to 1951 for me), Robert Giroux, Seymour Lawrence, Andrew Lytle, Jordon Pecile, Paul Porter, Katherine Anne Powers, Robert Penn Warren, Eudora Welty, and Monroe Wheeler; Hilton Kramer and Eleanor Langer kindly sent me photocopies of the Josephine Herbst letters. Peter Davison, when he was with the Atlantic Monthly Press, came to visit us in Toronto several times to help start off the book. E. Barrett Prettyman, Jr., has been a source of strength all along. Owen Laster, senior vice president of the William Morris Agency, has guided me as only one with his unique experience could have done. Ann Godoff, executive editor of the Atlantic Monthly Press, has helped with her keen insights; Nancy Lewin, her assistant, has been staunch and conscientious.

Remarkable assistance was given to me by the members of the Languages and Literature Department of the Metropolitan Toronto Reference Library. They were quick and bright and courteous with their accurate information. They made me feel that I lived on an inland lake that did lead to the wide seas on which Katherine Anne Porter launched her ship.

And one memorable October morning in 1982, Leon Edel generously gave me shrewd and wise advice as we sat in the sun at the window of the Windsor Arms in Toronto. I valued his words highly as coming from the distinguished biographer who had just published the letters of Henry James, the man who had written some of the best of his time. I tried to follow it in working with the letters of an admirer of James who has written some of the best letters of her time. Leon Edel warned me that toward the end there would be "donkey's work," as he called it, quoting Virginia Woolf, for which I might need help. For this I was fortunate to have the help of Marika Michael. Turning out the manuscript expertly on her word processor, she raised it to the work of a race horse.

Finally, I am grateful to the following libraries for permission to publish letters in their possession:

Newberry Library, for the Malcolm Cowley letter, from the Malcolm Cowley Letters Collection, and for the Morton Dauwen Zabel letter, from the Morton Dauwen Zabel Collection.

Pennsylvania State University Libraries, for the Kenneth Burke letter.

Princeton University Library, for the letter to Allen Tate, January 27, 1931, from the Allen Tate Papers; the letter to Caroline Gordon, August 28, 1931, from the Caroline Gordon Papers; and the letter to Mr. Dashiell of Scribner's, February 5, 1932, from the Charles Scribner Sons collection.

University of Delaware, for the John Malcolm Brinnin letters, part of the John Malcolm Brinnin Papers, University of Delaware Library, Newark, DE 19717-5267.

University of Texas, for the letters to Edith Sitwell, from the Harry Ransom Humanities Research Center, The University of Texas at Austin.

Vanderbilt University, for the letters to Andrew Lytle, the letter to Allen Tate and Caroline Gordon, March 6, 1932, and to Caroline Gordon, April 24, 1931, among the Andrew Lytle Papers at the Jean and Alexander Heard Library, Vanderbilt University.

Yaddo, for the letters to Elizabeth Ames.

Yale University, for the letters to Josephine Herbst, George Platt Lynes, Robert McAlmon, Norman Pearson, and Robert Penn Warren, from the Collection of American Literature, Beinecke Rare Book and Manuscript Library, Yale University.

I am always surprised that people cannot understand range and change and variety and contradiction and tragic feeling and a saving dash of frivolity and the deep sense of comedy, the salt of life that makes our daily bread bearable.

Katherine Anne Porter to Glenway Wescott
April 2, 1963

CONTENTS

CONTENTS

CHRONOLOGY

1857	June 28	Birth of father, Harrison Boone Porter.
1859	July 22	Birth of mother, Mary Alice Jones.
1890	May 15	Katherine Anne Porter born at Indian Creek, Texas.
1892	March 20	Mother dies.
1901		Grandmother dies.
1902–04		Studies at Ursuline Convent, New Orleans.
1904		Studies at Thomas School for Girls, San Antonio, Texas.
1906	June 20	Marries John Henry Koontz, son of Texas rancher, at Victoria, Texas. Her twenty-year-old husband works for the Southern Pacific Railway.
1914		Troupes a local Texas circuit singing ballads from Percy's *Reliques* and old Negro lays.
1915	June 21	Divorces.
1916		In Carlsbad Sanatorium in west Texas near San Angelo; in Woodlawn Hospital, Dallas, with tuberculosis in December.
1919	July 19	Six-year-old niece, Mary Alice Holloway, dies. Commemorates her in 1967 with *A Christmas Story*, "a lament in the form of a joyous remembrance."

	October	
	19	Travels by boat from New Orleans to New York.
1920		Writes ballet libretto for Pavlova, with scenery painted by Adolfo Best-Maugard. Performed in Mexico, 1923.
	December	Mexico.
1922		President Obregón appoints her organizer of the Travelling Mexican Popular Arts Exposition. Writes monograph for catalog.
	June	Sails to New York.
	December	"María Concepción" is published in *Century Magazine*.
1923	July	"The Martyr" is published in *Century Magazine*.
1925		Marries Ernest Stock, twenty-five-year-old Englishman, student at the Art Students' League, New York. Lives in Connecticut.
1927	August 21	Goes to Boston to picket for retrial of Sacco and Vanzetti.
	October	"He" is published in *New Masses*.
1928		Lives in Salem, Massachusetts; works on biography of Cotton Mather.
1929	February	"The Jilting of Granny Weatherall" is published in *transition*.
	March	Bermuda. Five months' work on biography of Cotton Mather. Returns to New York in September.
	November	"Theft" is published in *Gyroscope*, edited by Yvor Winters.

1930	Spring	"Flowering Judas" is published in *Hound and Horn*.
	April 28	Sails from New York to Mexico on the SS *Havana*.
	September 11	*Flowering Judas and Other Stories* is published in a limited edition of 600 by Harcourt, Brace.
	October	Edmund Wilson, Allen Tate, Kenneth Burke, and Elizabeth Madox Roberts sponsor her for a Guggenheim Fellowship.
1931	February	Awarded Guggenheim Fellowship.
	August 22	Sails from Vera Cruz to Bremerhaven, Germany, on the *Werra*.
		In Berlin writes "The Leaning Tower" and "The Cracked Looking-Glass."
1932	January	Paris, short visit to Madrid, then back to Paris.
	May	"The Cracked Looking-Glass" is published in *Scribner's Magazine*.
	June	Basel, Switzerland.
	August 20–21	Writes first draft of part of "Noon Wine."
	December	Lives in Paris, Hotel Malherbe, rue de Vaugirard.
1933	March 11	Marries Eugene D. Pressly, attached to US Consular Service, Paris. Lives at 166 boulevard Montparnasse.
	May	*Katherine Anne Porter's French Song Book* is published by Harrison of Paris.

1934	January	"A Bright Particular Faith," chapter of biography of Cotton Mather, is published in *Hound and Horn*.
	April	Spends five weeks in Davos, Switzerland, to cure bronchitis.
	July	"That Tree" is published in the *Virginia Quarterly Review*.
	August 13–18	Travels to Salzburg to see *Fidelio*, *Don Giovanni*, *Rosenkavalier*; goes to Munich to see *The Marriage of Figaro*.
	September	*Hacienda* is published by Harrison of Paris.
	December 15	Moves to 70 bis rue Notre-Dame-des-Champs, Paris, the house once occupied by Ezra Pound.
1935		*Flowering Judas and Other Stories*, larger edition with four stories added, is published by Harcourt, Brace.
	April	"The Grave" is published in the *Virginia Quarterly Review*
1936	February	Sails for the United States on the *President Roosevelt*. Works on Cotton Mather in Boston; returns to Paris in May.
	October 8	Sails on the *Washington* from France to New York.
	November 1–7	Water Wheel Tavern, Doylestown, Pennsylvania. Writes "Noon Wine."
	November 7–14	Writes "Old Mortality."

1937	January	Lives in New York City, 67 Perry Street. Writes "A Day's Work."
	February	Receives award of $2,500 for best writer, unduly neglected; jury gathered by the Book-of-the-Month Club.
	May 1	Marches in the May Day Parade, 57th Street to Union Square, New York.
	June	Week's visit with family in Texas.
	July	Olivet College writers' conference, Michigan.
	August	Drives from Olivet with the Tates (Allen Tate and Caroline Gordon) to their home, Benfolly, in Clarksville, Tennessee.
	September	Lives in New Orleans on the top floor of the lower Pontalba Building.
	December 3	Finishes "Pale Horse, Pale Rider."
1938	April	Her Guggenheim Fellowship is renewed.
	April 9	Divorces Eugene Pressly.
	April 19	Marries Albert Russel Erskine, Jr., of Louisiana State University Press and the *Southern Review*. Lives in Baton Rouge, Louisiana.
	June	Olivet College writers' conference, two weeks.
1939		*Pale Horse, Pale Rider: Three Short Novels* is published as book by Harcourt, Brace. Contains "Old Mortality," "Noon Wine," and "Pale Horse, Pale Rider."
	July	Olivet College writers' conference.

1940		Receives the first annual Gold Medal for Literature of the Society of Libraries. Presented at New York University.
	June 3	Yaddo, Saratoga Springs, New York. Begins *Ship of Fools*.
	September 12	*Flowering Judas and Other Stories* published in Modern Library edition, 5,000 copies, with introduction.
1941		Elected to the American Institute of Arts and Letters.
	December 21	Appears on the CBS program "Invitation to Learning" with Mark Van Doren and Bertrand Russell. Discusses *Alice in Wonderland*.
1942		Translates *The Itching Parrot* by José Joaquín Fernández de Lizardi from the Spanish. Writes an introduction, "Notes on the Life and Death of a Hero."
	January 23	Father dies.
	June 19	Divorces Albert Russel Erskine, Jr., in Reno.
	July	Travels to Indiana University, Bloomington, and attends Olivet College writers' conference.
	August	University of Colorado writers' conference in Boulder.
	September 12	Moves into her own house, South Hill, in Ballston Spa, New York.

1943	October	Harbor Hill, Cold Spring, New York.
1944	February	Washington, D.C. Is appointed a Fellow of the Library of Congress.
	September	*The Leaning Tower and Other Stories* published by Harcourt, Brace.
1945	January	Hollywood, MGM Studios. Works with Sidney Franklin on an Elizabethan film.
	October	To Paramount Studios; works with Charles Brackett on adaptation of *Madame Sans-Gêne*.
	December	All three of her books are translated into French, Scandinavian, and Italian.
1947	April	Lecture tour of southern universities.
	December	Works on adaptation of Chekov's "La Cigale" with Robert Rossen.
1949	January	Stanford University, Stanford, California, writer-in-residence.
	May 30	Receives honorary degree, Doctor of Letters, from the University of North Carolina.
	November 11	Moves to New York City, 108 E. 65th Street.
1950–52		Vice president of National Institute of Arts and Letters.
1952	May 7	Sails on the *Queen Elizabeth* for France to give opening speech at the Paris Conference, International Exposition of the Arts.
		The Days Before, a collection of essays, is published by Harcourt, Brace.

	September	Sails on *La Liberté* from France to New York; lives at 117 East 17th Street, New York City.
1953	September	University of Michigan, Ann Arbor, one year as writer-in-residence.
1954	June	Doctor of Humane Letters, University of Michigan.
	September	Sails on the *Ryndam* to Rotterdam; writer-in-residence at the University of Liège, Belgium.
1955	February 20	Sails on the *Andrea Doria* from Cannes to New York.
	July	Takes a house at Southbury, Connecticut, for three years.
	September	Her brother Paul dies.
1956	October 15	Begins a month's tour of fifteen cities, reading her stories and speaking.
	December	Christmas week in Waterbury Hospital, Connecticut, recovering from influenza.
1957	April 15	Appears on CBS television's "Camera Three" in a program celebrating Henry James's birthday.
1958	June	Receives an honorary degree (Doctor of Letters) from Smith College, along with Janet Flanner, Nadia Boulanger, Barbara McClintock. Senator John F. Kennedy addresses the graduating class.
	September 1	University of Virginia, Charlottesville, Virginia, writer-in-residence.

1959	February	Washington and Lee University, Lexington, Virginia. First Glasgow Professor—new chair of all the arts.
	September	Receives a Ford Foundation grant. Moves to Washington, D.C., 3112 Q Street.
1960	May 28–June 15	To Mexico; tour of duty for U.S. State Department.
	June	"The Fig Tree" published in *Harper's*.
	December	"Holiday" published in *Atlantic Monthly*.
1961	February 19–March 5	University of California, Riverside campus, Regents Lecturer.
	May 26–end of August	To Pigeon Cove, Cape Anne, Rockport, Massachusetts to finish *Ship of Fools*.
1962	April	*Ship of Fools* is published by the Atlantic Monthly Press. Book-of-the-Month Club selection. Hits million-dollar sales.
	May	Receives the Emerson-Thoreau Gold Medal from the American Academy of Arts & Sciences, Boston.
	June 3–23	Travels to Paris, Rome, and Taormina; returns to Washington.
	October	Receives an honorary degree, Doctor of Letters, from La Salle College.

	November 8	Sails on the *Leonardo da Vinci* for Italy. Lives in Rome.
1963	May 6–18	Naples.
	May 18–28	Florence.
	May 28–June 7	Venice.
	June 8	Paris.
	October 31	Arrives in Baltimore from Paris. Lives in the Jefferson Hotel, Washington, D.C.
1964	June	Lives at 3601 49th St., Washington, D.C.
1966–67		Receives the National Book Award for Fiction and the Pulitzer Prize for Fiction for *The Collected Stories of Katherine Anne Porter*; created Doctor of Humane Letters, University of Maryland; elected to American Academy of Arts and Letters, fifth occupant of Chair 49; receives the Gold Medal for fiction, National Institute of Arts and Letters.
1967	December	*A Christmas Story*, "a lament in the form of a joyous remembrance," is published.
1969		Joins the usage panel of *The American Heritage Dictionary*.
1970		*The Collected Essays and Occasional Writings of Katherine Anne Porter* is published.
1971		Moves to 6100 Westchester Park Drive, College Park, Maryland.

1976   October 18 Reads her "St. Augustine and the Bullfight" at the Poetry Center, New York City.

1977   *The Never-Ending Wrong*, a memoir of Sacco and Vanzetti, is published in the fiftieth year after their deaths.

1980   September 18   Dies at Carriage Hill, Silver Spring, Maryland.

WHO'S WHO

CYRILLY ABELS. Editor of *Mademoiselle*; Katherine Anne Porter's agent. Katherine Anne Porter wrote to me before Abels's death on November 7, 1975: "Cyrilly is the most lovely, gentle creature in the world, and I have never known any more courageous and generous—a lovely balanced mind—I have known her for thirty-five years and learning her nature in all its phases like the seasons changing year by year, every one with a new surprise that with every change you say, as if it were spring or winter—how wonderful to see this season again, as if you had never seen it until then."

ELIZABETH AMES. Head of Yaddo—the Spencer Trask mansion at Saratoga Springs, New York, maintained for the benefit of artists, writers, and composers—from its beginning in 1926 until 1970. Skidmore College awarded her the degree of Doctor of Arts in 1947; the National Institute of Arts and Letters gave her its Award for Distinguished Service in 1959.

SYLVIA BEACH (1887–1962). Owner of the bookshop Shakespeare and Company at 12 rue de l'Odéon, Paris. She was the publisher of Joyce's *Ulysses*. She introduced Katherine Anne Porter to her French translator, Marcelle Sibon, in December 1935, and they went over "Flowering Judas" together. She wrote her memoirs, *Shakespeare and Company*, in 1959.

GERTRUDE BECHTEL. Cousin of Katherine Anne Porter, sister of Lily Cahill, the actress.

DONALD BRACE (1881–1955), one of the founders of Harcourt, Brace and Company, 1919. He was Katherine Anne Porter's publisher and friend for twenty-five years. When he died, she left Harcourt, Brace.

JOHN MALCOLM BRINNIN (1916–). Head of the Poetry Center, YM-WHA, New York, where Katherine Anne Porter talked and read from her works year after year. At her last talk, in October

1976, he was her guest in the audience, sitting beside me. A poet and writer, he published *Dylan Thomas in America* in 1955 and *Sextet: T. S. Eliot and Truman Capote and Others* in 1981.

KENNETH BURKE (1897–   ). Literary and philosophic critic. He sponsored Katherine Anne Porter for a Guggenheim Fellowship in 1930. Among his works are *Attitudes Toward History*, 1937; *A Rhetoric of Motives*, 1950; *Perspectives by Incongruity*, 1964; *Collected Poems*, 1968. He was awarded the National Medal for Literature in 1980.

ELEANOR CLARK (1913–   ). Author of *Rome and a Villa*, 1953; *The Oysters of Locmariaquer*, 1964; *Eyes, Etc.*, 1977; and the novels *The Bitter Box*, 1946; *Baldur's Gate*, 1971; *Gloria Mundi*, 1979; and *Camping Out*, 1986. "Her grand talent it seems to me is for promoting an amused, witty, out-of-the way learning as a joyous adventure," wrote Katherine Anne Porter, citing Clark for membership in the National Institute for Arts and Letters on June 18, 1965. She is married to Robert Penn Warren.

MALCOLM COWLEY (1898–1989). Editor of *The New Republic* when Katherine Anne Porter was in Berlin, 1931. Among his works: *A Dry Season*, 1942, poems partly about the "lost generation"; *Think Back on Us*, 1967, a collection of his writings during and on the 1930s; *The View from Eighty*, his reflections on the life of an octogenarian.

HART CRANE (1899–1932). His long mystical poem, *The Bridge*, was completed in 1930. He committed suicide by jumping from the ship taking him home after a year in Mexico. His *Collected Poems* was published in 1933.

HELEN O'LOCHLAIN CROWE. Crowe was with Katherine Anne Porter in the first picket line for a Sacco-Vanzetti retrial in 1927. "I consider her one of the most remarkable persons I ever knew," wrote Katherine Anne Porter to Mary Doherty on October 21, 1932.

DANIEL CURLEY (1918–88). One of the editors of *Accent* (1955–60), he founded *Ascent* in 1975 and edited it until his death in Tallahassee, Florida. Among his writings are *That Marriage Bed of*

Procrustes (stories, 1957), *In the Hands of Our Enemies* (stories, 1970), and the novels, *How Many Angels?*; *A Stone Man, Yes*, 1964; and *Mummy*, 1987.

ALFRED SHEPPARD DASHIELL. Was managing editor of *Scribner's Magazine* in 1932 when they published "The Cracked Looking-Glass." As a journalist he wrote for various newspapers: *New York World*, *New York Evening Post*, *Boston Transcript*.

BABETTE DEUTSCH (1895–1982). A New York poet noted for her sensitive intellectual verse. Her works include *Banners*, 1919; *Honey out of the Rock*, 1925; *Fire for the Night*, 1930. Her *Collected Poems* was published in 1969; her critical works include anthologies of Russian and German poetry.

MARY DOHERTY. In the 1930s, worked for the Mexican Government in the Public Charities. She was the model for Laura in "Flowering Judas."

EDWARD DONAHOE. Author of "Head by Scopas" published in *Space*, 1934.

DONALD ELDER. Editor at Doubleday when *The Itching Parrot* was published, 1942. He wrote a biography of Ring Lardner in 1956.

ALBERT RUSSEL ERSKINE, JR. (1911–   ). Was an editor at Louisiana State University Press and of *The Southern Review* in 1938 when he and Katherine Anne Porter were married. He was an editor and is now a consultant for Random House.

REVEREND JOHN F. FAHEY. As a student for the priesthood at St. Mary of the Lake Seminary, in Mundelein, Illinois, he wrote to Katherine Anne Porter about his work on "The Writer and His Religion" in 1948.

WILLIAM FAULKNER (1897–1962). Katherine Anne Porter succeeded him as writer-in-residence at the University of Virginia in 1958. He was awarded the Nobel Prize in 1950 for his literary accomplishments. He won the Pulitzer Prize for *A Fable* in 1954 and for *The Reivers* in 1962. His *Selected Letters* was published in 1977.

ROBERT GIROUX (1914–   ). Editor-in-chief of Harcourt, Brace and Company during the time *The Days Before* was published (1952). He wrote Katherine Anne Porter that it was "a tremendously impressive statement about a life-time devoted to literature." He has been with the publishing firm Farrar, Straus & Giroux since 1955 and at present is chairman of the editorial board.

CAROLINE GORDON (1895–1981). Among the nine novels she wrote are *Penhally*, 1931; *Aleck Maury, Sportsman*, 1934; *None Shall Look Back*, 1937; *The Malefactors*, 1956; *The Glory of Hera*, 1972. Her *Collected Stories* was published in 1981. She was married to Allen Tate for more than thirty years.

LODWICK HARTLEY (1906–79). Edited, with George Core, *Katherine Anne Porter: A Critical Symposium*, in 1969. At that time he was head of the English Department at North Carolina State University. Among his books are *Laurence Sterne: A Biographical Essay*; *Cowper: The Continuing Revaluation*; and *Laurence Sterne in the Twentieth Century*.

ANN HEINTZE (1920–87). Daughter of Katherine Anne Porter's older sister, Gay Porter Holloway. She danced with the Ballet Russe in the 1940s and later taught ballet. She traveled with Katherine Anne Porter to Mexico in 1960 and to Italy and France in 1962.

JOSEPHINE HERBST (1892–1969). Her major fiction is *Pity Is Not Enough*, 1933; *The Executioner Waits*, 1934; *Roper of Gold*, 1939; and *Somewhere the Tempest Fell*, 1947. Of John Bartram and other early American naturalists she wrote *New Green World*, 1954.

MARY ALICE HILLENDAHL. Younger sister of Katherine Anne Porter.

GAY PORTER HOLLOWAY (1885–1969). Katherine Anne Porter's older sister. Porter dedicated *The Days Before* to her in 1952.

JOHN FITZGERALD KENNEDY (1917–63). He was not yet the thirty-fifth president of the United States when he addressed the 1958 graduating class of Smith College; during the ceremonies Katherine Anne Porter was awarded the honorary degree of Doctor of Letters. In 1956 he had won the Pulitzer Prize for *Profiles in Courage*.

FREDA KIRCHWEY (1893–1976). Editor of the *Nation*.

GEORGE LANDY. A literary agent who tried to arrange for the sale of "Noon Wine" as a film in 1949; Norman Mailer was interested in working on it.

SEYMOUR LAWRENCE. From 1955 to 1962, as director of Atlantic Monthly Press, he worked closely with Katherine Anne Porter during the writing and publication of *Ship of Fools*. Under his own imprint with Delacorte Press he published *The Collected Essays and Occasional Writings of Katherine Anne Porter* in 1970. He also published *A Christmas Story* in 1967, with drawings by Ben Shahn. He is now with Houghton Mifflin.

ALLAN AND BURRY LEWIS. In 1952, they presented to Katherine Anne Porter a playwright's outline for the dramatization of "María Concepción."

GEORGE PLATT LYNES (1909–55). Distinguished photographer and a friend to Katherine Anne Porter from the 1930s when they were in Paris until his early death. When Katherine Anne Porter had to choose a photograph for her publisher in 1936, she picked the one by him of which her *femme de ménage* had said, *"Ah Madame, vous êtes si jeune, si gentille, et si bien coiffée."*

ANDREW LYTLE (1902–). His books include *Bedford Forrest*, 1931, which Katherine Anne Porter recommended to her father; *A Name for Evil*, 1947, about which she wrote him one of her finest letters: ". . . the spirit and mind of man is truly indomitable, his creative will rises above and somehow does work in spite of the darkness and confusion of his instincts" (September 15, 1947). He wrote *The Velvet Horn* in 1957 and *A Wake for the Living*, his family chronicle, in 1975.

ROBERT McALMON (1896–1956). His autobiography, *Being Geniuses Together*, was published in 1938, though drastically cut. It was extended by Kay Boyle, interspersed with her own recollections, in 1968. When Katherine Anne Porter published a section of *Ship of Fools*, he wrote to her, "Liked Embarkation in Sewanee Review.

Dostoevsky and Glenway Wescott my eye! It's KAP, and if it resembles anybody it's Stendhal in its clipped neatness and saying just what you want to say" (January 24, 1949).

MARIANNE MOORE (1887–1972). Editor of *The Dial* (1925–29). Her *Collected Poems* won the Pulitzer Prize in 1951. *Like a Bulwark* was published in 1956, and *O to Be a Dragon* in 1959. She received the Gold Medal for Poetry from the National Institute of Arts and Letters. She made a verse translation, *The Fables of La Fontaine*, in 1954. *Tell Me, Tell Me*, 1966, collects poems and prose pieces.

FLANNERY O'CONNOR (1925–64). A volume of her stories, *A Good Man Is Hard to Find*, was published in 1955; her *Complete Stories* in 1971. Her novel *The Violent Bear It Away* was published in 1960; her letters, *The Habit of Being*, in 1979. Katherine Anne Porter said of her, "I loved and valued her dearly, her work and her strange unworldly radiance of spirit in a human being so intelligent and undeceived by the appearance of things" (*Collected Essays*, p. 297).

PAUL O'HIGGINS. A concert pianist before he became a painter's assistant to Diego Rivera. He taught Katherine Anne Porter music in Mexico in 1930 on her little rosewood piano made in 1820. Later he converted to communism and went to Russia.

NORMAN HOLMES PEARSON. A Guggenheim Fellow in 1948; professor of English and American studies at Yale, 1962–75. He was the editor of the *Complete Novels of Hawthorne*, 1937; of *The Oxford Anthology of American Literature* (with W. R. Benet), 1938; and of *Poets of the English Language* (with W. H. Auden), 1950. He died in 1975.

JORDON PECILE. Worked with Calvin Skaggs on two Katherine Anne Porter television shows: "The Eye of Memory" in 1986 and "The Fig Tree" in 1987. Professor of Humanities at the U.S. Coast Guard Academy, he has been Literary Advisor for the Public Broadcasting System series The American Short Story.

HARRISON BOONE PORTER (1857–1942). Katherine Anne Porter's father. "You write very well, you know, and I think I inherited my bent for it from you," she wrote to him on January 21, 1933. Damage from frost and tornadoes made him give up his orange grove.

PAUL PORTER (1887–1955). The brother of Katherine Anne Porter who is the model for the child with Miranda in "The Grave." He died in the year of the deaths of Donald Brace, Lily Cahill, and George Platt Lynes, all close and dear to her.

PAUL HARRISON PORTER, JR. (1921–). The son of Katherine Anne Porter's brother. She dedicated *The Leaning Tower and Other Stories* to him in 1944 when he was a corporal in the U.S. Army. "We look like mother and child," Katherine Anne Porter wrote to Monroe Wheeler on June 13, 1946.

EZRA POUND (1885–1972). Katherine Anne Porter named him, along with Henry James, James Joyce, William Butler Yeats, and T. S. Eliot as the great educators of their time. His cantos were collected in 1970; *The Waste Land*, *The Bridge*, and *Conquistador* have been said to be in their debt. For his fascist broadcasts in Mussolini's Italy he was to face trial for treason in the United States; he was committed to a sanitarium instead. Katherine Anne Porter visited him there on March 5, 1953.

JAMES FARL POWERS (1917–). The author of three collections of short stories: *Prince of Darkness and Other Stories*, 1947; *The Presence of Grace*, 1956; and *Look How the Fish Live*, 1975. His novel *Morte D'Urban* won the National Book Award in 1963. His most recent novel, *Wheat That Springeth Green*, was published in 1988. He has received fellowships from the Rockefeller Foundation and the Guggenheim Foundation.

EUGENE DOVE PRESSLY. Katherine Anne Porter's third husband. He was attached to the U.S. Consular Service in Madrid, Basel, and Paris, 1931 to 1936. He was a specialist in decoding.

WILLIAM ROSS. Was President of Colorado State College during the McCarthy period, when signature to an oath of allegiance was requested of the college's teachers.

EDWARD G. SCHWARTZ. Taught English at Syracuse University at the time that he compiled *Katherine Anne Porter: A Critical Bibliography* for the New York Public Library (1953). Essays he has published on Katherine Anne Porter are "The Way of Dissent," 1954, and "The Fictions of Memory," 1960.

MARCELLE SIBON. The French translator of all of Katherine Anne Porter's works. They worked together in Rome on *Ship of Fools* in December 1962. "We are going over the translation word for word, and it is amazing how clear and straight her work is, it reads back into English with not a shade of meaning lost," Katherine Anne Porter wrote to Seymour Lawrence on December 24, 1962.

DAME EDITH SITWELL (1887–1964). Both Yeats and Katherine Anne Porter saw reborn in her "the Swift grandeur and justice in wrath." Edith Sitwell dedicated "A Sylph's Song" ("Pomona's Daughter") to Katherine Anne Porter. Her *Collected Poems* appeared in 1954 and 1957.

STEPHEN SPENDER (1909–   ). A poet and critic, he was educated at University College, Oxford. As joint editor of the magazine *Encounter,* he published Katherine Anne Porter's "A Wreath for the Gamekeeper," included a decade later in her *Collected Essays.* Spender's *Journals* were published in 1985, his *Collected Poems* in 1986.

JAMES STERN (1904–   ). When the National Institute of Arts and Letters awarded Stern $1,000, Glenway Wescott said, "To James Stern, born in Ireland, in recognition of his long, devoted and faultless practice of the art of the short story according to its great tradition: in strict prose without trickeries, or exaggerations, nevertheless communicating a most constant intelligence and intense feeling." His stories are collected in *The Stories of James Stern*, 1968.

EDWARD R. STETTINIUS (1900–49). Chairman of the Board of U.S. Steel, 1938. Franklin Roosevelt appointed him Secretary of State in 1944. He accompanied Roosevelt to Yalta in 1945 for the conference with Churchill and Stalin. He was chairman of the American delegation in 1946 to the first session of the United Nations General Assembly.

ALLEN TATE (1899–1979). Edited *The Sewanee Review*, 1944–46; taught at the University of Minnesota, 1951–68. He wrote biographies of Stonewall Jackson, 1928, and of Jefferson Davis, 1929. A critic and anthologist, he is best known for his poems. His *Collected Poems* was published in 1977.

FREDERIC WARBURG (1898–1981). Of Martin, Secker & Warburg, which published *Ship of Fools* in England in 1962. He attained notoriety for publishing George Orwell's *Animal Farm* in 1944. Of his publishing life from 1936 to 1971 he wrote *All Authors Are Equal*.

ROBERT PENN WARREN (1905–1989). First Poet Laureate of the United States, 1986. Founder and editor of *The Southern Review*, 1935 to 1942. He has published ten novels (*All the King's Men* won a Pulitzer Prize in 1946), twelve volumes of poetry, and various critical works. "Your great endless Niagara-abundance of great work makes me feel like a trickling spring," Katherine Anne Porter wrote to him on December 27, 1976.

EUDORA WELTY (1909–   ). Katherine Anne Porter wrote the introduction to her first collection of short stories, *A Curtain of Green*, 1941. *The Collected Stories of Eudora Welty* was published in 1980. She received the Pulitzer Prize for fiction in 1973 for *The Optimist's Daughter*. Her essays and reviews were collected in *The Eye of the Story* in 1978. Katherine Anne Porter presented her with the Gold Medal for Fiction from the National Institute of Arts and Letters in 1972. *One Writer's Beginnings,* 1984, is autobiographical.

BARBARA HARRISON WESCOTT. Started the publishing house Harrison of Paris with Monroe Wheeler in the 1930s, for the printing of fine editions. They published *Katherine Anne Porter's French Song-Book* and *Hacienda*. "She was olive-skinned, with golden eyes and high cheek bones and a face like a young, beautiful female eagle," wrote Katherine Anne Porter to James Stern, on February 21, 1963. Katherine Anne Porter dedicated *Ship of Fools* to her.

GLENWAY WESCOTT (1901–87). His short stories were collected in *Good-Bye Wisconsin*, 1928. His novels include *The Apple of the Eye*, 1924; *The Grandmothers*, which won the Harper's Prize in 1927; and *Apartment in Athens*, 1945. His short novel *The Pilgrim Hawk*, 1940, has been published in the collection *Six Great Modern Short Novels*, with Katherine Anne Porter's "Noon Wine," Joyce's "The Dead," Melville's "Billy Budd," Gogol's "The Overcoat," and Faulkner's "The Bear." *Images of Truth*, 1962, a volume of remembrances and criticism, contains the essay "Katherine Anne Porter, Personally."

MONROE WHEELER (1900–   ). Harrison of Paris published his *A Typographical Commonplace-Book*. Nelson Rockefeller appointed him Director of Publications at the Museum of Modern Art, and Wheeler subsequently saw to it that the museum's publications defined the highest standard of book production. He organized important exhibitions. He is now a member of the museum's Board of Trustees.

MORTON DAUWEN ZABEL (1901–64). Editor of *Poetry: A Magazine of Verse* in 1926. He received a Guggenheim Fellowship in 1944 and occupied the Chair of North American Literature at the National University of Brazil from 1944 to 1946 and again in 1953. He received $1,000 from the National Institute of Arts and Letters in 1955. He became professor of English Literature of the University of Chicago on his return from South America in 1946. His principal works include *The Portable Joseph Conrad*, 1947; *The Portable Henry James*, 1951.

EDITOR'S NOTE

I took heart for the task of selecting from thousands of Katherine Anne Porter's letters those that would carry the story of her major working years, 1930 to 1963, within a single volume when I learned that she herself had selected from a thousand poems the twenty or so that she could read in public within a single hour. Limits perform their own function. A letter that illuminates her thinking, her writing, her philosophy, her temperament, her politics, her sources of sorrow, of joy (*"Interest unde quis gaudeat,"* she liked to quote from Saint Augustine, and in her translation, "It doth make a difference whence cometh a man's joy") often selects itself. Yet a passage or two within it may not be quite so telling. These have been deleted. Ellipses indicating deletion are marked by four dots. Less than four are her own. In the original, often a stream of dots flowed as she went thinking along. For clarity I have kept these down to three.

Her spelling has been faithfully retained to keep as close to the flavor of the original as printing will allow. She almost always wrote "its" without the apostrophe for "it's," and you will find this throughout. Other little ways of spelling: "aquaint," "developement," "judgement"—often the English spelling rather than the American—are kept. Occasionally she footnoted her letters as she went along, or added a note afterward when she went over them for her own records, for an autobiographical essay or a journal she once had in mind to do, and these have been shown, with asterisks or initials, as her own. My footnotes (indicated by daggers) I have kept to a minimum.

Usually Katherine Anne Porter typed her letters, with occasional rueful remarks about never having learned how to do it. This has had two happy results: that she could keep her own carbon copies (which a friend had persuaded her to do, though at first she thought it rather calculating), and that letters misplaced or lost by friends thus remain on record. Without a typewriter—when it was being repaired, when she was traveling, or when she was in the hospital—she wrote by hand, and apologized for what she feared her friend had to put up with.

I have often been privileged, through the kindness of friends and libraries who have sent me photocopies of the original, to see what both the original and the carbon look like, and they are almost always identical. In one case, the original has two underlinings that the carbon copy does not, and you hear her voice emphasizing *"at once . . . at once."* For this is how quickly she wanted her goddaughter to whom she was sending pearls to let her know whether the Irish customs charged any duty—duty that she would have wished she could pay in advance.

Through the years I have worked on this book, I would wake up in the morning with a phrase, a thought from a letter running through my mind and ask myself with alarm, "But did I get that into the letterbook?" What my spirit would hang on to, what held particular insights, what gave me fresh joy, I tried to retain in a book that I hope will enhearten anyone who reads it, anyone who takes it along on a journey, or keeps it within reach to see whether it is really true that Katherine Anne Porter has said, "Trust your happiness. . . ."

INTRODUCTION

When Katherine Anne Porter was born one hundred years ago, Queen Victoria had celebrated her fiftieth year on the throne of England and the Crystal Palace had been standing for almost forty years. Joyce was eight years old, Yeats was twenty-five, and Henry James had not yet written *The Ambassadors*, nor *The Golden Bowl*, nor indeed the autobiographies, about which she herself was to write so brilliantly on his centenary in 1943.

Yet she was writing her autobiographies all along. "All my letters, yours, too, are autobiography in a very pure sense," Katherine Anne Porter writes to her friend James Powers. To another friend, Glenway Wescott, she says, "But it's no use saying, this or that happened on such a date . . . for that is not what happened at all. My life has been so hidden and internal that just a record of events would be perfectly meaningless." This complex way of looking at things places her firmly in the century of Heisenberg and Gödel, when seeing and the way of seeing has something to do with what is seen, when nobody is sure of what it all is, after all. "But that doesn't let us off trying," says the writer whose last words in a famous short novel about a young woman who promises herself she would know the truth of what happens to her are, "in her hopefulness, in her ignorance."

This collection is a small sampling of Katherine Anne Porter's letters (she once wrote to me, "Someone has estimated that I must have at least ten thousand letters at large over the world"). The book was conceived as a whole—the letters are sometimes used in their entirety, sometimes in illuminating passages—to show range and depth of thought in a single volume. They will carry you, if you wish to read in sequence, from point to point during her major working years, 1930 to 1963. Little bridges form from idea to idea, from theme to theme. If you skip about, you may miss them. "I like having a sense of responsibility towards some one else," Katherine Anne Porter writes when she marries in Paris. When she buys a house in the country, she wants more than a place for her manuscripts and books and music and a place where friends will delight to come; she writes, "Housekeeping and duty and trusteeship: I *need* them all." We follow her to the point where she knows that the responsibility, the duty, the trusteeship must be to what is truly her own. There are other sequences you may not want to miss. For her to call Bermuda a paradise to one friend reads differently after she has companionably said to another friend, who is discouraged, "Paradise is a sell." You see the progression from her buying the house in Connecticut, to buying the mountain in California, to considering a place in Brittany where she can grow figs, to longing for a "Folly Cove" above the rocks of the Massachusetts coast. Finally, from Rome, she writes to a friend who also has no place of his own, "I do not own a foot of land or a roof anywhere, either, and in the very depths of my heart I probably don't want to."

This book begins with a letter to her sister: "Just now, this month, *The Hound & Horn*, a magazine published in Cambridge, has a short story of mine, called 'Flowering Judas.'" It ends three decades later. Katherine Anne Porter has been telling an old friend who has written only one story—one she wants to include in an anthology she has been planning—that she, too, for years was known for only one story. She talks to him as fellow writer, almost as though she had not written all the rest—short stories, long stories, short novels, and the novel Glenway Wescott has called "the book of the century."

From Paris, she writes to her niece, "I wrote to an old friend to ask permission to re-print his story, 'Head by Scopas' which appeared it must be thirty years ago in a little magazine. He has been in a rest-home in Mexico, had a complete break-up many years ago, thought his story was forgotten, and it has been terrible and touching and sweet to see what an effect my finding him has had on his spirits. He writes me constantly, sometimes two letters a day, and says the same thing over and over and over, with just the smallest variation or addition or omission, apparently quite hopelessly gone in his mind, and yet what gentleness and affection and charm he has, just as always. . . . Oh, it is heart breaking. . . . So I write to him all the time, and just as if he were perfectly well and sane."

This goodness of heart runs through her letters. "I have known in life so many strange, wild lost people, some of them very gifted, so many beings trembling a lifetime between madness and a kind of twilight sanity, such suffering and such cruelty and confusion, I have a good while ago come to the point where I love goodness and simplicity and the desire of the human heart to believe and to love. ... This is never to say that simplicity means simpleness. It is the most complex and difficult of all things to achieve." Too modest to realize that she herself possessed these virtues, she goes on to tell her nephew some dozen years later, "I know. ... goodness is supposed to be very dull, if not deeply suspect; but it isn't to me." Today, there are those who talk about *The Fragility of Goodness,* but they are the classicists, close to the Greeks, to whom Katherine Anne Porter always felt close, writer that she was of stories that are true classics. Her stories are a gauge of what it cost her to control the natural warmth revealed in her letters, a measure of how well she listened to Yeats: "Cast a cold eye/On life, on death."

Not that it is all goodness and gentleness and affection. She is fierce and independent and indignant, furious at carelessness and muddle, which she hates as much as she loves clarity and precision. She is outraged when she is asked to sign an oath of allegiance, and she writes a letter that could have scorched the hair of the president of the university who requested it. She sees into the corruption of the State Department, which coddles South American dictators who pass as anti-Communists. After trying to stay out of it, she rolls up her sleeves for the scrimmage over awarding the Bollingen Prize to Ezra Pound. She talks about the "troubles of people in our time trying to work in an art. ... I think sometimes the only trouble is with the artist himself. He doesn't believe enough in what he is doing to demand, and to take, the time and energy for it that he needs. ... Its our fault in the long run, my dear, if we cannot make ourselves and our callings respected a little, at least as much as if we were in the second hand clothing business, let's say." And money is as worrisome to her as it was to Mozart. Yet she tries to pay back every dollar she ever borrowed and manages, when she does make a good deal of money for herself and her publishers, to settle some of it, so much every month for the rest of her life, on her sister.

"My name is Katherine Anne Maria Veronica Callista Russell Porter," she tells the editor of a biographical encyclopedia, who has gone to the trouble to look it up and then has omitted the one she considers most interesting—Callista Russell, for a friend of her mother's (as a child, she had been called Callie for short). "Is this necessary or just amusing?" she asks. Maria Veronica was her confirmation name; Katherine Anne was her beloved grandmother's name, which she took for her own when she began to write. Her father once joked that they were probably kin to every Jones and Smith in the world: her mother was a Jones, and on her father's side, Rhoda Boone, one of her Boone ancestors (the many-times-removed grandfather had been Daniel Boone's nephew Jonathan) had married a Smith. The Jones grandparents were entirely Welsh, tall, thin, light-boned, and short-lived (her mother died at thirty-two, after the birth of her fifth child). Virginia was where the Joneses had settled in 1648; Pennsylvania where the Porters, originally from Warwickshire, had settled in 1720. Andrew Porter, fresh from Ireland, a blue-nosed Presbyterian elder, was descended from a soldier in Cromwell's occupying army who had done as soldiers in occupying armies do and had married the girl next door.

When she was about ten years old (she told me this when she was in her eighties, over drinks one night in her home outside Washington, high above the trees), Katherine Anne's father noticed that she was wearing a special dress. He wanted to know if it was a special day. She replied brightly, "It is the Feast of the Immaculate Conception of the Blessed Virgin Mary." "Do you know what that means?" asked her father. Well instructed by the Ursulines, Katherine Anne replied, "It means that the Blessed Virgin Mary conceived without sin." Upon which her father sent her into the library to "drive all the nonsense" out of her head by reading Voltaire and the Encyclopedists. A half-century later, she writes to her nephew, "I'm glad you had Forster to send you to Montaigne, Voltaire, Erasmus, and the rest. You had somebody in the family who had read them and had been formed by them from her tenth year, more or less."

By the time you come to the letter in which Katherine Anne Porter says she "can't account at all for the fantastic variety and unbelievable *levels* on which my life carried itself out," you have been moving among those levels. You have seen her gaiety of heart, her melancholy, her wearing through days and hours, her love of ritual, her meditation on love, her trust in reason. In New York, she writes on a sheet of paper from the Algonquin, "Two cocktail parties today, one at the River Club to say goodbye to Somerset Maugham, where were also Mrs. Vanderbilt, Alice Roosevelt Longworth, two Astors, one male, one female. . . . and Somerset Maugham who assured me I was the greatest American writer." In the country "even alone, one developes little rituals and ceremonies of common life, and I have a Coffee Fire every morning, besides other little reassuring stations of the day." Little rituals, ceremonies, birthdays—she always wants to know the day, the month, the year a friend, a grandniece, a godchild was born— progress to another level. "Lost entirely are the ancient sacred rituals and invocations to a higher power to work the divine change in man's efforts, adding to them the mysterious power necessary to raise them to perfection." She writes of love, "I have had great good of love—happiness and good company, hopefulness, trust; if they passed, so do the seasons and so does life and no one ever had to remind me of this." Of reason, she says, "I have no mystique of religion, no division of loyalties between church and state, but only a purely secular, reasoning system of political and ethical beliefs for my support." Years before, from Mexico, she had written to Allen Tate, "The artist who comprehends his time and the movement of the world in which he lives brings something better to it than mere agitations and controversy. He may join in these, but there is something beyond, and his value lies exactly in his sense of the beyondness—"

Transcending all these levels, of course, is talk about writing. "I have to sweep a track and make a dead run when I once start. . . . I depend. . . . on something that is *deeper than knowledge.*" And then, "If I take one episode as a starting point, it always leads to consequences which did not occur really. I believe that this is what fiction-writing means. . . . I must not use *actual characters combined with their actual experience.* I must either write fiction, or report the facts." And there are the extraordinary letters to her nephew about writing. "The best kind of originality is that which works within limitations of form, creating variations, and progressing, adding something new; it is a kind of organic growth and change. . . . everything human is his [the born writer's] province, and he sees the relations between all things, and will find himself neglecting nothing that the human mind has thought nor the human heart has felt." She tells him, "I am never so much interested in the kind of people the author chooses to write about as what he has to say about them and how he says it. Any character that seems to me presented in the round, a true portrait of a human being, with *illumination* which is the gift of genius to cast upon the deep places in human nature, is interesting to me; the author must be able to persuade me to accept his version as true, his insight as real." Encouraging a young writer, confiding that "over and over I have thought I could surely never write another line," she hands him what must have started him off again: "But it is the most wonderful thing of all that as you work, you do warm up some centers of energy and imagination and find yourself doing something you hadn't proposed and much better than anything you had planned."

The letters are full of what Katherine Anne Porter has to say about writers—of Forster, Joyce, Mann, Hardy, Wilde, Fitzgerald, Hemingway—where, as with everything, she gets to the heart of the matter. Of T. S. Eliot, she writes, "I think he is a very despairing man who has tried all his life to believe in something and has found it impossible, and he suffers from dryness of heart and lack of faith . . . But he has made good poetry out of these lacks and limitations." She also reveals her deep insight: "The greatest art comes out of warmth and conviction and deep feeling, but then, very few people, even geniuses, have all that."

Of course the letters are a gloss on the stories. There is a letter to someone who wants to make a film of "Noon Wine"—you read how she sees her people, how she would dress them, her shrewdness in trying to keep them safe from what Hollywood might do. To someone who wants to make a play of "María Concepción," she shows her fine dramatic sense, reveals the heart of her characters in a way that shows the one-dimensionality of what the adapter would do with them. She writes of "Pale Horse, Pale Rider" in a way that brings it close to Dante, to the dark wood, to the Adonis legend, to the Crucifixion legend. "Holiday" has taken forty years to write; what she has done, she tells a friend, is to interweave into her decades-old story what she could not do years before—what makes the story what it is. And all along we see her preoccupation with what grows into the novel. "You can imagine *why* I get so agitated and protest so much against so much, because I have seen so much *near to*—have been in the middle of the most apalling kind

6

of evils that it seemed to me most people took for granted—Almost everything in our society at a certain level is corrupt and wrong, old in corruption and wrong." And later, sending passages of her novel to a magazine to be published, she tells her friend, who is the editor, "Out of inertia, moral apathy, timidity, indifference, and even a subconscious criminal collusion, people allow others to do every kind of wrong, and even, if the wrongdoers are successful, finally rather approve of them, perhaps envy them a little. You will see all of this at work somewhere, everywhere, in this long passage I am sending you."

One of her friends, Robert McAlmon, told her, "It's always good to get your letters because you stay alertly awake, and not precious or full of mannerisms and theories, and anthology grouping about literachure." As she put it, "Letters I always thought were meant to be personal messages standing instead of talk between two persons who are not arguing, or trying to convert each other to anything, or writing essays for posterity or even the present public—so the free-er and easier the tone, the nearer it comes to a letter, seems to me." (This is astonishingly like what another great letter writer said three hundred years before. "All letters mee thinks should be free and easy as one's discourse," wrote Dorothy Osborne to William Temple.) Almost parenthetically, Katherine Anne Porter remarks, "I write at top speed with no effort, if I didn't I'd never get time to write letters at all." Sometimes she rewards herself after breaking through a knotty piece of writing. When a friend makes the classic suggestion that Katherine Anne burn the letter she has just written, Katherine Anne replies, " 'Better burn this letter,' indeed! . . . . If you don't want me to treasure such letters, better not write them."

Katherine Anne Porter did treasure letters from her friends. She went to the trouble on one occasion of sending back a letter to be copied and returned—she was too tired or she would have copied it herself. "It is too good a document for you to let go entirely . . . I cannot exaggerate how I value it, and I shall feel badly if it doesn't come back and soon!" This sense of the value of what a friend had written to her has much to do with her sense of the value of the moment, not unlike Henry James's sense of life as precious stuff. It has to do with her respect for life itself. She points out a paradox: "When I complain, it is only because the conditions of living seem to be so unnecessarily and stupidly painful. When I am raising the most hell, it is a paradox; because I love life so much, I can't bear to have it abused!" It has to do also with her sense of continuity, of seeing the words that she and her friends write to one another as forming a story that no longer belongs to the teller. When letters and manuscripts come from the East to the West Coast, she writes,

> Mss. and notes and journals and letters arrived from Saratoga Springs the other day, and reading some of it over I find the past much more solid than I had thought, and living much more continuous, which I had begun to doubt. . . . Things just accumulated, and behold, it has become history. . . . to be sorted and used as part of a story. I don't know that story any more than you do, especially not the end, and we will never see it, and I think it not very important whether we do or don't . . . It doesn't belong to us anyway.

I am probably the only person to whom she once said, "Don't write me a letter!" This was out of kindness. She had called several times in June of 1974 to talk to me about being her literary trustee. I had just told her that when the telephone rang I was about to write to her. We had been friends for over a quarter of a century—we had met at the University of Kansas at a writers' workshop. She knew that it would not be an easy letter for me to write; she knew my gratitude. Instead, she asked me to send her a sprig of the white lilac I told her I had picked on my way down to the lake to let the whole thing sink in. I have it still, for she saved it, along with the letter I was considerately told not to write, along with every letter she ever received.

She had a turn of mind like her beloved Dr. Johnson—things always turning into something else. She confesses she "reads him for consolation the way some painful souls read their Bible." (She even went sliding the way he did, though not in the Christ Church meadow but down a beautiful ski run in a large saucer with her goddaughter.) No sooner has she seen something one way— "Damn typewriters"—than she sees it another—"bless them." It is the turn of mind that reveals itself in the great stories—stories of the betrayed turning into betrayer, thief-catcher into thief, observer into observed, seer of fools into fool herself, a passenger on that ship. It is an amplitude and generosity that may find something in an interpretation of one of her stories so wrong as to be shocking, yet she would not for one moment expect the critic to change his mind to agree with her, for his point was well argued. When she is asked for an opinion of a certain writer, she comments, "I miss a certain generosity of mind." Then her sense of fairness makes her say, "It is not an ample talent, but not bad either."

Years later, Katherine Anne Porter even goes to the great Doctor to help her learn how to die. From her wheelchair at the window above the trees, she hands me a copy of the *Sewanee Review,* Fall 1977. The cover is the color of the blue dressing gown she wears. I begin to read aloud from the page to which she has opened it: "How to Die: The Example of Samuel Johnson."

But of course she had her own way of looking at death. She writes to me from Liège, "Your story of how your friend read 'Circe' to you at New Years gave me such a picture! . . . the whole scene, the mood of the company, was as fresh and untroubled as Homer's world! For the Odyssey is Comedy—no matter how many tears, how many shipwrecks and other disasters, how many deaths of heroes, all all is going joyously to the happy ending—Happy? all those slaughtered suitors and the fifty servant-maids hanging with their feet twitching 'like little birds—' Yes, this is a comedy and everybody's end no matter what, is a part of the purifying ceremony for heart and mind."

Katherine Anne Porter had a way of taking for her own the happiness of another and doubling it for both. "Let me be happy in your happiness, in which I believe most firmly." She delighted in the everydayness of things. Once, going up the long flight of steps to our house above Lake Ontario, I heard the telephone ring. It was Katherine Anne. I told her that Hew was still coming up the steps, carrying honey for which we had vague plans. We might use it for a cake—there was an Italian recipe I wanted to try—or just pour it over ice cream. "Oh! Oh!" she exclaimed with surprising joy. "You don't know how I love to hear this!" She spoke memorably of happiness. She tells Morton Zabel, "Trust your happiness and the richness of your life at this moment. It is as true and as much yours as anything else that ever happened to you." Indeed, she had said of him what could well have been said of her. "Morton is a dear old faithful, and I do love and foster that quality above all in this world. He has such a wonderful kind of generosity of feeling about his friends—really suffers when they suffer, I never knew him to show one smallest streak of envy or jealousy or self-consciousness of any kind in his talk of his friends." Of faithfulness, she writes to her translator and friend, Marcelle Sibon, "Maybe you could not imagine from my long silence how very faithful my love to you was, is now, will be: times change, our situations, but strangely my heart does not; affection does become for me a kind of habit of the spirit."

The letters show a playfulness that is as much part of her as her voice or her glance. In the spring of 1952, the day after she spoke to students at Cornell, we were having coffee together, talking about beauty and falsity, perhaps, or of good and evil—we could have been talking about anything, for one felt oneself with her: it was the effect of her genius. Suddenly, with a comic expression on her face, she exclaimed, "We had better be good—even if for the wrong reasons! It shows in your face!" I could have told her—and perhaps did—that what showed in hers said she had been very good indeed. There is this sort of playfulness in one of her letters to Monroe Wheeler, instructing him how to approach her door on rue Notre-Dame-des-Champs in Paris. "When you come to my gate, which cannot be too soon, you mustn't—unless I have got a new bell system by then—do anything so simple and conventional as ringing. First you press the button, just for luck. Then you must knock, and then kick, probably, and then yell. There are two bells, one a kind of dinner bell on a wire, the other electric which rings in the kitchen. Neither work except just by chance . . . But in the end I will hear you, I promise, and come rushing out, all smiles." This is something like the way she instructed me to come to her door on Sixty-fifth Street in New York in 1950, the first time I came to visit her. "Ring three times and ask for Joe!" she told me when I telephoned her from Cambridge, where we were visiting my husband's family. "That's the way we used to get into the old speakeasies!"

Look at the photograph of her at her spinet on her sixty-first birthday in 1951, and you will see how she looked when she opened the door to my three rings—not so very different, I imagine, from the way she looked, some years earlier, when Edmund Wilson was "mesmerized" by her beauty the first time he met her: the straight honest glance, the sharp eyes that missed nothing, the hair brushed back from the high forehead. If you want to hear the sound of her voice, slip a cassette of "Noon Wine" into your player, for it was about this time that she recorded it. She was afraid that she breathed in all the wrong places. But listen to the low, well-controlled, slightly husky voice as you drive along the countryside or sit at home. You will be surprised at how well she tells her story; you will feel she is sitting beside you in the car, as we felt the last time we drove to Washington to work with these letters in the archives of the University of Maryland. At home, you will feel that she is in the room with you, talking to you, as she does in these letters.

"I love memoirs better than any kind of reading except somebody else's most private letters, after they are safely dead of course," Katherine Anne Porter writes to her friend Jim Powers. She might merrily argue whether any one is safely dead these days. But she is safely alive. Not long ago, her name was proclaimed from the stage of the Kennedy Center to the hundreds there celebrating the award of honors to artists and to the millions watching on television. Walter Cronkite opened the evening by saying, "Katherine Anne Porter says the arts 'are what we find again when the ruins are cleared away.' " Some years before, Schuyler Chapin had quoted these same words, from her introduction to *Flowering Judas,* at the close of the Metropolitan Opera season. These public proclamations of Katherine Anne Porter's words would have brought a smile to her lips as she slipped three sheets of blue onionskin into her typewriter to write the novel that has been translated into every important language in the world—even, not long ago, into Hungarian.

Katherine Anne Porter writes to her friend Eudora Welty, "I am harder to amuse than Queen Victoria, though for very different reasons." This sampler of letters gathered to celebrate her birth one hundred years ago—published almost a hundred years after Queen Victoria's death—might well have amused them both, if for different reasons. Katherine Anne had once written to her father, "I hope we shall make a feast for you on your hundredth birthday and put a crown of flowers on your head the way the French villagers do for their brave ancients who have weathered so many storms." Katherine Anne has made the feast for us—no one makes better feasts than she does—and her own words flower into this crown for her hundredth birthday.

SECTION 1

New York, Mexico, Berlin
April 1930 to September 1931

All I ask of any man is validity; and there should be place for every type and kind of mind. I don't want to lose any testimony.

Katherine Anne Porter to Josephine Herbst
February 11, 1931

IN MEXICO, RESTING AND RECOVERING FROM ANOTHER BOUT *with her lungs (twelve years after her near-death in the 1918 influenza epidemic), Katherine Anne Porter works and waits to hear whether she has won a Guggenheim. Kenneth Burke, Elizabeth Madox Roberts, Allen Tate, and Edmund Wilson sponsor her. She tells Kenneth Burke that she loves making good wine and making feasts and wants a house of her own. "Is that being a peasant? I doubt it. What created the governing caste in this world but love of land and a strong foothold? For once gotten, even a peasant could in so many generations rise to nobility. If so,—this is the kind of circular syllogism I like—then the rich are all peasants in their souls, and the non-aquisitive of this world are the aristocrats." As a Guggenheim Fellow, she sails for Europe and starts the ship's log that begins* Ship of Fools.

To Gay Holloway   [78 Orange Street
                           Brooklyn, N.Y.]
                           April 1, 1930

Dear Gay:

You're a set of frauds, always pretending that I don't write to you, for I answered your last letter at once, and that was at Christmas time. No word from any of you until today. So there, and there, and yonder.

Your opening lines sounded like a popular song: to be sung heartfeltly through the nose, thus:

> *Wondering if you're well,*
> *Wondering if you happy*

add:

> *Wondering if you're gone to hell*
> *to join your great grand-pappy*

but its a fine tune, just the same.

We are, you know, a superstition-laden set, in spite of our rationalist upbringing. You WOULD write inquiring just when I had, really, no joke this time, hit rock-bottom in health with a great thud. My lungs have gone back on me once for all, it seems, and I am being ordered out of this climate, and shall go to Guadalajara, Mexico, within the next ten days or two weeks. I should have been gone six weeks ago, but I have not been able to raise the boat-fare. Now, by dint of a great, concerted scramble on the part of my friends, I am about getting the money together. After I get to Mexico, the rest will be fairly easy, as I have contracts from a new publisher to write a novel, and they will pay me a $100 a month for six months, and my old publisher—the one who still hopes to get the Devil and Cotton Mather, will give me two hundred more, and as living is cheap and comfortable there, I can very likely get through a year. After that, I hope, as authors do, for royalties. I have no intention of dying, I never have, but I saw the X-ray of my lungs and they are pretty funny looking. But I have survived twelve incredibly active years since I was pronounced "arrested" in Denver, and I don't in the least doubt I can survive twelve more if sufficiently interesting inducements are held out to me. Last year in Bermuda I had five secure, comfortable months, and was just about finished with Cotton when the money gave out and I had to come back here, where I have done book reviews and fought colds all winter, and have done only two short stories and a little correcting on my manuscript. Its inexplicable why I must write, but I must, so there's no more argument with that business.

I would send you some of my things, but I don't see what interest book-reviews could have. Just now, this month, *The Hound & Horn,* a magazine published in Cambridge, has a short story of mine, called "Flowering Judas." Its a magazine of small circulation, but I believe if you went to the biggest book seller in town there, you might find a copy, or have them order it. Its by far the best thing I ever did, and is in the mood and style of the novel, so I want you to notice it. I would send one, but I have only one copy and the thing costs fifty cents, and I'd have to go to New York for it, and I'm not able. I have been in bed three days with fever, and am just up now, wondering if I'll go down again or get out of this place soon enough to do me any good. I go by boat, that's easiest travelling, and costs less.

What I meant to say about superstition, several paragraphs up, was, we are always getting hunches about one another and sending messages at crises. It seemed odd you'd pick on this nondescript time to write me?

I wish I might come to visit you, but I can't, for I've got one book to finish and another to write within a year at least, and when I'm not working I'll have to be resting, and a dull time you would have with me. A little book, with six of my ten published short stories is coming out in the fall—a very small edition of six hundred, only five hundred fifty for sale, and the publisher expects to sell most of them here in New York, but I'll have a few copies, and you'd better keep the ones I send you, because they're going to try to make a rare item of it, and it will be worth, they hope, large sums in a few years . . . I don't know why they do this, except that they're taking me over, and wish to start me off as handsomely as possible . . .

It is not necessary to explain any more, is it, that one doesn't seem to make any money with an enhanced reputation?

I have a way of getting tired, so must stop this, and add notes for the others. I will write to Dad, and don't make him think this is anything serious, for I am not really nervous, and even if I knew that this was the beginning of the end, I still wouldn't be nervous, for it is not death that troubles me, but the boresome process of disintegration, and I don't mean to go through with it past a certain point. When I am ordered to bed for the last time, I simply don't mean to go there. That'll settle all this nonsense of slow dying, a thing I could never grow accustomed to. You positively are forbidden to get upset; I've had such an entertaining life I would be an ingrate to complain when it must end: and now it is too late to die young. I do want to get just a little real writing done, otherwise the whole thing will seem a little pointless, for that was really what I wanted all along, and I am just now at the place where it seems possible . . . If I don't, it will be a pity. But I think I can do it.

Its very nice to think that all the children are intelligent, and some of them attractive, and it is very probable that the manners will improve with time; if they are given something for their minds to work on, I should rather let everything else take care of itself. I could wish you had the camera habit, and would take snapshots of your children from time to time. I can't help but feel that we shall all live to see them quite, quite grown-up, and it will be rather nice. . . .

Love and affections,
Katherine Anne

To Josephine Herbst   SS *Havana*
9 O'clock Monday Evening
April 28th, 1930

With the band playing, and dancing going on on deck, and the soft wind blowing, and stars, and all that, Miz Herrmann, such as you don't need any description of, since you've seen southern nights of late. Well, here am I, in a pinkish, streamerish sort of dress, and my green shawl, feeling almost human after four days and nights of ocean travel, regular food, and hours of idling in a deck chair. I left them stars and that bum orchestra to come in and give you a few details about that final bloody stand in New York, when after eight mortal weeks of trying, I finally pulled things together enough to take the boat. But why should I rehearse that now? Like the bitterness of death, it is past, and I shall some day remember it as just one more thing. Now, I confess, I'm a little flat.

Like you, in Florida, I ask myself why I am alone on this trip, when everything invites the softened mood, the howbeit fleeting joys of this and that: but its nothing new to me. I always am alone at such times. My one or two real love affairs were always something that dropped on me like a bolt in the midst of poverty, illness, and the exact middle of a piece of work, and love, for me, has been rather more as if I were a bundle of wheat going through the threshing machine than anything else. When I came through, I was clean winnowed. Not for me—very evidently—the window dressing of romantic settings and the leisure to taste my joy. When such moments come, I sit on deck and wonder where my life has gone, and why the pattern should have been as it was.

Helen Black came to the boat last Thursday, and told me you and John were back. Did you get my last letter before this? I feared you might not. It will follow you home, I hope. It would have been grand, Miss Josie, to have a look at you after your vacation. You must be a fine sight. Friends came to the boat with flowers and little other gifts, and it seemed really like a Good-bye To All That. Ordinarily I just go down and get aboard by myself, hating farewells. This time I wished terribly to see everybody I liked, as if my roots were being torn up. It is impossible to believe—no one ever does believe—that this tuberculosis business is coming out badly. But I don't know; I do know only that I have an anxiety to set everything in order, to do everything I have planned, to be sure of my friends, in a way I never quite felt until now. No more delays. No more unfinished work. . . .

> With love and affection to you
> . . . Write to me, Honey.
> *Katherine Anne*

To Gay Holloway   Calle Ernesto Pugibet 78
                                       Mexico D.F.
                                       May 30th, 1930

Dear Gay:

Your awfully amusing and delightful letter came some time ago now, and I have been meaning to answer it, but there is so much happening every day, I think I should wait until I can tell about it. Now when I begin telling, it would just be a dreary chronicle of looking for a house, finding it, and trying to get it furnished enough to live in. I have spent just a month at this, too long a time, but I must try to rest for so much time every day in spite of everything, and it slows me up.

Well, I do have a house, anyhow. And if anything blasts me out of it under two years, I am a wretch who deserves no sympathy. When I remember all the damned houses and apartments that I have taken, painted and decorated and furnished and then within two months would be forced to give them up, I am weary to the bone of such wasted effort. This is oldfashioned, very Mexican, a separate house built into a block, with a wide, tiled, wasteful hall, a wide staircase leading up to a small covered balcony, and four rooms and a bath run around this balcony. I have a bedroom, living room, and a beautifully private work-room, and a guest bedroom. There is a little kitchen, and a big roof with laundry tubs on it. You know well the kind of thing. I have filled the balcony with potted plants and little trees and ferns, and soon each iron balconied window will be blooming with the merry little domestic Mexican plants; I have a funny mixture of furniture bought here and there in the Monte Piedad and in second hand shops and at the San Juan market. But it is all very clean and sweet and quiet. The rent is forty dollars American a month. It is just precisely the right thing for me, and I expect to be busy and happy there. I shall have a young servant girl to do everything about the house. I shall do nothing but work, and in the intervals practise on the piano. I have wanted for years on end to study music, and now is my chance. I know a magnificent pianist who teaches here in the University, and he will give me lessons for about half of what even ordinary lessons would cost in New York. . . .

A letter came from Dad, who seems pleased with his new house, but clean damnified by the perversities of nature in regard to orange crops, and so on. When wasn't he so, the darling? I often thought the whole world would not sleep o' nights if it knew by what perilous margin the food supply was wangled out of the stubborn earth. I *never* knew a good season for crops in Texas or Louisiana, yet somehow the grains and fruits and vegetables come through, and the horses and cattle get fat. Dad long ago decided he had a specially venomous Voodoo on his trail, and I think he positively enjoys it. He seems, bless him, to get along and be fairly comfortable. And I remember seeing, in childhood, whole cart loads of cantaloupes and cucumbers and green corn and heaven knows what, being fed to the pigs. That's just it, Pop would rejoin. When there *was* a crop, there was no market. Yet I know that planting things and watching them grow has been his chief delight. A born southerner, positive product of an agrarian culture. I'm glad he has in his latter days the health and spirit and above all the conscientious freedom to enjoy his hard likker and his reading.

I hope you were able to find that magazine. Just the other day a letter came from Edward O'Brien in Switzerland, asking permission to reprint a story of mine in his annual collection; this year *The Best Short Stories of 1930.* It won't come out until fall. The story is called "THEFT" and was printed in a tiny little mimeographed review called *The Gyroscope* which ran for four numbers last year, got up by a very good poet and critic, Yvor Winters. Only a few people saw it, and I wrote it in a dreadful hurry, but I liked it and am glad it is going to have a wider circulation. Watch for this book. I will only have one copy sent to me. If you didn't get the magazine, don't worry. I will send all of you a copy each of the collected stories, called also *Flowering Judas,* after the main story. . . .

Your baby sounds lovely, I hope she grows up sound and sane and full of energy. I have dragged this heavy load ill-health too long, I am very tired of it. I hope she may study music if she wants. Living is very incomplete without it. I mean to settle down and study the sixteenth, seventeenth and eighteenth century music, Henry Purcell, William Byrd, Frescobaldi, the nice Lully and Rameau stuff, and I have a little rose wood piano, made in 1820, with a keyboard no bigger than a harpsichord, which I got for fifty dollars here, and was just made for the kind of music I want to play.

It is a precious little jewel, and almost a gift at the price. But a very old Spanish lady is breaking up her house, and wanted to sell it quickly. Even so, it was an extravagance, the kind I mean to commit every time I have the slightest opportunity. . . .

> a kiss and a hug and all that kind
> of thing.
> *Katherine Anne*

To Kenneth Burke   Calle Ernesto Pugibet 78
                                    Mexico, D.F.
                                    October 6, 1930

Dear Kenneth:

With you, and Elizabeth Madox Roberts, and Edmund Wilson, and Allen Tate, to give me a "character" to the Guggenheim Committee, I feel it can't be *quite* such a lottery, but some of their choices of late don't encourage me much. And if you could lay an eye on the Fellows recently arrived here, you would be twice confirmed in your pessimism about the aims and ends of that organization. But thank you for your goodness even if it probably will be wasted, materially speaking. Morally it will have its repercussions!

Usually I am an enthusiastic, nay an aggressive, writer of letters. I own most of the vices of my sex, and I believe letter-writing is considered one of the more dangerous of these: but your letter came in the midst of domestic upheavals, an unexpected visitor, and a heavy attack of tonsilitis, which is as funny as the mumps, I suppose, to the by-stander, and as painful as hell to the victim. I remembered all the pains I had had in my whole life, a curious and to me interesting assortment, and I decided firmly that THIS was the pain I would under no circumstances consent to have again. The worst of it was not that I fell behind with my novel, but my letters piled up and I felt full of news. It has taken all this time to recover from the uproar caused by a young woman who took her Mexico as other persons take to cocaine, and all the train of evils following.

The planned departure is still a year off, and I shall need this much time to finish up the things I have on hand. And if you are my friend, pray that a little of the creative abundance of Madame Sand may fall upon me, without that woman's extravagances—for heaven knows she wrote with a shovel—because I have the feeling of a river in me, but when it comes up to the surface it is a very small trickle. What does one do about this? Maybe I am deceived, and it is only a trickle within also. But I fear I must die believing otherwise.

You are right about one's own back yard, and don't I wish I had one? But I don't feel strange or exiled anywhere, and I began something here years ago that very evidently must be finished, in the long, laborious unbreakable line of personal experience that begins God knows when and ends only when the last vestiges of your existence have been demolished. So I can't battle with my life, for here it is, and thus and so it was with me, and when I am finished with it, it will have been recognizably a life.

Mexico is changing so rapidly one grows dizzy watching, and all toward Chamber of Commerce ideals. At least, the show-Mexico, that surface now being exposed carefully by organized Tourists' Bureaus, Airways Corporations, Hotel Associations, Cultural Relations societies of all kinds. The Indian is poorer than ever, his heels are cracked as deeply, his face as despairing, he is more than ever a paintable object for the make-believe primitives. The Department of Public Charities holds enormous lotteries to pay the salaries of its officers, and justifies its existence by taking a half-hearted survey of the beggar situation, without doing anything about it. However, a great many maimed, diseased persons who would otherwise be beggars make half a living by selling the tickets, and the Department employs many worthy young politicians who would otherwise have to work, and in this oldfashioned way the thing limps along. The laws passed to protect Labor work out in this literal way: The law forbids factories employing large numbers of workers to move its plant to another part of the country, thus throwing its present employed out of work. The factories—I am using the cigarette factories as example—in the Federal District are taxed very heavily. Several of the factory owners have appealed for permission to move to another district where taxes shall be less. They have been forbidden to go. Upshot: They closed their doors on the grounds that they are operating at a loss. When I go down my street to the post-office I see several hundred workers sitting forlornly on the steps and sidewalk of the cigarette factory, locked out, but refusing to go away, while the owners and the board of arbitration wrangle, and several labor leaders ride once more the wave of publicity. I give you this concrete example of economic disjointedness for comparison with your theory—gradually there becoming practise—of employment and leisure.

There are other things here: The main streets are now lousy with Art Shoppes where you pay a peso for a blue goblet that you once bought in the market for ten centavos from the Indian who made it. The Indian still gets his ten centavos from the Art Shoppe owner. Various American art-lovers have scattered out to the old pueblas to teach the Indian how to "refine" his product and make it more acceptable to the market. One, at least, of the schools of Fine Arts gets its main revenue by manufacturing painted beds— with American canned paints—for the new country houses of the more recent politicians, and carving imitation Aztec statues for their gardens. Among the last, I was most impressed by a squat female figure with a hose attachment running up through the seat, arranged to spout water from one of the breasts. The place is stuffy with Hubert Herrings holding "seminars" and so on for God's sake. The famous free Fresh Air Schools subsist, evidently, on praise, for there are no funds for their support.

Shall I go on? The Crane (Fancy Plumbing) Foundation has a representative here taking those "surveys" without which life cannot go forward an inch, presumably; he is acting—in concert with others scattered about strategic spots in the world—on an official, but secret? dream of gaining moral power by boring into the country, like a worm, and establishing himself as the Mexican member of a little group of the Elect, such as Pythagoras and Plato put their faith in. They're going to achieve this by helping to establish Big Business Firms in the different countries, aiding all civic and moral enterprises besides, preaching the gospel of higher standards of living—including fancy plumbing, no doubt—and aiding the government they live under so effectively that they will become morally indispensable, and practically so powerful that this little company of Keymen will rule the world. "Picking other peoples brains is the first step to power," says one of the Keymen, ingenuously. And their program is to pick brains and pocket books so adroitly that the Foundation will get all the credit for noble works while other men and firms supply most of the brains, do their work and furnish considerable quantities of cash. A plumber's idea of ethics, I should say. Mexico is the God-sent stamping ground for this kind of disguised banditry. I suppose it is much the same everywhere, but here it is so obvious—every smallest step taken towards economic re-adjustment, or even mere alleviation of present suffering, degenerates at once into a little combine of grafters and careerists who collect money to finance the project, advertise it extensively, and so fatten—but the readjustment and alleviation somehow mysteriously fail to come. It is maddening to see.

In the meantime there are rumblings of upheaval in the real political circles: the military men who run the show. The lesser job holders are running for cover to the side which seems likeliest to win, and I suppose we shall have a little—or big—blow-up soon. Its a matter of time. The whole trouble is simply that this country is so menaced from within and without, nothing ever settles long enough to take shape. Its a vast and dreadful scramble for mere personal physical survival for everybody from the President down to the Indian selling peanuts on the corner, and everybody lives in the perpetual shadow of poverty or death, or both . . . No, really, Kenneth, it seems quite different from the United States as I look at it now. Or rather, all the human problems are distorted and magnified, so that the perspective is different. Poverty is a constant problem for millions everywhere, and death menaces us alike: but it seems more immediate and unescapable here, more universal.

Don't believe the rosy-edged tourists who come back fuddled with good liquor and sight-seeing—(this is a heavenly beautiful place—) if they tell you this is not a tragic suffering country.

If you think you ramble and take advantage of me, let's think no more of that.

Echoes of the Labor Day festival reached even here, and I wish I could have been there. I love making wine—I make very good wine, too—and making feasts, and I badly want a house of my own where I can keep my books and have a soft bed. There are 135 acres in Pennsylvania, with an old stone house on top of a hill, empty, going to rack, that I used to visit and imagine that I have five hundred dollars to pay down on it, and then I would sit all afternoon making improvements. They ran into time, labor, and money, let me tell you, but the place was perfect when I had finished with it. Is that being a peasant? I doubt it. What created the governing caste in this world but love of land and a strong foothold? For once gotten, even a peasant could in so many generations rise to nobility. If so,—this is the kind of circular syllogism I like—then the rich are all peasants in their souls, and the non-aquisitive of this world are the aristocrats. I love fireplaces and horses and automobiles and winecellars and lakes to swim in. But selfishly, for happiness merely. Do you mean that there is also an esthetics in the possessive? If so, I agree with you. And I should like to add something about the mythical relation in certain acquisitive natures—between their possessions and their own personal worth, but I am tired and can't think out the sentence that would make it clear. I think you will know what I am driving at.

The reviews of my book have been astoundingly friendly. I saw those in the *Times,* the *World,* the *Herald-Tribune.* And Allen did wonders in the *Nation.* I feel a little crushed by it, and say, "This is all very well, but I must do better than this . . ." But its a very fine way of being crushed, and I'll survive it better than I would have the kind of blow I might very well have got instead, except for this happy fortune of having fallen into good hands for a reading. What a letter, Kenneth. I hope you work through it somehow.

Sincerely,
Katherine Anne

To ALLEN TATE   Ernesto Pugibet 78
                                     Mexico, D.F.
                                     January 27, 1931

Dear Allen:

I think Caroline must have got my letter about the time you wrote yours, and then she wrote, and I had a fine time for a day or two reading the poems and the letters; your poems, let me tell you, were rather gay by contrast, for here we have had a steady, gnawing cold that takes the heart right out of me, and I think of Louisiana and Texas summers, and my summer in Bermuda, and if any one will listen I talk about heat so great one is pale and streaming and lives in straw slippers when one isn't getting in a tub of cold water, and not one of these Yankees believe me; least of all do they believe it is the most lovely and desirable way of life. Besides we have had earthquakes. I suppose you have heard. Oaxaca was almost destroyed, the papers here made very little of it, and I did not realize until I saw Eisenstein's pictures. A long record of broken walls and people kneeling or sitting stunned, motionless as the ruins behind them.

Here, about fifty houses fell, and about twenty five persons were hurt, and two were killed . . . But you might know I would see nothing of that. I was sitting here in my house at supper with a friend, who looked up at the electric light swaying rather wildly, and said with great calmness: "There's an earthquake." Then the floor began to heave gently under our feet like an anchored ship and through the open kitchen door I saw my Teodora swaying, barely able to keep her feet, holding the kitten, with a look of blind terror in her face. We went and took her by the arms, and my friend said sternly, "You can't kneel here," like a policeman, for she was going down slowly, and we groped our way down stairs in the darkness and out into the street. The lights had been cut off, and the city was dark except for a curious greenish, reddish light. My street was quiet, except for a family halfway down the block, kneeling together crying, "Jesus, Mary, and Joseph," in a long monotone, and Teodora was murmuring "Jesus Mary and Joseph" under her breath, kneeling and holding my hand. The earth rocked under us, I was dizzy, and we held on to the lamp post, but it was not violent: a long groundswell, dismaying because you cannot believe earth is moving under you like a sea. Nothing happened to us. It lasted for a little more than four minutes, the lights came on, we went back upstairs and stood on the balcony listening to the fire alarms, and the ambulances shrilling through the streets. We laughed with relief, and were proud of not having been frightened. But nobody thought of finishing supper, and all the next day I almost leaped out of my shoes when the walls creaked.

There have been little tremors since, I only know it because my head suddenly hurts violently, and then I see the electric bulbs beginning to sway as if blown as a wind, and the doors swing open and close again, but it passes at once, and shortly the streets are filled with newsboys yelling "Another earthquake!" But this has

28

not happened for four days now. Rumors come in of harmless looking mountains suddenly gaping and hurling out stones and lava, of a village overhung with heavy black and red clouds, of plagues broken out here and there . . . but all apocalypses take place elsewhere, as you know. I went to hear a concert conducted by Stokowsky, and to a supper party to meet Eisenstein, and this morning I went with Teodora to market to see if okra was really in season. It was. I spanked my kitten for climbing on the table, and practised Bach preludes for two hours on the piano, and have worked on the novel—that novel! My God—for four hours, and now I am going to bed because it is almost midnight . . . There were other things in the day but I don't remember them.

Donald Davidson alleging a political and social crisis as his reasons for giving up poetry would make me gloomy if I had not already passed the gloom stage through irritation to cold fury on this subject. It is strange to see happening in the southerners—some of them—the same thing that is happening everywhere else. Here, I listen to that kind of talk until I simply exhaust myself with rage. I will NOT sit down under it, and I have said to several that no man gives up the thing he cares for most, does best, and has a vocation for. If, I tell them sourly, they find they were mistaken, and are not painters or poets, or prose writers, it is just as well they have found it out, and waste no more time on it, besides adding to the multitude of aspiring mediocrities in the arts. But I think they are being disingenuous, to say the least, to pretend they are giving up art as a grand sacrifice to revolution, to devote themselves to humanity. If they are artists, they are cheating themselves and the race by reneging on the task they took up; AND (peroration) it is a dog-in-the-mangerish attitude to say to artists who know what they are doing and are sticking by the thing they believe in, that it is treason to society to work in the arts in this grand social crisis. If they have found a new interest, something they can do better, let them for God's sake go and get about it, and leave the artists alone. Also— (getting a fresh breath) a man can be a revolutionist and an artist, but it is not necessary. The artist who comprehends his time and the movement of the world in which he lives brings something better to it than mere agitations and controversy . . . He may join in these, but there is something beyond, and his value lies exactly in his sense of the beyondness—and so forth, but of course you'd hardly want to be so severe with Donald Davidson who is a good poet, and is probably going through a very healthy period of upset and aberration. But I am thoroughly sick of artists talking against art. There is treason if treason ever was. . . .

I hope you can persuade Andrew to prune the abundance of his prose, for abundance is a great gift, but remind him that no orchard is any good without the pruning hook freely used . . . and speaking of that, this letter is running wild.

The cabin was to come next, but I'll write about that to Caroline with many other topics; I want to write about your poems, but you know that I can't say anything further than I like this, or I prefer this, the reasons I give wouldn't mean much. I have a feeling that "The Oath" is the best poem because it has the most difficult measure, successfully done, and the best images, and if not the deepest then almost the deepest feeling, and for me the most subtle, hard-to-express idea . . . I simply mean that something so shadowy it can almost not be apprehended has been caught and expressed; the last six lines are as perfect as I could wish for . . . "The Twelve" and "The Paradigm" seem to me equal to what you have done before except "The Ode," the other two are good, but these three are wonders. Are you getting a second book together? I should think you might be, with these.

It was good of you to send them, and I wish I had something to send back, proving that treason to the social crisis is going on here and there, in some places quite shamelessly. But God knows I cannot get a paragraph to please me these days. If I didn't know it can't last, I should be terrified. I'm terrified anyhow, and have a recurring dream of Time as a thing past, done forever, I stand in a world in which nothing has changed apparently, but nothing more can come to pass because there is no more Time. And this dream has more horror than any ferocious nightmare filled with monsters, such as we have in childhood. But I suppose if I get scared enough, the thing will straighten itself out.

Looking at that, I hope no good old-fashioned Freudian ever hears of it. . . .

Affections,
Katherine Anne

To Josephine Herbst   Mexico, D.F.
                             February 11, 1931

Josie darling,

Your splenidorous letter came about an hour ago, and I am so
zipped up by it I run to answer . . . Not that the news about your
prodigal tonsils was so pretty, but everything else was. Are you
joking when you say your tonsils come back? I've always heard they
do, if they're not uprooted properly, and I have always been embittered about it. It would be tonsils instead of teeth, wouldn't it?
Good ole Mother Nature, the old bitch!

I hope you outwit the business somehow. Your spirits, I must
say, don't seem to cower under affliction.

There isn't an address above, you'll note, and that's because
I'm moving to a small town near by, Mixcoac, to a street named
Tiziane, and as my mail would have to go through two postoffices,
I'm taking a Box here; you'll find the number on the envelope. I
don't know it yet.

This town gets noisier and dustier and my house is badly
situated, so I don't get the air I should, nor sunlight. So I'm taking,
with Mary Doherty—the model, you might say, for Laura in "Flowering Judas"—and a young man named Eugene Pressley—Let me
begin that sentence again. I'm just barely out of bed and half-awake.
With the two named above I am taking an immense, rambling
country-kind of house, ten rooms, endless outrooms, a roof to
ramble on, a beautiful garden with a fountain in it, and a big fruit
garden with a small swimming pool. The house is in perfect condition, and I shall have a big sunny room on the roof to work in, miles
away from the rest of the household. I take my servant, a good
humored sloppy soul who has Seen Life—she was a woman soldier
for several years—and Mary is taking hers, a pinched but neat and
orderly old maid, and I hope they don't kill each other. Mary's
woman is a Totonac, and mine is Otomi, and these two tribes never
did like each other. Before this, I had an Aztec, and I don't like
them. We'll see how it goes. I have a charming but headstrong
yellow lady-cat, now kittening for the first time, and a perfectly
round, coal-black puppy of dubious lineage, though I think he has
terrier blood. He is a love and a curse, but he'll be all right when

he has a half acre to run in. Mary has a singing bird and two goldfishes. We'll see how this goes, too. Mister Pressley is No-body's Fool, but heroic, I think to venture. The bond is this: we're all mad for country and garden and sun, and there is plenty of room. Each one of us will have a private sitting room and bedroom, and plenty to spare for a common dining and living room, and the place is so big we can be where we like and not see each other. We share expenses, and our rent will be a little less than twenty American dollars for each one. There are baths and ovens and dressing closets and servants quarters and everything on the grand scale of a pros-perous Mexican family of fifteen members. The house is very sim-ple, running along all the rooms opening to the east on a porch with a glass roof. Fifteen persons must just the same have been crowded there, but the Mexican families are like your Russian people—like most human beings, I think—they love to live sitting in each other's pockets and hanging around each other's necks. (But I'll arrive by easy stages at your tremendous comments on Russia.)

Mary and Eugene will commute to town by electric train every day—about thirty minutes. Mary works for the government in the Public Charities—the net result of this revolution is that now sev-eral politicians have good jobs and can buy air-planes and ranches on the public charity money—and Eugene is Secretary of the Crane Foundation for International something or Other, I never quite inquired enough to get it straight. BUT anyhow—for I can't seem to wangle through this—I'll be in the place all day free to get my chores done—after all I merely have now two books in arrears instead of one—and the three of us have enough furniture to fill the place, and our shared expenses will come to about fifty dollars a month each, (about 110 pesos) where all of us are now spending nearly two hundred pesos each a month. Its a little private, anarch-ical venture at Communism, ha, ha.

Every one who pops in at the Tates goes away sending raptur-ous accounts of the place, but yours was the best. I am trying to pinch out enough money for them to build me a cabin, for I think once the young farmer is in he won't be easy to dislodge, but I shan't be able to occupy it for some time to come, if my present plans come out. I applied for the Guggenheim Fellowship, and if I get it I mean to spend most of my time in Russia, and Germany maybe, but I want to hear from you how Germany is now. I'd like a look at several other countries for the sake of getting a whole idea. It looks hopeful for the Fellowship, but I shan't know until the first part of March. If it comes through, I shall stay here until fall, maybe later, and then go straight on, I suppose, for I will never have enough money to make the visits I should like first. I want badly to see you and John, and the Tates, and the Cowleys, and Becky and John Crawford, and my father. But if I can't, I can't, and what I wish you would do is come on here now, because the hot season is going to be on us in about two weeks more, and you could sprawl on the roof like a lizard, and swim in the tank. God knows I'm going to work, but you'd be a puffick inspiration, Misz Stroller; that John comes too is understood, but mostly I'm thinking of your tonsils; even if Mister Stroller has no mortal infirmities, a little trip wouldn't hurt that old Stay-at-home a bit. I wish you had taken that Scribner money and come here with it instead of going to Florida. After all, you'd seen Florida, hadn't you? Here we had a devilish winter, too—the worst, of course, in forty years, though I seem to remember one just as bad ten years ago, and again seven years ago—but spring, which is to say summer, is upon us, and for hours everyday the sun is warm and the grand snow-covered volcanoes shine through the clouds around their necks.

Back to plans. If I don't get the Fellowship, I shall stay here until I've finished up, anyhow, and then I suppose I'll go to Tennessee and gouge myself into that cabin, and try to earn my living by writing. And if my books don't go well, there I will be . . . That seems to be about all. I thought if one got a cabin as a nucleus, one could add a lean-to on one side, and then another cabin criss-cross on the corner, and a cook-cabin some yards away with a covered path to it, and little by little have an honest rural retreat that one could really live in. We'll see.

I think your comments on Russia are the freshest and best I have seen. You really should write a few lines for Mike's magazine about it. And the contrast with the miserable, intriguing rotten-souled Poles;* I have only known a few of them, but they were all such as you describe. I think Communism is well on the way to world-power, but I suppose it will suffer sea-changes and modifica-

*These were the nobility and landowners and absentee politicians: Lubomirski, Radziwill, et al.

tions as it goes until the core is dispersed into something else which the generations to come will make of it. That's natural enough, but Communism is the next thing, I feel pretty certain. But it is odd that suddenly there is no place for people to live except in crowds . . . it seems to me room might be made, as for in time even the most gregarious soul is going to grow sick of jogging elbows every time he turns around. Russia seems to have this effect on most people who are convinced by what they find there; they begin to despise artists . . . but we shouldn't do that. We should only despise certain kinds; the piffling little souls who would be just piffling no matter what they did. These are hangers-on and campfollowers. I'm tired of the artist being considered a pet, or a pariah, or a prostitute, or a protegée—isn't that a swell line of alliteration? But those are the words I needed. I'm sick of the artists who think of themselves as any of these things. Unless writing, or painting, or whatever, is your life and nothing else will do, and unless you have the power to make this dedication effective, its no good. And I'm for putting the dabblers in those community kitchens and rock piles, where they belong. It wouldn't hurt the best artists to go there a while, too . . . Life comes first, an art not rooted in human experience is not worth a damn, but different kinds of minds have different kinds of experience, and all I ask of any man is validity; and there should be place for every type and kind of mind. I don't want to lose any testimony; it may be necessary for one man to sit wound up in his own vitals in order to find out what he needs to know, and his discoveries will be valuable if he is capable of telling the truth. Another must be wound up in the world around him . . . some must be active, and some contemplative. There are some kinds of work which require silence and concentration, like a very delicate chemical experiment. Others can be carried on under steam rivetters, and I shall never see why we must have one to the exclusion of the other, when we need both. (My! What a burst of Moral Maxims!) You are right, none of us live enough, and sometimes I think it is because we mistake hurrah and hullabaloo for experience, we get a sock in the eye and think it is a broken heart, something really important happens to us and we are in such uproar of movement we don't know anything about it until we find a quiet moment to realize it. I love living at high voltage, with speed and precision, but I want to be sure it isn't just speed and nothing else . . . I don't want to fool myself with slogans and the latest Ultimate Truth

. . . So far as I can gather from the intelligent Communists I have talked to here, they are over the religious crusade stage, and have grimly and realistically set about seeing their plan through, not because they think it is perfect, but because they really believe it is the next thing to do, the present situation of the world being quite impossible to accept. I like this, it makes me want to try to help. But I suffer here a good deal from the kind of puking little hangers-on that all movements must have, I suppose . . . those who refuse to wash their hands or put on a clean shirt, and think this, and an ability to live by "borrowing" money from their poor-fish friends who are silly enough to work for the capitalist system, makes them good Communists. I have advised several of these to go to Moscow and get their bottoms paddled. . . .

Have you read Kay Boyle's short stories. They are very gorgeous, but I feel as you do about Faulkner—there is something a little off somewhere in this talent, or maybe it is just that she is a little shrill and noisy because she isn't quite certain . . . If she goes the right way, she ought to be first rate. Or she may just fall into the egotistical self-exploitation that some very clever writers—women, I think especially—fall into. Like Becky West, for example, and a very good one. Her later critical articles—so fresh and keen and lively—got so mixed up with her black lace Paris dresses and her choice of perfumes and her romantic private life and her personal relations with notable people, that I couldn't read her any more. At last she has married a banker, I believe, and luxurious living won't be such a novelty to her that she can't keep from telling about it . . . I hope Kay Boyle gets over her toughness that is just a thin layer over what seems perilously like apple-sauce beneath, and that the inner fiber strengthens and warms a little. Then she's going to be grand. I'm reviewing her book, and I mean to praise it because she is good almost in spite of herself . . . She most certainly has something worth noticing. "Polar Bears And Others"—"Uncle Anne"—"Madame Tout Petit"—"On the Run"—these are I think enormously good. All of them are more than good, except "Wedding Day." Its just that suspicion of taint that keeps cropping out, and I can't quite locate the source . . . I haven't read a word of Faulkner. I can't get such books here, they are so expensive when they come at all, and I miss so much I want badly to see. Maybe I can get it at the American library, but its very small.

I read Caroline's story and I thought it good, but was anecdotal and the end seemed to me too abrupt, and the boy's last words a little too dragged in . . . It was as if Caroline herself wanted to say, "Aint that just like a Yankee?" and took this way of saying it. But what I saw of her book was good.

Josie, I'm sorry this letter is so crowded together but something has happened to the spacer, and it won't work except in single. Tussle through it if you can.

One of the best endings I remember in your stories is the old man standing on the staircase looking up at the place where the bunch of bananas had hung. I can't tell you why that gave—and gives—me the gooseflesh. And another is the ending of "I hear you, Mr. and Mrs. Smith." Did they get "Money For Love" translated into Russian? I think you put your finger in a word on what I felt about that book, but never really got it said. Pinched. As I read, I kept thinking of how your mind works, and how much you really know about people, and what you could say, and I hated seeing you deliberately paring to the bone, deliberately leaving out so much of your characters that I could not get to them. There was simply more in all those people than you chose to admit, I felt. And there wasn't any of the implications of more-ness such as made *Nothing is Sacred* such a beautiful book. Somehow you wouldn't give us the right to feel the more-ness in the second book. But in your short stories you always have this. Its the thing that makes them so damned memorable. Well, just hop on the way you're hopping, and it will be fine with me!

This is no letter, its one of these here now human documents . . . And it must end. Think seriously of coming to Mexico for a little visit. You'd be sure, here, of sunshine during the worst part of the Pennsylvania season. Even if the Florida sunshine puts up good competition, come along anyhow. The Mexican sun is different, for we're more than a mile nearer to it. The altitude is something to be surprised at.

Good bye, for the moment. Give my love to Mister Rover, tell him I hope he is purty as ever, and writing two novels at once.

Oh, hell, come on and visit.

Love,
Katherine Anne

After you once got here, your expenses would hardly be anything.

Forgot to tell you about Eisenstein. He's gone to the Isthmus.

Expect to see him again when he comes back. I enclose a caricature which describes him perfectly. He alternates between this grin and a look of most appalling solemnity. When he showed up the government, which is riding six horses at once, wanted to admit him, but at the same time show the world that this Mexico was no haven for Reds. or Bolshevikis, as they are called here. So Eisenstein was arrested and kept in jail overnight by one set of officials, and released next morning with bows, smiles and apologies by another set. He isn't a Party Member, and didn't appreciate the joke . . . (says he isn't, I mean, for he doesn't dare to do or say anything else). So the night of the dinner, we all went to the theatre at midnight to see the first run of his Oaxaca earthquake pictures, and when he left, I said I hoped to see him when he got back from the Isthmus. "Oh, yes, I'll see you," he said, "Unless they put me in jail or something, down there, with their confusing Mexican hospitality!" and the Mexicans present looked as if they had swallowed their oyster forks. He's all right. . . .

To Caroline Gordon   Apartado 2075
                            Mexico, D.F.
                            April 24, 1931

Dear Caroline:

News upon news, or so it seems from this vantage point. Edmund Wilson writes that he will be in Mexico in June. Janet Winters has a baby named Joanna, which of course you know. The news about that is Janet's calm way of disposing of the business in record time, a prize delivery, I call it, and her comment that it was hard to believe that she had really Joanna, "who is charming." And so home and no doubt back to the novel in ten days. This is the impression I received. Fancy writing letters with a five day old baby! Should not that woman be given a medal of some kind?

Peggy Cowley writes she is coming to Mexico in July. And others. But HART CRANE CAME! Did he! He bust in upon me one evening, screamed with joy over the garden, saw the big front room standing empty, declared he could live no where else in Mexico, and could he move out the next day? He was most lordly lit, and I thought it a drunken whim, and said, why naturally yes, and the next day he showed up cold sober with trunks and bags and in two days he was dug into that room with the victrola going, which has never stopped. He is wild with delight and enthusiasm. Gets out and waters the gardens and digs around the rose-bushes and suns himself on the tank ledge, and ramps up and down roaring fragments of Blake, Christopher Marlowe and Hart Crane. Goes to the market and comes back loaded down with grass mats and bandy legged tables. Gets up in the morning and feeds the turkeys and chickens First turning on the victrola. Goes four times a day for two litres of barrel beer wearing a red sweater and carrying a long blue glass pitcher. At the present moment he is pounding the piano, which I had not succeeded in moving out of the sala and now when I mention removing it he looks grieved. But its coming out just the same. Gene, my best young man, gets along with him up to a point. By supper time, Hart is usually nicely under the influence of beer—he seems to drink nothing else, and after two steins, Gene is apt to say, "Stop talking rot" when Hart gets explaining what all is wrong with my attitude towards Mexico. And so it goes. He wants to keep the house when We give it up, and that's a very good thing. This place is too lovely to let pass away entirely. And Its big enough, I presume, to hold us all until September.

All the Guggenheim Fellows for Mexico are here except Marsden Hartley. They must have taken the next boat. Such dispatch is not for me. But the novel gets on, I expect it to be gone by September 1. I've been remembering darkly all the things that happened in the country when YOU had Hart Crane in the same house, and I am still wondering how on earth this thing came about. The first night h⌐ got out and had a fight with a taxi driver and they went to the police station on a little matter of fare, another night he was raging about in the streets quite drunk, and a policeman came home with him, and we had—rather, Gene had—some pother to get the policeman out. He seemed to want sociability and a drink. Echoes of the riot ascended to my cloistered chamber, and the next day I lectured Hart in my most motherly Dutch Aunt style. He vowed that he had Made Resolutions—from this out I should see a changed man. So far, it holds. I would give a good deal to have again such ecstatic gayety and joy over Mexico as he has. He is happy in the sun as one of Blake's little skippling lambkins. We shall see!

I saw the announcement of "The Ice House" for the next number of H & H. God knows its time for them to have a good short story. The last, I think, was Kay Boyle's "Episode in the Life of An Ancestor." Have you read her novel? It is simply beautiful. At last I got hold of Faulkner's *The Sound and the Fury* and it curdled the marrow in my bones. I have never seen such a cold-blooded assault on the nerve-ends, so unrepentant a statement of horror as that book. And such good bold sound writing. That must be taken for granted, for only a very good writer indeed could do what he has done. It left me so shaken and unnerved I could hardly believe the face of the sun. Not, of course, that one doesn't read worse in the newspapers, every day. Not that I haven't myself seen a man burned at the stake. A few days ago a girl was taken into a beggar's flop-house here by two men dressed as policemen. They asked to leave her there because, they said, she was lying drunk in the street. When the keeper investigated the next morning she was dead, and a broken bottle had been forced into her womb. Not that things don't happen. But my *God!* There should be something in a work of art that gives you something to hang onto after the very worst has been told. Still, I want to read *As I Lay Dying.*

(See above. And the men were not policemen at all. They had taken off the uniforms in the alley-way as they left.)

It seems a long time since I heard from you. I do wish you had gone after the Fellowship business in time, and I hope you do next year. They seem to have a way of asking you to re-new your application from one year to the next. You'd undoubtedly have it the next time. But its quite a lot of red tape to go over again. I am still sending doctor's certificates and receipts for material sent and so on. Its been going on since last November. But I hope you'll send your application again, and maybe we would see each other in Europe after all.

(Something has happened again to this spacer.)

I just have a letter from Andrew, telling about his eightyfive mile advance towards Mexico when he was recalled about Forrest . . . I wish he would come to Mexico. There's a man would talk sense about it.

Honey, do drop me a line when you have a minute. Which means of course, do take an hour and write me a long letter. I want to hear about you.

love,
Katherine Anne

From the uproar downstairs, I gather that Hart—it is now seven-thirty—has just broken a lamp and is howling in French at the Indian woman because she hasn't heated his shaving water. He is at the saturation point, I take it. Does he always behave like this? Something tells me the sala is shortly going to be vacant again.

To Josephine Herbst   Apartado 2075
                                            Mexico, D.F.
                                            June 1, 1931

Josie darling,

I can scarcely wait to take the words to tell you my own sad history. By itself it is nothing, but viewed side by side with yours, I call it a marvellous and wonderful mess of coincidence.

Briefly then: (which means get ready for page after page). About seven weeks ago my right foot grew so lame and swollen and roaring hot with fever that I was fair crippled and went hobbling around suffering at the top of my voice, convinced that I had at least tuberculosis of the bones. I went to my doctor, who made X-rays of the chest and pronounced my famous T B gone again. But gone. Hardly a spot. No symptoms. "But," says he, listening intently through the stethoscope, "I certainly don't like the sound of your heart. I didn't like it last year, but I thought it was just nervousness. Now its something else. Would you," says he, "Kindly bring me a sample of your pee-pee?" I said, "Never mind my heart and the rest. What's the matter with my foot?" And he says (this is a bad case of total recall I have just now) "I'll tell you about that later." So I staggered back with the specimen, and he had it analysed, and then he said in effect that I was to take three large and dangerous looking capsules every day, and was never again to touch red meat,

40

ales, wines or liquors, only the breast of chicken, and green vegetables world without end. That I was to leave this altitude as soon as I could and live at sea-level more or less. Now here is the point: he said I had a hereditary disease, a very high faluting one, and did any of my ancestors belong to the nobility, by any chance? I said, "WILL you break down and tell me what I've got?"

Then he rose and took a large tome off the shelf, and said, "Doctor Alexander Sydenham" (now why should I even remember that name?) "was a great authority on your trouble and here's something he says that may comfort you a little." Then he read: "It may be truly said that more wise men than fools have suffered from this disease." I got all set up to hear some elegant polysyllabic name for my complaint; he said, "You've got the gout. And a fine classical case if ever I saw one."

And that is what it is, Misz Herrmann. Gout, which knocks your heart into a cocked hat and ties your kidneys up in bow knots, and believe it or not, I'm a solid mass of uric acid or worse. How I miss my dear old T B which permitted me to smoke my head off and drink myself under the table and eat a rare steak every day if I could get it. I have not had one drop of drink for five weeks today, my vegetable diet is already palling my palate, but after those capsules and an intravenous shot of something that had iodine in it, my foot has gone down to normal and that heart has stopped turning somersaults every time I run up stairs. To say nothing of the kidneys. They string along in the general welfare. But don't you think our histories make a lovely pair? Here I was eating red meat and giving myself the gout, and you eating green vegetables and giving yourself the hives, all to the greater glory of God. Moreover this doctor says that my T B hasn't been dangerous for years, it was the uric acid getting me down all along. And while I was congratulating myself that I had a heart of oak, he says why I haven't dropped dead only God knows.

Ah, dear—wouldn't you like to get at the real truth about health? My sole proof at present that this is not a wild goose chase is the undoubted fact that I am able to walk after limping for weeks, and that I feel in tremendous health and spirits. I don't know what you're planning to do with your old age, Misz Herrmann, but I have mine all settled. I'm going to sit in a big chair with one foot tied up in a large bundle, and I'm going to glare over steel rimmed specs and pound on the floor with a knobbly, brass tipped cane. That's what the gouty old uns do. And by golly, I don't blame 'em. Steel specs aside, I almost did it already during this siege.

What is there to do about sicknesses—our own, I mean, but to make fun of them? I wish I could ridicule my pains out of existence. Lord knows nobody could take gout seriously. Not seriously, but respectfully, you bet. The consequences of falling away from diet and treatment are too sudden and certain. The next day I'd be all swolled up and hot and full of shootin' pains. No thank you! But now we can lean on each other for moral support when the liquor is being passed around. For me this is bitter. I do love to drink. Did, I mean. Do, is what the hell I mean, Misz Herrmann. I feel like somebody got religion and just about to backslide again any minute. I'd pray against temptation if I thought it would help. The doctor hinted that coffee and cigarettes were better away, too. I told him plainly that I'd die without my coffee, and I'd kill any man who tried to take away my cigarettes. Still, I have cut out coffee except two large beautiful cups in the morning; the cigarettes, however, remain ever between the fingers. . . .

Nearly midnight. Gene just came in to say good night. I suppose it has been rather like holding out on something, Miz Herrmann, about the Blonde Young Man. He was much about the house when Peggy Cowley was here, and she liked him very much, and was advising me—in October—that really, something should be done about all this. Truth is, we are having an anniversary towards the end of this month. But I simply could not tell Peggy, even face to face, and there was nothing to explain in a letter. I think I wanted to know myself first what was happening, what was going to happen . . . I don't trust myself much in these things. Gene is really a grand person, but very quiet, extremely balanced, not very easy to know, and so far as I can discover, doesn't care much about anybody except me. He is Communist but not a party member, has no ambition, and simply cannot be stampeded into false situations or false behavior. He has been the same person twenty four hours a day for one year, and he loves me so steadily and infallibly I can hardly believe it. He has worn through my fits of nerves, my depressions, my illnesses, my general hellishness with a kind of super human patience and friendliness, if those words could half express the solid rock of love and goodness that simply never lets me down for even half a minute. I haven't been able to work, but it is not his fault. He found this house, did nearly all the work of fixing it, I have elbow room and all my time that I could use to myself if I could use it, now that my allowance is stopped he takes care of me, bawls out our Teodora if she comes up stairs when I am here, and makes my life as easy for me as I will let it be made. He has a realistic tough mind, a little too inclined to dismiss things not perfectly clear-cut, I think this is his youngness—he is only twenty-seven, and if I could find a fault with him, it would be for the clean sweep he is inclined to make of everything he doesn't agree with. But this doesn't really touch me, and where I am concerned he is very positive and very sure. I wonder at this sureness. I don't have it. I just feel its quite all right now, and the future may take care of itself. The one quality I value above everything in love—or any other relation—is loyalty. I never had it from a man—sometimes it was physical infidelity, sometimes that worse thing, a simple moral disloyalty founded on fear and distrust and vanity. This boy has the gift of being able to stake himself on his beliefs, and there is an indescribable grand dignity in the way he simply takes for granted the things that should go with love, and mostly don't. I can be easy with him, can love him as much as I want, believe as much as I want. So its really quite all right; I know that all sorts of things can happen, but this time I don't have to worry about any part in it but my own. Gene will come through, I'd risk an eye on that.

With me, its a matter of how tired I shall be if this struggle between work and health goes on, and precisely a matter of whether I shan't be forced in the end to live by myself because that is maybe the only way I can live permanently. Besides, I am older than he by just ten years, and its all very well now, but not ten years from now. Besides, I don't like a domestic life because I have to keep hours and engagements and have always a sense of responsibility for my moods and my time. All the little adjustments and compromises that he takes with such perfect calm very often gave me a pain and a grievance that is as acute as it is—maybe—hollow and selfish on my part. Yet, if I can pull through and manage to live for a respectable length of time with any man, this is the one. It would be a real victory for me over my really deep feeling that I do better to live alone. Yet already we are so grown into each other there is no possible reason not to go on. I can't quite think what I should do without him. He's a dear love, and that's that. . . .

I have a deep, incurable (apparently) painful melancholy, night and day, which just sits on my neck. Its nobody's fault except my own, if it is even that. I've had it for years, without any alleviations. So now I sit in the sun as if I hoped that would cure me. I think maybe work will cure me. Maybe not thinking about it will cure me. I cannot imagine what I am waiting for, or looking forward to. I have no earthly business writing such things to you, but it will probably pass, and this is the first time I have even been able to put it a little into words. The tussle to live has been idiotically, unreasonably hard, and I think this is a let-down when finally I came to the place where I could relax a while. Positively, it would seem that I miss the desperate strain, and the muscles of my mind won't let go. Anyhow, its not the kind of thing that lasts forever. I'll pull up and get going soon. I have to. This state of mind is too boresome to endure. Maybe Europe will be the change for me. But I know that journeys don't change the traveller much. And I know there is no getting rid of any part of oneself. I have to learn to live with me, which is a tough job.

My little piano is devilish out of tune and the keys stick, and I'm afraid it simply can never be repaired enough to depend on. But still I can wobble through several pieces, every day I practise at least an hour, sometimes more, and every day music opens its door another half-inch; when I get to Europe I mean to find a teacher such as Paul O'Higgins was, if there is another. I was nervous about beginning, but he made it possible, and in six weeks gave me the rudiments so I could go on learning by myself. My God, why didn't I begin with music when I wanted to at the age of twelve? But I wouldn't have the pleasure I have in learning it now. . . .

> Love and affections.
> *Katherine Anne*

To Hart Crane   [Apartado 2075
                                 Mexico, D.F.
                                 June 22, 1931]

Dear Hart:

First about the lunch. I was disappointed too, and sorry for
your trouble, for it is trouble to have food for people who don't
arrive. I waited too long at the Consulate, for of course they did
not have my passports ready as they promised. This was my third
trip to town, and I was so anxious to have it over I just sat and
waited. Then the day being spoiled anyhow, I finished up some
other tiresome errands, and had barely reached home when I heard
you calling at the gate. I started out to you at once, heard myself
being called, among other items, a whore and a fancy-woman and
Gene a fancy-man, so I just turned about and went in again . . . At
other times when you were in the same state, you have mentioned
my ancestry, upbringing, and habits of life in the same tone, with
a peculiar insistence that grew comic, but still forced me to believe
it was my existence you resented, rather than any superficial criticism such as friends make of one another.

This is a mystery to me, but not really interesting.

You know you have had the advantage of me, because I share
the superstition of our time about the somewhat romantic irrespon-
sibility of drunkenness, holding it a social offense to take seriously
things said and done by a drunken person. Therefore I have borne
to the limit of my patience with brutal behavior, shameless lying,
hysterical raving, and the general sordid messiness of people who
had not the courage to be as shabby as they wished when sober, for
fear of consequences, but must hide behind liquor and be treated
with indulgence. I have behaved badly when drunk, I know it, but
never to my friends, nor they, when drunk, to me. I believe a
drunken mood is as good a mirror as a sober one: your behavior
to me when drunk falls too consistently into the same pattern,
repeats itself too monotonously, for me to believe anything except
what I do believe: that for whatever reasons, and you are welcome
to any reasons you have, you bear a fixed dislike to me, of a very
nasty kind. At first naturally I did not want to believe this, then it
troublea me very much and I tried to get at the causes and cure

them; now I merely am finished, quite, with this whole affair, and refuse to have anything more to do with it. I have lived in Greenwich Village also, as you know, but I was never involved there in such a meaningless stupid situation at this . . . I have no taste for melodrama, and when I fight, it must be for something better than this.

I am by temperament no victim, and I wonder at your lack of imagination in picking on me as audience for exhibitions of this kind. I'm sorry about Peggy, but I suppose she has known persons who did not agree very well before now, and I see nothing in this to take sides about. I think that you like making mischief simply through idleness and restlessness, and you don't feel quite alive unless you are tearing at other personalities like a monkey . . . Let me tell you plainly that this bores me, I see through it, and I won't have it. I have heard the astonishing tale of your treatment of the Spanish teacher, and your gratuitous insult to poor Miss Kelly, and I am beginning to believe that a sanitarium for the mentally defective is the proper place for you. If this is true, I should be sorry at having been angry with you. But I think it is time you grew up and stopped behaving like a very degenerate adolescent. You must either learn to stand on your own feet as a responsible adult, or expect to be treated as a fool. Your emotional hysteria is not impressive, except possibly to those little hangers-on of literature who feel your tantrums are a mark of genius. To me they do not add the least value to your poetry, and take away my last shadow of a wish to ever see you again . . . Let me alone. This disgusting episode has already gone too far.

Katherine Anne

TO CAROLINE GORDON
Norddeutscher Lloyd Bremen
Au Bord des D. *Werra*
August 28, 1931

Caroline darling:

It simply was not possible to write until now. And here we are six days out, already striking across from the Caribbean Islands to

46

the Canaries: fifteen days, they tell me, from yesterday. Five days before, and probably ten to fourteen more from the Canaries to Gijon, to Southampton, to Bremen . . . Then by train to Paris, and so on down to Nice. We will have spent about five weeks on this boat before we are finished . . . A combination freighter and passenger ship, very steady, very broadbottomed and German in her style, doing sixteen knots an hour and keeping a level keel.

I thought of all possible ways to get by to see you, then go on and sail from New York and have it over, a week's voyage, without simply spending the whole first quarter of my allowance, and there was NO way. I wished to see my father too, and had great plans to fly over to Brownsville. But the money began to melt so alarmingly, I could do nothing but take the first boat and go on . . .

There is so much to say, but time to say it, too, at last. May bad luck overtake me if ever again I go through the hell of house wrecking which attends my every change of scene. I'm going to live in rooms, or a room, in inns, pensions, hotels: I don't know what, but never again shall I collect the odds and ends of a household until I have a roof of my own to cover them.

The cats were found good homes, the dog was disposed of to some one who wanted him, the baby turkeys and their mama went to Teodora, and the sticks of furniture were peddled here and there at five cents on the dollar, all this in the uproar of getting necessary papers together, write a last minute review; Lord, why tire you out with the list of things which make such a scramble at the last second? You know all about getting off to Europe as we seem to do it.

Of course there was a farewellish kind of party, which kept us up until four, and at six we rose to take coffee and make the train. I had wanted to go by day for a last look at the famous mountains and the tremendous railway to Vera Cruz which winds through and over cliffs like something at Coney Island, magnified several hundred times . . . The *Werra* was stuck on a sandbank at Tampico, and expected to sail late from Vera Cruz . . . this was the first set-back. Then my letter of credit was sent by mistake in another name, and I didn't know whether I had any more money until two days before leaving . . . We set off, with hang-overs, after receiving notice that the boat would sail on time, after all. Then the fog shut out the valleys all the way, so it had been quite useless to tear myself out of bed at such an ungodly hour, and to

sit miserably all day on an upright bench . . . At Vera Cruz a
storm came up at three in the morning, with thunder like the
crash of falling skyscrapers, and lightning struck the shaft of the
elevator just twenty feet from my room. It burst in my face like a
bomb, with an exasperated crack that almost deafened me. I lay
with my blood congealed and bones shuddering, and thought bitterly that really, this was the last straw . . .

After three lovely smooth days we drew in at Habana, and
there came on board 876 (exactly) third class passengers, all Span-
iards from the Canaries and ports of Spain, who were being sent
away from Cuba by public subscription because there is no work for
them . . . This is a very small boat, small as any old Ward Line tub
plying around the coasts . . . we have a cargo to the water line, and
1200 souls in space designed comfortably for five hundred . . . I
had thought of going third class, since there is no second class, but
when I saw the quarters I was glad I had not. Very miserable, hot,
not clean, and rooms for only about a hundred persons . . . Well,
they sleep on the deck in canvas chairs, very tired women surrounded by pale little children, very discouraged men who sit with
their heads hanging; they get sick on the deck, and the sailors turn
the hose on everything, and then they all pile back upon one
another, in wet chairs, on wet decks, with damp clothing . . . They
have no work waiting for them at the end, either. They are just
going from a place they are not wanted to a place where they cannot
be welcome. From misery through misery to more misery, and all
of them decent looking people who cannot find work and bread.

As a young occulist from Texas, on his way to Vienna for a
special clinic of some kind, commented: "It isn't as if they were
dirty Bolsheviks." I was so startled by this remark, as a voice from
the prehistoric times of the world, that I asked involuntarily,
"Where are you from?" It seemed, Austin, Houston, and Corpus
Christi, Texas. Still, so help me, they are talking that way in Texas.
I got him located by swapping names with him for a while, and it
isn't as if he were an ignorant hulk. He represents a great part of
whatever enlightenment that place has to offer. "They don't deserve their hard luck," he said, "It isn't as if they were dirty Bolsheviks." His wife is with him, and a nice young electrical engineer
from Kennedy, Texas, on his way to Berlin. My cabin mate is a
hefty Swiss girl, whose father was for thirty years a mining engineer

in Torreon, Mexico. A Spanish Zarzuela company—a kind of musical comedy troupe—is on its way back to Spain after the usual failure of hopes in Mexico City and Habana. The rest are Germans, Herr Doktors and Herr Professors and Herr Engineers and all that, with such typically German Frauen—vast, bulky, inert, with handsome heads and elephant legs, who drink beer all day long, swallowing a steinful in two drinks, smacking their lips and saying "Ja, Ja!" quite as the colored postcards had taught me to expect.

I am studying German attentively from the dinner lists, from stray signs and bathroom taps, and a grammar for beginners. But I really am reading up on French. And a short story is working around to be done on this long bee-line across the waters, which are getting very gradually a little more troubled. The ship's doctor says gloomily we are bound to run into weather. Pray that my sea-legs don't buckle under me. I have never been sea-sick except on one occasion when I went aboard sick already.

This is going to be a kind of log, Caroline; good bye until tomorrow.

Aug. 29. Last—it was Easter—a very gay festival—I found a blue Oaxaca pottery tea set for Nancy, a good one with pots and pitchers that really pour, and cups big enough for a girl like Nancy to take a mouthful from . . . Also a green glass water pitcher with three glasses of a sizeableness. Ever since then I have waited for some one to come by who could take it over the border and mail it to Nancy and nobody came. Thousands came, but no friend of mine. So I had a big tea set—coffee set, really—copied from it for myself, so Nancy and I should have dishes just alike, only different sizes, and they looked very fine, sitting side by side in their trays. I am carrying them with me in my suitcase, and maybe I shall see some one in Paris who will be coming back, and Nancy shall have her dishes yet. They are exactly for her and no one else. Give her my love and remembrance.

The attempts to make life on shipboard a little like life anywhere else is very sad. Life on shipboard should be something else. Night before last there was a dinner party for every one to get acquainted, and last night moving pictures . . . The people below deck were also recovered and in better spirits, and did the thing more successfully. They got out accordions and guitars, and sang and danced, making a tiny circle for the performers. The tired ones still slept through it all, and the full moon made their closed faces like silver masks. There was down there a huge fat man with a purple face and watermelon pink shirt, who got on at Vera Cruz. He had a voice like seven foghorns, and he roared and sprawled and guzzled beer and sang in a voice that drowned out the brass band and I think everybody looked forward with terror to so many weeks shut up with this noise. His wife and child came on at Habana, and he has been mute ever since, sitting around drooping like a grief-stricken elephant. Now and then you can see his wife lecturing him, coldly, calmly, patiently. He never says a word.

September 3. mid-Atlantic, and still going. There have been more moving pictures, and a dance. On gala nights we find at our plates little paper snappers, with toys inside, and a comic hat of paper with feather and ribbon. All of us put on our hats and grin vaguely at the others, who grin back, every body orders wine, the band strikes up "Wiener Blut" or some other Strauss waltz, and for the moment every one is acquainted with every one else. But nothing has changed, really half of us do not salute the other half on deck the next morning, and not from rancor but from indifference . . .

I think I have a very short short-story out of it: I mean to call it "Wiener Blut" and it is about a little fat man dancing a waltz . . . I have another in mind about selling out my house and leaving it, called " . . . And a Pleasant Journey" but the distressing thing is, nothing seems to come through. Everything forms vaguely and I catch it in random notes, and the ideas melt into one another. This has been a time of inner seethe—as when wasn't time just that? But I am done with worrying about it . . . or almost. Everything will get done, I feel sure of it.

Day before yesterday I saw three whales, enormous ones, swimming almost out of water, flashing white in the sun, spouting white fountains. There was nothing to do but scream "WHALES! WHALES!" climb up on the rail and almost fall overboard . . . They are a terrifying and gorgeous spectacle . . . Never before did I quite realize the immense lost depths of the sea . . . I used to swim about two miles out in the Gulf of Mexico near Corpus Christi, and whole schools of porpoises used to dive by, parting and sweeping around me and out to sea, and suddenly I would feel under me the awful waters and the unknowable life in them, and it seemed I would surely die of terror before I could get back to land . . . It was as dreadful as if you might be set down suddenly in the preglacial age in a wilderness of monsters . . . I love the sea, but as an old-fashioned Christian loved God—with fear and trembling . . .

The heat is lessening gradually, the sunshine is paler, every evening heavy columns of cloud rear up and shine red over the waters, and then thunder and broad lightning, and more wind, but no storms, Gott sei dank! (I learned that from the stewardess, who is always being grateful to Divine Providence for one thing or another.) (It may not be spelt properly.) The people in the steerage seem to be getting on rather nicely. We have everything on board . . . A woman who may have a baby before we get to Bremen, a new-born one who came aboard when he was two weeks old, a little dying man who sits curled up on his pillows and coughs all day, a hunch-back, a woman who weighs nearly four hundred pounds; and a beautiful Spanish bride with her devoted bridegroom—married the day we sailed from Vera Cruz. She is a lovely creature, as romantic looking as the princess in a fairy tale, with the grace and silence and naturalness of a fine wild animal . . . She sits and walks all day with her long hand lying loosely in his, smiling and dazed. He is the most utterly happy looking person I ever saw, with an irregularly featured sensitive face . . . They are really something to see. They do not dance, nor wear paper hats, nor drink, nor play cards, nor grin. If ever I saw two persons walking in Eden, it is now.

The dinner bugle is blowing raucously. I must powder my face and fly. Always I am hungry. . . .

September 6, Sunday. Last night I stayed up until after midnight, a new thing for me, because half my life I am asleep. Gene and I walked round and round the deck, stopping around sailors who were washing down everything with hose. All evening the Asturianos on the deck below were singing. A drunken man was improvising verses on any theme, or single word, the people gave him. He would mutter to himself a few minutes, and then break into a long cry, sing his verse, and wind up with a slow, flatfooted dance step. The crowd would shriek with joy. At the other end of the ship boys were having wrestling matches, as usual. At midnight, they were settled down and asleep. Some lay in chairs, some on benches, others curled like snails into hammocks . . . all with their clothes on, no covering except now and again a sheet. Many had their faces covered with towels to keep out the deadly night air, and one man, in blue overalls, hung his great crooked bare feet out of his hammock, his head swathed like a mummy. The most touching thing was the posture of nearly all of them . . . those shouting, singing, swearing Asturianos each lay in the pious attitude of a well-disposed corpse . . . on his back, hands clapped on his breast, feet crossed, and the occasional muffling white sheet gave the look of a cheerful morgue to the whole deck . . . At meal times they lift the canvas off the iron grating which gives light and air to the pit where they eat. And they sit down to mountains of fried potatoes, meat stew, piles of onions, bowls of cooked apples or apricots, huge pots of coffee. All those things are on the menu up stairs, only served in silver dishes and mounds of fresh napery, and in polite little specks, one at a time . . . Little by little I feel better about this voyage for them, because they are all looking better, and smoother, and happier, as does every face on board. The sea has been unbelievably friendly and beautiful, I am attached to this silly old ship. Fifteen days today.

If I were not keeping this kind of journal for you I could never believe it has been so long. This prelude is preparing me for life in an inn, a kind of community existence after my really anarchic freedom of Mixcoac. There, I was beginning to dread the appearance of a human face, any kind of face, the more clear space I had around me the more I needed, so that I managed quite habitually to keep two or three rooms between me and any one else, and I wanted the whole orchard to myself when I took a walk . . . Already I am accustomed to faces, all kinds, I sit here and write with the whole life of the ship revolving on the decks, and it is even comfortable to me.

There is a little hunchback man with downy dry hair and a shrivelled face who wears very gay neckties. On party nights he puts on his paper hat over one eyebrow and then sits on deck all evening with his head between his hands, eyes closed, listening to the music.

A Cuban woman about fifty years old, with short curled white hair and a waxy smooth face, follows various persons about, backs them into corners, and talks for two hours at a time, making strange desperate gestures, thumbs turned in flat to the palms. She leans forward and peers at the person she is talking to, as if she were communicating some dark important secret. She is very slender and was a tremendous beauty not so long ago. She tells every one the same: that her husband was killed fighting for the revolution in Cuba, that her sons are fugitives persecuted by the government. Her eyes are very dry and bright, she talks with a crying, complaining voice, eternally about her children who are lost, who have no place to rest, and how the government officials laughed at her when she went to them asking them not to persecute her children. Now they have exiled her to Teneriffe: it seems she is not married at all, nor ever was, but it is true that she has been very active helping the revolutionary students, and is being sent away, and her mind is unhinged. Cuba is her murdered husband, and the students are her children . . . There is a gang of university students on board, going to Gijon, but only because the university has been closed over their empty heads. Its all a great joke to them they must go somewhere else to finish learning the alphabet. All day they collect in knots and give college war-cries, then sing "Cucaracha": all about the unfortunate cockroach who can't run around any more because she lacks feet to run with: or has no marihuana to smoke: or no money in her purse: there are about forty verses in all, and they sing them through . . . Well, they have taken on La Loca, as they call her, have formed a Cucaracha club, elected her as president, made a verse in her honor, and escorted her around the deck, imitating her walk and smile at her back, prancing and grimacing, while she smiles at them, and makes a little speech: her hands dancing a ballet: "My sons were students who defied the government, and they were right. Youth must defy governments, even though it means persecution, exile, death. The young must not throw away their beautiful lives being stupid and living like half-dead things—leave that for an old woman!" She makes a very grand, old-fashioned bow. They shout and applaud, and wink at the other passengers. A stringy boy in Oxford bags like tucked up skirts lollops after her, at a safe distance and mimicks her frail complaining voice: "Youth, beautiful youth!" She walks on with them, her lace skirts flying, smiling blindly . . . Sometimes one of them will dance with her, and afterwards she stands talking, one hand under her breast, the other stroking her flank, a perfectly appalling expression on her face.

This morning the sky is pale and sunless, the water is grey for the first time. I woke up chilled under my single sheet, and put on a sweater. In an hour I had to take it off again, but we have crossed some line in the night, for it is early fall and not summer any more. Day after tomorrow morning we reach Teneriffe, but there is a rumor we shall not go ashore . . . just stop for a few hours. We pass Brest, le Havre, Boulogne, but do not stop there. The five passengers for Boulogne are going to be put off at Southampton to wangle themselves home as well as they may . . .

The ship's doctor is an old Heidelberg student with a grand hooked nose, a fine head, and two sabre scars across his cheek and forehead. He walks like an officer, and stands at attention apparently, for half an hour at a time, gazing at the water with the kindest, most serviceable pair of tan eyes you can imagine: they are almost maternally sweet and good. I went to him for help, having broken out with that dangerous tropical disease known as heat-rash. All over I was a welter. He gave me a lotion he had mixed for himself, being, he said, a martyr to heat rash. It worked like a charm. Was there anything else he could do for me? No, I was in perfect health otherwise. "You do not look to be a tough voman," he told me, "but it is possible you are very strong inside," and he tapped the front of his tunic. I said I thought I was fairly tough inside. He told me cheerful little anecdotes about his vife, like me a tough voman who did not seem so. She would insist on raising chickens, and they grew so tame they wandered all through the house, so that often she exhausted herself chasing them with a broom. He himself has a bad heart, and may drop dead at any time, but not, he hopes, until once more he can see that voman chasing herself with a broom after those chickens. . . .

Tuesday Night, September 8. Yesterday evening we sighted Palma, the first of the Canaries coming this way . . . It was a jagged rock-shaped, rock-colored mass rising abruptly from grey water . . . it is my idea of Spain—more Toledo than Seville. This morning I was waked by the engine giving three loud thumps, then stopping. There was Teneriffe—another long rock with peaked edges, with houses perched on levels hacked out with a chisel, apparently. Santa Cruz is lovely, and three things struck upon my eye: camels going loaded through the streets in company with burros, friars, fat and lean, of two orders, black and brown, slapping through the streets in their old-lady shoes and pork pie hats. And the milk-women in their short black dresses, bare legs, their heads swathed in a black shawl with a little round hat, secured in the back by an elastic under their knot of hair, carrying great flat trays loaded with battered milk cans. They have a charming walk, half-run, with rigid head and shoulders and wildly swaying hips . . .

We found a cafe called "El Quita Penas," (Forget Your Troubles) and sampled all the Canary wines from the great barrels along the wall. Malaga, Moscatel, Malavasia, Madeira, and the islands cognac, Tres Copas, and an orange liqueur something like Curacoa but not so good; with all this we ate a large Spanish lunch, and came away, just in the mood to hail a very small horse drawn veehickle something like a Victoria, but only half so large, and drive in great state to the very foot of the gangway, which was in the act of rising. We ascended just one jump ahead of the gangway itself, with shoals of hungry Syrians prowling below trying to sell us embroidered shawls . . .

It seems to me now I am having the loveliest time of my life—this is long after dinner, we are sober and the boat is rolling in heavy swooning swoops calculated to chill the pit of the stomach—so it isn't through a fog of Canary wine I write this . . . I was standing in a doorway surveying the sweet crooked streets with the soft, gay colored walls, feeling at home in the sound of Spanish all around me, when a brass plate across the walk suddenly announced that here was the Bank of British West Africa . . . A feeling that I was rather far from home came over me, just for a second. Tonight we are setting out off the coast of Africa; on Friday we will be at Vigo . . . news to me. This tramp freighter has changed her mind about where-all she's going about eleven times. We may even stop at Boulogne. The Boulogne passengers are invoking some old maritime law that says, when a ship takes on passengers for a certain port, she's bound to set them off there, and no where else, barring acts of God; so we're going to get a French visa at Vigo, and pop off at Boulogne if the Captain can be brought to see the light. When the steerage passengers swarmed up on deck with their bundles and laughed and wept at sight of their island, I envied them, and hope I might cry with joy to see some one place again . . .

When we left the harbor, the sea was so wild the pilot launch was almost swamped. The man at the wheel was drenched and had hard work to stay on board. The pilot came down the ladder like a spider dropping down his own web, swung into the launch, which almost capsized, took the wheel, and nosed her away; after a good sharp tussle, the engine went dead. The pilot just stood there, holding the wheel and looking up at the ship. I leaned out and waved my scarf at him. He took off his cap with a beautiful sweep and waved back.

The sailors have tied down the canvas storm curtains with hundreds of knots, the band is playing hoppety tunes, and those devil-possessed students are howling "Cucaracha" in the smoking salon. . . .

I haven't seen the map yesterday nor today, so to my shame I don't know whether we're just entering the Bay of Biscay or leaving it . . . Will let you know tomorrow, unless you're better at geography than I am, and know anyhow. . . .

More passengers are leaving . . . The ship is almost empty. About eighty first class, and the same number third. The Captain swears he will NOT stop at Boulogne. The Boulogne passengers must get off at Southampton: in little boats, with a keg of water and some biscuits, I suppose. We aren't going into the harbor even . . . But as you may have noticed, life on this ship is very uncertain, full of rumors, alarms, and excursions . . . One thing certain. We are on our way to Bremen, and will be set off there with due formality, armed with a ticket for Paris.

That reminds me. I read over your letters today, and have put in my note book the name of your little hotel, and we go there from the station . . .

(Hearing yelps outside, I put my head through the porthole to take a glimpse of Gijon. We are turning very slowly, and half a dozen launches are circling round filled with yelling friends of passengers, all waving, nearly all standing up in their bouncing walnut shells. A long row of Spanish ships are backed neatly into the dock like parked automobiles. Our gang plank is going down. Everything is grey and silent looking. My cabin mate looked out this morning while she was dressing, and said happily, "Oh, it looks like Europe already. Everything is so grey and misty!")

Which leads to the question about where I am going. It is really warmish near Nice, isn't it? Or Grasse? Kay Boyle wrote me that

Ville Franche was a good place. I mean to stay only a little while in Paris. Not more than two weeks. I wouldn't think of trying to stay in Paris; it would be foolhardy after all I've been told. . . .

Here ends this foolish note-book, made to amuse you a little and to remember my first Atlantic crossing by . . . It was a fairly good job, passing, as we did, Cuba, Africa, Portugal, Spain, with England, Germany a scrap of Belgium, and France to come . . . I feel like one of these tourists who rush through the world with eyes tightly closed, gaining momentum by the hour, counting on his fingers the lands he has travelled through . . . getting home with a souvenir spoon from each.

You cannot think how naively I should like to see the whole face of this world into which we are born strangers, and which we so often leave without ever acquainting ourselves with it . . . Then I think maybe one is always more at home in one place afterwards . . .

I love you very much, and never stop missing you. Love to Allen and Nancy. Tell Allen I have brought his extra copy of *Mr. Pope* all the way here with me, on the grounds that some day I shall mail it to him. I was re-reading some of the poems last night, and looked forward happily to the new book. These poems grow on me the more they are read . . . substance, and "tone" that mysterious and indispensable quality he attributes to the work of Ezra Pound also belong even more to his own . . .

Good bye for a short time

September 24. I don't expect you to be much astonished to hear that we are in Berlin. The French Consulate had not the faculty to grant visas to persons in transit . . . He told me this in French and I answered in Spanish, and we parted with mutual gestures of mystification . . . Then we did stop at Boulogne, after all! In the dead of night, with foghorns bellowing, the French pilot boat going twing-twing-twing under my porthole, the Spanish students disembarking drunk and roaring "Cucaracha." Then sharp quick nasal French voices on the deck above, and after a very short while, on we went, and I lay embittered, not knowing who to curse, that little worm of an agent in Mexico who assured me I could get a French Visa at any port, or the Captain, who assured me in Vera Cruz, while it was not too late, that he would not stop in Boulogne, or myself, who was fool enough not to prepare myself for any emergency . . . Still, it is done. So I decided to come on here, since I had always wished to, look about for a month, see if I could bear the cold if I had plenty of clothes and a warm house, and so come again in touch with the life-current of ideas and work, instead of just climate and a human vacuum . . .

The last of the voyage was very pleasant . . . When we passed the Isle of Wight, a great castle stood in a greensward, surrounded by little tender woods, and the grass shaven neatly to the lip of the sea . . . I thought as we passed along so near to the shores, that I was deceived again in my sense of smell, which brings me such strange whiffs on cross-currents of air. But it smelled of herbs and grass and grazing cows. I spoke of it to the Swiss girl. She said, "No, it is really true, I have passed here three times, and there is always that smell." At Southampton a little newsboy came aboard, and when I tried to buy a newspaper, I found that we could not understand each other at all . . . I do not know what dialect he spoke, but it was as foreign to me as German: broad, drawling, with vowel sounds I never heard anywhere else . . . In England and France, on this German boat, I felt as if I were passing through enemy territory . . . The English inspectors were saying something to our Captain, who replied in English: "Yes, this rule applies to German boats, I know. The Americans and the French can have everything." The Englishman sat silent with his eyebrows lifted . . . And the Germans said to me many times such things as: "We are not allowed to use the word champagne, but let me offer you some good German sparkling wine.". . . "We are not permitted to build air-ships of more than such-power". . . "Please don't say 'connoisseur'—we Germans no longer understand French." And so on. There is something real and undying in the hatred these two races have for each other. They hate in a way we cannot understand, I believe.

Well—at Bremen, some of the junior officers joined us after we left the boat, recommended a good cheap little hotel, and took us to the famous Rathskeller, where we drank beautiful Rhine wine and ate pig's knuckles with sauer kraut. I loved the enormous old wine tuns, each with names and a date—I remember 1580 something, painted, carved, decorated, with great bronze taps . . . but the whole place is a marvel of the most terrible German taste— great appalling blobs and festoons of carving, everything mixed up, writhen together with a horrid muscular energy without meaning or direction . . . I feel that this will bother me as I see more and more of it . . .

Went to sleep under a feather bed about 1 A.M. Got up at six thirty to catch the morning train for Berlin . . . took a third class compartment, astonished at its decency and comfort, with light and air and a little shelf table where we had coffee and bread and butter, and then hot broth and then fruit and more coffee, thus wearing away six mortal hours between sleep and nourishment . . . I was so tired by now I thoroughly wished to die . . .

Landed in Berlin, and checked our bags, got a map and a guide book, and simply roamed about the city until nearly evening. Then we picked a hotel from the guide book, came here, found a Mexican woman married to a German in charge of the place, who at once brought forth her Indian woman servant to wait on me . . . we have two stuffy rooms choked with feather pillows and plush table covers and knobby furniture and overstuffed divans, but praise God, the steam heat is on tonight; we get rooms, breakfast in bed, and maid service for twenty four dollars a month each, and that's as well as we can do in any pension we have yet visited—and they are not few . . . We have never eaten twice in any cafe, and have, by a simple hit or miss plan, sampled therefore about fifteen, with innumerable coffee shops and bars . . . No matter what the price, a platter of meat, potatoes, and vegetables is set before you fit to feed a starving family. The difference lies merely in the manner of getting it up. For 1 mark you get as much as for three marks . . . but it will be, meat, a gorgeous gosh-awful Gothic gob, potatoes, and vegetables cooked to goulash in meat broth . . . I foresee gout to the death, but I don't know yet what to do about it . . .

I know well there is a change coming over this German spirit: there are enough of these new houses with aluminum doors and window frames, thin firm concrete walls and lines of glass, orderly and bare as ships, their verandahs like decks . . . They are almost too bare and clean and pure, as if the builders were in an ecstasy of shearing away excrescences. In the shops I see beautifully designed furniture, clear colors, fine simple silver and dishes . . . There is a whole colony of new houses, built for the poor, for almost everybody is poor, where light, air, space, cleanliness, AND beauty have been the ends, with the greatest economy of means possible. I mean to see this: and some of the new films, and to hear some of the new music. Then I will be able to tell you something. In the meantime, I am bored with feather beds and figures of men and women who look like something by Albrecht Dürer . . .

But all of the persons I have spoken to, wherever, have soft voices and good manners. Their words of greeting and goodbye and thanks are very musical: it is all a great relief after the harshness, the nasty public manners, the shrillness and meanness of Mexico, where only the Indian gives any charm of being, and even that is the saddening courtesy and humbleness of a beaten creature who bows his way though life . . .

Write me once, anyhow, care the American Consulate General, Bellevuestrasse 8, Berlin, and by then I shall know where I am to be . . . I sent for my mail from Paris, and am trying to make up my mind to stick it through here, get my work done, and go south afterwards. It remains to be seen whether I can beat the cold . . . But a little time will show me.

Good bye and my love,
Katherine Anne

SECTION 2

Berlin, Basel, Paris
November 1931 to October 1936

I have a feeling of continuity, of things beautifully done for their own sakes, a strong live source of belief in life, that goes on and will allow me to go with it.

> Katherine Anne Porter to her brother Paul
> *March 8, 1932*

DURING A SEVERE WINTER IN BERLIN, KATHERINE ANNE POR-
ter writes "The Leaning Tower" and "The Cracked Looking-Glass." In
Basel she discovers marginal notes in Erasmus's own books and his Praise
of Folly. The following spring in Paris she marries Eugene Pressly. She
comes down with bronchitis and goes to Davos for five weeks to recover. By
summer she is well enough to go with Barbara Harrison to the operas at
Salzburg and Munich, where she sees people "swinging their arms in each
others' faces and saying Heil Hitler!" It is one day before the Nazi plebiscite.
Back in Paris, she lives in a pavilion on the rue Notre-Dame-des-Champs
where Ezra Pound had lived, although she does not know this at the time.
In the spring of 1936 she works on her history of Cotton Mather in Boston,
then goes back to Paris until October. "Paris won't be the same without the
feeling of you sitting there, a spot of sanity in an insane world, peacefully
working and strumming bravely on the Virginals!" her friend Jimmie Stern
writes to her as she leaves to move back to the United States.

TO MALCOLM COWLEY   Berlin
November 5, 1931

Dear Malcolm:. . . .

We're off on the wrong track somehow when strength and goodness can be confused with piety and dullness. I know and love some tremendously good people, and they are not dull, by any means; they have more spirit and energy, fullness and interest than the wicked ones. It takes more imagination to be good. (I use these words because they are easy and we both know what we mean by them). There is something shallow in viciousness, something scared and nasty. When good people commit wrongs against life they are aware of it, they have the grace to fight against their destructive impulses. They don't pride themselves on their meannesses and cultivate their wretched vanities, and love themselves so much they love even their own dirt. These are the things I hate in evil people, and when any one speaks foolishly of goodness to me, it is a judgement on them and not on goodness. I believe you are wrong in speaking of the "middle-class virtues" . . . Middle class virtue is a kind of code of behavior based on fear of consequences, an artificial line set up, but to [be] sneaked over if one can manage it with secrecy . . . Abominable. Virtue is something else: a spiritual aristocracy. You know it when you see it, and there is no arguing with it. If Muriel† has this, you'd better thank your stars and stick to her.

I'm saying it so badly and dully I may as well give up. The trouble is, you can't sum it up in abstract qualities, nor even name arbitrarily the elements of goodness. But it exists, it is real, it is capable of growth and culture, and the one thing worth having . . .

Katherine Anne

†*Soon to be M.'s second wife (KAP)*

65

TO EUGENE PRESSLY   Berlin
                              November 12, 1931

Can you guess how I amused myself last night? My throat and cough would not let me sleep, so I got out the map of the ancient world and my St. Augustine, and traced his travels, from Carthage to Rome to Milan back to Hippo, travels which he mentions so casually, but they must have been great undertakings in those times . . . Then I got off on St. Paul, and lingered on that fateful road between Tarsus and Damaskus, and traced the track of his epistles to the churches, and followed him around his route . . . This lead to Dante, I don't remember why, and though his travels were less, they were very important . . . so to Villon in his exile, and naturally to Dr. Rabelais . . . these two never out of France, but important travels, just the same. Then I went back to Catullus, and followed all mention of travels, and for two hours I wove about in what was then the whole civilised world—they traced, taken chronologically, the whole rise of Western civilization beginning at Nazareth, through Rome, Greece, Syria and Byzantium, over to Italy, down to Africa, (Carthage, exactly) and so on . . .

There are other fateful travellers, of very early and middle times, but I haven't the books by me and have not enough memory . . .

TO PAUL O'HIGGINS   Berlin
(in Moscow)   Winter, 1931

You are right that Art causes a great deal of trouble, and most of all, I think, to those who work at it. But I look forward to a world in which the artist has his place as a useful being, not for political purposes, but in his true function, which is that of a finder, a bringer, a giver of new forms of expression based on life, but seen with imagination and creativeness. First there must be bread for every one, but bread is not enough. Man eats his bread and looks about for something more, and the something more must be art (should be).

So it is only natural that the artist is now being crowded out a little, since art has been for so long only a decoration on life, and not an essential. Art must grow out of some profound belief, and the strange thing about beliefs is, it does not matter much what they are, or have been, the artist gives them beauty and meaning by his own vision of them. You would know what I mean if you could see the bronze sculptures around the portals of Sainte Chapelle here. The religion by which these artists lived, the conditions of their existences, seem now a monstrous nightmare. But it was all they had in the world and times in which they lived, and evidently it gave them some strength, something certain to go by, for these sculptures have a beauty and perfection far beyond the beliefs they celebrate, that comes of some perfect co-ordination between concept and execution; they survive now by their own value quite apart from subject or source, and are entirely self-justified. Any one who would destroy them for the sake of a political faith would be an enemy to the whole human race, no matter what hypothetical good he might bring to replace them. So I hope your government, (Soviet) while it is melting down the silver from the churches, is at the same time preserving carefully the true works of art, quite as we preserve the archaic Greeks and the ancient Egyptian things, all made in honor of gods that no one any longer believes in; but their value is no less for all that.

I think we must keep in mind that some day our now so new and exciting political faiths and mechanical devices will be out of date, and our descendents will be forced to reject them because they can no longer use them . . . but our architecture and our sculpture and our painting and literature and all our testimony of what life *was for us,* will be matters of great importance to them . . . We have no right whatever to try to mortgage the future . . .

TO CAROLINE GORDON   IN BERLIN, of all places!
Bambergerstr. 39 bei Reichl . . .
Monday, December 14, 1931

Caroline darling:

How I did enjoy your tone of fatality when you assumed that, under whatever cover, I had sneaked into Paris and was probably living there, a guilty fugitive from the I-warned-you's of friends . . . No, blight the luck, I'm still here. That isn't exactly just. Berlin is a pretty grand city, there are all kinds of things about it to pleasure a body, as Andrew says . . . Only, only, I am here so alone that all other alonenesses of my whole life seem crowded by comparison. Gene, whose financial prospects were sound enough when we left Mexico, was smitten low when we reached Berlin. Nothing to do but go to Spain, where he could find a job. He went, and is now loosely connected with the American Embassy as translator; a sad end for him if it were the end, but mean season he is looking for something else; and we are devilish unhappy separated, but cannot meet again until spring, for I will not if it takes my last breath, stir from here until I have got something done. He will by then have found an apartment for me, and be straightened out, enough, I suppose, to take on again the job of looking after me as he did last summer. I don't know what becomes of money, do you? For mine flees away, and even now Gene is sending me snippets to eke out until the next quarter . . . I don't know how he does it. In the spring I'll be in Spain, though. That's something. In Madrid.

Malcolm *never even noticed by one word* my several requests to review *Penhally* . . . Why Evelyn Scott, I wonder? Why didn't I think of the *Quarterly Review* until this minute? There might have been a place. I'm waiting for it with my last shred of patience; your first novel, and here it is months old, and I haven't seen even the jacket of it!

Your story about Jenny Wiley seems to give us maybe a thread to an old family romance . . . This Henry Skaggs was, I presume, that uncle Henry which my grandmother used to tell tales about . . . her father's brother. Remember my Grandmother was born in 1824. He may be an earlier one, but I think this one flourished around 1810 or 20; so I really don't know. He seems to have been rather stuffily on the side of law and order, as he appears once, name mispelled, in Bob Coates' book on outlaws as one of a posse that went bandit hunting on the Natches Trace . . . Oh, well, what I'm getting at is this: there is a Kentucky family named Wiley (they spell it Wylie,) kinsmen of ours because I distinctly remember Cousin (heaven knows what degree of relationship that cousin stands for, but it was a blood-relationship, I remember that) Altah Wylie used to come down from Kentucky to visit us, along with my great-aunt Keziah (nothing of the sort. She was my father's first cousin Keziah Skaggs—Great-Aunt Keziah was dead by then) and Rhoda Skaggs. God knows one falls into this elliptical, parenthetical style just naturally when talking about relationships. Now, did the Skaggs' and the Wylies, (or Wileys) intermarry after Henry's romantic (I presume) rescue of Jenny, or were they kin before? And was this Henry Skaggs from Kentucky? Because my kinsman Henry—one of them at least, the name seemed to hang on and recur—was from somewhere around Boonesboro or Bowling Green . . . Lord, I'll have to come down there and straighten it out, with the help of your bibliography on that period . . . You must be having a grand time of it . . . Don't you ever run across any Porters, or Rheas, or Wards; there are more names but I can't recall them just this minute . . . And oh, do save the picture for me! It was inspired of you to do it for me. Some day, I'll get there: maybe the last one, but I shall make it, and go all over and loosen the earth a little about the bones of my kinsmen . . . Let me see the story when you've done it?

I saw the story in *Scribner's;* it's a good story; you sound as if you hate *Penhally* and all your work: it's not so good as "The Long Day" or "The Ice House," because not so many stories are good as those . . . Still it has so much of your own kind of thing in it, I read it with pleasure and happiness . . . Its better to write everything, trust yourself and abide by it. I know this, but I don't do it. I am full of misgivings and reconsiderations except just now and then, when something forms and makes itself out of pure faith . . .

When that happens I let it stand and don't even ask myself whether it is good or not . . . So I have little bursts of joy at times, but not so often . . . for the most, writing is now just a horrible grim burden, I wouldn't do it if I were not morally engaged to do it; yet, I wonder sometimes if the mere moral engagement hasn't clamped down this smothering lid on me, as if I had to serve a term and then would be free . . . I don't suppose this state of affairs really affects the actual performance. One writes no worse for having to. But it puts a log and chain on my spirits, let me tell you. That unsurveyed but certain territory where I live; this is invaded, and I'm going to clear it out again as quickly as I can . . .

The log was written without pains, hastily from day to day as you saw it: women are, as you know, fabulous letter writers. It has been supposed (by men) to be their ideal form of literary activity. Malcolm wrote that you had sent him fragments, and "Darling," says he, "Your masterpieces are your letters," for which cheerfully I could have throttled my good friend Malcolm . . . Even if it is true, (God forbid!) somehow there was an echo of cheerful masculine voices down the centuries saying, "On his mother's side also our hero inherited some gleam of literary talent, for she was a writer of delightful letters." Now, I do not despise good letters, indeed, I love them, and if I write one now and then, I am glad of it. And I am pleased that it was a good letter, for I meant to give you as clear an account as I could of the voyage; to amuse you, and to console myself for not having seen you. And I am flattered no end that you show it to people. I have kept all of yours, as I think I told you, and have passed them around too.

If you get a Guggenheim, you would know by March or April. Then would you come straight on to Europe or wait until fall? Anyhow, whenever, I shall be here—meaning Spain, no doubt— but we will not miss each other again. That's the best thing about Europe. Paris to Madrid is nothing much. You'd probably be along the southern coast, wouldn't you? And till late summer we plan to be in San Sebastian, or I shall be, at least. Gene might have to be in Madrid except week-ends. How I do hope you get one. Jo Bashe is here, but I haven't seen him. And where is John Crowe Ransom?

You will find at the end of six months that *Penhally* has done something for you. It's waiting the six months that kills, of course: but I'm betting you will have something more of it than you expect. I never see any papers or magazines here except the *New Republic,* so I haven't seen any reviews, but that one. Gene sent me the *Scribner's* with your story, from Spain. I can't find the magazine here. In fact, the isolation is too great. And everybody in Berlin seems to have flu but me. That's boasting, and I know it, and well may I boast, for usually it's just the reverse. I wear wool stockings, wool underwears, and a wool jersey dress, and fleece lined over-boots and fur lined gloves in the street. I sleep under a down pouf in pajamas, and smoke only three cigarettes a day, eat all I can afford to, and generally wage a stiff battle against colds. My cough has disappeared absolutely. I am lost without it. But how cheerfully lost. Let's see how things come out. . . .

Its very late. I can't run the typewriter after 11 o'clock, which cramps me mostly, as I really like to work—just get wound up nicely, about 11.30 and on to 2.30 A.M. Its really ghastly, though I try not to think of it—living in one room. I've hated it always, but it grows more difficult. This place is probably as good as any, but no place is good under a strange roof with strangers.

Did you find German a difficult language to learn? Spanish seems like my mother-tongue after the tortuosities (that *should* be a word) of dies, diese, dieser, diesem, den, dein, der, etc—I shall probably never learn it, in spite of 2 lessons a week. My love to Nancy and Allen and to yourself.

Katherine Anne

To Mr. Dashiell   Hotel Malherbe
[Managing Editor *Scribner's*   11, Rue de Vaugirard
Magazine]   Paris—VIᵉ
                          February 5 1932

Dear Mr. Dashiell:

Yesterday I ran across a copy of *Ulysses* and saw again that phrase of Joyce's which had stuck in my mind: about the Art of Ireland being "the Cracked Looking glass of a Servant." I had remembered the word as *Mirror,* and so have called my story "The Cracked Mirror" when it should be "The Cracked Looking Glass—."

If it is not too late, I beg of you to have the title changed, and anywhere in the story that the word *Mirror* occurs, please have the proofreader change it to "looking glass."

This error of memory distresses me, and I hope you can help me straighten it out.

Sincerely—
Katherine Anne Porter

TO ALLEN TATE AND   Paris—
CAROLINE GORDON   March 6th, 1932

Great God, Allen, isn't that just like a poet. I never write more than one poem a year, and sometimes not even that. I didn't review your *POPE* because, after long pondering and holding of the head and beating of the brow, I decided that I knew nothing about poetry and it would be presumptious of me to try to give an opinion . . . I sent my little poem off to *Pagany* after much hesitation, and could hardly believe my eyes when I read the letter of acceptance . . . I got your letter forwarded from Germany, and keeping February 20th in mind, I rummaged through and through all the two hundred fragments of poems which testify to my grim determination to write a poem or die . . . there was nothing, I swear, that you would not have thrown in the fire with curses, or that I should ever have had the courage to send you.

And this is written at a later date, in another house, on a different typewriter to tell you that I have still been trying to write one, not that I think you could use it now, but just to prove that I could if I put my mind on it . . . but I haven't brought it off, and so I give up. You know well I would have if it had been possible. The bitter thing about it is, I may haul off and do one any day, and if I do, I'm going to save it for just this kind of emergency . . .

Later again. This is Sunday, March 13th. I found my calendar. Janice Ford just came in with news that knocked everything else out of my mind. About Caroline having got the Fellowship. She and Ford cabled last night and added my name, thank heaven. I was getting ready to rush out and cable you when she told me. Hurroar! Hurroarr! I was going to write to Caroline after this, but I must just go on . . . I read *Penhally* twice and its a monstrous fine book. An impossible kind of book to write but she did it! A book with a house for the hero and a strip of earth for the heroine, and human beings just a kind of Greek chorus, or the wind that passes over the fields and is gone; yet I remember them as having been alive, especially Alice and Lucinda Crenfrew and Nicholas. The scenes of the war . . . a grand warm book. The tobacco floor. Such knowledgeable scenes, one episode going on to the next so decisively. I'm interested in the technical thing because I'm finding it almost an impossible problem. The book didn't arrive until about three weeks ago. Meantime I borrowed Ford's copy, and then read my own when it came. I should think you'd both feel pretty proud of it. May my own be half as good.

Well, Miss Caroline, there's no use trying to deceive you, I am in Paris. Yes mam, I made it back. I came up from Berlin, stopped here ten days, fought a losing battle against my deepest inclinations, pulled myself out by the hair and went to Madrid to meet Gene. Madrid is a lovely enchanting city, and there was almost ready for me a kind of pent house full of sunlight, a roof garden, and so on. I gave one look at it all, returned to the hotel and went to bed and wept bitterly for eleven hours, thereby beating my own record, and drying up my tears for the rest of my life. Why? because I had seen Paris and could not endure the thought of being anywhere else . . . So I stayed two days more in Madrid, saw the sights, and Gene came back with me for two weeks. I had left here of a Sunday morning, and at midnight the Friday following we were both back. Gene liked Paris too, but he has a job in Madrid, so in May he will come back for a little visit, until he can see about a transfer from the Madrid to the Paris Embassy. I had lived in Berlin all winter without catching cold, after the first awful month. So I caught another cold in Paris, which hangs on, but I shall get rid of it when I am acclimatized. Ford thought I should have sun, and advised Toulon. I am sick of sun, climate and thinking about my chest. So, I have a room at the top of a little hotel next door to Ford, where I get full pension and service for 1,250 francs a month. It has steam heat and a fireplace. I have got a piano dragged up here and all my papers thrown around, and have dug in and shall not move a finger in travel until my book is finished. Also Ford sent me to Harrison of Paris and they gave me a chore translating old French songs to be sung. I was to select them myself. Part of my time goes playing them over and choosing. They run from 1280 to 1730. This will net me the vast sum of three thousand francs some one beautiful day. There are fifteen of them, but very short. They are not translatable really, I have to make a kind of rhyme that can be sung, keeping to the original sense of the things as nearly as I can. Tell Nancy I am learning to play the "Celebrated Menuet of Exaudet," and she can dance to it when we see each other again. If you come through Paris in July, you will find me here. You will find me here until the first of October. After that, I hope to have all done and shall go either to the south of France or the south of Spain . . . I imagine France . . .

Ford thought it would be fine for me to take his apartment, and I thought so too, until I remembered my lack of language, my ignorance of shopping, the fact that I should have to get up and build coal fires, and so on and on. Besides it would be too expensive, and anyhow I don't want to keep house ever again until I am settled somewhere once for all . . . I am as contented and happy and pleased and snug as ever I was in my whole life. I was miserable in Germany and I was fixing to be perfectly horribly miserable in Spain, and it occurred to me that this was not necessary. The first ten days here, en transit, I roared around and saw everybody: Caress Crosby and Sylvia Beach and the Fords and the Jolas', and who else? I made the rounds of the bars and cafes, and went to a Bal Musette, and bought a map of America 1631 on the Quai, and went to the Caveau Rouge and set up a Candle to Notre Dame de Paris and went over and touched the tomb of St. Genevieve, took a peep into the Pantheon (holding my nose not because of the illustrious dead but because of the Art there exposed), spent an evening with Emma Goldman in Le Select, and on and on. So when I returned it was in the character of one who was done with sightseeing for the moment and was ready to settle down. My God, I left out the Cluny and the Louvre; but the Cluny doesn't count, because I sneak in there every chance I get anyhow. And I shall go back to the Louvre for a few days with the archaic Greeks and the Italian Primitives . . .

In the spring I'm going for a week-end to Chartres and shall see Versailles. And I walk through the Luxembourg on most of my errands. Somehow I manage to get it in . . . But now I don't go even to tea parties; tomorrow I shall have lunch with Eugene and Maria Jolas. This last is a grand person. I like them both immensely, but she is tremendous. She was Maria MacDonald, from Kentucky, I forget just where, descendant of that upstart Thomas Jefferson and the family graveyard is at Monticello. She is ample and full of energy and resource: has two children in a nursery going at top speed, does all the heavy work of editing, and is taking on a small children's school at Neuilly so she can see for herself how her young are getting educated. This isn't half, and it isn't her activities that arouse my real admiration. Its the woman herself, sound and good and quick, a real oldfashioned "character" and independent as hell.

But they are leaving, and the Fords are leaving, and I shan't get much involved with such as Westcott and his crowd. I went to a party at Monroe Wheeler's after we had made our agreement about the songs, and talked all evening with Westcott and had not the faintest notion who he was. He invited me to lunch and I accepted; so soon, he said, as he had finished his book, which would be about ten days hence . . . so then Janice Ford told him afterward I hadn't known him at all and I haven't heard from him since . . .

All huddled up in a few paragraphs, it sounds like a noisy life, and it was for a while, but it isn't . . .

I know all you have predicted for me about Paris, but darlings, I am contented here and I have not been really so anywhere else, so here I stay till it wears off. Why I am happy I cannot explain, but I am. Full of energy and projects.

It is sad about the death of Andrew's mother; she seemed such a young sort of woman, it seems an early death. Give Andrew my true affection when you write to him.

Ford is having a nasty time with publishers, and agents. I don't know precisely what, but nothing comfortable. Janice is a little creature, thin, young and too much aquainted with hardship and trouble for her years, abrupt, courageous and baffled. Very mature in her feelings, uninformed, full of Jewish melancholy. She gave me a lovely painting of a tawny cat, and I bought a golden portrait of Julie in a straw hat for three hundred francs. She is nearly always good and when she is at her best is a really serious good painter . . . She hasn't an atom of frivolity in her, but a very caustic and clever humour. She does the most amusing sketches of Ford I ever saw . . .

Oh, well, I could go on and on, but what I'm really thinking about is that you'll all be here in July, blessed be God, unless you cut short and go to Toulon first. But you'll be here! Not across the ocean and half the world . . . Love to you both.

Katherine Anne

TO PAUL PORTER   30 Rue de Vaugirard
[brother]   Savoy Hotel
                                  Paris, France . . .
                                  March 8, 1932

Paul darling:

. . . . I suppose by now you have seen the letter to Gay in which I announced, after long debate with myself, that I was getting married. This report was much exaggerated. I came up from Berlin, stayed ten days in Paris, gathered myself together and went down to Madrid, where my young man had prepared an apartment and a ring. All the way I said to myself, "This is a great error, my good woman. You're in no mood to get married." I alighted from the train in a perfectly chilling blast of wind from the Sierras, was met by the blushing bride groom, we went for breakfast, and then to inspect the apartment, which was very charming, and then went all over Madrid, a beautiful, an enchanting city, and then I went to my hotel and went to bed and wept for nine hours because I know, always have known, that marriage is not for me under any circumstances whatever, and here was about the nicest person I had ever known fairly going to waste . . . In the end I plucked up my courage, said exactly what I thought, stayed on two days and saw Madrid, and came back to Paris . . . My young man came back with me, but goes again tomorrow. After all, he has a job in the American Embassy there and must get back. I know now I'll never marry him nor anybody else unless I go suddenly mad, and I'll never live in Madrid so long as there is Paris. I love this city, I should have been here years ago. I've had it in my mind for seven—ten years, at least, but Lord, how slowly and painfully I get what I want in this world! Not that Paris was the end of all this battle. But it is really a place to live, and I have already settled myself in a little hotel, with a very quiet room in a wing on the top floor, where I can clatter the typewriter at all hours, play on the piano whenever I like, have my meals regularly without thinking about them, and all for a little less than fifty dollars a month . . . Now, that novel is going to be finished and a lot of things beside.

I feel really happy, but gay and merry and pleased about things, for the first time in a very great while . . . Break the news to the family there aint gonna be no weddin' Wednesday week, down in old Bengal . . . (Do you remember Aldous Huxley's *Antic Hay?*) I'm certain they'll all feel it is for the best. God knows I do. It's been weighing on my mind all these months without my knowing really why I was so hellish gloomy.

The *Scribner's* story will be in the May number, out April 20th . . . Make voodoo for me that I get the prize. I'm beginning to believe in my luck, but that does seem a little fantastic. Already a publishing house here has made a contract with me to translate fifteen old French songs, a singing version, to be published next fall very beautifully, with illustrations. I shall send copies to your children and to the others, and I hope they will sing them . . . It doesn't pay so much (about a hundred twenty five dollars,) but it shouldn't be such hard work either, and will be something to fall back on when I'm sick of writing. If I could work steadily—something I have never been able to do—there are exactly eleven magazines which have asked me for stories or poems. Now some of this work can be done. Not all of it, for I don't mean to rush myself or write things I don't believe in merely for the sake of publishing. I never would do that, even when my case was pretty sad. So I shan't begin now . . .

Why have you never sent me even a snap shot of your promising young? I remember the first two so well, and now there's one I don't even know the name of, which I consider somehow disgraceful. I'm even a little dim as to whether its a boy or girl, though I have an idea its a boy . . . I hope that first little boy is growing up fine and intelligent, he was the sweetest thing I ever saw in a cradle, except possibly Mary Alice, whom I loved so much. The others, also, but I had a special feeling about that one because he must have looked exactly as you did at that age. Dorothy Ray must be half a young lady by now . . . Sister writes me about her children, and I have a small picture of Breckinridge trying to be a sky scraper, but what about yours? Gay says they're all talented and handsome, but what are they doing? And you and Connie seem to be making the one, the unique successful marriage—at first try—in our lamentably married family, for certainly if I had no talent for it, Gay had not either, nor Baby, at first . . . It was our famous bad judgement that Dad used to fairly boast about.

How's beezness? Speaking of Dad reminds me, for he cannot see, nor could he ever, any hope for the country or the family, financially speaking . . . His fortunes have been worse than my own, if that is possible. Every time I have a note from him I feel that total insolvency is waiting around the corner for all of us . . . It can't be as bad as all that. Did Mr. Hoover's Prosperity hit you very hard? It was odd that my first relief should come at the time of depression and danger, so that I was rich, for me, when everything was tottering.

Do write me a note after all these centuries, and tell me real news. I suppose I should say something about what I have been doing here: but after all, I have simply visited Saint Chapelle and gone to Jimmy's Bar and fallen into the aperitif habit for five o'clock, and I go to café with friends—Jolas of *Transition,* Sylvia Beach who published James Joyce first, Caresse Crosby who runs a publishing house, Ford Madox Ford, and so on. I have been to three or four literary parties, and am going to lunch with Glenway Westcott shortly, and t'other night at one of Ford's parties I won the first prize for a sonnet written in ten minutes—a great big Baba cake to be soaked in rum before eaten. So the next day I invited Ford and his wife to tea and some others and we ate the baba. My young man was one of the judges, and fought bitterly against my having the prize. He said loudly it was the worst sonnet—not only among the competitors, but utterly the worst he had ever seen, and if he had his way I would not even get the ribbon off the wooden spoon, which was the booby prize. He was right, absolutely, but they rode him down and he ate all he could hold of the baba.

I love going along the quay and shopping for old maps. I am going to get a collection of early American maps. There are many of them and very good. I have already a French map of America made in 1631, and a French map of Virginia dated 1640. They are beautiful and inaccurate and I mean to have a lot of them.

This doesn't give much idea of why I am so happy in Paris, though, does it? Well, its such a gorgeous dim old city, with remnants of all its history from medieval times still standing, still in use, still a part of life. I have a feeling of continuity, of things beautifully done for their own sakes, a strong live source of belief in life, that goes on and will allow me to go with it. I can live and work here without question, see the people I like, arrange my life as I want it without the terrible drain on spirit and energy that it costs almost anywhere else . . . I do not have to explain anything or listen to explanation, and I do not have that feeling of being at odds with society because I am an artist. Here the artist is part of the scheme, he has his place, he seems to be a human being, and not a pet, or pariah, or clown or prostitute; if he has anything to give, there are plenty of people with critical sense who will take a genuine, living interest in him, because they really feel that good art is important . . . That is somewhere near the reasons I feel happy here . . . I'm going to stay as long as I possibly can. I want to come home and visit, but I'm coming back, for I mean to stay in Europe—France most of the time, for at least five years. And then we'll see . . .

Give my love to Connie and all the babies, and my love to you.

Katherine Anne

I've spent days in the Louvre and in the Cluny Museums looking at Italian Primitive painting and Greek archaic sculpture, and wood carving from the 12th century and manuscripts of old music, and would you believe it, collections of shoes dating back to 11 hundred—well, for that matter, back to Roman times. But the 12th century ones are the most entertaining. You fairly wonder how, in such apparent instruments of torture, these people could ever get their minds on anything else . . .

To BARBARA HARRISON 30 Rue de Vaugirard
March 17, 1932

Dear Miss Harrison:

I regret extremely to tell you that I am finding myself quite unable to translate the songs, since most of them are quite untranslatable, and since I am not a fluent poet, writing small poems suitable for the music is proving a very heavy task. The idea of the book is a beautiful one, and I hope you will be enabled to publish it by finding some one else. I have not given up sooner because not until now have I become convinced that for me the undertaking is not suitable.

Would you allow me to suggest some one to take over my part of the work? I know a young man who lives here, is adept at translation, is a skillful adapter, besides being a poet of some gifts, and who would be very happy in exactly this sort of thing. I should like to see you at any time convenient to you, when I will return the books and explain more clearly the whole situation.

Very sincerely yours,
Katherine Anne Porter

TO ROBERT McALMON   Basel, Switzerland
                                              June 7, 1932

Dear Bob:

It isn't exactly t b, you know: it's what the doctors at the American Hospital described as A Condition. All I can say for A Condition is, it gives me as much trouble as an honest case of t b; the one doubtful mercy being, it shall probably not be fatal for years and years and years . . . No, let me be honest. I'm glad I'm not going to die unless something heavy runs over me. I'm happy as a pin-feathered lark that I can't POSSIBLY die unless I fall out of an airplane. I will never kick off this mortal shuffle until some one gets mad and shoots me . . . Oh, darlin', I've had moments and weeks and months when I couldn't even think of existence without cursing my head off, but how past all that is, for the time being, anyhow . . . I don't mind living in Basel. It's a *churming* spot. You'd perish here of boredom in fifteen minutes. And I may not stay here, anyhow. I'm thinking of going on to the Black Forest, or up to that little Montana you write about. I must choose somewhere and dig in, for I shan't be able to afford much more jaunting about either. If I go up too high, my nerves go jittery. If I stay too low, the lungs collapse. If I stay middle ground, the inhabitants all have cowfaces and scow bottoms and don't understand my German or my French or my English, and as for my Spanish, they never heard of it . . .

So there you are, now.

Suddenly I don't mind anything. Quite suddenly. I want to work and I shall work, and I shan't trouble about anything else until I've got all I want to say said as nearly as any of us ever can come to that state. I like Paris, and would like to stay there for a while, but a visit now and then will be about all. And the hell of it is, I don't go the rounds at all compared to any one you ever heard of. I never went near a bar oftener than once in ten days. I never fell off the stool once, when there were plenty around going down like plunk. I spent, in fact, just one third of my time flat in bed all wound up in down quilts and surrounded by bottles of Perrier. But its all over now. I am in good health and mean to stay so.

The project for the long short story sounds good. I have an idea—it was meant originally for a part of my novel, but if it works out I shall use it, for I can't possibly get everything into that novel I once planned to. More of this later. I was reading some magazine not long since, I think it was *Pagany,* maybe not; and it occurred to me that for a long time now almost all the stories I had read were almost as monotonous as the plot for a medieval Pastourelle: you know: a Knight riding through a wood, meets a maiden. He proposes to sleep with her, and she does, or does not consent. And that's positively all there is to it. This theme must have been used for five hundred little musical shows around the twelfth to the fifteenth century. Well, it seems to me now that a youth and a maid, or their approximates, meet, or go somewhere, in a wood or on a hill or behind a barn, and there they fumble around, and sometimes the thing comes off and sometimes it doesn't, and absolutely nothing new or even interesting or credible is added to our already complete knowledge of the mechanics of such things . . . Copulation as such is no longer a subject for good reading matter unless something occurs between the persons that makes it unique, memorable, something positively added to human experience . . . Damn it, *something* must *happen,* which is what most of these writers simply do not seem to realize. The new number of *transition* had some good stories: "Sub-tropical," by Bob Brown. "Balkan Journey," by Whit Burnett. —Well, I'm afraid that's all, for the stories. I suppose this is no moment to quote Chekoff. Tschekov, then. But he said something that's simply a fact. I can't quote exactly: but "the real artist is going somewhere, and he takes his reader with him. Like the ghost in *Hamlet,* he does not come and rouse our expectations for nothing . . ."

Even the love of man for man is not important unless there is something really to be told about them: two women in love can be fearfully tiresome. Its nothing new. Just telling how two dumb Lesbians finally got to bed is not getting us anywhere. . . .

Katherine Anne

TO HELEN O'LOCHLAIN   Basel, Switzerland
CROWE   October 8, 1932

Dear Helen:

Your account of Père Degeyter's funeral gave me a hunger and thirst after his kind of righteousness . . . I hope that when I am 84 or 96 and need a buryin', you will be there to say of me that I was virtuous and fidèle and courageous and *therefore* it was a joyous funeral! That is the very loveliest obituary I ever read . . . I really want to be good, it is so difficult and so rare. I think I have been cowardly and slack and very unfaithful, in almost everything, but still, I know better, and can try for something more . . . When I come up to Paris I shall take a wreath to Père Degeyter.

Even in what you tell me is a bad photograph, the ancient sculpture of the female form is prodigious . . . I should say La Chaise must have seen it and studied it much. I feel a little rebuked for having caricatured Madame, but it has been interesting to watch her expand through the years, until now I am convinced the final frontier has been gained . . .

If you are not aquainted with Erasmus of Rotterdam, you must be as soon as you can manage it . . . I'm sure in some library there you can find the first French translation—first good one, of the *Moriae Encomium, Eloge de la Folie, Nouvellement Traduit du Latin d'Erasme etc avec les figures de Jean Holbein, etc M.DCC.LXXX* these figures are not all by Holbein—his brother Ambrosius helped and maybe one or two other artists . . . Anyhow, you'll adore it, and add the *Colloquies* for good measure . . .

To Mary Doherty   Basel, Switzerland, of all places
[fragment of a draft]   October 21, 1932

Mary darling:

Your letter came this morning, sent from New York to Paris to here. . . . Gene, who never reads a letter, or hardly ever, was as happy to have yours: and read it twice over, as I did too . . .

The news of Hart's death, or rather, the manner of it, was a shock. He had told me so often he meant to kill himself, I doubted he would ever do it. He must have reached a stage of desperation beyond words to have done it. He used to frighten me half to death by threatening to cut his throat, or to jump from our roof, but even in my nervous shock I felt he would not really, but was merely determined not to let the atmosphere around him clear for even a moment. I have had no particulars at all, no one has written one word to me on the subject, and I have not written to inquire, for the whole situation, when I left Mexico, both there and in New York, had roused my complete distrust of every one, I felt that no matter what I said, in some quite horrible way nobody would believe or listen. The thing had been so frightful to me I could hardly believe it myself. You know how he talked and talked and slandered me, and in the uproar and confusion he created I simply felt it was useless trying to make myself heard. It was foul and outrageous, and as for me, his suicide has not changed the thing that happened. Death cancels our engagements, but it does not affect the consequences of our acts in life. And I have yet to see the end, no doubt, of what he did, while he has gone, escaped, without explaining, without once giving a sign that he realized the sin he had committed. I have several letters from him, written in sober moments after some of the worst episodes, and I wrote to him, trying to put down coldly on paper what I felt, asking him to read them over when he was tempted to repeat his insults, and to remember that I meant what I was saying, and was his friend who wished him no harm. I suppose these letters are lost, I wish I had kept copies, but I never keep copies of letters, and I have no evidence whatever that all the things he said and did against me were unfounded. And *why* did he? I ask myself this, and can answer only in part, and then the reasons are so tangled, so subtle, that when they are put into words they simply do not convey anything even to myself as I say them . . . and they may not be the real reasons. How can I know? I know that his feelings for me were very complicated, but I do not think his feelings for me had anything to do with his behavior there. He simply came into an atmosphere different from what he had expected, he told me what he hoped for in Mexico, he had been misled by stupid, frivolous untrue accounts of homosexuality in Mexico, and to find that even there he must observe at least the fundamental rules of decent behavior, infuriated him. He would not listen to me when I told him he could not treat the Indians as he wished to. Malcolm and others had told him that all Indians were openly homosexual and incestuous, that their society was founded on this, he would encounter no difficulties whatever. He told me he wished to let himself go, he had come to Mexico for that, he was sick of living in two worlds. I said, it could be done, but he must at least observe one or two small rules of human relationship. He was not willing, he would not consent even to this. He was utterly debauched and lost by the time he came there. The change in him in the few months since I had parted from him, on the best terms of friendliness, was astonishing. And what he would not understand was that I sympathised with his dilemma, I hoped he might find some way of living that would relieve his mind and spirit and body of their terrible tension, I had no prejudices against his sexual habits, but I had no intentions of letting my own life be destroyed by him, simply because I felt it was not necessary that our lives come to collision in any way. It was his infuriated determination to invade my life that I resented and resisted: and if I had it to do again, I would find a way to resist it more effectually.

We used to spend long mornings on the roof talking over all the things that troubled him, and he told me then, in those rather quieter moments, that he was beginning to feel himself hardening, that his brutal acts were brutalizing him gradually, he was frightened to find that he no longer had the power to feel except by the most drastic and cruel stimulants. This physically as well as emotionally. He said he feared he had gone as far as he could in the road he had taken, and there was no way back. He confessed that his sexual feelings were now largely a matter of imagination, which drove and harried him continually, creating images of erotic frenzy and satisfactions for which he could find no counterpart in reality . . . These are not his words, but the substance. He said, he now found himself imagining that if he could see blood, or cause it to be shed, he might be satisfied: and he continually talked of the little fourteen year old carpenter's apprentice—you remember that ghastly episode—as a virgin, who might bleed when deflowered . . . These things he said sober, so I will leave unsaid the things he shouted when drunken . . . I have no apology to make for my nausea with this episode. It sickened me, and made me ill for a long time . . . In Berlin, and even afterward in Paris, I was like a person suffering from recurring shell-shock. When I remembered even one thing of all the numberless nightmarish things, I would sweat and turn sick and go to bed for a day. Even so, it would not have been unpardonable if he had not turned so insanely on me, with such a bestial assurance of insolence, insulting me in my own house, the place I had gone to for recovery from illness, and a hope of some kind of peace for a few months . . .

I did not look at all upon him as some one who must be saved and spared at the expense of every one around him . . . I do not yet. But Hart was very acute in those matters and presumed outrageously on his immunity as a pathological case . . . There were and are yet in the world several persons more important to me than Hart Crane ever was, and many ways of life I consider much more worth saving than his: And besides, all this talk of "saving" him— he did not want to be saved, he could not be. All that was worth touching in him he put into his poetry, and it is this I wish to remember, and keep and foster. Not that living corpse, who wrote his poetry almost in spite of himself, and who, if he had stayed in the world, would have come to worse ends . . .

TO EUGENE PRESSLY　　　　　[Basel]
　　　　　　　　　　　　　　　It must be Thursday. November
　　　　　　　　　　　　　　　4? [1932]

Angel darling. . . .

　　I spent some time last night, after I had worked on Lizardi, about midnight, trying to clarify my ideas about God. And I decided one thing: that He has no concern whatever with our human affairs, with this body of our death. Therefore, one does not pray for mortal benefits, because He takes no part in them . . . But I wish one might pray for what one wanted in this world, and I have decided one can, really, and very effectively too, for a statement of our desires even to ourselves strengthens one, and so, I shall lose no time setting up those candles and praying my little head off, once I get back to that ancient seat of faith, Paris . . . and a church I have some faith in . . .

　　Praying that we'll really get to Paris and be settled together there happily. I love you truly, my dear beloved angel, I can't possibly live without you . . .

　　I'm making this a quick note because the sun is shining again warmly, and I want to take a long walk and keep in health and spirits . . . Write me when you can, I think of you every mortal minute of the day . . . But I work and eat and sleep comfortably, as if I were in training for a race, or something of the kind . . . Quite determined to do the work I have planned, so I shan't be always left behind when we make these changes . . .

　　Another letter tomorrow, darling. A kiss on your sweet mouth.

Katherine Anne

I created a work of art with the camera, maybe. It is entitled Madonna and Child with Milch Goat. If it comes out I'll send it to you.

To Robert McAlmon   Basel
November 12, 1932

Dear Bob:

.... Island life can gnaw in on one, no doubt about it. And if people develop hates, they take on a disproportionate importance, as if somehow the very smallness of the place acted on them, and made them sink in a little deeper ... I don't like hating in general, I have a few hates that wear me very well, and I don't want to take on any new one, or above all, any artificial ones. I don't blame you for just getting out. Thank God, that's always left. One can pack up and depart. Geography has never been properly appreciated in such matters ... You can look around and think, well, a new climate, and a different landscape, but the same world.

I spent eight months of self-elected hermit life in Bermuda, out of season, and it is really my kind of Paradise, all brilliant color and tropical sun and fruitfulness, and the British colonials there are the most reassuringly well-mannered and decent people ... I had a coral house and a ten acre garden, all terraces and roses and pomegranates and limes and bananas and palms and magnolias and a charming yellow haired kitten named Rufus, and I wrote at least six hours every day, and nobody hated me that I know of, nor I anybody, and yet, I burst out of there like the famous monk of Siberia "with the hell of a yell," you remember, and struck back for New York where I couldn't live on what I earned and the climate did me in, and was glad to do it ... And the Islanders went with me to the boat, sobbing, not because I was leaving them but because they wanted to go too ...

Paradises are a sell, darling. I suppose you must have noticed it. I gathered as much from your "Mexican Interval." ...

To Harrison Boone   Paris
Porter   January 21, 1933

Dear Dad:

Your long letter full of family lore was very welcome, I have copied out the essential parts for permanent record, so that if ever

I go to Kentucky I can weed out the kin from all the rest, if such a thing is possible by now, when all the families are so intermarried, I suppose everybody is at least distantly related to everybody else . . .

Now I have some questions to ask about mother's side of the house. You told me once that her father—whose name in full you gave in this letter—was the foster child of some one, a government official either of Tennessee or South Carolina, I forget which . . . I lost that letter, but if you will tell me again, I will copy it for reference and put it in my little loose leaf book. I am interested because the other day I met a woman from South Carolina who was by birth a Waring, married a Pringle, and asked me if my family—part of it—came from Charleston or anywhere near about, as the Porters and the Frosts were still there in force. Of course, I couldn't quite say, but she insisted that they must have been there at some time. Dear Daddy, you must think I've lost my mind or never had any to even think of disowning Dan'el . . . I'm much prouder of him than I am of any other ancestor I could possibly have, and understand perfectly Grandmother's pride in the Skaggs and Boones. They must have been fine people, and I would only be nervous for fear they would be tempted to disown their descendents if they could see them. Yet they have not done so badly. I am always hearing of or meeting Boones who are doing something a little unusual, and the old pioneer seems to have had energy enough to scatter down many generations . . . The Skaggs not so much. That is, of the name. But then, there are descendents of Boone, like us, who do not bear the name but are also pretty up-and-at-em. You know, I have very little patience with people who try to live on their ancestors, and southerners here wear me out talking about their families. But I do have a little private interest of my own in family history, and I wish you would write down for me everything you remember about all branches—for example, you never say a word about the Porters—You are the only one who really knows anything about all this, and I think it might be pleasant some day for the younger children to know at least who their great-grand people were. I will keep all you write carefully . . . You write very well, you know, and I think I inherited my bent for it from you . . . (Get yourself a softer pencil next time, honey! I will copy it on the typewriter.)

For example: Couldn't you just take your time and tell what you remember of your childhood, where you were born, what life was like, how we came to go to Louisiana and Texas—I remember something about a sugar mill in Louisiana, what you remember of conditions during and after the war, all the things that no one remembers now; it would be interesting. If it were full enough, I might even edit it a little if it needed it and get it published somewhere . . . But this is not the point . . . The point is to make a little record for the family. Don't write as if you meant to publish it, but put in all the most intimate things as if you were telling it to me . . . Do it as slowly as you like, and just write down things as they occur to you . . . Would you do this? It would just be something for your spare time, and I would be so glad to have it . . . It would help me, too, in a novel I mean to write after this one is finished . . . For example, I remember your telling once—this was when I was a child—how, after the war, you only had hot wheat biscuits once a week, on Sunday morning, and how you would grab a few, if you could, to eat later in the day. How you and one of your brothers got homesick for Louisiana and ran away, trying to get back to where the sugar cane grew . . . and all these things, which are lovely to me, and which I should like to hear again . . .

If you don't feel like writing so much, just write letters.

One thing more: there was a William D. Porter who was Lieutenant Governor of South Carolina, who lived in Charleston, about 1865. He also helped to found a school for the Sons of Confederate Veterans . . . Wasn't Uncle Bill named for some one in the family? I wonder if this man was a connection . . .

(Something else I remember that you told me when I was a child. How grandmother, I think it was, had a large number of blankets woven for the young men of her neighborhood when they went to the war. How one boy came back without his blanket, because his best friend had been killed, and when they put him in the grave, he looked so cold, the boy said, that he had put the blanket around his friend to be buried in. I remember so many things of this kind, but not the names or details. Tell me again. Also, there was a young Captain, or Lieutenant, John Porter, about twenty two years old, killed at the battle of Mansfield, Louisiana. Was this a younger brother or cousin of your father?)

Who was Brigadier-General John Jacob Myers, besides being

the husband of great-aunt Eliza? Where and how did he come by that uproarious title?

And so on. I wish I could come home and talk with you for about six months. Together we'd make a book, wouldn't we? However, dear Dad, it is not possible, just now. Europe is the best place for me, and even if it were not, I could not leave because I have not the money . . . The whole situation here is very bad, but it would seem not so frightful as in the United States now . . . Maybe it is because the United States always does things on such a grand scale, our collapse will also be many times greater than the disasters of other countries who have not so much to lose . . .

I have worked out of the frightful jam I got in at Basel, and my own prospects are fair enough. I shall not starve this winter, at least, and I hope you shall not; Paris has been deep in an influenza plague, but I got off lightly, with four days in bed and about four more sitting holding my head and wishing I had died. You know the horrible suicidal after effects of that disease. Much worse than the sickness itself. But now I am well recovered, and make the rounds visiting my aquaintances, who all came faithfully to see me, and afterward went down with it one at a time . . . I feel a little guilty, and yet with the city so full of the germs, they might have taken them anywhere else at all. When I was so desperately sick in Denver, in 1918, a young boy twenty one years old, whom I did not know at all, who happened to be living in the same house with me, took care of me for the three days before a doctor or a bed in the hospital could be found for me. Nursed me and gave me my medicine and came in three times every night to see how I was. Ten days later while I was unconscious in the hospital, he died of influenza. I cannot forget this, it is terrible that he should have saved my life and lost his own. In this case, I feel directly responsible, for he was a big healthy fellow who lived out of doors, and need never have come in contact with the epidemic at all. But as none of my aquaintances here were seriously ill, I do not feel so badly about them, since they run around, too, all the time to theatres and cafés and could as well have picked up infection in those places.

I hope the rest of you escaped, after Baby and Breckenridge got well. . . .

You were saying that you have very few enjoyments, and I wish you had more. Maybe it would interest you to write a little, maybe you are not as simple as I am, who love to listen to music on a victrola. I require so little entertainment, and still prefer reading to anything else. Do you still love to read? I could send you some books to amuse you . . . And that reminds me, I am sending that magazine in the same mail with this letter, with the story about Jinny Wiley in it. Caroline is not mistaken and neither were you. It was I who had the dates wrong. Caroline says that this Henry Skaggs was an old man about eighty years old at the time he rescued Jinny, and that it happened about 1780. So the old fellow would be possibly the father of your grandfather, I should think . . . Caroline didn't make him out such a hero as the actual story has it, but that was because she wished to make the woman the chief figure . . . But I said to her, that she should either make up her stories out of her own imagination, or if she must re-write history, not to libel my relations when she does it . . . She didn't exactly libel Henry, and she didn't mention his name, but I don't see why she couldn't have stuck a little closer to the facts just the same . . . However, its a pretty good story, altogether . . .

This *Hound & Horn* is the same magazine that published my "Flowering Judas." By the way, my story, "The Cracked Looking Glass," is to be reprinted in *The Best Short Stories of 1933* and O'-Brien, the editor is also going to try to get my entire book of short stories reprinted in a regular edition in England. This last affair will bring me a little money, as well as getting me a larger audience . . . I believe that is all the good news at the moment . . .

Do answer all my questions when you write, darling, and let me hear soon. If you have any more recent snapshots, do send them. I keep them all together, and have quite a collection. But I still hope to make, some day, a picture of you with my own camera which will be just like you . . . These are all so different I can't get more than a general notion of your looks. . .

Good bye, with a hug and kiss.
Katherine Anne

To Harrison Boone
Porter

Care Guaranty Trust Company
Paris
March 2, 1933

Dear Dad:

Your letter came today, when I had been thinking all day that I must write to you with news. You give your own news so casually; a new baby in the family, Breck takes shot at fleeing burglar, the orange trees are frostbitten again, etc; that I shall announce mine with equal calm.

This Saturday week, March eleven, at eleven o'clock in the morning, I am going over the Mairie of the Sixth Arrondissement (the part of town I live in,) and get married to Eugene Dove Pressly.

And there you are . . .

I enclose small snap shot of your new son-in-law, who is a monstrous fine feller. We have known each other for nearly three years, so it is nothing sudden. In fact he is the same young gentleman I almost married this same time last year, thought better of it, and have changed my mind again, because it becomes obvious as time goes on that neither of us will settle down or do anything until this is arranged. . . .

He comes from Pennsylvania, is of very good old Quaker and Presbyterian stock, pure Scotch and English descent,† a man of character if ever I saw one, and I should surely know a little something about human nature by now . . . I took these pictures of him with my camera last spring, and except that he is not dark as they appear, they are exactly like him, and I wish to point out to you a very fine head, my dear Pop!. . . .

Its odd about the way the cold strikes first one part of the world and then another by seasons . . . Here in Paris, famous for its hellish winters, we have had only two sharp fits of cold, and now it is like late spring, warm and showery and everything turning green. It is so unusual everybody speaks of it. All winter I have worn open brown sandals that I wore all last summer, and have not been

---

†In May 1950 Porter commented, "Gene told me only of his father's side—on his mother's he was German! half-German! and behaved like one at last."

uncomfortable. This after buying heavy shoes in terror, remembering the horrible winter last year in Berlin. And speaking of Berlin, I suppose you notice the news from there. The country is in a panic and people are running away. Did I tell you I met Goering, Hitler's right hand man, at a dinner party in Berlin last year, and he talked with me a whole evening about what Hitler was going to do, and I was skeptical, and thought, it is just politician's boasting. But it is all coming true, frightfully. Here, people go about saying that America may go to war with Japan, and if so, maybe to war with England, too, and it is too plain that this would be pleasant news to a great many people. But what do you hear there, and do internal affairs look any more promising? All the news we get here is bad, about banks crashing and unemployment increasing, and I wonder if it is really so tragic as it seems . . .

Getting married in Paris is quite a thing. First we went to a lawyer to be certain all our papers were in order, and he sent us to the American Consulate to sign our affidavits, and to the prefecture of Police for identification cards, and to the local arrondissement police to have our certificate of domicile stamped, and to the Mairie to declare our honorable intentions, and the honorable Mayor posted the banns in the wall case in the driveway of the municipal building where they must stay for ten days, and the notice is published in a newspaper, and then fifty—so far, only fifty—restaurant and hotel keepers, furniture houses, automobile companies, tailors, dressmakers, engraving companies, photographers, apartment house owners, etc. etc, have mailed us pounds of literature praising their several wares and offering us their distinguished services for a cash consideration in the approaching ordeal of our nuptials . . . It is merely an old French custom, and as I haven't a penny and Gene has a very modest salary, and we hardly know how we are to get a small flat started, and I shan't even have new gloves for the ceremony, and so on, we have spent quite a jolly evening or two over our fan mail; thinking, too, it would be humane for us to post a notice beside our banns saying: "Caterers to the nuptial victims, save your stamps. We're dead broke."

Fifty letters in four days, and a friend who has had experience says they will keep right on coming maybe for months . . . Marriage is a serious affair here . . . We have even received brochures giving every law concerning the state of matrimony, and little guides pointing the social etiquette of the entire procedure from the first meeting to the honeymoon trip and the bride's first entertainment in her new home . . . Its all really rather nice, and I should think would add considerable drama to an already exciting enough situation, but some how so little of it applies to us, we feel rather outside of this elaborate web.

Good night, darling dad, Its half past eleven, and time to stop the typewriter . . . My health is very good, I feel quite merry . . .

Love to everybody . . . Your letter today seemed also in better spirits, I think maybe the back of winter is broken and we are all getting the fresh life of spring. I do not consider you as really old, with your health and good constitution, I do not see why you should not live a very long time . . . I hope we shall make a feast for you on your hundredth birthday and put a crown of flowers on your head the way the French villagers do for their brave ancients who have weathered so many storms . . . There have been many times when I have been so entirely sickened of life it was very hard to work to keep on, a half dozen times I have been tempted to suicide, but I am glad I did not give way, for I have always felt that the last half of my life would somehow atone for the first half, and I still think it may . . . It is not possible to live in this world without suffering unless one is a born stone. But it is also possible to have a great deal of happiness in spite of the suffering. I hope you will have good health and live long, and I hope too to see you before so very long. It might be possible. If I sold one long story, I could make the trip . . . when I do, I shall make it.

> All my love and affection to my darling,
> *Your Katherine Anne*

94

TO ROBERT MCALMON   166 Boulevard Montparnasse
                          Paris
                          April 19, 1933

Dear Bob:

. . . . I'm very settled and happy about the marriage, dear Bob, it really gives some kind of solidity and form to my daily living that I seem badly to need, and Gene is really a pretty fine person. I think we'll make a good go of it. I don't know whether its because I'm so hopelessly female, or whether I share a universal human need, but I find more freedom and more scope for personal decision in action in having a kind of headquarters, or point of reference outside of myself . . . That is, I like having a sense of responsibility towards some one else, it keeps me from the danger of coiling in upon my own vitals like a snail; I know my own tendency to melancholia and perfectly egotistical self-concentration. I didn't marry to escape these things, but for the perfectly good reason that I have found a beautifully liveable person; but I find that I do largely escape them in marriage. Chronology has something to do with it, too: I am at that time of life when most conscious people make a final decision, a choice of some sort. If ever one is to settle a way of life, one does at my age. I shall be thirty nine years old next May. And evidently my temperament and my experience combine to urge me to gather up the ragged edges of thought and feeling into a compact whole that is recognizably my own and I am able to manage somewhat . . . Quite enough of this, I should say . . . But I think you are doing something of the kind when you suddenly find that you want to work whether you are published or not . . . Its really an important decision, and I am glad you have made it. . . .

                          With my love,
                          Katherine Anne

To James Stern   166 Boulevard Montparnasse
                                    Paris
                                    August 30 1933

Dear Jimmy Stern:

I think your short stories are magnificent, and the several persons to whom I have given the book to read think so too. My husband I think is a good judge, and so are Glenway Westcott and Lincoln Kirstein. Kirstein, who edits the *Hound & Horn,* was so enthusiastic he got your address and has probably by now asked you to send him a story. Do send him one, for such a sympathetic partisan should not be discouraged. He gave me a study called *Cecil Rhodes* by William Plomer. Rhodes, Rhodesia, and Rhodes Scholars hitherto had been of a mingled cloudy inconsistency in my mind, somehow symbolising rapacity, endless horror and cruelty, and ignorance: you can trace the connection easily. I know now as much as I wish to know about Rhodes, but of Rhodesia I shall read cheerfully on as much as you will write about it. Rhodes Scholars we may leave to God and Oxford.

"Inadequate book," indeed! How could you write that or even think it? Or maybe you meant, not up to what you can do, now that this is done, or not as good as you hoped for, or whatever you like. In itself, I should hardly know where to begin choosing my favorite, for every story is worth reading several times over and each has its own quality. I was delighted with "The Man Who Was Loved"—a gorgeous story. "The Heartless Land," and "Outcasts" and "Rule Britannia"—how could I prefer one over the other? I'm glad I don't have to.

September 7, 1933. . . . In all your stories I like the way you have taken the trouble to say what you wanted to say: I know you have, for only tough work will bring one to such ease of expression with directness and concentration of intensity . . . And the really complicated psychological predicaments you can build up in a group: The "Charles Congreve, Esquire" is probably the best of this sort of thing . . . I hope nothing happens to discourage or throw you off . . .

To Madrid? I hear that Bob is there, though not from him. If you know his address, send it me please, because I must get that manuscript back to him. *There is something good in everything he writes,* but oh, the sense of weary slogging in his style, the intolerable disgust and fatigue of his mind and heart, that makes every manuscript of his a long hard journey for the reader, too . . . And he really has got a look-in on something, a finger on a kind of reality, I *cannot* think why he does not work it out. A terrible pity and waste.

The roads to Spain and Austria seem now main travelled ones. We had thought of Spain for October, but Valencia and Barcelona. We probably shan't get there at all, but may go to Italy in December . . . Gene has only a month free, and so many places we have not seen! We may just stay right here, lacking decision to choose where we will go . . .

I hope you are working well, I look forward to the novel. Myself I do better in good weather—shameful confession. The weather here is perfect, and so I am working easily and quite happily . . . I am a grasshopper who has got to get my singing done in the summer, for no amount of thrift and storing against the cold will help me any . . .

Gene's translation of Adrienne Monnier's short story, "The Foolish Virgins," will appear in the *Hound & Horn,* and so will a chapter from my Cotton Mather book: "A Bright Particular Faith: A.D. 1700." Let us see something of your stories there too. The pay is smallish, if you mind that. I do, but what can be done about it?

Thank you for "The Heartless Land." Let me hear from you: forget charitably how slow I was to write, since I half-hoped by delaying to be able to say better what I think about your stories. But after all I can just say it is a fine job and I am glad of it . . .

Our best to you both,
Katherine Anne Porter

To Monroe Wheeler [166 boulevard Montparnasse, Paris]
Monday afternoon . . .
November 13, 1933

Dear Monroe:

The story has got away to a start: pray for me. Now it seems to me a better title would be "False Hopes." But something else appropriate may occur later on. The title does not have to be changed, but the story is growing into something else, and another title will not be out of place. It begins: "It was worth the price of a ticket to see Kennerly take possession of the railway train among a dark inferior people . . ." and goes on.

Sylvia called me up this morning to say that Louis Gillet, critic of literature in English for the *Revue des Deux Mondes,* to whom she had loaned a copy of *Flowering Judas,* was also interested in the Song-Book and went away with a prospectus in his pocket. If you gave him a copy do you suppose he really would review it, and if he did, would it make any difference to you? This is for you to decide.

In his latest letter, Lincoln says, offhandlishly: "Why don't you have a concert in New York with somebody very good singing your songs? It would be very excellent publicity for the book, and a great pleasure for all of us."

Bien, muy bien, but I have asked him how, situated as I am, one does such complicated things? There is a probable hope that "somebody very good" might be planning a concert there this winter, and would make a group of these songs. If this appeals to you, you might keep it in mind. Lincoln could help. He may even know that somebody. I do myself so wish to hear them all sung beautifull———y. Damn typewriters, bless them.

I write this because I am entirely sunk and shan't come up for air except with a new story between my teeth. It is going to sail with you on the 23rd . . .

Love to you both: I hope Glenway is working magic with his very last chapters . . .

Katherine Anne

All the Prospectii Are Gone!

TO MONROE WHEELER   166 Boulevard Montparnasse
                          Paris XIV
                          November 22, 1933

Written from the condemned cell last day before execution
and NO reprieve in sight . . .

Monroe, how can I tell you that the story will not be on the
Manhattan but on the Bremen? Just like that, I suppose . . . Like
the Baroness and the hat,* you remember that story? I have Shtroggled and Shtroggled; unlike her, I have lost. Yesterday I sat all day
in a sweat, and not one sentence would arrange itself. Today I have
an epileptic burst of energy, and tomorrow or the next day I should
think it may be finished . . . Dr. Johnson, whom I read for consolation as other painful souls read their Bible, or Homer, or Nietzsche,
or Karl Marx, remarks more or less that one who runs against time
has an antagonist who knows no casualties . . . You'll have the story
four days late. For me, this is being on time. I shall send a choice
of three or four titles, including the original one.

I am missing you dreadfully. I haven't gone to play on the
piano yet, but I shall celebrate getting this manuscript off by going
and tinkling gently at my Scarlatti Capriccio all one afternoon.
Reward of hypothetical virtue.

Monsieur Gillet of the *Revue des Deux Mondes* vows solemnly
if I will give him a Song-book, he will make a serious review of it
together with "Flowering Judas" . . . Maybe I'd better. I'm seeing
him at tea next Sunday at Sylvia's.** I haven't seen any notice of
the book here yet, when I do, I'll send clippings. Do you please
send me anything interesting about it from there. I suppose I should
keep a clipping service, but it is just now occurring to me that
keeping a record of things is probably a good notion.

Hasta luego. Vaya con Dios. I remember what you said over
the telephone about poetry for *Harper's,* to be sent to Russell Lynes

*Baroness Elsa (Freytag?) von Loringhoven, wearing a turban of
white crepe and fresh violets, a mourning wreath she had stolen,
from a door, not without twinges of conscience. 'But I won! Here
is the hat!'
**M. Gillet returned the Song Book to me without a word, and so
far as I know never read "Flowering Judas."

. . . I shall send some translations from Centenaire, if that's permissible—you will know about this—and two little original ones I have had a long time on hand. I don't trust my poetry out of my sight very often, but now I will. I have one also by Clement Marot beginning,

> *I am no more what once I was,*
> *And what I was no more shall be,*
> *My merry spring and summer days****
> *Have taken careless leave of me . . .*

But the trouble is, Marot's verse has alternate feminine rhymes which adds a muted syllable when sung, and this I haven't got yet . . . But it will come . . . in French the rhymes are maître, être, fenêtre, etc . . . In all English I find no rhyme for window—

Good bye for the moment. Give Glenway my love and remembrance. I have something to say to him about that voodoo of America he feared, but it must come after the voodoo of missing this boat with the story has been cleared off!

Don't stay away too long, either of you.

With my love,
Katherine Anne

Wrote to Donald Brace about this short story. I'm certain its quite alright, at any rate, now he knows.

***Amended: My jolly summer and my spring
                   Have taken thieves' farewell of me.

To Donald Brace   Care of Guaranty Trust
                                   Company
                                   4 Place de la Concorde
                                   Paris, France
                                   January 8, 1934

Dear Mr Brace:

. . . . You must have known when you wrote them how your comments on the fragment of manuscript [of Cotton Mather] would encourage me most marvellously. I am now making quite literally hundreds of minute corrections and verifications, besides some re-arrangement of chronology to make a more steady march. Shuttling back and forth and across is a fine device in fiction, but it can be most confusing in biography, I can't quite say why. So out go the fiction devices which crept in almost unconsciously. I shall be happy to know that the business of taking over the contract is really settled; and I hope there shall be no more difficulties . . . I believe I can promise safely there will be no more from me, at least.

Two things: On the same boat with this I am sending you a short story which I wrote quite suddenly last week, after thinking it over for some time. Would you try it on *Scribner's,* or *Atlantic Monthly,* or *Harper's,* or—if we must—on all three? *Scribner's* first. The *Mercury* won't have me, I feel pretty sure; there are several smaller magazines which would take it, but I should really like to have some money for it, if it is possible.

This is the first new story for the new collection. Please don't take it as setting a tone, or a pace, for there won't be any more like it; each one will be about quite different things and in different styles, so there's no telling what they'll look like when put together. We'll have to wait and see how they come out.

The second thing is a matter of asking your advice. Lincoln Kirstein asked me to write a ballet libretto for the new School and Theatre of Ballet he is organizing. I have the idea, and the plot, and the title *DOOMSDAY* . . . I want to reserve all my rights in it because I think it might make an opera later. So I wish to copyright it. How does one go about that? The ballet is to be produced in March, 1935. Writing a ballet libretto is nothing much, it's rather like a moving picture scenario . . . but the idea I believe is worth keeping for my own undisturbed use.

And a third request: Raymond Everitt doesn't seem to send back Gene's translation of the *PERIQUILLO*. It's a huge lumbering manuscript, and we have copies and Ford Madox Ford is going over it looking for places to cut out great slices even yet; so we do not really need that copy. But it has the illustrations from an old edition in it, so I would as soon know it was quite safe. May I ask Raymond to send it over to you to put in a safe corner? And this is really all. I can't think when I'll have another thing to ask of you! But you will see how literally I have taken your very kind offer!

With my best wishes to you,

Very sincerely yours,
Katherine Anne Porter

To Glenway Wescott   166 Boulevard Montparnasse
Paris XIV
January 10, 1934

Glenway my dear and dearer colleague!

. . . . Barbara writes she is still rotting in her bed, but there was a philosophically cheerful tone to the whole thing just the same. I wish I could explain why I have not finished that story ["Hacienda"], but ask me to explain why I was born and I can no more tell you!. . . .

It is now twice its original size, still growing, expanding in all directions, changing, a monster which most certainly I have created, but I do not know how nor why! And you shall have it shortly! You know, I spend my life thinking about technique, method, style—the only time I do not think of them at all is when I am writing! This is a kind of madness. . . .

Let me hear from you, my dear friend. With my love

Katherine Anne

To Barbara Harrison   Paris
                          May 23, 1934

Barbara darling,

"Hacienda" has broken through another knotty point, so I mean to reward myself by writing to you. Time is a mere fever-dream, Davos seems at once yesterday afternoon and years away . . . but the rest-cure and the visit I enjoyed with you are real, alive and merry . . . The trip began and ended in my favorite travel mood, pleasantly relaxed and mindless to Basel, and from Basel. Basel itself provided a certain kind of excitement; a very low kind, I think. I had just forty five minutes there, and had planned them very well, I thought. But a little viper of a customs inspector said I must not leave the train until my luggage was pawed over officially. Then he went away and did not come back. Twenty minutes later the passports inspector came, noted I had no visa, said I should leave the train entirely, valise and all, since I probably had not time to get a visa; and that I could take the next train at five o'clock. By this time we had been shunted a long distance back from the station, and there was no one to carry that white elephant of a bag. So the pleasant Frenchwoman in the compartment offered to help me lift it off the rack. It loosened suddenly, fell upon us and knocked us into the opposite seat. Then a youngish Englishman looked in and offered to help further. That brash gallant then lugged the bag, at a dead run, with myself running along beside him, all the way to the Swiss customs, where he dropped it on the long counter, and fled. I had kept murmuring, *"So* sorry!" or "How ridiculous!" or "It must be simply awfully heavy!" and such things, and he kept saying cheerfully, "Oh, I need the exercise!" or "It's *nothing*, really," or "Heavens, no, not at all!" then we shook hands in a flurry of mutual farewells and good wishes. "Do catch the train!" he shouted back. I doubted he could catch it himself. It seemed I would never find a taxi. Then I had to wait at the Consulate. But after all, I missed the train by only twelve minutes. Quite enough.

So I wandered out, having two hours, and found the Spanish wine shop, meaning to get at least a bottle of that seventy year old pale sherry for Monroe. The proprietor was out, would not be back until evening; the woman, after some talk, was able to remember me and the sherry in a group, you might say, but she did not know where it was kept. We went down to the cellar and looked, prowling among the casks and cobwebs. We pulled out shelves of crusted bottles and peered behind kegs, piles of coal, stacks of wood; I would recognize that particular sherry bottle anywhere, and it could not be discovered . . . So I went up and washed my hands and face and drank an enormous black beer. So back to the station, where I sent Gene a telegram, changed my Swiss francs, and sat in the station café drinking coffee and smoking and reading my London *Daily Mail*. Finally I went though the customs, where they did not open my bag, tottered back to the train—by this time missing my afternoon siesta seriously—and so, without further history, reached Paris at half past one—A.M.

After two days rest I was so far recovered that I transferred my curses from Basel and the Swiss to the lone French customs inspector, where they had belonged in the first place. Well, of course, I suppose that I should have got my visa on time. But its no fun cursing oneself.

Did you get your book from the Montparnasse book shop yet? Gene asked them about it the day after I talked to you, and they said they had sent it. My own Holbein is quite perfect. Clear, soft reproductions of fifty of his most handsome heads. I delight in it.

Nothing at all except work happens from day to day. From ten until five I live in that middle ground of my mind where exact memory deliberately attempts to mix and temper and change impressionistic memory: one without the other is nothing much, yet they will not fuse without struggle . . . After five thirty I am going to tea at Louis Gillet's, and his note says he is now writing "a little paper" about "the beautiful book of French Songs." It will appear in the *Revue des Deux Mondes.* He seems to be the editor of the English book pages for this revue; his father-in-law is permanent secretary for the Academie Francaise, and Gillet will be an Immortal yet, they say; and his words have such weight as these things carry with Frenchmen, and my few French friends seem to think it is a great thing: and that is all I know on this topic. But I do love to hear the Song Book praised, and if he does well by it I shall bless him. He is a Provençal with finely trimmed whiskers.

The snapshots were better and better, it consoled me to see that I was beginning to look human once more. It is painful to feel that one is actively, aggressively hideous. These later snapshots made me believe it is a curable affliction, like t.b. or bronchitis . . .

It is is *so* pleasant to remember, my Davos visit! and even better to look forward to the end of July, when you will be out and away, in Paris, maybe, or anyhow, well and free again. I do think that really I may get to Yucatan next February or March, and that you might go there also. These two pictures I send are the two kinds of Mexico that are still trying to live peaceably side by side . . . The stone head is one of hundreds in the Quetzalcoatl temple at Tepozotlan—the other, the doorway, is from the church there. Yucatan has even better temples, if the churches are not quite so good.

Give my love to Monroe, say he will have a thick manuscript to take back to New York. Only two more books after this long story, and then I expect to loll in that Heal chair for a week! Heavens, to think it might have been wasted on the tax collector! . . . This dislocated letter must end. At least, dear Barbara, it is not one you need have on your mind about answering, and that should be something in favor of dull letters.

With love from us both, and blessings on your head,

Katherine Anne

I have got the Lucrezia Borgia poem in a first-draft, but it must wait. Gene managed to read it fairly, and got it typed out. It should be rather nice. We'll see.

To CAROLINE GORDON   166 Boulevard Montparnasse
Paris, XIV
July 8, 1934

Dear Caroline:

We are settled cheerfully in a two room-kitchen cupboard-bath tub-alcove on the sixth floor of a large barracks, just across from the Closerie, around the corner from the Luxembourg, and our two windows look out to the south over a fine convent garden—one of those lovely combinations of formal walks, fountains, shrines, great trees, and orchard and vegetable garden. It is about time for the nuns to be climbing their trees again, taking in fruit. They have been cutting spinach and grass for weeks. According to an old map I have seen, the convent was here in 1551.

Our financial flurry due to tottering exchange is over, we muddle along nicely on our wages, and have solved the rent problem: 100 francs a month for this outfit . . . with electricity, hot water, Godin furnaces and bath tub already installed, for which we are paying a modest reprise. I think this comes under the head of good news: you might like to know that we have arrived where we do really live within our means, and like it.

I feel that I never get any work done, but I have sold one story, finished another which I have not sent off, finished "Hacienda" (sixteen thousand words more or less) for Monroe Wheeler, have got about a sixth of the novel done and off to see if some one won't print the fragment, and am on the last lap of Cotton Mather. So I suppose I haven't been idle, though I never seem really to work. I mean with that bleak, admirable professional regularity which I do so wish I could cultivate. The part of the novel which I have sent off is a section called "Legend and Memory": the whole book is called *Midway of This Mortal Life.* I think I must have talked about it to you here in Paris.

We are in the middle of a short but gorgeous hot summer. My energy and spirits rise spontaneously with the thermometer; I wish I knew of a place where the weather was like this for eight months of the year at least: I'd move there with the first cold snap here . . . Last spring after the very best winter I remember to have had in my whole life, not a sniffle or sneeze, in April I came down with bronchitis and had to go to Davos for five weeks. Just damn near died of sheer coughing, exhaustion and disgust . . . But Gene, who noticed that the winter is always a month too long for me, decided we would take vacation in that fatal month of March from now on, and skip for the hottest place in Africa. Try to break this bad habit, for it is that, of blowing up once a year. Since we know it isn't tuberculosis, we feel very up to the job.

The Fords left for England, stayed a while, went back south, where they are now. Ford I believe is doing a book on Provence, illustrations by Janice . . . Not a soul I know is here now, I see no one except now and then Sylvia and Adrienne, and that only when I pop into their shops. We used now and then to swap dinners, but

I don't cook any more, and won't go out evenings, except to some little restaurant, and so back home. I shall take up cookery again but not steadily, after this job is off. I have a fine femme de ménage who keeps this little cage as sweet as a rose, and I don't see how she does it on two hours a day. So I'd rather stay here than any other place I know.

. . . . Next year we're going to Italy. And the year after that, to China. And so on . . . I hope there'll be enough years . . . This August I'm going to Salzburg for five days, to hear Mozart and Strauss, mostly; invited by Barbara Harrison, or naturally I shouldn't be going. I feel pretty cheered up about it. I have a beautiful cloudy-blue organdie evening dress, very long and some-how very beautiful, though if I described it, it would sound odd. It's something in the way it is cut, all in a swirl, yet fitted smoothly about the hips and waist . . . It wasn't expensive, which makes it all the nicer.

Dear, dear—this will never do. I'm trying to catch up on letters, writing to friends I've owed letters to for at least two years. And I give myself just the hour between twelve and one noon for it. I get up at seven thirty, we eat a large farm-hand breakfast, mush and milk, bacon and eggs, fruit, pots of coffee, and we're through with eating until dinner time. So I am at work by nine o'clock, and don't have to stop until five. Sometimes I rest an hour between three and four . . . not always. But it takes all that time to do what seems to be so little, when I look at the day's work . . . This is not a permanent arrangement . . . just till this chore is done . . .

To BARBARA HARRISON   166 Boulevard Montparnasse
                            Paris XIV
                            July 29, 1934

Barbara darling,

The news from Austria is not very pretty, and the talk of a refugee or two makes it all very much gloomier. I suppose there will be Salzburg and the festival still: a young pianist who used to play over the radio there, and was, I think connected with the

Mozarteum, predicted there would be no music this year in that place, nor ever again. This may have been Russian gloom cross-bred to Jewish melancholy; I hope so. It can't be very cheering-up to have to run for your life because you aren't an Aryan. It may have been merely that he *hoped* all Germany and all Austria would blow up. They damn near have, judging by what I can gather from the newspapers, no two of which print the same lies, so its a little confusing.

I imagine you aren't even in Switzerland any more. It would be very sweet to hear that you were safely gone from Sanatorium for good and all; any other news over and above from you would be most cheerfully received, too. Are you disappointed in the story? That's a hair raising thought. But I can't think so any more—it did haunt me a little—because a letter from Monroe yesterday said he would be sending proofs in about three weeks, and added some interesting words about his frustrations in the matter of type, all lending the air of things getting done, which I love to hear about.

It appears that the Salzburg Opera Company refuses to play the music of Strauss, so what next? Mozart was safely Austrian, but what about Beethoven? What about Klemens Krauss and Reinhardt? I am quite selfish in my uneasiness. I know that all sorts of terrible things have happened and shall happen, it is quite plain nothing much can be done about it, so I can only hope that, if the Salzburg Festival must go, it won't at least go *this* year!

Let me have a word, let me know if I can look after anything for you here besides bringing a few things for you. I know you hate writing letters, we agreed about that, but agreement has nothing to do now with my wanting badly to hear from you.

Work goes slowly as death by headache, which it really turns out to be, I'm afraid. So I'd better be getting about it. It is no sort of life. Love and remembrance to you.

Katherine Anne

Gene sends his greetings, wants to be remembered, and hopes to hear you have really finished the cure!

To Josephine Herbst   166 Boulevard Montparnasse
[fragment of a draft]   Paris XIV
                                        August 3, 1934

Josie Darling:

As usual, Time does a grand sneak on me. I didn't realize how much of it has slid by until I happened on your story of the "Man of Steel" over at Sylvia's, in a *Mercury* dated, I think, just a year ago. It seems to me that almost your last letter was saying, "The story will appear next August . . ."

It is a very good story. Glenway Wescott once said, one was safe to write about any one, anything at all, because they either never recognize themselves as seen by others, or they pick out only the flattering things as applying to them, or they are so pleased to be taken for the subject of a story, they don't care what one says about them. As this is the first time I ever met myself in literature, I am still wondering which class I belong to . . . myself, I never used anybody I ever knew or any story about any one, complete. My device is to begin more or less with an episode from life, or with a certain character; but immediately the episode changes and the original character disappears. I cannot help it. I find it utterly impossible to make a report, as such. I like taking a certain kind of person, and inventing for him or her a set of experiences which I feel to be characteristic, which might well have happened to that person. But they never did happen, except in the story. Or if I take one episode as a starting point, it always leads to consequences which did not occur really. I believe that this is what fiction-writing means. Actually I think you have done much the same thing, because, while most of your episodes are perfectly recognizable, the *connections* and conclusions are very different from what happened, from my point of view . . . I mean to say, I know all the secret data of that unfortunate occurrence, what my own motives were, some things about the poor fool that explained some of the events, and so on. But you made a good and very logical story out of your materials, and I think it a good job . . . I have just finished a fiction version of "Hacienda," which will be published as a little book, and my struggles there taught me a great deal. For one thing, that I must not use *actual characters combined with their actual experience*. I must either write fiction, or report the facts. The combination for me is deadly. I cannot do it. I don't think my story is so bad, but I could have done better with it if I had not tried to stay within the frame of remembered events and actual personalities . . . That is merely the jumping off place for the imagination and that is where your story should begin, not end . . .

My novel started as autobiography, and after three pages I tore it up, named the whole first part "Legend and Memory" and began to write out of a fullness of *what I know in sum,* and not in detail or fact. And I have got by this not only more fact but more truth into what I am trying to tell; that is to say, it does no violence to the spirit of the life it is founded upon. That is all I can do.

TO GLENWAY WESCOTT 166 Boulevard Montparnasse
AND MONROE WHEELER Paris XIV, France
          August 9, 1934

My very dear Glenway and Monroe:

I suppose I shall always write you in the one letter, for though I never knew any two personalities more separately defined in my mind, still I can only always think of you, separate personalities that you are, as together.

This minute while I think of it, here is that song of Clemont Marot; my translation you have already for your *Typographical Book:*

> Plus ne suis ce que j'ai été,
> Et plus ne saurais jamais l'être—
> Mon beau printemps et mon été
> On fait le saut par la fenêtre:
>
> Amour, tus as été mon maître,
> Je t'ai servi sur tous les dieux—
> Ah, si je pouvais deux fois naître
> Combien je te servirais mieux!†

---

†*Katherine Anne Porter's translation:*

I am no more what once I was   *O Love, how I have worshipped thee*
And what I was no more shall be,   *Above all gods I thee adore,*
My jolly summer and my spring   *And were I twice-born I should be*
Have taken thieves' farewell of me.   *But born again to serve thee more!*

Well, you see what a lovely arrangement of rimes riche alternating with feminine rhymes it is, and my translation has no such deftnesses. I think the English version sings, just the same. If ever I find the original music book again—Gene has got everything battened down like a ship started on a long voyage—I shall send you the music. This is copied from a slip of paper I wrote out so I could work in bed without limp-backed books on my knees.

I never saw the Jefferson place—you me and (Monroe) Monticello? Or is it another house? I always loved the pictures of Monticello, and I always meant to visit Virginia where my mother was born. I did go once, about 10 years ago, to help christen a ship, at Newport News I think it was; we started drinking cocktails at seven thirty in the morning on the ferry with the advance guard of the reception committee, and I am now vague about where we landed, but I am pretty certain it was Newport News—and we were hauled around from town club to country club and out to Jamestown, where I spent some time tottering among the gravestones looking for the names of my ancestors; I did find a few, but I was so blind deaf and dumb on prohibition liquor and Virginia hospitality, it didn't really matter. I was almost as dead as they.

We danced to a jazz band which the Virginians believed to be better than anything of the kind in New York, and then smacked the little ship over the head with a bottle of champagne and named her *Carabobo* (Sillyface, literally, but its the name of a town in South America, scene of some locally celebrated battle) the moving picture cameras whirred, and the point of this reminiscence is that I never did really see even that part of Virginia I managed to land in. I hope to return some day.

After looking over a few reviews of recent prize-winning books and plays, I have warned Gene that if he gets the prize he will have earned his money twice, once writing the book and once reading what the critics have to say about it. To win a prize is to give a signal loosing the bloodhounds of the press. Its enough to blight a promising career. Well, on his own head be all of it! I have told him. God knows we'd like having that money. You remember an old song which says, very inaccurately no doubt, that Earth hath no sorrow that Heaven cannot cure. I know we have none that a little cash in hand would not clear up at once . . . Not that I feel we are in any way unique in this.

Glenway, my dear, with both of us I think this strange self-flagellation about being slothful must stop. I look upon you as a monument of productive energy and richness, and regard myself as virtually a total loss not only to literature, but the most daily and necessary human life. That is, if I don't really watch myself I fall into the most dreadful despair that is like a catalepsy. My mind fixes itself with terrible attention on a dark spot in space and remains cold and moveless, as if I waited for something that I cannot name, but something that I don't really want to happen. Its a matter of nerves and I know it, and when the mood passes and I feel a rise in spirits as immediate and direct as a barometer rising, the past is a mere blank; I have done nothing and thought nothing that I feel is worth remembering. This is a very clumsy statement of a situation that is very real and very difficult to overcome; indeed I do not seem to overcome it at all. When the rise comes, I work, but my energies soon begin flowing backward irresistibly, I am drawn back into that darkness once more. It terrifies me except that I know that to give way to terror would be somehow fatal and I rationalise my fears and reason with them and they can be controlled like a willful animal or child; a matter of being more stubborn and more quick than they . . . It comes to this, that I cannot conquer the causes of my fear, not even the fears themselves, but I do somehow keep the fears within bounds. I think even the word fear is not the right one. It is despair. I can and do dismiss myself as a neurotic, but that does not dismiss the condition nor its causes. And it is time for me to dismiss this topic. After all, I have been like this since I can remember anything.

What pleasant growths and changes you found at home—or reassurances—I think I might find too in my own family, judging by their letters. They seem most marvellously on their feet and at home in the world, not that they weren't always somewhat, but they do have an extra firmness of texture, calmness and humour neither frivolous nor easy. . . .

Flowering Judas came home in its beautiful new jacket, just three days ago, and I don't let it out of my sight. I wish now I hadn't kept a damaged copy, what possessed me? but there were so few, and I couldn't bear giving any one an imperfect book; certainly I could not foresee that any one of them would have such a binding, or I should have been more provident in the matter. It is entirely lovely, just my notion of a book, and I shall treasure it as long as I live, and will it to some one who will take it, in spite of those two spotty pages.

Your check is really being saved against my visit to Ameriky the land of promise, and the letter you sent me was from some one I hadn't heard of for seven years, so a little more delay surely cannot have mattered. I hope to receive the proofs in Salzburg, (this is all for Monroe) and it would be ever so much gayer if both of you were there, too. Veronica Jennings has been leading me around by the hand to places where I can get a hat that looks like a hat-on-purpose and not a mortal sin, and a dress that doesn't make me look like a governess or a frog. All to the good. And no fortune spent, either. . . .

With an office on Fifth Avenue, and your address on your letter paper, how enviably settled you seem. I'm still all at sea as to whether I should change this wall paper, and go mad among the upholstery, and try to make this place liveable, or whether we should just sit here like gypsies in a tent, waiting for the next move. I imagine we shall live here for years, but we cannot make up our minds. . . .

I'm glad you told me it rains every day in Salzburg. That's something to look forward to. It rains every day here, too. I could have hoped for a change . . . Speaking of Salzburg, a young Russian Jew named Serov† came through here the other day on his way to America. He is a pianist and I think a very nice person. He wanted an introduction to Lincoln Kirstein and I sent him on with it. If you should happen across him you might like him too. He lived two years in Salzburg, knows everybody, is a good musician, something very sweet and appealing about him. And extremely sensible and I thought intelligent. You will understand I only talked to him twice. Maury Werner wrote a book based on his life, called *To Whom It May Concern.* I never read the book. I believe he is going to play a concert engagement in New York this fall or winter.

Now my dear and dearest friends, this chatter must stop. You know if you were here or I were there I should be talking—and

†*Porter later commented: "He was the last, or maybe next to the last lover of Isadora Duncan—devoted, faithful, baffled—too young for her."*

listening too—I hope, until after midnight, so this is a mere hint of what I should like to do in the way of conversation.

So good night, with my love to you both.

Katherine Anne

Paris
August 22, 1934

Postscriptum.

Back from Salzburg. It was raining the day I got there and may have rained the day after I left, but for five days it was all sun light and blue sky. My train was late. I got to the hotel at ten minutes after six. Barbara and Doria had arrived an hour before. Barbara's father had missed the train at Vienna, wandering off to see about guns, or something. Just the same, we had showers, sandwiches, cocktails, got dressed and to the Festspielhaus for the curtain-rise . . . *Fidelio* with Lotte Schoene . . .

This is going to be a mere catalogue of events. You've heard and seen it all. Next day a quiet morning, afternoon ascent in funicular to the Archbishop's castle. Sightseeing, outright. In the evening, Barbara's father, with his new wife Doria, who had arrived in time for second act of *Fidelio,* wished to rest. Doria and Barbara and I went to the festive Alpin-Abend, full of peasant costume and dancing—schuhplaatle and step-dancing and not too damn much yodelling . . . Home, dancing in the street a little, lit up on one glass of white wine and natural spirits. Sleep. Third day. Off to St. Wolfgang's at ten in the morning, fine day of swimming and sun-bathing at the Weissen Rossli. Back to Salzburg in good time for *Don Giovanni,* with an Italian company. Dusalina Giannini singing Donna Anna . . . Ezio Pinza a splendid Don Juan. Sleep and beginning to need it. Next morning (17th August) Barbara rested in bed until nearly noon, I walked around and saw the town. At one we took the train for Munich, bare-headed both, in sandals and short sleeved linen dresses, but carrying a bag containing opera-wear. Drove out to Nymphenburg spent the afternoon seeing Badenburg and Amalianburg—oh, Amalianburg! but let us get on—and wading around in the green meadows apparently hitherto untouched by human feet, since the Germans love their orderly paths. Back to the Regina Palast to dress, and off to hear Figaro's

Hochzeit at the Residenz-Theater—Lotte Lehmann as Susanna ... Beautiful supper afterward at the Prysing Palast. Roast pheasant with chestnuts, Niersteiner-Domtal wine. Next morning visited four Asam brothers' churches—Some day I may be coherent on the subject of my first sight of Bavarian rococo, but not yet—serenely going about our affairs in a city with Hitler flags waving from every window—by order—a nasty picture of Hitler glaring at us from every taxi and shop and hotel window, and a confusion of loud speakers, set up even in the churches, working up the mass enthusiasm for the plebescite, which took place not too gloriously the next day. We also visited the room of ancient musical instruments at the Museum where a bearded little fellow with the thickest, stiffest fingers I ever saw performed expertly and casually on every instrument in sight, from a 1440 spinet to a modern and hideous electric moving-picture pipe organ, each tune being contemporary with the instrument played upon ... We went up in the gallery and I helped blow the bellows for a 1700 pipe organ with a heavenly tone ... So away, lunch on the train—we were always grabbing sandwiches at odd hours and eating on trains, back to Salzburg in time for *Rosenkavalier,* Lotte Schoene as the Marschallin, and a most manly young woman as the Cavalier. Gorgeous performance, with Mayr in his own role ... Sleep—and if I seem to mention sleep it is because I tottered to bed in a daze every night hardly knowing how I got there; but rose always fit and fresh and ready for more the next morning by eight. Next morning at nine-thirty, Barbara, her father and Doria off to Vienna. So I packed up, and then drove out and spent the morning at Hellbrunn, where we had all meant to go but there was no time ... Saw everything, then sat on a mossy bench and smoked a while, and so, after a farewell coffee at the Bazar, I took the 12-50 train back to Paris; and if I should group my memories in, let us say, five day periods, then surely I cannot recall any given consecutive five that were ever gayer and pleasanter than these. ...

Munich is probably not so pleasant as it was. People go about in restaurants and in the street swinging their arms up in each others' faces and saying Heil Hitler! and the *Figaro* Program had two pages of quotations from Mozart's letters under the caption, "Mozart the German" ... and Germans were forbidden to go to the Salzburg festival, or anywhere else in Austria; so it is all not very pretty. It was just that I saw everything in a fine careless holiday mood, refusing to admit any other . . .

September 18, 1934. My Angels, this is completely reediculous; the second part of this letter was written on August 22, or at any rate the day after I returned from Salzburg. The proofs must have arrived ten days ago, and were done up at once, in two readings. They go back on the *Île de France* with this. You will see how I have scribbled it up a little; and have agreed with your changes. I think the type is very beautiful, gives an illusion of speed, and I love a thin, clear type. Easier on the eyes—other extreme is German Gothic, the most blinding type I know. You do know that I leave everything in the way of paper and binding and margins and all to you with what confidence! It would never occur to me even to offer a hint. . . .

Two-thirds of my energies go in trying to save one-third for work. I suppose that is not unusual. I don't much care whether it is or not; in any case there is the devil to pay and no pitch hot, as ever.

The new apartment sounds pleasant; I always thought that section of the east side of Central 80's and 90's was a lovely place. I'm glad its coming back into fashion. And the things to happen sound exciting too. I should like to see Synge's plays again: especially the *Playboy;* I saw Moira O'Neill in it how many years ago! Its true I'm having out two books now, but later. I'm going to have an opera! A comedy, too, a real one; I hope . . . And we'll all go to that together maybe two years from now or the year after that! Nothing goes on here just now, and I've not even read anything new but Nijinsky, that appalling story by his wife in which she exposes herself so naively as the real villain in the piece. I never read a more cruel story. I began wishing with all my heart that somebody had thrown her off the boat on the way to South America . . . I note that she gives Lincoln Kirstein great thanks and credit for help. I wonder if he did it with malice aforethought . . . Men have the gift of getting themselves up rather neatly as the hero of their own life-stories, but women do give themselves dead away. The only one I knew who comes out admirably without even trying for it is Madame de Chateaubriand. She was so busy defending her husband and fighting his enemies and running her Infirmary she hadn't time to tell about herself: and meantime the most charming and unconscious portrait of a personality emerges.

Do forgive my being so slow. I shall wait now for the book; I know it will be beautiful. With my love and affection to you both; I'm missing you frightfully!

Katherine Anne

TO ROBERT PENN WARREN   70 bis rue
Notre-Dame-des-Champs
Paris, VI
February 24, 1935

Dear Red:

I hurry to answer your letter written December 22, which arrived this morning. Let me tell you the history of that letter. There is a young woman aquaintance of mine here who is a perfect bar-fly. About two weeks ago she was in a little Montparnasse dive, when another feminine night-bird, unknown to me, rolled in about two A.M. and remarked to the first young woman; "I saw K.A.P's name in a list of undelivered letters advertised in the newspaper last week. It was either the American Express or the American Consulate, I forget which." So the drunken young woman finally got around to mentioning this to some one else I know slightly, who in the goodness of his heart at last got round to dropping in yesterday morning and telling me this story. Gene decided it must be the Consulate. So he went to claim the letter for me in the Consulate Mail department which is one floor up, or down, from Gene's own office, where he has been for two years. In the American Embassy building. The letter had been there since the first of January. In another corner of the same room, my passport, special identity card, to say nothing of my marriage license, have all been issued to me with due notes on my change of name. If you can think of anything really appropriate to say about this, you know more and stronger words than I do.

But here is your letter, after its dusty sleep, and I was very glad to hear from you. It does no sort of good to have permanent addresses. The friends who know them seem never to pass them on to friends who do not. I have paid a hundred francs a year for three mortal years to the Guaranty Trust Company to receive and send on my letters, and I really believed I had sent out this information to enough people that about two or three times that many more could surely hear of it. But now, the above address is as permanent as anything can be in a world that slips pretty fast. Write me here, either as K.A.P. or Mrs. E.P. We have a delightful pavilion, with a little shrubby, gravelly garden, and a huge atelier . . . You know enough about European ideas of convenience to forgive me for boasting that the hot water really runs hot, the *chauffage central* positively keeps the whole place warm day and night, the house has three stories so we each have our own little apartment to a floor, and there is plenty of beautiful space, which has always been my idea of luxury . . . So if we don't stay here, it will be because Gene has been ordered to Peru or Constantinople suddenly. Its not a fine house, but sweet and oldfashioned, not really old, about a hundred and fifty years, but it looks like something brought in from the country and set down in the heart of Paris.

Of course, its too late now for your spring number, which disappoints me, though why I should be disappointed when even now I have no story ready, I can't say.

If I had known in time I could have sent you the section from my novel, *Midway in This Mortal Life,* called "Legend and Memory." But the *Virginia Quarterly* published two portraits from it, and have accepted for April a fragment called "The Grave." That leaves only three other fragments, "The Grandmother," a short portrait; "The Circus," which might not stand by itself, I don't know; and a very long middle section called "The Old Order." I am sending you a copy of this anyhow, for I should like for you to read it, whether you wish to use any of it or no. Beside this, I have only chapters from the Cotton Mather book ready, and I am afraid they are all too long—from twenty five to thirty pages each. But if you wish, I could send them to you for a reading.

Otherwise, I have on hand, trying hard to finish it, a fairly long story which I call "Pale Horse and Pale Rider," though I may find another title. What are your limits as to space for a short story? I know well enough you do not ask me to write stories of any given length, but I am learning a little about the problems of editors who have a set number of pages for their use, and if I know what your limitations are, I would then know at least that much about what story of mine you would be able to print. I wish you and all your associates good luck with your venture, it is very pleasant to think of another good southern magazine beginning. I hope—indeed, my mind is made up—to be among your contributors. Be certain I shall send you only what I consider my best.

But to think you are in Louisiana. Your arrangement there sounds ideal. I hope it wears you well, and really will give you time for your own work. And let me know where you are being published so I may look for your work. American magazines here are few and hard come by, and I'm afraid I buy only those which I know contain the work of those persons I like and admire. Give my affectionate remembrance to Cinina; I hope you are both well and happy and that you may remain so. Myself, I am altogether cheerfully, comfortably and I hope permanently married, now for nearly two years, and though I still think the Holy Institution as such is over-rated, marriage as an individual and private arrangement cannot be bettered when it really is successful.

Please send me a copy of the spring number of the *Southwest Review,* which I am too late for, and let me know the latest date for making the summer number. I'll do my best, with all my heart, much pleased to be invited.

As ever, your friend,
Katherine Anne

P.S. I just noticed in the *New York Herald Tribune* that your Louisiana State University Press has published a biography: *Alexander Porter.* For reasons of my own I am interested in this subject. You can too easily guess why. But the announcement carried no price list, which makes me think it was printed for private circulation, or in an expensive limited edition. Do you know about this, or could you find out for me?

The announcement describes it as the biography of a Whig Planter. So far as I have learned, no Porter of my line in America was ever anything else but a Whig, so there must be more to his history than that, worth telling . . .

Would you mind letting me know about this when you write again? Especially the price. You will know how that is.

K.A.

TO MONROE WHEELER   70 bis rue
                               Notre-Dame-des-Champs
                               Paris VI
                               March 23, 1935

Dear Monroe:

In Bermuda, I lived in an old house called Hilgrove, around the curve of Bailey's Bay as you go towards St. George. It had a hall, drawing room, dining room, kitchen on first floor, three bedrooms, two baths, nursery, sewing room, and something known as the morning room, on the second. It was terraced in three levels, with a ten acre wood, two rose gardens, a small banana grove, and a grass tennis court on the lowest level in front. I had limes for my sloe gin rickeys and pomegranates for my breakfast off the garden trees. It had bowers and rustic retreats and little stone steps running hither and yon. It was built in 1600 something and had been ripening nicely ever since. The original great benches and tables brought by the first Hollises—who were shipwrecked on that island on their way to Virginia—were sitting about, mingled with the accumulation of egg shell china and Spode and thin silver and hideous family portraits and horse-hair furniture ornamented all around with black walnut roses and grapes and Cupids . . . I lived there absolutely alone night and day for more than five months, in the heat of summer, and wrote eleven chapters of the Cotton Mather book, probably the last I'll ever get around to doing on that dearly loved but apparently impossible project. A good negro woman came in for two or three hours a day and cleaned up, and twice a week a little negro boy brought me fish he had caught himself, so he said. I learned afterward he had been stealing it off the lines of other fishermen, for which he was walloped first by his mama, then by his papa, then by his school teacher; and thereafter I bought my fish from a little regular cart which made the rounds—I learned to bake wonderful bread—I had always thought of bread as something that just happened, but Bermuda bread was so horrible I bought some yeast and a cook book and had hot rolls for breakfast, and loaf bread for my tea. I used to sit on the beautiful upper veranda and watch the ships come in. To swim I had only to go down the road a few steps and jump off a nice cliff into the sea; I would sink like a rock and then relax and float up to the surface again. It was the most beautiful place to swim I ever saw . . . A long sepia colored cloud mingled with mother of pearl lay almost without changing for half an hour one hot August afternoon: it was a pastoral landscape with a flock of sheep and small fluffy trees, and it moved just enough to give an illusion that it was real . . . towards the end of my stay I broke down and went twice to the Tennis Club, and once to a dance, and several evenings for motor boat rides when the boat races were on . . . Otherwise I was a hermit, and for as long as it lasted I loved it. Maybe I could not do it again, though I have had several periods of almost absolute solitude in my life, and they were always welcome and remain in my memory as pleasant, even when the situation was by no means so fine as that in Bermuda . . .

For me, that was Bermuda. When I arrived there in March, the last of the season, it was horrible, and I was so discouraged I could have wished to go away again at once. Damp and cold and no way of getting warm except by ungenerous little fireplaces that smoked and wouldn't burn . . . There were only a few very timid cockroaches, but *how* there were ants. But that passed, and the rest was Paradise. It reminded me of summer in Louisiana . . .

I do not in the least understand either why Harcourt and Brace are so careless about reprinting my book. They tell me also it is merely a matter of choosing publishers for England so then why in the devil don't they do it? I am getting them the manuscript together, and we'll see what they really do about it. I suppose I should turn enraged author and heckle them, but it is not worth it; after all I am not trying to make a career and there is no money in it, so what good? I am most miserably tired and fed up with all the machinery of the thing. I am not tired of writing, but I am about exhausted with the thousands of things that must be done before I can get to writing . . . They are real, there *are* lions in the path and they are not harmless after all.

About Curtis Brown . . . No, we must have nothing to do with them, either in England or America . . . This is telling all, but *you* mustn't tell. One of the Curtis Brown men wrote and offered to be agent for my short stories or fragments of novels, and I accepted and then it appeared that whey they really wanted was to officiate at the ceremony of buying my contract from Liveright and selling it again to Harcourt, or something of the kind, and H & B were much upset—holding as they do a contract with me for everything I write, if I ever write anything—and wrote me that I must under no circumstances take an agent for anything but stories to be published in magazines. Mr. Brace came to see me here in Paris, we made an agreement, and the man at Curtis Brown was furious and we had a most undignified, ignoble and low-comedy row about it . . . And the Curtis Brown people are still misled and misinformed, because I had no right to *Flowering Judas* or anything else in England. It must all go strictly through Harcourt-Brace . . . I have refused just five offers from agents in England in this past year . . . They, like Curtis Brown, refuse to handle my short stories, they want a book. I don't blame them. Its their business.

And oh God, what a bore it is. Harcourt Brace do nothing and they have got such a contract with me that I can do nothing for myself; so lately they pretended that they had told me months ago that if I would send them the manuscript of all my stories they would publish them . . . however, its quite true that even yet I have not been able to send them the manuscript. So they have a side to their argument . . .

Dear Monroe, why I should be writing this to you I do not know and I depend entirely on your friendly discretion, because I do not want and could not endure to have, any sort of disagreement or controversy with my publishers. They have done fairly enough, they are the best publishers I could have, I feel pretty certain, and I am being scrupulous not to overstep the contract which I signed with them of my own accord . . . so let it rest. This is just, I'm afraid, a pouring of complaint into a sympathetic ear . . .

It is strictly not true, just the same, that I have not wanted to publish the original *Flowering Judas* in England. It is just *that* I have most wanted, but the publishers on both sides keep roaring for weight and length, and demanding that I add more stories to it . . . So this I am doing . . .

I wish those fellows could learn to keep to the simple cold facts in cases like this.

I saw notices of Tchelitchew's ballet, and wished I might have seen it. Here I have seen and heard nothing, but there seems to be little to see or hear. The best thing I gather was a performance by radio of *Falstaff* from La Scala with I think Toscanini conducting, (No!) but of course I didn't hear that. Max Wald stumbled into it by accident over the radio some friends left with him, and was bemused and beglittered for days about it . . .

When you come to my gate, which cannot be too soon, you mustn't—unless I have got a new bell system by then—do anything so simple and conventional as ringing. First you press the button, just for luck. Then you must knock, and then kick, probably, and then yell. There are two bells, one a kind of dinner bell on a wire, the other electric which rings in the kitchen. Neither work except just by chance . . . But in the end I will hear you, I promise, and come rushing out, all smiles . . .

I wish that this very minute I should hear this kind of uproar, and open the gate and see Barbara, and Glenway and you standing there. It would be very merry.

So far I have been in fine health, but Gene has not. Two weeks of bronchitis, a complete death's head; but now recovered and back at the office.

April 1st . . . Dear Monroe, while I was writing this I received some very evil news; my brother was wounded perhaps fatally in an automobile accident. I forgot to finish or mail this. Let it go now . . . The latest news is that he is still in great danger, but he still lives, and I still hope . . .

Love to the three of you.

Katherine Anne

Since then, the Curtis Brown representative in England; Otto Theis, formerly with Liveright, and a young firm whose name I forget have written from London asking to be my agent . . . Quite impossible, all of it . . .

To Barbara Harrison
Wescott

[70 bis rue Notre-Dame-des
Champs
Paris VI]
May 31, 1935

Darling Barbara:

It IS important, being really married. Something quite mysterious and completely inexplicable to those not initiate. Its simply no
good trying to tell them. Its like trying to make clear why you feel
the way you do about certain kinds of music, to some one who
doesn't care for any kind . . . In a real marriage, something happens
to both persons that changes them for life, and what a change, and
how desirable a one. If this change doesn't take place, its no marriage no matter how many knots were tied and how much signing
of big books took place in the presence of witnesses. But the ceremony is important too, when the marriage has been made. An act
of faith, which is always quite mystical, or it wouldn't be faith.

The happiness in your letter made me happy too. I think I may
have explained to you, because I do know what marriage is, that
I never feel so unnecessary as when two lovers I know are stepping
off into their own fiery circle. They simply require nothing from
me, not even good wishes. Like those travellers in the Black Forest,
do you remember, going on their own journey, already absent,
really looking down remotely on the eager little man running beside the train calling "Glückliche reisen . . . Alle gut." They already
have their happiness and their good. Still, I love to wave and call
my felicitations to you. Happy journey, my dear married ones, all
good to you . . .

The wedding was such as I imagined, the least formality possible, the most personal kind of gayety. The only way. Your letter
came just half an hour before we went to St.-Leu-la-Forêt to hear
Wanda Landowska's Sunday afternoon Harpsichord music in her
small garden concert room. . . .

Gene sends you always his firm, steady affectionate admiration,
which is really his description of friendly love, and I love you as
always, but now with a kind of bubble of emotion about you, *so*
anxious for you to keep on being as happy as you are now; and with
a hopeful prevision of love for Lloyd, believing that all you think

about him is quite, quite true . . . Contrary to the opinion of cynics, Love is *not* blind. It is appallingly clear-sighted.

Katherine Anne

To Caroline Gordon   [70 bis rue
                             Notre-Dame-des-Champs] Paris
                             June 9, 1935

Darlin Caroline:

Your letter, dated one month less four days ago, arrived yesterday, which I think must be a modern record for transatlantic crossing. We are in the midst of the Pentecost holidays, such an important feast that my Sylvie, who is Arlesienne, goes home to her family for three days. She takes also Easter, of course, Ascension Day, Bastille Day, Christmas, and Three Kings' Day, and All Souls'. It occurs to me that this officially rationalistic France is as bound by religious holidays as Mexico. Anyhow, our little chore in the Foreign service does this for us: We get all the American as well as the French holidays; but mostly for me they mean, and so does Sunday, that I get stuck in the kitchen and the dishes do pile up. Just the same, this morning we pulled ourselves together and went to a little village about thirty minutes away by bus, l'Hay des Roses, and walked through an immense rose garden just coming into bloom. Oh at least a million roses, far too many, really. I should prefer about a half acre, with a dozen varieties very carefully chosen and tended. Some of those heavy dark red roses we used to have, some fine shell-pink-beige tea roses, Gold of Ophir, Gloire de Dijon, several climbing kinds, and a hedge or two of wild roses, and the whole thing surrounded by a carefully clipped wall of cape jessamines. I can see it, I know just how it should look. Some day I may even have it.

Ford, you know, is always praising the French by contrasting them with the benighted Germans and English who are just wild about nature, saying the French never know the names of flowers and think *grives* are something to eat . . . As usual, he is talking through his hatful of prejudices, and either doesn't know what he is talking about or doesn't give a damn . . . The French may not care for nature, but God, how they love a tree or a bush or a plant or anything they can set in the earth and train on a trellis and watch grow . . . They may not like nature, but they love a city full of leafage and fountains and birds. The whole town is just now like a garden . . .

Our own private estate has just about got out of hand. The Virginia creeper is closing in on Gene, he can hardly see out of his own windows, the ivy has gone wild, and lilac trees think they own the place, the chestnut is dense and shady as an umbrella, and there must be some hardy pruning around here come next clipping time . . . I send you a few pretty bad snapshots. The camera is really no good, how I miss my Rolleiflex . . . It's a hot drowsy afternoon, and I hear Gene over in the atelier playing Scarlatti's "Good Humoured Ladies" on the gramophone. Pretty soon we'll have some sherry. And I shall make hot biscuits for dinner. And that is about what living is like around here. I saw the Italian show—and saw things I shall never see again, I imagine—we went to hear Landowska play a gorgeous program of music of the time of Shakespeare, (What Music) and saw four thrillers at the Grand Guignol, and I went twice to the Horticultural Show at Cours La Reine, and that is a whole springtime of activity. For the rest, I just sit about in the intervals of small errands and household chores and think constantly that if ever, ever in this world I get two hours and a half to myself I'm going to finish one of those forty short stories I have lined up, or Cotton Mather, or the novel . . . None of this may ever happen unless I manage to distribute my time or grow claws. In "legend and memory" I am stuck right now in the middle of the history of great-aunt Sallie, who had a personality and couldn't find any way to express it, her family being what it was: they thought that if you had a personality it was quite natural, you went ahead and expressed it as a matter of course and what was there to get excited about?

This was not enough for great-aunt Sallie. So she changed her religion. She quit being a Cumberland Presbyterian (the Faith of her Kentucky pioneer fathers) and she became a Seventh Day Adventist, her husband's family being Methodist. And there-after she was a scourge to her entire community. As one of her relatives put it, "changing her religion put claws on Aunt Sallie." I wish I knew her secret. It wasn't *change,* I feel pretty certain, it was getting her bearings. I don't want to be a scourge to anybody, I merely would like to stop being a scourge to myself. My whole impression of her, after hearing her history here and there through the years, is that she had the devil of a good time and died happy. What more can one ask?

Well, I am in the middle of her history now, and I wish I could just keep going in a trance until I had finished. Its too much to ask, I suppose. I can only write anything once, and if it isn't finished then, its not apt to be . . . I made one draft of "Legend and Memory," Gene in his charity wrote it out for me in a fair copy, and I made a few corrections. I simply have to do things that way or not at all . . . that means I have to sweep a track and make a dead run when I once start. And that is a very difficult thing to manage for. But never mind, Caroline, I'll really do all I have planned, even yet.

You can't think how it pleases me that you like the part of my manuscript you have read . . . The people of the *Virginia Quarterly* liked it, and so did Red: and I like being approved by a jury of my peers. If the southerners approve, I know its coming off properly. Even southerners who do not really approve of each other know instantly what I am talking about . . . You do know that in this book, I am not looking up any facts, nor consulting with any one, nor going back to check my sources—*nothing,* I depend precisely on what I know in my blood, and in my memory, and on something that is *deeper than knowledge.* Your book was wonderful for another reason; you were back on your own territory, and you were writing of something you know, and you could go down the road a ways and ask a technical question if you needed to, and there is a most marvellous kind of here and nowness in your story. I cannot do that, I must depend on just what is in me, there is no one I can go to, I wish there were—

For example, I have curried a horse, and saddled him, and have ridden him, how many hundreds of times: and to this day I cannot really name the parts of a horse in a way that a horseman would approve, nor can I recall the names of all the pieces of harness I put on my horse, I really can ride but I do not know the names of the different ways of riding, this seat and that; I spent all my summers on a farm, and I do not know just when one plants cotton, or watermelons.

Now I don't feel in the least wistful about it, dear Caroline, though it does sound a little that way. No, not at all. What really makes me sad and angry is that I seem never to learn to use the typewriter. This is a lovely little silent portable that Gene gave me for Christmas, and it is quite perfect in every way, with a wonderful three-language keyboard—accents for all the usual languages, and I can't even hit the most familiar letters. . . .

Katherine Anne

TO ANNA GAY HOLLOWAY   [70 bis rue
Notre-Dame-des-Champs] Paris
June 30, 1935

Dear Anna Gay:

I've heard quite a lot about you, too, so its high time we were getting aquainted. When I saw you last you were completely round and pink with a kind of duck-fur on your head. Maybe that doesn't sound like an attractive spectacle to you, but I assure you we were all of us entirely fascinated with you. I have a snapshot of you sitting backed up against a log in the greenwood, still with no hair to mention, still round and very serious. And now you are a dancer making public appearances, know how to make your own dresses, or so I judge from something or other Sister Gay wrote me, and even if you can't spell—or so you say. I think you do better than I did at your time of life—it's just outright clever to be able to run a typewriter. So its really been a long time since we first met and its not going to be very much longer until we meet again.

Your mother has been giving me a fairly complete history of you ever since you began to dance. Did you know that I studied once years ago with Kosloff? But I began too late, and besides, I was going from the very first to be a writer, and I started early on that; I was just six when I wrote my first novel, drew the pictures for it myself, and sewed it into something resembling a book with thick white thread. I spelled it Nobble, I'm afraid, and the title was *The Hermit of Halifax Cave.* Heaven knows how I spelt *that.* Halifax was a place where we used to go camping in summers; I never had seen a hermit, and never have seen one yet, so I can't think where I got the idea. But that never stops a writer. I went right ahead and wrote my Nobble anyhow.

I am so glad you really knew early what you wanted to do and are going right ahead with it. I knew another girl who began dancing at three years, and she is sixteen now and dancing here in Paris with a very fine group. She was also trained entirely in Texas, Forth Worth, to be precise, and her work is beautiful. So I hope you are going to dance first in New York and then in Paris, and after that in Vienna and Milan and Budapest and London and everywhere else in the world that dancers go . . . I promise you faithfully I will look around here for books and articles about Pavlowa, and send them to you if I don't bring them very soon. Did you ever read *Theater Street* by Tamara Karsavina? She was of that first great troupe of Russians who came with Pavlowa to America. She was also a great dancer, but she retired early in England. I remember her well, she was divine. Her book is very good. I imagine you can find it in the public library. If not, let me know, and I will get it for you. When I come home I hope to persuade your mother to let you come and stop here with me and finish your training under a great old ballet mistress who trained some of those other famous dancers. It would be very good for you. We have a pleasant house with plenty of room, and a big studio where you could practise. Its across the garden and perfectly quiet, with a victrola in it. Paris is a beautiful place, and all sorts of things interesting to you are going on here. . . .

Gene thought your letter was remarkable, but of course, I didn't. I thought it was to be expected of a Porter child. But even for a Porter child it was a good letter . . . Write me another sometime, the sooner the better. Tell your mother *Howdy* for me. And all the rest of the family. Love to them all, but my special love to you who wrote me so sweetly and sent me your own love. I hope you go on growing tall and being happy and loving your work, for you'll have a very good life out of these three things . . .

Love, love, love
Aunt Katherine Anne

To Gay Holloway [70 bis rue
Notre-Dame-des-Champs] Paris
August 3, 1935

Dear Gay:

I add this to speak of things for Anna Gay to read. I can't find *Theater Street* by Thamara Karsavina here, but it is a very fine book, very suitable for her, she will find it fascinating, and I am certain you can borrow it from the Public Library there. It gives a fine picture of the old hardworking dedicated Imperial ballet, a picture of what kind of training it takes to make a *prima ballerina assoluta*. It has enough talk about *entrechats* and *pirouettes* to make her feel she is learning something, and the story of a beautiful woman who also had genius and goodness of heart will put fresh heart into our own dancer. She was a better dancer and a better person than Pavlowa, though Pavlowa was surely almost great enough.

There is another, but you'd better read it first. It is Romola Nijinsky's story of Nijinsky. It is much more sophisticated, and deals at length with Nijinsky's relations with Diaghileff, which were natural enough for them, but which might be bewildering to a little girl. But the talk about dancing and the story of Nijinsky's training is very good. The language is most discreet, the story of personal relations might just pass over Anna Gay's head. I don't know how much she knows, or how much you want her to know, and above all, how much you think you are concealing from her that she knows already—no wonder bright children sometimes pity their parents' ignorance—but I believe the book would not be bad for her. But you must judge.

I am sending her a small review in French, but the pictures of dancers and dancing might amuse her. She should both read and speak French. It would be a help to her if she is going to be in ballet companies, where half of the members are foreign, more than half, usually. If she took it up now it would come much easier to her later on.

I am writing a libretto for an opera, and a very good composer is writing the music. It has two ballets in it. Maybe some day Anna Gay will dance in them . . .

All for the moment. How are Leslie and Harry? I can only suppose that in the long run you named him that. He couldn't have given Son Holloway as his name on a marriage license, could he? Whatever in the name of God became of Paul's children? Have they faces, or not? If they have, why have I never had a single snapshot of one of them? I merely mention this to make conversation for the hundredth time.

Love and a kiss, and congratulations on reaching your stupendous birthday. I'll be along before you know it . . . I like being alive more every year. I hope you do, and all of you . . .

Going out to dinner this evening with my friend Glenway Wescott, who just popped in from Italy on his way to England and so to New York. He's delightful . . . Got to get my hair done up . . .

Katherine Anne

TO BARBARA WESCOTT　　　70 bis rue
　　　　　　　　　　　　　Notre-Dame-des-Champs
　　　　　　　　　　　　　Paris VI
　　　　　　　　　　　　　November 18, 1935

Barbara darling:

　　. . . . Today I wrote Cap Pearce to send you your copy of *Flowering Judas.* Imagine that I don't know your street number. Its my own fault, I suppose, so I'm having it sent to your place on Fifth Avenue. I have not written to any one for how long, if that matters. I get up at seven in the dark winter mornings (I don't want to break your heart) and creep back to bed which is the pleasantest place I have found, after all, all flattened out by eleven at night, and meantime I have been busy. So my silence does not mean that I have sunk into lethargy. For one thing, this is my special news for you, it has much to do with you. I am studying music—theory, harmony, with incidental struggles at the keyboard—and I have got a little virginal which is a direct descendant of the one we saw at the museum in Munich—saw and heard, you remember. And the ferment set up in my mind that day resulted in a small, beautiful instrument, copied by a fine craftsman, a minute and perfect reproduction of an ancient one. The keys are ivory colored boxwood and natural ebony, the sounding board is made of two hundred year old fir, prepared for just such a use as this. The thin strings are plucked with pared quills, condor quills, and it makes an other worldly music in its small pure voice. I adore it above everything I ever had or thought of having in my life; I tune it with a little key and cut quills for it and protect it from violent changes of temperature, and run do re mi fa sol la si do on it, and in fact do everything but play it. That comes later, much later. My musical training is not for virtuosity, anyway. Just the same, incidentally almost, in two years I may be able to play Purcell and John Bull and Byrd and Scarlatti and Fisher and Richard Lionheart (Had you thought of him as musical? I hadn't. He wrote at least one song that I know of, words and music.) I say maybe. And all the songs in our Songbook. These are my unreasonable hopes, and I do not see why hopes should ever be reasonable. They're no fun if they are. . . .

Does living in New York grow on you, as it did on Monroe and Glenway? The excitement seems to be there. Here it seems a little dull, even for those who manage usually to keep things in movement, and the idea of war has got into the air, and stays there, like a plague germ. War or no war, we stay. They have posted up in all areaways and halls long complicated directions as to what to do in case of air-attacks, gas or shells. Put on masks, turn out all gas and electricity at the house source, take to the cellar if you have one or rush to the nearest dug-out (situation not given) etcetera, you must be very familiar with all this. It seems an unreasonable amount of activity; besides, we have no masks, I don't know where the gas outlets are, and our cellar is a crumbling place at best. We'll wait and see. It is all very stupid, and may be more stupid before its finished. . . .

Note: My music teacher is blind and does not know one word of English, and I am having a wonderfully complicated time of it learning the do re mi system instead of the A B C one, with a theory and all in French, and ear training beside. He does not trust me and says, "Stop looking at the keyboard" when he is striking the note for me to name by sound, and I haven't idiomatic enough French to ask him why he thinks I would so cheat myself? But he has a fine method, very thorough, what I learn I really know, and it goes very fast . . .

With my devoted love to you

Katherine Anne

Did Lloyd like the European journey?

TO BARBARA WESCOTT   70 bis rue
Notre-Dame-des-Champs
Paris, VI
November 23, 1935

Barbara *Darling,*

. . . . Monroe, it must have been sent me a clipping from the *New York Times*—a review accompanied by a photograph, a passport one, which I sent in desperation . . . Imagine them taking that and not being able to find anything among George's work they liked. It reproduces so hideously I am suffering from shattered vanity. If I really do look like that, I do not want it published . . . Once I was really pretty and *photogenique,* and in those days I had no vanity at all . . . Now I am pained and almost incredulous at what the camera lens does to my poor face . . . The reviewer mentioned in passing that my material is "thin." Just how thick should it be, I wonder? How much material by the pound is considered a just weight . . . They still don't like "Hacienda," and I don't care. I like it best of the lot. If they keep on picking on me about it, I'm going to turn very stubborn and take it for my favorite story, and I'm working on another that will be just as chaotic as that. A little well regulated chaos will do them good, the smug little buzzards . . . (I don't really mean this reviewer of the *Times.* She did very handsomely by me. Only she didn't understand the themes.) Which reminds me of my favorite phrase in French, or English, either. It is from one of my Thiberge textbooks. Thiberge is the blind musician who has got up this exciting way of teaching music. Of course you know about him. He insists on "spontaneité rigoreusement contrôlé" and isn't that a wonderful statement of what must happen in any work of art? Great dancers, bullfighters, auto-mobile racers, painters, tight rope walkers, writers—all have it, or they couldn't be great. The potential ability to split a hair at one stroke. It always *looks* so easy and simple. So, well regulated chaos is just what I mean. . . .

I do not know whether Paris is really quiet, or the quietness is in me. There seems to be a great number of things going on, but the Flemish show was the only attraction that drew me out. The few persons I see prophecy mostly that there will be war, or there will not be more war than there is now, according to their wishes and their political slants. Communists and Socialists and such used to be the professional peace makers, now they are blood thirsty beyond words. I was just simple enough once to believe they were opposed to war on principle. Not at all. They're for war if it is their war.

If every party and faction which threatens to do its own kind of mischief here, really did it, there would be a marvellous confusion: but I think they will not get around to it this winter . . . There is nothing like a political, or a social-moral problem, to *date* a period, unless it would be hats . . . Hats and politics look pretty trivial next season when the fashion has changed . . . It is better to stick to more durable things, if you have a taste for permanence. I do have. Like Breughel, for example. All my life I have loved the Flemings and the late Medieval Germans better than I have the Italians, except Ucello, and I knew him later, and it is very consol-ing to find, not that my taste and judgement in art, but that my own choice for myself, was good. I still love them best. But some day I am going just the same to England, and to Oxford, and some way or another I shall get into the Ashmolean collection and see for myself that Ucello painting which I think must be the most beautiful in the world . . . *The Hunt.* You must have seen it often, lucky you. I have seen it only in black and white and the design is so stunning I did not miss the color, not being able to imagine it. And the writer, describing it, mentioned that the color was so superb one almost lost sight of the design . . . Do you remember it? . . . .

A gay Christmas to all of you. For years I thought Christmas was just another day, but of late I like celebrating it. We shall light a fire with the remnant of last year's back log, and set up the Mexican Bethlehem, and have egg nog, and exchange innocent, useless gifts, "a peach stone for a pigeon feather, a grasshopper wing for a sea shell." You won't recognize that. I'm quoting from one of my own poems, I believe the unpardonable sin in an author. But it came in so handily, I couldn't resist.

Goodbye darling Barbara. This must stop.

Katherine Anne

TO GEORGE PLATT LYNES   70 bis rue Notre Dame des
                               Champs
                               Paris VI
                               June 9, 1936

George darling,

The photographs are much too fine to be so prodigal with, so I mean to give them away carefully only to those who deserve to have some of your work, and who would be apt to appreciate it properly. I haven't chosen yet, I can't choose all at once, but I let them choose themselves as time goes on. One thing certain, Harcourt must see them—not all of them, of course, but the three or four that you, maybe, will help decide are good for publication. I have them all ranged round a wall, and look at them again, and have decided they are all too good to be true, but just the same some will be better in print than others . . . The one I have chosen to be myself, at last, is that three-quarter one seated among the topsy turvy landscape, numbered in your files 170 B. Glenway asked me which one I thought was the real one, with more of my own self in it, and I have decided on this one chiefly because I do so like the pose and the background and above all the camera work . . . and am probably no nearer answering his question than before . . .

The one which Glenway called Portrait of The Beautiful Mrs. Pressly (No. 175 B) may be, after all, the one for the general public, if I have a general public, which I doubt. My Sylvie picked it at first glance across the room, and gave her reasons: *Ah, Madame, vous êtes si jeune, si gentille, et si bien coiffée.* I decided then it was to be my official photograph. There are better things in it than that, but apparently these are the things that catch the eye. I have never in my life been half attentive enough to such things, and maybe I shall never be. Cousin Gertrude, (The Beautiful) broke all her engagements and would not leave her room, I remember well, because she had what we used to call a fever blister on her upper lip. A very small one, too. . . .

Dear George, I wish all of you were here, but more than that I could wish to be there. For the moment, affairs are so undecided, it is hardly time to speak of a change, yet we shall surely be out of Paris by midwinter. To London, or to Washington, or to South America. London or Washington would do nicely, but South America gives me sinking of the heart. I think I'll stay near New York and let Gene commute, from Lima or Rio de Janeiro. Gene has asked to be transferred, feeling that four years in one place are enough. Maybe. Well, I am already beginning to say Good bye to Paris. It seems a very short time since I came here.

There were so many things to talk about, little things that might be pointless to write, I felt, in getting away in such a fit of the jitters, like a woman leaning over the railing calling out to some friends on the dock as the ship moved away, "Oh, I meant to show you my new knitting." There were real tears in her eyes . . .

> With my love,
> *Katherine Anne*

TO TANIA AND JAMES
STERN

70 bis rue Notre Dame des
Champs
Paris VI
July 5, 1936

Dear Tania and Jimmie:

We were glad to hear you had left Madrid before the civil war started, it must be a depressing spectacle there now. I wish I could say, we are starting for Portugal at once, but we are not, at once or any other time. We are on the point of being sent somewhere else, we don't yet know where, though it may be Madrid. There is talk of it because Gene speaks Spanish and knows Spanish character and likes living among Spanish people. Nothing is certain except that we go somewhere or other about the first of October. It is possible we may be sent to Washington and transferred onward from there, like a bale of goods . . . I don't like being hauled about, I never did, so it is upsetting but not fatal. . . .

Since you are gone, France has had also a revolution, but a quiet one, no bloodshed and every one very proud of the *mésure* and *bon sens* and *comme il faut* of it all. The first Spanish revolution was like that, too. So we must wait and see whether here it is really the end, or only a beginning. I think nothing is settled yet, for the opposition is only silenced for the moment, not convinced by any means. I went to see the so called Victory celebration, and again walked with the procession of Communists from rue de Rivoli to the Bastille, and they were both astonishing performances, for order and gayety and good behavior. I wish with all my heart it could go on like this . . .

It seems odd that we are really leaving France. When we go, we shall have lived here just four years and three months of our more than five years in Europe . . . This is quite long enough to have formed habits of living and ways of thinking and feeling which will be hard to uproot and change. But I live so much in the present, having little faith in the future, and the past being now not very useful, I suppose the present will be enough anywhere, and places do not matter so much. But I did love Paris, and shall miss certain things I had here which I have not found anywhere else, and cannot expect to find . . . Gene is happy to be going, he gets a sense of freedom in action, and the illusion of a new different life in a changed scene. How he expects it will be different, or why, he cannot seem to say, and indeed, he appears to be very happy where ever he finds himself, and YET he wants to change. Myself, I think it is youth, simply.

Do let me hear that you will be in Paris before the first of October. I should so like to see you again. I see Darsey now and then, he brings me *New Statesman* numbers in exchange for my *New Yorkers,* which give us both a balanced ration of gravity and frivolity . . .

> With affection to you both,
> *Katherine Anne*

To Monroe Wheeler   70 bis rue Notre Dame des
Champs
Paris VI
October 5, 1936

Monroe darling:

     . . . . I don't know whether it is simply because we are moving
and changing, that we meet always people who are doing the same,
but everybody here seems to be fermenting, and nobody has any
permanent address more personal than a bank, a travel agency or
an office building . . . as vague sounding as Milky Way, Fifth
Constellation to the Right, The Firmament . . .

     We are sailing, bag and baggage, lock, stock and barrel, on the
Washington, the 8th of October. You wouldn't think it. Nothing is
packed, and the packers aren't coming until the day before . . . I
have a lot of empty suitcases lying about and spend all my time
muttering to myself and scratting hopelessly in a mountain of papers . . . It has been a cold and horrible summer, and a cold and
horrible fall. Being, as Glenway described one of his characters in
the "Deadly Friend," "weather-mad" this state of perpetual cold
helps a lot to reconcile me to leaving Europe . . . In fact, I think
I am ready to go, though I might have just stayed on. But Gene,
after months of indecision, resigned from this dull job and is going
to Washington to see about something else . . . We will be in New
York for about ten days—I will, at least. Gene is going on—and
after that I shall go somewhere and dig in for about three months
and try, once more, to get a set of stories finished . . . After that
I don't know anything . . . It is going to be lovely to be in America
once more, I am simply perfectly happy at the prospect, it is only
the present horrors of moving that distorts the landscape. . . .

     Until then,

Your always devoted friend
Katherine Anne

SECTION 3

Doylestown, New York, New Orleans

October 1936 to December 1937

. . . as I looked around me, I thought, these people are strong, and they are my people, and I have their toughness in me, and that is what I can rely upon . . . I loved them, really with my heart.

> Katherine Anne Porter to Josephine Herbst
> *August 15, 1937*

SECLUDING HERSELF AT AN INN IN DOYLESTOWN, PENNSYL-
*vania, Katherine Anne Porter writes "Noon Wine" in seven days and
"Old Mortality" in the next seven days. On May Day in New York, "I
got right out and marched with my old friends the proletariat," she tells her
sister, "from Ninth Avenue and Fifty-seventh Street to Union Square." A
few months later, living on the top floor of the lower Pontalba Building in
New Orleans, in the room that had once been slave quarters, she finishes
"Pale Horse, Pale Rider." "The* Southern Review *editors have been
snatching it page by page and having it set up," she says. One of them wrote
her that "the linotypers didn't like my story so far, because there are no
bawdy spots in it. The editor told them there weren't going to be any, and
one of them said, 'I thought this woman was a proletarian sympathizer.' "
At Benfolly, the home of the Tates, she meets Albert Erskine.*

To JOSEPHINE HERBST   Water Wheel Tavern
                               Doylestown, Pennsylvania
                               October 31, 1936

Dear Josie:

Arrived here in the profound state of melancholy and bodily misery that travel always causes me, found the front hall full of corn shocks, pumpkins, and seventy guests, male and female, making demure merriment in both dining rooms. I was shown to a very tiny room upstairs, no table, nothing but a big bed and a fixed wash bowl, with taps marked C and H . . .

The little girl of the house came and played on the virginal while mama was getting me a table and chest of drawers. The luncheon party turned on the radio, and we had a lot of swing music. A storm blew up. People roared up and down the hall outside my room. I was told I could have lunch when I wanted it. I waited until two o'clock when the party left. Meantime I sat down and held my embittered head in my suffering hands, and thought stonily that I would have lunch and get the hell out of here.

When I went down, the big tavern room was empty, tidy as if there had never been a party, the cheeild was playing with her remarkably fine dachshund puppy, the waitresses looked gay and fresh, the room was lovely, really unspoiled, and the most delicious food and coffee were set before me . . . Having eaten, I crawled back and found a big table, a comfortable chair, plenty of towels, plenty of coat hangers in the closets, and a big desk lamp instead of the little blinding ceiling light . . .

I began to unpack and settle down. I got out my papers and arranged them. I lay down and finished the novel I am to review. I wrote a note to Gene telling him how well I felt. At seven, there was more fine hot food. I went to bed at ten and slept until eight. Found my typewriter out of repair. Hell to pay . . . told the proprietor about it. He said, "give it to me. I'll have it fixed." So I walked into Doylestown and shopped. Bought scout walking shoes from a relative of yours,. . . . and noticed on the way that another Frey, or maybe the same one, is running for Congress on the Democratic ticket . . . The fields are beautiful. Saw a real estate agency advertising, among other things, five room stone house, stone barn, four acres of land, eighteen hundred dollars . . . Maybe one could get more land later . . . Walked back, had lunch; Found the house quiet, cheerful, life travelling at a fair, good speed with a rhythm in it . . . Settled down and went to work . . . So its all right. Costs more than I meant, $22 dollars instead of that hoped for fifteen. But the feel of the place alone is worth it. Owners young, healthy, good looking native Pennsylvania Germans, sensible and clever. Doylestown is an enchanting looking town, just a good walk, about a mile and a half; I can go in in the car at any time, but I think walking is better . . . as long as this weather lasts. All sun and benign cold and fall color . . . So now you know how it is, and I do thank you for telling me about this place.

Forgot to tell you the main thing, of course. Found this good typewriter to work on while mine is being fixed. Mr. Bachmann (proprietor) had got it for me, brought it back and set it on my table . . . So there's nothing to stop me, and here goes . . .

The big party yesterday was the annual Hallowe'en party of the Bucks County teachers; now and then they have such occasions. People drop in for meals, as they drive along the road. There is a little bar in the old tap room; Papa mixes the drinks and Mama gives the orders. There is a special tone of solidity, respectability, industry and a kind of prosperous thrift in this place that is very damn soothing to a broken wind-flower like I'm. It isn't going to be long now before I strike good firm roots in this very County and nowhere else.

Before I forget: I promised the editors of *Partisan Review* to send my address so they might send me some copies of the *Review*, and find I haven't got their address . . . Will you send it for me?

It appears that "Noon Wine" is going to get finished first. I'm in a fine fret of work . . . I think I should try to get two finished before I start seeing anybody, except Gene if he wants to come over for a week-end. But just the same if you come over to this part of the country you might just happen in for a good dinner. Day time hours are better for work if one can manage it . . . it can be managed here.

Good bye, darling . . . for the time being.

We had a lovely visit with you, and I hope this time next year you'll spend Hallowe'en with us in our house somewhere in Bucks County.

Katherine Anne

There is a W. (no doubt for William) Porter who runs an antique shop in Doylestown. Don't like his house, though. A terrible contraption, bastard Cape Cod in stone . . .

To Monroe Wheeler   Water Wheel Tavern
                           Easton Road
                           Doylestown, Pennsylvania
                           December 6, 1936

Dearest Monroe:

One of my favorite scenes from *Zuleika Dobson* occurs when the Duke, emerging one morning, sees an inharmonious arrangement of clouds before him. With a gesture he arranges them, they roll back into a more suitable composition. Your letter was such a gesture, putting the cloud—or fog—of the *Partisan Review* business in its place. It has now taken its proper perspective—but I am glad I wrote about it. Under pressure of excitement I am very apt to say exactly what I think, and it does sometimes have a fine, air-clearing effect.

. . . . Darling, I hope I wasn't being wistful about your lovely Stone-blossom. You know I shall have a house too, some day when the time is right for it; Cotton Mather may do the trick. I know just how it should look, and no doubt I shall be very pleased with it. In the meantime you have yours, and a lovely thing it is. The most delightful touch is the way the old French floor sank into that New Jersey farm house room with the fire place as if it had grown there. It is that kind of thing that makes having a house so exciting. And that spirited horse on your spring house that Glenway painted black. A man who sells antiques here has two, both different and neither so nice, and he wants ungodly prices for them. He assured me they were rare. I wouldn't know, your horse being the first of the kind I ever saw.

On my grandmother's farm, we used to have all the odds and ends that no one wanted in the other places, old secretaries, black walnut beds, mahogany chests, and sandwich glass. I remember the huge white hen with red comb which contained the breakfast boiled eggs. We thought it dowdy but practical. I could never afford to buy such a bird now. I don't really want one. I can look at one, and re-create a whole past, down to the least detail. I remember vividly things I had forgotten. I see windows stuffed with the things we sold en bloc to a second hand man for nothing. Short sighted, but I can't regret it. I shan't try to buy any of them back.

This is going to be a note-book. I took the first page out, went to dinner. Great huzzah and hullabaloo going on at the Tavern door. A hunter had come in with a 400 pound black bear. The bear appeared to be sleeping comfortably in the tonneau of a very new shiny car of the kind called Sports— . . . The hunter had got a deer, also, but had left him somewhere else. With tremendous excitement, all hands out from the kitchen, the bear was hoisted and hanged by the neck to a cross pole beside the front door. He is now a very painful sight, seeming to be in the last throes of strangulation. All of us are supposed to have our pictures taken with him tomorrow, so don't be surprised at anything of the sort you may receive. The hunting season has been lively. I have enjoyed the fine dogs, their excitement and intelligence about their jobs. We have had pheasant and venison and are now to have bear steaks . . . I never tasted bear, and I must say the prospect at present is not inviting.

As to work, I have had a let-down for the past two weeks; this happens, but it is not a mood I can tolerate, much less encourage. Good or bad ("hot or cold," remember the irreplaceable Bert Savoy?) they leave here on January first or a very few days after . . . The notion that *Harper's* might, by some persuasion, take a story of mine is very cheery-uppy. I'm money-mad, as you know, darling, and do think a twenty thousand word story is worth something more than I am apt to get for it from a smaller magazine. I have one, called "Old Mortality." It is in three parts, the first a story of romantic love and death, as patched together by a little girl listening to family reminiscence. In the second part, this little girl and her sister meet the hero of the romance, now grown old. Third part, one of the girls meets, when she is about grown, a woman who had been an enemy of the heroine. That's really all. It is to be the first story in the collection. If *Harper's* publish it, they would have to get it in by the April number at the latest, as the book is scheduled for April. The March number would be even better. Shouldn't I send the copy to you? It would be splendid if it could be made to happen, but we will none of us be too badly upset if it doesn't. The story needs a clean copy. Otherwise it is ready. Let me know about this, I will send it where you think it should go.

The title comes from a pastiche I wrote on tombstone poetry in my part of the country. My version runs:

> *She lives again who suffered life*
> *Then suffered death, and now set free*
> *A singing angel, she forgets*
> *The griefs of old mortality.*

Don't you think that sounds like a tombstone poem of the 80's? I was interested also to find, when I visited an old cemetry last spring, that almost all the mottoes and quoted verses were secular, and classical . . . Interesting, I think. Not religious, and not sentimental poetry, except now and then, but fine tall quotations from Shakespeare and Dante and Milton. Well, my story exists and is ready to be published and I hope your good friend can help the editors to make up their minds to mewards. . . .

We have almost hourly radio reports on the great romance of the century, and pictures from the cradle through some appalling phases of 1914 smartness of the woman who has shaken the throne of England. The whole thing seems to me to be carried out in the very best tradition, and the two principals are behaving very well. I notice that Buckie Kirk's sister and Mr. Simpson seem to be providing comedy relief, which adds the final Shakespearean touch. It makes me wonder, though, just what were the political underpinnings to the story of the Prince and Cinderella, and to King Cophetua's romance with the beggar-maid. I should ever so much rather see Edward King of England than Stanley Baldwin dictator . . . The newspapers seem to be carrying on much as they did in the Lindberg case, and God knows they haven't had such a story for a long time. I wish I knew the real story. There's so much more to it than just Mrs. Simpson, fine pretext though she has proved to be. . . .

> With my devoted love,
> *Katherine Anne*

TO ANDREW LYTLE   67 Perry Street
New York City
June 6, 1937

Dear Andrew:

Here is a word of homage to John Crowe Ransom. I wish you had told me a few particulars of the episode, only for my own information. It is fairly easy to guess the main outlines, however. Universities are about due for a thorough housecleaning and overhauling. The contest between Money and liberal learning has gone on long enough, and unless friends go to the rescue, Learning is going to take a drubbing . . . if it isn't about beaten already.

I am about at the point where I think there had better be a Great Schism: Education *must* be taken out of the hands of rich illiterates, third rate politicians, and put where it belongs: in the care of scholars. At present the whole University system is rotten to the core, and an appalling waste of time, energy and money . . .

Do raise the very devil of a row. This is worth doing, ten times over, no matter what it takes . . . I think the whole story should be written, signed and published as widely as we can manage. I wish I could attend the dinner, but meantime, good luck to your enterprise, my deep regard and respect to John Crowe Ransom, good poet, scholar, wit; to all my friends there, and their friends who are working, not only in defense of one man, but a whole principle of culture, and for the better education of coming generations . . .

Katherine Anne Porter

My dear, you will like this rhyme, which appeared here a few days ago; Published first in England where it would do the most good:

> *Milord Archbishop, what a scold you are!*
> *And, when your man is down, how bold you are.*
> *Of Christian charity how scant you are—*
> *Ah, Auld Lang Swyne, how full of cant-u-ar!*

Pretty *chic*, don't you think? Show it to Ford. He's good at that sort of thing. He'd enjoy this. . . .

Love,
K.A.

To Josephine Herbst

Care Tates
Route 6
Clarksville, Tennessee
August 15, 1937

Dear Josie:

.... We drove back through the Virginias, and I went sight-seeing to Mount Vernon, and Kenmore, a famously beautiful house that once belonged to ancestors of Allen, kin of the Washingtons, now open to the public; saw battlefields—Antietam and Appomattox, three days in sweet Alexandria, and could have just stayed on ... It was the first driving trip I ever took except with my sister and father in Texas, where we went also looking for places, not people; for the people we knew even if they lived were not the same people, nor were we; the places had changed too. But standing on the ground, I saw houses, gardens; and children who had once been ourselves; and could remember my father as another man, even while he stood presently by my side. Saw graves with familiar names and dates on them. At the Old Settlers Reunion in San Marcos they asked me to speak. An old gentleman announced me: "The littlest Porter girl, the curly haired one, is going to talk to you . . ." And an old lady said to me, "Honey, you were the sweetest, smartest little trick I ever saw when you were little . . ." and it was pleasant as could be but I had no regrets and no wrenchings of the heart for any part of the past, no not even up until the day before, and everything had moved back, taken shape, was something whole and finished and I could look at it with complete detachment, except for a pleasurable sense of possession; what had been was mine because I really could remember, and now understand, something of what had happened not only to me but to all these people, and I felt myself *part* of a society, and not alien or wanderer at all.

I talked with old gentlemen eighty seven years old who knew my grandparents and my dead aunts who were beautiful, they said, and they had such vitality, such impassioned memories, and had lived so fully and at such high tension I felt that everything I had ever written about them was very pale and out of focus ... It was a valuable time for me; they thanked me for coming and said how pleasant it had been to see me, and I told them truthfully I had got

149

a great deal more than I had given . . . I took snapshots of Dad with old ladies he had danced with in his youth. The things about these people that struck me was their look of race—real blood features they had, handsome noses, fine heads, and lively young eyes in their wrinkled faces. Our generation looks mixed and indecisive beside them. Well, God knows we have enough to make us indecisive. The problems they handled so competently for themselves were too much for us, the world I was brought up in taught me nothing about the world I was to live in, but as I looked around me, I thought, these people are strong, and they are my people, and I have their toughness in me, and that is what I can rely upon . . . I loved them, really with my heart. I liked the precision of their old fashioned language, their good simple manners that would be good manners anywhere, and their absolutely innate code of morals that shows itself in their manners . . . I feel pretty certain that I could live, now, in San Marcos, Texas, and have a good life and go on writing the way I have begun . . . I'd be willing to risk it.

BUT—they are a disappearing race, soon they will all be dead, and the young people are scattering out as fast as they can go. The land is impoverished, and the young do not care enough for it to bring it to life. I saw all our fields lying full of weeds, (my grandmother owned six thousand acres of good thick black land in that country once, and it was said you could plant a walking stick and it would sprout in that land) and the present owners don't know enough to plant the fields to clover for a few seasons to bring it back . . . that made me unhappy, yet I know part of the reason. No other country in the world so despises and mistreats the class of men who furnish it with food, nowhere is there such waste and contempt for the vital produce for daily living . . . No wonder the young are discouraged, but it is so shortsighted to desert their land and take to trades. Somebody must stick and produce food, but how can they, with great combines mechanizing the farms, getting a corner on crops, paying nothing to the farmer and keeping the prices up in cities? I know all sorts of persons who would call this sort of talk politically illiterate, and I suppose it is. I believe there is a cure, but I have not heard one proposed that I believe would work. I can only see the stupidity and its results . . . Anyhow, I am not writing about political theory, but of what I saw in the south . . . There are so many ills here, peculiar to the region and its people and its needs and its failings, and not one that cannot be matched by some other kind of evil in another section. So its positively no good to compare the worst here with the best somewhere else, which is the habit of almost every stranger who comes here to observe . . .

I don't know how long I shall stay here. We left Olivet two weeks ago last Saturday, and this is Tuesday or Wednesday getting into the third week. I never see a newspaper, or a Calendar, even my little watch has stopped mysteriously, no winding will start it; so time drifts somewhat, and though I meant to work, I am idle; that is, as to writing. There are so many animals, and I love feeding them and playing with them. Living day by day is pleasant, so I forget the future, in my short sighted way. And it is true that I cannot settle and work in any one else's house, no matter how pleasant or how promising the situation. I am not really a good guest, nor ever was. I feel myself to be at the disposal of the house-hold even though the members of it require nothing of me; and so waste my own time and no doubt theirs . . .

I am going to take to the road again very soon, and find a small inn, and settle there and write again as I did at the Waterwheel. That is really the best way for me. Meantime, I have had this lovely visit, and have enjoyed it. . . .

I should like not to live in New York and think I may manage it. Just how is not so certain. The first thing to do is to get my stories off, they will bring a little money and then I can look around and decide. I don't mind being homeless, really, I have always been and can probably not domesticate very easily. I want a *place,* and I love the south, but my feeling of security is somewhere in my own self, and not in any given spot of land or under any given roof. I am glad you found Gene looking so well. He is stubborn and refuses to admit anything, as usual, but this separation is the best thing that could happen to him. I feel that he is even more pleased than I am about it, if he would *only* face anything, once, but he is oddly conventional, wants to go through all the ceremonies of feeling, if not the emotions themselves. Well, it is finished and a good thing, and already I am as done with it as if it had never happened, though the effects are real; and I shall take good care never to see him again. I hate ragged edges to these affairs, they are as dangerous as badly repaired wounds or imperfectly stitched surgical operations. I put an enormous amount of energy, feeling and faith in that business. And then I did not put any more. For me it was as clear as that. I never dispute the end . . . It was a waste and could only go on for so long.

Well, dear Josie, let's keep in touch as we have for all this time, and we will be meeting somewhere soon in an unexpected way and place . . .

With my love as always,
Katherine Anne

TO MONROE WHEELER   543 St. Ann Street
New Orleans, Louisiana
September 29, 1937,
Eight A.M.

Monroe my darling

. . . . This place is full of tourists all the time; I walk out of my door into a crowd of them everyday, with the guide barking about the famous Pontalba family and its enterprises. Some member or other founded almost everything in the old New Orleans, even my Ursuline convent. Old black mammies, wearing the uniform of their legend, sit before the cabildo selling pralines and mammy-dolls. These women are not so old, nor as black as they should be, and one wonders (slyly, slyly) just whose mammies they might be. Al Jolson's, perhaps . . . It all reminds me of the Martinique cabarets in Paris . . .

I hope I do not ruin this letter for you by enclosing a little vetivert; add this to the smells in the street. It is all Louisiana in a little dried herb. It is good for putting among linen, and if you like I shall send you some for Stoneblossom. If you do not care for it, say so surely, otherwise you will be getting a bale of it. I hung a little bunch in a window for the wind to blow through, and wonder how on earth I could have forgotten it, of all things, when I remembered this place.

Monroe, my dear friend, you have saved me from so much by letting me have that money, in my relief I want only to write about pleasant simple things like breathing, and looking at the sky. Aren't you glad we are not Chinese, since when one Chinese saves the life of another, the rescuer is thereafter forever at once the responsible owner and the helpless property of the rescued . . . I think we were speaking of this once, and saying how no doubt a Chinese thought twice before he interfered in another man's destiny . . . even in charity. But we are not Chinese and in our good western way I am in your debt, and will repay you,† and the only added thing is that I have always loved you and shall love you as long as I live; and too, I hope not to trouble you again, who have quite enough without that; I should like to be a pleasure to you, rather than what I must have been these past few days . . .

Another letter very soon, when I know more how things are settling . . . I suppose the New York season is opening with excitement; tell me now and then what you see and hear.

> Hasta luego, with all my heart,
> *Katherine Anne*

To Glenway Wescott   543 St. Ann Street
New Orleans
December 3, 1937

Glenway my dear

Let me tell you what I have been doing and you will know better why I have not been writing to you when my delight is to send you letters such as they are. Just now, within this quarter hour, I have finished "Pale Horse, Pale Rider," and it would be quite useless to try to tell you what a thing it has been; this past month has been spent at it, quite literally, but it is done. The *Southern Review* editors have been snatching it page by page and having it set up, and here are the last dozen all ready to go tomorrow. Now I must begin at once on "Promised Land," which I hope to persuade *Harper's Bazaar* to take instead of the one I promised them, for it must be written next, no argument about that, and now is the time or never. I can't quite explain this steady energy, though I

---

† *cf. Note of November 3, 1944, enclosing check.*

have had fits of it before, and it is the best thing in the world while it lasts . . .

Perhaps being on my own, with a real necessity to make money, and a real desire to have some sort of control of things that happen, are good enough as causes. Being here may have something to do with it. Here is an excellent place for me to be, apparently. But I want to be back in New York in the late spring, maybe yet in time for Julius Caesar and the Elizabethan farce, but at any rate in time to see all of you, for that is my real errand, before you begin scattering places as you may. That is my hope, to see you three at Stone Blossom and in 89th street, and where ever else you may be. By that time my book will be out, and my hagridden conscience will be at ease momentarily, and maybe there will be more violets for me to transplant, or I can tamper a little with George's hawthorn hedge . . . Tell me, is that the pink-flowering thorn such as grew in the closerie at 70 bis rue Notre Dame des Champs? Did you ever see that little tree in full bloom? Promptly on the first of May it simply bloomed all over, and I thought it the pleasantest tree ever I saw, and some day I mean to have another just like it, I don't know where or how.

Nearly twenty thousand words, darling, laid neatly in rows on paper, at last . . . But most of them were written years ago, I almost know them by heart. I began this story in Mexico, went on with it in Berlin, Basel, Paris, New York, Doylestown, and now New Orleans . . . what a history. I need a method too. I hope you have found what you need, it is delicious news to hear your mood is better; I think you have simply emerged into another of your many phases, now you will do something else, whatever it is you have been preparing for. Bless you and bless you.

Maybe you will be glad to hear that in the rather dusty austerity of my attic, with no huswifly duties weighing me down, and a blithe disregard for my surroundings, I have developed my natural vanity again, and now go sleekly coiffed, curled, manicured, and spend three hours once a week in the hands of Julia, the Vieux Carré beautician who does the hair-dressing for the Petit Théâtre, also; she takes pride in me and turns me out smooth as a willow whistle. And I believe you will be glad to hear this.

I long to frequent you, too, my dear, and you are the only one I feel free to talk over the common predicament in which we find ourselves—literary predicament—One of the editors of the *Southern Review* wrote me today that the linotypers didn't like my story so far, because there were no bawdy spots in it. The editor told them there weren't going to be any, and one of them said, "I thought this woman was a proletarian sympathizer . . . but look at this story. Here's a couple dead in love and they don't sleep together."

And the editor added, "I think you may as well face the facts. You are not really a proletarian writer." . . . .

With my love,
Katherine Anne

TO ALBERT ERSKINE   543 St. Ann Street
                             New Orleans
                             Tuesday, December 14, 1937

Darling:

I've been thinking about your Christmas present. It occurs to me that I never heard you say you wanted anything. I know things you don't want, for example, a book. So I shan't give you Audobon's *Birds in America* simply bursting with pictures. You have already got all the leather things you want to carry in your pockets and don't seem to carry them. I should never dare to offer you an article of wearing apparel after the warning you gave me about ties. Besides you (probably,) know more about that sort of thing than I do. My knowledge is sound but academic, naturally. You've got a radio. (Don't give me one, by the way.) I've been looking through the gadget number of *House and Garden.* I could give you a pair of wooden brass bound liquor bottles, (I'm fond of them) but something tells me you would not really look upon that as any kind of proper present. Or a good dog. Would you like a good dog, darling, a Doberman Pinscher or a Setter or a Boston Bull? Or would you prefer a smoked turkey from way down East? Or a Dalmatian spot hound? What about a valet rack? It says: "The gift of gifts for a man, exclamation point. It saves time and temper by having his clothes all assembled for the morning rush." And then shows a picture with sure enough everything assembled. Its one of the ugliest things I ever saw, though. Would you like a ship's bell clock? Or a Swedish pottery silver inlaid cigarette box? Or a thousand packets of matches with your monogram on them? Or a pair of Mexican huaraches? (No, no, that's apparel, again.) Here is something to go with your Schick razor: a glare-less (hyphen theirs) shaving and make-up mirror (maybe you would let me use it now and then) with magnifying mirror and an outlet for electric razor . . . Now that ensemble would look like progress, at any rate. Darling, for God's sake, you can see how it is . . . What would you really like, really *like?*

There must be some one thing you would enjoy and be pleased to keep. But how can I guess?

It is nine o'clock now and I am going back to bed. Immensely, unbelievably, better after my rest. Good night, my dear love, my darling. I love you.

One thing more first. Caroline Durieux told me the other day that she had begun a new treatment for colds recommended by her doctor, one of those anti-body things, only now one does not take it as a serum by injection, but simply in little spoonfuls or tablets— I'm a touch dim on details—by rule, and once you have wallowed your way through the course, you are immunized for a year. The thing takes three months and must be done properly or its no good. I said I would wait and see how she came out, and then decided that I might as well try it too, beginning pretty soon. It is called Entoral, and wouldn't I like to see Consumer's Union about it before I begin? You buy it at any chemist's, for less than two dollars. I asked her if she thought it might turn out to be one of those drugs like the recent scandalous one whose name I cannot remember, and she said earnestly, Oh, no, my doctor recommended it. I reminded her that so did other good doctors prescribe the other deadly combination, but still my skepticism cannot outwit my hope. I am going to try it. Now *you* wait until you see how *I* come out, and it may be something for you . . .

Bright and early next morning, December 15.

"Darling," she asked opening her eyes and yawning, "Would you like a bycicle?" I never could spell that word, and can't pronounce it either. I have heard the English call it "BYCYcle" so much I can't get it right any more. I just noticed an advertisement for bicicles and the present question is still on my mind . . . (You will understand that I KNOW you don't want one?)

Your letter this morning was so lovely, I like long letters that are a little like talking. This morning I am up to stay up, and today and tomorrow will be the last two days I can work before the awful holidays swamp me, so I must make the most of them. I too have forebodings of those long two weeks—yet we did plan to see each other for New Year's Eve and Day, most certainly not two weeks off, and we are seeing each other Saturday, and this kind of pause to calculate our positions is a great consolation. Of course either or both may be nailed to the deck once we are there, but let's try not to be . . . I don't know about you, but its true my family can wangle me fearfully; I am simply caught up among them and tossed about as if I were a rag doll. . . .

I have written this before having coffee, but I slept so late that *you* will be having lunch by now. "Bright and early" for me meant a quarter to ten. Thank God for relativity . . . I love you, my blessed, my dear, my darling, I miss you most terribly, but you'll be here on Saturday, toory loo!

Your very own somewhat excitable but most faithfully adoring

Katherine Anne

SECTION 4

Baton Rouge,
Saratoga Springs, Reno,
Boulder
May 1938 to July 1942

. . . if only I can have my place to stay and be able to work to keep it pleasant and to care for it properly, I want nothing more . . . And everything I lost before in this world will come back to me there.

Katherine Anne Porter to Albert Erskine
January 29, 1941

EDMUND WILSON WRITES TO ALLEN TATE, JULY 24, 1939, *"We've just seen Sherwood Anderson, who is at Olivet, and reports that he and John Bishop and Padraic Colum and Katherine Anne Porter are putting on a show together—they* all *appeared and performed on one platform the other night—which is laying them in the aisles. . . ." This is the beginning of Katherine Anne Porter's years of touring the country to read and talk to students. She tries "to make a festive occasion of a reading of literature—to make serious literature a living part of the day." A year later when she is at Yaddo (which "invites artists with jobs to finish to come, and work quietly in peace and great comfort"), Paris falls. She walks the borders of the 105 acres she is buying at Ballston Spa and begins again next day at Yaddo with her travellers in* Ship of Fools. *They have "got back their names and faces by now and are thinking about each other, which will lead to almost no good."*

TO GEORGE PLATT LYNES   Kean Apartments
                          Chimes Street
                          Baton Rouge Louisiana
                          May 12, 1938

Dear George:

If you have happened to see in public print an announcement of my marriage, let me hasten to tell you the report is not exaggerated. And my slowness to write you the news myself is not just due to absent-mindedness, either. If it seems sudden to you, think what it must seem to me, who left New York eleven months ago meaning to stay away perhaps for a summer, or less: and who planned to go to Mexico with you: and who thought, finally, that it might be a good thing to stop in New Orleans for a while: and who—

Or perhaps I should start again on another train of much the same sort. I was ill all winter with an abscess in the lung near the bronchial tubes; have it yet, but under way to a cure. So found myself in Houston, Texas, of all places—oh *what* a place, George, never go there—in care of the family physician, a Viennese who specializes in the family chest, having treated seven cases like mine in my immediate connection. So I was no particular novelty to him, and he did nicely a very boring job . . . Meantime, Albert Erskine and I began making plans of our own. We were married just before noon on Tuesday, April 19th, in New Orleans, at the Palace of Justice on Royal Street. It was a highly secular affair: (I had my divorce just ten days before—) with Robert Penn Warren and his wife for witnesses. We had Planter's Punch in the St. Charles Bar first, and then, adorned with faint sprigs of bridal bloom, we went to the Palace to look for the judge recommended by the Italian Consul—Warren's wife is Italian—and she took on the business of finding the man to perform the ceremony. We found our judge hearing an all-Negro case; he suspended court and shooed us into a small office nearby, where an electric ceiling fan whirred and creaked, ruffling our hair, drowning our voices; and the deed was done.

"Now you are safely back home again," says Albert, "You will at once get the hookworm and malaria, and go to sleep, and wake up only now and then when there's a lynching."

But really the prospects are much better, dear George, and I hope you will wish me happiness.

Albert has a small patch of land just outside University—We sit here on the edge of the campus—6000 students male and female created He them to the confusion of the faculty—in a small flat meant for a bachelor of non-domestic habits, for the moment. But we spend our best times in the two acre wood at one end of the land. There is a young orchard, very young: and fifty gardenia plants, and wild cherries, young elms, a holly or two, an infant magnolia; the rest is just woods, a tangle, with now and then a moss hung oak or it couldn't be Louisiana. We work there, in company with an old Negro who has put in a corn crop on the cleared land. We seem to think we are going to make a Virgilian grove, Bayou style, out of our swamp. We love it. There is going to be a house there some day, we have no way or means of knowing just when. The place is full of birds: wrens and scarlet tanagers and cardinals and thrushes and mourning doves and Bob-whites and jays, and of course, of course, mocking birds. There is wild honeysuckle, wild roses, and wilder blackberries . . . Mosquitoes, chiggers, and spiders big as your thumb. And something quite unearthly in the slant of light between the thin tree trunks hung with all sorts of vines that I must have seen before but have forgotten. If you think of all the places I might have lived, even expected to live—but I live here. Of all the places I have looked at and thought, I may as well stop here . . . And *here* is where I have stopped. It's really strange and in more ways than I could explain, unexpected. But here I am. Wish me well, my very dear friend.

My Guggenheim Fellowship was renewed this year, a pleasant surprise and a pleasanter to know I shall really have the use of it this time. I am working well, you will be glad to know, and high time, too.

What is Mexico like by now? And what happened to you there? Tell me at least a little. I wrote to Monroe there, to the Wells Fargo Express, but there was no word since; where you are, there is interest and excitement; don't tell me your adventures were not unusual, I believe I know better . . .

Believe me that I did not mean to go away and not come back. And indeed I shall be back, but not this summer. And maybe next spring you will come south, and visit me in my woods, and even maybe you will like this country. It is beautiful and seems very strange to me.

> With my same love
> *Katherine Anne*

(Mrs. Albert Russel Erskine jr., imagine.)
Albert is business manager and assistant editor of the *Southern Review,* one of the editors also of the University Press. Is responsible for the appearance, set-up, format, what you please, of the S.R. and I think makes a fine job of it.

TO BARBARA WESCOTT   Kean Apartments
                            Chimes Street
                            Baton Rouge, Louisiana
                            June 15, 1938

Barbara darling:

Your letter was like you, and though I think and speak of you a great deal always, still you have been specially in my mind ever since. This time of year is a kind of anniversary time, any way. I remembered that you and Lloyd were having a third wedding day in April, and what a fine three years these must have been for you both. I think it was this month—or the next? that you were in Paris together that same year, and I remember the evening at the house in Notre Dame des Champs, and Kiki: seeing you and Lloyd together then made me very happy. Something lucky and certain and *right* in the very air around you.

When I left New York I really expected to be back in two months at most. But I stayed on with my family longer than I expected, thinking it might be the last visit for a great while. And then I went to Olivet College to lecture—not so stuffy as it sounds, it was the first time I had done anything of the sort, and I liked it in some ways. And there Allen and Caroline Tate reminded me that I had been seven years on the road to Benfolly—their place in Tennessee—so we drove back through the country, visiting battlefields and hot springs on the way, southern style. At Benfolly,

165

almost the whole editorial staff of the *Southern Review* dropped in to call for a week, and Albert Erskine among them. I have been assured that love at first sight is a trivial frivolous affair, but I do not in the least believe it. Its that or nothing, so far as I am concerned, and Albert agrees. We merely stared at each other in a daze for that week, and we did not meet or write a line for three months. Then he came to New Orleans to see me and it was all up with us. I thought it was madness, it may even be; but now, nothing seems more sane, no choice better, than this.

We have a tiny place in the country, and are clearing two acres of woods, meaning to build a small house there. We work there every afternoon, but really work, Barbara, clearing for a road, planting a small orchard. There are peaches, plums, pomegranates, figs, oranges, grape fruit, thirty young saplings all flourishing. There are oaks with moss on them, or this could not be Louisiana, and the place is full of birds—Audobon's birds, as Glenway calls them, and they really are his, for we recognize them by his pictures of them, and so many of them are there: orioles and thrushes and mocking birds and wood-peckers; jays and wrens and doves and owls. We mean to encourage them to stay.

We have a sharecropper. Wait until the *New Republic* hears of this. An old negro came and wished to plant corn in our field and we told him to go ahead, as we would never get in a drop of ours this year. So he did, with a hump backed mule and a spindling plow; and you never saw such a distressing weed-bed in your life. It gives me acute pain every time I see it. Next year there will be no weeds in the whole five acres. No not even in the woods. Five acres—what a pocket handkerchief of a place. But as much as we can manage, with our other work. There will be a garden, an orchard, a small crop of corn, fowl of various kinds, a duck pond; and a hedge of gardenias. There it is, and there we hope to be soon.

Promised Land is in its last stage, or so I hope heartily. And of course I expect really to get some work done now. Hope for me, my dear; for without it nothing would be of much good to me.

Mulhocaway must be something to see by now. And I hope some day to see it. Surely you will be going again to Mexico, and it is not so very far out of your way to Louisiana; some day, Barbara, I hope you and Lloyd will come in again as you did in Paris and let me see you again. I miss you very much, for to me, too (among so many) you are a special person, and irreplaceable.

Thank you for your blessing, it will bring us luck. With my same love to you both

Katherine Anne

TO ROBERT MCALMON   901 America Street
                          Baton Rouge, Louisiana
                          November 21, 1938

Bob darling:

. . . . You wrote once, "marry or don't marry, what differnce does it make?" but I was never able to adopt this highly developed point of view, it *does* make a difference to me, a great one. You may have heard by now in the roundabout ways that news can travel, that I divorced Pressly very soon after I got back to New York. He is now in Moscow at the Embassy or Legation or whatever the U.S. Government maintains there, and I suppose is no worse off there—with his peculiar temperament—than he would be anywhere else. At any rate, I came south, met Albert Russel Erskine, in August last year, and this last April we were married in New Orleans, and here I am, to my endless surprise, sitting quietly in Baton Rouge, feeling very well, very settled, very all sorts of agreeable things which naturally we both hope will last. . . .

Your last note was from Salzburg, one of my very favorite places. But now gone, I shall never see it again. Where were you during the Tschekoslovakian uproar? I wondered if you had by then perhaps gone back to Paris or even London. When I was in Paris, in the middle of all the excitements, I never felt so uneasy as I do now, waiting for newspapers and radios to tell me of the next stages of collapse . . . It seems to me your book is timely, a closing of accounts for a whole generation, a way of life. Let me tell you why I should especially like it. I have a group of books, of which perhaps you might say when I tell you the names, that the only bond they have is contemporaneousness . . . and so in one sense it is true. But there is something much deeper, I believe. I wish to do a kind of study and recapitulation, with these books: Kay Boyle's *Monday Night,* Williams' *White Mule,* Henry Miller's *Tropic of Cancer* or perhaps this latest one now on hand; Djuna Barnes' novel; *Every-*

body's Autobiography, Stein. Two recently translated novels by young French literary gents, for a comparison and contrast; and your own *Being Geniuses* for a running commentary on your times, and theirs . . . There may be more in this list before I get going on the piece; but this is a beginning. I was so delighted with your book, and whatever the publishers have left out that I remember in the manuscript, why with your permission I will mention that, too . . . Yours is a document I trust and the very thing I need to draw the whole thing together. . . .

A provincial Rotary-club-minded University is a fearsome spot, God wot, but I don't have to involve myself, and I don't. The tendency is towards a species of unreasoned, almost unconscious Fascism, with all the unimaginative vulgarity of such a point of view. A bore, to say it mildly, and hard to combat because the whole thing is too pervasive to get a thumb on. Well, after all, you are in the big middle, as they say in Texas, of the original disturbance, so these comments from the side line must seem a little vague to you.

I almost forgot to say, the story Hall re-sold for me is "Pale Horse, Pale Rider." I gathered that you liked it; I hope so. Your long story is good; you know I like the apparently rambling story that comes into focus at the end and makes the point quietly. I handed it over with recommendations to the editors; things go slowly here, it may be a month or two before we hear anything. A quarterly sometimes makes up its mind about material a half year or more ahead. Which means that even if they accepted it, it might not be published for three-quarters more. But please let me know where you are, from time to time, and how you do; now I am so far away it seems quite natural to remind you that I am really your friend and devoted to you. That I write so seldom means nothing at all except that I have very little sense of the passing of time, and come out of my trance now and then with a guilty start, feeling then really it is life itself I am letting go by so wastefully, and that I am neglecting my own heart when I lose sight of friends . . . I hope you are in good health. You said something about the old vitals folding up a trifle when you drink now adays. So do mine—or did, and for weeks upon weeks I do not have even a glass of wine. I don't seem to need or miss it, and dull as it sounds I do feel immensely much better; and I do like my new feelings of health and energy. Of course I went through such violent upsets and changes and came into a quite new way of living and a real change of climate; and it destroyed some old habits without my even knowing they were leaving me. Its quite all right though. The changes are surface; I am still quite surely the same.

Katherine Anne, with love

TO GLENWAY WESCOTT 1050 Government Street
Baton Rouge, Louisiana
July 10, 1939

Dear, dearest Friend:

First off: Somerset Maugham is a phony. P6H6o6N6Y. (That effect is accidental, but I think I'll leave it. It comes of pressing the space bar on this polyglot typewriter.) Phony, then. Years upon years ago I read *Of Human Bondage,* and that is a good solid, airless, beefy English novel, his masterpiece. For the rest he tells good, made-up tales that might entertain you if you hadn't got a God's other thing to read and were bored anyhow. He is a trivial, conventional minded, professional hack and I think it is perfectly proper that he should be elected Dean of English Lit. at once . . . He has all the qualifications, including the stipulated half-ton of half-good books.

Auden was here, guest in house for two days, two nights. I gave him my bed and slept on a narrow cot in Albert's room, a cot that once belonged to Jimmie Stern; I bought it off him when he broke up housekeeping in Paris. Auden had with him a young boy who looked like a combination young satyr and newly made eunuch, who sat with a blind, self conscious, sullen stare on his face, jolly well knowing he was simply irresistible in that pose. Auden says he has great talent and is writing well, but he advises him (A. advises the boy) not to try to publish for some years yet. They were really ideal guests with a gift for self-entertainment, played all the Mozart disks, lolled about, sipped mint julips, looked at all the books, examined the vegetation around the house, and were in short my delight and Albert's . . . We drove to St. Francisville and

Auden had his first glimpse of decayed southern grandeur at the celebrated Rosedown place; and at lovely Waverly the equally celebrated Mrs. Lester (queen of the Mardi Gras in 1912) gave us gardenias from her endless hedges . . .

Auden inscribed his books which he found on the shelves, and wrote a good letter afterward, asking to be friends for life; which I think is a nice prospect. He really is what you called him, a Stonehengish sort of fellow, I hope he does stay and that all ends well with this fine beginning.

About Maugham: and Jimmie Stern. About Auden, and Tennyson. Jimmie gave me a copy of Maugham's short stories, telling me what a great writer he was and how he Jimmie admired him. I said merely, My GOD, and took another sharp look at my friend Jimmie. Auden, here, was praising Tennyson, re-finding him, defending him. Now, really. Now Glenway, you know better. And what did he choose for praise? Some lyrics from *Maud. Maude?* I'll have no part of it.

Darling, this letter is being dashed off just after coffee early in the morning, and I simply hope it is some sort of answer to yours; I didn't see the *Coronet* interview, but shall get a copy. And as for the young Lyneses and the half-educated dog, don't I seem to remember that once before he committed a double nuisance on Barbara's white doe-skin (I think doe-skin) bedcover?

Twice, I suppose, in approximately the same place is too much.

Albert will answer your letter about the reprint, he called at once but the entire press personnel had moved out for its morning coffee, he has gone to the office and I suppose, knows by now. He feared the type had been melted down already. Oh, I do hope not. Your piece about me has become a kind of secret vice. I sneak back and tipple at it privately, hastily dropping the magazine if any one comes near. I get a little light-headed. I cannot believe it is about anything I ever wrote, and yet, there are the names. And how you do know about Hatch—

The money *is* nice, and always unexpectedly more. I was paid three hundred dollars each for the two they published, at a strict word counting rate. Red held out for decent pay, explaining to the board of supervisors that for once he wanted a high brow magazine that would make it worth while for high brow writers to write and send . . . almost the whole budget goes into that. And the S.R. is the only department of L.S.U. that doesn't need house cleaning by the Bureau of Federal Investigation. That would of course be a poor boast, I am not really boasting.

The excitement here has been a little wearing; everybody still believes—wants to believe—that all the preliminary arrests and indictments are leading up slowly but most surely to Leche, who has slipped off to Covington, his country place with its two WPA built barns, and is laying low and treading light. He'd better.

I read on in your letter and came to your statement that you were simmering up some remarks on Maugham . . . Do, darling, throw him to Forster. Now *there's* a man will never be Dean of anything if he lives to be a thousand. Much, much too good for it. . . .

Until we meet, then. But I do not feel so very far way.

> With my love,
> *Katherine Anne*

To George Platt Lynes   Olivet College
Olivet Michigan
July 28, 1939

George darling:

The family album, with only one member represented, is my singular treasure and you do know it. Here at this conference there are candid camera fiends lurking about; and my poor little female vanity has suffered perhaps fatal shocks, except that I am always able to remember what *you* can do, given only me for model. It sustains me, darling. I tell them freely I trust no one but you, and when they asked me for a photograph to hang among those of the other lecturers here, I said, "But don't take it here. I'll send you a Lynes." Pure pride and self defense. How I love those photographs, and know I should have really looked like that if there really was justice in the heavens . . .

I have news of you, or rather an impression of you, stitching away in Stone Blossom. Have you reached any vital spots yet? I remember yet how startled I was walking in for breakfast one morning, at what I thought I saw stacked up on the little corner divan . . . or settee; and next year it should be even more eye-catching.

We've been having scandals in that so-dear Banana Republic of Louisiana, as you must have heard; but the *Southern Review* goes on, and so do the Erskines, and we still hope you will come to visit us. We've had a rehearsal already, with Auden, and his young friend Kollman (for three days, and then they were off to Taos.) It was really gay, having them, so think how much gayer to have you.

George Davis hove in the other day, with a young musician and a black Persian cat, and hove out again presently. I sometimes wish I could plumb the depths or whatever it is of his gloom. But gloom gloom it is, all the way, and no sort of reason apparent. We are an assortment here altogether, but we assort rather nicely: Sherwood Anderson, who supplies the rough-diamond note. Padraic Colum and his wife Mary, with delightful Irish voices; John Peale Bishop, man of the world; me; George Davis (he lectured.) and a procession of transients from the moving pictures and the pulps, and Nannine Joseph, the agent, who as she says, sounds the note of sordid commercialism . . .

Ah, well, darling, I'm catching a train tomorrow, and this is being written between one interview and another with students who bring manuscripts under their arms; incorrigible, I am already engaged for next year, and for the spring tour besides . . . Its a change from Baton Rouge, where all is embezzlement and political malfeasance . . .

Good bye for a little, and again how many thanks for my gorgeous birthday present, quite the finest ever I had. . . . and don't forget I am your altogether devoted

Katherine Anne

To James Stern   1050 Government Street
                                  Baton Rouge, Louisiana
                                  August 13, 1939

Dear Jimmy:

      . . . . First let me explain about "Noon Wine." Maybe that
title was a mistake, though it seemed so clear to me. Don't you
remember the song is about a man who drank all his wine in the
morning and had none left for the rest of the day . . . Maybe I
went too far for my symbol, but it was for me a symbol of recklessness, of any rash act that would mar, even spoil, the future of
a man. And by extension this is true of Mr. Helton, and later, of
Mr. Thompson, too. Even if the reckless and unconsidered act in
both cases was the extreme one of murder . . . It *is* a little hard to
explain, though the connection still seems clear in my mind. But
you are not the only one who has wondered about it . . . but the
song carries a double symbol, for Mr. Helton is obsessed by the
memory of his act, and the song stands in his mind for the time
when he was innocent, and his constant playing of it is the symbol
of his constant brooding and remorse . . . so you see, it really has
a number of meanings . . . For of course he is not mad, never was;
a dislocated being, warped, out of balance, but not mad.
      Of course I didn't see the *New Republic* with your article, and
I suppose you haven't seen the Summer number of *Partisan Review*
with the Writer's Symposium in it† . . . I have a part in it, I wish
you would look at it sometime. I can get the *New Republic* at the
Southern Review with your article, and shall tomorrow.
      I did read "Traveller's Tears," since I read the whole book,
and the idea struck me as quite all right; the only thing wrong was
the American idiom, which was not well done because it was much
too mixed . . . There are about half a dozen (more perhaps,)
regional accents, besides the various argots of cities, besides the
drift of slang which changes from place to place and time to time
rapidly, and it is devilish difficult even for an American who listens
sharply as I do to keep them all straight. Your version, though, was

†*Her part in the Summer 1939 issue of the* Partisan Review *is reprinted in her* Collected Essays,
pp. 451–56 and in The Days Before, *pp. 123–29.*

a good example of a phonetic version of a strange language by a bewildered ear . . . and it is quite enough to bewilder anybody. The same thing happens when Americans try to write English idiom. It simply does not come off. You should have had your travellers English going back to England, or Irish going back to Ireland, or perhaps even Scots going back to Scotland, and you would have been quite safe. For the story told is applicable to human nature of any country, and it is certainly not a bad story. It is just that it should have been told "straight" and not in dialect. . . .

The heat here is something at present meant only for a native. Auden got here, stayed two days; admirable indeed, and *so* pleasant to have in the house. The simple manners of the hopelessly complicated person who *has* to be simple, for the first breach of simplicity leads straight to madness . . . Do not disturb him in his faith that mankind is Good. I should not dare to, I know. For myself, I know for certain there is Good *and* Evil. But every one must make his own discovery. . . .

Auden mentioned too the situation for writers here as opposed to that of England. Fewer ways to earn a living, he finds. (You have forgotten what you said in your letter, no doubt, but I am following it through and answering some things now and then. Ann Watkins should try to sell your novel in England, then, if "its no darned good for this country" and then I don't doubt it could be published here too . . . And so the most important thing till the last. My husband read your book and thought it very fine work. And I think certainly you should send stories here to the *Southern Review.* If you will, I shall talk with the editors about you, and I have already given Brooks your "Something Wrong" to read. By all means send one or several . . . You know there is nothing certain, but they are well disposed to you here. Auden praised you, too, which I fancy would have a little weight . . .

Affection to you both, and let me hear when you can.

Katherine Anne

To CININA AND ROBERT   1050 Government Street
PENN WARREN   Baton Rouge, Louisiana
                            May 1st, 1940

Dear Cinina and Red:

Today, ordinarily just May 1st, Mary's Day, Labor Parade Day, and Walpurgis Night, or Brocken night, in certain ancient Nordic countries, becomes a personal anniversary. Oh, yes, I forgot, May Day with ribboned poles in England and here too . . . This is also the day on which Albert and I have separated, and I think it better to send you a little announcement, to spare you the surprise of arriving here and finding the situation. It isn't much of a situation, even so, you may be pleased to hear. After a good deal of hesitation and real pain in the matter, we have very slowly arrived at this conclusion. The past week has been a curious one, a cloud of packing up, plans, beer and chess games to ease our feelings, music all day and interruptions to go out and train the garden up in the way it should go. Albert has also provided a system of locking up the place on the grounds that though I am not a timid woman, I should be, and in any case he wants to feel the house is safe . . . I am staying here, and Albert this morning after breakfast moved a few of his belongings to the Faculty Club. If his projected raise goes though, he will probably take a small apartment which we can do up very nicely with what he has . . . It is true he is coming back for dinner tonight, bringing a steak, but we are now in fact and in deed separated, and for life. Don't be troubled about it, we are not really doing violence to any thing in life, but making the best arrangement we can for both our futures. It is not that we are not friends, that we do not love each other, even. It is simply that the present situation is not good enough.

Now then. When you come home we shall both be here, quite as usual except not living in the same house . . .

Your postcards were delightful. We suppose that you will be starting back very soon now, the year has been short, hasn't it? I was shocked you did not get a renewal, Red, but we are hoping you may apply again next year. You have the possibilities for a renewal for exactly so long as you do not get one. Sooner or later they will give it . . . Moe wrote me a desperate letter saying in effect to reconsider my candidates—I had three good ones this year—if I possibly could, as the applications were mountainous and the committee hardly knew which way to turn. I wrote to him that I could not reconsider; my candidates were just as eligible as they were when I first recommended them, their gifts being not in the least dependant on the state of the Foundation's finances . . . No answer. But not one of my dears got a fellowship, either . . .

The weather is so heavenly now it seems odd human trouble is so pervasive and incurable. I know the fallacy of that feeling, I merely mention that it gives a keener edge to irony, like being murdered in a field of roses . . . Good bye for the moment, darlings, we'll all be very cheered up to see you safely home again. Your long flu-ridden winter reminds me of my first winter in Paris; just such a history, no different. With my love, as ever,

Katherine Anne

The medal trip was pretty gorgeous and oh, hecticker than any trip before—a combination triumphal tour and wild goose chase.

TO LODWICK HARTLEY 1050 Government Street
Baton Rouge, Louisiana
May 4, 1940

Dear Mr. Hartley:

It is possible I might not agree altogether with some of your conclusions about certain points in my work, but there is nothing at all for me really to challenge, for the analysis is your own, extremely well argued and thoughtful. I am so pleased to have serious criticism, it would hardly occur to me to quarrel with the conclusions.

Let me say I think your mild accusation of sentimentality in certain stories, or passages perhaps, struck me rather sharply. Of course, we know that sentimentality is a fighting word, like romantic, or whatever it is one doesn't want to be, or to be called. Myself I think half the evils of human relationship are rooted in sentimentality, which Joyce defined as (I forget the exact words) the feelings of one who wanted the pleasures of a situation or relationship without having to pay the price . . . That is good enough, no doubt, but my own view is that sentimentality is simply misplaced emphasis, too much feeling, or the wrong kind of feeling; giving a false and inflated importance to events. Now in "Pale Horse, Pale Rider," I think the situation in which my young people found themselves was desperate enough to warrant any emotions they could possibly have been capable of—in fact, my point was, partly, to show rather decent, not extraordinary, young and modest persons, facing a disaster too great for them to grasp. I think they behaved characteristically, holding on to their realities as long as they could, masking as well as they could from themselves the desperate and sinister nature of their predicament. The young girl was a little more conscious and articulate, the young man certainly of superior moral fibre and courage. You are quite right, that story is so completely autobiographical it amounts almost to a document, and if it fails, it is because I attempted, literally, the impossible—at least, I am afraid, for me. I attempted, among other things, to give an account of what is called the Beatific Vision, the strange rapture that occurs, and maybe more often than we can ever know, just before death. Not many survive to tell, and it is very difficult to tell even imperfectly. On another level, it is simply the story of youth in a war-world, of that touch on the spider web of life, as Hardy puts it, which causes the whole structure to shake. And there were other implications, but perhaps I did not make them clear, and if so, it is too late to explain them now. The time was then, and the place the story, for making all clear.

You are wrong about Laura.* She is a composite, five different young women of whom I was not one. But I was there, and I saw, and knew what was happening, and maybe that is a kind of autobiography too . . . The mention of "The Grave," and the quoted passage, delighted me truly, for that is one of my favorite stories, though I feel I might do it a little better now. I shall not try, for there is too much undone, and I have too many other stories planned that must be done.

Let me thank you for your article. Oh, yes, and let me say: I have never particularly stressed the feminine point of view, not

*"Flowering Judas"

being at all certain what it is; but if you, as a male critic, find this certain objectionable element which you define as feminine, (another word, I think, in philosophy for something, weak, devious and false) at the risk of being called a feminist, (slimy word) I wish to say that I do not believe that my faults are specially womanly, or my virtues specially masculine. After all, I am a woman of an almost boring normality, I run dreadfully true to form in most ways known as womanly. But I write as I do, also, as an artist, with an almost complete lack of self-consciousness as to sex. I don't know whether I understand women better than I do men: perhaps I don't really "understand" either, except in a few basic resemblances. Otherwise, each new human being is for me a new source of speculation, I have never been able to get them typed off and classified and pigeon holed, really I never know what one of the astounding creatures is going to do next. This makes writing about them an absorbing and hazardous occupation . . . I have some clues to universal human nature within myself: I trust them, because I have no better . . .

This letter is too long for that very old and good reason: "I had not time to make it shorter." It is being written at top speed, because I feel I know so well what I would like to say I should be able to say it at once. This theory fails sometimes. I do not depend upon it entirely, but in this case, let it rest. I have told you as well as I can at the moment, a little fragment of what I think.

With my best wishes to you, I am sincerely yours,

Katherine Anne Porter

To Glenway Wescott   Yaddo
                          Saratoga Springs, New York
                          June 14, 1940

Dearest Glenway:

Paris has fallen since you wrote your blessed letter, and I just saw, after writing your name, that I had written that date instead of the right one. This is the sixteenth, but it has been a long time since I heard the news, it has been a long life time of trying to realize the truth. It is no good saying we have known for a month that it was *almost* bound to happen; I am stunned quite literally in a way that never happened to me before. I can't sleep, I can't work, certainly I don't think except intermittently, and some things I know well are very important seem for the moment not worth even remembering. My reason or whatever element it is in me that continues, brings forth the most plausible arguments of consolation, and they are worthless. I know what has happened, and I know that our lifetime will not see the end of the disaster. But it is a majestic and terrible Nemesis, we know that the Furies do not come uninvited.

Ah darling, I can't write even to you. It is late at night now, and I have still been stubborn about working, but now I am going to take a tablet to put me to sleep—I don't know what it is, my doctor gave me them last winter and I still have a few—and tomorrow morning I shall wake up and begin again, and finish this letter because I want to write about *The Pilgrim Hawk.* Good night.

Here is the seventeenth of June. I slept and then had coffee and took a walk through the woods in the fine airs and colors of the morning, waving a handkerchief soaked in citronella to keep off mosquitos. The citronella ruined the air and my state of mind spoiled the colors, but still I am better, here we are . . .

The first thing is about a visit. This is a real monastery. I had not imagined anything so severely cloistered and delimited; all rules based on the general good of course, and flexible enough to make it possible for the individual to manage small plans of his own outside. I mean to say we are not confined to the grounds by any means. If you would come to visit me, you would have to stay in town about a mile and a half away. But we could walk on the grounds, and if Elizabeth Ames knew you were about we would probably have cocktails at her house. I have not mentioned the prospects of your coming because I should like to be certain. I will be in New York on the 12th of July on my way to Olivet, I thought of staying a day and night there, as I do not have to be in Olivet before the evening of the 14th. But I do want to see you before that. COULD you manage? If not, could you send me *The Pilgrim Hawk?* But that is not the best way, for we would want to talk about it. I wrote to Albert about it at once, you will hear from him. If the S.R. wouldn't take that story, tenderly as I am attached to one of its editors, I would renege on every good word I ever spoke of it. But there is no such danger . . . A story by you would be an event in any season, they cannot afford to miss it. Albert and Red I know about, Cleanth [Brooks] is less certain but also less important; Albert had the idea for the Hardy number, chose the contributors, (with one exception. Red invited me; Albert would have left me out in his anxiety not to appear partial, but once I was invited, he suffered agonies of anxiety for fear I would not make the deadline, which I did barely.) did all the editing and saw the thing off the press in so personal a way he was able to seize the very first copy for me. So it is really his number, in all editorial ways. He and Red make most of the manuscript decisions, and since Red has been gone a year, Albert has chosen all the fiction.

When Red gets back—he arrived on the *Manhattan,* but is spending the summer on various lecture jobs—the three are going to stage a palace revolution and have the masthead changed. They want to get rid of Pipkin who is complete dead wood; Red and Cleanth shall be editors and Albert remain what he is though he has not the title: managing editor. (euphemism for the fellow who does the work: Monroe, for example). Albert will also get a raise, long overdue. And they will have a new lease on life which I hope will last for at least five years more. All this is a way of saying that now you are writing, now you cannot help writing, I believe you have a place to take your work, start again on your new career on another plateau. For you write and think better than ever you did in your life, if I am any judge; better is a mild word. You are going now to flourish in the most ancient sense; you know we could not flourish in the first days, survival was all that could be hoped for . . . And here you are; it is the most splendid sort of triumph . . . Artists should flourish at least for a time, and we shall.

I must see the story, nothing else will do.

Dear Glenway, what wonderful praise of my debut as critical writer. The professional lads have always had me intimidated. I approached belles lettres with the humility of the neophyte, but still I knew well what I thought and wanted to say, and it had to be that or nothing. Cleanth, Eliot adorer, didn't see the paper until it was forever in print, and he almost had a prostration, which he wished to conceal and which took therefore monstrous and interesting forms of conduct . . . I admire Eliot tremendously, but not in the role of curé of souls, Church of England style. So high time I said so, and I have said so and I feel much better. This is my second: the first was the Katherine Mansfield piece in, I think, the *Nation.* But that was incomplete, they limited the space so, and I always meant to fill it out again with all I had to cut and publish it again somewhere. I have in mind half a dozen studies and articles, some day maybe I shall have a book of them. Your encouragement has given me the idea.

Well, to work, to work; these long days are splendid, they cannot last; sometimes I reassure myself; Nothing, nothing can happen today. ALL you have to do is to think about your novel: and my mind really does take a comfortable dive downward to the strangely silent and well lighted place where my life is stored and waiting to be used . . .

Let me know about a visit, that is what I would like.

With my love
Katherine Anne

To Cinina and Robert   Yaddo
Penn Warren   Saratoga Springs, New York
                                     June 20, 1940

Dear Red and Cinina:

From where I sit, I see the hills of Vermont shining very clearly this morning, and if I could see a little beyond them, why there is Bennington, I am told. I arrived here on the third of June, and shall stay until time to go to Olivet. If we do not see each other before, we shall do so then. Albert sent me on your letter, what a letter it is. I suggested to Albert that he ask you to let him send it to *Time,* (or is it *Life?*) which publishes letters of experience from all sources. Naturally Passinetti's name would be reduced to an initial, a changed one, and you could sign with an initial too. But it is a valuable letter; it is hopeful, too, in a strange way. Perhaps of all the places we have been hoping for a peoples' revolt against Fascism, Italy may be the first, yet. But the wrongs done already cannot be undone by repentance.

I have been a little benumbed since the fall of Paris, its no good saying anything now. I am hoping, maybe all Americans are hoping, that we will just hold our own fort now, do a little housecleaning of Nazis and Fascist organizations; and South America might help by cleaning them out there, too. It seems to be a popular notion, too—Here at Yaddo where *all* is peace and sylvan beauty—wonderfully landscaped sylvan beauty, of course—there was a Fascist cook who had a *crise* every time anybody said a word against her Party. And as everybody was always saying a word against it, there was riot. Finally the whole staff demanded that she be sent away, and she was. The present one is not so good a cook, but politically very satisfactory. She waves a butcher knife from time to time with threats against Hitler . . . The terrible thing is that this is a majestic sort of Nemesis overtaking a cowardly and divided world. If England had not backed Mussolini, in its fear of Russia, M . . . could never have kept his power. Having his power, if he had not supported Hitler at the crisis, Hitler could have been nipped. England, France and America combined in a race for trade in re-arming Germany, those three put the weapons in Germany's hand to destroy themselves. We are now selling to Japan all she needs to arm against us . . . I think we need not be surprised when the Furies come, having been so often and persistently invited.

I remember seeing a great Fascist parade in Boston, when I had got back from Europe after a good many years. Banners, slogans, Up Fascism, up Mussolini, with songs and marchings. I had got Europeanized in my point of view, I realized, as I stared with amazement. I wondered how far in the streets of Rome, Berlin, or Paris, a group of Americans, (even ten thousand of them, like these Boston Italians,) would have got with such a project. Can you see them, waving banners saying Up Roosevelt, American Democracy Shall Conquer the World, etc? Neither can I. They would never even have been permitted to gather, and rightly too. I remember my desolation at this sight, and the feeling that Democracy was bending backward, and would get a broken spine at that rate . . . There are Fascist and Nazi countries where Fascists and Nazis should live, and if they prefer the advantages of living in a republic, they should not be allowed to make the best of both worlds in any such way . . . In the last war I was all for tolerance. Now I should like to see boatloads of them simply deposited in the midst of those governments they are so loyal to. That is where they belong. I hope to see them there very soon. I am quite willing to help with the project. Goering once remarked that getting America would be an inside job. Its no good to be lackadaisical. We see what can happen, has happened to other countries.

Well, for twenty years the world has been piling up this monstrosity for itself, and now it is here, and its no good trying to shift blame or escape the consequences . . . The United States foreign policy has been of the criminal kind, and we shall all help pay for it.

The news this morning is that France does not accept the peace terms. That is good, that is right. Southerners who are after three generations still paying the oblique and heavy indemnity of total surrender, should be able to sympathize with the French point of view . . . I don't know at this distance what else we could have done, but France still has resources . . .

The Germans always coveted Paris so, and now they have it. I wonder how long it will take them to realize that they have not got Paris at all, but only another Berlin? Berlin is the best they can do, Paris will go with the French. That is something the Germans can never get through their strange heads: they still believe that if they can eat the heart of the brave enemy, they will have his qualities . . .

Good bye for the moment. Muy bien venida, and I hope you are rested by now, and comfortable.

With my love
Katherine Anne

TO ELIZABETH AMES   North Farm
                         December 27, 1940

Dearest Elizabeth:

This must have been the very happiest Christmas I ever had, certainly I remember none lovelier. And your party was the first real *Christmas* party I have gone to in many years: everybody seemed serenely gay and the faces were quietly happy. The music and the candle light and the lovely food and drink and the fire on the hearth, everything was perfect, but there was something else present too; I could believe the shepherds saw the star and heard the singing: and that the oxen knelt in their stalls. Albert was so delighted to be there, and sent you many thanks and good wishes; but you will hear from him presently.

Christmas day was perfect. We just lolled about rather, and listened to music. Albert brought me a new lovely Wedding Cantata by Bach, the Corelli Christmas Concerto, a Mozart Symphony, Beethoven's 8th, and a Missa Brevis by Buxtehude. We played them, and tried to talk enough and tell enough to make up for the long months, and in the afternoon we went to the studio and David [Diamond] played the songs he dedicated to me, and then prosaically enough we went to the Worden and had roast beef dinner. Oh, I forgot there were rum high balls at five o'clock. Albert and I were never dull with each other even when we were together all the time; we always sat in each other's pockets and talked, listened to music, played chess, and enjoyed each other's company. So you may imagine what this little glimpse was, to both of us. I am so glad you like him; he was delighted with you. Said, he had expected to see a charming woman, but he had not really expected so much as he found.

Elizabeth, it is perfectly true, that love is a strong fortress. We married for love, heaven knows there was nothing else, literally we lived by love and hope, and we do yet; but everything is arranging itself most splendidly, and we are so delighted with each other's good fortune. We simply do not thrive, either of us, when the other does not. Our lives are probably not going to be lived in the most conventional sort of way, but the bond between us is mysterious and deep, it gives us confidence and joy, we nourish each other even at a great distance. It is really love, I know that, and so beyond analysis or explanation.

My dear, I began this note to say, YES INDEED I want to come and see the old year out with you. And I want to call you up today, (Saturday when you will have this) to see if I cannot catch you for a little visit. Your week ends seem to be taken, mostly, but if you have time—There is something special, I think pleasant, and a reasonable hope, I want to ask your advice about. There is no grand hurry, its been in my mind for some time. But when we see each other, I would like to tell you.

> With my love
> *Katherine Anne*

TO ALBERT ERSKINE

Yaddo
Saratoga Springs
January 7, 1941

Dear Darling:

. . . . In this morning's mail I received a check for $10 from New Directions Press at Norfolk. I yielded to one of those impulses I have increasingly, (or rather, yield to increasingly) and wired him I was returning the check and please not to publish the manuscript. It occurred to me afterward it is probably too late, maybe it is off the Press by now . . . Naturally Mr. Laughlin's troubles with his fractious authors do not concern you, still I tell you as an item of news. However, if it is not too late, I shall withdraw the manuscript,† as I had an offer of two hundred for it. Naturally I didn't expect any such thing from N.D. Press, but I shall send Form Letter Number Seven To Publishers which I keep on file, reminding them gently that the *raison d'être* for their business, i.e. the Author, should simply be provided for in the budget from the beginning. It is no good to say the Press is not a commercial enterprise. Other bills are paid at commercial rates, printers and all, and the Author should not be required to foot the bills, in effect. However, don't let me waste this on you, belonging as you do to another department entirely. . . .

I gave a Twelfth Night party here last evening. Just Elizabeth and Rebecca and Mr. and Mrs. Slade and the Asch's and myself. I had two dozen tall green candles all lighted; we were all very gay, somehow, the talk was good, we listened to a little music, I gave

---

† *"Notes on Writing," published in her* Collected Essays, *pp. 442–50; originally published by New Directions Press, 1941.*

them egg nog Kentucky style and liver paste I made myself, and of course the usual big bowl of black olives and celery hearts. They came at nine and stayed until twelve. At twelve we took down the wreaths and laid them in the snow before the house and burned them. It was a most charming bonfire, and we all made wishes. I made one for you, too, my darling. I wore my red dress. I left the candles to burn down entirely, and went to sleep in their light. That is Twelfth Night tradition, too. They are supposed to light the Three Kings on their way to the Manger. . . .

I have not been working very well, but now the holidays are really over, and many things are settled, I shall get seriously into the routine, and there will be something to show soon. Truth is, I have been under such terrible nervous strain for so long, I had come to the point where I was frightened of a collapse: a real one; if I did not know I shall stay here and can be quiet a good while longer, I don't know how I could face much more. Looking back, it seems to me sometimes that I have *had* a kind of nervous breakdown, and may be just coming out of it. But I feel a little grim towards myself: breakdown or not, sick or well, dead or alive, come hell or high water, the point is to get the work done and try to keep one lap ahead of the bills. And if I do have to live a long time, maybe at last I shan't have to go to a home for aged paupers. You may laugh, it *does* sound funny, and it could happen. It is my one alternative to getting myself a house of my own and somehow enough to live on—so far as I know, it is yours, too. So you'd better look out. Only you've got longer to go. And you might marry rich, yet. But I shall never. Marriage for me has meant pure disaster, and a strange cruel starvation of the heart. I have no reason to think my fortune in this matter will ever change. But yours might. You've only failed once. And even it might not be called a marriage at all—at least not a fair trial. It ended the day it began, and the rest was just appearance. Darling, I really love you, and oh how glad I am we are separated. Now we can be at ease with each other. . . .

Katherine Anne

TO ALBERT ERSKINE   Yaddo
Saratoga Springs, New York
January 15, 1941

Dear Darling:

Here is a very snappy objet d'art George P.L. sent me. It was made in John Frederics hat shop, modelled, as you can see, by Keela, the Outcast Snake Maiden. I saw another one even stranger and more hair raising: she was wearing a small black feather hat, in the same pose. Try hard to imagine the grisly effect. . . .

The death of Joyce is a curiously personal shock, though I never saw him but once. That is not important, though. I read *Dubliners* in 1917, and it was a revelation to me of what short stories might be. I might never have begun, if it had not been for that book. I was no disciple, as you know; but reading it gave me *courage,* to go ahead and try on my own.

Send back my feelthy peecture, I like it. One thing I noticed about that barely human face. Both sides of it are identical. No divisions there, no split personality. If you do that sort of thing, you must have a one-track mind. You know how, by covering first one side of a full face photograph and then the other, you quite often see two different faces altogether. Not this one. No angel and no devil in her. Just plain clay. She grins a *little* more broadly on the left side, but not enough to matter.

Dear angel it is fairly early, but I am thinking of going to bed. I hope you are keeping well and eating properly and all. I love you, as I always did, but I have stopped missing you in the curious way I did. I don't expect to see you now, I don't even expect or wait for letters; I am just always pleased to see them. And I suppose I would miss them terribly if they stopped. But I love you, dearly dearly. Good night.

Katherine Anne

To Albert Erskine   [Yaddo
                                  Saratoga Springs, New York]
                                  January 16, 1941

Dear Angel:

. . . . During this little season of drought, I am doing routine work like collecting the short stories. As soon as "The Leaning Tower" is out, I might as well send in that manuscript. So I am having typed that section of the "Old Order" which you sent me, and shall return your copy very soon. I also did a little real counting of words on that whole manuscript, and it is always a surprise to me how short my stories are. They seem much longer as I read them somehow. But as it stands, I was optimistic about length. Everything I can pull together, including "Leaning Tower," comes to about 58 thousand words . . . I had hoped I might be able to publish what I have now as a book, but I see that "Season of Fear" must be added. This insistence on length and weight is going to ruin me. I have a dreadful time making up the wordage, and I simply cannot add a word if I feel it doesn't really belong there. I take out all my vices of verbosity, repetition and chatterboxiness in my letters and private conversation. They are vices, even there, but not so harmful, I hope. . . .

I'd better quit. I love you, my darling. This very minute.

Katherine Anne

To Glenway Wescott   Yaddo
                               Saratoga Springs, New York
                               January 23, 1941

Dearest Glenway:

. . . . Miss Pindyck, [Wescott's agent] I am sure, knows her horrible Limbo and its customs very well, if she undertakes to sell my story among the Big money magazines, I am afraid I can foretell her fate. I lived and worked in that Limbo once, and have had dealings with it, I know the place, and I washed its nasty smells off me carefully a great while ago. I do really shudder at going back into it. I made an exception of *Harper's Bazaar* on account of George Davis, but I have always been uncomfortable, more than a little apologetic in my mind, about stories of mine appearing there. Yet, if they would publish them as I wrote them, and I wrote them without regard to their tastes, and would pay me well for them beside, why, then what was lost except perhaps a little shade of my vanity in my fantastic and enviable reputation? I know that exists, it is exactly what I like, and I would not damage it by a hair . . . I have tossed a good many things considered generally desirable over the windmill for that one curious intangible thing that money cannot buy, and find to my joy that I was right, I have what I want and I have earned it, and look—I have taken money to live, and I have lived poorly, and there is no naming or describing what my life has been because of my one fixed desire: to be a good artist, responsible to the last comma for what I write; I have "lost" if you like, or "missed" entirely several kinds of good repute I should have been pleased to possess; but I could not have everything, I had to choose, and I did choose . . .

No need to explain this to you; and C.S., so far as concerns me, does not exist at all, what she thinks or feels about the matter is nothing, and my guess is that she can *do* nothing, short of destroying my manuscript, which I do fear rather. An accident might just possibly occur to it. But maybe when one must think evil of another, the thought goes too far of its own momentum . . . I don't trust her, I never did, naturally, but I did attempt negotiations with her because of her real desire to have another story. That she miscalculated badly her strength is again of no moment to me. I know my own, very well . . . I will explain to Miss Pindyck first, before she undertakes to sell my stories, that they are to be published as written or not at all . . . In the end, they can always be published in a book, and I have a good contract for that collection; and it would give me pleasure to see it in the *Southern Review,* or in any place where I need not be ashamed of the company I keep . . .

So there we are, dear Colleague; speaking of poor Scott Fitzgerald, who perished on that very road we are talking about. It makes me tremble to remember that really good talent, impoverished and finally destroyed by its own weakness for all the wrong things. The Beautiful and Damned, indeed; poor silly wretch, there was nothing at all beautiful in any aspect of his damnation—it was merely a little too cheap and nasty to bear inspection.

I dropped everything to write a little elegy for Joyce: it will be very short and personal, and probably will go to the *Nation.*

Ah, darling, let me talk for a paragraph about my house. The time has come when I must find a foothold where, as you might say, the rug can't be snatched from under me by just any old caprice of circumstances. My life has been a long history of my attempts to take root in a *place,* to have a place to go back to, at least . . . This has been so often thwarted and disappointed, it has become almost like a fantasy, a mere day dream, and I have resolved quite often to put it away, and think of it no more, and I have tried to persuade myself that such an apparently simple, natural, human situation was not for me, who am of all people you know, simple, natural and so human it annoys me, at times . . . But the truth is, I want to have a house of my own, where I can put my books and papers and little dear worthless belongings and I want to sleep and wake in that house, and work in it, and fuss with it a little, for the rest of my days . . . Well, a house of one's own is not easily come by in any case, perhaps. For me it has been simply impossible all this time . . .

About ten days ago (I had been talking to Elizabeth Ames about my wish for a house) I heard of a place for sale and I went to look at it; as we drove over the ridge of the road looking into the valley, I saw MY HOUSE sitting there behind tall maples, among a clutter of fretsaw porches and leaning sheds, a pure old good house seated on a knoll, surrounded by rolling land and pine woods and fine meadows. It is about 175 years old, has always been lived in and is alive. Good roof, good floors, stone foundation, fine cellar, attic space, not too large but not too small either; a good smaller tenant house, occupied, five hundred yards down the road . . . fifty acres touching on the Albany post road, my front yard facing a perpetual forest reserve of eight thousand acres of pine and spruce . . . 105 acres in all on my place. The great barn burned, and so it would be useless to a farmer without too much added expense. An old woman the last of her pre-revolutionary family owns it, and she is closing up her accounts . . . I can get it for two thousand dollars, such a price as I never heard of for so much, and an option of two hundred dollars will hold it for me until the first of May, when I shall really have my first serious money on my contracts. I arranged the budget this way to safeguard the fund, I am tired of Witch's Money that pours away and leaves no trace at all . . . Actually it is in perfect living order now, but there is only a pump over the well, the fine fireplaces are closed and they heat with real Franklin stoves, imagine.

Well, my dear, yes, apparently I have brass enough for anything. For in spite of my debts, other obligations, all, I am going to take it, and I am going to live there. It is my one sole good hope in this matter of a house. Elizabeth, who is expert in these matters, could hardly believe my good luck. She was enchanted with the house, and offered to buy at once from me the little one with a few acres . . . The point is, the rush for old houses has not reached this part of the country yet—may never. I have looked at old houses in Pennsylvania and Connecticut, Massachusetts, even a few days in Vermont, I have seen literally hundreds. I know at a glance what is there, and this is my house. That is settled. I am going to have it. But not at the price of letting Carmel Snow edit my stories. I can manage the affair without that . . .

The tenant house is occupied and the rent pays the taxes. They raise enough garden to supply both houses. A farmer has been renting the land for crops and will continue to rent it as long as I want. There is a stand of pine timber ready to be sold. There are apple trees and dogwood and lilac and hundred-year maples. I am going to live there for the rest of my days. Do wish me luck. I shall go there on May 15th, my birthday.

And now to work on *No Safe Harbor*. (!) With my devoted love,

Katherine Anne

To Albert Erskine   Yaddo
                          Saratoga Springs, New York
                          January 29, 1941

Dear darling:

. . . . Did I tell you? I meant to—that I am going to Olivet after all. I leave here next Sunday evening, arrive Monday morning, will be there for three weeks. Am taking along some manuscripts, as my schedule is light and I expect to go on working pretty well. Also I go to Smith College at Northampton, Massachusetts—for one lecture March 3rd. What I live for now is to get everything off by May 1st, and spend the whole summer working on my house, so that it will be sound and ready for fall and winter . . . The winter here has been beautiful, in some ways better than the summer, even. Yet I do look forward so to spring, to see my woods and fields in green, and to find out what flowers and shrubs grow there . . . Yesterday I went out and took the first pictures, and if they show anything: the light was pale and the camera strange to me: I will send them on. I saw a detailed map of the land this morning: where the spring comes out of a hillside I can have a large clear cold pool, facing and bordering it with just the stone around the place. I can also have a stone terrace in front and stone walks all around . . . It is going to be a fine and lovely place, better than I ever hoped for. I am going to join the Grange; just think of that; and go to farmer's meetings . . .

This place was founded in 1773, and has been in the same family ever since until now, and everybody calls it the Hill Place, or the Old Hill Farm. It is to the south of Saratoga, so I think it will be called South Hill Farm, and I am going to have the name on my letter paper. It *has* hills, too, so the old name can mean anything it likes. Something may happen to change my mind, it may just take a name of its own, but I shall let rest at present. My furniture is going to look at home in that house.

The Spencer's and the Pickmans—new friends? Connected with the college? Young? Entertaining? Do you find you get on with New Englanders? I do. They are ever so much more interesting than Mr. van Wyck Brooks makes them out. And I do so like this old oaken, ironbound character of the upstate New Yorkers. I get along like a house afire here, and feel wonderfully settled in my mind and heart. What a strange accident, after all. Think if Morton Zabel hadn't written that letter about Yaddo last spring. I remember how my heart sank at the whole prospect, with what bitterness I made up my mind to come here, only because it was the least evil of so many choices, all of them evil to me then . . . And here I am, really happy in some way that I never was before; really life is changed; if only I can have my place to stay and be able to work to keep it pleasant and to care for it properly, I want nothing more . . . And everything I lost before in this world will come back to me there. Just think, when I plant a tree now I can stay to see it grow, when I work and spend what I have on the house, I do not have to leave it just when it is becoming pleasant to live in. Just think, never again do I have to depend upon any one else for anything, and I can make what plans I like, then carry them out in my own time and way, and the house and the whole landscape around it will look as I would like them too, little by little, year after year. . . .

Katherine Anne

To Albert Erskine   Olivet College
                        Olivet, Michigan
                        February 25, perhaps, 1941

Dear Albert:

 . . . . It seemed to me natural that you would like the ballet, I wish I could have seen it with you, as we were together for your first opera. Let me tell you, the little Salzburg Guild performance was about as good as you may hope to see for sometime. The Met. will seem like a ton weight of brick beside it, unless the Met has changed its whole nature since I heard it last. I wish the Salzburg Guild had prospered (it didn't) and had made a speciality of *Cosi Fan Tutte, Coronation of Poppea,* and *Orpheus.* You would find me at every performance for years and years. . . .

I have been up again since day before yesterday, but in such a scurry trying to make up my lost classes, letters are accumulating. I go home Thursday morning after getting even a little with my schedule. Friday morning I shall be back at North Farm, a changed place, as Elizabeth writes she has had it painted and redecorated . . .

Ah, the house . . . the house. I put myself to sleep nights planning it; well, yes, the whole thing is going to be expensive, but that is because I shall put in plumbing and heating system at once, which means the cellar must be turned into a basement, and all that sort of thing. This will be about all I can do besides the preliminary tearing off of porches and taking partitions out and getting the place cleared for further work . . . The interior can proceed slowly, and should. I must live in the place for a while before I can see exactly what it needs . . . However, it is like this: For two years at least all I can have of money will go into it, but then, it will be mine. And if I did not do this, everything I can have would disappear like smoke and at the end I would be as miserable and placeless as I am now. After all, what else will I have, what else could I want? It is to be my pastime and my pleasure, my investment and the place I shall live in. Just having a painful and insecure existence has until now cost me everything I made and more; it seems a good bargain, to me, no matter what it costs.

It would be almost impossible to explain to you what my life is like, or how deeply unhappy I have been in my strange helpless situation ever since I came back to America, almost: I will end this, no matter what I must do to accomplish it.

You know I am capable of being cheerful and in fact I am cheerful, most of the time, in spite of hell. But just the same, like the man in Melville's story, "I know where I am," and I don't like deceiving myself—in fact I cannot deceive myself—as to what is true very deeply under the surface of things . . . I can't perhaps live in the house until summer: I don't take possession until May first, and then only when I finish paying for it, and that depends on my getting the novel done in order to collect the money or a great part of it. It is a marvelous thing to work towards, though: I feel pretty certain I shall make it. Then at best I do not see how it would be habitable for six weeks or two months: perhaps the first of July I can go in, I hope to be able to have visitors in August . . . I come to Olivet again in mid July and Joseph Brewer and Robert Ramsay will drive back with me for a few days swimming and races during the first days of August . . .

(My typing seems to be going steadily down hill, doesn't it?)

A two mile walk? I walk often into Saratoga Springs, two miles, and back again in a couple of hours, usually with *no* beer. Yet I am only a weak woman. I got up from flu and played badminton (don't laugh your head off altogether, please,) with faculty, and faculty, some of them, were at about my stage of development—I having smacked the little bird around perhaps three times before as you know—but there was a gym director who took all seriously and began licking us into shape as if we were going to keep it up a lifetime . . . I am going to have a badminton court and other outdoor devices at my estate, but as usual no doubt I shall be so involved in domestic duties I shan't ever be able to learn . . .

Last night I saw a chemical engineer invested with the hood of Doctor of Science, and was again promised my D.Litt., but I don't think I'll ever get it. And what does one do with it in any case? Only the hood is a very nice red and would look well in procession. But why should I ever go in processions? So perhaps it is as well to let it all go . . .

The house, the house . . . I mean to hand in the novel and the book of short stories in May, and then ALL summer I am going to work on the house and just enjoy it . . . What I can't get done by Fall I shall let go again perhaps until Spring . . . I am simply going to take time out . . .

There are extra chores to get in the way, though. I suppose I shall go on trying to do a lot of things all at once, as ever. I am going to write a preface for Eudora's first collection of short stories. And the *Periquillo* translation is accepted by Doubleday Doran so I must finish my preface for that . . . and *Accent* wants a chapter from Cotton Mather, and *Decision* wants anything I can send, which may be a chapter from the novel; my job now is to keep on my feet and keep working. And I feel pretty ferocious about it. I would slit the throat of a six months old infant who got in my way . . .

Dear darling, you know I love you, but you mustn't worry or think about not having written . . . Little by little the occasion to write will lessen, for us both; that is what separation is, even what it should be. The distance and time between us will almost imperceptibly be filled with other things, separate interests, new events, and this is very right. Don't trouble about it. Don't be afraid of hurting me, I am almost at ease. I don't suffer any more except when I see you, and just for that very little time I have the same illusion I had before, of real nearness and almost a oneness, but I do know it is illusion; still it is so extraordinary, I can only call it love, and perhaps it even was that . . . When *all* that has disappeared, there will still be something left, for you are very dear to me now without any expectations whatever of any further change except such as will take us away from each other; and my disappointment which was so bitter and deep in that love which after all, wasn't up to the real things of life at all, couldn't, after all, help us make anything together, is now in its place, a part of the natural sufferings of living; I can see it rather clearly now at a fair distance, and hope one day to do better . . .

I don't expect any answer to this, perhaps there is none, I did not say it expecting any. I know you are most comfortable when you can think of me as well and reasonably gay and good tempered and cheerful. Well, those are pleasant things to be and I rather enjoy them myself, but at times they are fairly expensive luxuries . . . one doesn't just pick them off trees . . . Believe me, one would have to be a natural half-wit to be gay in certain situations of my life, but the art is to maintain the *appearance* of it: or so my southern training reminds me. Some one told me the story of a southern woman who said her mother made her talk—when she was a little girl—for half an hour every day one summer to a peach tree in the garden, just keeping up a gay line of chatter as to a dumb guest at a party, never letting a fatal and hideous silence drop, but never saying an indiscreet thing or anything that could possibly contain an emotion or an idea . . . "It is the way," said Mama "to charm men. They don't want to be bothered with your thoughts or feelings."

Toujours gai, what the hell. That is proper for parties, but it can become a horror if one must die by such a formula too.

Which reminds me of a verse on a valentine (I suspect from Joseph.) It was a little blue lined filing card with a little red celluloid heart pasted in one corner, and the verse:

> *Now saints aint what they used to be*
> *And Valentines have changed, you see,*
> *But oh, l'amour*   (Hand printed
> *Remains toujours*   and home
> *So let's be gay and love la vie!*   made verse.)

Please see that this is engraved on my tombstone.

Now, do you see? With a little rehearsing. I might get back into form myself.

Let me look at your letter . . . Weather. Here also very sunny but suddenly cold this morning. I had a ten o'clock lecture with a flock of dead-pan students barely alive after caroaring around last night on late leave . . . This afternoon I have three private conferences, tomorrow a lecture. The nose freezes quite on the short skip from one side of campus to another. It seems colder here than in Saratoga, though the thermometer says not . . . We have snow too, but nice sparkly mica-dust kind . . . Now I just have time to run to town and mail this before lunch. So good bye for the present, my dear darling, I love you always, too, really always, though that is a big word.

> Love again.
> *Katherine Anne*

TO DONALD ELDER   Yaddo
                         Saratoga Springs, New York
                         March 6 1941

Dear really dear Don:

You endear yourself further to me every time you take type-writer in hand and make me a present of your view of things. I wish I could publish this letter: I wish I could send it around to people, or read it to the student body of this Republic . . . There is only one danger, a serious one. If the Big Stick Foundation For Commercial Seizure of South America ever got wind of your notions, you'd be snatched straight off your strategic job. You are strictly not the fellow they want in this business. They wouldn't want me, either; so let's keep vastly quiet and get in a few hot licks before they catch on to us . . .

As to the back-slapping rapacity of our business men vis-à-vis the dark inferior peoples. Its God's truth I still prefer them to the Nazis sitting on our elbows all over South America, though it wouldn't be anything new, as they've been filtering in there like certain germs through porcelain, for a great while now . . . I definitely prefer any evil we have in our life here to the kind of evil the Germans bring in on their bootsoles . . . If it comes to a showdown, I still think we have certain advantages: and I am all for knowing what they are and using them in this war. There are a great number of things wrong in this country, and it is the fault of all of us: if we don't while we still are able, fight the things we know are damning this place, then we are really in guilty complicity with them. . . .

This country is especially charming to me: Not too picturesque, not too dull, a good fair climate with four seasons, fine trees, good soil, good water, and a choice of plain solid old houses to work over . . . What more? My Aunt Anne and Uncle Gabriel used to come here—in the eighties—to the United States Hotel, for the races. My six times removed name-grandfather—Col. Andrew Porter—fought with some gallantry right over here on the Saratoga battlefield. My place, South Hill, is about two miles from it. I consider these two items quite enough family tie. . . .

Monroe and I were talking about something else. Everybody does a faint little piece on Sor Juana Inez de la Cruz, first first-rank poet in America, a Mexican nun who was a famous wit and beauty, who died at about forty nursing plague victims . . . She too has a strange history, and she really was a poet. I have translated several of her poems, and know a good deal about her life from documents I have examined . . . We thought perhaps a short story about her with examples of her poetry and two or three of her fantastically beautiful portraits might help the Good Cause . . . After all, she was the only great poet America produced until Emily Dickinson . . . However, this is for the future, and by future I would mean 1942, late . . . If you wanted a quicker job, I could translate Amado Nervo's *Life of Sor Juana,* though I do think it a little sentimentalized and incomplete . . . But this is only a suggestion . . . First, *El Periquillo Sarniento* . . . Literally, the Itching Parrot. Are you keeping that title? It strikes me as having something of its own, and I like it. . . .

With my love.
Katherine Anne

To Glenway Wescott   Yaddo
                        Saratoga Springs, New York
                        March 6, 1941

Dearest Glenway:

. . . . At Olivet I read "The Moral of Scott Fitzgerald"; nothing better could have been said, ever will be said, on that subject unless you say it. And oh, what there was to say . . . Your style is growing so flexible and expert it doesn't look like a style any more at first glance: your years of being a "fussy stylist" will repay you and all of us. I looked for the "malicious mourning" you described, perhaps I expected something you did not mean, but the tone seemed to me sober, the right gravity and tenderness: in those days I was sternly anti-Fitzgerald and all the wretched man represented: I still am. The reasons for his ruin seemed then, and seem now, trivial and shameful. Dear John Peale Bishop used to gaze at that career with wonder and even strange envy; but I always believed it was because he had a wife who regularly pointed and said, "But why can't *you*" etc etc and in any case John Peale has come through nobly, intact, after what I call an awful beating, and I admire the man extravagantly . . . Perhaps no one should be praised for any virtue, it is inborn, like beauty; but like beauty it can be marred, even lost altogether. So maybe it is right to praise a man who *keeps* his virtue, and grows in it. So I praise you, my dear greatly gifted one, by indirection. You haven't changed direction, or nature, or even style, you are just going to be more of the same, more and better. I haven't the *New Republic* by me now, but I did like so specially your discreet warning, dropped in at the right place, to American writers who are going to be in for a horrible period of wangling by all the emigré writers and the weight of stampeded Europe suddenly on our necks . . . I think the third number of *Decision* is utterly abominable . . . and the perfect example to be held up by the nape, showing plainly what you mean . . .

I haven't seen Bishop's *Selected Poems* yet, but I shall soon . . . *What* about the new magazine? I can get no word of it from anywhere. Believe me it wants to be something on its own, I have real anxiety about that project . . .

Joseph sent you fond messages in return, he counts on you

greatly for Olivet this summer. I am going back, too . . . This is in haste, too, everything half said, but with my same faithful love and *what* faith!

Katherine Anne

TO DONALD ELDER   Yaddo
                         Saratoga Springs, New York
                         April 9, 1941

Dearest Don:

My things arrived yesterday, they are in warehouse here and tomorrow morning I shall go down and take out my manuscripts and papers. So the missing volume of *El Periquillo Sarniento* will be sent you at once, and I shall begin working somewhat on the preface. I cannot promise to have it in at once, because I am really getting towards the end of the novel, and I can't stop at present. But it would appear that it need not be altogether July before I can send it. It might be the last of May.

I do hope you will be there to see the end of it, but that is only a way of saying I hope with all my heart *you will be there* for as long as you want: I believe in miracles too, I know they do happen, the impossible comes to pass oftener than we think . . . But suppose there aren't any more miracles? I would feel much better if I could find out which side we are fighting on . . . that this war exists at all is due to one thing, or another: subhuman stupidity on the part of the English and American and French governments, or subhuman malignity: either way I don't feel reassured. I have never been able to decide which is the most dangerous . . . I clip a letter from the *Nation* which struck me rather pleasantly. It seems to me the man makes a point. What I fear is, his war with Hitler may incapacitate him for taking up again his war with Messrs Cameron and Luce . . . Still I like what he says and the way he says it.

Won't it be a jolly war, with Mister Luce cheering on the valiant cohorts, Mister Ford managing the Commissary (though his sumpter mules seem to have balked) and Miss Clare Booth as Head

Vivandière of the whores de combat. No, Don, that is no place for you or anybody I know. If the Axis wins now, it means this generation and a few more are damned. If the Allies win, it means that England and America will fight it out in the next generation, and we are damned anyway . . .

Or maybe that's no way to talk. But looking as far backward in history as the records go, and as far forward as I can see knowing something of the logic of events and the law of everlasting consequences, it seems almost silly to talk in any other way.

And I don't any more mind our being so hated by Germany, Italy and France, but what does make me nervous is the way Great Britain hates us. No good can come of *that.* Donald Davidson, I think it was, once remarked that the human race can survive an infinite amount of destruction. That is all very well for the human race, but my interest is in the individual, and not only that, but our exact contemporaries here on earth *now,* and though he meant the thought to be consoling, I do not find it so.

Whether anything happens or not, but more especially if it does, if you felt like it, why not come up here for a few days? You could stay here at North Farm; there is nothing to do but walk about in fine weather, listen to music, read, talk, sleep, if you like: or you could work all hours if you were in the mind. If you must go, there might not be time for this, or there might be so many claims on you. This is not one. But I could wish you a little while somewhere with friends, quiet, complete freedom . . . It seems very natural to me that you are unable to work now. With all my determination to work—for what else can ᴉ do?—it is next to impossible. I do work, but with such a division of mind and heart, it goes heavily, I ask myself what it is worth. Still I must finish if I can what I set out to do. And above all now I am glad of all the people who keep singing, and playing instruments, and who dance, and give plays and write their books planned before. What would we do, what would become of us without them? So I hope some one will be glad of me, too, and read what I wrote, here in this time. In all ways except my suffering and feeling of being, too, without much choice of my own directions, I am exempt from the immediate danger of being torn up and dragged here and there bodily, as you are. I am ashamed of this, I do not want to be more fortunate than my friends. But I *am* more fortunate in that one particular, so if I don't work, my conscience won't let me rest, either.

With my love,
Katherine Anne

I had in mind for years translating the writings of Santa Teresa, but you should do it, I hope you may, and I never shall. There should be a life of her, too, a real one, in English.

To GLENWAY WESCOTT   Yaddo
Saratoga Springs, New York
May 4, 1941

Dearest Glenway:

. . . . This afternoon, I left everything and went back to South Hill to go with a cousin of the former owner and walk over the boundary lines. . . .

There is a fine road in the place, and another old "wood road" as they call it, made in pre-Revolutionary times for the wagons to go up for wood cutting . . . It is wild and goes up hill and down, they hadn't got much notion of saving themselves or their horses, in those days. Well, Glenway: I am in love beyond anything with that little piece of earth, I shall love it till I die, and so, since you are to outlive us all, "I hope so"—you must see that my ashes are scattered properly there, too . . . You will have ashes in your hair, my dear, by the time you get through sifting your friends out around their favorite trees . . . But never think you will be unhappy. I remember my father at eighty in the little country graveyard where all the friends of his youth and members of his family, and wife and a little son, were buried. He walked about in a gentle dreamy mood and would say, "Why, there's John . . . let me see, I was five years older than he. And just to think, he has been dead twenty years." And so with a long list, and at the end, he was thoughtful and spoke well of the dead, and could hardly believe they were gone, and he still here. But he was not unhappy, not triumphant, either; he just thought himself a lucky man, for he loves to live, and I think he is right.

Tonight I am sunburned and tired, we must have walked eight miles, or so the cousin said, and part of the terrain is quite difficult; but it was delight, all of it, and so now I am going to sleep early and begin again tomorrow with my travellers, who have got back their names and faces by now and are thinking about each other, which will lead to almost no good.

With my love,
Katherine Anne

To Paul Porter   Yaddo
[nephew]   Saratoga Springs, New York
                               July 24, 1941

Dear Paul:

When I wrote the date I remembered that tomorrow is your aunt my sister Gay's birthday. So I must send her a little telegram.

It is done. Your letter was a happy surprise to me, to have it at all was charming, but even better to know you remembered me, and our talks; for I enjoyed talking with you, yet older persons quite often feel timid about expressing their ideas to the younger ones, for fear of seeming to be giving advice, or being a bore . . . but you seemed so interested in those things that seem more real than any other things to me, music and literature, and painting. It is not a bad choice of interests, in the light of eternity or even of merely a long life, which I hope you may have, for you will find they outlast everything else, and are as good to have and to know on the last day as the first. And you can never, no matter if you devoted all your time to music, writing and painting, reach the end of them. I can't know how you would feel about that, but it is the kind of prospect I like best.

"I think it may be permitted to a lady of my years to *reeemi-nisce* a little." That is a quotation from a speech made at a literary dinner by an Irish friend of mine, Mary Colum. It suits me so well now I take it over. When I was your age and younger, it seemed to me I was on a desert island quite literally. No one to talk to about the things that interested me, and not only indifference, but an active hostility to the way my mind was growing, and the direction my life had to take. Not only was I not helped in the least, but I was hindered. It took years of the most exhausting effort for me to struggle out of that situation, and all my work and development were retarded and warped; I had to fight almost to the death even to arrive at the knowledge I needed if I were to survive at all; for I hungered for music and all the arts as if they were bread, and they *were* bread: for their sake for years I had very little of the material food, and I do not regret one day of it . . .

Well, this is to let you know what happened to me, so you will understand me better: and let you know also that already I understand this much about you and your situation . . . Perhaps it is no good to generalize ever, but still it doesn't seem untrue to say that all the young are lonely: or we can say, all the young who are thoughtful human beings. While you are trying to grow up, really to be a mature human being, and not just a case of arrested development (which is the case with a frightening number of people in this world) and finding your way every day through new experiences, trying to get the education you need for your own particular uses, you are almost bound to feel isolated. You have to find your own place and your own people, find your friends and your enemies, for yourself; and if you really read great poets and listen to great music and associate in that way with the best people in the world, you will get a set of values that will assure you that both your friends and your enemies will be the right kind for you; and you will be, in a deep sense, independent of both. I am glad you are setting out to do some good hard thinking for yourself and never be afraid to think . . . just go ahead and pursue a train of thought straight out to the end, wrestle with your problems as Jacob wrestled with his angel, and never, never pity yourself. That is one bad habit of youth that can be broken early, and you start now, from scratch. All life worth living is difficult, nobody promised us happiness; it is not a commodity you have earned, or shall ever earn. It is a by-product of brave living, and it never comes in the form we expect, or at the season we hoped for, or as the result of our planning for it . . . So don't feel sorry for yourself. That is important. If you have a good mind and an active body and imagination enough to know what you want, you need never pity yourself unless your wants are base and cheap, which they are not. I'd be delighted for you to write me anything on earth you want to write, and your letters will be treated with the most complete confidence; it will be as if you wrote and then burned them, except of course, the fire does not answer back, which I shall do . . . Perhaps the habit which distinguishes civilized people from others is that of discussion, exchange of opinion and ideas, the ability to differ without quarrelling, to say what you have to say civilly and then to listen civilly to another speaker. So let's consider the Round Table as opened, and write whatever you choose to write. I may not be the most prompt correspondent, at least until I get the novel done, though it is nearly finished, and yes, it is that same one; but the title is changed, because another book was brought out lately with the same title, and my publishers asked to find a new one. It is now called *No Safe Harbor,* and you will get a copy when it comes out in the Fall. When I said I hated letters, I meant only those hundreds of meaningless ones that pour in and take time and waste energy. I didn't mean letters from my Nephew Paul, at any rate . . . I will write long letters at fairly long intervals . . .

Sorry. Aunt Gay has got me mixed with two other authors. I never did write an article about Thomas Mann. My first opinion to you: Mann seems to me, in his critical writings, extremely labored and rather turgid. Also, his so-called major opus, *Joseph and His Brethren,* I find completely unreadable . . . A friend of mine, Glenway Wescott, himself a splendid writer, remarked not long ago that Mann is the dullest genius he ever knew . . . In your place I would not worry trying to read him if you find him hard going. He *is* hard going for a good number of persons, and some of them pretty good judges, too. But there are things of his I think remarkable: long stories, and if you want to try him again, get them from the library. Ask for his collected stories, which contain *Death in Venice, Disorder and Early Sorrow,* and *Mario the Magician.* His early novel, *Buddenbrooks* is, I believe, his best. *The Magic Mountain* I simply can't get through . . .

If you like, I will make you up a reading list of things I think are really first rate and good reading besides, some old, some new. There is a splendid writer named E.M. Forster who is not widely known, and he wrote a beautiful novel called *Passage to India.* Try for it at the library, I recommend it . . . If you buy it, it has been reprinted in a cheap little series called The Penguin. I think it sells for twenty five cents . . . I will send you a list of publishers who reprint good books in cheap editions, if you want to own a few, and I will look around and pick out a small number to send you, as present, when I find out more or less what you would be interested in . . . So let me hear from you, about this and any thing else at all. I remember that you had a very good, sound, musical voice, and I hope you are still singing, for there are a number of fine songs I should like some day to hear you sing . . . When you read anything that interests you, I should be glad to have your opinion.

Now I must go back to work. Thank you for your good letter, I enjoyed it and was proud of it. With my love,

Aunt Katherine Anne

P.S. (of course.) I notice you wrote on the letterhead of a Law Firm. Are you working there? Tell me family news too. I hear that Dorothy Ray is going to have a baby, and that everybody is very happy about it. I hope it will be a fine intelligent baby. Is Patsy as beautiful as ever?

Note: On Sunday afternoon, August 3, from two o'clock until 2;30 Eastern daylight time, I *think,* I will be again on the "Invitation to Learning" program, Columbia Broadcasting system. This time we will talk about Stendhal's *The Red and The Black.* I hope you can get it on your radio. I don't know what hour that will be in Texas, but I'd love to think you were listening . . .

Good bye again, with my love again
Aunt K.A.

TO PAUL PORTER   Yaddo
                                  Saratoga Springs
                                  August 5, 1941

Dear Paul:

I won't try to answer your letter just now, either, but I send you these books of New Writing from England, and I advise you to ask at your library for the collected poems of William B Yeats

. . . W.B. Yeats, I believe one says . . . As you can see, everything is in flux, as it always is; try to find your own way among all the conflicting opinions. I sent for these books for myself, and then decided they would be very good for you to see . . . What you do find in them is a certain simplicity and clearness of phrase; try to learn to say boldly but simply what you think, and all the rest depends on what you yourself will learn about language. I marked passages that interested me: that does not always mean I agree with the person, sometimes it means that I don't: but I do like for everybody who has something to say to be able to say it, and I like them making their points. You make yours, too. Just use your mind, my dear, and your emotions will take care of themselves.

Your feelings are very right, I think you can depend upon them; that poem about the idiot Negro is a good sign. Read some of the published poems of these young Englishmen: I think you will feel better . . . Your poem is faulty in spots, but it has wonderfully good things in it, I wanted to edit it but restrained myself, because you will find your own way and shouldn't be hampered just now by personal criticism such as mine would be: you have time, darling, just be brave and think things out.

Read Virginia Woolf for what she has to say about the way an artist has to get his education: a very mixed affair, having to do with all sorts of things outside the curriculum. And read the young ones who fight with her. It will all do you good. And listen to great music—darling, I hate Wagner, and have hated him all my life, but if you like him you should listen to him. I love Mozart, and Purcell, and Beethoven, and then, in a lighter way, Scarlatti. Gluck I love, and all the old music. Wagner I think was like Nietsche and Schopenhauer—Nazis, supermen, mad as hatters and they should all have been in strait jackets: I loathe the lot of them.

If this had all happened just now, you could suspect it as being part of the present war feeling. But it is not true. I hated Wagner long before the first World War, when I was a child. That fellow seemed to me even then to be saying something I did not agree with and it has turned out to be very true . . . Listen to Mozart, darling, who was the best composer who ever lived, listen to him with your mind and your heart, and you will see that Wagner was a loud and noisy charlatan, a shell-game man, a rotter. When I was a child I hated the way he would take a commonplace theme and blow it up, like a balloon, and work it over and repeat it and in the end, just give me a pain in the neck . . . I hate him yet. And now, he has become, for me, with Nietsche and Schopenhauer, a part of Hitler's Germany. No, I won't have that fellow. And I am glad I rejected him when I was eight years old, a long time ago. My elders took me to a lot of Wagner concerts and operas. I remember them well. I didn't like them . . .

I will write you later. In the meantime, pull yourself together and tell me what you do . . . That lawyer's office, Well what about it?

With my love
Aunt Katherine Anne

If you want your poem back I'll send it later. I would like to read it several times more, then maybe I can be able to critcise it for you, if you want . . .

I dated the books on your birthday, since I would have sent them then if I had known the date . . . July 29, 1921, you were born. Lord, surely nobody is young as *that*.

To Paul Porter   Yaddo
                                     Saratoga Springs, New York
                                     September 8, 1941

Dear Paul:

. . . . Don't be distressed at my attack on Wagner. As I think I said, you should listen to him as much as you please and as long as he says something to you. There was and still is a mighty army of until-death-do-us part Wagnerites, they are an international company and not the worst company in the world either. I know he was a great composer and I can't listen to him. But that has never stopped anybody else who wished to listen to him and don't let it stop you, either. It is no doubt a result of my experience, I lived in a world that was highly Germanized, through a long generation of people who worshipped Nietzsche, Wagner, Schopenhauer, Hegel, and my instincts were simply against what all of them seemed to teach; and I think I see now pretty plainly that what they taught, or what their teachings led to, was what we call for the present, Nazism.

It is impossible to go into this at this very moment, but for example, if you should some day decide to read: (1) A biography of Wagner. (2) Wagner's Letters. (3) A Life of Nietzsche. (4) Nietzsche's *Thus Spake Zarasthustra.* (5) Schopenhauer's Philosophy, any volume you can find. (6) Hegel, any volume, or a condensation; and then read Hitler's *Mein Kampf,* and you will have no trouble in following the line of argument . . . I shouldn't worry about Bach unless you want to hear some of his secular cantatas, The Wedding Cantata, The Coffee Cantata or the Peasant Cantata, his gay antic music; or unless you have a chance to hear a really good performance of the great B Minor Mass; or Wanda Landowska playing on the harpsichord the Goldberg Variations. I have these and the cantatas too, so wait until you get here if they aren't to be heard in the record shops there.

I have stacks of Mozart too, the quintettes for viola, for clarinet and some piano concertos and a symphony or two, all performed by great artists, and so you will hear them some day not far off. I have a good collection of ancient music too, so you can begin at the beginning around 1200 A.D. and work through the centuries at your leisure, hearing music grow and change . . .

A word about your friend? in the office who insists that unless you know (what was it, mathematics? or theory and composition? or harmonics? or what? it doesn't matter) music scientifically it is affectation to say you like it . . . That argument is the last resort of people who lack an esthetic sense. I never heard a working artist say such a thing, and never will, because the artist knows better. It is exactly the same as to say you have no right to like a color because you do not know the chemical components that went into it. As if to say you had no right to admire a great masterpiece of architecture because you have not learned the principles of architecture. Music is essentially sound, organized and arranged on a set of principles, it is based on science, as all arts are; but it is meant to be listened to by any one who can hear it, and the one who hears it best is the one who is gifted with a good ear, and who can first love it and delight in it before he has any musical knowledge whatever . . . It is this natural delight in music that is the very best foundation for a true understanding of it, for it will lead you on to study it, to discover its principles, and I do know that the more you learn about it, the more you will be able to hear, and the more you will enjoy it. But to begin coldly, drily, to dissect music in order to be able to listen to it is the special snobbism of uncreative people, and there is no one who sees through them more quickly than the artist who has done the work. I think that this fellow is really the affected one of you two: let us go further and challenge him with a fallacy equal to his own. I shall say, for example, that he has no right to say he knows music unless he is able to compose a presentable piece for the piano. That is not true, but it is as true as his thesis . . .

I began to read with excitement and interest when I was very little, and I read far beyond my years, and I got my education, the kind of education I was able to use later, in just that way. Suppose some one had come along and stopped my reading on the grounds that I did not know how it was done and could not understand all I read? You see what a fool's argument that is.

I am sending you a reading list I got up for students at Olivet College. They were all studying to become writers, and I tried hard to make them see that writing cannot be taught, it can only be learned, and that by the hard way. I have marked on this list the things best for you, but I put in a good many things to fit special cases, trying to find something that would do for all kinds and levels of talents . . . The ones I have marked seem to me the very best. You have probably read a great many of them. They all are *good work*, professionally speaking and of course you know already which are the really great ones.

Don't be frightened when you hear of young men of twenty already getting their things published . . . I marked that published poem to encourage you, not to upset you . . . I did not think it so superior to your own, the one you sent me . . . I thought Virginia Woolf's last essay extremely good, sensible, true—not the whole truth, where will we find that? but valuable because it was the considered opinion of a firm honest artist, and I thought the ones who attacked her had not read her carefully enough, or thought enough about the whole situation. They were trying to prove a political belief and this got in their way in considering what she was saying. That is, they were so anxious to make their own points they disregarded all in her argument that did not enable them to express their own opposing opinion. But that is the interesting thing about all discussion, and these pieces are worth reading. They are all well written and expressive. They are not to be swallowed whole, but I don't need to tell you that.

Sometime in late October I expect to have a copy of a new book of short stories by a writer I consider very seriously gifted, Eudora Welty from Jackson, Mississippi. (I will send this.) I wrote a preface for it, the first I ever did for any book except my very short one for *Flowering Judas,* which is another kind of thing altogether. I did not say everything I wished, but there are some paragraphs in it that might interest you, and the stories are extremely worth reading. She is very imaginative and bold and complex, yet not in the least "experimental" in the current sense of trying to break out of a tradition and start something new. Any writer worth talking about, no matter how original he seems, can be placed within a line of tradition: there was somebody before him who prepared the way for him. The tradition you belong to is something you can't select for yourself: your own temperament will simply lead you into a certain path. The best kind of originality is that which works within limitations of form, creating variations, and progressing, adding something new; it is a kind of organic growth and change. But the substance and quality of that change depends on the substance and quality of the artists who help to make it, and that, darling, is where *you* come in. Grow as well and as fully and effectively as you are capable; if you write, be a good writer. I think you are remarkably well begun, so trust your imagination and use your intelligence, and know all that you can about all the arts. Musicians and painters don't seem to know, and don't care, about literature or any other art except their own. But the born writer is a different sort: everything human is his province, and he sees the relations between all things, and will find himself neglecting nothing that the human mind has thought or the human heart has felt . . . I believe on these grounds that you would do best as a writer. A talented person usually has several talents, and it is a good thing to try them all, first because that is the way to discover what you can do, and second because you learn about all the arts in that way. Is your art school any good? Wouldn't it be a good thing to study music, too? Not only to play the piano, but to know theory and harmony? But you will know which you want to do. Meantime, write as you can; I wish you could have gone to college, and of course it is not too late yet, but that is not of the first importance except that you get clues and directions that would help your further study.

Your letters are very splendid, and when I get back that envelope I want to say something about the personal things in it. But those are after all your exceedingly private concerns, in the sense that no advice or comment of mine would help or change. Your own personal temperament will be perhaps with you, as mine was with me, a major battle, but trying to understand other human beings will help you understand yourself, as you know your own faults you will be, not less critical, I hope, for the critical faculty is simply the faculty of discrimination, which is most important, but less exacting, less demanding. But you are right to reserve your opinions, and to choose no companionship at all rather than the kind that will sap your energies, blunt your mind and keep your imagination from having a field to play in . . . My fault was, for years, a blind kind of affability to all sorts of really dreadful little people, I always gave them credit for my own level of intelligence, my own kind of feelings, it took me a great while to learn that most people you meet casually are simply not worth a moment of your time. And my instincts knew this; and little by little I learned to recognize who were rare and special persons and who were not: and this rarity, this specialness, will appear in the most unexpected places in the most unlooked for shapes . . .

Dear Paul, I am going to work now. I started this letter last night, and continue it this morning. I love writing to you, never think it is a trouble. The only trouble is, I might just go on until it was a book, and that won't do. Remember: try to plan to come here next spring or summer or whenever you can make a space of free time. It is possible, since you must have a job, that you might as well have it in the East, and you could manage to go to school here too. If you want to study music and go to art school, you might as well do it in New York. But think this over. It is important.

With my love,
Aunt Katherine Anne

To Paul Porter

Yaddo
Saratoga Springs, New York
December 16, 1941

My dear, really dear Paul:

The whirl *was* rather a one, and it all seemed elegantly worth doing and gave me the feeling that I was getting somewhere at top speed, and the end was in the very nature of things good . . . All that stopped as if some one had thrown a hammer into the machinery on December 8 . . . Feast of the Immaculate Conception of the Blessed Virgin Mary, and birthday of Mary Alice, Gay's first baby, who died before you were born . . . A very well loved baby she was, and her birthday a happy one, for she was the first baby of your generation in our family. And that reminds me that the New One has not got her present yet, but she will. Your letters are packed away again, I moved over to another building on this place to be nearer headquarters for the first snow, which is now very deep and beautiful. So, send me her birthdate again, I want to have it engraved on a little silver cup for her . . . And all around the rim I am going to put that line by John Skelton (tutor to Henry the Eighth, and I think later his poet laureate) to a young lady he knew; "By Saint Mary, my lady, Your mammy and your daddy Brought forth a goodly baby." Don't you think that is lovely? Her name: should it be Patsy Anne, or Patricia Anne in full?

I will like any letter you write, and we will write chitchat when we feel like it, and other kinds of things when our minds are working that way. I have started you several letters and never got one finished but I have worked of late until I feel hollow and immaterialized. Still the work is done and sent away, and I shall rest a little over the holidays.

I am going to answer questions and fact-like things first.

My books are packed away and I cannot remember where I got the Breughel book. But I am going to be in New York on the 20th of December and I can find one . . . If not exactly the one I have, one as good or better. They do exist. If Patsy wants to give it to you, I will have it sent directly to her C.O.D. If she finds something else for you there (Van Gogh is worth having, a good Picasso book would be nice) I'll give it to you myself. There will just barely be time the way it is flying now. If you get this in time wire me collect here about it.

Speaking of the 20th. On Sunday December 21, at half past eleven Eastern Standard Time, I will again be guest of the "Invitation to Learning" program, CBS, with Mark van Doren and Bertrand Russell, talking about, of all things, *Alice In Wonderland.* If you wish to hear the slightly rumpled voice of your devoted aunt, then will be a chance.

I suppose the Harvard Classics are really a good compact working collection, a sort of spine for a library and I hope you are going to be around to read them from cover to cover . . . Send me your poetry and the painting too. You know I want badly to see them, anything at all you write or paint . . .

Paul, I think you are very like me in temperament, but you write better and are more balanced and use your mind better than I did at your age, and in every way so far it seems to me you have done rather better than well: so you will do well as to the war, also; for we are alike in this, too, we are really tough and resistant at the core, and I have known danger—real, physical danger as well as other kinds, and my courage rises with the degree of danger I am in . . . Also you have it in you whether you know it or not, to face and live through long wearing trying jobs of work; and I have the most complete confidence in *what you are,* as if I could look ahead and foretell what you shall become by just what I know of you now. You would be inhuman if you did not value your life, there would be something seriously wrong with your nervous system if you did not know fear. I think all your reactions so far as I know them are instinctively right and very normal. It is true that you do get no doubt a higher degree of shock than one with a more bluntly articulated nervous system, but then your brain is clearer too, and you are already thinking it through, and extremely well. My dear, it would be no good for me to say any of the usual and perhaps proper things to you about this. You know what I think about the whole system of war, and I say now, again, that this world catastrophe is a criminal thing *because it was preventable,* and I have seen the whole thing from the beginning until now, step by step, and the half dozen separate places where it could have been stopped. I am far past surprise now, I have not been surprised at anything since Munich . . . It began, (I mean actually as to this present thing) when

England did not protest when Mussolini went into Abyssinia . . . well, before that. When Hitler moved into the demilitarized zone and France could have driven him out in a week, but England would not back France and France would not move without England's consent . . . When France and England refused to back Loyalist Spain . . . When England tried to treat with Hitler at first, to strengthen Germany and weaken France and keep that famous balance of power. And so on . . . All a horrible dirty business in which no humane principles were at all involved, only the same old power politics played by the same unscrupulous men, almost the very same, who ran the first World War . . . Very well. But it has come, it is here at last, we are all in it, it is our lives they were gambling with, and we are given a choice now to fight to be an independent country or to be a defeated one . . . No choice at all, I would say . . . We know which we prefer . . .

Your life is very precious to me, I love you dearly as if you were my own child, with the love of the blood kindred which is the most lasting and the deepest of all human bonds, and I have been very happy to see the directions your mind has taken, and the way you were growing and so swiftly. I have great pride in your gifts and promises; you are irreplaceable to us, all of us in the family, you are our hope for the future. It is all very well for you to resign your plans, give over your life, say the individual does not so much matter now. But I cannot and will not say it or think it or feel it for one moment, and there is no power that can require it of me. The individual is all that matters, and the evil of war, as of Fascism, is precisely this destruction of identity, this notion of herd life and mass death . . .

I believe in our form of government, I think it the best ever devised in human affairs, in spite of the abuses, in spite of the perversions that have deformed it in practise. This war will decide whether we are going to have another chance for a real democracy here or will this country be turned over again to the Morgans, the Fords and the Standard Oil company. First we have this war with the foreign enemy, and then there is a second war to be fought here afterward with the internal enemy . . .

Let's do the very best we can in both wars . . . You are facing something I shall never be called upon to face, but you may believe that I do not intend to live safely with you in danger. There is plenty of work in plenty of busy places for me, and I mean to be in one of them. I never did ask any one to do anything I was not ready to do myself; if you risk your life I shall risk mine, for one is worth no more than the other, and the blood of those who have died for me lies heavily upon my conscience even now. But there comes a time when the uneasy conscience demands action and no more words.

Still I write to you now because you are beginning your manhood on the very edge of the most disastrous epoch the human race has ever known—not worse in kind, really, but only by the overwhelming weight and size of it—in which quite literally the whole human race is involved. And if we are ever to speak and to say what we mean, this is the moment—almost the last moment . . .

Look about you and see the possibilities for getting into Officer's Training. It will give you more responsibility and you would be happier for it. Don't be afraid of yourself. I'd be very uneasy and disappointed in you if you didn't think and feel pretty much the way you do. I find you quite all right.

With my love,
Aunt Katherine Anne

I am having the publisher send you a book of short stories by Eudora Welty, a new writer, with my introduction and preface . . .

TO BABETTE DEUTSCH   Yaddo
                           Saratoga Springs, New York
                           December 30, 1941

Dear Babette:

You may not remember me, but I hope you do, for I remember you very well. The other day New Directions Press sent me a copy of your translations of Rainer Maria Rilke's *Das Stundenbuch* and I must write to you about them, for you have done such a beautiful and grave and good work in them. They read aloud most marvelously—I find best for me "Put Out My Eyes . . ." "The Sovereigns of the World Are Old." . . . "All Will Grow

Great . . ." "Already Ripening Barberries . . ." and oh above all the last great lovely one—"Do Not Be Troubled, God, Though They Say Mine . . ."

I know a little German and comparing as I went, I do not see how these poems could have been more honestly and exactly translated, and yet with a music in English. I love Rilke particularly, in almost every thing, and it was so very pleasant to see that some one I knew a long time ago had been able to bring him out of one language into another so clearly . . .

There is only one word in these poems I mention that I would want changed, and yet I do not know the word to put in its place. "Then on my *blood-stream* I would carry you." Literally so would I thee in my blood carry . . . For some reason the word blood-stream has for me associations of science and the laboratory, and I hesitate when I come to it, every time . . . It is one of the most impassioned and noble short poems ever written, and it really shakes the blood—not the blood stream. Do you suppose you could find another word? Or do you defend this, and if you have time, tell me why?

This is a little matter of one word . . . Instead of mentioning it, I should be thanking you for what you have done, and I do thank you, here and now. I was reading them again tonight, and it seemed to me quite wrong that when a poet had done so well, and given so much, the reader should keep his pleasure and benefit to himself. Silence in such a time is ungrateful.

After all these years I hope your life is what you want it to be and that all you work for repays you.

A good and happy New Year to you and your family

Sincerely
Katherine Anne

To Barbara Wescott
Yaddo
Saratoga Springs
January 14, 1942

Barbara darling,

I wish I had known you were going to New Orleans, for then I would have asked you to go and look at Jackson Square and the lower Pontalba for me. I had an apartment in that old house in 1937 September to January 1; and that was an important time in my life, and I have very deep feelings about that little square which is so lovely, with St. Louis Cathedral on one side and the old French Market just around the corner on the other. I wrote "Pale Horse Pale Rider" in that big top story room which had once been slave quarters for the whole building, and Albert used to come to see me there. It was an immensely deep and painful and happy time, full of the past and the present and I couldn't see to the end of my nose as to the future . . . Well, that future has come to pass, and as Cotton Mather used to write in his diary, "Lo, see what was in it." Not that I hadn't some right premonitions, nor that I am sorry for anything.

One day, walking along Royal Street, I saw a sight seeing bus drawn up at the side walk, and a man was shouting at me, "See the Cabildo and the old Slave Block: see the old Ursuline Convent and the Pontalba Buildings, see the historic old French Market . . ." and I thought: "Well, I went to school with the Ursulines, and I pay my rent in the Cabildo, and I buy my food in the French Market and I live in the lower Pontalba—really, you never picked on a more unlikely customer . . ."

I saw the Bellingrath Gardens with azaleas in bloom. But azaleas and gardenias I had in my own back yard, too. Any little azalea bush just looks like a basket of something got up by a florist, and it is merely a question of magnifying it to infinity. That is the sweet thing about all blooming trees, they start from infancy in the same shape and style, you have only to wait for it to grow greater in girth, the real nature will be just the same . . . I had white azaleas, too, which I love.

There are lovely houses at St. Francisville, too, in Louisiana. There is a house in Charleston which belongs to a branch of my maternal grandmother's family—it is called the Pringle mansion, and two little Misses Frost, aged perhaps ninety by now, who own it, let you in and take you around and show you its faded glories for the sum of one dollar . . . They are cousins of mine. My mother's mother was Caroline Frost from Charleston . . . well, they skip straight over the Civil War and speak only of the Revolution, as if it had happened day before yesterday . . . The little old ladies may be dead by now. I saw them about fifteen years ago . . . Sarah, and I forget the other name. Aren't the little old houses lovely? That, or something by Wright is my choice. My little house here is something like the houses I knew . . . Not quite so finished, there was a plainer life here, no carved shells over the doors, nor fine panelling, but still the air is something like.

This Yaddo is the most loathesome example of something that broke out like a pox all over the east and north; built out of war profits: the whole imitation Jacobean and English manor house stuff was built by the new rich who got their money out of that war. But these people had something more: their story—their personal story—is very human and full of suffering and strange . . . They are buried up on a hill here, a woman, her husband, and her life long lover: the two men business partners, besides; and the three graves lie together very sociably, Katrina in the middle, with not a date to indicate when they lived, and not a word on any tomb to say what their relations had been, actually.

Well, I shouldn't like it . . . my taste is for something rather more clearly defined: but that is the way it was with them, and there they are. And here I am. It is hard to say why this country is so pleasant, but I like the way it looks, the color of the air and the shapes of the land, in all seasons, all weathers. The only other place I ever felt so about was Paris. I woke up every morning happy to be there, feeling in the most unaccountable way at home . . . I go out to visit my house, and walk about in it and sit on the steps and look at the meadow and the woods and the road and think, if ever I feel at home again it will be in this place, this very stone I am sitting on now . . .

Darling I imagine you are idling a little now, moving more slowly for the time being, taking care of yourself and being taken care of, so I write you at length because probably you have time to read letters and to do all sorts of leisurely things. Yes, twins would be nice: a boy and a girl at one time, a real family. But John

Peale Bishop says twins have a way of ganging up on you—they form a hermetic society of their own and at times exclude even parents . . . They take each other's advice and fight each other's battles and admire each other above all living beings: a kind of mirror life they seem to lead, so maybe one at a time is more comfortable for everybody in the long run.

My family is reproducing itself at a great rate. I have now a grand nephew nearly two years old, and a grand niece nearly three months old, which sets me definitely once for all among the Gammers. I feel quite at ease there.

It makes me very happy to know you will like the dedication. Let me go on to the end of the novel, and look again at the mss. of the short stories and the Journals . . . I would like you to have the best one, though maybe I am not able to tell which that is. But of three one at least is bound to be somewhat an improvement over the others . . . We'll wait a while . . . I know the novel has been continuously interesting and even exciting to me, and what you say of it is important to me. Maybe it should be that one. Well, I'll go on with this monologue in private.

Heavenly luck to you and perfect health: yes you are the type that would go all out of shape early, with very small waist and narrow pelvis and long legs. But thank your stars you've got something in the way of a figger to go back to, not every one has . . .

My nephew described his young sister just eleven months after she was married. He wrote that she looked like a pouter pigeon whose chest had slipped . . . But the baby was a great success and she is already beautifully in figure again. Three cheers for the marvelous human frame, I say.

With my love to you both, or all three, rather. Lloyd and the thrilling Incognito. I miss seeing you, I never really expected not to see you oftener, but next summer I must come up for a look at you and the family . . .

Katherine Anne

To Freda Kirchwey   Yaddo
                                     Saratoga Springs, New York
                                     February 5, 1942

Dear Mrs. Kirchwey:

The Trotskyites are most marvellously adroit in their manipulation of human sympathy, they have a finished technique of making catspaws out of humanist liberals, socialists, believers in justice, et al. How frequently I am called upon in the name of simple human decency to speak in defense of some martyrized Trotskyite, though by doing so I find myself enmeshed subtly in far reaching commitments that, now especially, put me in the position of seeming to support seditious activities. I can see pretty clearly how this is done, it annoys me to the bone, and yet, I am cornered; for I cannot stand by and watch one set of men oppress another set, even if either set, once in power, would undoubtedly oppress me and my kind without conscience.

As for anti-this and that. I am anti-Fascist and have been since I first knew the meaning of the word, now more than twenty years. I am Anti-Nazi and have been since I was in Germany ten years ago and saw the beginnings of that party in power. But this does not make me a Communist, nor a sympathizer with either faction. I am anti-Stalinist, as well as anti-Trotskyite. I think my opposition to the present Communist regime in Russia cannot be interpreted as opposition to the alliance of our own government with Russia against Germany. I never thought a military alliance called for sentimental alliance too. I resent extremely the popular fallacy that military alliances are based on love between governments, or even between peoples. No such thing; and not necessary and not even desirable. Russia and China were the natural allies for us, they have been for nearly a quarter of a century, we should have secured them and strengthened them long ago, but we did not, and for very sinister reasons . . . Let that go now. The point is, Communism in Russia, for Russians, is not in the least objectionable, to me. The people I hate and find detestable in their political morals, political tactics, and general life point of view are the American Communists of either wing; I think their acts are treasonable at this time, and even if they are anti-Fascist, they are also anti-American; the sole reason that they are not as dangerous as the Fascists who find so easy entrance into this country is, they are not so numerous and they are more easily watched.

It seems to me that we have a good many more important things to protest against in our own internal affairs; we should be sending signed letters to Washington about the presence in this country of known spies and agents who are unmolested while a trial of little spies is carried on with hullabaloo . . . We should learn more about the activities of the German Dye Works (I.G. Farben) in this country and the exact nature of its connection with Standard Oil: we should insist that all firms, Italian, German and Japanese as well as their allies, that have been put on a banned list should really be suppressed, and not continue to advertise their wares by radio— Bayer's products for the first that comes to mind . . . The actual present state of trade relations between all countries should be examined and made public. About two years ago the United Chambers of Commerce in America stated clearly that so long as business was to be had in Germany, they would do business with that country. And if Germany won, naturally they would carry on business and trade with her . . . There is no reason to believe these men have changed their minds or their methods . . .

I could wish that your weekly, or another, might run a feature analysing the propaganda stories from Axis sources which are published as news items without comment in nearly all newspapers. This is a real source of infection of the most subtle kind.

Well, dear Mrs. Kirchwey, I did not set out to write you an unsolicited article. But I confess I am wearied out a little with the noisy minorities who keep up such a continual clamor about their wrongs they manage to drown out the voices of those millions of equally good, equally important, from any human point of view, and equally suffering people whose only crime is, they have no political axes to grind and were not clever enough to join with some political faction. I know the Trotskyites are having difficulties. I know the Jews have been most outrageously abused. No human being fit to be called by that name but resents and resists their wrongs. But they are so self-centered they lose sight of the larger disaster, and they can almost cause the rest of us to lose sight of it too; what I am most interested in is a clean-up in the State Department, and a wide public campaign among Americans who believe in the democratic form of government, for the millions of good, honest anti-Nazis and anti-Fascists who are neither Trotskyites or Stalinites; we should spend our time and energies helping these people, above all, we should help them get admission into this country where almost any sort of enemy is allowed to come and live freely, even now, even in time of war.

This is a private letter. I suppose I choose you to write to because the Letter to President Camacho came this morning and set my mind running again on the deplorable situation of all those people who have no one to speak for them, or to act for them effectively. I know there are dozens of organizations committed to one or another form of immediate relief and these are certainly valuable. But there does not seem to be any organized body of investigation into the *root* of the evil, which is here at home and in our own state department and business firms. I read the *Nation* and I know you are immensely keen and quick in these questions; but you need more support than you get, as you very well know. And the way to get it is to draw together the great body of truly Democratic, truly loyal American public opinion, in an organization of people whose good faith is beyond question and who have the right to criticise this government because it is theirs. I belong to that group and we are larger than you think, perhaps. It would be worth finding out just how many of us there are.

Meantime, I have signed that letter, for I can't see men like Victor Serge and Grandise Muniz in danger without protesting. I know David Siqueiros very well, he was a killer from the beginning, and his subsequent career does not surprise me in the least.

Sincerely yours,
Katherine Anne Porter

To Mary Alice
Hillendahl

Yaddo
Saratoga Springs, New York
February 6, 1942

Dearest Baby:

Your letter which came just this minute is the first word I have had from any one about Dad's death and burial . . . But evidently you are the only one who had anything to tell . . . I don't usually care for pictures of funerals either, but I am pleased to have this one of Dad's flowery grave to put beside the one we took of mother's with all our flowers upon it. . . .

Darling, try to remember that Dad was a most unhappy, frustrated man for all his life, at least all of his life that I remember. He had good gifts and a good mind, but there was some psychological blockage in him, he had evidently got some kind of blow to his pride or his mind early in life, and though it is nothing at all that we can blame him for, much less condemn him, still there is no reason to deny it, or despise any accomplishments of the rest of us or compare lives. For myself, I know very well that I have contributed something worth having to the world, I have done first rate work and I am proud of it, and I have the right to be, for I did it absolutely without any help and without any preparation except what I got for myself, without any encouragement or belief from my family, and without health or money . . . And I think part of my will to overcome obstacles and to use my gifts came out of my real horror at seeing the way our father simply could not, for whatever mysterious reason, use his own gifts. Many thousands of men have had worse obstacles than he, and have overcome them triumphantly . . . He could not, and that was his misfortune, and ours, but it was nothing to blame him for or to be bitter about. I used to be, but I outgrew it as I went on . . . And all I have done and all that I shall do in the future will give honor to the family and the name, and I am glad of that, too. Even if the family doesn't think it of any value, still there are many thousands of others who do think so, and I must be contented with that. I am a good artist, and I have a fine reputation, and that is what I did for my family and for the world. And I think Dad was proud of me, even if he didn't really know or care much what I was doing.

It is such a blessed relief to know that the end was quiet and gentle: you had told me so many things about his terrible bitterness in the last year or two, and the painful things when his mind began to go, and though of course we all understood what was happening, still that did not help much in just the everyday long pull; I know that. And your very last letter before he died told how you had to tie his good hand because he threw things at the servant . . . But do you know, I don't mind remembering that he was furious and full of resistance even almost to the last; I only would regret if regret were not useless that all his vitality could not somehow have found a good outlet in a life that would have given him some satisfaction . . . But its all over now, my dear, and I like to think that you and Jules are going to rest and be easy in your minds, and have a peaceful pleasant life doing the things you enjoy at home and with your friends. Jules' picture is fine—he doesn't seem to change or get any older, he just stays put, God bless him. Give him my love.

From your letter I suppose the funeral took place in a church? The flowers are simply lovely, my little roses are quite lost and I am glad it is so. But I sent Talismans because he had chosen them to take to mother, as I believe I told you . . . I had such an urgent feeling that I ought to come home around Christmas, but Baby, it is literally impossible. I simply did not have the money . . . I have had a few delays in finishing work, and so delays in receiving money, and so I could only hope he might live at least until spring, when I had planned very carefully to allow enough to get there for a few days if no more . . . But now, since some things happened as they did, I am glad I missed that. It would have been so unhappy and so useless.

Try to remember that though Dad's last years were wretched, part of the trouble was in him, it was an accumulation of his whole life's bitterness and frustration overwhelming him as he lost strength, and that though he certainly was not helped any by his unhappiness and his quarrels with his children, still he did have those strokes and those accidents, and he finally did die of old age and exhaustion. After all, nearly 85— It was time to go, that is an unusually great age. Try to remember exactly how things were, how you felt at times, and don't be bitter if you can help it . . . Try to forget and enjoy your own interests and make your own life as nice as it can be, for you have a great deal to live for and to be happy about. Forget Gay and Paul, let them go, don't let what they do spoil your life, it is not worth it.

It is a strange thing: but I have been seeing some cousins of ours, in the Skaggs branch—Lily and Gertrude of San Antonio, and they were telling me tales of the family, in several branches, Porters and others—and this peculiar family quarrelling and division and bitterness runs through branch after branch, generation after generation; so it must be in the blood, and if we know that, we can guard a little against letting it get the better of us . . . Perhaps this is the most useful part of knowing something about one's family history: it helps us to understand ourselves and be on our guard against the inherited vices of temperament. I remember how our grandmother's sons just turned away from her grave, divided up her property and belongings and never afterward had anything to say to each other for years and years . . . That is not the best way, but it is better than staying together and hating and quarrelling.

Well darling, try to rest and be well. You look much thinner in your pictures, and awfully well. You have come through wonderfully, and I hope you just go on from good to better. I don't know when I shall be in my house, there is no use trying to begin there now until early spring, though it is really almost finished, but when I am settled you and Jules must come and look over the proppity . . . God knows I hope it turns out to be a pleasure to me, for my life-blood has gone into it . . . But what else could I do? I must have a place to live, that seems little enough to ask after a life-time of work and homelessness. But we don't always get what we feel we have earned. I know that. I don't do much day dreaming any more . . . Life is real and Lord, is it earnest?

Write me when you feel like it, honey, I am always happy to hear from you . . . Just talk along and say anything you think. I like that.

With my love . . .
Katherine Anne

Let me know when that important second grandchild is born. I hope Old Timer's nose won't be too badly knocked down.

Tell me about the expenses of the funeral. Will the insurance Gay carried cover everything? If it doesn't I want to do my share, even if you will have to wait for it a little while.

To Glenway Wescott   Yaddo
                        Saratoga Springs, New York
                        February 6, 1942

Glenway darling:

After all your trouble, and after I had read again with what loving absorption the whole book of the *Grandmothers,* I changed my mind . . . I want to use the two stories of Grandfather and Grandmother Tower . . . I trembled with indecision too, about Great-Aunt Mary Harris . . . These are heroic stories, after all, about heroic people; but I decide once for all for the Grandparents Tower . . . Do you feel well about this? I was so glad I had the book again, to reconsider. The story of the Mother is as good as ever it was to me, but I found something in the others that for some reason had not stayed in my mind, and yet I cannot see why now . . . they are really superb . . .

Your letter in two parts was so welcome, and I meant to write at once. But I am swamped in things beside the novel: trying to do editing jobs for fees and all the clutter of making a living while writing, writing some things almost to order, but not things that can be harmful either . . . this is not complaint, I just mention a fact of life . . .

My poor little old tired mad father died and was buried on January 24th. The telegram was delayed somehow and I did not hear until three o'clock in the morning of the day of the funeral . . . He had been a wonderfully handsome man, intelligent and strangely in advance of his generation in so many ways of thinking, and yet also of the old fashioned eighteenth century humanistic school . . . I am his child by temperament and knew all about him by instinct . . . But the last year was terrible, his mind suddenly vanished, and he was angry, violent, embittered, alienated completely. I am glad I did not see him so; and yet, his children have all agreed that it was better: we could not have borne it if he had been softened, beaten; no, he shouted and threw the first thing he could lay hands on, and spoke outright some scalding and awful truths . . . that is better. Yet now I feel so tenderly about him, as if he were my child, newly born and I the older. At the end, all the women he had known became merged and universal, he called his youngest daughter Mother, and confused his mother and his wife in his memories when he struggled sometimes to tell what his life had really been to him . . . And he kept asking after that pretty girl he used to dance with, and at last my sister discovered he was talking about his sister Anne, who died before I was born. (Remember Amy, in "Old Mortality"?) Our mother died when our youngest sister was born, and our father died in that sister's house, and was buried on her birthday, the day our mother began to die all those years ago.

Well, darling, I can think of nothing but that father, folded away to sleep forever, after so much turbulence of mind and spirit: we are all very quiet as if we were resting and recovering too from his long weariness . . .

The country is beautiful here now. I will be in New York again for the "Invitation to Learning" broadcast, *March 22,* and this time I hope to stay over for a few quiet days, and see my dear household on 89th street.

> With my love
> *Katherine Anne*

TO DONALD ELDER

Yaddo
Saratoga Springs, New York
February 28, 1942

Dear Donald:

When that Dope Goering remarked en passant that America would be an inside job, well, I could only hope it wasn't so. But now I lie awake nights fearing it may be true . . . God knows the air is full of signs and portents. Did you happen to see that perfectly wonderful profile of Harry Bridges in a *New Yorker*—good while ago—in which he described the methods of the FBI? It was frightfully amusing, and I mean frightfully. I laughed with my hair on end.

But in spite of all the terrible things going on, there seems to be a fine healthy lot of shouting about it, and people do seem able to get Deatherage out of his job and send Viereck to jail and perhaps keep Dennis from getting to the bar (legal) and even by radio I hear some very tough talk (From Natchez to Mobile, from Memphis to St. Joe, . . . I've been in some big towns, and heard me some tall talk . . .) and if all of this is not enough, its a good sign and I still believe there are enough of Us to make trouble . . .

Blessed Forster. I have loved him for at least twenty years, he is one writer I can read over and over. It is very likely I have read even *Abinger Harvest* half a dozen times . . . Where did you find that paragraph you quote? I should like to have all of the essay. Where can I find it . . . I don't really believe the artist is rat or parasite or outlaw, I think he is looked upon as such by the very people we must try hard to scuttle . . . I'm not disagreeing now either with Forster or you, but I've seen some awfully big towns and heard some awfully tall talk by financiers, army and navy people, diplomats, and the filthy rich international crowds and they really are all of the things they call the artist and the intellectual, and considerably more. It is curious too how insecure they feel. It is that fear, that sense of insecurity, that makes them grab office and grab money and grab every kind of power they can get, it takes everything there is to make them feel easy in their minds. This fear is back of their intolerable greed. They want to keep labor on starvation, they want to corner the food market, they must control utilities, because to share these things would be to share power, and this frightens and outrages them . . . The other day I listened to a debate between a University professor, an economist and a Socialist, and Rukeyser a capitalist . . . The Professor was cool, calm, civil and kept landing punches in vital spots. The other fumbled, growled, roared, went into cold furies and hot rages, and fell back on name-calling and personal insult when he couldn't answer . . . It was a wonderful illustration of what I mean . . . One man was talking for any number of people beside himself, not thinking of his own profit particularly, and the other was fighting for his own personal advantage and nothing else . . . It made an astonishing difference in their voices and manners.

Well, I have done so much editing and preface writing lately I have been thrown off the novel, but am back again and shall try not to be interrupted by anything until it is done . . . please don't let the gestapo discourage you too much from getting some kind of job in defense work . . . Don't let the Nazis get everything. As you know it is a part of their strategy to get office or jobs in key places, and it wouldn't surprise me if FBI didn't do a good deal to help them. For this reason FBI would naturally put as many stumbling blocks in the way of such as you as they can devise . . . Get over or around them someway, Don. Make it your business to get over them . . .

As soon as the novel is off I am going to try hard to get in to some place where I can do something useful too . . . No good just letting them run away with everything . . . We live here too . . . This is our place, and we aren't planning to go anywhere; so I want to help make the place a little liveable, at least. I am in such a cold and grim fighting mood I'd just enjoy a good fight with the FBI or almost anybody on the other side . . .

If ever we believed in anything or hoped for anything good in this world, now is the time to say so, and to act upon our beliefs. The trouble is of course that we really are civilized, peaceful people, and the whole horror is so indecent and so unnecessary. But here it is, and I don't propose to sit down under it. . . .

I am going to plant about four dozen peonies, all colors. These peonies at Yaddo have been blooming every year for thirty years. I am putting in an asparagus bed—one year old roots, 150 of them. I am going to plant white lilacs and mock orange all over the place, and a hedge of primitive roses, rosa rugosa. I am going to plant sweet smelling things near enough to the house that when they bloom the perfumes will come into the house at night and keep me awake for joy . . . I hope other people love flower smells near the house. When I was a child I used to get up at night and sit in an old swing under an oak branch just to smell honeysuckle and roses and cape jessamine. But anyway, what I mean to do is this: everything shall be hardy and long lived and sweet smelling, or good to eat and long-lived like the asparagus, and there they shall be for the future, I hope for a great while after I am gone, and I hope many others will enjoy them besides myself. It is really an act of faith, and I know that faith makes the difference between life and death. So I hope you can come up and help me plant a few things, and give me advice about where to put furniture, a thing that baffles me. I'll let you know when with as much notice as I can give. . . .

Love again,
Katherine Anne

TO GLENWAY WESCOTT   Yaddo
                          Saratoga Springs, New York
                          March 31, 1942

Dearest Glenway,

Of course the social occasion is over by now, but the serious business is only beginning, so I want to say now what I would have said then if I had wit enough to play gin rummy and think at the same time.

1. If Tiresius really believed that women have more pleasure than men in the act of love, may it not mean simply that he had always been a better woman than he was man, during all those laborious changes?

OR

2. Being ancient at the time he gave this judgement, he may have concluded, in the way of the old and impotent, that the whole show was over-rated, a base kind of delight better left to the inferior sex.

OR

3. It may explode for good the myth that he ever was a woman.

OR

4. It may be true.

AND this might just mean that I am not as good a woman as I might be. You may well imagine how my pride boggles at this last clause.

I have been the theoretically happy object of the "love" of many men. An unbelievable number of men have said they loved me, and I still believe that two of them really did love me. Maybe that should discourage a spirit like mine, yet I am not discouraged. Of all the men I said I loved, I loved truly only one. So laugh if you like, but that is the truth. Of these men, it was the last I loved—always. And I knew when the last really came, I did know he was the last . . .

It would have been so delicious to have heard your lecture after sitting in at the dress rehearsal, and to have been mentioned by name and to have said my little say. And I miss the other pleasant things that would have happened too. But I called up when I reached the hotel to find out how certain things were going here, and I knew I must get back, for indeed, quite simply, my life depends upon it. I cannot somehow speak of my difficulties when I am in the midst of them, and they are great and many now and I must really work this time as never before if I can expect to come through them. Its dull darling: not enough money, too much work, too much alone and no one to do anything to ease me up just a little . . . Now then, I got myself in this place by myself, though I did not mean precisely this. One never does. I had not forseen how alone I would be and how burdened. . . .

With my love
Katherine Anne

TO ROBERT PENN WARREN   Yaddo
Saratoga Springs, New York
April 15, 1942

Dear Red:

I know that you and Cleanth did the work of an army in defending the *Southern Review.* You were good to write me as you did, for maybe I should not have written what I did. But oh, it was so bitter to see you use the last resorts and ruses and yet to have them fail too. And I never swallowed anything with such difficulty as I did the whole attitude and behavior of those horrible people: for I never believed any thing but that they meant to do just what they did in the end, and they simply dangled hope before you until they were ready to strike . . . I suppose the parallel of the things happening in Europe, the whole thing from Spain on to Munich and on to the fall of 1939 was always in my mind, and the disheartening sight of our government's relations with Vichy France—imagine, our still sending supplies to them which were used by Nazi Germany—and I could see too clearly the relationship between one thing and another, from great to small. As John Crowe Ransom says in his notice in the latest *Kenyon Review,* the SR was one of the casualties of the war. But I think, a casualty planned by the enemies in your own house. That is the dreadful thing about it. But you know what is going on as well or better than I do. The people who for seven years have been waiting the time when they could destroy the SR just took the first really good chance that came. It would be very interesting to know what other things were cut off the budget, and what amounts.

Well, it is done, and there is one thing they can't destroy: the record of seven years superb work. That stands. And that is where they fail, always. They can't destroy the record.

Your collection of poems is so fine I would feel impertinent to praise it. Every poem, every line, is splendid. It goes so far beyond anything you did before, and I am very ready to say it is the best poetry ever written by an American. Mind you I have the greatest respect for our best poets: they stand very well in good company. Such a little book and such a huge shadow it casts. I liked everything about the way it was brought out, too: the dedication, mindful of association; and Albert's really beautiful job of designing. I have two copies, yours unbound, and a bound one from Albert; the last, the last of so much, and the beginning of so much. In the end is the beginning. There is a terrible weight of life history in that poetry, and in the whole book. You cannot think how grateful I am to you for writing such a book.

Lambert Davis writes me you are now nicely wrapped up in a contract with Harcourt Brace, and that is good news. I hope they did well by you. It is a very good house, may you have a long lease there. Also he says you will be in New York about the first of May. I shall be there from the first to the fourth or fifth, mainly to go on radio Sunday the third, and then to straighten out some publishing affairs, and I hope to see you and Cinina. We should be able to keep track of each other, having the same publisher. I will leave my address with them for you, you do the same for me.

I think you are truly philosophical about your material affairs, after all it is a pretty serious thing to have bought a house and to have put so much into property and then to leave it, probably for good. I suppose I was reckless too, for this house is weighing me down and still I am unable just to do the last things necessary to live there. Now I am going to Reno to get a divorce, which I would have done before but I simply was too swamped with work. That will take six weeks at least, there will be about a month between that and my season at the Rocky Mountain Writers' Conference . . . Davison said you could tell me something about that, but then, you have already. His offer is not so very good, $400, but with living expenses, and I thought perhaps a total change would be good. Something may come up to prevent me, but I cannot now imagine what it could be. It means I shan't be in South Hill until about the middle of August, after all . . . It seems fantastic, all this confusion, doesn't it, after all the years of working towards stability and some kind of order in life . . . And the breaking of personal ties is the hardest thing about it.

Yes, I like Zabel too, I did enjoy seeing him here. He sent me a marvelously gaudy post card from New Orleans on his way to Baton Rouge.

I just glanced at your review of *Opinions of Oliver Allston,* and Red, would you believe, I had the idea to do my piece about him in just that way: as if Oliver Allston had been a real character, and then come down on *him,* not particularly V W B, but of course, I only made the notes, and fell by the wayside. I am going to read your criticism later on, when I am in bed. Now I am so tired I am afraid this is an incoherent letter, but if I don't write now something may happen to prevent me again . . . I have been wanting to write.

The novel has stopped entirely, what with my troubles about the house—no money, that is the trouble—and the pressure of work, and a scattered mind, and the having to go west just now, and all. But it will begin again when I can get a little more sleep and a slightly more easy mind . . .

See you in New York. Give Cinina my love, she must be in something of a state, too.

> Yours
> *Katherine Anne*

TO GLENWAY WESCOTT   Yaddo
                            Saratoga Springs, New York
                            April 19, 1942

My dear:

No rough treatment, no wounding, none, but only the gravity that comes of having to admit once more to a friend some bitter truths I have already admitted to myself.

Your letter came at a magically opportune moment, for I was going through bales of letters and papers which contain the record, all of it that can be contained on paper, and it is horrifying how much time has been lost in just that erosion of small worries, involvements with the small worries and needs of others—but it is not mean or poor, I believe, and yes, it is the sordidness of this Fader episode that has, as you say truly, demoralized me a little. My life has been a disaster, but it was not ignoble . . . I felt in this business as if I had strayed into the lower East Side and had been pelted from the push carts by hoodlums. Something quite as irrelevant as that.

And this is a week of peculiarly complicated anniversaries, of which today is the grand climax. On the 16th of April, Albert drove to Houston to take me back to Louisiana with him. Could not wait for me to come by myself. Sent telegrams from every town to mark his progress towards me. On the 17th we drove back to together. On the 18th we celebrated his birthday with SR friends in Baton Rouge. And today, four years ago, the 19th we went, with Robert Penn Warren and his wife, to New Orleans and were married. And in this very season it comes about I must be packing up to start out again, to a strange place on my way to get a divorce, and day by day, in the most extraordinary manner I have been getting all his letters, more than a thousand, all by special delivery and air plane, with telegrams as punctuation, together, and I would inevitably come upon a letter written in those days, those times . . .

Would you think that might be gloomy? No, it has lifted my heart and made me very gay again, for we were right, it was love and it still is love, and though now it seems to me that my sufferings are growing so great and so mysteriously deep and pervasive, as if they wished to be greater than the place where they live, as if they were determined to show themselves outside of me, as if I must wear them publicly, still all that happened between Albert and me was great and good, deep and with living fire in it, and we neither of us would have missed it for anything else we can imagine, and we can't deny or regret anything now. So these days I have been saying really good bye to that past, to Paris, before, and all: but it is none of it dead. After the novel I am going to work on that journal . . .

Oh yes, it is better to lose everything at once, for in such a loss only the irrelevant things fall away. Nothing is lost after all. . . .

I know that a house is not freedom in any loose sense of having all your time, your energies, for yourself. Who would want that? But it is knowing where your mss and books are, your music to play instead of being boxed up in a cellar, a place where friends will delight to come. Housekeeping and duty and trusteeship: I *need* them all. Not too much, naturally. Too much would be as destructive and wasteful as my present homelessness . . . I need a practical daily life, and it seems to me I have not been particularly idealistic . . . Ah, wait now until you see South Hill ready to be lived in.

Your advice that, in case of disaster I should begin again, instantly, to rebuild and reclaim, is just what I do, darling, always; I have always done that; I have even thrown things away and instantly began to replace them. By *things* I don't always mean materials . . . But this time, I say no, I will not lose this because this is what I really want and can have and must have and I am not willing to do it again, because I have already done it too much . . . And so it shall not be lost.

Again, something seems to be happening to my energies: they are coming back, my head is clearing, I am able to see farther than the tip of my nose, and I am full of courage, which comes and goes in me with the tides and the moon. Also, this clearing and burning of papers and putting things to rights gives me the sense of getting life in order for a new start, or a continuance so strong it will seem like new . . .

Meantime, I am in the midst of the most appalling apparent confusion but I can see the firm core of order in it, I know what it will be like when it is finished . . .

I have all your letters together now, and this one goes with them. Someday maybe you would like to see them again? They are a record, too, and a superb one . . .

Now I wait to hear that George and Monroe are safely back in 89th street—of course they are or will be so soon. I am trying to make it possible to be in New York a few days before the broadcast, there are a great many people to see about last minute things, and I hope you will have some time for me, too. Then to Reno, with the novel and an anthology and a translation for company, and on to Colorado, and—this is absurd, to Indiana University for a series of lectures, and so home again, and this time, home indeed.

I have said farewell and meant it sincerely to unlamented loves. It is most melancholy, don't you find? Why to Devil's Island? Why?

> With my love
> *Katherine Anne*

In these days, reading as I put things away, I could see the plot very clearly, perhaps for the first time . . .

To Elizabeth Ames   303 Hill Street
Reno Nevada
May 9, 1942

Dearest Elizabeth:

The New York business was finished well enough, the trip was very long but not so tiresome as I feared. I arrived Thursday at half past one and by four o'clock was settled in an incredibly inexpensive comfortable little furnished apartment: one bed sitting room— the bed folds up in the wall and becomes discreet panelling in the day time, little bath, wee kitchen.

A woman I met on the same errand as myself asked her lawyer about a lawyer for me, who would be more reasonable: she is divorcing a famously rich husband, expense no object—and I went to the recommended one. He turned out to be from Kentucky, he knows my family there, knows old timers in Texas who were friends of my grandmother, recognized my name when I gave it, and promptly took over my affairs as his own. He is about seventy five years old, has one of the oldest flying licenses in the country, and told me he hadn't travelled in a train of cars (train of kyars, he said) for twenty two years. He flies about ten thousand miles a year. He has a daughter who writes and who takes advice from Archibald McLeish about her Art. She is coming to see me and I must get in the habit of dropping in afternoon for a little snifter of sherry or whiskey. Meantime, proceedings have started and the grounds are perfect: separation for a certain period of time. No grisly false charges, and a private hearing . . . His grandfather was a celebrated surgeon, and bosom friend of Henry Clay. He has had some famous horses and his office is full of pictures of himself, his family and friends on horseback. Also picture of Daniel Webster, Henry Clay, Uncle Joe Cannon, Old Hull when he was young and fresh out of the backwoods of Tennessee, and beautiful drawings of his very good looking wife and daughters. His fee is just what I hoped for, $100 and I began by explaining frankly to him that I had been told he would make reasonable fees for those not able to pay a great deal. The average fee is $250, no limit upward, but just what the traffic will bear. . . .

With my love,
Katherine Anne

P.S. I send you a copy of *Story* with a piece called "The Enchanted" by Laurette Macduffie Knight. I saw her for only a few minutes with John Woodburn, she is a pleasant, sedate young looking woman with gray hair. Woodburn had asked me to read the story and write to you, in case there should be vacancies unexpectedly among your guests—meaning those men who must go to war. I promised before I read the story, alas. You know me, impulsive. The work seems to be honest and careful, it is certainly a pretty good story, but I think superficial, and I miss a certain generosity of mind. Compare what Eudora can get out of a southern small town, and this . . . The difference is in the caliber of the artist. It is not an ample talent, but not bad, either. I find two other stories of much greater interest. If you have time, read "This Lucky Man, Our Friend," by Eli Waldron, 27 years old, from Oconto Falls, Wisconsin. And "Where The Sun Died" by Jerome and Abe Selman. Both apparently very young, from New York. These are painful stories, but they have the spark. The younger ones have got into the deeper stratum of human suffering.

To Donald Elder   Reno, but not for long
                                   June 14, 1942

Donald Darling:

.... Well, and I have done a good deal of work on the novel,
and do more, every day. And I read at night the trial of Clement
de Fauquemberge and make notes. Lord, how many notes . . . I
never tire of it though. I read a half dozen contemporary histories
and journals along with it, and how I love Old or Middle French
. . . Even here in Reno it doesn't seem like a strange language. And
I wrote, or re-wrote, the whole scene of St. Joan's capture at Com-
peigne, with every act and move of that moment, even to what she
was wearing and what part of her dress the soldiers took hold of,
and exactly what Guillaume de Flavy did: he just ordered the *pont
levis* raised and left her stranded . . . I think he betrayed her, all
right. But I have also the arguments on the other side and shall give
them too.

How pleasant to think of you, a Young Executive, and on a
good salary too, not just sitting there either but doing something.
Your plans to see that Littrachoor gets its dues is naturally the kind
of thing I like best to hear, and I will set you on the trail of any
young hopeful I may find . . . I have a theory though—remember
Ford Madox Ford's favorite maxim, which he said came from the
Chinese: "It is useless to look for the sacred person of the King-
Emperor in a low tea house." Well the really serious good young
writers can't afford to go to conferences, they are a small, dark and
hidden band who emerge, one at a time, when you least expect it,
from some hidey-hole where they have been fighting it out for
themselves . . . Still I have seen some good promise in some of these
summer mills: and will remember you if I see it again. But our
future Tolstoi or Flaubert or even another Henry James is lurking
out on the marge, and we shan't snare *him,* or at least not this
summer, I imagine.

I too take great joy and vanity in my goggles, which help me
to see so nicely and hides my face at the same time: the perfect
disguise . . .

The glimpse I had of Albert at his work was strange. For he
has no more business selling advertising than you have. He is a born

editor, an acute and sensitive critic, he designs books beautifully, and it is really a shameful waste of gifts that he does not have a good authoritative editorial job . . . However, somebody is bound to catch on sooner or later . . . He did all the choosing of fiction of S.R. and found for himself half a dozen perfectly good young writers, the first two I remember being Eudora Welty and Michael Seide . . . If a publishing house really wanted a first rate talent scout, that is the man . . .

About that ill-fated advance: I can pay it back in the fall. Maybe not all at once, but in several installments . . . You are very sweet about it. I just hope now we shall be able to make a really first rate job of the translations. By the way we have never changed the contracts have we? That can be done when I get back . . . And you know, I sat down and really figured it out, and as I had asked for the five hundred additional on that contract, which would just have covered what I needed, and as after all it was not advanced on that, why, nothing was solved in the long run. But the immediate cash was a life saver, and I shan't forget that, even if it would have been a huge bite out of something else I hadn't meant to touch just then . . . It doesn't matter now. My God, this has been a grisly time, but it will end. Your tremendous phrase about the sultry and murderous East struck me doubly because here the atmosphere is so very light and thin and cheerful and you hear nothing about the war except the radio, which chatters all day and succeeds only in making it all rather unreal . . .

The FBI finally tracked me down to ask questions about friends. I was really happy to be able to tell them that so far as I knew they had no political consciousness whatever . . . They ask the strangest questions, don't they? And as you said once about this very thing, it is surprising to find how little one does know about the actual life of one's friends. What do they do all those long times when I don't see them? Where are they? What goes on in their heads?

When my FBI man finally gave up and decided to go, I said, "Well, this is a dirty kind of business, I don't like it much, do you?"

He looked surprised: he was young, good looking, very tall, the typical FBI sleuth, I am told, and after a short pause he said, "Well, it has to be done." I think so too, but I wish they would be a little more acute and get the right people . . .

I must stop now and pack up a little, getting ready to go. To go again . . . It will be nice to settle down and live in one place some day, long enough to grow at least a bush of some kind.

With my love,
Katherine Anne

To Elizabeth Ames

E. Davison, Care Writers'
Conference
University of Colorado
Boulder, Colorado
July 1, 1942

Dearest Elizabeth:

The 19th of June passed safely and well; the grand fourteen hour flight across mountain ranges and millions of greenacres was a really joyful thing, even when I slept I knew where I was and loved every minute of it; the conference at Indiana was altogether a success, and I saw a good old friend, John Crowe Ransom, and met some very good new persons: and there received an offer from the Louisiana State University to return to Baton Rouge and take R.P. Warren's place (as if it could be done, as if—what idiots they are) and the inducements are so persuasive, same salary as Sarah Lawrence, only five hours work a week, all the rest of the time my own, I am tempted to take it. I asked to be released from my agreement with Sarah Lawrence, because I can see, freshly after my recent teaching experience, that that job is going to be gruelling hard work and probably means I couldn't do any writing at all for nine months . . .

Well, South Hill is on my mind and my heart, but this is not the only year, and after all I must still earn that place, and must do my work too, and I am being extremely calm about it. I made every effort in my power to bring about the kind of life I would have liked, and would not take No for an answer, in spite of the obstacles, and it may all happen yet, but not just yet, I can see that . . . Of course, something even better may come up—the radio job, for example, in which case everything will be changed again, and

241

in such an ideal way I don't allow myself to dwell upon it or have hopes. I just sit here in a girl's chapter house on the campus and write Novel . . .

Its a green and rainy world all over, the weather has been beautiful everywhere, and I never saw so much bloom. Every sort of tree and shrub and vine capable of producing a flower has out-bloomed itself altogether this year, and people are blooming, too, at least in this western country. It is as if the shades of catastrophe had brought all of us to some kind of feeling that now or never we had better get on our best behavior and keep it on, and there is a good solid kind of self possession and sensible facing of the situation. It is also very pleasant to see the young ones on these safe campuses, really working and studying, making their seven A.M. classes looking fresh as milk, hearing music, and riding, and carrying on their courtships frankly, and every day another boy gets his questionnaire, and the boys and girls go around singing merrily "Last Call For Love."

I guess the world will go on, Elizabeth, and somehow in this country, I can't believe these people are villains or martyrs, I can't see them at all as ruined or ruinous. They are getting pretty informed politically, too, and there is not the taint in the air of Fascism that I smell always in the East and the South. This trip has been wonderful for me, I am getting the "feel" of something very American and very strong and good . . . The students of course, come from all over the country and they are a fine cross section of the young generation: I am inclined to think perhaps the nicest young generation the human race has managed to produce so far.

Every train is really a troop train now, and there were only two women on the plane, and the faces of the soldiers are completely grave and thoughtful . . . Of course, you see them huddled together sometime carrying on a giggling conversation full of "And I says to her and she says—" and all too obviously they grab their fun where they can get it, but the real tone is pretty grim, and these boys have grown up several years before their time. . . .

With all my love
Katherine Anne

SECTION 5

South Hill, Washington

September 1942
to December 1944

The great old classical habit of the interior life of the mind and spirit is now perfectly in disrepute. But it is as good as ever it was, and more necessary than ever.

Katherine Anne Porter to Donald Elder
December 1, 1942

"WITH MONKEY WRENCHES AND CORKSCREWS AND HAIRPINS *and icepicks"* *Katherine Anne Porter takes the furnace apart one icy January day. She cannot make it work. Repairmen make the house warm again but another winter at South Hill is out of the question. Yet "the activity, the illusion of life, that house gave me tided me over a difficult time . . . and I think it is not wasted in that sense." She goes to an inn on the Hudson with books (Yeats, Montaigne, Samuel Johnson, Aubrey, Donne, and Coussemaker's* Histoire de l'harmonie au moyen age) *and virginals which she practices an hour a day, and works on the novel. She is invited to take John Peale Bishop's place as a Fellow in the Library of Congress. She campaigns for Roosevelt and selects songs for a demonstration; "listening to them for the past two days has given me such a lift of the heart I feel almost happy for the first time, really, since the war began."*

To Paul Porter   South Hill
                            R.D.3
                            Ballston Spa, New York
                            September 18, 1942

Paul darling:

.... I will send you a copy of *Fiesta in November* as soon as my copies arrive, and you can send it on home afterward, and I will send the *Accent* with (note well,) "Affectation of Praehiminincies" (slipped up myself) in it. That word has got so many people down, apparently not a soul but Cotton Mather and I know what it means. Pre-eminencies, of course, but only half-clawed out of the Greek root and with C.M.'s own inspired spelling. But I got the word from his own diary and loved it. In the book, farther on, it comes but in proper context and explains itself. My book, I mean; and it shall be finished some day. . . .

My dear now and then only a true truism will properly cover a certain situation, and so let me remind you that you are more apt to be lonely in a crowd than anywhere else. And more especially in a crowd of strangers where a kind of artificial intimacy is imposed by the conditions. You are just in the same fix as a boy on his first day at school, if you remember that: and the chances for finding a perfect friend are always very long indeed, it is possible you may never find one, and if you did, you might not be a perfect friend to him. The important thing is to know how to *like* people, and to know that every single soul of us is isolated, in some part of his nature, in his own kind of loneliness. In that loneliness you must learn to live, that is where your own life will develope, that is where you do your work, that is where you learn everything you know, because that is where you take your experiences to remember and examine and understand them. You will probably be in love many times, and you will no doubt have many friends, and not one of them will be perfect, no more than you can be. But there will be something worth having and something memorable in all that happens to you, and little by little you will find the very things and the very people that are for you. Look how suddenly you found the books and the music and the quiet place, and just the day before you didn't even know they were there . . . I loved your letter about the brawl, the beer-woozied feelings all rampant, the poor lonely fellows trying to have a good time on nothing much, and making nothing much of it; and your insight as to why the singing together didn't do so well was really astonishing. So don't worry about your letters. Just write what comes up first; for one thing, that is a fine exercise in learning to write, and second—only second, mind you— it gives me some extremely good letters from you. Truth is, that is the first consideration, because if you wrote in style, thinking about whether or not you were saying something intelligent or just merely the right thing, it would be very sad for me. Letters are written to one person: in this case to me—and they should be just free and spontaneous. I like to know your moods and what goes on as it happens; "set pieces" as professional authors call carefully composed passages, wouldn't do at all.

Tomorrow ends the first week I have spent in this house, and it does not look like the same place. My room is lovely now, full of white wooly rugs and my nice waxed pine furniture, chests and tables and my dark blue silk covered easy chairs: the guest room is nice, too, rather manly in tone, done up with you in mind: and the sun porch is really a place now to sit in the afternoon for coffee and cigarettes and a look at the view: now obstructed alas by some débris and some unfinished flagstone paving. I wish you were here to look at things and talk over plans: I could do with a little advice and help just now. How I wish, too (one may as well wish reck-lessly) that you might be sent East for training. There's an air field just over here about seven miles away. Why couldn't you be trained there? But we are not being consulted just now in these things. I'm only saying what I'd like if I had my druthers, as a little Negro I used to know in Louisiana says. (Remember how they say, I'druther?)

Well—as to drinking. I don't know why beer and wine taste so good and are so heavenly to have, but I do know they are. But five bottles of beer in one sitting is a lot of beer for anybody, three are all I ever attempted at my boldest, and your four seem to have done wonders for you. Drink for fun, darling, for sometimes it is fun, and try not to drink just to knock yourself out, because as you have said, it builds up a headache and sometimes makes trouble and in general is no good, no good at all. And be careful who you drink with, for drinking with the wrong people is a really dreary business.

Some of the gayest times I remember were just being out with a
few good companions, doing up the town, drinking a little here and
a little there, and talking and having a wonderful evening, on
nothing but the right company and a few drinks. You'll find the
company: I trust your judgment and feelings. And oh, that speech
of yours to the fellow who didn't like your face, and that line "I
looked him straight in the eye in a roundabout way . . ." That
belongs in the *New Yorker*'s Neatest Trick of the Week department.

Good night. I must get to work. A little squinch-owl has been
coming every evening and sitting in a maple tree outside my window and complaining in a little monotonous squeak, hours on end.
I wonder what's on his mind. With my love. I think of you all the
time.

Aunt Katherine Anne

To Robert Penn Warren   South Hill
R.D. 3
Ballston Spa, New York
October 8, 1942

Dearest Red:

. . . . You remember the time, Christmas in Baton Rouge,
when you and Albert were talking about the *Southern Review* and
you suddenly thought up the Thomas Hardy number, invited me
then and there to contribute, and gave me in effect a year and a half
notice? Well, this James business is only ten months away, but I
swear I'll make it. I still owe a Proust article to *Kenyon*, and its
coming up too. And both are going, with the Hardy piece and
others, into a whole book of such things I am preparing . . . About
James: I have been mulling around trying to find exactly the point
to take hold, and your suggestion is going to help me decide. Here
is my first thought, first definite one, I mean, and will you please
tell me what you think of it. James and Childhood. His treatment
of child characters, such as Maisie, the two children in "The Turn
of the Screw," and others I cannot now recall, but will soon, related
to his own book of memories, *A Small Boy and Others*; the point

being, in my mind, that James' child-characters are to me almost the best in fiction, an extraordinary understanding of the young mind and nature, the situation of the child in an alien adult world; and that his own remarkable memory of his experiences and feelings and states of mind as a child is naturally the source—his children are deliciously Jamesian, subtle and intelligent as he was, and as more children are than most adults seem to be aware of: James' children live in a strange world, as James did in childhood, and continued to do so all his life: a world of wonder and mystery which he labored steadily and with perfect concentration to understand and explain . . .

Something on that order, Red. But this is the first time I ever tried to put it into even little sentences, and I never really thought it clearly until an hour or two ago, so I send it for what you may think it is worth . . . But there are so many phases. I am full of notions and theories as to James' real attitude towards Europe, especially England; one could write another book on his *Art of The Novel* alone, and so if you wish to assign me a facet of the subject I'll take it up cheerfully. I have spent years upon years of my life in that society, I don't think any phase would really be strange to me, I would undoubtedly find something to say no matter where we began . . . So let me know what you think . . . I'm delighted to be asked to contribute; and you know I'll do my little damndest . . .

Well, love to you both, and with the good hope of seeing you here at South Hill . . . by the way, this is the house letter paper, present from Albert who designed the lettering. I have simply bales of it, thank God . . . I hope Minnesota proves to be just what your first impressions tell you. First impressions are often signals from the deep that we should credit oftener than we do . . .

Katherine Anne

I refused finally both offers: from Sarah Lawrence and L.S.U. because it seemed so unreasonable not to live where I had planned, if there was a possible way. And the way is possible, I can live here.

To Paul Porter   South Hill
                          R.D.3
                          Ballston Spa, New York
                          November 19, 1942

Dearest Paul:

Your snapshots came, and a little later that framed photograph signed to the sweetest one, and you know I don't mind in the least being one of your interchangeable sweeties, perhaps you did just as well to send it here instead of there: those words are dynamite planted in the wrong mind; a girl could get no end of ideas, with consequences, as you might say, in eternity. Well, that was a narrow squeak, and now mind you don't start putting your letters in the wrong envelopes.

I liked three of the little pictures so much better than I did the other three, The one holding the pipe and looking out from under your visor—what's that medal looking affair on the boozum? Are they handing them out already and what for? the second, the stalwart pose, grimly at attention, and the hatless one, strictly serious, still with that pipe . . . They seemed to resemble you as I remember, and the lighting and photography are better, too . . . The framed one alas, after all that uproar, I liked least of all. Your Great grandmother Porter once regarded a youthful portrait of herself with dissatisfaction saying, "It gives me a deceitful look. I know I was *never* deceitful—" and you, my dear nevvew, in this photograph, look sly—just the kind of lad who would write sweetest one on a picture for a girl and then take it back . . . No, prudent is the word for that. Where did you get such a quality? It is very refreshing to see a grain of it come into this family, who never had any, never even inquired the meaning of the word . . . Cultivate it, moderately. You have the real family look, though, I would recognize you if I had never seen you and didn't know who you were . . . They are extremely nice looking pictures and I am happy to have them . . . As to my promised snap shot, we have never got the films off to be printed yet. They are in color and must go to a certain place and for some reason they do not get sent. Federico is so proud of his films he must show them to every one who comes, on the white wall with his projector, and I suspect he does not like to give them up even for the week we need to get the prints; but they will come, and they are quite flattering.

You seem to be getting settled at a fine rate, who wouldn't be in Supply if it means a room and all the pleasant things you mention? Still you do not say why you will not be in active service—so-called, for you seem to be active enough, directing camp set-ups and settling pleats in officers' tents . . . Does it mean, or can you tell me this, that you may not be sent to one of the fifteen fronts? Or—this is a thought—will you just be sent there without a gun? Do explain as much of this mystery as the rules allow, for I am interested. It makes a great difference to my state of mind about you.

Dear me, if "normal" characters bore you in fiction, perhaps it is time for you to be reading Kafka and Rilke. I recommend *The Journal of My Other Self,* by Rilke, a noble and beautiful book, and when I send it I will copy from one of Rilke's letters his own comment upon it. I read that and his *War Time Letters,* (letters from that other war, but all of it is true for now, too). He is a great poet, and even translated from German his beautiful, complex but clear style comes through . . . Also Kafka. Perhaps *Amerika* to begin with, then *The Castle,* if you still wish to go on. You are very right, *Fiesta in November* is nowhere on a level with either the Mann or the Joyce stories and I would hardly know what to say about these, considered together, for "The Dead" is written in English and we can only have a translation of "Mario and the Magician," so it is hard to judge of the styles, which would be most important to me. They are both great stories, and I am never so much interested in the kind of people the author chooses to write about as what he has to say about them and how he says it. Any character that seems to me presented in the round, a true portrait of a human being, with *illumination* which is the gift of genius to cast upon the deep places in human nature, is interesting to me; the author must be able to persuade me to accept his version as true, his insight as real. Joyce does this, but so does Mann. Joyce's people live in a stagnant society, emptied of nearly all meaning, he wishes to say that all they think and feel and desire is false. Mann's is a parable of Fascism, the magician is the fraudulent prophet, the active principle of evil unscrupulously at work on the minds of men in a time when society is unsettled and on the point of breaking up . . . Mann comments and points out meanings and wishes to influence you as you read: Joyce tells his story and lets the reader draw his own conclusion. I do think that Joyce despaired and that Mann does not . . . One can be moral and say no man should despair or if he does he should keep it to himself. But I don't agree. Joyce's despair has been very instructive, and he was a great artist we should be much poorer without . . . I think you are at that stage of your developement where you read for all sorts of excitements that are personal and not particularly based on literary judgments, but this seems to me quite all right too. The discrimination comes with time and reading and thinking things out . . .

As for "normal-abnormal" the lines are hard to draw, but for me, I have known in life so many strange, wild lost people, some of them very gifted, so many beings trembling a life time between madness and a kind of twilight sanity, such suffering and such cruelty and confusion, I have a good while ago come to the point where I love goodness and simplicity and the desire of the human heart to believe and to love. These are all very rare, and they are not accidents, and they can be possessed only by exceptional and great natures. It seems all too easy to too many people to be "abnormal" irresponsible, evil. A true search for the meanings of things will lead one away from this . . . This is never to say that simplicity means simpleness. It is the most complex and difficult of all things to achieve . . . Perhaps it is not possible to achieve it altogether, but it is always worth trying for.

Dear Paul, I must stop and work a little. Work has been going badly, and I have not been well: even spent a few days in bed and saw a doctor, who is going over me with all kinds of tests tomorrow, but I think nothing much will come of it. Nothing much ever does. I will be ill for a while and then I will recover, as I do, with only the time lost for it . . . I am feeling much better now and have even gained a pound or two. So you are not to think of this, but I was not able to write as I would have liked. I have such an enormous amount of work hanging over me, and so many things get in the way, I feel rather swamped at times. But I still think I am going to get the use of my time and energy, if I plan and manage properly.

With my love,
Aunt Katherine Anne

I think I prefer the largest snapshot, bare headed—"the strictly serious" because your face looks quite calm, self-possessed, and it shows off better the good shape of your head, too . . .

YOUR POEMS, good heavens. I almost forgot to tell you I think the ballad is best as a performance, though the sentiments are light to say the least . . . Nearly always I prefer your prose. But don't let that stop you from writing poetry when you feel you can . . . Even if you never become a poet, writing poetry helps to form a prose style. All the great, and all the very good poets, always have wonderful prose styles, too.

To Paul Porter   [South Hall
                                R.D.3
                                Ballston Spa, New York]
                                November 29, 1942

Paul darling.

I know that by now you must have had a longish letter, but I want to send another word saying I had got your anxious little note. Truth is I was not well and had an enormous amount of work to do: and Doctor thought I might have incipient tb and should probably go to a sanitarium. I was firm about it: I would go nowhere. Here I would stay and here I could get well if anywhere . . . After a week and some consultations they reversed their decision: pronounced it tracheal bronchitis, which should worry no one, not even myself: that is a family failing . . . I am being very quiet and taking good care of myself and everything is going beautifully well. So don't think about this any more . . .

There was something you wrote about several letters ago which I meant to answer, but I am always a letter or two in arrears with all I should like to write to you . . . About your sitting with the nice young negro and your extremely mixed emotions . . . It has pleased me very much to know your feelings about the negro, his treatment, the unfairness of his restrictions in this country, and I was delighted with your answer to that midwestern fellow who had sworn he wouldn't associate with negroes . . . Well, when it comes to the show down, we should be glad, for that is our chance to find out once for all if we really mean what we say or have just been talking. For years now, I have been in places where now and then I meet negroes on terms of implied social equality—it always occurs in very advanced and sometimes self consciously "liberal" circles, and I am usually warned beforehand, because I am a southerner, and the northerners can't seem to get anything clear in their heads about us and the negroes . . . I always go and sometimes it seems to me I am the only one who really feels at ease and the negroes feel at ease with me . . . I have no trouble at all, it comes naturally to wear the same face and use the same voice and talk about the same things that I do with any one else. I eat with them and have danced with them. It is true that these particular negroes are superior people, poets, musicians, teachers, editors, happens they belong to the class of people and practise the professions that I seem to prefer, and the truth is the whole race question seems absurd, inhuman, barbarous at any time, but quite incredible when you actually know the same kind of interesting colored people that you know among any other race . . . I think at best there is perhaps a certain tension that exists yet between even the most intelligent persons of the black and the white races in this country. There is too much evil and sad history, too many painful memories, between us . . . But it can be overcome, outlived, not by denying the past, but by understanding it, and by not opposing the changes that can be brought about gradually by education, by generosity on both sides, and by a resolute putting down in ourselves all those old and ill conditioned prejudices that have become almost second nature . . . Man is not perfectible, but he is capable of improvement, and part of his improvement must consist of developing his sense of justice and honor. There are inferiorities and superiorities among human beings, not all are equally endowed at birth with good gifts of mind or spirit, but no man should be oppressed because of his natural limitations, and above all no man should be subject to restraints and limitations of his gifts because of his race or color . . . This is true, darling, by any civilized standard of thought or feeling, and let me warn you that you have come on a bitter time, when defense of civilized feeling and thought is going to be harder than ever, for there is a kind of pall falling over the human race, a real threat of return to brutal mindlessness and darkness . . . Be careful, watch yourself, go for help and support to the great and good who have lived before you and who can advise you . . . You know good and evil and you also know right from wrong, so you have a responsibility upon you that you can't side step or deny, and oh, how fortunate you are my dear . . .

It isn't anything so simple as just being able suddenly to be amiable and friendly to individual negroes, it is a whole complex of ideas and feelings and it extends to the farthest reaches of your life in every act and thought. Some day you will know so well just what you are and how you feel and where you stand you won't have to stop to think for a moment, but will find youself with the certainty of something better than instinct working for you almost unconsciously, like a good painter who no longer has to think about his technical medium; or like a critic who can judge at a glance the exact worth of a poem or of music . . . So go ahead, you've made a good start . . .

Well, darling, you see I am back in my old form, writing my thoughts as they come: not as well as I might, if I took more time, but at least I do say what I think, just as the words come. And this was something I wanted badly to write you about . . .

With my love
Aunt Katherine Anne

TO DONALD ELDER

South Hill
R.D.3
Ballston Spa, New York
December 1, 1942

Dearest Donald:

Muriel's book is very fine and unusual. Its deep interest for me was her way of telling a story of intellectual adventure, of a history lived almost altogether in the mind. There haven't been so many in this country, and few enough in the world, and yet they are the most exciting of all lives, the deep and narrow ones lived in devotion to some one idea or occupation. I have read it twice, and it will always be something to read in again. I don't share many of her loves and enthusiasms, I think her hero is something of a monster, but monsters are wonderful to write and to read about . . . I do not breathe well the air of New England Puritanism as you know, and I hope it does not smother out everything else in this country, as it threatens: their mean old God is offensive to me; the Adamses are none of my heroes. But she has done a fine job of them, at any rate, and makes them seem portentous and sometimes admirable. For one who thinks Thomas Jefferson was really the only first rate man this country has produced, that is a great admission. I should have been glad to review the book but I am no scientist or mathematician, and I think some one in that line will do better by it . . .

I am going to be in New York soon, but only to see a doctor, a very special specialist; alas, I am at that point where doctors will begin to hand me around to each other, but this one found something he thinks he can manage, and we expect the other one to find something else *he* has a cure for, and so on. It sounds dull and may be . . . But I am coming down and going back again, no time for anything else, but am going to stop with Glenway and Monroe over the week end at Stone Blossom. Christmas was always a painful season to face, something happened to that lovely season so long ago I have forgotten what it was that spoiled it for me. But this year yes, there must be no nonsense of personal feeling. And maybe here, with a green pointed tree brought in from my own wood, and a fire, and long quiet snowy evenings, after writing letters to all my friends, Christmas may come back. I'd like to go to midnight Mass: the last time was at St. Etienne du Mont, but with the wrong people. It is after all people who spoil or make things for one. Foxes who gnaw. By all means if you have yours thrown out, never expect me to send you one. I have after all this time thrown out mine, and now I can smell a fox at sixty paces on a down wind and I think my foot work is better than it was, too.

It will be odd if Albert goes to Doubleday, for I know Harcourt Brace was interested in him: but John goes there instead and Albert maybe to Doubleday. I hope it is a pleasant association. He has a fine critical sense and should be somewhere where he can use his judgement without too much interference. He has been doing some work for Fischer, a firm I don't trust politically at all . . . I don't like "refugee" publishers who were once willing to publish books dedicated to Goering, with Heil Hitler on the title page . . . A man who stays to do that would have stayed to do more if some personal difficulty had not got in his way.

But then, really I don't like anything much. The Austrian legion being turned over to Otto. Darlan accepting Dakar in the name of Petain—(that is one of the foul sell outs of this war, the Darlan thing, and no explanation explains in the least) and I don't like the Franco business, and I don't like the threat of peace with Italy, a Fascist state, while we continue to make war on other fascist states. And I don't like our not having rubber because Standard Oil and other monoplies refuse to allow free manufacture of the suppressed kind. And it is not really encouraging to see the growth of the Luce power; what is that appointment of Mrs. Luce to the important international post—a gruesome joke? I wish it were. So Willkie seems a rather bland and gentle influence, after some other things. But he is a symptom too. I hope he is never president, but I can think of worse now. I know man is not perfectible, but he can grow in grace. But I don't believe in conversions really, in the sense of changes of heart. Don't cite Saul of Tarsus. He was the same man after he changed his name and his religion, and he did a great deal of evil, as he was doing before, only in different ways and towards different ends . . . Yet perhaps a man may choose between the good and the evil in his own soul, and perhaps he may see the light. But I think not Willkie. He is just shrewd and a good observer and he will do and say the right things to get along . . . I have seen everything in this world that I hated, despised, and opposed, win out, one by one, sometimes slowly, sometimes suddenly . . . I shouldn't expect a change now . . . But that can't keep me from hating and despising and opposing them to the end. They can't win altogether if we simply don't let them . . . But are there enough of Us? And just where are We?

You know I do approve of your Spanish studies, I couldn't do otherwise without cutting the ground from under my own feet, with my Medieval French and all. "Escapism" is a dirty word used by all subversive people who resent your not falling in with their plans. It is a very transparent term of abuse for people who quietly pursue their own tastes and interests. The great old classical habit of the interior life of the mind and spirit is now perfectly in disrepute. But it is as good as ever it was, and more necessary than ever.

Languages, poetry, history, music, and the attentive study of the human heart, good behavior to the human being immediately next to you in this world: I suppose these activities can never be organized, I suppose their voting strength is nil, but they are the only interests worth wasting a breath upon, and I say this with perfectly dogmatic certainty. "And in this faith I hope to live and die." Everything else is a disgust and weariness to the soul.

I am finishing this letter begun last night at six o'clock in the morning, in darkness outside, with a fine light and a good cup of hot coffee; this coffee is precious treasure, for when it is gone it is gone; and meantime I pay no attention to those piffling instructions as to how to make it last: boiling, which spoils it for me: a teaspoon to a cup, which would be a watery nasty brew: re-brewing, a loathesome idea. I just dip in freely with a big spoon, and make excellent drip coffee such as I was brought up on, and have my one hot, strong, aromatic cup of coffee. It won't last much longer, and then I'll take to tea if there is any, or just quit the whole business, and get up and start the day as my cat Friday does, on warm milk and a biscuit. Well, for cat-biscuit I will substitute bread and butter—and when the butter gives out, bread. When that gives out—but I won't think further, it isn't necessary. Everything can go, foul substitutes and ersatz can elbow out the sound good things we had, but the important thing is for us never to be bludgeoned into thinking this is all right, a proper state of affairs, never to be sold the idea that oleomargarine is really as good as butter, no matter if we have to eat oleo for the rest of our lives. And always to remember that all the reasons for this state of affairs are beastly and evil . . .

It has been snowy weather here, did I say so before? I haven't reread the other side of this page. Now there is a high wind blowing, but this house just stands in silence and immobility, not a creak, not a flapping shutter, not a quiver, warm and sweet smelling. You will be here some time, and after that, you won't rest until you have got your house in Martha's Vineyard . . . It has been the most complicated and difficult undertaking of my life, but worth every bit of it . . .

Love
Katherine Anne

To Paul Porter   South Hill
                                         December 30, 1942

Dearest Paul:

. . . . That was a fine impression you gave me of the group
singing carols under the street light, and of the two boys drawn
together by some vague but real sympathy and need of human
warmth . . . And of course you were there, too, which is what they
didn't know, seeing them. That is what the artist does: he sees, he
is the witness, the one who remembers, and finally works out the
pattern and the meaning for himself, and gives form to his memories . . .

I have been absolutely alone here, except for the Russian
Polish neighbors down the road, whose children drop by and say
Good Day now and then, since last Wednesday morning. I spend
some time every day polishing my house a little, it is getting into
fine order. I read, and write letters, and rest, and think, and plan
my work, and my energies seem to be coming back, and my mind
is getting into a good steady rhythm. I needed this quiet and this
solitude, there has been a great deal of pleasant but quite aimless
excitement and too much distraction. Now with this preparation I
mean to begin the New Year with real work; wish me luck. There
is so much to do. . . .

Aunt Katherine Anne

To Paul Porter   South Hill
                                         R.D.3
                                         Ballston Spa, New York
                                         March 31, 1943

Paul darling:

I haven't been agreeing with you or praising everything you
do by a long shot, as you know, and I speak up pretty frankly saying
what I think. Its a family trait. But I do, at my stage of development,
think it better not to get into wranglings and hair splittings if they

can be avoided, but save your breath for the larger issues . . . Also, I do really think you have good, sound talents, and if you aren't able to back up your judgments (for they are judgments, not just impressions) yet, that is simply for lack of the confidence that comes or should come with experience. And you have had no real challenge, either. If you had run the gauntlet as I have, almost from the beginning of my life as writer, having to fight and defend every idea and every statement as I went against a varied mob of the most conflicting and opinionated persons who could really give me an argument, you would, believe me, not only learn just what you think and believe, but *why:* and you'll find the words and arguments, too . . . That, or go under . . . But time enough for it . . . Go on thinking privately and working things out. . . .

Our cousin Lily Cahill came down to visit me and the guest room was christened after all by a member of the family as it should have been, and we drank very good Bourbon before dinner, Southern Style. Old Forester. Some day when you are feeling rich, get a bottle and treasure it. Its the best Bourbon going . . . I suppose treasuring a bottle of likker is very bad form in the army, if possible at all. But in any case, don't throw it away on somebody with a tin roof to his palate. Pick some body who knows the taste of good whiskey . . . If you aren't able to do this, I promise you a bottle for your birthday. What day is that, by the way? Don't forget to answer this . . . I am divided between June and August—I believe August. That is a long time to wait, though . . .

Oh dear, the romantic touch (that gossip) is such a gloomy proof of a sad truth—men like em hard, gorgeous sophisticated, sly, catty, etc etc—at any rate in a certain period of life, that very time when one is most apt to marry and then its too late for anything but a divorce or a long life of wearing horns and liking it . . . By all means do stay away: but if that's your style, you're by no means out of danger: There are others, many of them, oh, how many, you'll trip over her double if you don't watch out . . . Love and leave all such, darling, try not to marry one.

I am working on a long study of Henry James based on his autobiographies; it is very interesting to do, also very difficult, and I had better be at it. He is the very greatest artist and novelist this country ever produced, and his *Art of The Novel* should be a Bible for young writers. My devotion to him grows as I study his life, the most admirable life I know, lived as it was in the mind, the imagination, the heart, and the most unwavering fidelity to his own knowledge and convictions . . . With no support, almost no encouragement or understanding from anybody, he just went on being an artist from his cradle to his grave, and the record is so honorable I wish every writer in the world could know of it. But people go on writing the same old clichés about the man. I am going to do my little bit towards breaking up that rubber stamp . . .

With my love
Katherine Anne

TO PAUL PORTER

South Hill
R.D.3
Ballston Spa, New York
May 21, 1943

Paul darling:

The past month, when you have not heard from me, has been so full of so many different kinds of work I have been too exhausted at the end of the day to write even a line: even to look at the typewriter again made me more exhausted. This jungle of mine suddenly bloomed out in an interesting combination of beauty and horror, and the favorite nightmare of my childhood promised to come true, literally. I used to dream—never let Dr. Freud hear of this—in the south, that the canebrakes had, during the night, grown up to the house, thick, impenetrable, silent, covering and closing all the doors and windows; I would be alone there and no way to cut my way out . . . The nightmare you told me of is quite the most terrible I ever heard, my canebrake seems small by comparison; at least I can cut back these weeds and burrs and care for the flowering trees and shrubs and the violets and irises: But your dream is already true, for indeed, the man being destroyed *is* numb, unconscious, does not realize what is being done to him. And he will never really die, either, he will just go on moving that arm even after it is cut off. He is mankind, you know. There is a good deal more to it but all the political and social and human concepts that are stirring somewhere very deeply in your mind are in it, it really means something, that dream, it is trying to tell you something you ought to know, and *do* know, but it hasn't come clearly out into the open yet. I wish I could talk to you, and not only about modern poetry. . . .

I don't send you things to read on the grounds that you must agree with them or like them or anything of the sort. I want you to know what is being done and published, and to be able to criticise, choose, disagree, and get your own tastes and point of view established *by opposition* as well as liking. To know what you don't like and won't have is a long step to being able to choose what is good and right for you . . . I think most of the little poems just scattered here and there in the small magazines is plain rubbish: imitators of Eliot, of Tate, of even Randall Jarrell, or James Agee . . . But these are good poets even if they must seem obscure and hard to understand . . . When you work them out, they mean something, they have something to say. And some of the great things of the world, even if they have a surface simplicity, are very deep and difficult to come at fully . . . When I first read Eliot it was nearly Greek to me. Now I wonder how it could have seemed so . . . By the way, I have an extra copy of Eliot's new poems, *Quartets,* and I am sending it on, together with a magazine containing his essay, "The Music of Poetry," which is good sound sensible criticism and comment on modern method . . . That should help.

I'm sorry, but I did send the Jane Austen book, and it seems to be lost . . . Of all those I sent, that was one you should have to keep. I'll just send on another, but not this minute , . . .

My birthday was the fifteenth, and friends came down over the week end to help celebrate. Paul Cadmus and George Platt Lynes. We made photographs and hung bird houses in the trees, and ate wonderfully—I take pride in having fine food without even touching my ration books—We played gin rummy and sunbathed, and watched the spring coming in, gathering mou.ˀntum by the hour: you could almost hear things growing—a low sweet simmer, with now and then a chorus of little growls, which would be the violets fighting their way through the humous . . . Your modest violet, I discover, is a born fighter, never happier than when knocking the spots off of circumstances. Nothing can stop a violet when he decides to come up. So I promptly have transplanted three thousand of him—an army, really, to a little border, and am going on transplanting them until a neat clean border, eighteen inches wide, will run completely around the house. There are quite enough violets growing here for this project, there remains only the question of how long I can hold out at it . . . But it can go on all summer and until the leaves disappear again. It is fine monotonous work which keeps the hands very busy and the mind goes right on meditating about Henry James—I am doing a big essay about him for the *Kenyon Review*—or Eliot—an essay about his new book for *Partisan Review*—and I am getting very tough and thin and healthy with all the work in the fine moist spring air . . .

I was really living for this season and now it is here, and I am making the most of it.

The war news is really prodigious, it could hardly be more encouraging. I wish things were going half as well at home. There is nothing wrong with the fighting men, the Army, the Navy, the Marines and the Air Corps are all doing just as we expected: its the politicians I don't like . . . But if I got into that, this letter would never end. The American people are all right, too, once they get it through their careless heads that this is real . . . Its just those politicians. . . .

Your poem, in satire on the methods of some you have been reading, and which made sense after all, as you say, was not, it seems to me as true as your dream . . . this is not a time of revolution and progress, remember, but of the direct reaction. There is alas no hope at all, I am afraid, on any further "breaking down of class differences," for a long time to come. There is an awful lot of talk about *Jeffersonian Democracy* going the rounds, but I happen really to be an active, practising, Jeffersonian Democrat—you know, it is a real system, which extends from international affairs down to your relation with your nearest neighbor: and I am not fooled by any of it. Practise and not theory was Jefferson's idea: now his idea is used as a mask by those in power to disguise their real intentions towards the people . . . I only hope the real Democrats will get into action in time to save the remnants of what we are fighting for . . . But back to the poem, you must keep in mind that the use of symbols to express thought is a great tradition, it is perfectly all right to say a thing obliquely, or in symbols, but the symbols should be commonly understood, and the poet must make it clear he is speaking in symbols . . . But then, if you read my work you should know where I stand without any doubt: clarity and precision and more clarity and precision . . . Say the most complicated thing you know in the simplest language—it still won't be easy . . .

Darling, I must stop now and get to work, firmly . . . The rain sogs on and on: you suffer from dust and grit, here things will get mildew if this goes on . . . But there will be good weather, and meantime, I am going to have another cup of chicory with a little coffee in it, and turn out pages of essay today. With my love, my dear, as you very well know

Aunt Katherine Anne

. . . . My dear I must mention something so silly and comic you would like it. There is a woodpecker who comes every day and tries, for half an hour at a time, to drill a hole in my metal roof. Always in the same spot, always seriously and at top speed. If there were bird psychiatrists, he should certainly be sent to one . . .

TO ELIZABETH AMES   South Hill
R.D.3
Ballston Spa, New York
May 29, 1943

Elizabeth darling:

Shannon got out at last, running the state police blockade with only a post card from me saying Bring Food, Bring The Champ, and heroically he did both. The Champ now stands in the front yard, daring me to come on. I back it in and out and back again around the trees and postbox a few times every day; the only thing I regret is not being able to leave it until the last day of school as I meant to, but this situation which is really not so bad at the moment, could well grow very bad in a little while if I am not able to drive myself about when we are once more allowed to run our little errands . . .

For the last two days I have been trying to do a quick job for the *Nation* which they asked for in a hurry, 1500 words about Laurence Sterne . . . it must be a quick job because I shall need the money and have no time really for it, but it must be as good a job too as I am able to make, so a good deal of midnight electricity has been burned, as well as quantities of fine free daylight.

I think it was Rilke, wasn't it, who wrote to some one that there comes a time in the world's grief and disorder when there is no consolation to be found even in nature which goes on being so lavish and beautiful and indifferent to human evil and suffering. These are not his words but mine, but he mentioned it as a discovery during the last war, and I discover it again in this one. Everything has bloomed in a procession, first the swamp was full of cowslips, and then the sturdy fighting violets battled their way up through the mould, and they go on, the grass has been violet dotted for two weeks . . . I picked them by the hundred and transplanted hundreds if not thousands into borders . . . Then the house was full of apple blossom branches, and now lilac, white and purple, and sweet honey smelling blooms are coming out on little stray trees whose names I do not know: and this morning I found five budding flags, and a clump or two of narcissus gone wild among the knotted grasses have just the same brought out a few perfect big blooms . . . I found a tame strawberry patch and cleared it. I found horse radish all over the place and gathered it up and put it together in one cleared spot, and asparagus is scattered about, two feet tall before I discovered it, but the tips are good. I marked each root with a tall stick and a stone beside it, so I can find it early next spring for transplanting. Rhubarb showed up in giant size back of where the barn was, and it is delicious simmered in honey . . . I fight bordock with butcher knife and hoe, not one shall come to seed this year if I can lay hands on it, and I can . . . But I think the dandelions win the campaign this spring, they were the lesser evil as compared with bordock, next spring I shall take a turn at getting rid of them. This time I merely gathered about a bushel of the flowers and started a huge crock of dandelion wine . . . There will be wild strawberries for jam, wild cherries for cherry bounce and jelly, bushels of apples in the fall: I have loved all this all my life, it has always delighted me, and oh, my hopes of a good country life at last. What became of them? What has become of every thing? Death sits on every doorstep now in one or another of his many

shapes, and spring gives me among millions of others a heavy heart
. . . This house should have people living in it, it is wrong for me
to be here so utterly alone, but who is there to come here? And
these fields could feed any number of people if only there was some
way of retrieving them.

Your remark about the British war film and the American
flops: next Sunday in the *Herald Tribune* I have a short review of
the Brenner-Leighton book on Mexico, in which I take occasion for
a little side-swipe at the high-powered Hollywood aspects of this
war as photographed by such fakes as Zanuck et al—they still seem
to think this war was put on to give them a chance to make trick
shots with plenty of atmosphere . . . I mentioned MGM but Zanuck
and Warner Brothers are the worse offenders . . . They are cheap
and nasty bastards, they have made a cheap and shoddy thing of the
moving pictures in this country, and they have no business whatever touching this war from any angle . . . They slime over everything they touch with their own natural beastliness, and they make
any decent person sick at the stomach more than ever . . . I suppose
however, he and his like will be sent to England or the war fronts
. . . If they could get scenarists like Leonard and give them their
heads, and real photographers like Walker Evans and Paul Strand
and a dozen others, the pictured record of this war might be somewhere near worthy of it . . . but no hope, no hope at all . . . The
Bitch Goddess Hollywood rides this country Roman, as the cow-
boys say . . .

I don't apologize for my strong language: if I could, I would
use stronger. . . .

As to Carson and Rebecca, from a realistic point of view it is
just as well they were brought back this year, or they might have
thought I had something to do with keeping them away. They
should know better, but likely they wouldn't . . . You know well,
Elizabeth, I do not begrudge them Yaddo and all the good they can
have there, even if I had been consulted I would have voted for
them, not because I think their work is good, I don't—I think it is
worthless—but because I see no point at all in adding anything to
the miseries and confusions of this world; and my personal feeling
about them is very simple: so long as they do not get near enough
to me to behave as they so barbarously do to me, (for God knows
what mysterious reasons, for I never harmed either of them, and

asked only not to be bedevilled by them—) I cannot care what they do or where they are. I think—and this opinion was formed on a first reading of Carson's first book long before I ever saw her or any one who knew her—that it was a peculiarly corrupt, perverted mind, a small stunted talent incapable of growth: and her further work has borne this out in my mind . . . It is a bad school; nothing good can ever come of it. But this is my opinion as a professional writer with a definite point of view, and I give it freely as those who admire her work give theirs. We all have the right to speak . . . And this is not personal. It dates from far back: from Louisiana days . . . I realize that she works an appealing personality and her youth and misfortunes to the hilt, and she is getting away with it in great shape . . . So, as Al Capone used to say, "Its all right if you can get away with it." I think youth and misfortune should be helped on purely human grounds: but its no good getting literature mixed up in the business . . . That has been my only regret in the matter. There must be splendid young writers who need help worse than she does: she has had a Guggenheim and a National Arts and Letters prize, she has a home to go to, and she is a rotten writer . . . Its a bad combination.

Well, I hope that question is cleaned up on once for all . . . I am going to try to get in before the 7th, no doubt hunger will drive me, but first, three little manuscripts must hit the mails . . . and speaking of mails, today is Saturday and I don't know if Monday is a Post Holiday, as well as a general one for others, but this letter will lie in the box a good while; in time though it will reach you, with my devoted love and my thoughts really all the time, Elizabeth, about you and Margery, and the long days there for you both . . . To think that when we are young—we look forward to some kind of fruition, a field of repose and quiet, some gathering of strength, some harvest for the long effort we make: so at least I did. What an illusion. The road is uphill all the way, isn't it? But no one ever tells you that when you are young, and perhaps it is just as well.

With my love,
Katherine Anne

To Paul Porter   South Hill
                                   R.D.3
                                   Ballston Spa, New York
                                   July 20, 1943

Paul darling:

I meant to answer your letter, your last, to me so important
one, a good while ago. But I have been swamped in a kind of quiet
nightmare of too much work, too much distraction, too many other
little (that is the worst of them) things that must be done, which is
where the distraction comes in of course: and every day I would
think that now or very soon, I would be at a point of quiet and
enough leisure to write you as I would like. It doesn't come: so let
this be, not an answer, but just a word to say that I do know, very
well and very deeply, just what is happening to you, just why your
state of mind is what it is . . . It may seem like a very brutal paradox,
perhaps it is in one way, but only on the surface, for me to say, I
am glad you feel the way you do, given exactly what is happening
to you, your special experience: if you felt otherwise, my dear, or
worse, did not feel or think at all, what a wretched thing that would
be for you, and for me, too. For I have rather got in the way of
depending upon your instincts to be "right" in exactly our sense,
and for your mind to be of a certain cast, and for you to be affected
in certain ways by certain experiences. I could not be surprised then
that the Detroit disgrace struck you so hard as it did: it struck me
almost as hard, at this late day, when you might think I had had so
many shocks of that kind I would be a little calloused, if only in
self-defense. And then, that episode had, as things of the kind will
have, an effect reaching far out beyond its immediate territories.
We can't have had many illusions by now about the actual attitude
of the great majority in this country towards the Negro: towards
any unfortunate minority, but towards the Negro doubly—but also,
such a crisis as this "smokes out" the deep and hidden feelings of
people around us whom we had never suspected of any such thing:
it gets between us and even our friends, or at least, individuals we
had liked and trusted, up to a point. But there is one thing left to
learn, a point for you to work towards: as before, when you were
full of faith and confidence in the goodness of everybody and

everything—this exaggerates, of course: you had already got some distance from that before you went in the army—you were illusioned, for of course the evils were there, had been there since the beginning of man's history, *and always more or less* the same kind of evils, based on the same impulses in the human heart, now you are illusioned again, in the shock of your new discoveries if you fall into the error of feeling that all and every one is evil. You are in a very bad place to learn anything much about the humanities, and at the very time of your life when you could best have learned about them; and you have the natural instincts and the mind to understand them. But they still do exist; as you were a little consoled to see those pictures of the sailors and soldiers who helped the Negroes and tried to protect them, remember too that they were sent there for that purpose: they were under orders, and that from superior officers and from the government: so there is a definite power in our country that can and will, at such crises, not allow the weak and helpless to be always and altogether crushed. I know and you know there is not enough of this power, it does not get into action either quickly enough or effectively enough, and that is because it has so much opposition to overcome *within the government itself:* yet the soldiers did go, and they did help to protect the Negroes and stop the attacks on them. . . .

Dear Paul, there is so much to be said, above all, so much to be *known,* it can hardly be touched in a letter. I wish I could talk to you, if only to tell you what I learned a good while ago, at first hand, in Mexico, in Europe, all the years I watched this present situation gathering itself, all the forces slowly getting under way, in every country in the world . . . And absolutely *everything* was a symptom, some of them so small it was hard to make people see why they were important, why they did belong to the great pattern of destruction that was being so terribly formed . . . I wish first that you might have had a different sort of work, something that would have really used your mind and your capacities, even in the army. But that is not what an army is for, not what a war is about. The individual is lost, and wasted as individual. If you seem useful where you are, that is where you will stay. The point is, not to let it destroy you. It all seems a trial rather beyond your years and all outside of what you were really intended for, and to me this of course is the immense wrong and waste and catastrophe of the whole business. Every talented, gifted, valuable man I know is in the army, and most of them are privates or non-coms doing the heavy work, as nearly completely reduced to machines as they can be, silenced and under the same conditions as you. And if we were to be overheard saying what we think of this, I suppose it would be called by a very ugly name. That the name would be a lie is of no importance. It is terrible and strange to me now to remember how I have loved this country and what hopes I have had for us as a people: and now I have a horror of the way I see it going . . . There is no doubt at all that the Allied Nations will win this war, and any American who did not wish this, and who would not help in it with the best he has, would be a madman, simply. It is not losing the war I fear. My fear is that the very thing we are fighting in Europe is seeping up here among us like a kind of miasma out of the very earth under our feet . . . Winning the war with bombs and tanks and armies is easy beside the long war every human being that was brought up a free man must fight perhaps for the next half dozen centuries . . . There never was such a concerted assault on human liberty as we see now, since the first idea of human liberty was ever fought for. And our worst enemies are here at home, most dangerous because you can't walk over them with an army.

But then you know all this by now: you most certainly had a good notion of it, years ago, when you were sixteen and in high school. I remember the things you said, even if you have forgotten them, maybe. You were very well grounded then in ethical and humane ideas, anything learned so early cannot be stamped out, you know. Because I love you very dearly, I could wish you had not to suffer. But that is only the natural feeling of all the older generation towards its own young ones; and in turn we all must live as we can, and life is in no case easy or free from suffering, much keener and more bitter if we are really capable of thinking and feeling, if we really are aware of what happens around us, and within us. Your education has simply begun, in the toughest kind of school, but you are going to find all of it of the most immense value to you. Believe me, I am not taking your shocks lightly, or just saying the easy thing. It is just a truth of the most bedrock variety. Know your world, and your time, my dear. Try to keep your head clear.

And that brings me right to my usual paragraph of Aunt K.A.

good advice. Yes sir, stop drinking instantly until you get your nerves under control. Nothing on earth can so knock out a sensitive nervous system as too much alcohol. I hope to hear that you kept your resolution nobly—or anyway you could manage—and that you found—I am not expounding theory, I am talking about something I know—that no matter how hard a situation is, nothing is actually unbearable if you have steady nerves, have eaten properly and got enough sleep. Just set yourself to that as a positive regime. If you are got up at all hours, all the more important to sleep when you can; Darling, I'm trying to say, take care of yourself. You can do it, somehow, and must. Or the future won't be in the least what you would like it to be . . . I think you are very right to discipline yourself as severely as you please in the little matter of losing all that money. But I don't care to add to your woes, and it is a very sad thing to me that I can't just send you a little check for the difference. I know you wouldn't want it, wouldn't expect it, it might even not be "good" for you, but that doesn't, any of it, make much difference to me. Well, I learned once that there aint no such thing as a *friendly* poker game, and nobody gets me into anything more serious than penny ante—five cent limit now. But one has to earn the privilege of being such a sissy by growing much older and being able to do something else so well you can make your own rules. Don't gamble, darling, until you can afford it . . . You are, so far as I know anything about this world, and you do know I get around, rather—in as tough a spot as you could well be, morally and in a good many other ways; I wish I could help, I mean actually and materially and presently. But I can only help by waiting, and watching, and depending upon your own heart and mind, which I believe in thoroughly, to make something recognizably intelligent and full of form and meaning out of the materials of your life and experience as you go along: for this is your life for the present, this very year and minute: shortly it will be the past, and I want you to have solid ground under your feet when you come to look back on your past. And Oh, Paul, isn't your birthday about here? Don't tell me it is gone? Let me know. What would you like? If you don't answer this question I am apt to send you handkerchiefs, merely because you said once you could use them. Would you like a book of Vincent van Gogh? Or Degas? The new Hyperion and Phaidon Presses have a color photograph reproduction which I don't care for so much as the old method, and there are not enough in color, for me, but these two books do exist and I can send either. Let me know. They are certainly better than nothing!

Well, my dear nephew, my very favorite relative, this turns out to be a sort of letter after all. Still not the one I hoped to write, but there is too much to say always. Here a Polish Russian family is cutting the hay in my meadows, they have carted off eight big loads, sitting up like birds in a nest. I am well, but harried, as a literary woman must always be.

With all my devoted love
Aunt Katherine Anne

To Paul Porter

South Hill
R.D.3
Ballston Spa, New York
August 1, 1943

Dear Paul:

The Eliot poems got away today, and no doubt some time or other the essay and perhaps even an article or two will follow. There are some good critical explanations being given, and you may need them for a second reading. This is just a note to answer some of the questions about my own work.

First, my book of short stories has been in the publisher's hands now for more than a year, he could have published it at any time, but wanted to wait for the novel. Thought it better business—after all, publishing is his business, not mine—to have it in that order. And the novel was so long in getting finished, I don't know now if they are going to be able to publish it this year, after all the announcing. They have been announcing it in the catalogue for two years . . .

My James essay is gone to *Kenyon Review,* will appear in the James 100th birthday number in September . . . The Eliot is gone, and is featured in the *Partisan Review* for September also. I will send you copies the day mine arrive, so don't think you will ever be allowed to miss them. I am sending now a copy of *The Nation* with my review of a book on Laurence Sterne. And when my next books come along as they do you will be sent copies. So, at ease.

Ah dear, how pleasant it would be to a writer if only he could know that after years of neglect and evil criticism during his life time, and all sorts of complete misunderstanding of what he was trying to do, he would find his hundredth birthday being celebrated the whole year long by other writers, whole books of real praise, but good critical analysis, too, the kind of thing he would like . . . If that should happen to me—though I haven't been neglected, on the contrary—*you* will know, though I never shall. You will be a venerable author (or painter) of sixty nine or something yourself by then, but still, you should still be around . . . So maybe you can help celebrate. And if no one else does anything, why, you can celebrate by yourself . . .

I have been leading a strictly non-literary career today, helping my Polish neighbors give their dogs worm medicine, feeding Lily orange juice and chicken soup—she is in bed with a high fever— (lungs) baking bread, pulling weeds, transplanting irises, and in general being domestic, which I really don't much care for, never did, never will, but there is not a human being of any size or shape for miles around to call upon. Everybody is getting in what crops they can without machinery, without help, and no way to get them to market anyway. There are only four male humans on this road, one old fellow of seventy, a young man half-invalid, unable to work, a man of fifty who runs a farm with one hand and works in a munitions factory with the other, and a little boy of eleven . . . The army or the factories have all the rest . . . All the women, too. So, what is done I must do; the house is very pleasant and shiny and nice, but the landscape is going rapidly back to jungle. Its a beautiful farm, too, very fertile and good in every way; well wa- tered, rolling land, woods, good fields: no, this is not an advertise- ment, I am not trying to sell it to you. But farming will have to wait on literature, just this once . . .

"Mood" is a perfectly good word, my dear: not "arty" at all. It has a real meaning, and nothing else can take its place. Perfectly good words can, if we don't mind, be spoiled for us by careless or wrong usage. Be respectful of words. They mean something.

I thought your piece—the one you sent—had been too badly tampered with for me to tell much about your intention. But it lacked altogether the tone of your letters, as if you were trying to "write down" and I suppose you might have to, but if you must, then don't write for that paper . . . It won't help you to learn to write at all, and if you cannot write sincerely and seriously and say what you really mean, it is much better not to waste yourself. Instead, you should keep notes (under lock and key, God knows) and try, when you write, to get to the very bottom of your feelings and thoughts and as well as you can, say what happens in your mind—your deepest mind, not just the surface . . . You haven't got the touch for the kind of thing you would have to do to be acceptable to that paper, apparently, so, I should think, best lay off. And darling, after that pome you sent me, never leave me hear another squeak out of you about the "obscure" poets. I get the idea, y'un-nerstan, but my, what curlicues. . . .

> Love again.
> *Aunt Katherine Anne*

To Paul Porter   South Hill
                                        R.D. 3
                                        Ballston Spa
                                        August 28, 1943

Dearest Paul:

. . . . I wouldn't think Mr. Eliot would stand a chance in your present flurry. Don't think of him. He'll keep. You did give a very fine criticism of his method, though . . . It is just that innocent sweetly simple air of his, the use of all those plain words, one after another, with such deep implications and echoes and associations, that do finally assault the mind very subtly. He's a good poet, though. He is really saying something, even if you can't sympathize with his reasons, or altogether understand his feelings . . . I think he is a very despairing man who has tried all his life to believe in something and has found it impossible, and he suffers from dryness of heart and lack of faith . . . But he has made good poetry out of these lacks and limitations . . . The greatest art comes out of warmth and conviction and deep feeling, but then, very few people, even geniuses, have all that.

I must stop. This was meant to be a line chiefly to tell you I will be on the radio Sunday Morning, 11:30 to 12 noon, Eastern War time, Station Wabc, Columbia Broadcasting System, "Invitation to Learning," and we are going to talk about Laurence Sterne, his *Tristram Shandy* and *Sentimental Journey.* You have the *Nation* piece I sent you by now, I suppose. It was that piece that caused them to ask me to be on this program. You might just happen to have the moment and the luck to get that station. Its nothing, except you will hear your learned Aunt discoursing in her slaphappy style, and if I thought you were listening it is just a pleasant kind of communication, even if a bit one-sided. I would like it if you could tune in too . . .

> With my love
> *Aunt Katherine Anne*

To Barbara Wescott   Harbor Hill
                        Cold Spring, New York
                        December 24, 1943

Barbara darling:

. . . . Your new adventure with Black Markets, Jim Crow and all, does make the old Europe seem amateurish in its criminal activities. But you can imagine *why* I get so agitated and protest so much against so much, because I have seen so much *near to*—have been in the middle of the most appalling kind of evils that it seemed to me most people took for granted. Almost everything in our society at a certain level is corrupt and wrong, old in corruption and wrong, and Black Market and Jim Crow are just terrible symptoms! Everything is on such a huge *scale* here!

Christmas Eve. I've been listening on the radio to war news and carols alternately. In bed still, but certainly on the way out now. Doctor gave me one of the sulfas and broke up whatever kind of flu it was this time. Good health to the three of you, I hope you have found sun and warmth and ease and freedom—

> With my same love
> *Katherine Anne*

To Glenway Wescott   Harbor Hill
                       Cold Spring, New York
                       December 27, 1943

Dear Glenway:

Forster decided, you remember, that life is a game of piquet.
You see mine, at a certain distance, as a bramble bush. My notion
is to combine the two and say that Life is a game of piquet played
in a bramble bush in very bad weather . . .

The American Indians, certain tribes of them, had a habit of
staking their war captives out over a red-ant bed, and leaving them
in the hot sun until their bones were picked bare. It used to seem
to me at times that Life (always with a capital L, mind you,) was
rather like that. Now let's make another combination. Suppose Life
is a man fastened over a red-ant bed, in a bramble bush, having to
keep a cool head and play piquet with his captor who will set the
man free if he, the man, wins. I forgot to mention the weather,
which must always be bad on these hypothetical occasions. You see
how we could go on from terror to horror to catastrophe.

Luckily for us, Life is not like any of these things at present,
or so I hope. Let me speak only for myself. I have had influenza,
for the first time in four years. That infinitely resourceful plague
manages to think up a new one now and again, and keeps one jump
ahead of the doctors. But this time I took one of the sulfas, and I
was in bed ten days yesterday. This morning I got up deliberately
just after breakfast, found it could be done; I am dressed very
prettily with my hair in a curl or two, and this time last week seems
now like an unpleasant dream. I shall write a few notes and lie down
again, but the illness is over, I feel certain. I am a little pale, and
my face has a new expression which I cannot quite make out.
Distinctly remote, disengaged, full of mental reservations. No
doubt I shall find out what these are before long.

You know, my dear, sometimes I think you believe me to be
one of those appalling people full of illusions who get badly ruffled
up because nothing is quite perfect. But this may be a feverish
notion of my own. I am not restless, but on the contrary have the
same kind of abstracted patience I always had, as to surroundings,
people, everyday life, and all that, but my nervous system is, has

always been, shaky and hard to keep in balance. Yet I trust myself very well, and even this nervous system, for it has had some fine solid tests and strains and doesn't, I find, get any worse, which I think is important. This fall and this winter to come are a great improvement over the last, to put it mildly, as to work, as to health, as to state of mind. My reason for thinking of leaving here were simple: we had agreed on a date, the first of January, for the finishing up of the novel. It is not finished, so I have not kept my part of the agreement. I think that is quite enough to make me very uneasy, and it has so made me. I am sure that my reasons for not finishing are entirely human, no doubt natural, perhaps acceptable as excuse, but I don't like them just the same and I don't like excuses. It is also quite horrible to me to find myself in a situation where I must be regarded with various kinds of dismay by my dearest friends. Really it is not so bad as all that, and it is very unbecoming to me, and a fearful piece of tactlessness on my part, to arrive at the role of Problem at this stage of my journey. But damn it the fact remains that I have muffed on the grand scale the whole material question of living, and to set this straight is going to be my whole concern as soon as the last pages of this book are off . . . I have simply not had the force I needed if I was to do everything I expected of myself. But don't worry about me, don't pity me. No matter what might happen, I merit better than that. I believe I shall get the work I have planned, done, even yet. My mind is a good sound lasting instrument and it lives a life of its own, very independent of time, bodily change; there are some fears in me, but not in that place where I truly live. But that it has stood a long siege I will admit. You know that every force of instinct, and every psychic evil in us fights the mind as its mortal enemy, but in this as in everything else I have known from the beginning which side I am on, and I am perfectly willing—indeed, I can't do otherwise—to abide by my first choice to death. For death it must be in the end, so far as the flesh is concerned, but what lives on afterward can be honorable. Even now I have lived to see almost everything I hoped for come to ruin, and everything I have believed in and fought for become matter for contempt, but that in no way at all touches the heart of my belief and my hope.

It is too like me to get up out of bed in a sweat of mortal weakness and begin trying to make clear a whole view of life which is completely inexplicable even to me who live it because its truth or falseness cannot be known until the end; if I do hold firmly, and do my work, and not fail in what I know, why then, we'll see. And meantime I shall lie down again, and go on with the fantastic row of apothecary's powders, pills and potions all of them in the most poisonously brilliant colors, amethyst and sapphire and emerald and London Purple, each with its own mission of soothing, or elevating the spirits, calming the heart or stimulating it, loosening the phlegm and tightening the nerves, stopping the cough and lowering the fever. I plough through them faithfully, and as for the sulfa, I had to take a tablet every four hours for two nights and two days, and never once did my mind fail to wake me at the right hour, on the hour like a little radio station. Once I slept stubbornly, had to be waked by a sharp rapping at my door. It was four in the morning the whole house asleep and quiet. I sat up knowing instantly Who had done it.

Thank you for your dear letter. I hope Barbara and Lloyd and Deborah got off safely. Barbara is enchanting about her baby, but then, about everything for that matter.

Love
Katherine Anne

I know of nowhere to go that I would not take all my cares with me, so I stay here—

To Andrew Lytle   Harbour Hill
Cold Spring, New York
January 14, 1944

Dear Andrew:

. . . . It seems to me your sense of honor has been invoked and exploited in a very hard bargain. Turkeys are very delicate difficult things to raise—I know, I have raised them in small quantities—they need immense care at first, you must have been put to great expense in equipment and housing etc . . . of course, I suppose you will be paid well for them, I hope to God this is so at least, but what is the penalty if you don't produce an even grand of turkeys? Will your lights be taken away? You can see how this has really seized my attention, I'd love to have any further little bits of information you can give . . . Questions of honor aside, you can't make turkeys live by contract. They have rules of their own for that.

Back to the other troubles of people in our time trying to work in an art; to begin with, nobody respects the work of an artist; people resent very much his needing any time to do his work. There is not much money in it, at first any way, and the idea that it should be treated as a profession at least, with a place to work and hours during which one shouldn't be disturbed, is very upsetting to the kind of people who would never dream of disturbing a life insurance salesman while he was getting up his accounts . . . Again, I think there is a great deal of resentment based on the fact that a man working in the arts, is supposed to be enjoying himself—he is one of the few persons in the world doing something he really likes and wants to do, so the notion that he should be paid for this use of his time is outrageous, to say the least. It is almost plain thievery for a man to take money for enjoying himself . . . as for myself, I have done all my work on the margin that was left after I did housework, cooking, jobs to get money to pay my expenses, my part of them if I were married, that is: for I have never been taken care of for a day in my life since I left my father's house. I have not only paid my own way, but I have, in marriage, always to carry the double load of making money and doing all the work—I have never cut from any relationship until the burden grew so intolerable I simply could not support it any longer . . . I have in my life time lent over two thousand dollars to various aquaintances. And not a dollar have I ever got back, or even an acknowledgement of the loan. But I am paying back every dollar I ever borrowed . . . I tell you these things Andrew, because I think it is time to break up the legend that I was skipped through life as irresponsible as a deer, all luck and lightness. Nothing could be farther from the truth, and I often wonder how any body could read even one of my stories and not know that it could never have been written by an irresponsible or frivolous person. I do not complain in the least, I understood from the beginning that I was not choosing an easy life, I expected even worse difficulties than I have had, and believe me, I think my life was worth everything it has cost me. If I could go over it again, I would take the same road.

I suppose these things are a little on my mind for out of Washington lately came rumors of the foulest and most irresponsible slanders and nasty stories about me, from that center of infection we both know too well, and suddenly—for it is nothing new to me that I am slandered, and not only by that particular set—I have lost patience, and decided not to keep silent any longer . . . I think we are all guilty of criminal collusion in any case, to allow, as we do, such tongues to run on so foully, unrebuked . . .

Still, take my letter as good omen for your year; for you know I am a good friend, perhaps have never said so, maybe will not say so again, for it is not the custom to say such things. Any wickedness would seem natural, but good words are suspect, as you know. Still, I am your friend, and I wish you well with all my heart. And oh, how I do hope to see *The Voice of The Turkle* very soon . . .

I remember very well in Texas the country people always said turkle and turkle dove . . .

Andrew, the more one has in mind a certain kind of thing, the more difficult it is sometime to free even half an arm for it . . . Naturally everything and everybody in the world come first. And there are some engagements that no one wishes to renege on, one doesn't live in a moral or emotional vacuum . . . I think sometimes the only trouble is with the artist himself. He doesn't believe enough in what he is doing to demand, and to take, the time and energy for it that he needs; such time and energy as would be granted without question to a man in any other calling. Its our fault in the long run, my dear, if we cannot make ourselves and our callings respected a little, at least as much as if we were in the second hand clothing business, let's say . . .

Let me hear from you. With my same old affection . . .

Katherine Anne

To Barbara Wescott   Harbor Hill
                         Cold Spring, New York
                         January 19, 1944

Barbara darling:

Things have been winding up here in rather a huzzah and hullabaloo, for half my energies are usually devoted to consideration of ways and means and what and the hell does the future hold, if there is a future? The novel is finished EXCEPT for a nasty tough little spot in the exact middle of the Captain's party, which I am going to write in the next time I catch my breath and a few evenings. Otherwise, I do think the time here has been most remarkably well spent, if writing the book was the point, and it was . . .

But promptly with the New Year came the annual flutter of offerings of jobs—last year it was teaching—three almost at once this time, and just this minute I have sent the telegram which settles the question. I was two days ago offered a fellowship in the Library of Congress, tenure of seven months, salary three thousand, work of a sketchy research nature. I am leaving here on the morning of the twenty fourth, to get settled a little by the first of February. My other two offers were less promising: Mrs. Barnes has a magazine called *Common Sense,* I don't know why, because its editor seems to be a kind of America Firster: she seemed to want me to do editing, in a literary way, but it all grew so vague I finally refused to go up even for a meeting to discuss matters. Chiefly afraid of their politics. I dislike American Fascists even more than I do the European kind . . . Then Henry Allen Moe asked me if I would go to lecture on American literature for three months in the University of Mexico, to begin March 1 . . . This seemed much better. But the appointment seems to come from somewhere behind scenes, all my efforts have not sufficed to disclose whodunit, what I am really expected to do, what I should be paid, or anything. They just keep on saying they (whoever They are) want me to go to the University of Mexico to lecture, etc . . . So I just wrote and resigned from all that, and took Mr. Macleish's (is that spelled right?) job and am off, God help me, poor woman.

Truth is, my heart sank at the prospect of writing about other peoples' books. And Mexico is so much a matter of the past, and I do not want any of the past back, or to go where It is recalled to me. I never lived in Washington, it will be new, I never had a fellowship in the Library of Congress, and I shan't have to write a line of anything except my own work. So I am very gay at the way things have turned out . . .

I don't know if you are at home again, but the two weeks you spoke about must be up. I almost hope you have decided to stay on a while, and I'd love to think of you and Lloyd and Deborah still basking in each other's exclusive society. Darling do let me know how you are; and if this reaches you late, after the 24th better address me at Washington. More later when I am slightly more coherent. All my love

Katherine Anne

K.A.P. Reference Department Library of Congress, Washington D.C. Until I know where I shall find a room.

To Paul Porter   The Library of Congress
                          Washington 25, D.C.
                          March 27, 1944

Dear Paul:

    . . . . Everybody talks his or her head off, free speech our proudest liberty is still going strong here, at least. But when you think it over, it was all just personal opinion, nobody gives anything away. They criticise and wrangle and complain, but just about bureaucracy, which is safe enough . . . Of course, there are little hotbeds of mischief makers, fake refugees, Vichy French, royalty from "neutral" countries, and so on, but the government knows who they are and where they are, one hopes it is safer to keep them here where they can be watched . . . The very thing about people that makes the human race interesting is also the thing that makes it so hard to get anything done without the most horrible confusions: no two people think exactly the same way about anything, and very few people are capable of faithfulness to a love or an idea, and everybody in the long run loves himself the best of all. And there is a natural Judas sleeps in the heart of too many. Every kind is here, and they are all trying to get a little foothold of power some way . . .

. . . . The other day I spent hours in the National Gallery here, looking at a very fine collection of paintings from all over the world, all ages, beautifully hung and lighted, and really, you were at my elbow all the way. I wanted you to see them, I have seen so many and now it is your turn.

With my same love,
Katherine Anne

To Barbara Wescott   3106 "P" Street, N.W.
Washington, D.C.
July 23, 1944

Barbara darling:

. . . . Well, I never forget you for a moment, because you just live along in my mind as being, my feelings don't, can't vary, it would be monotonous if you knew how steady and how fidèle I am without even trying, or even knowing I am until I am suddenly startled into knowing by your letter. My winter was a strange kind of nightmare of illness and fever and struggle to keep on my feet, I got caught in that plague and simply couldn't get out again, and my mind grew very disturbed of course, and I did have morbid notions that I was probably going to die and have to leave my little projects all dangling; and really, no amount of reasoning, or sense of absolute proportion, could overcome in me the feeling that what I have been trying to do has some kind of importance, however minute: and that my life does count a little, and I must account for it in the end. Truth was, it was pure physical infection, a germ, then sulfa twice, and afterward a little abscess that had to be treated with shots in the arms, and so on, *such* a bore, and really, I had a kind of shame at all my weakness. . . .

I have a charming and gifted young man very much in love with me, and you know that is a kind of illumination. He is too young for me, of course, they always are, always will be, no doubt: but you will be glad to hear that, after long time and far overdue, I have arrived at years of discretion in this matter, so never fear I shall do anything foolish. I am running the show this time, and it is plain that everybody will have a better time that way.

O I wish I could come to see you, and maybe I can. I couldn't adore Debo more than I do, but it has been sad for me not to see her grow. I think my book of short stories will be out about September 7, that is the date they aim for, and my publisher wants me to come to New York for that occasion. That doesn't appeal to me much, but the chance to see you does, and it will bring me that near. Would sometime around that date be good for you?

Next day: Went down last night and was interviewed on the radio by a funny little boy who asked the silliest questions. Today Robert Penn Warren arrives to take up the Chair of Poetry lately vacated by Allen Tate, and there is going to be a long lunch at a long table in a very plushy office for him, with no drinks and food brought in from the Senate Cafeteria. Dull food, need I say? and me so partial to my vittles.

The heat has set in again, and it is all that was threatened, but I just remember how it was in New Orleans, to say nothing of San Antonio, Texas, and this begins to seem quite natural, just summer again, you might say. And I prefer summer on any terms to the best sort of winter.

Last evening I went out to the Shoreham to sit on the terrace with some cousins of mine who are in the army—he was a military attaché in London all the years of the bombings-out—and was neck deep in people named Bowes-Lyons and Lascelles, and the Latvian minister whose wife is a Polish princess, and American generals, and they all talked and talked about what they want after the war, and it was strange to see how little they are concerned with saving what they had. All, except the American generals, have lost or expect to give up shortly their goods and estates, and the women don't exactly know where their clothes are, (this includes my cousin Helen, who just dumped her household gear into storage in London and is rapidly and cheerfully forgetting it) and genuinely it was pleasantly surprising to see them all so calm and detached and abstracted from things. But they are all dead tired and worn to the bone, and they have a deep interest in food. They eat as if they were catching up on something . . . The Latvian and the Pole, his wife, however, were very firm about not wanting Russia on their necks any more than they want the Germans. And the British were firm about their policy in India. And the American generals were very firm about private property and the ideals of democracy, and so I thought, maybe when the devil is sick, the devil a saint would be . . . Let's wait and see how they feel when this is over . . .

Angel, I do so want to see you, and so, please let me know if I can come up sometime during the book coming-out. Your letter was lovely, and if I had some self-accusing feelings about the novel, it is not because I think you require or expect anything of me but what I can do, or will be able to do in time, but because I was disappointed and wretched about all the delay and strange baffle-ments of that long illness, and did almost despair. But I think I am tough, really, and will manage to stay on for the finish of what I have planned, and your book is going to be as good as I am able to make it, and it will be a whole book, even yet.

> With my same love,
> *Katherine Anne*

To Glenway Wescott   3106 "P" Street, N.W.
                         Washington, D.C.
                         August 27, 1944

Glenway darling:

"Ne tremble pas, carcasse!" Thank you and thank the Greek hero, and thank good Henri IVth for that motto. I add it to my little collection: "It doth make a difference whence cometh a man's joy." (St. Augustine.) "In my end is my beginning." (Mary Stuart.) "Take good heed, and look well to the ending, Be ye never so gay." (Everyman.) and, above all, "Ne tremble pas, carcasse."

Now then, with that final broadsword added to my other armor and harness, I should be well defended for all emergencies. The first three, of course, are just good solid maxims for the use of the artist. The last one is for his use in action.

It was for long the custom of the female carcass to give up one

tooth for each child. Then science rushed in and prescribed lime
and calcium for the pregnant diet, and teeth don't fall as they once
did. But who is to find the lime and calcium for our kind of gravid-
ity, if that's a word, and it should be?

Naturally I am excited about your review . . . No matter how
it looks, (to the public) I intend to do something about the C. of
W. [*Children of Wrath* as *Apartment in Athens* was then called] but
perhaps the right time will be when your preface to the new edition
of the *Grandmothers* comes out: I should like to see you re-issued
altogether [in a] uniform edition of The Works, but that I suppose
is too wild a hope for the present.

This is a G.I. typewriter and therefore doesn't really work.

I don't think Barbara is expecting me on the 5th now. I wrote
her about the changed dates, and how I couldn't leave here until
the 13th, and then the publisher is putting me up at a large public
caravanserai so the reporters if any can find me easily, for a few
days. So that brings us fairly on to the 18th or 19th, and God knows
what shall have happened by then to change her plans. My own are
fairly fixed—or maybe I should say, my hope which is to see her,
and you, for even a day, and longer if it could be managed. Your
jail birdies seem to think the war is over, don't they? This is a
reference to an old military joke: about the sergeant who kicked the
major and the private who kicked the sergeant, you remember—I
thought they were under a kind of parole and not free to dash away
when they choose. Red Warren has a Japanese servant from a
concentration camp, who is very good and faithful up to a point,
and then refuses to allow him guests more than so often, is pertina-
cious in demanding holidays and overtime, etc. So apparently we
are really not to have any more slaves, and a damned inconvenience
it is going to be, too.

Oh yes, I feel the sap rising slowly towards a general leafing
out again as to the novel, and I think I shall just go to Yaddo and
sit down to it once for all. This time, shall we run a race? And WHY
do I not see an advance copy or page proofs or something of
Children of Wrath? I am on edge with excitement about it.

I am sitting out the last few weeks here, mostly staying at
home and packing up very slowly, full of the happiest moods and
feeling very well indeed. I shall be alone in the house for the last
ten or twelve days, leaving here on the morning of the 13th. So

if you can, come between the second and that date. It will be lovely to see you.

> Your devoted
> *Katherine Anne*

TO PAUL PORTER

Yaddo
Saratoga Springs
October 22, 1944

Paul darling:

Perhaps I should begin this letter with a message of practical cheer; we are so given to disregarding the material aspects of life, that is to say, we often forget to mention them, it is time I dragged them in by the ears. And such ears, my child. Your book, my book, our book, [*The Leaning Tower and Other Stories*, dedicated to Corporal Harrison Paul Porter, Jr.] is selling—selling seriously and steadily. In four weeks your famously insolvent aunt has, without turning a finger, just sitting here at Yaddo immersed in politics and the coming election, has earned—and I do think it is earned, over a long period of work—more than six thousand dollars on that little tome. In four weeks. There might be another thousand piled up by now, but I simply don't inquire any further. One thing good about it besides it just being a good thing in itself, is this: publishers' royalties don't come due for six months, so I can't get my hands on it to squander it, (as if I would, never fear) and I must continue to live on what I have such as it is until late spring—April, to be precise. It sounds like the foundation of a little fortune to me, of course; the most money I ever saw in one slab was two thousand five hundred—for as I keep telling my students, when I talk about literature in the colleges—serious writing was never and is not now a get-rich-quick scheme—and I am sure I feel richer than Mr. Morganthau this minute. For the truth is, I have never felt poor. The difference is now, I feel solvent, which is quite another thing. I have no debts, either—not a nickel. So it is all clear except the income tax and that doesn't come up until way the end of next year . . . The income tax doesn't bother me because the more you pay the more you have left, strangely.

And did I tell you this? The Army and Navy printing project—I don't know its official name—is going to print one hundred thousand copies of a selection of my stories gathered from all three books. About January, for distribution to the forces overseas and to Army and Navy hospitals here. I made the selection last week and apparently it is on the way to press. The fee is small, she said largely, leaning back on that six grand, $500 as my half—other half to publisher—but ah, if they had only known, they could have got it for nothing, I would have been so glad to know that a hundred thousand copies of any book of mine was circulating. Luckily, nobody told them this, so I get half-a-cent a copy. This is yours, darling, to help you stay in France and go to the Sorbonne, or come home and do what you want here: a little starter, but there will be more. Tell me how you would like it. Have you got a bank account at home? If so, I can just deposit it to your name there. Or buy Treasury Bonds, or War Bonds or anything you like. Merry Christmas, my darling.

I send you a clipping, reprint from the *New Yorker.* I just think it makes pretty good sense . . . I belong to a very lively organization of liberal Democrats, National Citizens Political Action Committee, and am one of ten chairmen on the Womens Division; and I think you would approve of me if you could see me campaigning for Roosevelt—making speeches, raising money, harrying the voters to get out and register, ("Vote as you please," I say to them, "but *vote.*") telling them we aren't just voting for ourselves this time, but for all the soldiers who won't be able to this year, and for all the wretched voteless people of this terrible world. Well, this countryside happens to be a honeycomb of the loyal opposition, and I am helping to get up a big mass meeting (it was my idea. My being made a chairman seems to have aroused my latent sense of organization) the first Democratic demonstration ever held in this neck of the woods. We are going to have singing too—real singing by fine singers: records of marching songs and popular songs of all the Allied Nations, great full chorusses, with an amplifier. I have been helping to select these songs, and listening to them for the past two days has given me such a lift of the heart I feel almost happy for the first time, really, since the war began. They are all brave good songs with beautiful melodies: American, English, Greek, Chinese, Russian, Negro, Polish, Cheko-Slovakian, everything we have been able to get hold of. And a dozen people, men and women, young boys and girls, are going to speak about three minutes each . . . no long-winded ill-tempered wrangling, or name-calling. Just as clearly as we know how we are going to say what we mean by a democratic form of government and a democratic way of living . . . It will all be over by the time you read this, and we will know the best, or, by our lights, the worst. But there has been a great rather sudden swing of popular feeling here towards the President, and the Democrats are feeling pretty hopeful. Were you able to vote? The laws of some states make it quite impossible for the soldiers to vote, others make it possible. It is going to be very interesting to have the figures on the vote of the Armed Forces. I suppose they will be given after the election . . .

Well, I registered yesterday, and it turned out that I couldn't register in Saratoga Springs, but must go eight miles in the country where I pay taxes on the farm. Darling it was extraordinary. The registry took place in a large, prosperous red barn, simply bursting with grain and corn and smelling sweet as the weather itself. I slid back the big door and looked in, and there were half a dozen farmers in their best country work clothes, fine heavy windbreakers and good tough corduroys and boots and hunting caps with ear flaps, and checkerboard shirts, good healthy stout countrymen in middle-age, sitting around a table made of pine planks spread on sawbucks, a lighted lantern in the middle, for it was a dark day of pouring rain. They called me by name at once, which surprised me for I don't remember ever to have seen one of them before. And when I went to mark my choice and drop it in the box, one of the men said, "Miss Porter, I'm sorry to tell you you haven't paid your school tax yet." I said, "I'm sorry, but I haven't had a notice and I forget when it is due. Can I pay it now?" He said, "Not here, just stop at the white house on the right hand side of the road before you turn into your road, and pay there." I said, "I suppose you wouldn't let me vote if I didn't pay it?" He gave a great roar of laughter and said, "I'm a Republican myself, and I shore don't believe in letting Democrats vote." He knows I am a Democrat, because the local papers have been writing up my activities. So I loffed heartily too, and said, "That is just why the Democrats are not going to let the Republicans get in again. We believe in everybody voting."

They all laughed out then and cracked their fists down on the

Katherine Anne Porter's mother, circa 1888; she died when Katherine Anne Porter was two.

Katherine Anne Porter at the age of eighteen months, seated in her grandmother's lap. Beside her is her sister Gay.

Katherine Anne Porter at the age of eight, 1898.

Katherine Anne Porter at the age of nineteen in Corpus Christi, Texas, 1909.

"This photograph was taken in Mexico, in Mixoac, ancient Indian town, near Mexico City, against the wall of my house in morning sunlight— late summer 1930—no make-up, no re-touching—Manuel Alvarez Bravo was then young, just setting out on his life work. He has become a famous photographer," wrote Katherine Anne Porter.

Eugene Pressly, Mexico, 1930.

Hart Crane, Mexico, 1930. He killed himself in 1932.

"Sitting in my Mexican study when I got news of my Guggenheim to Europe," wrote Katherine Anne Porter, 1930. Photograph by Eugene Pressly.

Barbara Harrison and Katherine Anne Porter in a carriage at Davos, Switzerland, May 15, 1934.
Photograph by Monroe Wheeler.

Sherwood Anderson wrote, "At Olivet with a lady I much admire," July 28, 1937.

Marcelle Sibon, Katherine Anne Porter's French translator, 1936.

Caroline Gordon in the dining room at Benfolly, the Tates' home on the Cumberland River, Clarksville, Tennessee, 1937.

Andrew Lytle at Benfolly, 1937. "He doesn't really look this gaunt," noted Caroline Gordon.

Allen Tate and his daughter Nancy at Benfolly,
1937.

Albert Erskine in Baton Rouge, 1938.

Dad at 80 yrs.
Mission Texas

Harrison Boone Porter,
Katherine Anne Porter's
father. Photograph by
Katherine Anne Porter.

Katherine Anne Porter, Albert Erskine, and Monroe Wheeler in Baton Rouge in the summer of 1939.

George Platt Lynes, Edith Witmore, and Katherine Anne Porter at the opening of the Museum of Modern Art, May 10, 1939.

"*Elizabeth Ames took me for a long drive during the hours that Dad was being buried and we visited South Hill and I took this picture that day — It was wonderful and quiet there and very reassuring,*" noted Katherine Anne Porter on January 24, 1942.

Charles Shannon, Solomon Islands, July 1943. He had an affair with Katherine Anne Porter that year.

Christmas in California: Katherine Anne Porter and her niece, Ann Heintze, in 1946.

"You must have one, even if only for a good joke: you'll never see me, you never did see me in Fifty-Eight Thousand dollars worth of high class trash, and it is a sight, the once-in-a-life-time-if-at-all sort of thing," wrote Katherine Anne Porter to her niece of this Vogue *fashion photograph taken by George Platt Lynes. July 28, 1947.*

Katherine Anne Porter's niece, Ann, cutting her wedding cake. Pictured are Ann's new husband, Walter Heintze; Katherine Anne Porter's sister Gay Holloway, the mother of the bride; and Donald Elder. Taken at Katherine Anne Porter's home, 108 East 65th Street, in 1950.

Monroe Wheeler, 1951. Photograph by George Platt Lynes.

Cyrilly Abels, circa 1951.

Katherine Anne Porter at her Paris spinet on May 15, 1951, her sixty-first birthday.
Photograph by Arthur B. Long.

Katherine Anne Porter at the Paris Conference, International Exposition of the Arts, May 1952. To Katherine Anne Porter's right is Glenway Wescott; to his right, Robert Lowell. Andre Malraux is at the front table, at the left; at the extreme right is W. H. Auden; to his right, William Faulkner.

Marianne Moore at the time she translated The Fables of La Fontaine, *1954.* Photograph by George Platt Lynes.

Eleanor Clark Warren and her daughter, Rosanna (Posey), 1954.

Picture of Roxbury Road, July 1958. Southbury, Connecticut.

"I made this picture of Paul with his camera and flashlight in the evening, January 2, 1956," said Katherine Anne Porter of this photograph of her nephew. Southbury, Connecticut.

Katherine Anne Porter, Monroe Wheeler, and Glenway Wescott in Southbury, Connecticut, July 14, 1956.

Katherine Anne Porter with Flannery O'Connor and one of her pet peacocks, April 1958.

Katherine Anne Porter honored at Smith College with Janet Flanner, Barbara McClintock, Nadia Boulanger, and Mary Parsons, June 1958.

Robert Penn Warren and his daughter, Rosanna, 1960.

Samuel Southwell, Cultural Attaché, Guadalajara, greets Katherine Anne Porter arriving from Mexico City, November 30, 1964.

Isabel Bayley talking with Katherine Anne Porter at her eighty-second birthday party, May 15, 1972.

Katherine Anne Porter, Washington, D.C., 1970. Photograph by Robert Phillips.

Katherine Anne Porter and Eudora Welty, circa 1972.

Tania and James Stern at Tisbury Station on Katherine Anne Porter's eighty-fifth birthday, 1975.

table, and I rushed out and stopped at the white house on the right hand side of the road and discovered that my school tax was over-due since early September. Well, Paul, perhaps I am not giving you much of a notion, but the whole thing pleased me immensely, I think I never felt so close to this country, nor somehow so much a citizen, nor so free, in a mysterious sense of that word, as I did, driving along home through the dusk; in this world of such ac-cumulated horror and terror and endless death, here was a whole country getting ready to elect a President of their free choice, marking our parties and dropping the paper in a sealed box—all over the country in red barns and little houses and along country roads and in the great cities, and nobody (beyond mere human curiosity) has the right even to ask another man how he means to vote. I have asked many people, and many people have asked me. But we can answer or not as we choose. You know, we would have taken for granted that this was the most ordinary and usual sort of liberty—(mind you I don't forget for a minute about the Negro in the south or *any* of our millions of poor and neglected) but now, in this present world, it seemed to me for a moment something almost miraculous. And if we have millions of poor and mistreated, still we have fewer than we had, and there are millions who are really working to see that the number is reduced steadily. So to put it mildly, I felt pretty well, and do now; a great part of it is no doubt because I am actually working too, here and now, not just talking, as I have for so long. I think the talk helps too, but I like to roll up my sleeves now and then and pitch in. You know—you have listened to me too long not to remember—how pessimistic I can be, how bitter about the way things go too often, you know that I have got a good idea of what is going on politically in the world. But my belief is growing that our political and social evils are remediable, if only all of us who want a change for the better just get up and work for it, all the time, with as much knowledge and intelligence as we can muster for it. Half the wrongs of human life exist because of the inertia of people who simply will not use their energies in fighting for what they believe in. And finally the wrongs roll up into world catastrophes and millions of deaths and a terrible set-back for all mankind . . .

My dear, I cannot tell often from your letters whether you have been getting mine, but I suppose so, or they would come back to me? I don't expect you to "answer" them, there is nothing to answer, really, we just go on keeping our little diaries and sending them to each other, but mention that you had a letter when you do get one . . . I haven't been writing as often as I meant, and yet your letters are the most valuable thing in the world to me. Your description of the French countryside and those marvelous old people along the roads, makes me homesick again for that blessed country. Your postcard portrait of the old woman is beautiful: you are right, age is a better estate there than here, and it is perhaps because the French were always wise about ways of getting old. But you had a great-grandmother whose face was as noble and more beautiful than any of them, and her courage was as good. And this country is full of fine old heroes, even if they are scattered about and we don't seem to see them so much . . . But France is admirable, and her people made it so. I hope you can stay there, or rather, return there, after the war. For I suppose you will be sent home and mustered out, or whatever they call it, but never fear, you will be able to go back. I shall see to that.

You never mention yourself, in the oddest way. When I think of the way you used to grouse, (not often, but plenty when you did) you seem to have got into a rather abstract way of thinking about yourself. Are you warm? Do you get your food regularly? Would you like a big sweater? The husband of one of my friends asked the other day for the heaviest sweater she could find, *tout de suite,* he was freezing, we figured out, maybe in Normandy. Do please ask for anything you want. I saw a lovely Mexican silver lighter advertised the other day, guaranteed. Would you like it? the advertisement said one could send lighters to soldiers without requests, but I don't want to weigh you down with gadgets. Just let me know what would be really useful to you . . .

Well, I still haven't written you what I want to write, I don't seem to have the words for it. Take my love for granted, dear child, depend upon it, and let me make it helpful and comfortable to you. Let me do for you whatever I am able, and remember that it will give me great happiness.

With my same love
Aunt Katherine Anne

To Paul Porter   [Yaddo
                              Saratoga Springs]
                              October 28, 1944

Paul darling,

Your latest letter reached here yesterday, dated October 13.
And so I travelled a few miles further with you through the French
countryside, seeing again through your eyes what I saw once. The
part of this country I am in now is not as familiar to us as the France
you are in for the first time. Indeed, you were never here. This
morning we were at freezing point, but the air is still, the fall colors
still high and brilliant, and the sky is a true jewel blue. Everything
glitters and shimmers, and the sunlight falls so clearly into the
woods they are illuminated all through; you can see great distances
through them. After my years in Europe, I was almost blinded by
this American light; and when I finally reached Texas, I took to dark
glasses until my eyes could get used to the shocking but beautiful
colors. As a painter, I imagine you will notice this difference even
more than I did.

My dear, as you move further and further away from us, and
I must expect silences for a while, I miss you more constantly and
everything becomes more a matter of holding out grimly than ever
. . . Where are you today and what are you doing? As I can imagine
only in the most general way, and you undoubtedly can never tell
me—not yet, anyway—at least I can tell you what I am doing, and
I think it may please you.

I am helping to campaign for the President in this moss-grown,
rock-ribbed upstate New York, with half a dozen speaking engagements at various big meetings. Believe me if I had not been a
Democrat before, these people would have made me one by sheer
repulsion. In Saratoga bands of young toughs, horribly like the
Hitler toughs I saw in action in Germany in 1931, go about at night
painting the word *Jew* in big black letters on shops and housefronts.
They painted the word by mistake on the house of a Christian
doctor, who has just let it stay there, adding the words: "No Jew,
but no Fascist either." We held protest meetings and persuaded the
local editor, a Republican, to write an editorial against this, and at
our rally, to be held on the first of November, we have invited a

Negro preacher, two well known and respected Jews and a local labor leader, besides American citizens of many national origins to sit on the platform and some of them have promised to make little speeches . . . The President spoke by radio last night, a wonderful great speech which made all the mean and slanderous campaign against him seem pettier than ever. Yesterday I was called by telephone from New York to come up and help speak at a meeting where four or five thousand people are expected. I shall go to a Negro Democratic meeting here tomorrow. So do know I am doing my little part as well as I can, with you and all like you in mind.

Our book goes on bravely, people really do buy it. Have you got your copy yet? Reviews keep coming in, all friendly so far; you have seen enough to give you a notion of it. I am not writing at all, just now; promising myself that the day after election I will go back to my mss. and stay there. I will write you often, even if just the little V-mail things. Remember a postcard with three words on it will be enough for me from you during this "busy" time; I don't worry about you, that would be too pointless. It is just that you are never out of my mind. I wish I could do something quite practical for you: send you something you need, for example. Please note my questions in the letter before this. Not the V-mail note—the other. Alas I lost track of numbering my letters long since, I can only hope that you are getting them all. With my same love

Aunt Katherine Anne

To Monroe Wheeler†   November 3, 1944

Open this carefully, darling, and don't faint, upon or after Date Written, it will really work. Try it! I know you never expected to see this again, and sometimes I was discouraged about it myself! All my love and thanks and remembrance again!

Katherine Anne

†*Monroe Wheeler noted: "This envelope contained a check for $300.00 that I had given Katherine Anne to move her possessions to Baton Rouge, La. when she married Albert Erskine."*

To Robert Penn Warren   [Yaddo
                          Saratoga Springs]
                          First day of Winter,
                          December 22, 1944

Dear Red:

    . . . . I meant to send a copy of L.T. to Denis [Devlin] and to Leger, but I don't seem to have their addresses. Could you send them me, or could I send the books in your care? Also I wanted to send one to Tommy, but his whereabouts eludes me also. It was pleasant to know that Leger actually read my scrap in the *Sewanee Review.* Bunny Wilson finally broke down and admitted that in all these years he had never read anything of mine, looking upon me as just another lady-author, and not being a girl-poet, he couldn't bother. (the last clause is mine, of course.) And some time ago, I had letters to the same effect from William Carlos Williams and earlier, Sherwood Anderson, both of them saying in effect they had looked upon me as a pretty girl making a career in literature via S.A. These simple lads never seemed to realize what they were saying.

    Oh yes, I think Denis is a good poet and has a fine book in hand, and I do agree he should leave out a few early ones. Is there anyway of getting him to do this?

    Darling, I will try to get that Blake piece written, really try, because I would like to do it, for you and for me. It is a most beautiful collection.

    I think Archie [MacLeish] has left something he could do and that was very becoming to him, to take on a heavy career of grief, frustration and sorrow [Assistant Secretary of State for Public and Cultural Relations]. But I hope to be mistaken . . . which positively reminds me of something. I have signed up to go to Hollywood at last, and will be leaving sometime the first week in January. To work with a producer named Sidney Franklin, so far as I am able to make out through the barrage of trans-continental telephone calls and three page telegrams, as a kind of literary adviser, while he teaches me the technical side of producing. Well, it stands like this. They asked me for six months at fifteen hundred dollars a week, straight. I said, No, fifteen hundred for the first thirteen weeks, Two thousand a week for the next thirteen. At this they halted, drew back two paces, went into a huddle and came forward again muttering about options. Now, they pay me fifteen hundred for thirteen weeks, with option to go on at two thousand, BUT I must then sign up at that salary for six months every year for three years. So I said, all right, maybe. I am waiting now while they arrange transportation, and anyway, darling, its a roof, as the saying is, over my head, because they also undertake to find me a hotel room or something of the sort. They want me to fly and I want to go by train, in a little room so I can stay in bed and get some rest . . . I suppose something could slip even now, but so far it seems to be going forward rather smoothly . . . My words about Archie's troubles and changes brought on this train of thought.

I am going because the money is very tempting and my aim is to grab out some of it to put in bank against the wet and weary future . . . the news got out prematurely in the local papers because a blab-mouth woman here in the house overheard the talk by telephone and took telegrams for me by telephone from Western Union, and then told the reporters without asking me whether or no. So last night I was in the Worden Bar with friends and people got up from the dining room and came in to look, and today I am going down to a book shop to sell tickets for a China Relief project, and now they expect a thousand people where yesterday we would have had fifty come to buy. It will be nice to get to California where fifteen hundred dollar a week writers come a dime a dozen. As Elizabeth Ames said, if I stay around here they will be organizing pilgrimages to Yaddo to touch me for luck.

Well, Red, its done. This is the third offer I have had and it was easy to refuse the others, but now with three books and the novel nearly finished, and after all these years, I feel I have made my point, and I can take on Hollywood for a round or two. My belief is that at the end of 13 weeks they will be glad to kiss me goodbye forever, and I'll get back to South Hill for spring and summer, very lovely here. If I go through Washington westward, I'll stop over a few days. But I don't know yet how I'll travel . . .

A happy Christmas and good New Year to you and Cinina . . . It is wonderful to know she is getting up; I really enjoyed staying in the hospital, I look back to it as a holiday, I would like to go again for another two weeks . . . but I promise myself that after Hollywood, I can afford to take to my bed for a little cure if I still need it. I hope Cinina is on her feet for good, and finds the world fresh and interesting . . . My same love

Katherine Anne

SECTION 6

California
April 1945 to July 1949

I find the past much more solid than I had thought, and living much more continuous, which I had begun to doubt.

Katherine Anne Porter to Josephine Herbst
August 16, 1946

WORKING FIRST AT MGM WITH SIDNEY FRANKLIN, THEN AT *Paramount with Charles Brackett, Katherine Anne Porter learns that Hollywood is not for her. She buys a mountain, sells it, and realizes "I am romantic in these matters, and my judgement, let us admit freely, is even worse than in husbands . . . I am good for friendship and for writing. Nothing else at all. . . ."* Flowering Judas, Pale Horse, Pale Rider, *and* The Leaning Tower *are translated into French, Scandinavian, and Italian. With Eleanor Clark, Glenway Wescott, Morton Zabel, and other friends of the head of Yaddo, Katherine Anne Porter defends Elizabeth Ames, who is assailed "on the very grounds of her virtuous and serious attempt to direct a working democracy." After being writer-in-residence at Stanford University, she moves to New York.*

To Monroe Wheeler   333 25th Street
                       Santa Monica, California
                       25 April, 1945

Monroe darling:

Things are tottering along very nicely here now. I left MGM
at the end of the thirteenth week, promptly on the stroke of the
hour. It had been explained to me, to my mystification, that the
essence of an option was to give to the taker the whole choice in
whether or not the contract should continue after a certain time
. . . It seemed to me fair enough for a while, because it seemed
certain to me that at the end of thirteen weeks they would be glad
to kiss me good bye for ever . . . My agent then assured me that
this was by no means the case, and every time I thought of the
interminable future my heart sank . . . About the middle of my term
I began gnawing away at my bonds like a fox with his leg in a trap,
and by the thirteenth week I had Mr. Franklin persuaded that I was
not that woman he had been praying for to come to his assistance
. . . I can't work with Franklin. The man is a Christian Scientist, and
his pictures are simply horrible, fuzzy, sickeningly sentimental, they
never touch any kind of reality sides, top or bottom and I kept
wanting to toss a monkey wrench into his mental machinery all the
time we were talking over any kind of scene. I would hear myself
saying, "For *God's* sake, human beings don't talk like that." or
something of the sort, and there would be a stiff silence and Franklin would turn an alarming scarlet and look as if he were going to
have apoplexy, though he is really a thin ascetic-looking man who
shouldn't have such a tendency. Then, the censorship drove me to
drink. The explanation here is that it isn't Hays—he just usefully
keeps tabs on public opinion and reports to the producers just who
objects to what, and where they can expect to run into trouble if
they do this or that. Here, they blame it on the women's clubs, who
run the local censorships all over the country. Therefore, public
opinion has nothing to do with it, really . . . But I couldn't endure
it, from whatever source, and couldn't conform . . . I finally reached
the point where I felt it was not corrupt politicians or even black
marketeers or Fascist tendencies in the State Department that were
troubling this country but the Women's Clubs and the Catholic

church. They really do run things out here, and do a twenty-four hour patrol on the job. So I was losing my sense of perspective and my wish to live, and got out just in time. Things ended nicely, politely, with handshakes all around. Franklin, who had been horrified at my salary, suddenly began to worry about my future, what on earth was I going to do now, where was I going, did I have any money? I was happy to be able to tell him I was relatively rich and wasn't going anywhere . . . My agent couldn't believe either that I wasn't broke and wildly in debt. All his other clients are, he said . . . Apparently people go a little foggy minded out here. Well, darling, I had my turn at Hollywood and it isn't for me, any more than ever it was. Now my publisher's agent and my own are busy peddling my stories and declare they will sell something. Maybe they will, and if they do, it would be nice. If they don't, things will remain as they have in the past . . . I never had any such expectation, and haven't now.

Enough of this . . . Now I am fairly well settled for a while, and am reading over the novel and trying to get back into it. I have been so wrenched about by one thing and another this past year and a half, its a wonder I am not all in pieces. But still I am not, Darling, I miss you incredibly, I wish something pleasant and unexpected would bring you here, since I can't come back there for a while. You will be glad to know the doctor appears to know what he is doing, I am getting better, no doubt of it, and indeed it is not so difficult to live here as I found it in other places. There is wonderful sun and you could sunbathe all day in the back garden. A pretty dream, and just by looking out of the window I can see you there very plainly . . .

Let me hear how you are, and with my love always

Katherine Anne

To Edward Stettinius   [Santa Monica]
[telegram]

30 May 1945 to Stettinius, Stassen and Connally at San Francisco, Fairmont Hotel.

We who have soldiers giving their lives in what they have been assured is a war against Fascism, are appalled and discouraged by the spectacle of our American government supporting openly at least two Fascist Governments, Argentina and Franco-Spain. I ask you as a representative of a Democratic people to use your great strength and influence to oppose the admission of Franco's Fascist regime to the World Security Organization, and to support firmly the Mexican and other delegations who are fighting Fascism on our home territory.

Katherine Anne Porter

To Cinina and Robert   201 South Bentley Avenue
Penn Warren   Los Angeles 24
     5 July 1945

Dear Red and Cinina:

. . . . My life has been a long and quite bitter and determined tussle with health: trying to get well of just being sick of living, I should say; but this ailment can take more forms than Proteus ever thought up, and some of them do give way before the marvels of science. I shan't name all the distresses of head and chest nerves, but I have had almost constant treatments—and at last in a kind of wit's end decision, they gave me penicillin. It cleared up almost everything but my mind. That has been going from bad to worse ever since the President died, and my view of the European situation confirmed everything I have feared all this time. You know all that I know and more too. But I see enough. First, Italy, where the Allies are hanging on like grim death to all tried and trusty Fascists, hoping they will still be able to keep the Italian people from freeing themselves even a little. Then they invite the only really Nazi-

Fascist country in this hemisphere except our State Department, which is a country by itself, a state within a state—to come to San Francisco. And wanted to bring in Franco, but didn't quite dare. However, I hear by radio that Churchill will see and arrange things with him before the Big Three conference . . . And now the Italian Fascists are going to sit in. And England has already turned her guns on the people of Greece, trying to push back on them the wormy little king they threw out in 1922. I have only one question to ask of the mob who is running the show now: why this unkind discrimination against the German Nazis? After all, they are the strongest and most convinced ones. Why leave *them* out of the Peace Conference?

I have Thomas Mann on the subject of the peace, too; I always was for a tougher peace than Germany is going to get, I'm afraid, but if I hadn't have been, as you say, he would have converted me instantly. He is a dangerous kind of German, and this country is full of his kind . . . God, how get well? and what for?

Eleanor Clark is indeed a lovely gifted person, and having a very hard life of it too, trying to come out on some kind of firm ground in all this. I have liked her immensely for years, and am always happy to see her. The last I heard she was still at Yaddo, fighting it out with that novel. She'll win. . . .

Speaking of California, which the Californians around here refer to as the Southland, which throws me off a little, I just happened to notice how I am dressed, and none of you-all ever saw me like this. I am wearing a thin tailored black shirt with a really elegantly made-to-measure-pair of black slacks, a wide white canvas belt, white platform canvas sandals, and three rows of white china beads around my neck. It might look odd anywhere else, but here it is just right and I am going down to that place and have myself made a couple of summer outfits in cool stuffs and colors. And I haven't been anywhere yet that I couldn't wear this outfit or one like it and be quite all right. That may say something about the range of my social life, too. But I don't seem to want to go anywhere at all, and there are about half a dozen nice people who come in to see me now and then, and that will be enough for me. The place itself is beautiful, you never could show me too many blooming trees, plants, shrubs, too much grass, too many flower beds . . . I can do nicely with perpetual good weather and perpetual bloom. I don't think life is long enough for them ever to grow monotonous . . . And I have absolutely no moral scruples about being as comfortable as I can. It isn't half comfortable enough at best. And I should like everybody else to be comfortable, too, in whatever way he likes. I'm fed up with the hard way. It got me nowhere and has ruined my health. So to hell with it. . . .

Love again
Katherine Anne

To Barbara Wescott   201 South Bentley Avenue
Los Angeles 24
28 July 1945

Barbara darling:

. . . . In the last two weeks I have been reading Bynner's version of Laotzu, Auden's poetry, *Apartment in Athens*—it must be for the sixth time—and *The Kreutzer Sonata,* which I hadn't read since I was nineteen; it seems to have gone mostly over my head at that time, or I had since got it mixed with two other Russian novels, for it read like a new book to me. It is the most appalling study of male egoism I daresay ever written. The only thing, (and I have felt this about Tolstoy in every book of his, even *War and Peace*) is, I wonder uneasily now and then if that is what he really intended to do . . . Sometime when you are reading again, soon I hope, read that and tell me what you find in it. I do have so often that same exasperated, baffled feeling after reading so many Russian novels—Dostoievski even more so, I think—of just wanting madly to get into the book myself and take some of the characters by the nap of the neck and knock some sense and logic into their maggoty heads . . . So with this infernal unconsciously evil man in the *Kreutzer Sonata.* But Tolstoy was so bemused and confounded by his forty-year-long battle with his wife, he never did get really straight on sex; a born sensualist whose morality ended by corrupting him instead of humanizing him. I saw just now a portrait of him by some very good artist, who had caught the combination of goat and devil in that superb old John the Baptist face.

We have weather here, too; just the opposite number of yours. Drouth. I am running up a no-doubt fabulous water-bill trying to keep the brash vegetation, which rushes up during the rainy season, from just turning into dry sticks. It is very distressing about your crops. After all I come of a respectably long line of folks who spent a good deal of time watching the weather, and it made all the difference to them whether they got their cotton, corn, sugar cane, hay and so on safely under cover at the right moment. Otherwise, they didn't live, simply. So I watch the weather too, and am distressed at news of flood or drouth or untimely heat or cold as if my own fields were threatened: and they are too, for everybody is affected by what happens to the land; though almost nobody seems to know it, or to care if they do know. And I think I hate most of all the cruel waste of human energy and effort. . . .

With my love, and a hope to see you soon!

Katherine Anne

TO ALBERT ERSKINE   201 South Bentley Avenue
                                     Los Angeles 24, California
                                     11 August, 1945

Dear Albert:

My French translator, Marcelle Sibon, who was reported to me as having been shot as a hostage by the Germans, has turned up alive. To see her hand writing was like seeing a welcome ghost, and I wish I could see many ghosts of the kind. The point is just now that she is a fine translator, and is doing all three of my books and all are to be brought out in rapid succession in Paris during the next year . . . In a letter today she asked me to recommend books that might be suitable for translation, and I thought at once of *Angel In The Forest**, which for me, as I think I wrote you, is the book of the year, if not of several years . . .

Do you suppose it is translatable? Remember Mademoiselle Sibon is *very* good. And do you think it might be interesting for the

*By Marguerite Young

308

French? If so, and if Miss Young has no translator, and does not mind my choosing one for her, would you send a copy to Marcelle for me? Have you anything else on your list that might appeal to the French? Marcelle knows a great many publishers, and if she did not do all the books herself—indeed, under our plan, she could not possibly—she would know the best translators. With her and several others, I mean to take a hand in getting certain books of ours by our really good writers—whom Europe never hears of—translated. They deserve something better than Steinbeck and Saroyan . . . Of course they do have some of the best already, but not enough. And never until they have wide reputation. I want the new interesting ones to be known in Europe . . . Marcelle's address is at the end of this letter.

It is beginning to look as if today is a Day† we have all been waiting for . . . I never felt soberer or less like celebrating anything in my life, but it will be wonderful to draw a deep breath after all these oppressive and horrible years.

Unbelievably, my health changed suddenly for the better. My doctor in desperation gave me penicillin, and everything that has troubled me all these years—except, as I said to him, my state of mind about the European situation—cleared up as by miracle almost overnight. I am in a delicious state of well being, though still being filled up twice a week with vitamines and calciums and so on. The only troublesome thing, my hair is turning dark, and shortly I shall not be able to recognize myself any more . . . This if you please when I had finally despaired, and was ready—not ready, but trying to be—to die. It seems strange now, but it was real then and is still real, but in the past . . .

One snippet of gossip I meant to write you months ago: almost the first person I met here was Margaret Tallichet, and she is the youngest and freshest and prettiest thing I almost ever saw, invited me to come and spend an evening with her and the children but I was then ill, and never could set a date. She has that dewy, cherished look, you would take her for all of a virginal twenty three years: and complained that her husband's absence in the Army had got in the way of her plans for a family. "But we'll make that up when he gets back," she said, gayly . . . Its rather nice to see some

† *V-J (Victory in Japan) Day was declared officially on September 2, 1945.*

one get precisely what she wanted, isn't it, even if I for one can't quite imagine why she wanted it . . . But that serene beauty which comes of fulfillment of whatever kind can't be assumed. It really does come from inside.

I have been absolutely alone since the first of July, in a pleasant, smaller house, doing as I please, sunbathing, working, sleeping, listening to music, reading, seeing almost literally no one, and I do thrive on that life when I can get it. Its much too good to last, but I make the most of it.

Do let me know what you think of the translation projects. And write me here before the first of September, as I shall be on the move again, God knows where. Wherever I can find a house. I mean to stay on here now until the spring, as being so well and strong and now, from today, somehow so much free-er in my mind, I'll just have a good winter for once, and get some work *finished.*

Yours
Katherine Anne

Address: Mademoiselle Marcelle Sibon
   5 Quai Voltaire, Paris, France

I am doing a review (by request of Margaret Marshall) of your Mr. Willison's *Saints and Strangers.* That is a good useful interesting book. Nothing can ever make me love the Pilgrims but I do admire good solid history. I knew Toni Willison in Paris years ago, she called me up here and wanted me to come to dinner, but I lost the address and everything, and then forgot—(God knows I have not been much interested in aquaintances old or new) and now can't find them. Would you be so good as to send me their address here?

To Monroe Wheeler   Paramount Pictures Inc.
West Coast Studios
Inter-Office Communication
3 December 1945

Monroe darling:

Look where I'm, exclamation point. Rounding into my sixth week of a stretch of fourteen, and not even groggy yet. This is better, entirely. I am working with Charles Brackett—who did *Lost Weekend,* and a French professorial sort of person named Jaques Thery on an adaptation of *Madame Sans Gêne* for Betty Hutten—or have I told you this? In case I didn't, one evening at six o'clock they called me up and asked me to come to the studio all set to plunge in up to the eyebrows in the script. I asked why they couldn't wait until Monday, it then being Wednesday and they said, Golly, NO. Tomorrow at eleven a.m. you be here.

So I hastily broke my neck re-arranging my life for an indefinite period, showed up all eager on the hour, was greeted, kissed, handed around, lunched, patted on the head, shown my office, and about three o'clock Brackett said, Come on Darling, I'll drive you home . . . On the way he remarked casually that I needn't come back until I was sent for, they just wanted to be sure they had me, or words to that effect. So I sat out two weeks, drawing my wages with heavenly punctuality, then I was asked to drop in sometime if I felt like it. I felt like it the next day, and sat in a cribbage game with Billy Wilder, Thery and Brackett. They carry on a game every day about noon. (Do you play cribbage? I saw the prettiest little ivory board the other day and thought of you, I don't know why. Except that if you play cribbage you really need it.) They also got me into a discussion on the subject of abortion, with the Catholic censor, who was objecting to something in another picture of Brackett's. Then Mr. Thery remarked that when he was finished with me, I'd be able to write any scenario I wished with one hand . . . I sat around the office catching up on my correspondence and telephone calls, and went home about five. Not until last Monday, one week ago today, did I begin coming here every day, and four of them I have spent listening and watching Thery talk. I sit in a big arm chair and he gallops up and down the room before me, constructing a play. He really can construct one, but it has nothing to do with Sardou, or *Sans Gêne,* or fact or fiction or anything human . . . I keep interrupting, "yes but—" trying to tell him he is off the rails completely, but he never listens. If I do get the right of way, he stops and stares out the window and day dreams until I finish. Then he shakes his head as if he had water in his ears and starts galloping and talking once more . . . He has constructed and thrown away one play every session, and we are just where we were . . . This morning I came in at 11, and had a message from him he would be working with Billy Wilder today—he works with half a dozen writers and directors . . . So here I am darling, catching up on my correspondence some more . . .

But nobody else seems to be in the least worried, so I'm not either. I do know, there is evidence for it, that pictures do actually get made, somehow, and no doubt one I work on will finally emerge, too. It could be very interesting, a good comedy, but Thery is not funny. His way of working reminds me of a pack of cards somebody sent me once, called "Add-a-Plot."—No, Deal-A-Plot. You shuffled them and laid out five, and selected a hero, repeat for heroine, for theme, for treatment, and so down the line. Then you were supposed to go ahead and make a story out of what you had in hand . . . I feel that if they would let me alone I could get a decent play out of Sardou . . . but that is not the way it works, so I am just floating along. Only trouble is, my name will be on the damned thing, and I'm afraid Thery is the one who will really be responsible. But that is a long way off . . .

Darling what are you doing and how are you? And how does every one? I picked up an Astrology Magazine idly the other day at a stand, and saw Glenway's fortune being told in it, so I send it on. I consider this as being real fame. His name must be a household word for an astrologer to have heard of him . . .

Tell him I am in no sense running a race with him, still I *have* been lately translated into the Chinese . . . Of course I suppose he was years ago.

Social notes: Heard Maggie Teyte. Went to dinner with Adrian and Janet Gaynor. Sunday Lunch at Brackett's house. Met Judy Garland at Robert Lewis' for dinner. She said shyly as a child that she was a fan of mine from way back. I told her I was a fan of hers, too. She was pregnant as could be or almost, and had just come from an all day session being Marilyn Miller. She had got to the point where a stand-in had to do the faster dancing. I see Sylvia Sidney now and then and like her . . . I lost thirty dollars (more or less) playing poker with Richard Hagemann (that conductor) at Robert Nathan's house; nobody told me he was a semi-professional shark and I didn't come to and begin playing real Texas poker until it was simply too late. At one time I was more than a hundred dollars in, but I did a fast scramble and saved some of it . . .

At Clifford Odets' I met Charlie Chaplin and his latest child-bride, pregnant, of course, and knitting a blue baby blanket. He is an odious little beast, amiable as hell and what good does that do? Then later, a couple of weeks ago, I met dear Paul Green there, and we got into a religious discussion and I had mangled his tender heart before I realized that he really is religious in the most simple Methodist way, or at least, wants badly to be . . . I had Thanksgiving dinner with Bernardine, Rosemary and her pleasant husband whose name I never can remember, and the baby is a charmer . . . This whole territory is simply crawling with babies. The most philoprogenitive place I ever saw . . . No matter where you go— except perhaps Mike Romanoff's or La Rue's—fond parents trot out a basket of young, and every body takes turn about holding the baby on one side and a cocktail on the other.

You are supposed to have love affairs here, whether you like it or not, and I am afraid I am going to get a really sinister reputation if somehow I can't get a rumor started that I am sleeping with somebody—it doesn't seem to matter so much who . . . I have practically been driven to hints that I am being faithful to an absent One, but that is considered more than a little odd, too. Complete strangers will come up to you at parties and ask: "Are you having a love affair? Are you happy?" This runs along side by side with the most neo-Victorian domesticity, celebrated glamour girls will talk all evening about their infants, their beautiful false eyelashes quivering with cozy emotions . . . The houses are really fabulous, all looking like something run up for a super-spectacle by MGM, with twenty foot square bathrooms carpeted in pink velvet and so on . . . The most beautiful and in some way simplest house is Adrian's . . . About a million dollars worth of utter simplicity, but he really does get away with it. . . .

I am really saving a little money this round and high time, too.

The agent says he plans to get me just one fourteen to twenty week contract every year, if I can make up my mind to behave myself. Poor dear, my behavior is going to be a real shock to him. Its odd the different things one is to different people. To my dentist I am just a couple of rows of teeth. To my agent I am a fair-to-middlin good property and every week I don't work he considers he is losing money on me. I shan't tell him now and ruin his Christmas, but he is going to lose a small fortune on me . . . and my dear nephew often addresses me: My Darling Wailing Wall. If I could see you for an hour I'd be Me again, as you are You perpetually, no smallest shadow or anything or anybody else . . .

> With my same devoted love
> *Katherine Anne*

843 6th street, Santa Monica.

I have a nice Navy Lieutenant who is a kind of Nightclub Beau, so he was up yesterday, from San Diego, wild to get going as usual, and at four o'clock this morning we were still falling in and out of taxis between an assortment of the oddest little joints, and if this letter doesn't make much sense, it is because I am hung-over like a cliff . . . but this doesn't happen often darling. I usually keep sober because somebody must be able to tell the taxi driver where to go next. And life is fairly sober all around anyway . . . but pleasant and there is quite a lot to look forward to . . . love again.

TO EDNA AND ANDREW   843 6th Street
LYTLE   Santa Monica, California
                            27 December 1945

. . . . Well, Andrew, on January 10 Caroline is divorcing Allen, at his request, and when I think of the marriages they tried all through the years with such bitter concentration to break up—I know of three, myself—it isn't irony at all but just exactly the slow overtaking of poetic justice that it was their own marriage they were breaking up all that time . . . It has been rather grisly—I have been getting both sides in a series of letters—to see how blind they have been and still are to what they really have been, have done, are doing and being. I cannot realize that two people could live together so long and know so little about each other. Apparently each one of them just cast the other in a rôle, and played out the grim false comedy to its end . . . Allen did what seems on the surface the most conventional vulgar thing; fell in love with a girl twenty years younger. And Caroline found herself in that most ordinary and sickening of womanly situations: deserted in her menopause for a young girl by a husband who suddenly has a panic because his youth has disappeared and he must retrieve it somehow, even if only by a symbolic transference . . .

Its odd how people who weren't really conventional in other ways will suddenly behave when confronted with the awful realization that their lives are at least more than half done, and what was it all about? I love my time of life, and live in it with more ease and satisfaction than at any other period . . . I seem to have arrived at the age God always meant me to be, but I also had everything suitable to me as I came along, and life is better for me now than ever it was. So it really hurts me to think of those savage, ruthless people, who never hesitated to wound their best friends in the most unpardonable ways, now burning up in a hell fire they built for the others, and must endure themselves . . .

Caroline was at Princeton, couldn't bear it—went to the Lowells, and you know what a time the Tates and the Lowells have put in together. Today I had a letter from Marcella Winslow, saying that Allen and Caroline were frantically trying to get Caroline established there with her. The very notion filled Marcella with horror . . . Caroline is a walking death to any human way of being, and I know I would not have her near me ever again for anything on this earth . . . those rages she always had have increased to a point that looks like madness. . . .

To Albert Erskine
843 6th Street
Santa Monica, California
17 February 1946

Dear Albert:

George Platt Lynes just buzzed in over the mountains, and told me he had seen you in a record shop and that you had said something about sending me some records, and I said, Well, that is odd, for they haven't come. And he said, They were Isabel Bailly records, and *I* said, Golly.

For they did come, the only two records of hers I didn't have, and couldn't get either here or at the Gramophone shop. And darling, you should have sent a card, because I took it for granted they were sent by some one who had sent me two others—*Let The Bright Seraphim* and *Flocks in Pastures Green* etc—and so I wrote him one of those fulsome little notes of thank-yous, and now everybody is going to have red ears . . . maybe not you, of course, but I have and so will he . . .

It is very pleasant to me to know that we are finding the same music at the same time—I have a really lovely collection, and my Purcell albums are filling up beautifully . . . Do you know Lily Kraus? Her Mozart Fantasia is wonderful. And there are two singers, Blanche Thebom and Kathleen Ferrier, who do Handel and Purcell, and you would like Boyce's *The Prospect Before Us*—he is about contemporary. With Purcell, and this is a ballet suite. And Suite No. 1 by Isajas Reusner, just before Bach. The last side of this is a heavenly little Canon by Pachelbel who was a little earlier . . . Purcell's *Comus* ballet is out, too . . . and on and on. There is a shop here—there is always one everywhere almost—which gets the most fabulous shipments from England and France. And I have sent a list to my translator, Marcelle Sibon, in Paris, and expect some fine things from there . . . I am still trying to get *The Magic Flute,* and John Palmer told me you had asked him to try to get this for you from the Navy shop in San Diego. Well, I had asked him to try for me, too, and I hope you had better luck than I had . . .

It is now midnight, and I am writing this through a slight rosy haze of Chablis—we drank a bottle each over dinner . . . I did up a chicken in white wine with hot biscuits and we ate ourselves all out of shape and then listened to music. I am so sober these days, a spoonful of alcohol sends me over the moon—I notice there is a very nice one outside—and tomorrow I shall be hung over like a cliff. But it is fun occasionally. I love being sober, the mornings are so gay and fresh. I get up saying Hurray, here is another day . . . Tomorrow I don't know about . . . but I can guess. It is going to be awfully like old times, I am afraid . . .

All this my dear is to thank you—fulsomely—for the records, they are ravishing and I love them. How did you happen to think of me? Please tell me if you have not got the *Seraphim* and *Pastures Green* records, because I can get them for you here and would so like to send them . . . Be sure to tell me.

> With my love
> *Katherine Anne*

TO GEORGE PLATT LYNES   C-Bar-H Ranch, still, but not
for long.
Going to Santa Monica in two
days.
28 March, 1946

George darling:

. . . . Shall I tell you something perhaps a little surprising? I own a mountain. I bought it yesterday. I saw it for the first time day before yesterday. You know my constitutional *faible* for falling in love desperately at first sight. Apparently it works for mountains as well as for men, and God knows, even for mice. That remains to be seen. I feel so sane and happy and quiet about it I must just be mad once for all. It is about five thousand feet up, perhaps a little less, a good road—for mountains—all the way, in a government reserve. There is a valley on my mountain, with two fine springs—I bought it for the air, and the view and the water. (thirty thousand gallons a day, pure and cold.) My tract is eighty acres, but I have a man tunnelling the springs, the pipes were laid already, and when they are finished, the government grants me eighty acres more. It already has a little house and a little barn and some oddments like that on it, but I am going to build a rambling adobe business there later. I can have my own electricity with the water power, a swimming pool and a big irrigation reservoir. I am just telling you the practical things about it because I wouldn't dare to try to tell you how beautiful it is, and how, once having seen it, I could hardly leave it. . . .

So now I have only to finish this play, come east and settle about South Hill, go to Washington to the annual meeting of the Fellows of the Library of Congress, go back to Santa Monica and finish the novel, and I'll be all set to start my 'dobe shack on the mountain. That is my year's program. . . .

I'm feeling awfully free, untrammelled and independent, darling. My elbow room extends thousands of miles in every direction. Even after three hours on my mountain, I come down being very critical of mere desert air, and the confined little lives going on down here . . . One thing more—a government bombing range is near by—not too near I hope—so I can even sit in on the dress rehearsals for our destruction. Isn't that a splendid inducement?

I hope you'll be coming back soon. In any case, I'll see you; either here or New York in April.

> With my love
> *Katherine Anne*

To Albert Erskine

843 6th Street
Santa Monica, California
9 April, 1946

Dear Albert:

Happy birthday (18th) and would you mind kindly pulling yourself together and letting me know if anything special is happening to you. I don't know if it is mere extension of my own mouvementée career, heaven knows things are in a spin here, but of the kind I like: but are you doing something out of the ordinary, or even having it done to you? I have had the oddest feeling. I'm not doing this by astrology, numerology, mind reading, or any other esoteric means. It just rather keeps coming over me in waves that you are in unusual situations—not one, several . . .

I am taking a plane out of here on the 25th, and will be at the New Weston hotel until the morning of the 29th—unless I am in the country with friends part of that time—and then off to Saratoga Springs to settle up about South Hill. I have sold it to George Willison, he went up and looked it over and was pleased and took it. Just like that . . . I break even and a fraction over for luck, and a good thing too; for just a week before I bought a mountain and want to start building a house on it this fall. This kind of activity gives me the divine illusion that some day I am going to have a place to live, and in the meantime, I am all ready putting myself to sleep nights planning my house . . . It is beautiful, spacious, full of light and mountain air, the machinery all works, it glows and glitters with cleanliness and order without anybody turning a hand, the colors are all perfect though I can't quite see what they are, and no unpleasant person has ever yet knocked at that door . . . You never saw such a house, and neither did I, and perhaps nobody ever will. And yet it exists and I am living in it . . . and I mean to make a good try at putting it where others can see it, too.

I hadn't any faintest intention of buying a mountain, but I went to the Mojave Desert to finish up that Paramount job, and one day while out driving with some people I saw it and was hardly able to leave it even long enough to look for the man who owned it. Its not never-never land, either, it has two great springs (thirty thousand gallons of cold water every day, and a good road to it, and fine fertile land, a valley on a mountain top) a man is putting in the irrigation system, and another man is planting tomatoes (share-cropping already, how the traditional customs do come out) and I got it reasonably because the owner has a gold mine and wants some cash to work it . . . At the moment I bought it I didn't have a check book, or any money, I scratted round and raised $9.50 and borrowed fifty cents from somebody to make it an even ten, and he wrote me a receipt inside of a folding match thing, and the next day we went to the bank and put the thing through in good order . . .

So now I shall have my things sent on from South Hill, and visit a little with friends, come back here and finish the novel, and in the fall start the house . . . It all seems quite natural and simple and there were no difficulties.

But what is happening to YOU? Or is it that just all the Aprils or springs, anyway, when I knew you were seasons of uproar, upset, change of one kind or another—or so it seems to me now, from so far way . . . Well, anyway let me hear if only to prove what my strange little hunches are worth.

Yours,
Katherine Anne

To ALBERT ERSKINE

843 6th Street
Santa Monica, California
22 April, 1946

Dear Albert:

It could be simply the joyous and hopeful hubbub and brouhaha of my own affairs during the past month which gave me the impression that every body else—for some mysterious reason, especially you—was also making vast far reaching changes and all—from where I stand now—for the better . . .

Your changes seem to have come about more calmly and gradually, for all you tell me is news to me of course and good news . . . You seem to have four jobs at least and I am glad you are getting paid for three of them anyway—or so I hope. Honors first, and then money, if at all—such was my experience. Maybe it is typical.

I want to remind you of something I want to ask you when I see you and mightn't think of it . . . Apparently I have got an account with the wrong record shop—the Gramophone—there . . . Because all those records I mentioned to you I have utterly been unable to wring out of them in the past year or so . . . So I want to talk about your shop the Liberty and go there—it is the Liberty, isn't it? And you are please to tell me what you have and if I will be able to get some of them . . . Especially I want the *Magic Flute,* Damn it . . . I will bring my list and comb every shop in town before I go . . .

Monroe called me by long distance and invited me to the country for the week-end, so I'll just be getting off the plane in the morning and leaving for Stone Blossom in the afternoon of the

26th, and will be back Sunday the 28, and Monday the 29th for lunch will be fine for me . . . But I will be stopping at Monroe's instead of the New Weston for that time. He cheerfully told me he had cancelled my reservation it would be wasteful, which is true. I am going to stay over until May 1, to go to George Lynes' farewell dinner at the Soby's, (he is coming out here for a couple of years—) but I'll call you Monday morning or if you get to it first, call me at Monroe's . . . Its an engagement, up to now, and I can't see what would get in my way. You might just get bogged down in Boston . . .

My nephew Paul is here with me now and really he came out of the war wonderfully well. I have got him staked out in a little cabin on the beach and he is just resting and thinking it over in a pair of bathing trunks . . . He is music mad too so we spend days and evenings listening, listening . . .

See you soon.

Yours
Katherine Anne

TO PAUL PORTER

Hotel Algonquin
New York 18, N.Y.
21 May 1946

Paul darling:

Two cocktail parties today, one at the River Club to say good-bye to Somerset Maugham, where were also Mrs. Vanderbilt, Alice Roosevelt Longworth, two Astors, one male, one female, besides the Nelson Doubledays who were giving the party—and of course Barbara and Lloyd Wescott, Glenway, Monroe, me, and Somerset Maugham who assured me I was the greatest American writer; and a spate of other names you often see in the newspapers. Then we were out of there and on to Monroe's party for Jean Casson, where we did cultural relations with France and Russia and Java, and to my taste an immensely better party—

Well, where else have I been and what been doing? Lunch, with Albert Erskine and the Willisons, and all the South Hill business is settled. The other evening Ann, Walter and I went in back stage to see Cousin Lily, who looked lovely. Tomorrow afternoon I am going with her to see Laurence Olivier in The Old Vic *Oedipus Rex* and *The Critic.* (I keep writing and saying *The Rehearsal* because I think Buckingham's play is better and funnier but nobody else seems to think so, so I don't expect to see it in my life time but I'd like to). Tomorrow is lunch with Harold Ross, of *New Yorker,* also.

Well, people keep coming up for my autograph, but today they brought *Leaning Towers* to be signed, a change for the better ... I am seeing friends, sweet Eleanor Clark for dinner tomorrow night, and last night Paul Cadmus just back from Washington, cooked dinner for Monroe, Jarry French and me, the most fabulous chicken in white wine and sour cream and sherry and herbs I ever tasted. He just tossed it off, he doesn't pretend to cook—I may say I hung my head, all that Cordon Bleu stuff seemed so *wasted,* somehow.

Everybody seems to want to know about Christopher—do you see him? Do you see George?

By the time you get this it may be too late to answer, but I'll be seeing you soon anyway, and I hope you are managing things well and not being any more annoyed by outlandish folk than you like to be just for the hell of it!

All my love
Aunt Kat

Jared French's new painting scared the socks right off me. I'll describe it when I see you.

TO MONROE WHEELER   2058 Watsonia Terrace
                               Hollywood
                               13 June, 1946

Monroe darling:

Just twelve days ago I fell off the plane into the arms of George, who came all unexpected to the airport, and there, you might say with no hint of scandal, I have been ever since. . . .

What I meant to tell you though was something about George's coming-out party in Hollywood society. He had been coming out quite a lot already but the Adrians gave a big dinner party for him and in true Hollywood style, didn't let him know he was honor guest until he got there, which is much on the level of a stranger dedicating a book to one without asking, isn't it? (this occurs because it has just happened to me and the hell of a horrible little book it is, too—rhymed.) I don't remember all the guests, but there were Mei-Mei and Irene (Sherov?) and Bernardine, all three of whom George appears to have escorted, and a large assortment of moving picture and other celebities; and George as guest of honor was supposed to be seated at Janet's right, but somebody else wanted to sit beside Janet and just sat there, so George wandered off and took the first free chair. ("Well, darling, I *warned* you these people are real savages and won't observe even the tiniest little rule," I interrupted at this point in his narrative.)

He gave me a look and went on. It was a dull party apparently from the beginning, and Adrian has a theory—he told me so himself—that no group of guests or any evening at all should be allowed to take its natural form and progression, but must be controlled, whipped up, restrained, urged (by him, of course) until it takes on creative meaning. One fatality is the habit of two people who like each other to get into private conversation . . . So when things were pretty far gone to hell he got up a game. I think it was a word game, something like a charade but they call it something else. Never mind. At this point George, who had been doing a slow burn on one account or another all evening, rebelled openly, refused to take part, gathered up Mei-mei, Irene and I think Bernardine and walked out. The gals had some small feud or argument among themselves and yowed and yipped at each other all the way home. So you might just chalk up one more wasted evening, mightn't you? By no means . . . The next day George went to a huge cocktail party at Sir Charles Mendl's (who may have been celebrating Lady Mendl's Constellation flight out, out of this country) and there on all sides, by known and unknown alike, he was praised and patted for his fabulous heroism in walking out on an Adrian party . . . Nobody in the whole history of the human race had dared to do such a thing, though many had yearned to . . . Oh, what sophistication, what aplomb, quel savoir faire, wotta boy, in fact.

("Darling, I *told* you we are living in a suburb," I said.) And George got good and mad, just plain old fashioned American mad, at suddenly finding himself a celebrity (I'll never recover from Allen Porter's story about Mrs. Ford) for the wrongest reason any body ever heard of. What could have been more natural, he thought, than to have quit when he got so bored he couldn't even raise his eyebrows . . . However, a good spit in the eye is what Hollywood loves above all else, so George is a made man. Janet called George up and was plaintive, not indignant, which should give you the idea.

When I first got home before I knew I was going to bite the dust thataway, I invited George and Paul to go to *Henry Vth* with me. The date arrived last Saturday. It seemed best for us to meet at the Players' Restaurant, which is as nearly central as anything is around here; for George was going to Santa Monica to a roaring big cocktail party at the Hamilton Garlands (beautiful, rich, happily wed, I can't think where George got the idea that it would be perfect if they got a divorce so Mr. Garland, whom I have never seen and do not expect to see, could marry me. However, it is a beautiful thought) and Paul was going to be somewhere else. So I took a taxi and arrived five minutes before the hour set. Paul came in twenty minutes later, having travelled miles by foot, by hitch hikes, breathless and swearing to God he was going to stop trying to get around in this bloody place. He had two dollars in his pocket and I asked him why he didn't take a taxi as far as that would carry him, but he is not a boy to toss his money around like that. It is perhaps as well. We ordered martinis to soothe his heaving bosom, and then came a telephone from George saying he was bogged down in Life and Theda Bara, but was even then rushing towards us with speed and would we just go ahead and have dinner. We did, and the time came when we were going to be late for the show, so I decided that in such emergencies the thing to do was for the assembled company to march on to the next objective, and the lagging troop could follow the trail. So Paul galloped off to hail a taxi, and in rolled George, hair on end, having fought traffic for fifteen miles, and no dinner, and then we had to look for Paul, and at last we set off for more miles and got there in the middle of the Globe theater part, which was not doing so badly. Well, we WERE there, and how that picture did repay all the huzza and hullabaloo, which is after all only the normal way of getting around Out Here, as this region is so aptly called. It is quite simply glorious and we want to see it again, and at once. It happens to be set in my particularly loved and familiar period of French history, and I must say, Shakespeare's account from the English point of view of what led up to and away from Agincourt is strictly from nuts, or am I an incurable Francophile?

Well, where were we?

This is a profoundly unbalanced picture of what goes on really. In the intervals of George's dashing out and dashing in, meeting hundreds of people and apparently not liking one of them, Dick Sisson comes out and brings two beautiful Klees, and exchanges for two of George's for a while, which I think is a charming custom among owners of paintings. We play music for hours on end, just the kind we like, and we get in a lot of conversation . . . Lunch in the patio is always quiet and pretty. This blessed minute—Monday morning, 17 June, 1946, at exactly five minutes after twelve noon, George is sunbathing on his terrace and he was doing the same thing yesterday and the day before and almost every day I have been here. As for me, I have lolled in perfect ease and accumulated new forces in what would be called here, in just ordinary conversation, mind you, my "psychic reservoir" whatever the hell that is. I feel enormously better, it has been a most charming visit, and I am having a hard time making up my mind to quit this lovely safe bed (seventeenth century Spanish with a high, wide and inordinately fancy painted headboard, all over flowers, red laquer and gilt . . . I love it.) and go home and Face Things again . . . But this time I can take it easier, which was what I couldn't do two weeks ago . . . It has all been lovely and I have rested here with the confidence of old friendship, and so scandal, by way of our dear Bernardine, has reared its unsightly head. I know really nothing of Bernardine's private life, but I do know mine and it is of the kind she would describe as dull if she really believed it. But she does not . . . When I told her last spring that my favorite and very dear nephew Paul was coming to visit me, she mentioned then to George that beyond doubt he was no nephew and she seemed to wonder why I took the trouble to be discreet. When it was finally established that he [is] indeed close kin—we look like mother and child—it then became really interesting, a plain case of incest . . . I have never believed that incest was particularly interesting or prevalent. But God, who knows? Well, when I came back and went to visit George, naturally he mentioned it, and so it is settled. We have embarked upon an illicit lia——I find I can't spell it, but you-know-what. Well, Bernardine came to see us in our new love-nest and asked us what we had been doing and we said, "Playing records" and she asked "What, already?" or something of the sort, and beamed upon us gruesomely . . . Oh can you imagine? And what does one do with such an unteachable woman? Well, we decided it would do us no harm. I am going home today but not on that account, you may be sure. And George is disturbed about all kinds of things in this place, but not about that. Truth is, we think it is funny. . . .

Vic and George are now having lunch downstairs, and I am staying up here because I don't want to dress. Vic is the assistant in the Vogue thing, and I peeked over the stair rail for a glimpse of him, his luck being of the order that could possibly be communicable by a glimpse of his living person. He was one of the twelve photographers who went ahead of the Army to photograph the entry into Paris, and eleven of them were killed . . . It was such a flash I hardly got even an impression, but he seemed medium height and medium colored—I really only saw his shoulder and the top of his head. But still he was there, the one in twelve, of twelve fated men. I wonder does he wake up every morning still hardly believing he is here?. . . .

Love again
Katherine Anne

TO JOSEPHINE HERBST   843 6th Street
                           Santa Monica
                           16 August, 1946

Josie darling:

Eleanor wrote me from San Francisco that she saw you at the Grist Mill on her way west, and she wrote the best sort of news about you—that is, that you were reassuringly your splendid self, and the same good talk and the same *being* "all the things that I always liked in her, only more so as we go on," she wrote. I thought that was the kind of thing I like to hear about you. In South Hill I saw again your books in a row on the shelf, and your inscription to me that said I had always been the same person in all circumstances since you had known me. I was pleased with that again. And you seemed so much the same girl only that you had finished some things begun a long time ago, and on these conclusions you were on your way to something else. Eleanor didn't say what you were working on, but I hope you are working. . . .

A two hundred pound steel cabinet of mss, and notes and journals and letters arrived from Saratoga Springs the other day, and reading some of it over, I find the past much more solid than I had thought, and living much more continuous, which I had begun to doubt. I am glad now I kept all this, though I had no particular plan in doing so. Things just accumulated, and behold, it has become history . . . I found a lot of your old letters—I certainly never destroyed even one, so they are all around somewhere, and really, you are certainly among the best letter writers in the world, and I couldn't give up even one now for anything— and an honorable record it is too, darling. Never be afraid if they should fall into any hands at all. But they won't. I have made my will and have a literary executor, and unless you claim your letters now, which I hope you won't, they'll go in with the rest, to be sorted and used as part of a story. I don't know that story any more than you do, especially not the end, and we will never see it, and I think it not very important whether we do or don't . . . It doesn't belong to us anyway. . . .

With my love,
Katherine Anne

TO MONROE WHEELER   843 6th Street
Santa Monica, California
18 December, 1946

Monroe darling:

Your letter was lovely, and I've been quoting bits from it to George by telephone, and when I was at dinner there the other evening, he showed me his letters from you and Glenway, and I remarked that we behaved as if we were stranded on a desert isle grabbing occasional bottles out of the sea with your messages in them . . . I really am at a loss to explain *why* I feel so in a vacuum here. It does seem to be a kind of *far niente,* but not somehow so very *dolce* . . .

Your account of things at the Museum, and the Falstaffian army of intellectuals, U.N. ones, makes me feel like taking a train and coming there if only for one look: it does seem the kind of thing I should not miss, and yet I have seen it, on a smaller scale, in several other countries. Another glimpse would only confirm too hideously what I already know, and I should probably feel like blowing my brains out . . . Oh, I know they are clowns, but I don't think this world of human beings is altogether just a circus to provide a ring for them to clown in, and after a little while the fun turns pretty nightmarish . . . Think of it, that gang is making the decisions of life and death for the whole human race . . . And there is not one among them that I would trust to decide even the smallest least important problem that I can imagine in my own life . . . I would not trust one of them even to be able to see what the problem really was, much less to have any honest intentions of really settling it properly. So much for that . . . It sounds a little like despair, and it may be . . .

I didn't see any pictures of Henry Moore in the papers, of course: but did see those of Raymond Duncan in his curtains, and also one of Edmund Wilson—looking by now like a cross between Winston Churchill and Herbert Hoover, God help him—with his new six-foot wife, just after he was kicked in the pants by a Reno reporter . . . Apparently he has decided to stop being Bunny and be a big Wolf . . .

His nasty book shocked me because it was so grossly ignorant and insensitive, and I had all this time been thinking of him as rather a *sensible,* intelligent man. To find out at this late day he is a mere goon is sad . . . Still he does not leave a gap in my life because I hardly saw him once in a year and thought of him perhaps not that often . . .

I hadn't heard about the projected sale of Harcourt Brace. I say simply what I have said before—when Donald Brace goes, I go; that is, if I can break away. They made it impossible the last time I tried, but maybe by now they wouldn't mind. I don't exactly dislike everybody else in the place, I am just indifferent, I think they are a dull lot.

My mountain is not quite sold, but I had a cash offer which, after all fees and expenses are paid up, would give me just eleven hundred dollars profit . . . Well, I am not in the real estate business, though you might think so from the way I go on. This is the third place I have bought and sold in nine years, total profits about four thousand in that time. I do not look upon this as a get-rich-quick scheme, I was quite honestly trying to get a place to live, but I am romantic in these matters and my judgement, let us just admit freely, is even worse than in husbands . . . I am good for friendship and for writing. Nothing else at all, and I began to suspect this a good while ago. I cannot think it matters much whether I live in this flat the rest of my life, but I do want to keep my friends and get my work done. . . .

If I get the novel finished, I mean to go to Paris too, I had set next April as perhaps the time I could go, but then, it is nonsense to plan so far ahead . . . And I shan't go unless I get some kind of job of writing to do there, maybe a series of articles for some magazine, but I have not even given a thought about where to begin prospecting for such a chore, and so it is all very vague. But Marcelle and Henri Calet and other nice people write me I am a great *succès* there, I should come and cut a few fresh laurels before they wither, and so I imagine the succès is something like at home— *d'estime,* which you know I do not despise . . . The few reviews I have seen from Paris are really remarkable. They just broke down and took me in and said I was good and that everybody should read me: and invariably they took a smack at Hemingway, Steinbeck, Faulkner, and who is that other one? Saroyan? Caldwell? both, I think, and the only thing that bothers me is that they mention them all in one breath, not really being able to pick out Hemingway and Faulkner from the others . . . At any rate, they all say I am the best of the lot and wonder why I wasn't translated before. I repeat all this with the utmost vanity, as you can see, because it is just true that I hoped the French would like me, and this funny little triumph made me happy.

Social life here is very odd—or at any rate, the kind that comes near me. Adrian and Janet have long wanted me to come to dinner with a horrible beast of a woman named Ayn Rand who wrote a trashy fascist-minded book, and I have side stepped of course. So not long ago they asked George to ask me to come, still hoping I think for some disturbance of the peace for an evening's amusement, and I explained again to George that They had no right to introduce such a creature to me, or expect me to know her. George found another and politer excuse and it has all blown over again . . . Then, the editor of a foul little newspaper here in Santa Monica called suddenly and explained that the Ferdy Grofé's were giving a big party on the 21st for literary celebrities, and they had asked him to make a list of those in Santa Monica, with telephone numbers, for them to invite. Then I had a call from Mrs. Grofé and she had two reasons for inviting me: it was a party just for celebrities and there was going to be ham for supper, too . . . It is an odd little *sequitur,* don't you think? Darling, I cannot tell you how desolate this kind of thing seems to me. I thanked her very much, but I had another engagement. . . .

Love again, your devoted
Katherine Anne

TO CININA AND ROBERT   843 6th Street
PENN WARREN   Santa Monica
                                             22 December 1946

Dear Red and Cinina:

. . . . Albert sent me a novel—*Under the Volcano*—which he is devoted to, and I can't say just what I think now, because I read it only once and want to look at a good many things again, for it seems to me to show a real brilliancy. But oh God, how to the eyebrows am I fed up on the ubiquitous hero-heel with the soul of a sick jelly-fish—he never can believe in anything, an impotent Don Juan, an amateur theologian wrong-side-out, who asks God to destroy this world because that is the only way he will ever be able to get his nose out of a goblet of mescal or whatever his particular form of self-indulgence is. The poet manqué wallowing in a Baudelairian bed of Flowers of Evil . . . Christ, as the characters are always yelping, and I find it is catching . . . Yet there is something to the book, only I am left in deep doubt of one thing: is the author deceived by his *hombre noble,* or not? And if that is a noble man then what was Dante, Sir Thomas More, St. Francis, Erasmus, or even in the end just the Prince whose name I can't remember now, in *War and Peace*? He makes an ass of Hugh, proving his desire to help was just insufficiency; but if you are a poor soul, isn't it rather better to feel pity for other poor souls and try to help, than just to sit down and wallow in your own distempered guts as our hero-heel does?

Well, of course, its all a question. Albert asked me to tell him the truth, and I mean to do it, if I can find out what it is . . . I don't like the book, there is a taint in it I have smelt before, and never liked. But I am going to read it some more, and meantime will probably temper my language a little, too. But this hero—he is Cain, he is Judas, only gelded morally, psychically, spiritually. And so by doing nothing he assists all evil. . . .

Katherine Anne

To Robert Penn Warren   843 6th Street
Santa Monica
27 February, 1947

Dear Red:

. . . . Nobody would be happier than I to contribute even one little green leaf to a garland for John Crowe Ransom, on his sixtieth birthday, (and *we* should live so long) for I'd bring him a whole Sarah Frost camelia in full bloom if I could—but golly, do you realize that I never opened my mouth on the subject of poetry except in the most unprofessional way and among friends I could trust? So I am stuck with a unique task; but I am going to do it if it kills me. Truth is, I am appalled and intimidated by the critical essays on poetry I read in the reviews—those boys have really got me licked, if they but knew or cared. Poetry is something I read and love, I really only read poetry and criticism and letters and documents, but the awful truth is, if you sat me down with pencil and paper and said, "Write in five hundred well chosen words what you think of this—" ("Captain Carpenter," for example—) I should be stymied.

Years ago, I loved and do now, "Captain Carpenter," "Blue Girls," "Dead Boy," "Bells for John Whiteside's Daughter"—and also I was fond of Allen Tate's "Ditty," but he was severe with me about that and also "Captain Carpenter" . . . So I decided there was no pleasing these poets, you could never pick their favorite poems and it was better just to keep quiet and gnaw your favorite bones to yourself . . . (This was really *then,* it must have been 1926). But I don't want to go into personal reminiscence and sentimental feelings, drooling like Ford Madox Ford; God knows, there is a time for that, but is it now? I think not. So I shall pull myself together, and read all the poems over again and try to do something that will not disgrace us . . . Still, I have an awful hunch that you are right when you say I'll provide a slant you just couldn't get anywhere else.

I sent a telegram to a dinner given to John Crowe Ransom when he left—was it Vanderbilt University? *Tant pis* for Vanderbilt. That's a vulgar name, and the heads of the Institution lived right up to it in that episode, I remember . . .

Let me tell you something about poetry which will probably explain something. I read it first when I was about ten, and I cannot even think of it now without a rising of the hair: "Fear no more the heat of the sun . . ." remember that? . . . .

About your doleful dumps, there is no cure except within yourself, which I think is always damned bad, sad news. But about Cinina's cold, being material, being subject to medical science, let me brag: I haven't had a sniffle since Doctor Nelson shot a venomous looking, emerald colored fluid into my arm, which makes now two mortal years. It stung—stang?—like a bee, for fifteen minutes, twice a week for three months, but it worked. So I wish she could try it . . . Look, for two thousand years we haven't learned a damned thing about feeling or behavior or morals or anything that matters . . . But medical science and machinery are quite workable, and we may as well enjoy their benefits. And in any other time, I should by now have been a toothless hag probably on crutches with arthritis or gout or dropsy, and frankly I'm delighted not to be. And I owe it to medical science which pulled me together and balanced my tottering chemistry and shored up my wavering teeth and kept my waistline intact, and I may be a born heathen but all this gives me a consolation and pleasure which no religion I ever heard of has ever been able to afford. So, in short, I wish Cinina could find a doctor who would inoculate her against colds, for I don't like to think of her having colds, even if she is well cured of her old malady.

So do survive this spring, for everybody's sake.

> With my love to you both
> *Katherine Anne*

I am invited to lecture at LSU and also Sewanee this spring. LSU has made me two offers to run the "creative writing" dept, since I left there, and I lived there for two years and not a single invitation to talk to the students . . . isn't that absurd?

TO GLENWAY WESCOTT 843 6th Street
Santa Monica
19 March, 1947

Glenway darling:

I just wrote to Eleanor in effect: Hosanna, huzza and hullabaloo, with alarums and excursions, three cheers and a double tiger with a pickled onion—so deeply do I feel the implicit justice of the committee's—that is to say, your—decision in the matter of that sacred little grand. I am sure they have, as the British say, laid out the money well. And now let's hope she gets the whole good of it.

Well, so much for literature. Let us now unbend and talk about familiar things.

Your other—and wonderful—letter discussing Eleanor, her character, her history, struck me as a thing not to be answered lightly. You know I usually do answer lightly in the sense that I just begin and let the topic carry me whither it will. But this time I took notes, and of course, lost them. I kept telling myself that a letter is not a short story, and unpremeditated outpourings are best. So I gave up, not being able to be unpremeditated on this particular subject. And yesterday afternoon I found the notes, here transcribed:—

About Eleanor: I don't know about the St. Leger episode. I know there was something between them, but what? Relations were strained between us on Eleanor's side in Washington because the Tates—who have singly and together the most irresponsible tongues in the world, the most slanderous minds—had persuaded Eleanor that I was her enemy. The truth was that Caroline was her enemy because Allen had the prurient curiosity about her which passes for sexual attraction with him, and Caroline hated her for that (typical wifely attitude, I suppose.) I often wondered why Eleanor, whom I liked so well, kept dodging, or so it seemed to me. I am easily discouraged in such matters, so gave her up. At least a year and a half later she told me about all this, and wept. I said, "What awful nonsense, and why didn't you know better? Don't you know the Tates? Don't you know me, at all?". . . .

As for cynicism, who could be more suavely and obliquely cynical than St. Leger himself? Whoever treats with him honestly would be sorry, I imagine. Still, I wish you would tell me about this.

Why should we demand of Eleanor such virtues as, in so many instances, we demand of no one else? Look, my dear, at the utterly impossible human beings we have taken for friends—Cocteau for one on your part. Hart Crane for mine—and so perhaps we should be willing to lower the standards a little too for our present candidate . . . As for her not being willing to say Thank you, why darling, she said it to me when I offered to sponsor her, in the most complete simplicity and goodness . . . not that I wanted thanks. I did it for her talent, not for her.

I remember in Washington once, when I broke out against St. Leger and his Fascist works to Eleanor and Denis Devlin, they both rose up and defended him with fury, and I was all but floored. Denis I can understand, in Eire diplomacy as he is, representing a toy Fascist state, but Eleanor—well, my scunner against St. Leger was not against his poetry—some of the most awful black mean souls I know write very good poetry—Tate, St. Leger, Eliot, even Robert Lowell in spots—but against his political chicanery in Washington . . . It is not enough that Washington can welcome a Vichyite in time of war, the State Department can take his advice, God, no—they must also make him a fellow of the Library of Congress in order not to appear to be paying him for his real work . . . You may well imagine how annoying I found all this. Well, where were we?

As I was all for hanging Ezra Pound, on the grounds that a poet should also be considered a responsible citizen when he takes a political stand—so I shouldn't at all mind seeing St. Leger consigned to a dungeon—because he is a mischief-maker. But about their poetry, what I want to say is this: Denis (not a first rate poet, but good, interesting, rather elegant) St. Leger (not first rate either but impressive) Eliot (a dry damned soul who packs an awful wallop) are still lifting their voices like a pack of mournful hounds for everything in this world that was and will be our damnation: Religious mysticism (in Eliot's case, the Church of England makes it slightly comic) myth, the voice of the blood, the will of man to be deceived, the dark, shapeless, half-idiotic mutterings in its sleep of some protozoic thing that never emerged from the first slime of life: so, I read them and think, Yes, they are clever. They really do know the language so that it makes good music but filthy nonsense. Yet good music does not make nonsense and good poetry does not, either . . .

The notes end here, you'll be glad to know. So let us onward to better and higher things . . . I don't know about George needing the young. (do you remember your letter before last? I'm talking about that one now). Is he old? Then what am I? I suppose I should give a conventional shudder, but I can't, I like my age. I don't need young OR old. Every one of value to me has his own value, his age is where he happens to be at the moment. It is true that for a great while men much younger than I fell in love with me, and I fell in love with them, too. Love always comes out of need, but I often wondered rather despairingly why some one nearer my time didn't love me, for then we would have something to build a life upon. But they didn't. And no one loves me now, and that seems quite natural too . . . I have had great good of love—happiness and good company, hopefulness, trust; if they passed, so do the seasons and so does life and no one ever had to remind me of this. I have had so much love, I do not want any more. But all of us have the right to share in everything we love until our last day: but how we love and what we love, who loves us and why, surely change with our times, and what is strange about that? You tell me about that good, kind, easy love you had for such a little while, but what have you had beside but a great love full of suffering and accidents and changes, that has lasted you all your life until now? What surprises you that this little boy couldn't possibly do more than please you sweetly for a while and then blow up with fire works, all drama, all youthful misunderstanding and disappointment? Look at him again. What was he? It is possible you *did* wrong him. You once advised me not to put on some one more responsibility than he could take . . . You were right, too . . . I think you were never young in that sense, as I never was either; but you had great good fortune to find some one who was not young in that sense either: that is to say, you met your match early, one who could not defeat you nor be defeated by you, and everything after that must be just experiment— just experiment, my dear. So I am glad you had your gayety and sweetness, but it is expensive, and you mustn't pay interest too in sickness and restlessness. If it was a drug, disintoxicate yourself. Love is not a drug and you know it.

(Note: I keep thinking I will call up George and ask him what red-head that was. Tread light, good friend. Wait at least until the bandages are off your fingers before you put them in the fire again.)

My last glimpse of Monroe through your eyes is perfectly right, perfectly natural. He *is* terrible, thank God. I think all of us can depend on that.

Whatever his image of your potentialities may have been, whatever any one expected, you have done that and more. But it is no good trying to persuade you . . . What I hear of his health and what you say troubles me. Do you suppose the time comes when we must face futures without those who made the past for us? It seems so soon. With my love.

Katherine Anne

To Albert Erskine   843 6th Street
                              Santa Monica, California
                              18 May, 1947

Dear Albert:

Your letter and enclosure of mine reached me on my birthday, and that was only one of a series of odd little coincidences of dates. For I went South in mid-April to lecture at LSU and Sewanee, being promoted of course by our old friends Cleanth and John Palmer, and so it happened that the 19th of April found me in Baton Rouge, and except for the fact that I was coming down with flu, Cleanth, Tinkum and I had meant to spend that day in New Orleans, and quite without planning, too. Well the little tour was a modest triumph and a pleasant reunion with people I like and who like me, and still I could barely keep on my feet, having got a high fever: I held up until I got to Sewanee, had a beautiful evening there, then went to the hospital for five days. Then up two for an evening with John, who was by now suffering from frustration of his plans for a gay round of things, but I must say he behaved like a hero and was goodness itself all through. I travelled by train, having had so much trouble last year, engine trouble all the way to New York and really dangerous storms all the way back, I decided my luck at flying was running out. But this trip meant eight gruelling days getting chilled in Pulman berths, and did me no good either. So I got back here on the 6th of May, had dinner with Wm. Wyler and Margaret Tallichet on the 7th—they were getting off to Europe—and on the 8th went to bed and called in doctor and nurse . . . Nurse left yesterday afternoon, Golly, I have been washed and spoon fed and plied with sulfa and bossed breathless—but it did work, I am up, feeling a little lost and forsaken of God and man, but it will pass . . .

(The occasion with the Wylers was, that he is considering taking "Old Mortality" for a picture, but as every one says—there are a half dozen people surrounding him who are working on him to take it; he is slow, slow, it takes half of eternity to get a notion through his bean, but once he gets it, hosanna . . . So we are hoping he will get it. He simply said at parting he hoped when he got back we would work together, and I said I hope so too, and we swapped a show of teeth and a handshake. So keep your fingers crossed. It would settle my financial whatnots for life . . .)

Margaret—called Talli by her friends, and she is admitted to be the nicest and best liked woman in this place—has her third baby, a boy this time and she said she was glad because Wyler wouldn't feel so outnumbered by females in the house . . . They live in solid state, with Japanese servants all over the place. Immense amounts of silver and furniture and rugs and so on, but I thought she looked like a little girl at the table, somehow I felt she had little to do with all that luxury, it is given to her, she lives in it without much sense of *being* in it. I may be wrong. Yet it is undoubtedly what she wanted . . . Or anyhow, beyond question the best she could ever have had. Her two little girls wear old-fashioned pinafores and long curls, and they curtsey, and after they went to bed she remarked that she always felt that at least twenty people had left the room when she got rid of them . . . She is seeing Paris for the first time, and expressed apprehension that Wyler would just take over and run everything and she would never get to see the place for herself . . . which about sizes up her situation.

Well, you see you didn't need me to put over *Under the Volcano.* From all I hear and have seen, it was a real hit, and I was glad for you, but still have my reservations as you still have your judgement of it . . . It is a better book than most that have come out in its time . . . My real chagrin came when Helen Taylor sent me a page-proof of a novel called *The Left Hand is The Dreamer,* asking my opinion. And I wrote her that I thought it about the nastiest little job I had seen for some time. So now it is a best seller, practically neck and neck with *Forever Amber* . . . It is worse than F.A. though, because it is pretentious as hell . . .

In Baton Rouge rumors had come through that you and Taylor were going into publishing on your own. I did hope it was true, for from the first you had said to me that what you really wanted was a publishing company of your own . . . I think you will have it yet, but this is really a shaky moment to take it on . . . When Bennet Cerf was trying to get me to come to Random House in 1940, he remarked that really, publishing business was just peanuts. That year he had hit the million dollar point for the first time. "Compare that with steel or oil or the automobile industry," he said . . . Apparently he has kept this in mind and is doing his best to get publishing into the big industry field . . . Let's hope you will do well there until the time comes for you to go on your own . . .

I am enjoying a feeling of anarchic freedom after my five weeks of guesthood, making schedules, keeping engagements, catching trains, and being sat on by doctors and nurses. This morning I made my own coffee exactly the way I like it, and went down to look at my roses and camellias and azaleas and gardenias and tuberous begonias, and they thrive. Only the roses are in bloom now, with the begonias coming on. But oh, my roses . . . they are enormous and perfect, and though they look real to me at any distance, a nearsighted being came in a day or so ago and peered and said, "Why they look artificial." Not to me they don't, after all the spraying and watering and mulching and watching every leaf and petal unfold . . . My camellias were triumphs also, if you don't mind a little pure shameless bragging, and the gardenias promise nicely . . . Tinkum has a hedge of gardenias from the two I gave her when I left Baton Rouge, just cuttings from the parent plant five feet high now. So I took fifteen cuttings and have preserved them all the way, and shall make a little hedge here, the third generation from those first two that I loved so and was so happy to see in bloom if only once . . . Mrs. Blanchard also showed me a hedge about fifty feet long and remarked "That is Eleanor's wedding bouquet." The south is nicer now, everything seems to be more comfortable, the negroes are better paid and look happier, the place is building up. The Tennessee Valley and all Sewanee is one of the beauty spots of this world . . . I was happy there for the first time since I was born, and had a real pull towards the place . . . anywhere, Louisiana, Tennessee, South Carolina, Alabama. It wouldn't matter . . . but I can't live there, I know it, I never could, its no good being sentimental . . .

Tinkum and Cleanth are going to sell their little house when they move to Yale. LSU which ignored me the two years I spent in Baton Rouge, paid me four hundred dollars and expenses to come back for one evening, and I never was so interviewed and photographed and radioed and misquoted in the student paper in my life. They were so friendly and gay and interested it did not seem like the same place . . . I have also had two invitations to come there and take charge of the "creative writing" (whatever that means) dept . . . Funny, isn't it?

Well, I have about thirty letters to write, and as for those four pieces of work I was on in January, only one is finished and another coming up . . . But I mean to get through with everything, including that seven-times-blowed-up novel. Odd thing is, no matter when I get a few pages done, over the years, it is just the same thing—tone, pace, style, you can't tell where the breaks came . . . So I guess it is all right. But I am in a ferocious mood now, and would throw my own bother (stet! But I meant to write Brother) down stairs if he interrupted me at work. I've had that, thank you, and I'm thoo, as they say in Texas . . .

Yes, we'll take up our discussion some other time. Meantime I do wish you the very best of luck, meaning simply that I hope your work will be appreciated, and that you have a chance to do something that you like.

Yours
Katherine Anne

How do you like being thirty six? My God, how young you were when we first met. But I must say you fooled me—you seemed a lot more mature than you turned out to be, but still, that was not YOUR fault . . . You have got a long way to go to catch up with me, but don't hurry . . . One thing nice I find: I like my age, and its a fact you never reach the place you set out for, but continually are on the way, with all sorts of plans and unfinished business and the most endless hopes. I still believe I shall be given time to get a great deal of my work done, though . . . Of course I do—that is where divine hope comes in . . .

To Andrew Lytle

843 6th Street
Santa Monica, California
15 September, 1947

Dear Andrew:

. . . . I read your book [*A Name for Evil*] and my hair, wild at best, tried to break its moorings entirely. But first I must say this: we are in opposite schools of thought (interrupted here. It is now morning of 16 September) as to the causes of the present disintegration of what we have looked upon as civilization. To begin with, I cannot possibly consider Western European Christianity as the highest civilization this world has seen. It has been most horribly bastard, a badly assimilated mess of Egyptian, Judaic, Greek sifted through Rome, mixed very imperfectly with tribal beliefs and customs of the ancient western world; every religious notion of the entire old world seeped into Christianity in Europe and has roiled and stank there ever since like maggots in a corpse. There were beautiful and wonderful things in European civilization, and this, to my sincere conviction, is because the spirit and mind of man is truly indomitable, his creative will rises above and somehow does work in spite of the darkness and confusion of his instincts. My own conviction is that the so-called subjective mind, or the unconscious (I know this is the jargon of modern psychology, but we do know what we mean, we must call it something) is a moral imbecile, a total ignoramus; and that the real struggle in the nature of man is to conquer, to shape, to try to explain by intellectual processes, and to justify by almost any means, the dark, bloody, irrational faiths of his sub-cellar being. You may say, this is an argument against the intellect: I say simply that the intellect has this function, and that it has been partially unsuccessful is simply to say that it is also human, and limited. But I say to the end that it is the best thing we have, it is all we have, if we are to be saved, that is to say, if we ever save ourselves, it will be through the workings of the intellect which gradually will free itself, and be able to use instead of being used by, the forces of instinct. I shall here leap over a long train of reasoning, for I don't want to put you to sleep, and conclude: "modern" man (man is always modern) in trying to *be* God has merely reached the reductio ad absurdum of his original absurdity in *creating* a God in his own image. I believe in God under no matter what name we call him; That is to say, there is a Power "that moves the sun and other stars" and we can daily see the working of a law in what is visible to us of the universe. This law is irresistible, absolute, we are subject to it without any will of our own, and to question it in the sense of rebelling against it is puerile nonsense. To inquire into it is our natural right and good mental and spiritual exercise. But no one has ever been able to explain in terms of religious dogma one single point that satisfies me in the least, either in heart or mind. All systems of religious belief and social systems founded on them are trivial, downright silly, compared to the limitless grandeur of the plan of which, only now and then, the spirit is given some tremendous and consoling surmisal.

God as conceived by man is a purely human invention, what can you expect of him other than what we do get? And as for the special disasters of our times, I cannot see that man is behaving much worse than he always has, in any religion, any system of society, only at millennial changes you may have observed that there is an added shamelessness and desperation due to his knowledge, forced upon him by events and yet hardly acknowledged by him, that *he has failed again* because of his refusal to take upon *himself* the responsibility for his own acts. His God has failed him again; that is, his attempts to identify the will of God with his own human desires and willful beliefs has thrown him again into utter confusion. At this point, even more than the outright criminals now in power, I fear those petty theologians who are preaching a "return" to blind faith, to religion, to what they call God, frantically assuring us that our only salvation is to put our heads back in the noose. They are trying to avoid the true issues, and make us swallow again the old stale theological messes we have vomited up once, after two thousand years of being poisoned by it. At a time when the world situation is on the point of breaking up into fragments, (only to be re-assembled in a slightly different shape, but of the same materials) because of the division in our minds between spirit and substance, we are urged to make this division absolute, so that religion will have no responsibility for human wrongs, no earthly concerns; in fact, it condones and supports the most awful human crimes so they are committed in defense of religion. I know nothing about the true nature of God, and I have never known or heard of any one who did: but I have a private theory. He is not a petty criminal on the human order. And if he is concerned with human individual souls, he does not know the difference between the Pope and the beggar sitting on the church step. And as for the putrid little social snobbisms of this world, it is an insult to the very idea of Divine omnipotence to attempt to justify them or support them by claiming they are based on a caste system ordained by Him.

Well, there are hundreds of things to be said about your book and no doubt they will all be said sooner or later by somebody. I will just slap down my first impressions. I think I never read anything—not even excepting the "Turn of The Screw"—in which a murderer took such a winding long roundabout way to his crime, nor so elaborately provided an alibi not for the world but for *himself.* That love is an evil murderous passion Christianity has from the first insisted: that sex is vile St. Jerome perhaps more than any other succeeded in convincing us. That men and women when they are mismatched can hate each other is a human phenomenon a blind man could hardly miss.

Interruption. It is now September 20.

This reminds me of my favorite story about Fray Luís de Léon, who was accused of preaching heresy (around 1560 or 70) at Salamanca. So he went off to prison where he stayed for a great number of years. Then he was freed, and returned to Salamanca, ascended his chair and began his lecture: "Gentlemen, as we were saying yesterday—"

However, the Inquisition is not after us, so we may speak freely; I'm sure that if it were, almost none of us would have Luís de Léon's courage.

Two of the most terrible love stories in literature happen to be rather brief ones: a chapter in *The House of the Dead* called "The Husband of Akoulka," and the "Turn of the Screw." Dostoyevski's hero merely beats his wife to death with fists and clubs, and you know where it landed him. Like the wife in your story, she was also innocent; but he *wishes* to believe evil of her because that would justify him in his acts. Your hero has a beautiful young wife, whom he loves on the lowest possible level, sexual attraction without tenderness, and with vanity in her beauty. His hatred of her and his hatred of the land are based on the same motive: he feels himself challenged in his manhood. On the physical level it is fairly simple, yet after years of fairly harmonious sexual living he must finally rape her. She offers him no living rival against whom he can tilt a lance—how the old symbols do creep in—so he must provide for his own justification an all-powerful spirit of evil, the Devil against which no mortal can contend successfully (without Divine aid, of course, which he neglects to call upon.) By this device he is free to corrode her innocence in his own mind, to invent his own slanders of her secretly, to proceed subtly and determinedly against her.

What is the second ghost who comes but his own good angel—(I can't keep the old gobbledygook of theology out of this, either) fighting however ineffectually in defense of his victim? A ghost of his own blood, a man who has learnt in eternity, and maybe that is what eternity is for, the nature and meaning of love, that is to say, love purged of its evil imaginings. He wants to play God, as you say, to his wife, to the negro serving man, even to the land, above all to the land, and they instinctively and rightly resist him. When his wife finally, out of her fatigue, her clearness, and her pure sense that something threatens her, speaks a most human word of practical criticism he takes her for an enemy, he makes it another point against her. The wonder of course, on the human level, is that her patience lasted so long, and why she had not spoken so long ago. Naturally, it is the Demon Lover who has opened her eyes to his dishonesty, his malignancy.

He has made every condition of living as difficult for her as he can, and in his total shamelessness he never once regards her as a human being created by the same power that created him, but must invent her for his own purposes. From the moment she speaks, revealing her self as separate from him with a destiny of her own, one realizes that her fate is sealed. She as victim had had her warning from the beginning, and her early instincts for flight were good. Then she is lulled half asleep by her very incapacity to grasp the nature of her danger, and when her last chance comes she does not even recognize it.

Everything is almost too symmetrical, if my reading is in line: Even to the destruction of the unborn child with its mother: the child which is the one reality, the one assurance of the future in the natural sense, which the man destroys because he loves nothing, and believes in nothing, not in the past, nor present nor future. And I think it is no good to say that such a man would find salvation in some kind of belief in a God outside himself. A man cannot create an idea of God better than himself—a glance at some of the Revelations is enlightening—and this reasoning madman who knows even his madness is false, a mere trick to fill up the void in him with romantic invented situations and sentimental murderous confusions, would also see through any God he might be able to invent.

You speak of the false romantic temperament. My notion is that all romantic temperament is false, based on falseness; and there is always in it a deep-in-the-grain vulgarity. When, after flights of language, high flown acts, it finally comes now and then to ground, it exposes its grossness. For example: This man, among all the complexities of his self-absorption, resents the fact that he is expected—by society, perhaps, certainly not by his wife—to maintain her in a style *worthy of his feeling for her.*

My God. Not because she might enjoy a pleasant life with him, and he with her, not of any generous wish on his part to do as well as he can, not just for her, but for them both; not just because of his feeling for her, which is a monstrous compound of vanity, cruelty, and self-consciousness, but for the sake of their mortal destiny together. All the way through he admits his enjoyment of their hard-won luxuries and *menus plaisirs,* in the end they seem more important to him than they do to her, but in some way you show the reader plainly—this reader, anyway, that he really resents *having to share them with her.* The notion of making her life pleasurable is unendurable to him. He wishes to make her suffer because that makes him feel his power over her. He cannot, in a word, endure to do anything that will solve the problems of human living on a natural human level, where they belong. I feel that he is one of so many little souls who have no destiny—did you read *Under The Volcano?* there was another one—was not capable of having one, but sees that people who do have one somehow have hold of a secret of life; and he sets out to be important, come hell, come high water. Is that not vulgarity, the very essence of the romantic temperament?

As I said, there is a lot more to it than this, but for the present this must do, for I am writing at top speed before I am stopped again by something or other, and the relation with his wife is all netted together with the other relations, so that one can more or less explain and stand for the others. When I noted that even the land resisted him, that is of course my error. Land exists, it has its own nature, it can be used or abused; it will respond according to its treatment. We have seen too many deserts made to bloom not to know this. But his intentions towards the land were as evil as those towards his wife; and he excuses himself *to himself* by pretending to believe that it was cursed by the last owner who had brought it to perfection. You make a wonderful stroke when the negro says, after the curse, that he expected to see the fields blighted in one stroke, but no, the next day they were as yellow as butter . . . And this is right because nothing mortal is ever brought to perfection. If our unfortunate hero had worked with love and knowledge, and waited, he would have brought in many a crop as good or better. But no, it was easier, it was more romantic, in a word, it was more fun, to sit down under a curse and become a murderer . . . Really Andrew, you are as remorseless with your hero as he was with his victims—you don't leave him a single way out.

Well, we have no evils now that were not prepared for long ago,† by people very much like ourselves, and no doubt we are preparing our share of doom for the next comers. Our present evils are no greater, except in scope, in mere volume, than they were in those now so-called golden ages of faith when man blamed his evils on the Devil and his virtues such as they were on God. He behaved just as badly but only gave different excuses for it. We have always a preponderance of evil because Man loves it, he cannot live without it. Times change, but human nature does not. There are periods, I believe, that are somewhat better than others—I speak always and only on the level of human existence in this world, here and now—but they do not last for long, the scales crash inevitably on the side of evil, because that is the line of least resistance. Did you ever hear of the world falling into the state of good? If Evil is the true God, it is because Man prefers it so. He has only to choose. And he does choose. But he will not accept the responsibility of his choice. He prefers to call it Major Brent because he cannot, cannot—oh why can he not? this to me is the riddle of the universe—face the truth of his own motives . . .

Well Andrew my dear, I didn't mean to write you a book. You see why it took me so long to get going . . . I knew how it would be . . . It seems an odd time of day to try touching at top speed the dark insoluble problems of man's hatred of this life—which he claims came from God, or at least some of them do—and which has nothing wrong with it per se but his view, and his use of it . . . like

---

†In a draft for this letter Katherine Anne Porter wrote: "We have a little easy habit of blaming everything on our times. Our Time is not pretty, but you know, I am a student of western history, especially from St. Jerome, Augustine, Origen onwards to the death of Erasmus. This is my stamping ground and I am at home there. We have no evils now that were not prepared for then."

those fields . . . like that wife . . . I must give it up for the present, but you see how the theme of the book did touch me off . . . and speaking of theme, you mention that your difficulty in finding a title comes of your book having a theme . . . Dear Andrew, I have a theme, too, deeply only *one,* but capable of many variations . . . Did you not suspect this? Look again some time when you have time. No, lack of theme is not the reason for finding titles easily. Some people can and some can't, and it has nothing to do with theme or anything important. Its a knack. You either know what your story should be called or you don't, and if you don't, you have to worry about it a little . . . Some things, thank God, are as simple as that or we'd all go mad.

One last word about Paul Engle and his saying that his ancestors had been good shoemakers in Germany for five hundred years and his feeling that as a poet he was a change for the better. I think we shall agree that to exchange a good shoemaker for a mediocre poet is no bargain at all, and he forgets apparently that the large majority of great artists of Europe came from peasantry or humble artisans or at least families of modest estate. The trouble with the arts I think is that they have become middle class. Its a fact that Paul might have been a better poet if he had stayed in the shoemaker class in Europe. (I know that poets were some of them high born and all learned men, I'm thinking of painters and composers, mostly) But maybe not. We know that Europe flourished for centuries on the blood and bones of its peasantry, and we are seeing the end. In this country we did not begin that way, nothing in our tradition supports the idea, one does not found a peasantry, it grows. It will never grow here, and should not, this country must work out its destiny on other foundations. This is a millenial change, out of all this destruction something will survive and build again, out of old and new things, we cannot tell what they will be. Its no good saying we are lost unless we can restore certain things that are past. The history of Western Europe is a shambles, if you like—there is little of it I care to see take root here: but great things came of it which the future can use. I am not one of those who thinks the human spirit has died on its feet because the kind of world I knew is passing. The future will be a shambles too, no doubt, and with great things in it. I am sure there are as many great minds and souls to be born yet as have already been born, and they will be, not the world's Redeemers, but the redeeming features of this on the whole rather unsatisfactory world.

In the meantime I have only to be as good an artist and human being as I can manage with my limited means. Women in general feel no call to invent God, or to be him: and for myself, I never got any satisfaction out of trying to persuade myself that the Devil tempted me, or God led me. I just choose to call my dual, warring impulses by other names, and blame the all-too-often defeat (for I aspire to goodness with at least half my mind and heart) on myself.

Do let me hear from you. Is the book doing well? I hope so.

> Your faithful friend
> *Katherine Anne*

29 September, 1947

To Elizabeth Ames

843 6th Street
Santa Monica, California
13 October, 1947

Dearest Elizabeth:

. . . . I was so amused to know about the Powers baby coming on into life in the stately scene of Yaddo—a place of pregnancies by definition and purpose, but I think this is the first *literal* one, isn't it? Does she write, too? I hadn't known it. J.F.P. is applying for a Guggenheim and I am happy to be one of his sponsors. I gave the final decision on whether or not his first story should be published in *ACCENT,* and have not got over being glad of it, for I believe he is gifted. I hope to God he doesn't crumble up on the second round, as so many promising ones do. In artists as in race horses, I like the "mudlarks" with heart enough for the long heavy track. But whether he does or not, he certainly has started well, and that is all we have to go by, and it is worth taking a chance on. . . .

Do you ever see *Harper's Magazine?* They are publishing "Gertrude Stein; a Self-Portrait" in December, and I hope you will see it. In it I did try to say something of my long considered opinion of that whole school of undisciplined, self-absorbed, pretentious "geniuses,"—I see more clearly now than ever that they were just the boils on the neck of society indicating a morbid condition. I did so like a crack of Bernard Shaw's (I saw it somewhere, the other day) about Anatole France describing himself as "a man of genius." Shaw: "Any whore can always call herself a daughter of joy.". . . .

My social life is nothing, for going out is very wearing. I am not ill, but everything tires me, and there is almost no one I wish to see. So I read immensely: Matthiessen's *The James Family* is a stupendous achievement, I am joyfully sunk in it. That family is our great glory, we can all share in it. 19th century America produced some wonderful great souls and noble ideas, we were really on the way to getting civilized, and I don't for one minute believe it can all end in darkness: the human aspirations are not easily destroyed. I have seen some good French pictures lately, and every one of them says; "Look, look again, Germans, here is what you have not been able to kill." I saw *Cage of Nightingales* and then *Zero de conduite* and both of them just so clearly compared the civilised attitude towards all life compared to what they have just suffered and survived . . . I could have wept for joy because there is so little to keep one's hopes alive with, yet that little is so firm and so beautiful and so deathless. So, in spite of very black moments, that is surely enough to live by.

> With my love
> *Katherine Anne*

To James F. Powers

843 6th Street
Santa Monica
5 November, 1947

Dear Mr. Powers:

. . . . Of course I have always known that you were in prison as a conscientious objector, and I should have been there myself in your situation, even if no doubt for rather different reasons. (I am assuming that your being Catholic had a great deal to do with it, and if I am wrong it would be good of you to tell me.) I am violently opposed, have always been, to war on every possible principle. I wrote and published before that if it came, it would be a crime, and I went on saying it was a crime and I still say so. But my real objection to war is that it is never fought for the reasons given to those who are to die in it, and no matter whose the military victory, none of the conflicts are ever settled. If our war had been really meant to destroy the roots of the terrible totalitarian idea of government, Nazism, Fascism, Communism—I should have been most ardently for it and would have considered any objector, no matter how conscientious, as an enemy to body and soul of humankind. But if we had not known before the foul complications of this war, indeed we would have to be very blind and stupid not to see them now . . . In prison it is possible that you found your problem simplified, yet I wonder how many of your fellows did you find to have very dubious motives? Out in the world, let me tell you, I kept running into Germans and Italians especially, some of them many generations in this country; some of them refugees, for whatever reason. And while denouncing Hitler or Mussolini specifically, in general they talked pure Nazism, pure Fascism; they could not hate this country enough; with perfect cynicism they were here to save their skins: and in my objection to the war they saw only aid and comfort for their side, and a treason in me to my own people. So my position has been difficult, for I am really an American, a believer in the Democratic theory of government—no matter if in practise it fails at a thousand points, we have, even now at this desperate looking moment, a more livable society than there is anywhere else at the present, and I am very much inclined to stand by it, for the deepest reasons of the heart and mind. As a Catholic, I was always anti-clerical; as one who left the church for purely political and moral reasons, I am horrified at the growth of power of the church in this country in the past twentyfive years, co-inciding perfectly with the growth of Fascism everywhere. All the ancient plagues of Europe are converging upon us, and even these serio-comic so-called witch-hunts are the preliminary skirmishes between Communism and Fascism in this country, dreary parodies so far of the tragic situation in Europe. I fear Fascism most, for it has the Pope at its head, and is Protean in its forms, and I hear people talking Fascism and acting it without knowing what name to call it by. So I hear them—and not only Catholics—defending

Franco-Spain and Argentina, and clamoring on the most sentimental grounds for immediate restoration of Italy and Germany, and simply refusing to remember what really happened . . . So you see, for me, merely to oppose war and to refuse to take part in the one waged by my own country is not so simple. I have no mystique of religion, no division of loyalties between church and state, but only a purely human, secular, reasoning system of political, moral and ethical beliefs for my support, and I assure you I know well this is a frail superstructure built over the bottomless pit of natural evil. People of my point of view are called naive, we are called optimists, we are called innocents, our belief in the possibilities of the daylight virtues rouses such fury and malignance on all sides it is at times a little disturbing, if I may understate to a fault: but I am none of the things I have named; I know the nature of evil and its power and its reality, and I mean to keep my little superstructure in repair, hoping only there will be enough of us to do the same, to ride out this fury and still have enough left to rebuild and go on building . . . The question is so deep, so tangled, it is almost impossible to follow even one smallest thread of thought to its source, to explain even one point of reference. Confusion is a technique deliberately applied to every phase of the situation, even the meaning of words has been so perverted one hardly knows how to use them any more. We hardly have a language in which to communicate.

People who work in an art do find themselves doing the oddest variety of things, don't you find? Your history of yourself matches mine in this: "a reader of old books—" I am a long-time student of medieval Europe—"a would-be saint and ascetic"—oh the years I spent almost literally sleeping on a board and living on bread and water nearly—then also I have had such funny jobs trying to live, and helped to gather the first show of Indian Mexican art for this country, and was up to my eyebrows in the Obregon revolution, and was perennial guest picket in all sorts of strikes—being pro-labor on the grounds that it was pro-human. I do find that power corrupts, the aim of the down trodden is not to establish equality, but to be the down-treaders.—I was in jail so many times that under the Baumes law, I believe it is called, I should by rights be in for life by now. (There was a law that if you were jailed was it three, or four, times? You went to the clink for good. I don't know why they overlooked me but let's not bring it up again.) And I lived in

Germany just when Hitler was coming to power, and in France in time for the Fascist coup of February 1934, I believe. Or '35. I have journals and so forget dates with a feeling of safety. I have rebuilt an old American house, and have worked in the pictures—a failure—after twenty five years of saying I would never; and now sit with mss. rising about my ears, getting over a three years' illness, or so I hope, trying to finish a novel and growing very fine camellias and azaleas and gardenias and roses and carnations and irises in a crowded little back yard.

There seems to be a great deal left out, but this gives you the notion . . .

Thank you for your letter, and tell me how you go on, and believe that I wish you all good in your work and life.

> Sincerely
> *Katherine Anne Porter*

To Kay and James   [8706 Sunset Plaza Place
Powers   Hollywood 46, California]
                          14 December, 1947

Dear Jim and Kay:

It is not astonishing that you have become, sight unseen, first names to me when I am told the charming news that your daughter has been given my name. May she be pleased when she learns about it, and may you three find great joy in each other for a long life time. I can't tell what to wish for her first, but everything at once: intelligence and compassion and beauty and health and firmness of spirit, and gayety. . . .

Jim I enclose a note from Houghton Mifflin, the same kind I get every year; it might be interesting to you, and if so, write them for the circular, (I have lost the one they mention) saying that I advised you to do this. And use my name as sponsor if you decide to enter the contest. You do not have to have a completed mss . . . only an outline and description . . . With as many complete pages as you wish to show . . . It *might* come to something. Meantime I have written a letter to the Guggenheim Committee: but that does not interfere with this. Eleanor Clark got the National Institute of Arts and Letters prize at the same time with the Guggenheim . . . The Institute prize is another thing I have in mind. When the time comes I mean to put up your name . . . We should get *something* out of all this . . .

Another thing: Luigi Einaudi is certainly not a Communist, and—to me equally important—he is not Fascist either. It is true he somehow compounded to live in Italy with Mussolini, but he appears to have been rather bold, wrote some things that might have got another man a quart of castor oil, or a rope and a lamp post. He is my Italian publisher, I notice, and seems to be the best choice of perhaps not a very wide field. The trouble is, we don't need to fear getting involved with Communists: we do know who and where they are, and what they are up to: no one is a Communist through ignorance or by accident. It is political theory which you must know and believe in to practise. But Fascism comes out of the very virus of evil in the soul of man, it is the oldest evil under a new name. It has exactly the same goal as Communism but under a thousand disguises, and I hear perfectly "innocent" people talking it without knowing what they say or where they picked it up. And this is much more to be feared. I much prefer a running fight in the open to an enemy ambushed in the church, in the state department, in the press, in the very air we breathe. It is a true poison, and—unless mankind in general grows less maggoty-minded than he is—I don't doubt that in this war, the totalitarian idea under the name of Fascism will win over the same thing called Communism. That we must choose one or the other is the falsest of all alternatives. I know several better things to choose, and I reject both, have from the beginning and will to the end . . .

So, Einaudi is certainly not a Communist. He is just not a hero who got himself killed by the Fascists. He is of the kind called by both sides, a "survivor" and he seems to have landed right side up, and is going to go on publishing. In spite of my presently very narrow situation, I have plans to go to Italy a little later on—it is best to look at things for oneself, if possible . . . I am hardly in the position to require active heroism from any one, for I have not been faced with their dangers yet. When I see how I come out, it will be time to criticise others.

As to the other questions, yes of course we will talk about all that someday, and in the meantime it is better for friends to take each other's good faith for granted. And please take this hasty letter now for a mere token of what I should like to be able to say, and what I do indeed feel, about all the painful questions of our most desolate times; and a kiss on the top of the head to my darling little namesake.

A serene Christmas and good New Year to you three,

Yours
Katherine Anne

I have been invited to stop transiently with a friend, the address will be on the envelope.

Later about Ezra Pound. So much to say there. I know this though: if ever I committed treason, or any other crime, personal or political, it would infuriate me to be considered insane. I insist on being held absolutely responsible for my words and deeds. I know the meaning of both, and would loathe being waved away as a nit-wit. To be an artist does not mean that one is outside of the manifold predicaments of human beings. They should have hanged Ezra—(and he wouldn't have been the first poet put to death for political beliefs) or they should have set him free. They have lifted the ban on Jane Anderson, a real bloody horror of a fascist traitor, one of the lowest types of international double-dealers, but then, she was not an artist. This offends me very deeply. Let's talk about this too sometime . . .

To George Platt Lynes   At Purdue University
                                           25 May, 1948

George darling:

. . . . It was a long job of work getting across country, even if I did take a "rooomette" and stay in bed the whole time. That is, I meant to stay there. Did you ever get trapped into a roomette? It is a narrow little tomb with a bed that lets down when you operate levers, covering the toilet seat and locking the washbowl shut, and when it is down there is not enough space to get out of bed unless you unlock your door and back your little undefended fanny into the corridor. You then, if you crave to faire le pipi or wash your face, give one hell of a heave upward on your bed, and it swings up and hovers threateningly over your person while you are stooping over looking for whatever you dropped out of bed—glasses, books, tissue-handkerchiefs, or slippers. Having retrieved these, you back out into the corridor again, weighed down by a heavy curtain which parts in the middle to expose the seat of your nightgown, haul on the lever, and the bed drops suddenly. You pull your head back in time to save your neck, the thing crashes and rumbles into place, you crawl back, clutching your belongings. If you overlooked any thing, it must all be done over again. Well then I would lie there exhausted and ring for food, which always came, tidy and hot, with a nice negro waiter who remarked with cheerful envy: "You look mighty comfable in there." I didn't argue. But for the first time in my life I felt like crusading against any further inventions in the name of *confort moderne.* The roomette MUST be the last word. . . .

All my love, darling,
Katherine Anne

To Monroe Wheeler   Stearn's Hotel
Ludington, Michigan
11 July, 1948

Monroe darling:

. . . . In Kansas, we were all housed in a barracks which called itself a Catholic Fraternity house, full of the aroma of what Baron Corvo described as hot boy and very little else. Food at the Union House was a long mile away, we finally wangled kitchen privileges and fell over each other in the morning making coffee. Caroline Gordon is an impassioned mushroom hunter, and we had divine mushrooms on toast for breakfast twice. We also brought in watermelons and ate them around a long table in the evenings after work. If I seem to remember food, it was because it was so hard come by and generally so poor, I dwell upon every edible mouthful. Allen

Tate was there the first week, the second week they brought in Erskine Caldwell, who stayed at the hotel and was a very unhappy man. Some one asked him if he had ever been to one of these shindigs before and he said, "Yes, but this is my first time in the Big League." We were awfully nice to him, and I tried to forget that I had attempted to strangle him in the cradle, as twere, by getting his first mss rejected at my publishers. Long ago, long ago, and look at us now . . . He came and listened seriously to all the sessions and remarked that it was news to him that writing took all that doing . . . The students went around asking bitterly "What is HE doing here?" but he stuck it out manfully and his eyes—the true goat's eye, cold-grey, at close range I almost expected to see the slit pupil—now and again seemed to have a watery, wistful look. It may have been suppressed yawns, of course. I don't know what became of him in the last day or so . . . It is hard to explain, but the thing was a huge success, we all worked like hounds in smothering heat and every kind of discomfort, but the tone was all right, just the same, and we none of us would have missed it for anything. However, as Jake Kilrain remarked about his bareknuckled bout with— was it Sullivan?—we weren't licked, Nature gave out. Meantime, I found out what is wrong with the American University System. It is the so-called Extension department, and the teachers who are intimidated by the box office . . . Caldwell was brought in because he was the only writer in the group Extension had ever heard of, and they said they needed a drawing card . . . At the Chancellor's dinner I sat way below the salt with Extension to the right of me, Extension to the left of me and across the table, and picked up an education in the seamy side of University life. If I were capable of it at this late day, I might be disheartened entirely. But then, I feel I always knew where the wrong lay, just as I did about Hollywood, really. Yet it is a good thing to get out and have one's mind nudged again in such matters.

At Columbia, Missouri, I ran smack into the Old South in late but lavish bloom, being the guest for a week of Miss Florence Willis, whose family managed somehow to hang on to money right through the disturbance and then some of them had the presence of mind to marry more money. Her sister, for one, who so far forgot herself as to wed one Ames Butler of Boston, son of the Old General (Spoons) Butler, who won his title fairly by stealing all the silver he could lay hands on while occupying the South. Well, when Miss Flo's sister got married, a Texas cousin sent a single old handsome serving spoon as a wedding present, with a note, "Here is one your father overlooked." And Virginia cousins sent a fine chest of silver complete except for spoons. Miss Flo is about seventy now, and lives like a fighting cock in her charming house which is a small museum of beautiful European loot; she lived for years with her sister and brother-in-law in an Italian castle which is a national monument, and she keeps her quarts of emeralds and rubies and diamonds and pearls in the bank, along with pounds of old carved coral, moonstone, opal etc period jewellery. Wanting to show them to me, she went to the bank and brought it all back in a market basket with a sack of potatoes, a bunch of celery and a few onions distributed on top to fool everybody. As everybody in town has known for years that when Miss Flo is seen carrying a market basket it can mean only that she has been to the bankvault again, it has become a fond local tradition, and she fools nobody but herself. She has an Australian lad in a white mess jacket who brings breakfast with the snap and expertness of a British officer's batman, which he was, and a black cook who calls her Missy. She drinks good old Bourbon over ice, and we started before lunch on the first drink. I saw drawings and photographs of her in several stages of her gay youth, and she was a high-style, high-stepping beauty, of the kind any man would be glad to marry if he had the slightest chance. She is beautiful now in her age, and when I asked, one day after the third whiskey, if she ever got tired of people asking her why she never married, she laughed and said, "No, because I think myself it was odd, but I simply never fell in love, imagine. And I was too romantic to marry without it. But I always liked men, I couldn't have enough of them around me. Really, I *love* men, but not to marry." And someone there who knew her history well said that until she was well past fifty she had the most eligible men simply turning somersaults around her . . . From Miss Flo's house to the barracks at Lawrence was quite a jump, but the kind of thing my life is fullest of. . . .

With my same old devoted love
Katherine Anne

To Rev. John F. Fahey   [Palo Alto, California]
5 October 1948

Dear Father Fahey:

You are the first to call my attention to Mr. Sylvester's article.† If you are "surprised and saddened" I must say I am merely surprised and annoyed at the strange liberties taken with my name, my beliefs and ideas by some one who obviously knows nothing whatever about them . . . I have not read the article and do not intend to; long ago I decided not to be troubled by anything published about me and my work, short of actionable slander. For to enter any kind of profession or public career, no matter how unpretentious, is to invite such attentions, alas. So much for Mr. Sylvester.

To answer your question: I am not a Catholic and cannot be judged as such; and have made it a rule never to discuss religious differences with any one, for I believe firmly in absolute freedom of religious faith and expression for every human being of every known and (to me) unknown denomination; and I am truly disturbed by any threat from any source to this freedom. I claim also my inalienable right to my own private thoughts and feelings on this subject. And this I hope shall offend no one.

None of my works are "autobiographical" in the sense of being personal history, that mere reportage which all too often passes for fiction. Again, it is almost impossible for an artist, whose work is the transmutation of his living experience on all levels—spiritual, intellectual, moral, psychic, emotional—into symbolic interpretation, to explain how he does it. Or why his mind works that way: or what numberless forces, influences, ideas and memories shaped it through the years. But if you anywhere read cynicism or nihilism into my work, you have misread it altogether, and I am

†"*Problems of the Catholic Writer*" *by Harry Sylvester, Atlantic Monthly, January, 1948. In draft of letter to Father Fahey, KAP wrote: "Certainly one of the great functions of any art is communication; certainly it has a moral function; but its real reason for being is that it preserves unbroken the line of continuous human feeling and satisfies the esthetic instinct from age to age on the human level: so that a work of beauty and nobility remains forever new and never loses its preciousness as work of art, when the creed and forms of government and the very race and the language of a period have disappeared.*"

sorry for this. No true artist on no matter how humble a plane can be either cynic or nihilist. His task is one of love.

Thank you for your very kind letter.

Sincerely yours
Katherine Anne Porter

To Monroe Wheeler   [Department of English
                           Stanford University
                           Stanford, California]
                           9 November 1948

Monroe darling:

.... I did feel a little better when I set out for Chicago. Got through the lecture all right, with Morton Zabel looking after things. One thing unusual: Morton told me the tickets were all sold in half a day after the announcement, and the hall which holds 1200 was packed and rows of chairs in back, and it was a good crowd—in my view, that is—quiet as mice except when they laughed at all the right places, and a long flood of applause when it was finished, and I remarked to Zabel that from now on I was going to demand a paying audience . . . They do much better by a speaker altogether . . . an oddity: Robert Hutchins came, sat far back, went away without coming near me, and remarked to some one as he left, "Well, I suppose I'll have to take up writing seriously." Whatever that meant. . . .

Nobody could find me a house, after all, and I couldn't find one for myself, and I was only allowed to stay a week in the guest room at the Womens' Club on the campus. After that another visiting fireman was booked for it. So, I could go back to San Francisco to the little theatrical hotel where Ann stays when she is there with a Ballet company—all the dancers and the lesser singers stay there—or take a room at 6 dollars a day in Palo Alto—on *my* wages—or could sit under a bush or trek over the hills through the redwoods and jump in the bay. Having by now eleven assorted pieces of luggage, no room would hold me and it. So comes along somebody with a cabin to rent about sixteen miles from Stanford, up winding mountain trails into an apparently trackless forest full of squirrels, and stray cats left here according to the old humane custom by departing summer people. . . .

Day before yesterday I heard the familiar urgent wail of The Cat at my door, opened and said, according to formula, "Come in, I was expecting you," and there walked in a small tiger tom, about six months old, thin, with the pointed anxious face of premature sorrows, a being obviously the end product of a long line of errors and misfortunes. He is long and lean and graceful by nature, but his little belly was ballooned with famine, his slanted golden eyes dilated with fright. But he swarmed around me, broke into an enormous purr, curled his long thin tail at the tip, gave a few little leaps to show what a gay spirit he had, and worked like a trouper to make himself charming. Indeed, he was delighted to find me, I am sure of that. And why not? He is now lying sprawled in the best armchair before the fire, warm and clean, full of beef and milk; he has washed himself carefully, and his nose and paws are a pretty geranium-pink. Every time I move around the room he rouses and gives a big snoring purr and falls asleep again. He found his own bed—a pile of cushions on a corner couch, and he is so at home he quarrelled and argued for fifteen minutes through a window screen with a grey squirrel who ran up and down a tree trunk just outside and seemed to be daring him to come out and fight. Well, God help me, I have another cat. His name is Rufus. Tiger toms are traditionally fine hardy tough fellows and I don't doubt he is going to grow up to be a curse and a nuisance with split ears and fur mostly in rags from fighting. But here he is . . . He goes back to town with me when and if I go . . . I may just be stuck in this place. I'll be sure to let you know. . . .

Well, the house is warm enough now for me to take a bath and make myself decent for the day. I am wrapped in a dark blue quilted cotton robe with a red striped handkerchief tied around my head, and fleecelined booties, or bootlets, or something. Anyway, not boots, not slippers, not mules, not shoes of any kind. Yellow chamois objects lined with fleece. Thar's cold in these here mountains, stranger . . .

The kettle is simmering, Rufus is asking to be let out, I must see if the bread is rising properly . . . After a while I shall go out and scramble up and down these paths through the woods, it is the sweetest smelling air in the world . . .

Wasn't the election a big surprise? I had really given up, and now have a red face that at last I had let myself be misled by Luce and Hearst and company . . . This is the fifth time a President has been elected with the whole Press against him in full cry. The first four times I wasn't fooled at all. Perhaps this time it was because I don't like Truman really—it has come to this merely, that I preferred him or anybody else at all, to Dewey . . . I suppose we haven't a very good president, but better than we might have had, anyway . . . I haven't seen a newspaper or magazine or listened to radio for eight days, so anything that may be cooking up will be a surprise to me if I ever hear of it . . . Only one thing I mean to know about in time: when will the Sitwells be here, that is, on the Coast?

Look at this:

> *"In the streets of the City of Cain there were great Rainbows*
> *Of emeralds: the young people, crossing and meeting."*

Write me sometime, my darling. It will reach me.

With my love
Katherine Anne

TO PAUL PORTER   [Palo Alto]
                                        19 November 1948

Paul darling:

. . . . One point interested me: your saying that magic meant only the power to fool some one . . . I take it you meant that this is the Hollywood perversion of its meaning, as everything else is perverted in that place . . . Lost entirely are the ancient sacred rituals and invocations to a higher power to work the divine change in man's efforts, adding to them the mysterious power necessary to raise them to perfection . . . This was real, and is still, but the secret is lost or nearly. And indeed, such as Hollywood never knew that it ever existed, nor would know its use if they had heard of it . . .

Read *The White Goddess.* I never had such a picnic with any
book for years upon years . . . I am going to have my classes read
it, study it and set them off on a wonderful wild goose chase after
all the myths and symbols: they'll be educated for the practise of
an art when they're through, if they have it in them. If not, they'll
be less ignorant of the deep history of man, at least . . . Also, the
book is a model for following a line of thought through thick and
thin. . . .

More later. All my love

Aunt Katherine Anne

To Monroe Wheeler   [Palo Alto, California]
                           12th Night, 1949

Monroe darling:

All a-palp with antiquarian excitement, I opened the little
book, looked at the date, admired the tiny goose quill writing,
seized my reading glass expecting God knows what, and made out
the following, which I copy for your Commonplace Book exactly:
(page 235).

A gentlewoman in London streets having on, an old gowne,
whose many taggs and tafsells did sufficiently proclaime its antiquity, as she went along, was espied by a merry fellow who thought
to have put a trick upon her, and to that purpose went acrofs the
street to meet with her, & took ye foare part of her gowne and
kifsed it, at which the Gentlewoman asked him what he meant.
Madã saith he I doe but reverence thy antiquity; O Sir, said she, if
you intend that, you might better have kifsed my ta: for that is ten
years older.

This was most exquisitely noted down by one John Crakan-
thorpe in his book, (Anno Dom: 1658,) and I'll bet it was a good
old standby of a joke even then. The record begins really with a
list of books, showing that the writer favored history, travel, and
religious controversy. And the last mentioned date in it is 1687,
which accounts for the different kinds and shades of ink and the
varying thickness or thinness of the goose quill, and the change of

handwriting which at several points almost made me believe several persons had written in it . . . But no, its the same man, from pages of *Ulysses* in Latin to Pages of the New Testament in Greek to the complete odes of Horace to scandals about the Jesuits to moral tales from Erasmus and Thomas More and gossip about Clara Farnese and the then-Pope, with its political consequences, and so on, for 239 pages, and yet, the book falls open at the only improper story in it, that I can find, at any rate . . . I can't account for it; but it is odd and nice and very human to see how he starts out all Latin and Greek and winds up all typical everyday 17th century conversational style and gossip. For he *retells* all his yarns. Ah yes, darling it is a peculiar present in the old sense of the word: peculiarly the kind you would give me and the kind I would like . . . I've had a lovely time with it. And now I wonder if it was a custom for gentlemen to carry these little books, jotting down the things that interested and amused them, to show to friends, to break the ice with strangers, to remind them of proper topics of conversation? I never saw one before, but I know there must have been others . . . A Common Place book, after all.

Before I go on to another page, look, this is my new typewriter; same kind as before, with the same keyboard, almost. It had to be done specially in spots, and the man taking the order insisted on my having an exclamation point! !!! I told him it had taken me four years to discover that the other machine didn't have one, and there were other things I preferred. However, it is astonishingly complete, but I have already found out on this one that my nice pounds, francs, and dollar marks are missing. Even so, I can still write in English, Spanish, French and German, so long as I don't mention money. And it does really look as if I shan't need any money symbols now even as much as I need an! Well, here is the keyboard: (Imagine, this is only my fourth typewriter in all the time I have been writing. 23456789& ! QWERTYUIOPA SDFGHJKL:ZXCVBNM?/+é"'(−è_çà)qwertyuiopasdfghjkl;zxc vbnm,.= Messy, what?

I loved the news about the Sitwells, and above all the heavenly account of Marianne Moore on the Manor House week-end. What a divine thing she must be and how have I missed even seeing her all these years? But maybe I get a truer look at her through your eyes, for obviously there is that between you in friendship which does not come just because it is called, and which takes years and recollections. So I shall like her as I have, in her poetry and in your stories about her.

On the 20th of December I left the mountain, and came down on the little truck which also carried my *richesses*—yes, we do have the same notion of what are the true necessaries of life, and I love that line in Sitwell's newest volume, "at that time I had nothing but the bare luxuries." So the truck was heaped with such as crystal clocks, and crystal lamp bases, and hand made gloves and Paris perfumes and all those books, and many more, and here I am, clean to be sure, well lighted to be sure, not too warm, true, in two pawky little rooms under somebody's garage, with an electrical device or two in one end of the bedroom on which I prepare from time to time a little food . . . I think this last, last detail is somewhere outside of decency—but shan't go on with it, for so it is, and there is nothing to be done about it . . . My books, my music, all my little things, are in storage, except what I picked up in recent travels—and it seems so wasteful, having all I need to be quite comfortable, but no way of making use of it . . . There was a plan here to limit my class to twenty, but thirty eight showed up for the first session day before yesterday, and many who cannot show any work wish to listen in . . . I was for letting everybody come that wished, in the beginning, for they many of them will drop out, and in the end I will have the ones who really should be there . . . I feel strange about being here, but California is the only place in the world where I have not been able to feel at home even for a day. So it would be nonsense to go on trying to live here, no matter what kind of climate I need . . . there is another kind of climate I need worse, and it is not here . . . I have made no friends here, and that I think is some sort of evil sign . . . It never happened to me before, certainly not in a stretch of four years. (Exclamation point!) I except of course Winkie [Margaret Winkler of Westwood Book Store], but she seems somehow as much a foreigner here as I feel . . . Well, this is a dull topic. I know there are some people worth knowing here but who? where? Well, we'll see. . . .

My classes seem to be going well: they still crowd in and listen very silently and with very acute expressions on their varied but usually quite pleasant features . . . So I suppose it is all right. And now, every time I go to wait at the bus stop in front of the University BookShop, some student is sure to come by and call out my name and ask if he or she may drive me to town . . . And each one tells me how glad he (or she) is that I am here, and how when they heard of it they could hardly believe their ears, and so on, and it is pleasant and yet, somehow no consolation at all for being here . . . Well, I am going to stop this owl-like hooting of despair which is just loneliness, I feel sure . . . God knows what, but I don't doubt you have had more than enough of it.

I see by the papers that Glenway is extending his sphere of political influence; the National Commission of Unesco is God knows a body that should either be curbed somewhat, or have at least one person on it who knows what he is doing. Short of just pulling the whole thing up by the roots and starting again somewhere else with something different, I do think the substitution of Glenway for Canby is a streak of light on what has been up to now a practically viewless horizon. Oh GOD, what sinkings of the heart I have when now and again for my own good, that is to say, to remind myself of what I am up against, I sit in on little conferences of people who really have the power, whose trade is the manufacture and distribution of something they call culture, which is an unspeakable mess of political propaganda, salesmanship of "Ideologies" and is somehow connected with international trade and distant raw materials . . . So I do think even a token representation of just one working artist on that commission is so much to the good . . .

Sample of higher education: the other day a young woman in the advanced fiction class said the most wonderful picture she had ever seen in her life was *Wuthering Heights.* I told her she should read the book, too. She was thrilled. "Oh," said she "Did they make a *book* of it?"

We have been having freezing weather—the coldest in 60 years, I believe, which completes my year of meeting everywhere with the hottest, coldest, dryest, wettest weather known to living man: indeed 1948 was somehow an excessive year, and almost every one I know now says it was a painful one in one way or another—so my long *supplice* in that period was, just once more, my share of the universal bafflements . . . May we all do better this year, my darling, you especially, though I didn't hear you complain of 1948 any more than ever you did of any other year . . .

With my love going right on through the ages

Katherine Anne

I didn't send even a card for the holidays. Shame on me!

TO ALBERT ERSKINE [768 Santa Ynez St.
Stanford, California]
14 March, 1949

Dear Albert:

I had to ask John Palmer for your address, as I forgot just where Random House had moved to except that it was just around the corner from the New Weston. This letter is about very odd business, two kinds. First: Several collectors have written me lately wanting to buy mss. of mine, and it occurs to me that they must be lying around in the files of various magazines? I thought of the *Southern Review,* and was trying to locate "The Old Order," or The Hardy piece, or "Noon Wine," or "Pale Horse, Pale Rider" . . . I know where "Old Mortality" is: I gave it to the poor little ole poverty-ridden University of Texas, who pleaded so touchingly, while I was in Baton Rouge . . . So much for that. It seems I could now turn a relatively honest and certainly easy penny on the things if I could lay hands on them . . . John seemed to think you might know something to tell me? I had asked him as the last editor of S.R. Then on his travels he spoke to Cleanth; and Tinkum seems to think there may be something cash-convertible in the "hot attic of Allen Hall." Well, what do YOU think? It is fairly plain that if I expect a living, it will never be from publishing, but just the odds and ends: lecturing, anthologies, mss sales, etc . . . So help me in this if you can, and all my thanks.

Second: After all the huzza and hullabaloo about cancelling the *Flowering Judas* contract, I now have word that, instead, *Flowering Judas* will just be allowed to breathe its last decently with the sale of the last copy of the present printing, and will then revert to

HBCO, and *Pale Horse, Pale Rider* will be substituted in the Modern Library list on exactly the same terms as *Flowering Judas* . . .

Well, well . . .

This is all I have been able to get from my side of the fence at this distance, and I suppose they imagine it is all perfectly clear. Well, it isn't.

So please, not in the way of business, and kindly forbear to regard me in the regular commercial lights (in the cinema industry my agent describes me as "a property,") and think of me as a human being and tell me confidentially what in the streaming hell goes on. I am writing this to you confidentially, and will keep all you write me in confidence, and remember, I make my living feeding vampire bats, who pay me a small royalty per pint. So please tell me WHY things are being done as they are, and what I am to expect.

I live now by a little Calendar all marked with strategic dates for six months ahead, and so when putting rings around dates I came to April, I notice that your birthday and of course all the other anniversaries around that time fall this year on exactly the day of the week that they did in 1938. This may have happened before, but I never noticed, and it occurred to me that I really never did know how many years must pass for a day and a date to coincide on any anniversary . . . The eleventh year? Eleven years since that very odd sort of time. One-fifth exactly of my badly-managed but not absolutely wasted life—Really it has been rather nice. Of course part of this comes from the fact that I have been pronounced in solid good health, positively no illusions; and no denying at all, this is a great help to a calm spirit . . . My first semester has passed very well, the lectures are fun: I just open my mouth and say the first thing that occurs, and it goes with a good deal of zing. The Grooves of Academe are taking quite a beating, you'll be pleased to hear.

But when this is finished, I shall talk no more. I have already refused five lecture engagements and shall go on refusing them from now on. I mean to be a writer, in the long run.

Do just sit down to a private typewriter will you, no secretaries, and write me a private letter about this funny business and I'll be very cheerfully glad to do something for you sometime if ever you are stuck someway, which God forbid . . .

John says you had an operation on your knee and that it is all healed and proper again. True? I hope so . . . My God, it chills one a little to think what happens—just a little playful leap over a fence and then, trouble for seven long years. I hope it is all over . . .

Yours
Katherine Anne

To Eleanor Clark [768 Santa Ynez Street
Stanford, California]
22 March 1949

am sending short telegram to John Slade

Dear Eleanor:

Your letter was really shocking to me, as I had not a hint of anything of which you write. I have tried to compose a telegram but there is too much to say, and a special delivery letter will I believe reach you in time to add my name to the list of Elizabeth's friends against this contemptible attack on her.

As you say, the right thing to do is to stick firmly to the political aspects, and keep the whole line of inquiry firmly on that straight line. For we know well that the strategy of her attackers will be to muddle everything, to confuse the issue, and bring everything down to the lowest level of personal slander. They wish in fact to make a scandal, the more public the better, and I wonder how they dare, for they do stand on very shaky ground indeed.

Well—When Agnes Smedley left Yaddo she wrote me a letter which I still have, telling me the story from her point of view of course, but making one thing very clear indeed: that Elizabeth Ames had asked her to leave Yaddo for the precise reason that her political beliefs and activities were discreditable and dangerous to the reputation of Yaddo: and according to Agnes, Elizabeth rebuked her very severely for using Yaddo as a base of political operations. If this act of Elizabeth's seems a little belated in the face of Agnes' long residence at Yaddo and the perfect openness of her lectures, writings, it is very important to remember that Elizabeth's prime article of faith on which she based her whole directorship of Yaddo, was that no one should be discriminated against because of

368

race, color, religious or political beliefs and you remember how carefully she invited Chinese, Negroes, Jews, Hindus, all nationalities in fact, and she never inquired as to religion or politics. And if Yaddo was to have any meaning at all in the terms of its own charter, she was right. And that she is being assailed on the very grounds of her virtuous and serious attempt to direct a working democracy is, I think, much to her credit: and we—any and all of her defenders—owe it not only to her but to ourselves and to everything we believe in to "confound the politics, frustrate the knavish tricks" of those really contemptible beings who are making all this muddle—

You are right in saying there are elements in their behavior that appear to be pathological; but we still are in the difficult position of having to deal with them and the situation they are creating as if they were normal and responsible; at least until they expose themselves as otherwise, plainly enough to be seen by others. If they insist on maintaining that they are responsible, mentally and morally, then I am all for a good heavy libel suit in which their appetite for making trouble shall be fed up nicely to the eyebrows. It is true that Lowell has had one complete breakdown, and his history is of extreme instability, to put it mildly. But Elizabeth, alas, never did inquire into the mental state of her guests, either . . .

Glenway popped in here yesterday and spent the afternoon and we had dinner and oh such talk and I did so enjoy his company. I read your letter, which came at noon, and I wish you would talk this over with him, for he was instantly on our side, and he might have some good sound advice to give, and help. We spoke of you with our usual tenderness and affection, and we said admiringly, "really how the woman writes, a little shimmer of light comes up from the page," and so you see. . . .

Love
Katherine Anne

To Albert Erskine   [768 Santa Ynez St.
                                  Stanford, California]
                                  25 March, 1949

Dear Albert:

All my thanks for your explicit story of all the goings-on about
the *Flowering Judas* contract. Of course, it was also about forty other
little odds and ends, a most interesting little exposure of business
methods when mixed up with malignant personal motives . . . Just
along with your letter I had another from Miss McCarthy at HBCO
adding the bit of information I had not got yet. She had written that
Pale Horse was going to be substituted for *Flowering* etc., *on exactly
the same terms.* This interested me financially, as *Flowering Judas* got
a five hundred dollar advance (so much as that? I wonder.) paid in
four installments. So naturally I looked forward eagerly to a repetition of this, even with the hope that by now Random House was
so rich it could afford to pay the whole thing in one whoop.

Ah ha!, as the characters in *On Approval* are always exclaiming,
I might have known there was a bug in it. I know too, that advance
money is really a delusion, that is to say, I get no more until it is
paid out in sales, but still, living from hand to mouth and day to day
as I do, a nickel in the hand is more useful than the same nickel next
year. What do I know about next year? I've never been there. I
don't know any one who has. Well, anyway, booksellers I know
have always told me that *Pale Horse, Pale Rider* outsells two to one
the other two books on the HBCO list, so maybe it will do much
better than *Flowering Judas* did. But the fact is—you can see it, in
fact you have said it in effect—my affair has been very badly
managed and I am being quite effectively done out of an advantage
I might have had long ago—that of two books on the ML list
. . . When you tell me you have long wanted to add *Pale Horse,* it
really makes my heart to sink, for it is at least three years since I
first asked at HBCO *why* they did not offer you that book . . .

Really, it is so disgusting, isn't it? And what, what should I do?
I always did need somebody to help me manage my business, but
I never had anybody; even looking back I can't see where there was
ever any likely candidate for this highly insecure position, and mind
you I don't complain. It just seems sometimes a little odd. And so

far as the ragged edges of this little imbroglio could be mended and trimmed off even, you have done nobly . . . You know I am very happy to feel that you did what you could and would have done more.

The trouble at HBCO is, that when I wished to speak to Reynal my old friends there asked me not to: it could, they said, only make ill feeling, of which there seems to be already more than enough. But I still cannot see why they allow me to be used as a club and expect me not to notice it . . . And this reminds me of the way you have been choked off, also, and prevented from stating your views and motives to this same person. What is it, a system? Why are we prevented from seeing him? I am meditating a little letter, carefully thought out and set down in fair words, without mentioning any body or any sources, to him: marked *personal* and let's see what it brings forth. Not just yet, though—I have too many other things to do. I should be working of course, trying to finish books, and really my God, I feel as if my energies were just being gnawed away at all the edges by such things as this . . .

I hope your knee is repaired for good; it has been hard for me to realize how disabled you have been all this time. Let me know how it goes—I'll tell you if anything new happens, and do you let me know from time to time what goes on.

Yours
Katherine Anne

To ELIZABETH AMES   [768 Santa Ynez Street
                           Stanford, California]
                           1 May, 1949

Elizabeth darling:

Of course I'll come to the house party, it sounds a splendid notion . . . By now I feel certain you have accounts of the dismal hangover of all the recent wild events, ending naturally and properly with Enemy No. 1 now placed where he has belonged for at least twelve years: in a hospital for the insane . . . He was never anything else, but I wearied of saying so, for nobody would listen . . .

Coincidences went on and on: the two neatest, I think, were: Glenway was here when I got Eleanor's letter, he flew home the next morning and hit the deck fighting. I alarmed Morton Zabel, he alarmed me about the business, and our letters crossed in the mail. Then, Lowell, fleeing to his faithful allies the Tates in Chicago, naturally provided Morton with a first hand account if not view, of his actual going over the final border to total madness . . .

The thing that amazed me most, however, was the defection or whatever you call it, of Newton Arvin. I remember when he came out of the rest home after his nervous breakdown, you let him spend a long convalescence at Yaddo, when he treated the rest of us as if we were interlopers and nuisances interfering with his cure . . . On second thoughts I do not know why I am surprised . . . in a milder degree, he is only following Lowell's example.

Well, enough of this . . . At this moment, I have the radio going, and the Catholics are holding a public radio meeting against Communism, telling of miraculous appearances of the Blessed Virgin, and praying in chorus for the whole world to come to God, that is, to the Catholic Church. And they chill my blood as much, in a way more, than the Communists, because the Church is Fascist, and somehow, religion and totalitarianism seem more popular in this country than atheism and totalitarianism . . . Militarily, we may be in danger from Communism, but morally we are deeply in danger of being taken over by Catholicism . . . It is growing incredibly impudent in this country . . .

Forget your enemies, Elizabeth, and remember your friends. This episode was perfectly in keeping with everything else that is going on, and little by little individuals who have been lost in the general fog of political and every other kind of confusion, are getting sorted out and it is rather a bitter relief to know what is what and who is who . . . Now you need never have your confidence abused again. You should know the signs of the vampire bat from this day out . . . Just don't warm them and nourish them, my dear . . . Not Democracy, not human charity, not even the charter of Yaddo, requires it of you, at least I should think, not any more. . . .

The Catholics are now winding up their religious exercises with a choral singing of the "Star Spangled Banner." I'll swear, I believe when all is said and done, I prefer the Communists.

They hate the country and will break up everything if they can, but at least they *don't* sing the "Star Spangled Banner" at their meetings . . .

Well, well.

Goodnight, bless you. With my love
Katherine Anne

To Monroe Wheeler 768 Santa Ynez Street
Stanford, California
6 July 1949

Monroe darling:

. . . . The perfume came yesterday as I was leaving the house on a dreary errand: getting off a letter to Archibald MacLeish, another to the editors of the Sat. Rev. of what they regard as literature, a note to the Librarian of the Library of Congress, all about the stinking row about the Bollingen Award† . . . I am so melancholy about the whole thing, yet I really believe it is a very good thing to smoke out the literary Westbrook Peglers—I used to call only Bernard de Voto that, but I see he is a crowd and a big one—and after my usual hesitations, and hopes to keep out of low scrimmages, I finally rolled up my sleeves and went in . . . We'll see whether they publish my letter or not. If they don't, I want to send you and Glenway a copy. . . .

8 July. I took this letter out of the machine to write a word for a student who is trying to get a Fellowship of some sort so he may go on writing . . . He writes well enough by middle-brow magazine standards—I am using this term in Russell Lynes' sense, and *Harper's* is one of the better examples of what he means—he can undoubtedly get published; but there is no reason on this earth why he should ever have begun writing at all, no reason to encourage him, and yet I do for two reasons: he is a shade better than his next

†*See KAP's* Collected Essays *pp. 209–215, for this letter about Ezra Pound and the Bollingen Award to the editor of the* Saturday Review of Literature.

contender, and also I am surrounded by vampire bats who do not go without their dram of my life-stream. I find that I can be blackmailed and in the most curious way. I have to be extremely careful not to say to any one that his or her work shows promise or some imagination or what ever it does show, because instantly this blood-seeking look comes into the eye, and the next thing I know, the subject is clamoring for letters to editors, letters sponsoring his candidacy for this or that wandering sum of cash, or demands for help in re-writing his stuff so it will be at once saleable—the unconscious cynicism and total lack of scruples really do dismay me . . . It is not that I am surprised that they exist and seem to be nine-tenths of human motive at least in this business, but that I should have got myself mixed up in such a mill. Well, seventeen more lectures and it is over . . . But I meant to say, if I show signs of fight about recommendations, they say invariably—"but you encouraged me, you said I was doing well . . ." God forgive me, maybe I did . . . What is impossible to make them understand is that that would be only the beginning of their apprenticeship. They don't even know the meaning of the word. It is just merely sickening, the whole racket, and my proper place is as far away from it as I can get, a step I am preparing to take as of next fall.

There are some good serious people here with talent, and it is very noticeable that none of them behave like this . . . They shouldn't be here, they are being cheated and misled, but the real ones will get out I hope safely.

This seems to lead us back to Litt. D's somehow. My honors do always have a seamy side to them, and maybe this is true of them all. I remember when I was given the Gold Medal, with Clifton Fadiman making the main address—M.C. I believe he was officially—and Pearl Buck handing me the object, which you have seen. The best description of it was spoken by Lloyd who looked at one side and then the other, and handed it back: "It's a brute," he said. I was so lost in the shuffle that time I almost got thrown out by the headwaiter because the committee had neglected to provide me with a ticket, and so on and on . . . Also there had been a preliminary skirmish between the University and my publishers as to who should pay my expenses for this wild goose chase, and they finally, grudgingly on both sides, divided the damages. They had both expected *me* to pay them, the big optimists. Well, all this taught me something but not enough . . . Last January I received from the Chancellor at N.C. the most courteous and stately letter possible indicating that they were delighted to honor me, would be so honored if I should accept, etc—all perfectly in form and reassuring, lulling my instincts for flight at such prospects. This time, I found out too late, there was no question at all as to who was to foot the bill for my expense. It was me. *La petite je,* as a student of French here is fond of saying. At the last moment, HBCO consented to make an advance on something called general royalties, and my hood cost me four hundred dollars or nearly, which cut me to the bone financially and destroyed my margin of subsistence for a year at least . . . I have nearly gone bankrupt on this job in any case, not being able to do other things to make a little extra money . . . However, this is not really the worst. Dear Randall Jarrell had been snagged as my "sponsor, guide and friend" though the ex-governor of N.C. claimed afterward that it was HIS idea to give me the degree. I'll never know. Somebody else told me something quite different. So the first thing Randall told me, on the way from the air port, was, that it was a strange piece of funny business, because another literary figger, also female, was being made Doctor at the same time, a local woman who writes feverish local history novels so bad there is no rank assigned to them at all. As the day went on, and the next day after the ceremonies, at lunch and cocktail parties, bits and pieces began to emerge . . . It seems last year, for political reasons—the lady has powerful family, and political connections—the governor, now ex-governor, had proposed her for a D.Litt.—you will understand that the University is run by Politicians; but she was voted down . . . So this year, I was proposed, with her name added, and it was somehow put over that we were to be voted in—or out, as the case might be—together . . . the old bill-with-streamer technique . . . Now she might have turned out to be a pleasant nice person. But in fact she was a Teep of super-dimensions, a pure mixture of Louella Parsons and Elsa Maxwell; God, you should see them rolled into one, and above all, hear them. So with identical grave ceremony and high-flown citations for services to literature, we received our identical hoods and got identical applause; and at lunch following, I was seated at the right hand of the Chancellor, she at the right hand of the present Governor, but my ignorance of protocol in these matters forbids me even to speculate on the meaning of this. If there was any meaning to anything anywhere at all, which I doubt, strongly. The only thing that worried me was that the Governor was the best looking and the only interesting man present, and you can imagine how that annoyed me . . . I could hear odments of the Governor's conversation being wasted on the Teep, while my Chancellor was solid meat and bone from top to toe . . .

Just the same, the flight there and back was sublime, perfect weather and no engine missed a beat. I thought I was taking a cross-continent plane, but it turned out to be the Bounding Broomstick; we made fourteen landings in twenty two hours. In the south they use the planes for busses, making fifteen minute flights between towns to play golf or have lunch, and air travel takes on the most familial tone. A fat old lady at one point was brought on in a straight chair, and at the next town was taken off in another. I was told she is nearly ninety and goes up every week-end to visit her son and his family . . .

Are you tired of this? Sequel to foregoing. My students here are not given credit for their work with me because I have no degree. Or had not . . . There seems to have been a special faculty meeting on the subject and it was decided that to give my students credit would establish a bad precedent . . . This for the first two semesters. Before the third semester of course, I did have a degree, but nothing has changed . . . My students still don't get credit. I am of a mind to write to my Chancellor and tell him that Stanford does not recognize degrees conferred by North Carolina, and that my only motive in informing him is my hope that it will be the beginning of a beautiful friendship between these two great institutions of higher learning . . . I am mean enough to think of this, but not low enough to do it . . . So much of my virtue lies just there, that I refrain from doing such mischief as I enjoy contemplating sometimes, and so I miss a lot of divertisement of a questionable sort. . . .

I must stop this minute . . . Living here is so silly, somehow. So crowded with emptiness, nothing seems to belong to me or become me, the center is dispersed, everything is wrong, and now I suppose it will take the rest of my life to set it right, if ever I can at all . . . I can trace this line of disasters, I think, and can hope that is my clue to repairing all the wrongs. We'll see. I live from one day to the next, but not idly, I am getting ready for a change, this time, I hope, not another mistake . . .

> With all my love, you darling
> *Katherine Anne*

Poor Malcolm Cowley never was anything but cold oatmeal from the neck up, and even warmed with likker it is still oatmeal. I wouldn't trust him for even the simplest insight or memory of any sort. The parade of names in this Chambers-Hiss business has been remarkable. I have been so annoyed about the Fascists I almost forgot to notice the Communists . . . I knew that M.C. in his sloppy way leaned towards some vague notion he had of Communism, but the only effect it ever had that I could see was to just add confusion to his natural chaos. Lucky that cause which hasn't Malcolm, I would have said. Let the Communists have him, by all means . . .

To George Landy   768 Santa Ynez Street
                               Stanford, California
                               22 July 1949

Dear Mr. Landy:

Your letter of the 15 July reached me this morning, having taken the long way round through New York. My publishers sent it on.

I have always believed that "Noon Wine" could be made into a picture, but I could wish it might be done by Robert Flaherty with no strings on him. One trouble, as a thoughtful Hollywood producer, a friend of mine who does very successful popular comedies, said, "It has no love interest . . ." My own view is that if the relations between Mr. and Mrs. Thompson are not seen in the right light, then the whole thing will be wrong . . . I have thought in this regard of introducing something in the way of young hopeful love, as contrast to the older tragic one, a girl for Arthur, a schoolmate who grows up with the situation . . . However, this is the kind of thing to be worked out as one goes along.

Perhaps you heard the radio version—or Mr. Mailer perhaps did?—made for NBC's "Theatre," with Beulah Bondy as lead. I have a recording of it, and it is almost pure disaster from my point of view. To begin with, the structure of the story is destroyed and the whole point missed. Which is enough. And the music is completely inappropriate. The little Scandinavian drinking song really exists, it is beautiful, and any incidental music must be based on that. In any case, I am having the radio version suppressed until drastic changes can be made. That contract, by the way, interferes with nothing in any other field at all . . .

One can do little about suppressing or changing a picture once it is launched. So many persons in moving pictures have expressed an interest in this particular story, but it is a fact that none of them has known quite where to tackle it. It would have to be a "serious" picture, (I wish it might be done in France! that is to say, with French seriousness and vitality) and you know well how such a prospect scares Hollywood people off. Also I would not allow propaganda, nothing about the down trodden farm worker, nothing about the unenlightened south, no "tying-in" with any special argument of any kind whatever . . . The story is about Man caught in the network of his own mistaken motives, of human beings in a moral predicament, and it could be transposed to any language, any period, and place in the Western world since the twelfth century at least and need only change of scene and costume, and local custom. So none of the messy garbled psycho-analysis or half-baked sociology that Hollywood has just discovered can be made to pay off . . .

I say this first because it is of first importance, and any one who accepted the story, and any one who worked on the script, would have this fixed rule to observe. Within that limit, they cannot go wrong . . . It should be kept in the time and place of its present setting, also, for the sake of the speech used and the manners of the people . . .

I should like very much some notion of the kind of interest Mr. Mailer has in the story: his attitude towards the whole thing, what he sees in it, how he regards the human beings in it, especially the three men whose lives collide so fatally: they are of almost equal importance: what he plans generally to do with it. I suppose this would call for a short synopsis; he will know best about that. I should expect to be consultant all the way through, as my friend Robert Penn Warren is doing at Columbia with Robert Rossen.

As for the financial side, I should want a lump sum for the story of course, a salary or a fixed fee as consultant, and—I know the difficulties here, I have discussed this with the most hardened experts before—a percentage of the profits of the picture no matter how small. My percentage, I mean. The company has the right only to make the one picture . . . no final sale. I know a few histories about that, too. (I have three different writing contracts with three of the main companies and you need not spare me the facts of life. I have a pretty clear notion.) Everything must be limited as to time, and one sole picture. After that all rights in the story return to me . . .

But I do not want to sign away my story and then see nothing left of it but perhaps the title and my name as author when in fact I am nothing of the kind. And I do not want a picture "based" on anything I have written. So I wish to be consultant. You know producers have a tendency when dealing with people in obscure ways of life to treat them with contempt, reduce them to Tobacco Road types, or to ignore economic facts altogether and show them in California ranch palaces with the heroine in a pink organdy by Irene. My Miss Ellen Bridges afterwards Mrs. Thompson undoubtedly wore pink organdy when she was young, it is just what she would wear, and she ran it up herself on her own sewing machine . . . What Hollywood never gets through its head is, it might still be very pretty and attractive.

My people in "Noon Wine"—of the family and neighborhood—are decent, self-respecting members of a small conservative farming community in South Texas in 1898, and onwards, and I wish them to be presented as they are, dressed as they should be, treated with human decency, their ways understood . . . It is in these things that I shall be useful, and shall earn my money.

When you have thought this over and talked to Mr. Mailer, and believe that you may be able to handle the story advantageously for all of us, do let me hear from you further. If it should come to contracts, everything must be handled through the office of Mr. Robert Giroux, Harcourt Brace and Company, 383 Madison Avenue, New York 17, N.Y. My publishers who also handle all other rights for me, except my contracts as writer with moving picture companies. These are handled by whatever agent happens to be able to place me.

Thank you for your letter. It would be rather splendid all around to have a good picture out of "Noon Wine" . . . If you see Agna Enters give her my most friendly greeting, please; and if you have her address, please send it me? I haven't acknowledged her last Christmas card—they are charming—because I don't know where she is.

If you write before August 15, the address at the head of the letter is right. Anything later should always be sent care of Harcourt Brace etc.

Sincerely yours,
Katherine Anne Porter

SECTION 7

New York, Paris, Brittany, New York
July 1950 to September 1953

I think joy is just as instructive as pain, and I like it better. I never meant to suffer any more than I could help; my nature was meant for happiness, a daylight art and living.

> Katherine Anne Porter to her nephew Paul
> *July 18, 1951*

"I LOVE TO PRAISE WHAT I LOVE," KATHERINE ANNE PORTER *tells Eudora Welty, "and I won't for a minute believe that love is blind— indeed, it gives clearness without sharpness, and surely that is the best light in which to look at anything." She sails on the* **Queen Elizabeth** *in May of 1952 for France to open the Paris Conference, the International Exposition of the Arts. She writes the preface to her collection of essays,* **The Days Before,** *in Brittany, hearing the sound of water and seeing the light from the mill stream dance on the underleaves of the trees. She tells her French translator, who is reading as much as she has written of her novel, "My people are in general perhaps a little more stupid than I meant them to be, but that could come of limitations of my own." At Finistère, on the very spot Tristan and Isolde landed, children will "take you to the rocky promontory where, if you kneel down and gaze a long time, you will see the roofs and spires of the drowned city of Ys. Well, I surprised them—indeed, I surprised myself—I saw it, clearly."*

To Marcelle Sibon   108 East 65th street
                            New York 21 N.Y.
                            5 July 1950

Marcelle darling,

Once I become really discouraged, it can threaten to settle into a permanent state. I know well that the world highways are open once more, have been for a good while, friends see you in Paris and bring me news of you; there is reason to believe this letter will reach you, as I intend to insure it: YET I am still somehow unconvinced, after all those letters I wrote you which you did not receive, and all those little exploring notes saying merely, in the best tradition of Irish unreason, "if you don't receive this please let me know." Even I believe several packages didn't get there, towards the end—the end of my tether, I mean.

Yet I had your letters, some of them with distressing news, about your accident, your illness, your weariness, that set me desperate to get at least a word to you so you would know I did at least know what was happening to you . . . It was and is painfully mysterious . . .

I have all your letters, and even remember without reading them again some of the things you said, things needing badly to be answered . . . One thing: your feeling that I was silent through some kind of disappointment with the sales of my books. Great God, as if I ever expected any sales! Or as if you or I had the faintest connection with that aspect of the thing . . . I hope you think better of that by now. It was lovely to hear that you had a prize for your translation of a book by Stephen Spender, not so nice to hear that except for that, you would have got a prize for your translation of one of my books . . . Plainly, one of the committees seemed to say, no matter how good you are at your work (and everybody agrees you are superb, and I don't know a young American serious writer who doesn't hope to secure your interest as translator) it would manifestly not be fair to give you *two* prizes. Such logic is beyond me . . . And what irony, too, for do you remember long ago in the little garden in Notre Dame des Champs, you showed me a letter from Stephen Spender, wrote that he had seen your translation of *Flowering Judas,* and would like you to consider translating his things. And we talked about it, and I had just read *The Burning Bush* and it represented everything I detested both in mind and heart, and I advised you that the fellow was not good enough for you. I still think the same . . . But which translation got the prize? Darling this really appeals to my sense of humor; and sometimes I warn young writers not to depend upon my judgement: if I praise them they will fail surely; better pray for me to attack them, they will most certainly have a successful career.

Young Ransom wrote me you were charming and so very nice to him. Young Goyen brings me a late glimpse of you, but says the same with added notes on your lovely, live mind—neither seemed to notice your situation as either old or fat—Well, if you are old and fat, I am old and thin, older than you, I know that well, no beauty and never was . . . I have here thumbtacked on my notice board above my desk that smiling beautiful photograph you gave me just before I left Paris. It did not flatter you at all, and so I did not appreciate its beauty until later, when I was not able to compare it with the original. Now I will accept it as your likeness, but once I knew it was not beautiful enough by half . . . I suppose I look as well as ever I did, but that was nothing much, and I feel no sense of loss. What I should like to hear from you is that you are well and have a little more freedom from all your cares and overwork. There does seem to be a point at which it is just waste energy to drive oneself any further, one can reach it rather suddenly, too.

I was cheerfully distracting my mind by growing roses, ca-mellias, azaleas, carnations, irises, in tubs in my back yard in Santa Monica, when the owners of the ugly little house, of which I had the upper half, descended and waved me out, on the grounds that they wished to live there themselves . . . I sold my flowers, put my household things in storage, and set out on a year's lecture tour across country in universities and colleges . . . I lived in deserted fraternity houses, odd little hotels, guest rooms of faculty members, in busses, airplanes, ferries, and trains: I even slept on a bench under a shed at a Ferry landing in Michigan, and I talked myself blind, deaf, and dumb, (I say nothing of my audiences) completely across this continent, which is larger, wider, hotter, colder, rougher, smoother, uglier and more beautiful than one thinks while sitting safely somewhere looking at its map. Also it is full of the most intelligent, stupid; sensitive, coarse; dull, witty; charming,

boring; educated, ignorant; wicked, good; malignant, kind; stimulating, tiresome; handsome, hideous; attentive, indifferent; sensible, silly; unconscious, highly aware; generous, mean; well bred,
base, and generally varied people drawn from every nation on
earth, any one could ever expect to see in this world . . . I was
fascinated by the utter variety; yet in the end I was pleased, a little
placated, a little convinced (for you know my pessimism, and well
founded, don't you agree?) by the scales somehow tipping however
lightly to the side of the human virtues . . . I saw more people to
like than otherwise, and it is a fact that the pleasant ones rather
defended me and kept the unpleasant ones at a distance, where, I
must say they stood making faces and hostile gestures . . .

Just the same, I began to feel like something in a travelling zoo
and refused all offers for the next year and this, and went to Stanford University in Palo Alto, California, and lectured there on
literature for a year . . . Stanford is not a good university for the
humanities, especially for literature . . . It was not a good year and
I rejoiced to leave the place . . . But now, I have accepted for one
semester at the University of Chicago for next spring, and that shall
really be my last . . . I do not feel at home in the academic world,
and I feel sure it is not a good ambience for the artist . . . what
business have we to be teaching when we should be doing the work
that may be taught in the future? So I have refused every offer,
though it is true I can make two or three times as much money
lecturing as I can writing. Yet, writing is my work, and I shall leave
teaching to the better qualified: After next spring, that is . . .

I came to New York last fall, by luck was able to take part of
a large, oldish house here with friends, and brought together my
scattered possessions—imagine that I have here my Paris chairs and
such things, made like new and my treasures—and have all my
books and papers under one roof after too many years . . . and am
now realy finishing my novel, also doing some critical writing,
reviewing and so on . . . New York is noisy, dirty, huge, crowded,
the very worst you hear about it is no doubt true . . . but there are
other things to balance all this, I love a world capital, and this is
indeed a center. Nearly all my friends are here, or nearby, or will
pass through sooner or later, and I am seeing dear friends I have
not seen for years . . . Editors and publishers are here, they can call
me by telephone and invite me for lunch or whatever they are

offering; and all the peoples of the earth have brought the aura of great state and glory to this city. It would just be nonsense to waste time hating or opposing it. But then, I know I should have been happy in Babylon . . . My delight in Paris was that I had only to put my head out of the window of the little funny dear house in Notre Dame des Champs to feel all the living currents of the world blowing across my face. I had not to go looking for anything—it was all there.

I live here as quietly as I did there. One may, by ignoring door-bell and telephone for days at a time, live in the silence and solitude and not unpleasant trance which for me, must be the prelude to doing any kind of decent work. This seems very natural to me, I thrive on it, but it is hard to explain to friends who live a life of continual movement and change and seeing hundreds of people—mostly people very like themselves—going to the country week-ends, vacationing regularly in July or August, keeping themselves always in a state of stimulation—such a life would kill me; indeed, when I tried to live it, thinking it was the proper thing and expected of me, I damned near did perish, and learned better barely in time. Yet I dearly love my few and adorable friends, and see them as often as I can without getting again on the treadmill.

After the semester in Chicago, my plan and hope, having then the novel finished, is to be again in Paris for a month or two. I have had for years in mind a large project of translating something from French or middle French, a series of documents from the fifteenth century, but I know I need help—your help, exactly. So we would if you like make a joint affair of it, I know where to find a publisher, and there remains only for me to get us some money, which I will do when the time comes. So I shall come with my *projets* under my arm, and hope you will not be too engaged with too many other things, and maybe this long-cherished plan will come alive . . . This will be only one of the hundreds of things we have to talk about?

Meantime, my dear, maybe you could not imagine from my long silence how very faithful my love to you was, is now, will be: times change, our situations, but strangely my heart does not; affection does become for me a kind of habit of the spirit, and sometimes I am amazed to find how many years have passed, how long we have been good friends, because in that steady climate without seasons which is the nature of my love, time seems to have stood still. And now, once I have broken through my own silence, which closed in finally after so many discouragements which had nothing to do with us, but a mere postal system, a mere passing failure of practical ways and means, you will see that I write as long and rambling letters as ever . . . Do tell me how you are, about your health, what happens to you . . . I am in better health than for a long time, I think because many burdens I had and many troublesome things have been finally disposed of, I am free to work and know where I shall be for a year or two, so why should my health not be good? And so it is . . . May I hear that yours is too, and that everything goes better with you . . .

I say nothing of the near prospect of this country being at war again soon, if we are not, actually, already. Though the officialese jargon seems to call it something else . . . What is there to say? Those of my generation have known nothing but war, why should we expect to see anything else? I am very strangely unmoved by the whole prospect as if all the emotions I had to give were spent on the other wars, and now—still I cannot help having a very small pin-point glimmer of hope that this may not be war, but the preventive measure the despatches claim it is . . . I did always believe that if the U.S. and Great Britain had backed France when France was all for going up and throwing Hitler out of the Rhineland, all the disaster that followed would have been prevented.

With my same love as always, yours
Katherine Anne

TO JAMES STERN   108 East 65th Street
                        New York 21, N.Y.
                        15 July 1950

Dear Jimmy:

One post ahead of your note, a note from Ernestine: saying you had written her that "strong arm methods had committed Harcourt." No doubt her words, not yours, but good news in any case. It is not surprising that for months one may urge questions of

literary merit, injustice of keeping a writer's mss. in a dark cup-
board, unfairness of not allowing him to seek other publishers—
well, all the little modest formless arguments of simple decency,
and then have the whole thing suddenly decided by some one else
offering to pay good cash on the barrel head for this unprized
property . . . That happened to me also, and in the very same
publishing house. I stayed where I was because I had no reason to
believe things would have been any different in any other firm or
anywhere in the world . . .

Henry Green was lucky; at least he was given a gorgeous start,
and if he isn't going to go on being a best seller, at any rate he has
got his own kind of readers to keep for good; my London publisher—tied alas in bowknots of ancient friendship as well as business with Donald Brace:—Jonathan Cape his name is—took me on
because there was no way out, but sat down from the start saying
in effect, No Hope! And except for a rare and delightful word such
as yours, about your family knowing my stories, it would not occur
to me that a soul in England had ever heard of me . . . Yet stop.
Did I tell you Ann's account of my fame in England—London at
least? She was there with the de Basil Ballet Russe de Monte Carlo
(all the *Russes* being American girls like her, and de Basil not
having seen Monte Carlo for twenty years perhaps) and a young
British writing man led her around to literary teas, and introduced
her with a set speech ". . . the niece of the American Elizabeth
Bowen."

In Paris, my dear translator Marcelle Sibon wrote that *Pale
Horse, Pale Rider* had been allowed to drop silently into the limbo
of uncared for things; she could not account for it, because the first
book had sold well. I still think writers would do better to care a
little more about what *kind* of readers they have than how many;
but this my firm life-long conviction is greeted usually with jeers or
skepticism or both, and I am reduced to the silent stubborn cherish-
ing of a private notion of a Jehovah's Witness in wartime.

Ah, wartime—that reminds me. Things are going normally.
When we are years late getting into the scramble, we are rebuked
bitterly for letting Europe, Africa and Asia go to hell in their own
way. When this time we are in at the drop of the hat, we are more
bitterly rebuked as war mongers and invaders of European affairs
. . . I am reading up on the subject to find out who and what the

Europeans blamed their mistakes and disasters on before U.S. became a world power—which wasn't really until just before World War I. I have been working on the thing for about twenty years, but now and again I am given a fresh surge of interest by present world affairs . . . Things are going to change, no doubt for the worse, they always have, according to the chroniclers of all times since the fall of Rome, and naturally we are most of us going to be dismayed, we always are; I confess for one I am dismayed, but then I always was. Having totally misunderstood the nature and purpose of war—due to my bad Jeffersonian upbringing—I have always opposed it on the grounds that it never is fought for the reasons given and never settles any grudge, neither the official one or the real one . . . Still I always believed that if England and America had backed France to chase Hitler out of the demilitarized zone—remember that old hat? how quaint it all seems now! the whole filthy business of World War II could have been avoided . . . Of course, everybody should have started earlier except that almost no one wished to . . . Now we'll see if quick action works for the best, as a *rule:* this is another time and another place and too much damage has been done all around to give us much hope for anything, *yet,* though this is war, it is not full war, it is a preliminary skirmish; and as usual, we have green troops insufficiently provisioned giving the most amateur kind of performance, and the whole world knowing well that our sources for war have hardly been touched even by the War II, that we really have those bombs, and that we do mean business. I do wonder therefore at the strange timidity with which this country always approaches war. We never do anything to forestall or prevent it, we behave just like Europeans in that; and yet never know when to strike, or where . . . Yet, except for our own self-indulgent and senseless Civil War, we have managed to keep the peace—by all sorts of methods, you may call them anything you like—on this continent, a relative, uneasy peace, but peace—ever since we settled down as a nation. I think it is not bad, and I have hopes for better. But then, Jimmie, I am a native of this place; a huge network of families cannot be three hundred years in a country without getting a mysterious feeling of identification with it: one is not a summer soldier, or a peace time patriot. I find that love of country is much like any other human affection—for better or for worse, in sickness and in health, through good and evil report, and anything less is not even worth thinking about. So I am getting all ready again to wade through the sewers of hatred and slanders and blunderings and villainies and general stupidities of the whole world, my part of the world not excepted or excused . . . Still if I could choose a country, which I cannot, where would I not find the same evils? With this one difference, that my heart is here, and would stay here, no matter where I went. I could wish we had better administration of the government than we have, we have a rotten habit of electing some odd birds, but no American really makes the mistake of confusing his government with his country. I like our form of government, but it could do with an improvement in details . . . It is not really as corrupt and cynical as it was, say, in Harding's time, but the scale is larger, and the people in general know more about what goes on. We have a foul press, 90 percent, but the people know it and are not led by it. Even these few little consolations keep me from despair.

Well, my dear, all this comes no doubt of my summer habit of getting up at five in the morning, never hearing a radio, seeing a newspaper perhaps once a week, and sitting at this machine slogging my way through the novel, with intervals to do a review now and again. I have long long silent days, no parties, no alcohol, no theatres, no week-ends on the country—what DO I have then? Life never seems more brimmed up with the kind of thing I like: New York is no problem to me nor ever was as you know. Let the visiting firemen battle with the place—I never knew a place easier to live in except Paris.

Love to you both, I'll be happy to see you back here, let me know when you come . . .

Katherine Anne

To Barbara Wescott   108 East 65th Street
                              New York 21, N.Y.
                              Monday, I think the 7th? of
                              August 1950

. . . . Darling yes, I am shucking off those wrappers one layer at a
time you will be glad to hear. Life-blood, death-blood, what does
it matter? How else would I have spent my life, which is meant to
be poured out in one cause or another? In some ways I have lived
like a prisoner to an idea, in curious, stubborn, frustrated devotion.
But it is very possible that these were the conditions required, it is
just true that once we make a choice, numberless other possibilities
must be put aside, and if the choice was a true one, then all the other
things are not missed or regretted . . . I remember once poor
William James nearly blew his cap over a certain philosophical
theory that if you once accept a way that seems to you good, then
you must accept all that goes with it, the evils implicit in it too.
Reading Renouvier restored his equanimity. I never read
Renouvier, did you? I never quite understood his excitement. I too
and do take for granted the double aspects of any choice. Yes, I
have had the strangest sufferings, and the most mysterious set-
backs, and the most idiotic mischances, but then, they have been
well overbalanced by those things that I take for good, in the sense
that confidence in what one is doing, no matter what the end may
be, is good. The end is not in my hands.

    Your sweet letter charmed me. I love you as always, a thing
I hardly think needs saying by now. Yet words being my trade, "my
solitary sedentary trade" (Yeats?) I do now and then rely on them
to say what I feel, and believe that they really do work. Your words
work, I know that.

                              Katherine Anne

To Dr. William Ross   [108 East 65th Street
                              New York 21, N.Y.]
                              March 4, 1951

Dear Dr. Ross:

I cannot possibly sign the oath of allegiance you sent me, and I'm sorry I was not told in your first letter that this would be required of me, for a good deal of time and trouble would have been spared both of us.

This is the first time I've encountered this dangerous nonsense, but I have known from the beginning what my answer must be. My memory goes back easily thirty years to the time this law was passed in Colorado, in a time of war, fright and public hysteria being whipped up by the same kind of people who are doing this work now. Only now we're worse for thirty years of world disaster.

I believed then, and still do believe, that this requirement of an oath of allegiance was more of a device for embarrassing and humiliating honest persons than an effective trap for traitors and subversive people. We, all of us, do quite a lot of ceremonial oath-taking on many important occasions of life as an act of faith, a public testimony of honorable intention, and it is the mere truth that an oath binds only those persons who meant to keep their promises anyway, with or without an oath. The others cannot be touched or controlled in any such way. We all know this so why assist at such a cynical fraud.

I'm entirely hostile to the principle of Communism and to every form of totalitarian society, whether it calls itself Communism, Fascism, or whatever. I feel indeed that Communism and Fascism are two names for the same thing, that the present struggle is really a civil war between two factions of totalitarianism. But Fascism is older, more insidious, harder to identify, easier to disguise. No one can be a Communist without knowing what he is doing. A man may be a most poisonous Fascist without even in the least recognizing his malady.

It is not the oath itself that troubles me. There is nothing in it I do not naturally and instinctively observe as I have and will. My people are the old stock. They helped to found colonies, to break new trails, and to survey wildernesses. They set up little log cabin

394

academies, all the way from Virginia and Pennsylvania to Kentucky and clear into Texas. They have fought in all the wars, they have been governors of states, and military attachés, and at least one ambassador among us. We're not suspect, nor liable to the questionings of the kind of people we would never have invited to our tables.

You can see what the root of my resentment is. My many family branches helped to make this country. My feeling about my country and its history is as tender and intimate as about my own parents, and I really suffer to have them violated by the irresponsible acts of cheap politicians who prey on public fears in times of trouble and force their betters into undignified positions.

Our duty, Dr. Ross, is to circumvent them. To see through them and stop them in their tracks in time and not to be hoodwinked or terrorized by them, not to rationalize and excuse that weakness in us which leads us to criminal collusion with them for the sake of our jobs or the hope of being left in peace. That is not the road to any kind of safety. Nothing really effective is being done here against either Communism or Fascism, at least not by the politicians because they do not want anything settled. Their occupations and careers would be gone. We're going to be made sorry very soon for our refusal to reject unconditionally the kind of evil that disguises itself as patriotism, as love of virtue, as religious faith, as the crusader against the internal enemy. These people are themselves the enemy.

I do not propose to sit down quietly and be told by them what my duty is to my country and my government. My feelings and beliefs are nothing they could understand. I do not like being told that I must take an oath of allegiance to my government and flag under the threat of losing my employment if I do not. This is blackmail, and I have never been blackmailed successfully yet and do not intend to begin now.

So please destroy the contract we have made, as it is no longer valid. I know I run some little risk of nasty publicity in this matter. I hope not. I am not in the least a martyr. I have no time for heroics and indeed distrust them deeply. I am an artist who wishes to be left in peace to do my work. I hope that work will speak in the long run very clearly for me and all my kind, will be in some sort my testimony and my share of the battle against the elements of corruption and dissolution that come upon us so insidiously from all sides we hardly know where to begin to oppose them.

You may say this is a great how-do-you-do about a small matter. I can only say it is not a small matter when added to all the other small matters of the kind that finally make an army of locusts.

Dr. Ross, I thank you for your courteous letter and hope you will take my word that this letter has nothing personal in it. That towards you I intend nothing but human respect in the assurance that I believe I understand your situation which must be extremely difficult.

What has this kind of meanness and cheapness to do with education? What is wrong that undesirable applicants for the faculty are not quietly discovered and refused before they are appointed? Why must a person like me be asked to do a stupid, meaningless thing because one person with a bad political record got into your college once? No, I can't have it, and neither can you. The amusing side of all this brou-ha-ha is I really did not expect to have any occasion to mention the flag or the laws of Colorado or the Communist Alger Hiss or even the Fascist Senator McCarthy. I meant to talk about literature, life understood and loved in terms of the human heart in the personal experience. The life of the imagination and the search for the true meanings of our fate in this world, of the soul as a pilgrim on a stony path and of faithfulness to an ideal good and tenacity in the love of truth. Whether or not we ever find it, we still must look for it to the very end.

Any real study of great literature must take in human life at every possible level and search out every dark corner. And its natural territory is the whole human experience, no less. It does not astonish me that young people love to hear about these things, love to talk about them, and think about them. It is sometimes surprising to me how gay my classes can be, as if we had found some spring of joy in the tragic state to which all of us are born. This is the service the arts do, and the totalitarian's first idea is to destroy exactly this. They can do great harm but not for long. I am not in the least afraid of them.

With my sincere good wishes, and apologies for this overlong letter,

Yours,
Katherine Anne Porter

To MARCELLE SIBON   108 East 65th Street
                                 New York 21
                                 19 April 1951

Marcelle darling:

The heart keeps its strange tenderness, and the mind seems to go on in its special way; the spirit does not fail particularly, but I can't help noticing that little Brother Ox has a way now and then of sitting down in harness, balking utterly, refusing to carry any more the weight of these other three. I was pained when you told me of your new illness, an arthritic state, and your regret for the lost integrity of your body. Since my twenty-fourth year I have known I carried in me a malign thing, the enemy that I have all this time had to deal with, so that my feeling about my body has been always that it was just a little overburdened, had something more to do than it should have, speaking in fairness. And if it fails from time to time, I am not surprised—only annoyed and mystified and sometimes a little bored.

So if I tell you that I have had pneumonia three times between April 1950 and February 1951, let this stand for all delays, silences, unfinished projects and plans not quite carried out. I have not much interest in my own illnesses: they recur, I get well or nearly, and so on. But when you wrote me about your accident and then your illness, I was dismayed, for you have always been the healthiest person I know, in every way, and if you are ill, I feel that great measures should be taken at once, there must be something done; who is looking after you, and what are the doctors doing? And how are you now? I feel that helplessness that distance gives to one, the not quite knowing, the wish to be near and *do* something; I would know what was needed if I were there. Yet look—for months I have not been able even to write the letters I wanted to write, and time has slipped away while I held my hands cupped over the present moment, trying to salvage it in order to have tomorrow at all. And have been worse than useless to myself and to my friends . . .

But this has been an odd kind of time: within just the past few weeks I have had half a dozen friends from very remote pasts, (one has a dozen pasts or more, all running parallel in the memory) to return, or rather to show up suddenly out of a benign fog, to look for me, to speak, to remind me of something pleasant and good that we had together once: it has been charming, we have not disappointed each other in the least, and the abyss has closed up with hardly the faintest seam between us . . .

. . . . I met Stephen Spender, one of your "stable" and alas, was no more impressed by the slack and boneless charm of his person than I ever was by the slack and boneless character of his writing. Oh Marcelle, how bored I am with charm of this sort! I feel one has only to poke a finger through the surface, and all will prove to be apple-sauce, and mildewed apple-sauce, besides. Do you remember William Goyen? His *House of Breath* did very well, I was one of his sponsors for a Guggenheim Fellowship, which he has just won, and is now on the edge of finishing his second book. I thought well of the first, as you know, but hope for much better in the second. Of course he longs for you as translator, but then, so does every one . . .

You may be surprised at this bank order which drops out. Not at all, it is perfectly natural. I want two things. I never knew your birthday, and wish to give you a birthday present, and never knew what to send, time and distance making such changes in one's tastes and wants. Second, I long for a whiff of my beloved Essence pour Bains, for I have just used the last drop of what you sent me. So please, with my love, spend half of this for essence, and the other half for something pretty, or useful, or both, for yourself, "to remember me by," as our country idiom says it; if I were there, or you were here, I should find something for you, but look at how things are! And above all, will you please tell me what day of what month you were born, for I consider this very important, and should have known long ago.

Marcelle, I long to see you again, I have for a great while; but lately I have such an impulse just to get up and fly to you, as if you had invited me this moment; I have never seen you in your lovely apartment on the Seine, where it seems to me so many persons I know have seen you, and have told me about you there. Will you write me if even only a short little note, saying how you are, what happens to you now, and even what you are doing, and what you expect to do this summer; you have always worked too hard and no doubt still do. I could wish you had not had to do so much, but I will not weary you with my anxieties that are useless because they cannot *act*. I would say, take care of yourself—what irony. One cannot take care of oneself beyond what the possibility of the day allows. So let me tell you again that you are dear to me, and I wish our friendship might have been lived a little nearer to each other. It has been rather wonderful to me to see what our lives were like when we first knew each other, and what they have become.

> With my same love as always, yours,
> *Katherine Anne*

To Elizabeth Ames   108 East 65th Street
New York 21, N.Y.
6th May 1951

Elizabeth darling:

Its all straight in my mind about the meeting for the 17th, and I wish I might have been going to them all along. No doubt at all the impossibilities that presented themselves come out of a very deep trait of my character: I am just no committee person, and have no sense of what I should do, and feel, perhaps rightly, that things will do just as well without me. I never have, in the whole seven years that I have been a Fellow of the Library of Congress, managed to make it back to Washington for the annual re-union. I never went near the National Institute of Arts and Letters until they simply elected me a vice-president, and Glenway being another, he keeps nudging me, and I pull myself up and make an appearance at the most crucial bouts of policy, but without him I would never have done it. Its a gift, the ability to run organizations, and I haven't got it, with all the good will in the world and a real desire to be useful. But I'll be with you on next 17th May, all right.

Elizabeth, its high time I told you what really happened to the fork I took away from your apartment that time, if you remember. I had hoped to wait until the replacement, which turned out to be not so simple as I hoped. Well, first, let me tell you, not long ago I read a line of Ogden Nash's broken-backed stanzas that struck me most pow'fully. It was a lament for the dear past when he knew how to repair the household gadgets when they went wrong, and for his present utter frustration when faced with these mysterious hermetically sealed contrivances you can't get at when they go bust, and even the inventors and manufacturers don't really know how they work. The line that struck me was:

"I am no longer the head of my house, the man who does all
and knows all—
I have now become merely that One who put the bubble gum
in the Dispose-all—"

Well, I am the one who, reading all the directions and following them painfully, with special note of the warning about closing the hatch so as not to drop silver into the grinder, simply dropped a Tiffany entrée fork, marked with Mr. Peabody's initials, into the growling maw of that really wonderful invention—I *don't* want to seem ungrateful, I love labor-saving devices and would be happy to have more of them than I have. Yet, in one blinding instant, without having even seen the fork disappear, without indeed having seen the fork at all, there was a most shattering metallic commotion set up inside the thing. I shut it off; Dr. Swanner came up and fished it out, it was simply tied in a bowknot, or perhaps more like a pretzel. So I took it away, and went to Tiffany's with it, and you know what they are like. Nothing surprises them. I was told the pattern was obsolete, that it is not in stock any more. It was brought out in 1888; and they still had the moulds, and might bring it back some day. I should think they might, it is such a beautiful shell and leaf pattern. BUT, they take orders for such things only before May 1st, so I got my order in safely; AND they deliver the silver around October first next. So it is all arranged, paid for, and a new fork, engraved exactly like the old, will be returned to you next fall. What a how-do-you-do for one split-second of awkwardness; I am very sorry, darling, but this is all I could think of to repair it. . . .

I expect to see Eleanor here in a few days, and will be very glad of it. She is having her battles too, but if you have seen her *Hadrian's Villa,*† you will see that she is coming on nicely. She is a stubborn, suffering spirit, but she does manage to transmute all into something better, she does not suffer for nothing . . .

†*cf. KAP's* Collected Essays, *pp. 77–80, review of* Rome and a Villa.

Angel, this is getting to be one of those letters of mine, I'll stop it right now. I'd love to see you and talk, and hear you talk. Let me say once more that those three days I spent in your house were the sweetest I have known for a long time, and I remember you and that time with tenderness. And I did some good work too, in your apartment, in spite of being smacked down so suddenly. I got something started growing there, and it is going on very well. That little space of freedom was what I needed to get me back into the feeling of work. I have been most awfully derailed by all the moving and the pneumonia and the endless distractions of trying to live in this house which is always in a whirl: I shall never try to share a house, even with separate floors, with any one again . . .

> Bless you, Elizabeth, with my same old love,
> *Katherine Anne*

To Paul Porter   108 East 65th Street
                              New York 21
                              18 July 1951

Dear Paul:

Oscar always did make me queasy, I always thought him one of the most tiresome men ever born—there is in English letters only one other that bores me as much, Lord Byron—and I sent you the copy of *De Profundis* for the reason I gave in the inscription. It was one of the most discussed and inaccessible of documents, and needed badly to be printed and read especially by young men, and especially young men writers; I hope it does its good work in dispelling the miasma which has poisoned the literary and moral air for two or more generations . . . You must know without my saying what I think of the whole smelly mess; and I am glad to know the effect it had on you—a healthy one. The whole letter, its whole effect, is of rottenness to the bone—the end, which you realize is only a pervert's love letter, the aim of which is merely another meeting and a beginning again of the same foul situation, is of course the point to be noted in the whole thing.

I have got your birthday books packed and will try to get them to the post office in time for the 29th. Should be able to do that. I am sending the five volumes of English Poets, prefaces by Auden—an unusually stinking and opinionated sodomite, but does know how to select poetry—the full collected edition of Yeats' poetry, to the very last; Pound's *ABC of Reading;* and the three very expensive and valuable in all ways *History of the Inquisition* by Dr. Lea, who has never been successfully challenged much less refuted, in his findings and conclusions. Also, he has the noble generosity, scrupulousness, and good manners of the real old-fashioned nineteen century scholar, observing all the graces, but managing nevertheless to get everything said. It will be a liberal education to you in just that sort of thing, which has vanished from scholarship as from the rest of the world. . . .

I never thought much of the Kraft-durch-leide school either—I think joy is just as instructive as pain, and I like it better. I never meant to suffer any more than I could help; my nature was meant for happiness, a daylight art and living. But it is true that my life has been almost unbearably difficult most of the time, and I have had around me so many people who were mere parasites on the good of my life, draining it away for themselves and giving nothing back, and far from knowing how to live in order to have and to give happiness, did not even know how to be decent in their human relationships. In the end, I find myself remembering very little happiness: and the fewest possible number of real friendships, but those very true and good.

Your picture of the Negro woman fishing—my dear, you did better in words than the camera could have done. And the fallacy of your wish for Cartier Bresson to snap the vision for you is this: you should have had your own camera along, and have known how to take it yourself. As a writer, you have better than a camera if you will use the faculty, discipline it, channel it, respect it and get down to the practise of it. I do hope you are methodically saving some money, it doesn't matter how much, but just tithe yourself and get a little backlog so when the time comes you feel you are really ready to work steadily, and have completed your apprenticeship, you will have something to rely on . . . This is the advice of one who has poured all her resources down the sink, which should give it the value of the Horrible Example, like the old-time Salvation Army drunk. . . .

With my love,
Aunt Katherine Anne

TO GLENWAY WESCOTT   Care Brooks
                            Forest Road
                            Northford, Connecticut
                            19 Sept 1951

Glenway darling:

The revolt against the novel as a form seems to be in the air: I don't know if you started it, but I have heard a number of writers insist they are only writing "a book," refusing to give its shape or intention a name. Well, the novel has had a long, glorious run for its money, maybe Henry James did carry it to its extreme possibility, discouraging further attempts at it, for a while, at least. Then too, any little bootstrap writer can master the "form" and turn out something that really is a novel, technically speaking, even if it is empty and useless as a grasshopper shell. By the rules, Joyce never wrote a novel, nor for that matter, did you. I don't know whether what I am writing is a novel or not: I'll leave that to those who judge.

But—(some one told me not long ago that my most maddening habit was to listen attentively to an argument or statement of a position, nod agreeingly and say, "Yes, of course—but . . ." and then launch into the opposition. I hate being made self-conscious in these things, BUT, it looks like I am doing it again!) But, then, I think the whole present curious attitude towards the novel is caused by a confusion between "shape"—that is, the technical devices used in the making of a novel, the set of rules by which almost any one can make a novel, easily recognized as such, and "form" which is simply another thing; form is not a question of technique— it is a matter of internal structure, the working of the individual artist's imagination upon his material, it is an inborn sense; if one

403

has it, one has it, and no amount of trying or taking thought or mastering of various techniques will either give it or compensate for it or conceal the lack of it. So no matter what you do, what kind of book you write, it will have form if you have it. So you see the Bowleses and the Windhams and the Beuchner's and the Sansoms and the Greenses, both of them and God knows who else of the battered little crew turning out their novels, really shaped like novels; and no serious artist could be blamed if he decides *that* technique is now rather too slimed over to touch again . . .

I still don't think that is any reason for doing a campaign against Henry James. I can see why such as they might hate him, his whole life and works is (singular because the life and works is one) a standing rebuke to their frivolity and emptiness. But James has never wronged you. You belong on his side, not theirs.

I wish I could have heard some of those passages at Blooming-ton, Allen thundering, etc., for I have heard you both, but not from the same platform. It should be enlivening.

You are right, I asked for the Forster papers, but they had gone to Auden. I am to have your Colette, though. I came here to visit with my dear Tinkum and Cleanth Brooks rather suddenly after long planning and talk about it, and they have a beautiful old house with fireplaces like yours, in a landscape that makes me feel as if I were sitting in the midst of an illustration from a History of New England—even a little old cemetery with winged skulls on the red granite (or sandstone?) tombs. Will be back in a week or so. Try to work, but cannot. I feel sometimes as if I am dying of my dislocations and anxieties—they have gone on too long.

Please tell me which passage gave you gooseflesh? I cannot imagine which one it could be! With my same old love

Katherine Anne

To Paul Porter   108 East 65th Street
                                  New York 21, N.Y.
                                  13 October 1951

Paul darling:

Maybe you should always write your letters so, saying the first thing that comes to mind, telling what interests and pleases and troubles you most in that minute, for letters I always thought were meant to be personal messages standing instead of talk between two persons who are not arguing, or trying to convert each other to anything, or writing essays for posterity or even the present public—so the free-er and easier the tone, the nearer it comes to a letter, seems to me. Anyway your account of the party was gorgeous and of course I believe that none of you were drunk. One of my most favorite songs in the oldest days was Bert Williams' "I don't have to *make* my shimmy shake, I can strut my stuff on tea!" I still believe the best gayety comes with a minimum of likker, anyway. I am in a book, a vanished novel by a vanished novelist of the bath-tub gin era, disguised as a little brown-eyed Mrs. Whoozit (don't remember the name) who always came to the party sober and gay as a cricket, and went right on being gay the whole evening on two drinks and went away gay and still sober, having had the best time of anybody. I wouldn't have known it was meant for me if the author had not told me, and yet, it was true, only I had not thought it was anything to write about. The less I drink at parties the better time I have. . . .

Your praise of my little piece about love, really, charmed me. There is so much in one's mind that doesn't work itself into fiction and I love to write for the sake of writing and saying what is in my mind at the time. I take this out in random things, reviews, articles—we are happier and do better work if we let our minds range freely through *all* our interests, not trying to sustain one tone, or level or mood; and everything we do helps everything else; by writing we keep limbered up, like an athlete; and the constant exercise is to see just how much of what we really think and feel and know we can get down visibly on a page where we can *see* it: thoughts just running around in the head are not much good to anybody, least of all the writer unless he can snare them and put them into becoming words. I do always manage to say something near what I mean in any little old piece, and with everybody goin round shootin they haids off, why so shall I. Its fun. . . .

Honey I'm in the dead middle of a review of Forster's new book, which I mean to mail tomorrow evening, so this must end. Francis Steegmuller—who wrote *Flaubert and Madame Bovary* sent me a new book about Gide by the boy named Victor who hated him so—Victor was Gide's name for him—and also there has been published all that Gide left out of his journals about his wife. He recorded an evil malodorous life, and it looks as if he has left an unusually stinking corpse. The really revolting thing that comes out and out is his "morality." His religiosity. And strangely, he did so many good things. Yet the Chinese—really the Chinese, this is not just a saying—have some proverb about when a good thing is done by an evil man, the thing brings evil with it. Something else about a right thing turning wrong when done for the wrong motives . . . The net result of his life and work seems to me to be incalculably evil.

Bye-bye—back to Forster, who is another problem, belonging also to the Afflicted Brotherhood, but somehow triumphing over his disabilities . . .

Let me hear how you do. You sound as if you were getting a raise a month: how much does that make now? You'll be able to get married soon if this keeps on. High time for you to be thinking about it, and you seem to have snagged a likely candidate. Just try not to let her find you out until the deed is done.

> With my love
> *Aunt K.A.*

To Eudora Welty

108 East 65th Street
New York 21, N.Y.
8 November 1951

Dear Eudora:

Scratting through my baskets of paper, your gay letter of just eleven months and four days ago, today, came up with a little tag pinned to it: "To Be Answered At Once."

A good deal of history, general and particular, has bustled by since then, but your letter is as fresh as this morning; and I called Duncan (I've forgotten how to spell Dermot Irish-style) Mr. Russell, anyway, to ask if you might not be in town again just now, for I had heard lately that Elizabeth Bowen was, and your letter told so wonderfully of her visit south with you; and I hope you still have in your head the notion of a little visit: You, Mrs. Bowen, and me, clustered around a table here in my house—I have a remarkably suitable table for such a cluster—with a bottle of some kind of restorative—Bushmills for my choice—not just sitting there, but doing something. Bill Goyen flew up on some kind of an errand, saw more people and got more gossip in three days than I do in a year, living as I do in almost the exact center of this island; and his dear project was to invite Mrs. Bowen and me for drinks somewhere. He was called back suddenly—he had meant to stay a month—to his mother, who is dying slowly, but dying; and he will probably stay south with her. So, that Mrs. Bowen and I shall ever meet seems most improbable; I can think of no reason why we shouldn't, but we don't. So I rather hoped you would be here at this time, though any time in the world would do nicely.

This is really to say, do let me know when you come again, for it is absurd the way we keep on missing each other. A little our own fault, I'm sure, for always being up to the eyebrows in ten thousand things at once. It is fairly certain in my mind that you are in the middle of a new book; tell me. I am more or less at the end of a very old one: but publishers don't seem to remember that I have done several other things since I started that business. Health, tiresome topic, is good enough, better than for many years. A new wonder-drug—new to me—has done its little miracle and I shall be all-right until I become immune to it. By that time maybe *They* will have thought up something else.

Gossip: Red Warren is happily divorced and is a newly-born soul. Albert Erskine is separated, getting divorced, I believe. On the other hand, half a dozen young pairs I know are preparing to bring forth a basket of young shortly, among them my last-year married niece Ann. She and her husband returned from four months in Europe with the merry news. I am pulling myself together to go to a party or so for authors who have books out, and a couple of gallery shows, and a theater opening or two; but Lord, my heart is not in it. I am harder to amuse than Queen Victoria, though for very different reasons, and for society I love only the company of a good familiar friend or two at a time, and talk; this grows rarer and harder to come by, everybody complains of it, but still we must all run like sheep from one mob-occasion to another, and there is no time left keeping friendships warm. Dear Eudora, I miss you very much, and have: so the next time you come, let me see you.

With my same love,
Katherine Anne

To Gay Holloway   108 East 65th Street
New York 21, N.Y.
15 November 1951

Sister darling:

Naturally human curiosity will get the better of me, and I write to Tante Ione if only to find out what that "important" something she has for me can be: I wonder what image of us she has in her mind, for I was about fourteen when we saw her last; and I remember her best as an incredibly soft, white-skinned, downy bride of nineteen, with sky-blue eyes and the slowest Mississippi accent in the world. Also her diamonds, which struck me as of Golconda or a rajah's treasure at least, and her clothes, like nothing *our* family had worn for two generations at least: and perfume. In fact, she represented *This World* in all its glory; all the luxury and delicacy and pleasure and idleness—(she was the idlest girl any of us had ever seen, couldn't do one single solitary thing except dress her self) that then seemed to me the most desirable of all things . . . Well, well—

I think I shall never see her, for there is no use disturbing this memory, nor disturbing hers, either, whatever it may be; but it is sweet of her to invite me for the winter, and I wish it might be done. Nothing is so easy as that, though; even the smallest change of base for me means the uprooting of a household and unbelievable expense. But winter has struck me; I've been flat, staying in bed taking penicillin and pyrobenzamine and sleeping tablets, for eleven days,

408

just. Got up this morning—indeed, have been getting up and having breakfast every day, but oh, with that effort! got up, I say, resolved to stay up, at about ten this morning. It is now three, and though I haven't done anything, and don't know where the time has gone, still, I have been up, which was the point. I think the worst is over.

Really, I'll never in the world get used to the way you-all down there never tell me a thaing. Wouldn't you think that young Paul might have said something, for Patsy was his favorite sister, indeed he was simply infatuated with her beauty; but I did not know that Patsy was even divorced, much less going to get married again. One of you did mention that she had left Pete and gone home, but then, she had done that so often, I paid no attention. Even now you did not tell me the name of the man, nor what he does, nor who he is: in general, we are such disastrous marriers, I shan't be too optimistic until we see how it comes out.

Today I am giving up two things: cocktail party at my publishers for George Willison, whose book *Behold Virginia!* is out today; and the opening of the Stravinsky ballet *Apollo* tonight, which should be wonderful. Cocktail parties I abhor, always did; but I regret missing the ballet. Next Monday I have the funniest chore. There is a darling old hostess here, Mrs Murray Crane— (of the "paper" Cranes, not the plumbing) who is the very last, I imagine, of the very-rich ladies who ran *salons;* she keeps a whole list of literary affairs going tandem: huge evenings of poetry readings, lectures, short plays (with a stage set up in one end of her sixty-foot drawing room) and literary teas (with real tea) and literary Mondays; these Mondays are subscription affairs, a group of ladies raise fifty dollars among themselves every week to pay some writer or other to come and chat about the higher things of life to them.

I am the chatter for next Monday; its nice work if you can get it. For me there could be no easier way of making a living than to be paid for talking, (which I have been, and well paid too, for years) if it didn't take all that travelling, too. But this is just around the corner on Fifth Avenue, and I mean to take it very easy. I go to her big evenings about twice or three times a winter: the literary talk doesn't interest me much, but I see pleasant people there, and supper at 11 o'clock, and home, sober, a little after midnight. That kind of hostess is disappearing from the world rapidly, which is a pity.

A few months ago, my friend Glenway Wescott got the brilliant notion that it was time for me to have another public honor. So he got William Faulkner and Thornton Wilder to second him as sponsor and put me up for the National Institute of Arts and Letters award. I am vice-president of that gloomy society, which I thought was enough. Well, other people put up their candidates, and who did they turn out to be? William Faulkner, Thornton Wilder, Ernest Hemingway; and one of them will get it. Still, I'm one of the Big Four, as Glenway reminded me. As writers, I honestly don't believe that any one of them is a *better* writer than I am; but they have all turned out bushels of work, have had conspicuous public careers, are better known than I am, and besides, are men, which is what will really clench the matter. The point is, I TOLD Glenway I didn't want the Medal, I've got a Medal as big as a saucer and ugly as hell, and I somehow agree with Flaubert that honors degrade, and I've never had one yet that didn't cost me money or trouble or both. I know that Faulkner doesn't give a damn about it, either, and I seem to remember that Hemingway refused to belong to the Institute when elected a member. So I can't think he wants it. That leaves Wilder and maybe he would like it—I think he belongs to the *Legion d'Honneur,* and in general he impresses me as liking such things. I stayed away from the dinner when the nominations were made, but Glenway said some very highfalutin speeches were made for me, and a really beautiful one by Marianne Moore, who is my favorite living poet, and one of the most delicious persons alive.

Well, darling, I'm just telling the news such as it is; after my lying in bed away from everything, I seem to have time to write about what goes on in my narrow circles.

Friday, 16 November, 7 A.M. I had got to this point when Ann came in, bringing me in her red hatbox a hot dinner: lamb chop, fresh peas, lettuce and aguacate salad. The day before she [brought] a large thermos bottle of clam chowder: and before *that,* enormous broiled beef and salad and fruit . . . Bless her, she is really having a chance for the first time to do what she feels like doing, and the really maternal side of her nature is showing itself most beautifully: she is full of the tenderest and warmest feelings, yet of course not softish: keen-edged as ever; still, a strange difference, new and quite charming, in her; even in the expression of her face. I told her not to come today, Guinelda will be here with me. And I have to go out this morning, to have my eyes tested. I haven't had my reading glasses corrected for five years, and it is now time. For some reason I could not sleep at all last night, and finally gave up, got up at five and made coffee, and have tried to work a little, but it is no go. I was determined not to take any more sedatives, for they should be kept for real emergencies, but it is true that I have been under great tension for too long, and can't seem to let go as I should. But I do what I can, and try to be well. It just occurs to me that today is just one year since I went to St. Luke's hospital, and really, I am much better off in so many ways than I was then: for one thing, I have got this sad, heavy year behind me, I don't have to live any of it again; and so many things seem to have settled themselves for me; mainly I feel more hopeful about my work. But I have grown almost superstitious about saying anything about it; I have only to mention a plan or a hope and it seems to go up in smoke.

Have you set the date for your coming here? Let us know as soon as you decide, we are all excited. I shall be glad to have my letters† because I am writing something about my life, a series of three articles that *Harper's Magazine* asked for, and my letters are really like a journal; I wish I could get a lot of them back, years and years and hundreds of them to dozens of people, for my history is in them, I feel certain; and memory, without a few records to look at, can be very unreliable. But I rather wish you wouldn't destroy all your little keepsakes, I'm afraid you will miss them. If you have any little pictures of Mary Alice or Harry when they were little, I am sure Ann would like to have them.

I have just come to the line about the spoofing letter from Brother Paul. Of course, he has had it all made up in his mind that I was the devil of the family, and forgets that I was more bedevilled than devilling, quite often. However, every family must have the scapegoat to blame everything on, and I was elected. I'll be delighted to have the letter—he used to write very funny ones. . . .

Bless you, my darling, I love you.

Katherine Anne

†*Katherine Anne Porter commented in 1973, "I received the script of these letters and papers on June 26, 1973 after my sister was dead nearly 5 years, and—enough!"*

To Paul Porter   108 East 65th Street
                                  New York 21 N.Y.
                                  7 December 1951

Dear Paul:

. . . . Donald Elder and I were talking last evening and agreed
that a distinction must be made between innocence (which belongs
to childhood and inexperience) and *purity,* which one can keep in
spite of all suffering, evil experience, and worldly knowledge—for
virtue is something that can be worked for and won and held only
by really grown-up minds. Did you notice what I said about innocence and stupidity in the Colette review? (You slipped there, you
didn't look attentively enough. Her stories are NOT about love.
Think again.) I was so pleased to see (in the Jarrell review) that you
think in the same way, and have said a very good bold thing—that
grown people have no right to self-pity: that is really what it comes
to . . . Suffering is as natural as joy, part of the whole human
experience, but it is very perverted to seek it, or coddle it, or
mistake its meanings and its causes . . . I like the Jarrell review—you
put a firm thumb on the very thing that has disturbed me in his point
of view. But your last line gives us all away who like his poetry; we
do water and tend too much that insidious little "black rose of our
sorrow." MUST not cultivate black roses (or blue, or green ones
either).

I think I shall read the Herman Hesse *Siddhartha.* Never did,
being thrown off by the kind of persons who did—you know who.
And then, they have a knack of turning every idea they touch into
a great dead jellyfish floating in an ocean without shores . . .

                                  With my love
                                  Aunt K.A.

TO PAUL PORTER   108 East 65th Street
                                  New York 21, N.Y.
                                  15 January, 1952

Paul darling:

. . . . My New Year was odd, but in a way I liked. I started
out in all simplicity for a small gathering at Eleanor Clark's (her
Rome and a Villa will be out in April, why don't you ask to review
it? Its a great book.) And there were mostly musicians and composers—Sylvia Marlowe the harpsichordist, Eleanor's best young man,
Alexei Haieff, one of the very best young composers; Samuel Bar-
ber, Gian-Carlo Menotti, and so on—a roomful of talented people
all being nice to each other, and friends had sent two magnums of
champagne, and there were other delicacies, and a pretty supper,
then people began scattering off to other parties, and we—Alexei,
Eleanor and I and a young man whose name I never did learn, went
on over to Mrs. Murray Crane's—to her enormous Fifth Avenue
apartment full of butlers and maids, and there daughter Louise was
having open house, with more champagne. I met more people I
knew, and a lot I didn't; then we went on to Eleanor's married
sister's which was a dancing party with a real live jazz orchestra, and
there I met a lot of terribly nice rather brokerish and *Fortune*- editor
types of man who danced and hugged and kissed me quite a lot, and
told me how beautiful I was, and fed me things off trays and rushed
me drinks and of course, I am now at the age where I can do with
any amount of that sort of stuff . . .

Then we landed on East 65th just down the street from home,
but way over on the river, in Todd Bollender's house—he is a
dancer, and the place was full of dancers, and there I seemed to
devote myself to consoling Munción, a part negro, part Spanish
dancer, a very good one, but he was totally sunk under a sense of
the General Incurable Awfulness of Everything, and I was very
earnest about trying to convince him that, though Things were most
certainly Awful, they simply could not be as Awful as That. However, that was a gay party too and gay people; and then, quietly, I
found myself at a quarter after 7 A.M. having cornflakes and milk
at the big new Longchamps in the big new apartment house very
near by, with Eleanor and Alexei and the young man, and then was

set down at home feeling sober, but sleepy. I slept until after four that afternoon, and came to with the most delightful impression that I had had a wonderful good time, and that this was almost bound to be a fine, happy New Year, started as it was like that . . . The very oddest thing I find is this: usually in such a long night, with such changes and so many different kinds of people, something is almost bound to happen that leaves a few little scratches that begin to fester next day. Not this. Not a soul was too drunk, no one was ugly, no one wanted to quarrel, every where every body seemed to want to be gay and pleasant, and every body was . . . At Louise Crane's midnight struck, and the whole big party just rushed together touching glasses and kissing and crying out, "Happy New Year, Bless You!" Nobody wept, not even for joy—there was a curious Elysian Fields serenity everywhere we were. . . .

It is, one supposes, not good news about you and Nione; but one doesn't suppose it is final—nobody gets off as easily as that. Or maybe this is the final break after a dozen preliminary breaks, each one meant to be final: and it is true, no matter what you gain in the future doesn't change at all what you have lost. Alas, too, it is very hard to say goodbye and make it stick. One or the other won't let go so suddenly. I was always one for the sudden-descending axe and the clean sweep, but most people—maybe I should say, most men, or modify it further and say, the men I knew who said they loved me, *never* wanted to call it a day and quit for good. No. They seemed to want a kind of twi-light tapering off, with temporary little reconciliations and dramatic leave-taking, on and on, until one is really dead of sheer fatigue.

But here is the strangest thing: when in whatever way my love for any one has been slaughtered, it stays dead. I think now with amazement how, how COULD I ever have loved such and such a person? Yet I did, it is no good trying to deny it, and it was serious, or it was nothing. But even when the love is gone, and nothing but this amazement lasts, I still have that anguished sense of loss, which is not really for anything I lost, but for what I had believed I had, and now know I never had, because it did not exist in that love, in that person . . . This is awkwardly said, but the best I can do with it at present. I can't remember ever having tried to say this before . . .

(And don't you try saying it better or different, for I'm going to pop it straight into the second chapter of my autobiography I'm working on now . . .)

(This thing of having two writers in the family could get right stuffy that-a-way.)

I wish of course that people in love did not feel that their state gives them the right to behave like cannibals and thugs to each other: but then, though love may now and then have his head in a "cloud [sic] of stars," he is usually sunk to the navel in a hog-wallow, and it can be confusing, even to the most spiritually advanced! And then, most love is just an extension of self-love, anyway—each one using the other quite unscrupulously to get what he or she wants; and in the very lowest cases, giving at the same time as little as each can manage. Its a mug's game, really, when it isn't a case of murder. So much for love. Your admiration for the intelligent, sensitive young wife who sits knitting baby-things and listening to the men talk, (dropping a word of Sybil-wisdom from time to time) is touching. If ONLY women would get out of the way, if ONLY they would knit and keep their eyes down, how sweetly simple life would be for the men! I remember something Bill Goyen wrote me once from Yaddo about the "Good kitchen women" there (the cooks and waitresses) of the kind he loved and "feared was vanishing from the earth." Jesus! Oh, if ONLY the females would keep their place, knitting and having babies and cooking, and let the great gorgeous male ego spread its tail and strut before them, they only lifting from time to time their dazzled eyes, how pleasant life might be. No criticism—no needs or wants of their own to disturb the masculine self-absorption, no demands, no nothing: just a bag of humble instincts too rudimentary to require any attention—well, how bloody selfish and stupid can even a man get, I do sometimes wonder? . . . So much for that.

Your reviews are really good, and I am going to put them in an envelope and send them to Harvey Breit, who might just send you a book or two for the *TIMES* . . . Its worth trying for, anyway. Oh, *how* I agree with you about the Siddhartha legend, all of it. I don't think much better of Christ, either, and indeed, they have dismaying points of similarities.

Darling, I'm glad you had Forster to send you to Montaigne, Voltaire, Erasmus, and the rest. You have somebody in the family who had read them and been formed by them from her tenth year, more or less, and when you asked me for a reading list I must have included them. But Forster lacks something I have, and that is the vision of the Fiery Rose. He is a good little being, but on the small order; he is on the side of the angels, but he is also a homosexual, which cramps his style a little. I could have wished your first influence could have been a whole man, or a whole woman: but maybe that is too much to ask in a time—I complained of it thirty years ago—in which almost nobody knows his hands from his feet, and thinks that is a very exciting way to be.

I always thought we ought to know our hands from our feet. Perhaps this was my mistake.

Your darling Aunt Gay; one can hardly ever tell whether she is enjoying herself or not, she has so got herself into that state of the woman who asks for nothing, expects nothing, and finally gets nothing of course, since that is what she always insisted on having.

I think, beyond all the maternal feeling, and the pain of having lost her first two children, the children of her illusion, that she has a terrible sense of relief at having known the worst, suffered the final disaster, and has come out onto the rather lonely plateau of old age free at last of all the parasites that sucked her life away. She is apparently left quite stripped—they took away all her furniture, she seems not even to have blankets enough, she needs everything, and she does not in the least seem to know that it was her darling son who assisted at her despoiling; she insisted that he was a dear love, and I suppose he was, to her. I am glad he is dead, for it frees her from that wife of his: and I now feel that I can send her a warm bed jacket, or a rug for her floor, or any little thing, a bottle of perfume, even—and it won't be snatched from her; really, Paul, how low can life fall? How evil and cheap can people make life for each other? But she has an immense vitality, I cannot imagine why she has spent a whole life defeating herself as she has, when she had such capacity for something so much better. She was sweet here, but is so set on her martyrdom no one in his right mind would think of trying to interfere . . .

Don't love yourself too much: it is wasting your affections on an unworthy object. . . .

Bless you, my dear good child, and good night.

Aunt Katherine Anne

To Andrew Lytle

108 East 65th Street
New York 21
Candlemas, or Pancake or
Groundhog Day, 1952

Dear Andrew:

And I forgot entirely to eat pancakes this morning! What can
we expect of our luck if we overlook all the rituals of flattering and
misleading if we can the hellish spirits of confusion which haunt the
air like gnats? Still, there came your letter, with news and prospects
of seeing you in Florida. I'll speak of this first, for it seems so timely
and promising. I am engaged for March 7 next in Jackson Mississippi; Friday, March 14th, Greensboro North Carolina—then a
long pause, and Friday, Columbus Mississippi Friday, April 18.
Could you work in Florida immediately after the first two, or just
before or after the third, or something like that? For though I shall
probably have to fly back here at least once between engagements,
it would be a pity, expense and energy being what they are, to have
to fly back twice. . . .

I am also plagued by the Little Peepll: you know, the kind
that used to live in the woods and dance in rings in the moon-
light. Time was when you could get along with them by setting
out bowls of milk and hanging a horse shoe over every door and
window. But they've moved right in with us now, and you never
heard so much scuffling on stairs, and hot-jazz blasting the roof off
of nights, and panty-waist accents; and in an atmosphere of interior decoration and burning incense sticks . . . They have not of
course, lost their nocturnal habits, their parties begin at midnight
or after, and I do hardly remember when I have had an uninterrupted night's sleep. It is fantastic; This whole city now simply
swarms with every little pervert from every little town from every
point of the compass in this land; of course they are always here
and in every other city, but they are really taking the place—
speaking of termites. I think a real male in this place must begin
to feel pretty besieged from all sides: the women like him, of
course, but the pansies like him even better, and call all real men
"male impersonators," and regard them as their peculiar prey
. . . I should be telling you, who was in the theatre here . . . but

417

I was always able to ignore them; and for my carelessness, and lack of observation, I find myself sharing a house with the most depraved and tiresome set of half-humans I ever saw. . . .

I have always thought it was Yeats who said, Be careful what you wish for in youth, for when you are older you will get it. Not long ago I saw that same advice attributed to some one else, I forget who. Well, I have a number of things I never dreamed of wishing for, most of them rather trying and not what I like at all; but it is strange, that, however, imperfectly, incompletely my deepest wish was fulfilled, still it was fulfilled a little, I didn't miss utterly the point of my life, it hasn't been all failure. We can't have all we want, because we do not even know what that *all* might be; but I did want to be an artist, and live within a certain devotion and belief, and—with a shocking margin between intention and achievement—still I have so lived. I could wish I had lived it better, and had more to show for it. But this doesn't in the least mean that I don't still think I *can* do better, and more. Time is not run out altogether yet; but if I worked eight hours a day for ten years I could hardly finish all I have begun, and it *is* late, but not later than I think . . .

Well, somebody told me Caroline was praying for me, too; but she herself told me I was the worst damned soul she knew, because I had been shown the light and rejected it . . . I always thought religion is no help to the naturally wicked. It is only an enhancement to an already existing virtue. I'm sure Caroline always believed all her friends were damned or should be, and I am fairly certain a great part of her pleasure in her religion comes of having, now, official confirmation of her belief. HOW she will enjoy eternity, leaning over the gold bars of heaven watching US crawling and howling on the floors of hell.

Well, she can have it . . . Do let me hear again soon. It would be fine to have a lot of talk, but if we can't letters must serve! With my same old affection, too!

Katherine Anne

To Eudora Welty   108 East 65th Street
                               New York 21, N.Y.
                               13 February 1952

Eudora darlin:

All the prospects to the south are fair, and we'll have a gay time
no matter how or where-at. I am clamped firmly between the two
dates, 7th at Jackson, 14th at Greensboro, and unless I decide to
fly to Gr., I have a twenty-two hour train trip with three, or is it
four, changes, which means I must leave Jackson Wednesday midnight at latest. Get to Gr. late next evening, and must be frash and
brash Friday early . . .

Well, D. Trexler has, or will soon, reserve me a room in a
hotel there, and it does look to me like we'll have a very short week
for gallivanting down the coast. But I'd love to go, just the same,
if only for overnight or two, but you do know I am the highly
distractible sort, and it is no good for me to start out thinking I
should be able to write anything amid such changing scenes. I'd just
ruin my fun, which I begredge in advance. So, if you can take time
out, or if you have enough concentration of mind and character to
work a little anyway, in flight, let's plan at least one little foray, but
I'll stay at the hotel when I'm in Jackson, since they are giving me
it for free, shame to waste it!

What do you think of this? The mainest thing is to see each
other, catch up on our gossip, tie up floating ends into little bowknots, and just enjoy our visit. That should be easy.

Then, I had first planned to go somewhere along the coast for
three weeks and work, until the other two engagements turn up.
But now I have some kind of arrangement with HBCO that makes
me appear to be a species of literary adviser, I scarcely know how
to begin to tell you; one day a week, and that day Wednesday,
though I suppose almost any day would do. At any rate, I am paid
for it, so it will be to a certain advantage to get back here between
engagements; and as for work, who knows? At the moment, not
having enough on my mind, I have undertaken to collect under one
cover quite a lot of my writings now scattered in magazines and
newspapers; they will bring it out in September, more or less.
Editing and putting back all the stuff I had to leave out for reasons

of space—dear me, I *could* have written a novel! Theoretically, of course.

Oh I did have a strange feeling right from the first day of January that this might be a nice year, more on the law of averages than anything else—just simply high time for one! I was ill with same-old-thing from last October to middle of January, but now gaining, spiritually a little certainly, and ten pounds bodily—up to 112 from 102, and now I hardly clank at all when I move.

Good God, I never dreamed you and Red Warren didn't know each other! Personally, face to face, I mean. He loves your work, says openly in so many words you are a "pure genius" which everybody knows but I like to hear it said. . . .

Yes, do your best magic on the weather. I suppose light wool and such will still be appropriate? I never had the right clothes for ANY occasion in my life, and its too late to start worrying now . . . My same old love to you.

Katherine Anne

TO MARIANNE MOORE   [108 East 65th Street
                        New York 21, N.Y.]
                        Easter 1952

(With a present of twine, scotch tape, pencils, mss. envelopes and carbon paper)

M. darling,

I saw blooming white cyclamens and thought of you *specially,* and also remembered something you said once about presents:—how they were generally useless and unfitted to your purposes, etc. It happened I was out shopping for my own desk-and-word-ridden life, such as it is, and decided for once you were going to get a present you could use, one time or another.

It is Easter, my dear, or nearly! Happy spring to you—I am the old-fashioned life-intoxicated kind that sticks my face out of the window early in the morning and even New York looks and smells beautiful, this time of year. Three blocks away I can get a whole street's width view of Central Park and its still a muddy brown color, but I am not deceived or disheartened: *it* is spring, and every growing thing knows it, and is getting ready!

> Yours
> *Katherine Anne*

To Eudora Welty   108 East 65th Street
New York 21, N.Y.
15 April 1952

Eudora darling:

. . . . First, bless you for the mss. you gave me of your radio speech—I was as happy about it as you were unhappy; it is beautiful, and it is true in the sense that *that* is the way you think and feel: I can settle for that, easily. Maybe we are wrong to be uneasy about writing about the friends whose work we like. I love to praise what I love, and I don't for a minute believe that love is blind—indeed, it gives clearness without sharpness, and surely that is the best light in which to look at anything. In fact, I long to believe you are right about me!

I just remember my visit with you, the delightfulness of your mother, our fine escapade to the Gulf Coast, the Sunday with your friends, all, all together in a shimmer of greenery and warmth; I am so glad it could happen. Then, in Greensboro, how everybody was gay and things went well. We talked about you until you must have heard echoes; Peter Taylor especially thinks you hung the moon, and I was joyful to agree with him!

Angel, I am getting off to Paris on the 7th of May, and won't be back until the 12th of June† . . . being sent to that International Congress for Cultural Freedom. I balk at such titles, and I don't know if its a good sign when people get together to talk merely to prove they've still got freedom of speech. Just the same, I aim to put in my two-bits worth. Red Warren was invited, but Yale won't let him go. Faulkner naturally was implored, and I see by the papers

---

†*KAP noted later, "Really did not come back until the 22 of September 1952."*

he's supposed to be going, but if he does, everybody is going to get a big surprise . . . Allen Tate, Auden, myself, Glenway Wescott—in place of Red, God forbid—James Farrell, are expected really to get there . . . We'll see. . . .

Happy Easter to you, and my same love

Katherine Anne

TO ELEANOR CLARK   Moulin de Rosmadec
                                     Pont-Aven, (Finistère,) France
                                     8 May [June] 1952

Eleanor darling:

Not death, but *the end of the earth,* is what I have been really wanting all along. And now literally I am there: well of course, even literalness can be relative; it is fifteen kilometres to Concarneau, where the sea does pile up nobly against a very stubborn shore. Pont-Aven however has the feel and the air of awayness—for one thing, I am the only foreigner here, and I must say already it is plain what an advantage that is with the people of the place: they find it easy to be human with one foreigner. And then, the ease of their good manners! I am still be-blurred and confounded with the French money, I grab out great pawfuls and forget how to count, how much the object I hope to buy costs, and give no doubt an impression that I am not quite bright, which is certainly true in that instance at least. (Further than that I refuse to go along). So, yesterday, myself trying to buy a few maps, cards, and newspapers, was scratting through my money as I usually do only with my mss., and the woman across the counter, in her airy lace crown and white pleated pointed, lacy bib, her bright blue Celtic eyes really smiling (they do, you know) simply reached over into the depths of the yawning handbag, took a sheaf of notes, spread them out before me and counted them over, and sorted them out, picked out the sum she had named for the stuff, and handed the rest back to me, saying 'Have all confidence, Madame. I have counted this correctly.' Being a true Bretonne, her accent was nearly as strange as mine, in French.

Then, I started to visit the little church, built to honor the memory of the dozen or more Pont-Aven boys who died in the war of 1870, and I asked a very old woman, wearing *her* special widow's headdress, if it were all right for me to go in the church without a head-cover. 'Ah, Wooee, wooee, natuerellamawnt,' she said, so nearly as I can put it down, and she made one of those strong affirmative gestures, a jerk upward of the bent arm and down again, as if to say: 'Who ever heard of such nonsense?' I went in to visit, a very poor, humble little place, full of twilight; I looked about for an altar to make my one religious devoir, which is always to light candles for every friend whose name I recall at that moment: the list sometimes surprises me, pleasantly. In Paris not long ago Robert Lowell (of all people, you'll say, and how right!) and I lighted an enormous candle together in St. Germain-des-Prés, and that light was charged with messages to the very tip. I'll tell you later about the Battle of Paris. I heard some one there, let his name go to dust, who remarked horridly about the conceit of those who fancied other people needed their prayers. I was shocked as only one can be who hears, of a new, totally undreamed-of wickedness. In my whole life, even in my deepest mind, it had never once occurred to me that we did not all of us need each other's prayers, that is to say if you like, love and good wishes. Afterward, through the whole lunch, I kept staring at this man, I could not keep my amazed eyes off him, they went on returning of themselves to view again an unbelievably atrocious spectacle; and at last with a deep sinking of the heart and a dreadful depression of the mind, I had to admit the world was full of people like him, and getting more and more: that he was not just being clever and nasty—he meant it. Well, I am happy to be in Brittany: and I will let you know later how people here feel about this question.

This place is a fifteenth century grain mill turned into an inn, and Pont-Aven is undoubtedly a tourist way-station at least, because the stone gates are draped with plaques of recommendation from the authorities of tourism, official reassurances about the cookery, the accomodations altogether, and they were not put there for fun. For me, it is all beyond praise. The millstream rushes on one side, the little river on the other: I am already used to the sound of falling water, I should miss it, after three nights of going to sleep by it. The place itself is full of old beams and wide planked floors: I never saw old wood brought under the discipline of wax more utterly than this. Even the great round covers for the millstones on each side the little staircase, are polished like rosewood. The sunlight falls on this table, now, half past ten morning: I sleep in one of those big rabbit-nests of a bed, with Brittany linen sheets thick as canvas, but softer. The drink is what you would get anywhere in France, except for Brittany cider. I have yet to be converted to cider of any region or nation. So I let it alone. But the food! Such cream, such sweet butter, such Belon oysters (eaten plain, not even a drop of lemon juice,) such little broiled lobsters, lamb chops, veal chops, little filet beefsteaks—well, natural carnivore that I am, I try not to growl with joy! The fish are all so varied and wonderful I shan't try to tell about them. And then, besides, the real wonder is simply freshness. A kind of bloom of freshness on everything, from the crusty dark bread to the last little strawberry. Even an egg—one had forgotten what an egg tastes like: or how it should smell, which is even more important. It is very intimate, primeval-biological, and pure!

Let me add what I started out to say: this is not the season, the tourists come later. Yesterday at dinner a wedding party came in: the most beautiful young girl and boy you could ever see, and their families, part of them, no doubt—not more than a dozen in all. They were all dressed in Sunday black, the bride in pure white with white flowers. They sat round a long table, and drank exactly one magnum of champagne, exchanging toasts inaudibly, gravely: and departed as they came, two by two, soberly gay, without having spoken a word that one could hear. The proprietress said, "They do these things very simply here, but still, that is the way they do them!" which I love for all kinds of over—and—undertones . . . finality, complete acceptance, really no reservations, and familiar, affectionate humanity.

That is too many long words for what I heard, but all I can do for now.

Eleanor I began this yesterday, stopped to work a while, went over to Quimperle for dinner with a young pair I know here! He is French-Egyptian-Turkish, she is Spanish-Jewish brought up in Long Island, both naturally speak English. He is manager I believe of a Paper Mill here owned by a friend of mine—. Well, the trouble with everything is, there is too much history unless one simply ignores it entirely. They are very nice young people and live in a huge decayed chateau sort of house with enormous stone fireplaces in every room, (every one of which smokes violently, I am told) and they showed me the garden, and I said, "I can live here if this vegetation passes one more test. Can you grow figs here?" They took me through another great stone and wrought-iron gate and showed me one of those patristic, biblical fig trees under which the happy and lucky of old times were invited to sit in peace and plenty. It was loaded with enormous green figs nearly ready to begin ripening. There are camellia trees obviously more than a hundred years old. Azaleas, rhododendron, gardenias, besides the roses and such I have seen in this garden at the inn. Honeysuckle, mock-orange, magnolia, white lilac, and so on. I said, "That settles it." The girl said, "Yes, but it rains all the time." I said, "So it does in Louisiana, too: I remember more rain than anything else." I looked at a huge ugly ragged palm—I dislike palms of any species—and said, "Are there mosquitoes?" "Sometimes," they answered. So I said, "Well, I suppose I COULD as well go on back to Louisiana." But oddly, I can't quite explain, it seems *so far away,* not exactly from here, for the warm Gulf Stream that starts there, more or less, comes right on across and breaks on the coast of Brittany: no wonder Tristan and Isolde drifted in with it: this is the real scene and climate of love, rather than the Côte d'Azur where no one would think of dying for a little thing like treachery, or adultery. No, Louisiana seems far away from Paris, let's face it. I am as far away from Paris as I ever mean to be again for more than a few days or weeks—oh well, maybe a few months when I go to Italy—and this Brittany for some reason has struck me sweetly, with its soft moist climate, rain, deep sunshine and washed freshness. I think it is perhaps as simple as this: it looks and feels like something I knew and loved somewhere else, a long time ago.

There is of course a huge undying worm at the heart of this rose, and its shape is human, what else could it be?

To Robert Giroux Moulin de Rosmadec
Pont-Aven, (Finistère) France
(Brittany to us.)
10 June 1952

Dear Bob:

How I happened to come here is a longish but not in the least a sad story, and I am so happy and comfortable and at ease in my mind, I hardly recognize myself. It is a little inn, only three bed-rooms, I am the only staying-in guest, for the little bar, restaurant, and terrace-garden are the real attractions: it is crowded every evening with very nice gay people who fold up and go home at eleven-sharp: there is no nightlife, I am the only foreigner in town—at least the only one who speaks English; and I have heard two radios—the one down stairs which talks and sings gently to itself now and then, and one in the paper-shop around the corner, which never raises *its* voice, either. You have the feeling that they are barely tolerated by the populace, and know it, and pipe down so they won't get thrown out. Even the birds sing discreetly and the bells ring softly. This leaves the whole field to the Brittany wife, and does she make the most of it! They kneel in half boxes with cushions beside the mill stream, and at fixed places all along, where the stone steps end in a platform meant, it appears, just for washing. So they kneel, wearing their handsome headdresses, immaculate pointed collars, and wash and wring and bat the family linen around, and gossip at the tops of their shrill voices, with the energy of machine guns and the wild joy of gulls gone mad before a storm. Now and then a man joins one of them on some errand of his own: he is just as quick and loud a talker as she is, and they turn their batteries on each other full force, looking each straight in the eye, and unless you saw their intent, quick, smiling faces, you would think they were threatening at least to drown each other at once. It ends as suddenly as it begins, and the beautiful musical silences of the river and the wind in the trees take over again. Old women—and if you never saw a Brittany old woman, you don't know how old women can get, and look—sit huddled on window ledges or benches beside doors and bob their heads at each other, and talk—with passion, with an intensity of tone and face and gesture I shan't even try to describe: well, it makes me feel a little thin-blooded and no doubt emotionally inadequate—think of getting that steamed up every-day, a dozen times a day about things and people you've been seeing every day for maybe seventy years. I do think its pretty grand, but I'm not up to it.

As soon as I finish the preface, I feel like writing a real, out-and out travel piece: just all about going somewhere and looking at life roaring all around me. Try to do it while all is still fresh and new, and while I am still a visitor, who could pick up and take off on an hour's notice. Meantime, let me answer your letter about the book. First your praise of it makes me very happy; that you find a shape and direction and connective tissue in it is of course the important thing: I had fear of irrelevancy, or a kind of randomness. Yet I hoped that my life which really had a continuous central interest, preoccupation, would have shaped itself as it went, could *not* have taken any form not its own, would not too much misrepresent the true intentions of my mind. Well, I am not saying it very well, and trust you to know what I mean, just as you do see the life that is in the book.

Now then, of course, leave all three of the Gertrude Stein pieces in. Yes, I agree—*The Days Before* alone is best, no subtitle. As to the title to the Hardy piece, I'd love to duck that missile-word 'stuffy' and let it sail on by and smack Red or Cleanth or Albert, but the truth, horrid truth, is, that the title is mine. I thought it up all by myself, not a soul helped me. Albert—to whom I was married at the time—had such a hell of a tussle to get it away from me at all, he threw it on the press without looking at it half an hour after I had handed it to him through a window at our house: I don't think any one ever even noticed the title until now. Imagine, I can't think of any other, and I can't even remember what the present one is. Maybe I can change it in the proofs—may they come quickly—

. . . . You have not said what you plan as to sending the book for review, I admit I am anxious to have good writers review it: even if they don't like it it is better than being turned over to little fifth-stringers, so I hope you will scatter page proofs—pretty please, *not* galleys, what I have suffered fighting galleys all over a table, armchairs, and the floor! I will put on a separate page a list of the first persons I think of to send a copy (page proofs, I mean of course) and I wonder did you think of offering it to Messrs. Trilling, Barzun, and Auden for their book club? I hadn't until this split second. What do you think? And will it be published in England at once, or will Jonathan Cape Inc., just let it drift on a year or two and die of inanition? Oh, WHY can't I have Secker and Warburg for publishers in England? And while I am all tuned up on this subject, Oy, oy gewalt! WHY can't I take the Denyse Clairouin Agency, Marcelle's friends and agents, to manage for me in France? I have met the two partners at Marcelle's house, along with several critics who had written wonderful reviews for my books, (Marcelle showed them to me, I didn't even know they existed!) And Flamand says there is no reason why they should not sell if handled properly. (Of course, Flamand is running true to form in one thing—he wants to bring out *No Safe Harbor* <u>before</u> *The Leaning Tower,* then he plans to buy the other two from Editions Pavois and reprint them. You are right, Marcelle is a working angel with wings that never tire: also she knows just what she is talking about, she is truth itself, and we would be very short-sighted not to be guided by her in anything having to do with publishing me in France. Her motives are perfect, she loves my work, is a personal friend: everything began with that, years ago. And she enjoys her prestige as the best translator in France, with her ribbons and medals and prizes: she wouldn't be French if she didn't appreciate a public career with honors. And she would like to help make me famous: and besides, we would both make a little money, which neither of us is foolish enough to despise. She has made nothing out of my work so far: and yet she persists, and never falters in her efforts to get me on a sounder footing here. So let's for God's sake get my business out of Mrs. Bradley's hands—if it was ever there; she has been and is more than ever, useless—and let these good energetic interested folks go ahead. I have long since despaired of England—it is just too late to try to retrieve anything there. But we can do better in France. DON'T put me off about this. Pay attention. Oy, oy, GE-WALT!

I see there is a lot of space left. Here are the names I thought of: Margaret Marshall, Harvey Breit, Glenway Wescott, Eleanor Clark, John Crowe Ransom, Allen Tate, Robert Penn Warren, Cleanth Brooks, Kerker Quinn *(Accent)* Eudora Welty, Peter Taylor (Woman's College University North Carolina) Philip Rahv, (Barzun, Trilling, Auden) Jordan Pecile, address Telluride Association, Cornell University, Ithaca: Andrew Lytle, University of Florida, Gainesville, Florida. All the main literary quarterlies, *Sewanee Review, Southwestern Review, Kenyon Review, Accent,* etc. In fact any University publication: remember I have trouped those circuits for years and students know me. I'd like James Stern and J.F. Powers to have copies, though I believe Powers is in Ireland and Stern still in England. I can't find either address, though I have had both.

Perhaps this is enough for the present. By now, it is morning of the next day since I began this letter, and here is another lovely day, cool and sunny and green, with that sound of water which is the most quietening sound in the world, and every time I glance out of my window, I see the light from the mill stream dancing on the underleaves of the heavy-headed trees . . . No use, I am no better than a little furred, four-footed animal in the spring, in the country; you'll see that my entire preface is going to be quite different from what it would have been if I had written it in New York in that bloody prison on East 65th street, with Trouble breathing down my collar. That was real, but this is real too, and the kind of *real* I like and don't have enough of. But I go to sleep at ten or eleven, wake up to my breakfast on a tray at 9, by half past nine I am up and scratting around happily among my papers like a bird scratting leaves, and I have the whole day, and tomorrow and a good many days after that, just to live like this: it will be a cure of many things, you'll see: it can't last forever, maybe should not, but it is here now and not a day too soon. . . .

Thank you for your fine letter. Yours

Katherine Anne

To Burry and Allan   Moulin de Rosmadec
Lewis   Pont-Aven, (Finistère) France
                               18 June, 1952

Dear Burry and Allan!

The outline by Mr. Apstein came yesterday morning, I have read it twice and thought about it; there are some very good things in it, but I am glad to have seen it, for there are also a few things I feel are quite wrong: not from the point of view of construction, but from misreading of the real meaning of the characters and a distortion of their relations to each other.

Let me go into this quickly. (1) Maria Concepción is a much stronger more important person than she seems in this outline. Where ever, in the story, a scene has been given to her to illustrate her character and feelings, in the outline it has invariably been softened, omitted, or the emphasis shifted to another. Example: the scene where Lupe offers her prayers, and Maria Concepción refuses. And the cruelty and insolence which Old Lupe uses as the right of an older woman to a younger, is absolutely misplaced when Mr. Apstein takes her speech, 'Did you pray for what you have now?' and gives it to Maria Rosa talking to Maria Concepción, an outraged woman with a knife in her hand. This whole scene between Maria Rosa and Maria Concepción really shocked me with its falsity. To begin with, Maria Rosa talks like a tough girl in a Hollywood film, and she would not have been allowed to finish a sentence no matter what it was. And there is nothing in the story to say that she had become hardened in the gangster's moll sense. I have known many Indian army women, one of them was my cook for a year, and they are tough, all right, and brave, but not debased as women. They lived hard lives, earthy, realistic to the last degree, but not mean ones. I mention that she was lean as a wolf: but she falls screaming in the road when Juan is arrested. And she loves Juan: the scene where he visits her when she is caring for the baby should make this clear: and Juan prefers her to all other women: he says so himself, to Givens. Maria Rosa is a small soul, who pays for her adventure with her life. But she is not a nasty bitch, as this outline makes her. Maria Concepción is strong. In the outline, her decisive act of taking up the child herself, which is typical of her, has been taken away: its meaning is lost if Old Lupe is the one who makes the decision. Maria Concepción has been firmly keeping old Lupe out of her business from the first, and it would not be for Lupe to mix in at that point.

In the same way, there is a dreadful commonplaceness to the scene where Maria Concepción runs to the road calling after Juan. This is just a cliché I hope never to see again in theatre or picture. And our heroine would never have done such a thing. The whole point is, that Juan and Maria Rosa escaped secretly, Maria Concepción knows nothing until they are gone utterly. What makes Mr. Apstein think that if she had seen her husband running away with another girl, that either of them would have got away? This is the really ruinous moment in the whole thing. We can't have this.

About the murder scene: if it takes place on stage, the hut should be dimly lighted from the low doorway, and perhaps from streaks of light through the straw roof. Maria Rosa should be where Juan left her, on the straw mat with the swaddled baby. Perhaps Old Lupe could be hanging a charm on his neck, or giving Maria Rosa some medicinal brew to drink, and scolding her, not violently or vulgarly, just the old-fashioned wise-woman rebuking the folly of a girl who so lost her decency as to go running off with another woman's man, making scandal. But there is no question of casting her off. She has come home, she has behaved wickedly, she is a nuisance, in fact, but Old Lupe expects to have her around, just the same, and the baby will be brought up, and Lupe will scold to the end. Juan will go back to his wife of course, where else would he go? and so Maria Rosa has made a fool of herself, that is the worst of it. At any rate, Old Lupe has to go to the stream to wash, and her last word to Maria Rosa is that she can expect to get up from there and do her part of the work, and support herself from now on. Maria Rosa is meek but not abject, she talks back a little but not enough to get herself a good slap in the face. Lupe goes, and Maria Rosa is silent, still, holding the baby. Then begins to cradle and sing to it. Maria Concepción enters swiftly as a Fury, goes straight to Maria Rosa, and there should be in the half-light a brief struggle of the utmost violence and almost in silence, broken low speech, throttled screams. It is over and Maria Concepción goes in the same haste and fury in which she came. There should again be silence, with the baby crying in very small whimpers. The thing has happened so suddenly that Maria Rosa never has a chance to try to defend herself, hardly realizes *what* has happened.

Now then, this is only a suggestion as to 'treatment' but at least the characters, temperaments, and situation of every person in the scene has been maintained and developed . . .

One more point: Maria Rosa would never show her curiosity about another woman's husband above all to that woman herself. And the point of the story so far as Maria Concepción is concerned, is that she had never had a hint, nor a suspicion; her first sight of Juan and Maria Rosa together comes as an absolute shock. Even if there might have been some remark among others, even if the neighbors had noticed, Maria Concepción would be of course the very last one to learn about it. This is part of her bitterness: that from an easy taken for granted faith in the validity and efficacy of her church marriage, in one instant the whole thing falls, there is nothing left: and the ruin was as complete as it had been when her house was burned by an enemy she had not suspected.

Of course, all this seems to me so utterly clear and obvious, I am almost embarrassed at writing it again, explaining it. And I know that an outline is just merely that: everything remains to be filled in. But I believe it is better to catch these shades of misinterpretation *now:* and I confess I was dismayed by a few little quick-and-too-easy scenes in which the persons become simply *types,* and that they are not, above all.

Please above all, where the speech is kept intact from the story, (perhaps as in the scene where Juan and Maria Concepción eat supper and he instructs her) let the rhythms and turns of phrases be unchanged. And—you will think this is endless—please to note that in the story, Juan is flattered at the attentions of two such desirable *women:* not *females. Hembra* (female) among the Indians is not used much for women. There are almost invariably called *mujeres* (women) or were when I was there, a good long time ago, and these were country Indians, which is important.

Now then, I am exhausted, and must stop, and do fifty other things. Trying to finish my preface, must work on the novel, and suddenly I have to decide about storing my furniture or coming back to New York or staying here, and I no longer believe that there will ever be for me again even a day that I may have just for my own work. It seems odd, for after a life time, one should be able to manage it! . . . .

Yours,
Katherine Anne

TO MARCELLE SIBON
Moulin de Rosmadec
Pont-Aven, (Finistère)
20th June 1952

Marcelle darling:

. . . . It is wonderfully exciting and stimulating to know you are liking the novel as you go . . . It is true, there are almost no final solutions; I think of Charles Bloodgood's famous saying to William James, "What has been concluded, that we should conclude about it?" More or less: that is a memory quotation and not quite exact, but the meaning is there. And the doctrine itself belongs to Renouvier.

My people are in general perhaps a little more stupid than I meant them to be, but that could come of limitations of my own. It is just true that numbers of people are appealing enough as human beings, touching to the heart in their troubles and confusions, honest enough really in their intentions, but full of fears and cruelties and just plain lack of rock-bottom intelligence: and their sensibility is so often just touchiness and frightened vanity . . . I say *to them:* I belong to this human race, and believe deeply in its strengths and virtues as well as its evils and weaknesses. I do not want to be unjust to myself in being unjust to my characters. They all are alive for me, too: I have to treat them as if they are all going to come and confront me some day and say, "Why could you not have told the truth about me? And if you could not, why did you pretend to?" But there are some hateful creatures in the book, I know they are hateful and I will not be guilty of criminal collusion with them, any more than I would be in life. . . .

Katherine Anne

433

To Allen Tate

Hotel d'Isly
29 rue Jacob
Paris VI, France
11 August 1952

Allen, hon!

How're you doing by now? Not a word from you since I was in Brittany, and here I've been back in Paris more than a month, and its less than a month from now that I must be getting back to New York, and still not a moufful of news from you. Now I feel oddly that this letter is being aimed at space in air where you were, and you may just have evaporated yourself, temporarily of course, a rest from the things of this world. But of course you have done nothing of the kind. So do let me have a word of what goes on with you now.

Brittany is now a green island in my memory, as sweet a country as ever I saw, Tennessee, Louisiana, Connecticut and Capri rolled into one, all the beauties of all or any of them and none of the faults. Of course I was there in the heavenly time of year, in the places famous for climate and landscape and human history: but I visited around quite a lot in the region, Finistère, Morbihan, and its true, there is a very ancient enchantment still floating in the air of that place. Why not? Its true, little children sell you thread—lace and shell necklaces on the very spot where Tristan and Isolde landed, and will take you to the rocky promontory where, if you kneel down and gaze a long time, you will see the roofs and spires of the drowned city of Ys. Well, I surprised them—indeed, I surprised myself—I *saw* it, clearly. It is there, by now apparently turned to pale coral, and webbed with giant sea-weed, at depths beyond the reach of sunlight yet lighted as if by phosphorus: all stillness and silence and the very place to go when dry land gets just too tiresome. And the child said, "When there are storms you can hear the bells tolling down there, and that means a ship is sinking and drowning men are calling for help."

The people nearly all look Irish, as they should, and the Brittany tongue is gutteral and muted and evasive, and sounds as I imagine language did sound when human beings were just discovering it. Yet facial types, costumes, change from region to region, even from village to village. In one small seashore town there persists a most beautiful race, with smooth fine black hair, very white skin, and deep-sea blue eyes: I've seen Danes with coloring like that, and of course the Irish. I wonder who it belonged to originally. When you see it in its perfection as I did in that little Brittany town, you forget every other kind: it seems the most beautiful coloring in the world.

Paris is no longer the Paris of last May: it is the Paris of August, with every other shop closed for the month, busloads of tourists erupting every thirty minutes into all the places they are supposed to be, and by God, the're going to BE there or know why! The natives, as I have heard them called by these same visitors, are all somewhere else if they can manage it. I am in a tacky little room in a very decent little hotel on the corner of Bonaparte and Jacob, not expensive and the people are wonderfully amiable and pleasant; I am on the second floor, a very few little steps to climb—remember when you and Glenway carried me handy-pandy up the stairs for the Figaro lunch?—that was fun for everybody I hope! I loved it.—and so I might as well be on the sidewalk, as to noise and lack of privacy. The noise is so obstreperous day and night that last night—and I can't account for this at all—I was waked out of deep sleep feeling terribly lost and uneasy, out of some dream of fright or mental disturbance, and could not imagine why. It took me a few seconds to realize that there was absolute silence all around me. I went to the window and looked out, and so far as I could see up and down and round the corner, there was not a soul in sight, not a moving vehicle, nothing. How come? I'll never know. Then a young man, weaving a little, came round the corner; he wore tennis shoes and was perfectly noiseless, but he *was* talking to himself in a fretful mutter, and several times he hit himself a resounding smack on the brow with his palm. So the silence was lessened a little, and I went back to sleep.

Well, while I am gone, that entire mausoleum in East 65th street has disappeared, friends and family have moved me lock stock and barrel into a groundfloor apartment, in East 17th Street, and there my plunder sits, covered and nailed down until I get back. It was that or a most horrible confusion of sending furniture to storage and papers to Harcourt Brace's vaults, and I cannot face any more such rendings apart and re-assembling what is, after all, the more or less necessary machinery of my daily existence. I am told the place is very good, a whole little floor with a garden patch: it will do, I am sure. But there goes Paris, for a while at least. It is just strange that, no matter whether I plan and make my changes for myself, or they are done for me by others, I have no real feeling of being in control of my life: I never had it to any great extent, but things really seem to have got away from me ever since I came back from Europe, all those years ago. Nothing has gone well since: yet I still believe—a little, and a little less every year—that conditions need not be so hopelessly unwieldy. What I really need more than anything at this point is only what all of us needed all along: a regular income, just some small foothold on which I can base a course of action. My alternate feast-and-famine sort of life, very modest feasts and very grim famines, ends by wearing me down. I am now trying to write some pieces for magazines that have invited me to, and indeed the only kind of writing that pleases me at this moment is just a kind of diary, writing every day about just sights, sounds and notions. Still, I can't imagine who would be interested in it, though I read that sort of thing myself with delight. So maybe I had better write it first for myself as I do write everything anyway, and trust to my luck that some one else will like it too . . . I just did this morning an account of a strange meeting between a cat and a dog on a street corner yesterday. Never before had I seen such an essential display of pure catness and dogness, and afterward I realized that in my dealing with them both I had also displayed something essential deeply akin to, and very different indeed, from them both: I suppose humanness. It was strangely enlightening.

Robert Lowell wrote from Vienna, more or less on his way to Salzburg: Ray West also from Austria. I have not looked for the very few friends that might be here. I am in my hermit phase, and like it. Tell me your news.

With my love
Katherine Anne

To Ezra Pound   117 East 17th Street
                                 New York, N.Y.
                                 21 October, 1952

Dear Ezra Pound:

For you to accuse me of being led in any particular by a van
Doren is extremely lowering to my self-esteem, to say the least: and
I should like to argue with you about it, except that I see the utter
uselessness of trying to do so by letter.

I was delighted to have your note, and nothing could be more
welcome than your invitation to drop in and discuss things, more
particularly those points of which you disapprove.

Still, I must even now say one thing: I have known your work,
and loved and respected it, for more than thirty years: and did not
even in the beginning need any one to tell me what to think about
it: you came just at the right moment for a lot of us, and so many
of us discovered you each one for himself, at a time when for the
general public, or even the literate informed public, your name was
just a rumor. The writers everywhere, even those who did not write
to you, (as I did not) knew you for their own: and perhaps you do
not even now realize—for such an intangible would be very hard
to grasp—how deep your influence and example was for such writers as myself, finding our way pretty much alone and looking everywhere for help and direction.

I am really sorry if you feel that my view of your work and
career and temperament are wrong, or based on a misunderstanding. In this single case of the letters as published—and no doubt
they have been edited with such an effect in view—I found again
certain qualities I had already found in your poetry and more than
all in your critical writing: intransigence, impatience, a fanatic devotion, an immense range of gifts—and do you think I have not
admired all this, and that all of it was a stimulating, inciting blast
of fresh cold air into the airless world of the arts at that time? You
helped not only to break up old decayed ideas, but to replace them
with freshness of thought and feeling. So, please read again my little
piece, and notice how I quote from the letters as I go, and illustrate
from them, and try to follow the thread of your own thoughts and
experiences in them. If I am mistaken, why then, the responsibility
must be mine, and not van Doren's, or anybody else's.

God knows I am not much of a dropper-in, Washington seems a good distance from here; but for a long time I have wished so much to come to see you, for I would like to think we might have something to talk about. My friends come and go, bringing me news. Robert Lowell, Marianne Moore, etc., even those charming young women of the Caedmon Press, who probably want you to make a recording for them. So I expect to get there too, and correct my errors of interpretation of your point of view.

On November 9 here at the Poetry Center I am going to read poetry, and several of yours: "Hugh Selwyn Mauberley" of course, and several of my favorite translations from the Chinese and Provençal—we are just going to have a kind of poetry-binge. . . .

Thank you for your note. Sincerely yours,

Katherine Anne Porter

To Paul Porter
[117 East 17th Street
New York, N.Y.]
11 November 1952 Morning

Paul darling,

. . . . My dear, you must never suppress anything you read about me or my books; I like to see everything, no matter what. The publishers have a news-clipping service on me anyway, so sooner or later ALL the chickens come home to roost, a few with knives on their spurs, now and then with poisoned claws, but mostly a very fine thriving friendly lot. From the first until now I have had the most unbelievably good reviews, more constantly friendly I daresay than any other writer in this country. And I suppose my books are the least-sold of any serious writer here. Look at Hemingway. The reviewers and the critics have needled him steadily for twenty years, and the worst thing he writes becomes a best seller overnight. If the newspapers could kill, he would be dead years ago. Red Warren said to me, about his students all over the country, that they either adored me and found no fault at all, or just didn't get me and so let me alone, without any hostility. "You haven't got any opposition," he said. "No enemies that I can see. That's bad. You need somebody to attack you, and provoke a big row . . ."

Well, as publicity, no doubt it would be useful. But, though I don't think I am soft, really, I can do without it. Perhaps the warmth and friendliness of the people who read and review my books now takes the place of any private happiness, or life of my own. The three readings just finished at the Poetry Center were lovely for me; small audiences, but profoundly still, attentive, listening; then great waves of applause at the end, and then the smiling swarming around, with books to be autographed, hands to shake, smiles and pleasant words to exchange; it is the way, by now about the only way, I have of touching the world of living people. This might possibly be made to seem sad. It is not. Life itself is just sadder, and lonelier, and more difficult as one grows older, I believe this may be true of every one; and I feel lucky in having this interest, and this work, and this way of touching the minds and hearts of people around me. What do those people do with themselves who have nothing but just their own little concerns and interests? It is a kind of living death . . . more and more the small secondary things, amusements, interests, little pleasures, are disappearing; I need less than ever amusements and distractions.

The friends I really love and who love me seem to be the only company I need; and I am at the point where it [is] just impossible for me to bear any longer the aimless idle people who pester me because they have seen my name in the newspapers a few times. They are a tribe, and dangerous parasites. But I have learned a little better how to defend myself. Well . . .

This is Armistice Day, and this government is busy building up Germany for the second time, and recognizing Franco, and injuring France and England our Allies, and, I don't doubt, preparing another great war and a great depression to follow, in good republican routine, just as they began to prepare on this day thirty-eight years ago. On that day I came out of the death-stupor of influenza, and realized that I would live, after all, but it made such a change in me, that near-dying, and *knowing* just what was happening, it is as if I had had two lives—one on the other side of that illness, and the second one ever since. I have not a word to say against life; when I complain, it is only because the conditions of living seem to be so unnecessarily and stupidly painful. When I am raising the most hell, it is a paradox; because I love life so much, I can't bear to have it so abused!

I hear a big band, no doubt leading some idiotic parade, roaring along outside. Still playing John Philip Sousa's tacky tuneless tunes, sounds just like that band in Denver thirty-eight years ago . . . Great and good things have a way of happening seldom, one at a time, and never twice alike. Dullness and silliness and dowdiness and meanness just go on repeating like a flock of parrots forever and ever. Amen, God forbid. . . .

Bathe your eyes in boric acid water, rub lumps of ice on them, and try to sleep. Rest them a little.

> Love again—
> *Aunt Katherine Anne*

TO ELEANOR CLARK

> After September 14,
> Department of English
> University of Michigan
> Ann Arbor, Michigan
>
> August 30 1953

Eleanor darling:

"Better burn this letter," indeed! I have read letters a thousand years old, and older, with that note at the end, and I intend that people shall read this one in time to come, who knows for how long? If you don't want me to treasure such letters, better not write them. But that of course, could spoil everything, and of course what I should do is what other people do, just say nothing and tuck the letter away to be discovered among Those Papers.

Rosanna must some day be seen as her mother saw her, as I was shown her, the most delicious portrait of a baby that I know. I feel I know just how she looks and is, I shan't be surprised at all. And there is another picture, this time by telephone, of the littlest angel playing an invisible lute . . . Lucky darling infant, who has a mother and father who really look at her, and can see her, and make others see her too.

Now I was never one to think that new parents should try to hide their rapture, as if they could, any more than new lovers—its just a new kind of love, and the rest of us can only be glad of it, and try not to mind that we haven't got something of the sort, if not the same, why, nearly as good. As my belief is, there isn't anything else nearly as good, I just say, Joy and Halleluia, colics—if it is colics—and all!

Darling, in all matters of the heart, I belong to the company of the Old Believers, so you must just be easy; let me be happy in your happiness, in which I believe most firmly. As for original sin, let nature take its course. I always believe we'd have less of it if we weren't told about it too early. . . .

With my love,
Katherine Anne

TO ANDREW LYTLE   [117 East 17th Street]
                         New York
                         August 30, 1953

Dear Andrew:

. . . . Your view of the University system as a machine is surely right, and of course in dealing with a machine, every kind of ruse and strategy must be employed to get around its works: you did make me see that the people who after all run the machine—who *does* run it, by the way?—have found devices to make room for such as you and I for teachers. I never liked compromises, my definition of a compromise being a solution that pleases no one, never believed them necessary; have always seen the systems of expediency and improvisation as being the root-evil of life in everything. I am simply not able to be cynical, and it makes great difficulties for me and for some of those around me. Of course, if I had any sense, the important thing is that I take this good job and the good salary that goes with it, and I suppose I should have swallowed the neglect and suffered the suspense and upset as part of the job. But I didn't feel that way, and still don't.

In the matter of asking for credits for my students, it could be argued that the assignment of credits was not my affair, I was there to teach and let the machine grind on in its own way. But I cannot see it! You said I should not have mentioned my lack of a degree to the Michigan Committee. I was bitterly criticised at Stanford for not having mentioned it, as if I had purposely committed a fraud. I had not thought of it, even, because I did not know such a question existed. So, after I got there, I found myself in a nasty situation which I did not want repeated at Michigan, not for any amount of money . . . I see no reason at all why I should not put my cards on the table, and let the other players do what they must do in that case. I have in fact no intention of flattering anybody that their messy little ways of running things is any good; this is a bloody messy and horrible world because simply most people in it like it that way. I happen not to like it, and I shall go on saying so at the top of my voice to the end. Not that it will make any difference except to the health of my nervous system. I did just the same make one small effectual effort towards order and clearness, in my writing; that I did do, and that is all I was able to do. Ever since I was old enough to know anything at all, I have known that the evils of life are implicit, there is no cure for them; but the one thing we can do is to know what is evil, and never be seduced into calling it good; or even to "go along with" it for the sake of—well, going along!

My what a fuss I do make about taking a little lecturing job in a university, but of course, no one thing is ever just that, it is connected with everything else, and I have turned up so many stones and planks, every sort of thing from radio and moving pictures to buying a house to love and marriage, and the same crawly organisms come romping out, and don't think I don't know they are in my blood, too. I am a part of this filth, something in me against my will and my spirit, consents to it: or I wouldn't be in this world. Well, let it go . . . it is very hard sometimes not to despair altogether, and of myself first, because I know myself best!

One evening after I had been reading poetry at the YMWHA, Red and Eleanor came home with me, and we were repeating verses to each other, and I said Sir Walter Raleigh's sad little poem ending with "But from this grave, this earth, this dust, My God shall raise me up, I trust." And Red said, "There is a certain amount of doubt there. I think he meant, 'I guess.'" So I revised it: "From this unholy, sordid mess/ My God shall raise me up, I guess." But alas, I don't believe even that.

But my dear, friendship is a lovely thing, and that comes of human nature, too: and poetry. And music. And the lovely bright morning, and the hope that today one will do maybe just even a little good work, good work of any kind at all. And I am not going to be contentious and difficult at Ann Arbor at all, but just do as well as I can, and get along with the people there, and help to make life a little pleasant as we go; but then, we can do this without once denying any principle we live by, nor once giving up a single mental reservation as to the real meaning of things . . . not simple, not easy, but the only terms in which life is possible, I do believe *this!*

> With my same old monotonous affection.
> *Katherine Anne*

To Donald Brace   117 East 17th Street
                                 New York 3, N.Y.
                                 9 September 1953

Dear Donald:

I thought of sending a telegram or calling, but maybe a note is better . . . I am so very rushed and distracted (not in the sense of mentally unhinged, just too damned many little things to do at once) that I couldn't possibly be good company; and this decision of mine, which is considerably more serious and far-reaching than is necessary for me to say, is a real closing up and farewell to my whole life until now; even though it is impossible for me to have made any other move—except one—and I feel quite serene in my mind about it, still there is a good deal of melancholy too, and I really cannot talk about it, even to you. Perhaps least of all to you, for the most obvious of reasons. So let's have lunch together some other time, somewhere else, maybe, under a better star.

It has taken me a good while and a tremendous lot of painful thought and very reluctant facing of facts to do what I am doing but in the end it was very clear that I could no longer endure the life I had, no doubt, brought on myself; I had to make a radical change for what I hope is the better, or commit suicide. I have been very near to it this year, and I do not in the least intend to do it until

I have exhausted all means to make some sort of bearable existence for myself . . . Nobody can help me, not effectively, not the kind of help I need, which is some kind of continuous, dependable way of life, in which my mind would have time to settle and work without fear of crisis from outward circumstances; the incessant worry about *how* I was to manage a living without anything definite to look forward to.

Well, I am exhausted, and in one way, this could be an act of despair: but it is not so desperate as the only alternative I can see, so let's look upon it as a minor, incomplete victory. Really, it only comes to this: so far as writing as a profession or a probable means of existence is concerned, I am through. We can both see that it is no good. The only thing I want in the world so far as publishing is concerned is to get out of debt to Harcourt Brace; and even the spring royalty statement took quite a bite out of it, and I am hopeful that the next one will have good news, too. A friend of mine in the Westwood Book Shop in Westwood Village near Los Angeles just wrote they had sold two hundred copies of *The Days Before* already and are still selling them. Its a very little bookshop, so I thought that sounded hopeful. I was told that the first printing of six thousand had been about sold out, and a second printing ordered, I don't know how many . . . What I am trying to say is, I suppose the debt would pay itself out in a few years just with what we have in print, with the various little fees from this and that. But I am anxious about it, and so I talked with Catharine Carver about the short story anthology, which I am sure she relayed to you; and the text-book department seems interested if I can do something to specifications . . . I should very much like to know what these requirements are, for this is to be strictly a paying-off job, and I want it to be something that will sell. I think when I am free again of debt and the weight on my conscience of what I have done to my work and myself and after all, to my publishers by getting into this appalling oppressive muddle about money, I shall begin to feel easy in my mind and shall write again; I read over the things I so long to do, the notes and preparations and I still believe in them, and want to finish them as far as I shall have time; but time is what I needed, that is, free time really to work out my plans, and not just do what I could on the ragged edge of my energies after doing jobs to make a living. But I have no plans in the matter at all.

Now then, maybe that was all I was going to have, and in any case, it was all I did have, or was able to manage for. If I have been a very bad manager, then that was my weakness, and nobody's fault but my own. And what I am doing now is on my own head. It is an odd little reversal of the rule: one lives in the world to a certain point of age and experience, and then retires to the cloister. I am leaving my cell, closing the door,—it was very noisy and crowded in there, anyway—and coming out really to live in the world, and forget all this nonsense about being an artist. I am an artist, will live and die one because I have no other choice, but it is clear that that, too, is strictly my own business and of interest to very few people. I was not out to prove anything, anyway. I just followed my instinct and did what came natural. But alas, what came natural to me seems to be a very outlaw state of affairs in the practical world, and I have fought the situation until I am exhausted. Imagine all this hubbub and to have got four little books out of a possible twenty after all these bloody years . . . Could you blame me if sometimes I feel rather a fool?

I don't like feeling like a fool, so I am going to take up teaching in universities, and from now on, I don't intend to be without a job in one institution of education or another; I am already looking around for next year . . . I got this appointment merely because the regular teacher is taking a sabbatical year.

So now my dear Donald, good bye for the moment: I am getting away in the usual incoherence of uprooting once more, and the great consolation is that this time, it doesn't matter; I am not going to try to write, I don't need to be settled and secure, it makes no difference at all what I do or where I go; meantime I shall be making an honest living and next summer if I live I'll take a trip to Italy, a place I have not been . . .

In spite of the clouds of melancholy which do now and then float up from the abyss, I can't help feeling a certain lightness of heart. It is just a relief to be able to make a plan and carry it out myself, even if only once.

This is really a private and personal letter, I'll write again to whoever I should write to about the text book, my wish is not for a new contract or any advance, I want to substitute this for, say, the Journals; but I must know first just what the textbook department believes it can use . . . This is business and nothing else. We've got to get that sinister row of red-ink figures to the lower right of that royalty sheet wiped out

My God, here I sit writing with fifty little chores piled up . . . No more today. With my same love and old-time affection, I hope we can stay friends in spite of all the nuisances of time and change and publishing. After all, I am not running out on you. I am still accountable for all that money, and it will be paid.

Yours
Katherine Anne

SECTION 8

Ann Arbor, Liège, New York

September 1953 to May 1955

Where just do I stand? . . . on a profound conviction that goodness, which I love, resides in the individual, and that personal virtue is no respecter of class or person—it finds its own place and sits down there.

Katherine Anne Porter to her nephew Paul
October 28, 1954

"AUDACES FORTUNA JUVAT" IS ENGRAVED ON THE SILVER *bowl Katherine Anne Porter leaves at home in New York when she goes to Ann Arbor to teach; two stags with broken horns and two with unbroken horns are her crest. After suffering an attack of angina pectoris at the University of Michigan, she thinks for a moment she is going to die. But she has no wish to call anyone, "for I thought of every one I know and love somewhere at work and occupied with his life, and there was no point in disturbing any one!" Indeed, fortune does favor the brave, for she is sent to Belgium "as a sort of minor ambassador of American literature and civilization . . . but if I have any such thing to offer, it has nothing at all to do with being American, but with being human." Illness brings her back to New York from Liège before her Fulbright year is over.*

To Glenway Wescott   Hopwood Room
University of Michigan
Ann Arbor, Michigan
26 September, 1953

Glenway darling:

You have heard all this by now, but I want to tell you again how dramatic, yes, literally like something done on cue on a stage, even if no one in the cast but the Messenger knew his lines—was the delivery of your dear telegram at Giorgio's dinner party. Well, there we were, gaily full of cocktails, the main dish a festive affair and a community project at once, (Giorgio and I hovering, tasting, conspiring, stirring and muttering incantations over it) and so we sat down in pale candlelight in the open hall. The door of the elevator burst open back of us, and a large, seedy, melancholy character actor in sagging seedy melancholy clothes surged in, holding a telegram and pronouncing my name in a rising tone. Flurried I went to get my reading glasses to sign for the message. Meantime some one took it and read it aloud, with the right inflections. We were all up and circling about, mysteriously excited. The man got back in the elevator. It would not work. We knocked on the door and made gestures, towards the buttons. He pressed them here and there. He opened the door, he came out. I seem to remember perhaps Monroe going in—or was it George? and trying the machinery. The man went back in. Door closed. Buttons. Nothing happened. Then we got him started walking down stairs, and settled down again, or nearly. Odd thing was, the only words he spoke to me while I was looking for pen, glasses and a quarter at least, were: "Good thing there's an elevator." I agreed.

The look on his shapeless, battered face through the glass when he believed himself trapped in the elevator, his helplessness—I cannot forget it. I think his experience of life—such a nerveless creature, messenger boy at his time of life—made him fear dimly that perhaps we were playing a joke on him, or really meant to drop him into the cellar. . . .

Yours
Katherine Anne

To Robert Penn Warren   Hopwood Room, Angell Hall
                           University of Michigan
                           Ann Arbor, Michigan
                           16 October, 1953

Red Darling:

I took the 20th page of my outline for term paper in contemporary poetry out of the typewriter after reading your letter; its now or nearly never that I'll answer it. You know too well my Eager-Beaver temperament; I meant only to give a little side-trip from the regular tourist route of the poetry course, and having discovered that 99 percent of my students had never read any poetry at all except a few "modern" ones, I settled on the lyric as the thing, and jumped them back to Catullus and Petronius Arbiter, am taking them on a roller coaster ride through the medieval Latin poets straight into late middle English—well, a couple of the snappier things of Chaucer's, to Lydgate—my what a long stretch there, and what a fall—Skelton, and then the Elizabethans, Seventeenth century, Eighteenth, Nineteen, and so, in no time with their hair in their teeth and a roaring in their ears, we are soon fetching up in the beautiful hurley-burley of our times. And it seems to me wonderful how well the good poets of the past thirty-odd years hold their own in the English lyric! I'm not carrying the gospel or anything of the kind, but I just thought it would be nice to give them a little of the background. I began with 85 students. This morning, the fateful thirteenth session, exactly fourteen have fallen by the wayside, but the rest seem to mean business, even if they are a little confused and I still have to explain to them that this is not a joy-ride no matter what it looks like. It has a shape and a direction and when they get through, at least they will have read more poetry than they ever dreamed existed, and that is really my point. Some of them give yips of agony from time to time, but they do come through, as I keep telling them they must. Arno Bader says it is a fine thing for them, but the University did not bring me here to kill myself with so much work. They said, "The class is yours. You can do anything you like with it," so I did. Anyway, its not dull or so they say.

But I am about exhausted, and on Saturday night I go to bed and stay there until Monday morning. I live in a little hotel, have breakfast sent up, have taken a Sabbatical year from everything except what I should be doing, for once, instead of that and ten other things besides.

Your plans are most attractive, what story would you like me to account for, if I can? I did by request a sort of story about "Noon Wine" for my advanced class, only five students, trying to give sources . . . But you choose. For the second book, account of composition, I don't remember ever having written anything like that, except a very slight thing for Whit Burnett's *This is My Best*. What would you choose for that, or should I choose? Let me know. I'll be coming out of the woods soon I don't doubt, and want to do something beside face these amiable-but-sabre-toothed tigers of mine five hours a week without counting all the conferences, which really do break my bones—always did.

I am sorry that Austin Warren is not here, but it is because he went to NYU that I am here: he recommended me, I am told. Then Mr. Bader took his classes and gave me *his* (Bader's) and next semester, they said, I should have *criticism*. I said, NO! I want the short story! So we are thinking about that.

The weather here too has been wonderful as paradise's own climate, only maybe a little too warm. But I am told to soak it up, for the winters are terrible . . .

I saw your picture in the *Herald Tribune,* a smiling one, the first ever I saw of you smiling, and your eyes were so fixed on one point, something that delighted you, I just took it for granted you were looking at Rosanna and Eleanor in some particularly charming composition. Or maybe Eleanor was sitting by, and you were *both* looking at Rosanna like that . . .

Why do young babies take to food so reluctantly? Why do their innocent little midriffs have to be racked by the very stuff on which their life and growth depends? A wicked warning of nature, to teach us early that she has tricks up her sleeve for us, and is to be trusted only so far? But I am happy to tell you that Rosanna's new blooming every morning will go on and on, years upon years upon years. Real beauty is long-lived and hardy, like real love or genius. . . .

> With my love
> *Katherine Anne*

To John Malcolm   Ann Arbor
Brinnin   22 November, 1953

John Malcolm darling—

When I was writing to Marianne just now I tried to describe the way you looked when we saw each other at The Poetry Center, and I almost did it—that you were "transparent with exhaustion" . . . It would have been like seeing a ghost except that your eyes burned so—It was wonderful of you to be able to come, and go through the evening which must have been an almost unbearable ordeal, and I expected nothing of you, nothing—even in a trance as you were, you were exactly yourself still, which is quite enough.

It is good of you to say I did well, for I was numb with just plain bone-tiredness when I went on, but thank God for the second wind that comes when we need it! I fall in love with my audiences, you know, and I believe they feel it—Any way I do sincerely wish to give them a happy evening, or why should I *be there?* I do hope, sometime we will be able to spend a little quiet time with each other—what a pity in Paris, that lovely place and weather, and such a wretched topic! Will do better for ourselves the next time! With my love,

Katherine Anne

To Robert Penn Warren   [Ann Arbor, Michigan]
                        22 February, 1954

Dear Red:

. . . . Rosey-Posey is clearly setting out on the athletic life; a motor-trip across country in dead of winter is a test, but her triumph does not surprise me. I am longing to praise her to her face (I don't think praise is as harmful as we were brought up to believe. That is a Puritan notion: anything that makes us happy *must* be harmful to our morals!) I wish for Rosanna that she walk on rose-leaves to

the sound of silver flutes all her life. It will be *very* good for her!
She will be even more beautiful for it. . . .

Love to the three—

Yours
Katherine Anne

TO MONROE WHEELER   [Ann Arbor, Michigan]
                          April Fool's Day, very early in
                          the morning, 1954

And I DID fool 'em, a little ahead of time, Monroe darling.
I'm still here, and a little better for just seven days of pure rest and
quiet: its people in crowds that get me down, I feel pretty certain
by now. Anyway, they did put me through the wringer at the
hospital; a wonderful hospital, the very best far and away that ever
I was in, with three first-rate doctors and a cloud of young doctors
who trailed them as witnesses and students—it is a great clinic and
medical school, I gather—and I haven't been so investigated since
I was born. They know all now, and like the good scientists they
are, confessed they didn't know very much: the human corpus is the
more a mystery the more they learn about it. But they did a noble
job of making tests, and came up with some good advice, which,
boiled down to a sentence, is only what one is bound to hear, if one
hangs round long enough: SLOW DOWN! Oh very well. I'll slow
down. In fact, it might be fun. At last they decided it was a slight—
slight, mind you—attack of angina pectoris, the kind of thing that
can carry you off in one split second or hang around and nag you
for forty years. I feel sure mine is the forty-year-kind. I've had it
twice before, just two years ago this coming April and May, about
three weeks apart. I was in hospital nine days then, yet got up and
went to Paris between attacks, you remember, and have lived to
have a third. So I can't seem to worry. This one, by bad luck,
happened in class; I was talking along easily about Henry James, his
particular genius for carrying the story forward by conversation, all
that seemingly casual and disjointed talk nudging the reader for-

ward without his knowing; when the well-remembered pain about the size of the palm of my hand started just under the lower ribs slightly to the left and spread and expanded and grew agonizingly all over my midriff and up to the shoulder and into the jawbone and down the left arm, and I broke into a sweat and put down the book I was referring to at times, and folded my arms and put my head on them on the table, and after that everything was very dim, except I could feel, more than hear or see, a hub-bub, and the next thing I knew I was in an ambulance—the siren mooing hideously brought me to—with an oxygen mask over my face and a very sweet-faced, pleasant voiced young interne patting my forehead and chin and saying, "Now do you feel better?" So with great originality I asked with perfect sincerity, "Where am I?"

After that it was just routine. But for my sins there is a full-time student newspaper being run on this campus, one of those semi-professional affairs with AP service and Drew Pearson's column, and a flock of young vampire bats learning to be reporters; so they reported a heart attack, and the local radio picked it up, and the Radio too, has national affiliations, and so—well, I have had letters and telegrams from all over this country, from friends and strangers, and from Rome, Paris, Brussels, London, Bremen, New York of course, long distance calls to the doctors; a stranger sent the card from Bremen, saying he had read the notice while travelling, wanted to say how much pleasure reading my stories had given him. A woman who had a conversation with me eleven years ago on the train between Baton Rouge and New Orleans wrote she had never forgotten me, but this was the first good excuse she had to write. A man wrote that he had seen me on the *Queen Elizabeth* in 1952, somebody had pointed me out, and he had hoped to be introduced, but it didn't happen . . . and so on.

Well, darling, once, it seems like centuries ago (in Denver 1918), I read my own obituary, all set up and ready to go with only the day and hour blank, and I remember how *impersonal* I felt as I read it; and this has the odd feeling too of having happened to some one else, some one I don't know. Yet there is one odd circumstance: of all the messages, there was, except for you and Glenway, *not one* from any writer or "colleague" as Glenway so charmingly calls them. Not a word from the entire membership, for example of the National Institute—not from the Sitwells, nor

Eudora, nor Red and Eleanor, nor the Tates, nor, except Cyrilly, from any of the many editors who have published me. (Harcourt Brace naturally,) In fact, I cannot name them and it wouldn't make any difference if I did; the teetotal silence from the entire banked heirarchy of my contemporaries and supposed friends has become, as time goes, really impressive. William Humphrey, a most gifted young writer, my candidate for a Guggenheim this year, wrote me a sweet little note. No one else . . . Everything came from former students, strangers, and not-writing friends, readers . . . with the exceptions you know.

What do I make of this? Absolutely nothing . . . I was amazed at what happened—all that spate of kindness and gentle feeling from all Europe and this country; how could I expect anything like that? But since it did happen, then the strange silences began also to assert themselves . . . Never mind. I mention it because I thought of it. . . .

This has been a wonderful winter, I think nothing could have been better than my coming here; there is just really nothing wrong at all—there are some better-than-good people here on this faculty; and it is strange about Universities. These people have really first rate minds and civilized feelings, they should be able to do more than they do, but there is a kind of harness on their talents, they are not able to break out of the curiously cramping situation of mechanized—could almost say, industrialized—education. But I am free as the air itself. . . .

And besides: I had to pass up an appointment to lecture in Cambridge of all places this summer, because I was already engaged here. I am sorry for this, it would have been pretty to lecture in Cambridge: but, *They* say, maybe next year. This has to do with my appointment on a Fulbright fellowship to the University of Liege, (Liége? Liège? I expect to know this time next year!) for, they said, a *very* light round of occasional lectures, a little social life, and nothing else. Allen Tate, who got one last year, had been over the same route—that is, a preliminary lecture at Oxford—Oxford and Cambridge alternate each year with this summer term—and on to the University at Rome . . . for me, Cambridge and then Liège. They haven't said what the financial allowance is, but assure me soothingly it is quite generous. I hope so. Of course, this scandal about my heart attack may knock the whole project into a cocked hat. . . . So my angel, if nothing happens to trip me up, I'll spend next year, beginning middle of September, in Liège, of all places. Simply a place I never thought of except in the wars, when it seems to be the first place attacked by the Germans. Well, at the rate this government is getting its old sparring partner back and ready to fight again, I may yet live to see the Germans coming into Liège a third time . . . I wonder what insanity in our politicians make them believe—can they believe it?— that Germany is going ever to fight for anybody or anything but Germany . . . Germany is NO ally, never was, never will be. And here it is, the great bloodsucking, blood-shedding monster, already grabbing world trade from Great Britain and France; Golly, Monroe, if I were a nation, I'd hate like the devil to be an ally of the U.S.!

Darling, I'm getting to feel that you will never be able to get through this letter. Maybe some quiet evening in early bed, if you ever have any such time. I feel so *reaching-out* to you—better be glad I am not there, I'd talk both your ears off. But no, I'd listen, to your story of travel and especially of India. I've always felt that Santha Rama Rau was not too typical, in spite of her splendid saris and Hindu good looks. Glenway, if he has not already, can tell you the delicious encounters we had with Hindus at the Festival in Paris: well, *he* had them, really, and handed them on to me; that is, he could put into words that really unfathomable, unbridgeable difference and distance between us and them. Darling, I sometimes wonder if it wouldn't be better if nations could let each other alone on the fundamental issues, like religion, customs, manners, ways of feeling and thinking . . . Must we go around understanding everything about everybody, insisting that everybody understand and perhaps even approve of us? It does not seem to be necessary. The only common ground for people of all nations is art, we can exchange that and it does refresh life for every one. Trade and commerce surely could be carried on freely without trying to change, influence, direct, the essential lives of others . . . I really detest and distrust this leveling, scumbling, mixing up of things not meant to be mixed, all boundaries destroyed, the denial, somehow, of the right of people to the privacy of their own thoughts and beliefs. . . .

And yet O my God, look what I am about to do: I am being sent to Belgium as a sort of minor ambassador of American litera-

ture and civilization—that is what it says, right there in the proposed appointment—and that must mean I am to try to be some sort
of example of something in us, our society, that is worth knowing
and believing in: but if I have any such thing to offer, it has nothing
at all to do with being American, but with being human. . . .

Darling I love you. That is the whole simple secret. In turn,
I trust your friendly love, so unchanging, so completely it is odd
perhaps even to mention it, except that it pops into my mind, and
this seems to be a moment of the kind of unselfconsciousness one
has when—no matter if it was not really true—one believes oneself
to have looked for even a moment into the open grave. It *is* true
that I thought just for the smallest flash that I was going to die. It
passed so quickly you might think it left no impression; but it did.
A split-second of dismay, and then, complete calm and quiet and
no regrets, not even for all that unfinished work—no uneasiness of
any kind, no wish to ask for anybody, darling, not even you—for
I thought of every one I know and love somewhere at work and
occupied with his life, and there was no point at all in disturbing
any one! This was just no cause for trouble, not even to me. It was
a lovely way to feel, angel, and it hasn't left me, and I hope it stays
by me from now on, because I'm going straight back into the
brouhaha, but this time, I'll have a better sense of proportion!

Love again!
Katherine Anne

To GLENWAY WESCOTT   25 Avenue des Platanes
                          Cointe-Sclessin, Liège, Belgium
                          23 October, 1954

Glenway darling:

I wrote your mother, and you will see the letter and so stay by
your resolve of silence; I have made my explanation of why I was
so long answering her.

When you and others younger than I, by I forget how many
years, out a good number, complain of getting old I think with
dismay, But what must they think of me? Not at all, Am I then really

so old? nor, Am I then so signally showing signs of decay? In the first place, I have had such a struggle to survive, so many illnesses that nearly crippled me when I was young, so many intimations of mortality before it was time, I have felt more decrepit when I was twenty four than I ever have since—and again, I do not have a proper sense of time—it does not chop itself like stove wood into decades convenient for burning one at a time—it is a vast drift in which I float, eddying back and forth, spun round now and then, moving always towards no fixed point but that one day will dissolve and drop me into the abyss. But then again, I did not have youth as you did—no golden time, nothing to remember with joy and love and regret; not a day of my whole life that I would want to live again . . .

And then, I can't trust other peoples' eyes or judgements in the question. When I was sixteen, a woman of middle age, when told *my* age, said, "Ha, she'll never see eighteen again!" And when I was twenty eight, a man, not at all malicious, guessed my age to be forty. Oddly enough, when I was fifty, another man, (Charles Shannon,) guessed my age as forty again—and I told him about the other guess, and wondered if I was ever going to escape from that particular age. Long ago, I decided not to worry about my visible years—others were so happy to do that for me. Did I ever tell you my very favorite story about age? Glenway, this really happened. I was having lunch in the Commissary with Charles Brackett, Clarence Brown, and Billy Wilder, and a few tables away little Margaret O'Brien was lunching with her mother, her director, her governess, and who else? and these three men at my table looked her over as if she were a pony they were thinking of buying, and one of them said, "How old is she now?" and another said, "Six years old," and there was a pause, and then Charlie Brackett said, "She looks older than that." There was a kind of nod-around among them, and the moment passed . . .

I can tell you one thing—I am really old now and it is not so bad . . . What worries me is that time is running out and I have four more books I want to do, and I wonder about this frantic hope of mine that somehow by taking all these jobs I could save up enough money to get a head start and do them. At this point, all other obstructions and obstacles are cleared away, no man will break my bones with his "love"—all my vampires have disappeared, I could do it now if only I am given ten years or even less, with enough money to live on without having to go on with this gruesome public sort of life; but well, let's see. Of late I was asked to do some autobiographical notes, and I have done bales. But its no good saying, this or that happened on such a date, mentioning names and places: for that is not what happened at all. My life has been so hidden and internal that just a record of events would be perfectly meaningless.

This enough about me, and God knows enough about age. You are really at a time of most sustained crisis; when we parted after the dinner party at George's, I said, "I hear you are sunk in . . ." hesitating but meaning to say, I had heard you were sunk in a piece of really private writing that couldn't be published until everybody mentioned was dead . . . somebody I forget who told me this portentously . . . But you said, "Yes, I'm sunk . . ."

Maybe you are, and maybe it is nearly time for you to surface again, and I wait for that, in extraordinary confidence. . . .

I want to put up Eleanor Clark for the 1000 award, before somebody gets her voted in as a member, and will you second this? I mean to ask Marianne, and can you suggest some one else? I just feel she should have it. Is it too late for this year? . . . I am interested though only at this time in trying to get that money for Eleanor . . . *Rome and a Villa* surely merits that, to say the least.

There darling, how lightly with the assurance of an old friend do I add another pound weight to your burden, but you will forgive me, and maybe even forget.

It is five o'clock, I am in a dowdy little furnished apartment where the keys don't turn, the gas cocks stick, the bathroom gadgets work half-way, the neighborhood is tout-petit bourgeoisie, the furnishings are from the Belgian branch of Sears Roebuck, the place is suburban, the wild yellow leaves are flying in a high bitter wind under a smoky sky, and I feel I have come to world's-end, and what was my errand here? There is nothing I wish to say to anybody here, does anybody want to listen? But it does look as if here, in all its unlikeliness, the place and time had met for me to sit at this table—three and one half feet square—and write something of my own . . . I am melancholy to a point I have not known since Germany, Berlin in 1931—These heavy dark northern countries—how they oppress me. Still, I am here, tethered, if not actually nailed—nails seem more likely for there is a real pain in it . . . and then, I look back, and remember, and for how long has life just been for me an endurance contest, how many times have I said, "I will live through this, and to the next thing . . ." This is really no worse than I have known before . . . It is only NOW, and the other was *then*.

With my love, my dear, and write when you can.

Katherine Anne

To Paul Porter   25 Avenue des Platanes
                                  Cointe-Sclessin, Liège, Belgium
                                  Thursday 28, October, 1954

Well, you *said* you would like a letter!

Paul darling:

While my hardy, good tempered, heavy-footed femme de ménage is tromping all over the place and talking a streak, I'll begin at least a letter to you. It might just be the day for it: I seem to be on the edge of coming out somewhere, almost even. The very first day since I left Hoboken in a cold mean rain that did not let up the three thousand miles of Atlantic, nor at Rotterdam, nor straight into Brussels and for a week after. I found I could never be warm except in bed, so I stayed in bed most of the time, in a little cabin with two cabin-mates; very nice women, both, and they seemed to think as well of me; and we gave quite an object lession in civilized behavior under rather sordid conditions, and parted kindly, and swapped postcards afterwards. The German girl, Fulbright exchange Professor in Science, was going back after an exciting six months in California. She proceeded Doctor at the age of twenty three: is now thirty, and what happened to her? Well, she was engaged to a German in Frankfort, but she met an American in California, and got engaged to *him,* too: and seasick as she was nearly all the way, lying staring at at the ceiling all day and half the night, she was caught in a crossfire of cables, the American refusing to say farewell and demanding that she return immediately or he would be coming after her—the German refusing to believe a word of her escapade and promising that he would break up that nonsense, that "mood."

She lived on hot tea and toast, with an occasional sip of champagne from the case of Moët Chandon the American had sent with her, amid the wilting white chrysanthemums the German had ordered by cable to the ship. She is a beautiful young woman, need I say? The dark, warm, intense kind of German.

Once in a while I would come out of my book, or my drowse, and study her prostrate figger across the cabin from me, all of six feet away, and think, "at this distance, it LOOKS like Life, but who can be sure?" and when she now and then rather timidly asked what I should advise about her predicament, I thought of my Jenny on the boat from Vera Cruz, remember? listening to the Swiss girl, and that is not altogether fiction, and here it was again; only this time, not a poverty of romance but an embarrassment. Finally I managed a worldly note: "You don't seem to be enjoying yourself, and that is a pity. You could be having a delightful time out of this!"

"Oh, no!" she said, shocked, "I am much too serious!" I said, "In that case, there is nothing for you to do but take the one you love." She said, "Yes, but which one is that?"

When she left the ship, she was in the same fix. Her little square parchment card read, *Dr.* Ingeborg Raben. But it is not for philosophy, after all. . . .

I have done a little scattered meditation—never believe you can't meditate in fragments—about Art, my darling, Art, *tout court,* and what about it? For here is a whole population which has lived and reproduced itself in the shadow—under the wing, in the bosom—of centuries of tremendous art, architecture, poetry, music, and this whole suburb consists of rows of houses in which people live without a book, without a picture, without music except the radio, who are no more touched by it than if they had been brought up in a sod house in Kansas. And—this is irony so obvious I blush to mention it—I have come all this way to land in the dead middle of the sort of surroundings I have been appalled at all my life, the dullness, the dullness, the—well, the dullness. And a professor at the University found it for me, and assured me it was the very best, the high choice, of at least twenty he had seen. . . .

Already I am engaged for readings and appearances of one sort or another in Brussels, Antwerp, and here, and there will be other things. I am quite sure I can do everything required, I have done it all before, but in some way I am benumbed, as if I were walking in my sleep. I should like to write—to finish the novel, to write a long story, to get up the poetry anthology, and I expect to do these things, but it is just true that in some way I am simply indifferent to the bottom of my soul—there is a point at which endurance and patience turn into despair, and the only thing that makes me believe I have not really reached despair is that the thought of it frightens me . . . So I think this is just fatigue pushed a little past my limits, and it will pass. I sleep better, for one thing, almost by an act of the will. No sedatives, almost no alcohol—I take a good slug of Bols' old reliable Genever, very aromatic and pleasant with a sliver of lemon rind and plenty of cold water, every evening before dinner. And dinner is usually just a broiled filet of beef—real filet, mind you, which costs about the same as hamburger at home—and a salad; the food is of course abundant and fresh and good everywhere, and it seems absurdly inexpensive after New York . . . There is really no reason why I shall not be rested and accustomed and able to get on with what I want to do—but it is just this, I am tired of this monotony of change and uncertainty and perpetual waste of time and energy; well, in a word, I am tired, and this time to the bone . . . Poor Yeats was amazed because he had expected the aging of the body, but he had not known the heart could grow old! I had not known that the love of life and the will to live could be reduced to such a tiny flicker in me . . . So I must stop now and hold myself very still and be quiet and let life flow back again . . . it has gone very far out, this time. . . .

The potato is going on nicely, and I have put the fish in the oven . . . I want to say something about people in general, without regard to what class they belong to, or how they live. I have not, since I came to this country, met with anything but kindness and courtesy, it does not matter from whom—and the family across the street took in my misdirected mail and took the trouble to find out where it belonged—and when my trunks were delivered there, they paid for them and had them sent to the right door. And then the husband, a retired Colonel, when I asked him what I could do for him, said he would be pleased to have any postage stamps from foreign countries. Of course he collects stamps, and his wife told me with tears in her eyes how the Germans destroyed his wonderful stamp collection which he had begun when he was a very small boy. (Another thing I *love* is, that every person who has spoken on the subject feels exactly as I do about the Germans. And if you could see even now the never-repaired ruins, or even more, the marks of repair in wonderful old houses, you would understand, if you don't already, which I think you do.) The girls in the shops, the policeman, the taxicab drivers, the waiters, all have a simple kind of decent manners which seem entirely natural, as if they had never had to be taught. So where just do I stand in this matter of peasant and aristocrat, and to hell with the middle classes? I'm afraid where I have stood since I was able to think or feel at all—on a profound conviction that goodness, which I love, resides in the individual, and that personal virtue is no respecter of class or person—it finds its own place and sits down *there;* and maybe it is just that, as Mazy Augusta works with *gout,* so I prefer virtue with *style;* and this is what the middle class lacks . . .

Very well, darling, I am now *remplit* to the neck with buttered fish and baked potato, water-cress and *red* wine. The Moulin-à-Vent was already open, and it "went" wonderfully. Also, my French conversation coach showed up suddenly, a magnificently impressive man, weighty and serious, grey at the temples, black-eyed, authoritative as hell, a teacher at the University, who has manfully volunteered to be the one who is to get my disordered syntax in some sort of Christian mood. We are to go yackety-yack at each other twice a week from now on—Saturday and Monday at 11; halfway through our talk he dropped into French and hauled me after him, and I felt somewhat like somebody being pulled through deep water by the strap of my bathing suit. But I could follow and in five minutes I was attempting to swim by myself . . . So maybe when you see me again I'll really be speaking French, something I cannot claim ever to have done, even during those five and a fraction years in Paris . . . Truth is, I never wanted to think in any language but English, but that's nonsense, no doubt. . . .

Good night, and pleasant dreams . . . I've been having some odd ones, all on the same theme . . . lost in mountains, foundered in deep still waters, abandoned—I don't know why or by whom, it never seems to be *people* concerned—all very simple, I'm sure, takes no great amount of imagination to see through—bewildered in fogs, yet no real peril, no fright, it all fades away gently. Well, tonight I shan't dream,,, I shall just go to sleep. . . .

There were three square envelopes, and behind them concealed a short, or letter size, airmail letter from Sister Gay. She leaves for Connecticut today, or rather after midnight of the 30th, will reach New York in time for breakfast, and so into the wilds of Connecticut; her own kind of letter, like nobody else's, and casually she drops a paragraph in the middle saying that Jules had been six weeks dying; but had made it at last; and was buried three weeks ago today (that would be 23rd of October;) that she, Sister, had been exhausted staying up nights with M.A. who came and kidnapped her every evening. But that she, M.A. was carrying on very well now, and was extremely well provided in the way of money. I should hope so! It would be painful to think she had got *nothing* out of her silly life. I don't know if it is because I saw too much of them, knew too well what they were up to, but just for sheer pointlessness I never knew a life—the life they had in common—to equal theirs . . . Still, poor wretch of a Jules—Remember those old marble slabs in church aisles in Mexico—no, you never saw Mexico, did you? which go on saying monotonously in rows: "Here Lies Juan (or Maria) Fulano deTal, in life a sinner, in death, nothing." Poor Jules had a worse fate, for in life he was nothing—nothing . . . If he had never lived, there would not even be a hole in the air where he might have been . . . He wasn't even a sinner—just badly behaved!

But poor mortal wretch. . . .

Yes, Virginia Woolf's Journals are painful reading; but her husband left out so much that should be there to give a real portrait of her—Of course, she suffered hideously, (hijjusly?) but sooner or later every living creature does, and the point is not just the mere anguish of things, but what kind of feeling, what plane of awareness, that goes into it . . . Think of all the suffering in this world which comes to nothing, nothing—but she was Virginia Woolf, and nothing in her experience was meaningless. How I love that brave great artist, with her thin skin and rattled nerves and tough spirit, and then, her genius, after all. That is the final undeniable fact about her, the only thing that made her Virginia Woolf and nobody else. She can't be explained away on any grounds—there she is, one of the wonderful beings of our time, who finally could not bear this world another hour; and I am haunted by a vision of her figure, tall and gaunt as a tower, leaving her stick and her cloak on the bank, and walking into the water on that cold March day . . . Think of any one being so lonely as that! I still shed tears about her, for some

reason her death hurt me more than any I have known in my time
. . . In all this death, imagine . . . but it is simply no good saying
that, or trying to think that because death and suffering are everywhere, one still has not the human right, the privilege, to feel what
one does feel about a certain given being. She was great in so many
ways, and that is simply a quality I love, and I grieve when I see
some one who possessed it go into the dark. . . .

> With my same love—
> *Aunt Katherine Anne*

To Morton Zabel   25 Avenue de Platanes
                              Cointe, Liège, Belgium,
                              29 November, 1954

Dear Morton:

. . . . I live in a little bourgeoise house in a bourgeoise suburb,
full of furniture such as you find from pole to pole, it looks like a
respectable home in the middle west or in the south, with allowance
for climates. Framed chromos on the wall, different pattern of wall
paper in every room, every curtain, and chair and table covered
with a piece of material in a different pattern. Furniture straight
from the Belgian branch of Sears Roebuck of forty or fifty years ago
. . . but there is hot water and steam heat, quiet, privacy, and a sweet
good woman who has the lower floor—it is her house, where she
was born and brought up and all her family—the elder dead, the
young ones married and gone, and she gets out and puts her gardens in shape like a professional gardener, then goes off to her hat
shop for a long day's work . . . I can do with this sort of thing very
well, I have nothing against it . . . what I need is this neutral air that
doesn't press on me too much. . . .

Ah well, Morton it has been a tremendous thing for you, this
year, and as you say of the weeks in London, "dense!" How can
you absorb it all? And some day, not in a letter, God forbid we
should get into such a talk on paper, I want to ask you what you
mean by "reality?" yes, I know, that sounds as if I were going to
look you solemnly in the face and ask—"What do you think of

eternity?" No, it won't be like that at all. But twice you have written with dread of returning to Chicago where the past is waiting for you, and to grief and remembrance, and you always call it "reality." You have taken your past everywhere with you, because it is in your veins, and you have never been for one moment out of "reality." Trust your happiness and the richness of your life at this moment. It is just as true and as much yours as anything else that ever happened to you. . . .

I won't forget that picture. I'll get a copy of it for you. I liked it because it looked like my grandmother—the only one I knew—and I loved her very much, and was happy to see that something of her had survived in me. . . .

Ah well, I *am* being dull. I have worked at this typewriter all day, and there is a wild storm going on, high crashing wind and black black night, but I can hear the trees creaking, and the windows strain at their locks, and there is for me always a kind of hallowe'en excitement about this kind of weather. I shall give up this day for gone, for finished, for used up, and have supper, and a glass of hot red wine, and so to bed, for tomorrow is going to be a very rushed sort of day . . .

I just looked out, and saw a high bonfire down in the next garden, and at first I thought the garden house was on fire. But no. It is half past eight at night, and two men are out burning leaves imagine in a wind like this. But then, if these people paid any attention to the weather, they'd never get anything done. So they rake leaves in a pouring rain, plough in the mud, and burn refuse at night in a high wind, and so on: and these Flanders peasants, in their fields, with their fat haunched horse and oxen, look still very much as they did when Breughel painted them.

Good night. Aff'ly aff'ly yours
Katherine Anne

To Glenway Wescott   27 December, 1954
[Post card from Rome.
Particolare del Chiostro di S.
Paolo]

Glenway my dear, I'm glad I never saw Rome until now, for
how could I dream anything so new and fresh and gay could happen
just by finding another city? I am now making plans to live here for
at least a year after my Liège appointment is up! Monroe tells me
you are collecting your papers for a book!
Best news of the New Year!

> With my love,
> *Katherine Anne*

To Isabel Bayley   Grand Hotel Moderne
                        Liège (Belgique)
                        22 January 1955, Saturday

Isabel darling do overlook the blotty start if you can—This pen
up-chucks like a baby—How do you like my green ink? Got it in
Rome, the only color they had for my poor inadequate Parker 51,
and I thought it might cheer him up, and sit on his stummick more
lightly, but no!—He spits it up, too.

x x x

You see where I am geographically and I am not certain,
whittling down territory, whether I should say, also topograph-
ically or cartographically. Anyway, personally, I am sitting in the
middle of a big fine soft bed under a good light in a warm clean
room, and no typewriter, but plenty of poetry books, writing
paper and ink—it was this or hospital; so Dorothy Deflandre of
the Foundation in Bruxelles came down, gave me my choice; I
said, never again never hospital! and indeed all I need to get well
is just what I have now—

x x x

It probably started on that very beautiful December 21 when
I was boosted literally into the helicopter—the only passenger,

469

and my first flight in one, and we simply bounced straight into the air about, I should say, 300 feet and swung along as if we were running on a slack wire—we bounced gently all the way to Bruxelles, where I changed to the plane, and so to London. I fell in love with London, it was on first sight overwhelming, but I felt at home! Newby met me at the Waterloo Station, took me to Hotel Connaught in Carlos Square, left me—I was of course exhausted. I went to bed at once.

It may have been the sudden change from the squalor in which I live in my unspeakable little flat, but it did seem as if the British are the only people who have really whipped the question of comfort when they finally put their minds on it. My room was full of beautiful really fine old furniture made to live with—pure linen on the bed, silk down comforter, warmth of air just right, and when my tray came, real silver and linen and good porcelain—luxury in fact, and so simple, all of it, in a way I can't describe—I tell you this because Newby had been uneasy about where to put me, and I said in effect—just so its clean and warm! and I must say he did himself proud way beyond the call of duty and I slept, ate a dinner—that was the tray!—of Roast beef Yorkshire pudding, with Guiness Stout and Bass' Pale ale half-and-half. . . .

Next morning—since I wrote last, I have had (1) a shot of Vitamin B's—1 and .12—in what is known here *tout court* as *La hanche*—swallowed 2 ampules of liver extract and strychnine—(and iron!) and have had 11 hours sleep . . . Also, dinner from Le Chapon Fin, a fine restaurant loosely connected with this hotel, and I have a new deesh—a feesh deesh—to tell you about. On my own responsibility I had a half-bottle of white Burgundy-Meursault, and a Remy Martin after dinner . . . I am in fact wallowing in luxury after my awful miseries out in my bloody suburb—

The dish is called *Sole Albert Premier* and is really fit for a king . . . I know there is no sole to be had on the American Continent unless it is flown in ice from England or France or Holland, but we do have flounder, which masquerades as sole, and does nicely. Flounder is a good fish, and we shouldn't let people call it sole.

I have just hit my first snag in giving this recipe. A fish with sauce calls for a broth (Court Bouillon?) made of the head, bones, etc. of the same fish—I mean another of the same kind of fish—oh well, hell, here goes—

Flounder Albert Premier for 2.

Get one large flounder and 2 smaller ones. Filet the two smaller ones and stow away in the ice-freezing shelf of the ice-box.

Break up the skeletons conveniently, and with the heads, cover barely with cold water, salt, pepper; simmer until flavor is extracted. Strain broth—at least 3 cups full—and—

Sorry—I should have said first, have your fishmonger skin these fish for you, but keep the heads. Put the main flounder's head in the broth, too.

All right. Meantime you have put the big flounder, whole, into a dish—a kind of flat dish which can go in the oven. Your oven has been heated to a good 400°—Put a lot of butter on your flounder, and pop him into the oven for as long as it takes you to make a *roux* of an ounce of butter and a rounded tablespoon of flour, which you mix gently into your fish broth on top of the stove until smooth but *never thick.* Pour this over the flounder in the oven, and leave just long enough for the sauce to bubble and clear a little. (Note— almost everybody overcooks fish.) Remove it from the oven. It is ready—At this point I hear you ask, "Well, whats so different about that?" and I reply *"Nothing!"*

But now, you lift out your feesh onto a suitable platter—and you mix into the sauce about 2 ounces (or more, plenty of caviar!) of the very best caviar—fresh if you can get it, very quickly and lightly; then you put your fish back in it and spoon the sauce over it and (I wrote *him,* but that seems too personal, somehow) and mess it forth, as the medieval cook books say. At the last, you have worked quickly and it is all still perfectly hot, but the caviar must not cook, of course—the sauce should be abundant—

There are no herbs or wine nor excessive seasoning, not even black pepper, in this Platter. It is concentrated yet delicate pure natural flavor, very slightly thickened, and then that strange surprise of caviar coming *after* the first savor—If Albert Premier didn't decorate and pension the fellow who thought it up, he was simply not the king I thought he was—Don't be shocked to hear that I ate this delicacy with *Frites*—fried potatoes, but *Belgian* fried potatoes, like no others; they fry potatoes as other people roast chestnuts, or pop corn, and go about the streets eating them hot out of paper cones.

Maybe you'd better have Baked Potatoes, or just crusty *hot* French bread.

x x x x

Well—your story of how your friend read "Circe"† to you at New Years gave me such a picture!—I saw a sunny room with a winter landscape glittering with light at the windows. There was even a fire-place with a leaping fire in it—and half a dozen of you—Now why? You mentioned only the reader and Hew and yourself. You didn't *name* Hew because of course I'd know he was there—and the whole scene, the mood of the company was as fresh and untroubled as Homer's world! For the *Odyssey* is Comedy—no matter how many tears, how many shipwrecks and other disasters, how many deaths of heroes, all all is going joyously to the happy ending—Happy? all those slaughtered suitors and the fifty servant-maids hanging with their feet twitching "like little birds—" Yes, this is a comedy and everybody's end no matter what, is a part of the purifying ceremony for heart and mind—I'm happy to know about this reading—You know it was so mutilated by the magazine that published it first, it was nearly without meaning. I restored it for The Greeting,‡ but *still* I wished to write in long passages from notes—and shall yet, but there was not time—I hope to do this yet—and isn't it most beautifully presented? That marbled paper! The dark sea with foam capped waves and the blood of heroes and monsters streaking it! About the type—I wonder, too! Let me know what you find out! ———

Just had a letter from Dorothy Deflandre at the Foundation. They plan to move me to Brussels—but first, they are paying my hotel here, and are getting ready to send me to the South of France for a vacation. They seem to say 3 or 4 weeks. Can you imagine? And even these two days here of quiet and warmth and food have nearly restored me! I wouldn't have been so bitter about McAgy if that news came now!—but do you know, whenever I attack *anybody* for *any* reason, even my best, most sympathetic friends always take up for him—When I was married to Albert Erskine, I asked him once *why* he never supported me when I attacked somebody, and he said simply—"I feel that anybody you attack needs

† *"A Defense of Circe"*; *cf.* Collected Essays, *pp. 133–40.*
‡ *KAP printed "Circe" in the form of a small book as a New Year's greeting for her friends.*

help!" This brought me up short, and I did realize how furiously unjust and outrageous I can be when I do turn on somebody. I am sure you are right about McA.—even if you were not, I still didn't need to try to pull him up by the roots and throw him in the fire—but the truth, or as much of it as I can grasp at the moment is, that he began by not keeping his word and causing me simply frightful effort and expense at a crisis when I was already about to cave in with worry and fatigue—So you see, I was quite ready to blow up at a second run-around which came again at a time of illness.

Well angel I am sorry and I hope you will forgive me and not form a severe judgement on my character. I have had a terrible struggle with my own temperament, and at this point I can only say, I should love to be good, really good, and I do try, but God! It sometimes looks like a lost cause! I do know there is such a thing as a just and righteous wrath, and anybody not capable of it against certain wrongs simply lacks a faculty—but it is pretty difficult to raise in its pure state about one's own wrongs—It really belongs to the long war in defense of others—I hate certain evils quite simply and without apology—I hate them and I fight them and shall—but that shouldn't get in the way of my containing my rage when somebody, poor devil, not in the least knowing what he is doing, strolls by, and adds that last straw to my load! Angel, I'm going just to cut this short! Otherwise, nothing to stop me just going on for another eleven pages. Bless your heart. Kiss dear Hew for me, and my love to you both.

Katherine Anne

I'll give you the new address when I know what it is.

473

To Donald Brace   Liège
                               30 January 1955

Dear Donald:

. . . . Of the changes taking place at Harcourt Brace I knew exactly nothing except that some important re-arrangements were being made, and your account is the first I've had and shall no doubt be the only one. It sounds like a radical re-organization all right, and if you are pleased with the new regime, why certainly I am; and indeed, it looks as if the firm were taking a nice long new breath, for just yesterday on about a day's notice I signed the agreement for the paper-covered re-print of a selection of my stories for HBCO; my only regret is that it can't be a big volume with all three books rolled into one, and that it couldn't have been done several years ago. But that was only my wild dream and is no doubt beside the point. I'll settle for this; though I wrote to Catharine that I thought the selection was limited, I should like *all* the southern stories; that is, besides the six under the heading *The Old Order,* and "Old Mortality," I want "He" and "Granny Weatherall"—they'll help give backbone. I should even like "Magic," the New Orleans story, a kind of little low-life gloss on the gay New Orleans Amy knew, and would you please mention this, if you agree, and speak to Catharine about it? The way it is now, the selection seems a little half-hearted, incomplete.

But just the same—I'll be pleased to have more readers!

                               With my same love—
                               Katherine Anne

To Robert Penn Warren   Edith Cavell Hospital
                               Bruxelles
                               4 February 1955

Dearest Red:

. . . . Eleanor did tell me about the new baby, and I am wondering if you really have had the naming this time? I love

474

Daniel, Gabriel—either will be fine, I always liked Ezekiel and
Zachary, too. Its been a long time since I knew any boy named
Gabriel or Zachary. I love Theophilus, too—For a girl you can
hardly beat Eleanor—it is a royal name . . . Then there are unusual
but pretty ones like Chantal, Bertrade, Amparo, Antonia, Marina—
Duchess of Kent may have made this a little fashionable, I don't
know —and sweet little ones like Suzy—remember your character
who thought *all* women should be named Sukey? Not a bad idea
at all!

Oh you are right, boy babies must be nurtured carefully so
Rosanna may have the widest and most varied pick possible . . . But
if your next is a boy, you will find that your sex has, in infancy as
well as later, an indefinable but very real charm—for women, at
least. (If you have not known this already?) The real advantage of
boy-and-girl, sister-and-brother is that they get on to each other's
quirks of temperament early; They can't say, "Nobody told me"
when later on the other sex turns out to be intractable! (as it will,
as it does.)

Just think, I have time to be writing a letter by hand. I should
be doing that "Flowering Judas" piece. But it is all in notes in a
wicker basket trunk at the Club, and the typewriter too and I'll do
that while I'm waiting for an apartment. Its just I've been so bedevilled with travel and change and trying to lead three or four lives
at once—I have engagements for Paris—3 separate rounds, one at
the Sorbonne—Rome, Spain (not set *where* yet) Brussels, Ghent,
Utrecht, Rennes, Dijon, Grenoble, Luxembourg, Lille—I can't
think where else—and though some of them were postponed just
now—they are all supposed to come up again. I forgot Stockholm
and Copenhagen. I just read poetry or one of my stories and talk
a little as I go—It goes here just about as it did at home; in fact,
my dream of a lecture a week at Liège and then time to write, has
gone to hell utterly. I simply can't *physically* do that much! I signed
the contract with Bantam just the same—Donald Brace held it up
considering co-publication for three months, then decided against
it, just three months wasted—but I mean to do it, and on time. Bless
you for suggesting it to me! They have been very nice. . . .

The thought of your father suffering by himself because he
didn't want to be trouble to any one is very painful; and must be
to you. It was very heroic and characteristic, maybe he did what he

wished to do, it takes very pure courage, surely above all at that age, to know death is near, and not ask any one to know what is happening. It is customary to say, one is born and dies alone. Not true about birth, at least, which mother and child most certainly share, and not just in the body. Death is a solitary thing, yet the living *should* take their part in love and help, there is a sharing and how happy you must be to have been told even at so late an hour, and to have been with your father to say good bye to him. I love his toughness of spirit, but he shouldn't have expected *you* to be tough about him. But then, I remember the wonderful passage in *Brother to Dragons* (Red, I keep thinking of that title as *Blood of Dragons!*) when in his father's company the Poet had begun to understand the nature of happiness—I am sure everything was clear and right in his mind, but I understand the nature of loneliness. . . .

> Love again
> *Katherine Anne*

To GLENWAY WESCOTT Gallia Palace
[postcard] Cannes
  20 February, like April in
  Texas! 1955

This hotel is delicious Edwardian rococo and I love it. Should be at the Embarcadère in an hour but the *Andrea Doria* is not in sight—12:30 noon all ships are late on account of storms. It storms here like mad every night, and glitters and shines, all blue, all day! But the harbor is so choppy 3 little American gunboats moved over to a quieter corner last evening. Will see you soon.

> Love
> *Katherine Anne*

To Edith Sitwell   117 East 17th Street
                                  New York 3, N.Y.
                                  24 March, 1955

My dearest Edith:

The splendid *Collected Poems* came to me in Liège at a moment
of the utmost darkness, the morning star suddenly shining through
the cold and murk of that dullest of towns, and my long slow giving
way to illness. So imagine! the book would have been enough, but
your inscription and above all, the dedicated poem—such a gift
would make happiness happier, but in that special time, it worked
miracles of healing! And my little song—"Pomona's Daughter"—
I'll never believe it is not one of your diviner lyrics—delights me
to the heart . . . you could never have chosen one for me that I could
like better, and altogether, it was a gay surprise: I had never
dreamed of such a thing. So bless you forever!

I had to resign from my appointment as Lecturer at the University of Liège, and come home, and once here, must be quiet and
take treatment getting ready for a very uninteresting *surgical inter-
vention,* as my Belgian doctor says it; God knows I shall spare you
my symptoms, and would indeed conceal the whole disgraceful
episode if I could, except that now and then it seems better to
explain a little why I am somewhat in hiding for the present. Ever
since I have known you were here, I looked forward so much to
seeing you again; I hope you are staying on for a long time, and
in any case at all, I mean somehow to see you, when the more
boring aspects of my enslavement to doctors orders are past . . .
Meantime, I work on my collection of poetry, to be published in
the fall: am trying to finish a new story, and do odds and ends in
the two or three hours a day I am allowed to be up and about. I
have been reading *Letters* of W.B. Yeats—very incomplete but a
fine gloss on his poetry and "public" history: and here is a passage
that you may know about, but I have never seen nor heard of it until
now: (this is on page 776, letter to Wyndham Lewis, September,
1930):

"Somebody tells me you have satirised Edith Sitwell. If that is
so, visionary excitement has in part benumbed your senses. When
I read her *Gold Coast Customs* a year ago, I felt, as on first reading

The Apes of God, that something absent from all literature for generations was back again, and in a form rare in the literature of all
generations, passion enobled by intensity, by endurance, by wis-
dom. We had it in one man once. He lies in St. Patrick's now under
the greatest epitaph in history." For what it is worth, let me say I
cannot quite agree with him about *The Apes of God*—but it pleases
me to have agreed with him about you, all unconsciously until now;
for I wrote almost the same thing—in more words of course! just
about twenty years later, even to seeing re-born in you the Swift
grandeur and justice in wrath . . .

My dear, this is only a way of saying, I love you, and I am glad
you are here, within speaking distance at least,

I'll write again as I am able.

Katherine Anne

To Paul Porter   117 East 17th Street
                                        New York 3, N.Y.
                                        21 May, 1955

Paul darling,

. . . . The sad news is that George Lynes was operated on
yesterday morning, an exploratory operation, they called it; and of
course as we all feared, George too, it is cancer, and already so far
spread over one lung they didn't even try to operate, but closed up
the wound, and there is apparently nothing further to do but nurse
him and wait for the end . . . It is really a shock; I had dinner with
him on the 2nd of May, and at that time he told me he had been
spitting blood for the past ten days, and was going to see a doctor.
On the fifteenth of May he called me and said he had been in the
hospital a week, being given all sorts of tests, and on the 16th I went
to see him and took him flowers; he seemed very quiet, and said
they couldn't make up their minds and were going to perform an
operation just for a look. And yesterday morning it was done, and
this morning Russell told me the bad news. I had called the hospital
over and over, and got nothing but "satisfactory" but this morning
the nurse hesitated on that word, so I called Russell . . .

Paul, on the 16th the doctors dismissed me in effect, and I felt so wonderfully well I walked all the way from Park and 77th to York Ave and 68th (to the hospital) and on the way stopped to buy flowers, a mixture of green-streaked tulips and little blue and yellow irises; and then passed a little Catholic Chapel, St. Jude's I think it was, and just for luck went in to light a candle for George—and walked straight into a funeral, with the coffin lying bare at the foot of the altar, and I listened to the Mass for the Dead, and I cannot tell you how painfully it struck me, though of course it is a little Chapel in the hospital district, and no doubt a funeral in it every day. But years upon years I have been stopping in at strange churches at all hours and in many countries; and I just never happened upon a funeral before, except in St. Denis, (near Paris) more than twenty years ago!

Well, darling, it is on my mind because he is an old friend and a very faithful and affectionate one, and he was forty six years old this last April 15th, and for the first time in years I did not observe his birth-day . . . That is much too young to die, and I am appalled at the ordeal he has before him—but I shan't write any more about it . . .

You stop smoking, do you hear me? No back-talk, just quit. Don't do as I do, but as I say, this time! Give up all the half-way measures, and quit. . . .

With my same love,
your Dutch
Aunt Katherine Anne

SECTION 9

Southbury
August 1955 to June 1958

I write of the base aspects of human character out of a loathing of it, really—yet it is there, all mixed in with the good and the desirable.

        Katherine Anne Porter to Seymour Lawrence
        April 5, 1956

WHAT KATHERINE ANNE PORTER CATCHES IN HER LETTERS AS *she works on her novel looking out on the Connecticut countryside is the sort of thing Henry James caught in his notebooks. And there among her birds she says, "I am a Franciscan." She asks her editor to save a good writer who is mildewing in a New England writer's colony. Seymour Lawrence does, and the book he published of Tillie Olsen's stories is still in print. Between letters of encouragement to fellow writers ("We are here to believe in and help each other") she goes on a barnstorming tour of fifteen cities for a little nest egg. She links arms with Janet Flanner in the academic procession at Smith College. As the degree of Doctor of Letters is being conferred upon her, she hears, "She has made for herself a unique place among American writers of fiction with short stories and longer tales . . . The best of them are among its permanent classics."*

To Glenway Wescott   [Roxbury Road
                                Southbury, Connecticut]
                                4 August, 1955

Glenway darling,

Your letter to me, and Eleanor's letter to you, and your letter to her gave a lovely effect of a three-cornered conversation. I added a note to your letter to Eleanor and it is going to her this morning. I did forget to tell her about the irises.

I am sitting in a glassed-in sundeck upstairs where I have established my workroom, and have green landscape on all sides (but one, after all!) and this house is beautiful and amiable in a modest yet somehow ample way. Paul came down with me and stayed three days and worked like a longshoreman, and left me perfectly installed and in order, even waxed and polished far beyond, not my raising, as we say in the south, but my habits of late. It is a misty cool day, and I feel well and happy and hopeful for the first time in so long, I had begun to fear my melancholy was rooted in some incurable sickness of character, but no—it was sheer continued misery at my dreadful way of living . . . I need at least a presentable house in a reasonably good location, and I can, apparently, do with the lack of a good many other things. I want you to come and see me. I have a really elegant guest room: I asked Paul to choose anything he wanted and to set it up just as he pleased, and he did, and I am really house-proud about it! So come and sit down in it soon.

You remember I said, at Stone Blossom, that no small consolations or ameliorations of any kind could any longer help me: I had to make a change from the foundation. And this I am doing, have indeed done a great deal just in the massive move to this house and the settling down to solitude and a facing of this table and this machine by eight o'clock in the morning. This morning, earlier, but I had slept enough . . . I do not know if Monroe's new system will work with you, it would drive me mad in two days, because I want desperately to write, but I cannot if my mind is so distracted and my time so shattered as it has been. Now, the days are tremendously long and slow and there is no sense of loneliness or isolation. I can hear the motors on the road at the foot of the hill—the New

York bus goes by my driveway, dogs bark, far away—cows go moooo from time to time, the birds keep up an intermittent sweet little twitter: but there are thrushes and robins, and now and then, morning and evening, they sing their whole repertoire like opera stars. I love them.

You need to find, somewhere in that house, a workroom that no one has occasion to pass through or come near. And no one to ask anything of you until two o'clock in the afternoon. You know perfectly well what it takes: uninterrupted meditation and long hours of steady work. These are *impayable* luxuries for the most part, and several times in my life I have had to rip myself up by the roots and take to a strange place where I can get something finished before the world catches up with me. I am going to defend myself here against all the familiar threats . . . I have begun my career of saying No to invitations, for example. And so on angel. Don't let me be a bore.

But do let me say out of my long love of your work and faith in it, that I hope some power in you may operate to put you to writing again . . . some change of heart or mind. We do change, thank God, even if only going on to become more or less than what we were before . . . I have to stop darling. I am doing a little preface for a translation of the *Retrial of Joan of Arc*, [by Régine Pernoud] *has* to be in Harcourt Brace's office by the Fifteenth next, and I have barely three pages of rough draft, and I don't fool myself anymore that I'll strike it out red-hot at the last minute as I once did . . . No, this is steady labor, and I must get to it . . . Bless you for liking the "Adventure" . . . [This became "St. Augustine and the Bullfight."] I realize I didn't say enough about Alypius and his career. I am mending that error in the version I mean to send to John Lehmann . . . I mean to write a number of incidents in my life in that way . . . it is what I can do now, it satisfies me while I am working on it . . . Not a word was changed this time by any editor, I was so outraged at the mayhem committed on "Circe," I made it a matter of life or death that not a word should be changed. But I shall add some! Bless you! How does Barbara do, now? I called the hospital the day of the operation, they said she was "doing very well indeed." I hope so!

K.A.

To Gertrude Bechtel   [Southbury, Connecticut
                                     September 20, 1955]

Gertrude darling:

Tuesday, 20 September, 1955, seven minutes after five afternoon here in the East. I suppose about half past three in Texas, and
Paul's funeral took place—will take place at four o'clock Texas
time. So I sit here struggling with Time while we are called once
more to look as well as we can into Eternity following the new
ghost—oh what a tired little shadow my brother was before life let
him go! I think of his soul as a small fiery particle flying away from
us; already, for him, death and not-being-born are precisely the
same. I had not seen him for so many years, and the news came so
suddenly, just when I began to believe the good news about the
operation was really going to go on being good, and the funeral is
taking place so hastily, there was no question of my going home;
and though it is very sad crying by oneself in a strange house my
brother never set foot in, yet—and I don't doubt this is selfishness
bitterly as I ache in mind and heart, I still am consoled to remember
him as he was before the long supplice of his dying set in. There
was nothing I could do, he did not miss me; poor man, he was
swamped and deluged and God knows I think, almost literally
smothered to death in family, yet God knows too he loved them
and he could not have lived either without them. Yet, at this very
hour, I should be there; this is the momentous first death that breaks
into a generation: we have come a long way together, the four of
us, not a circle at all, but a real squared arena, so like each other
in small irrelevant ways, so deeply unlike in everything that makes
for happiness in a family. It is not really the first death, but the other
little boy died at fifteen months just a few days before I was born,
only Gay remembers him dimly. He was only a name, and a little
ghost I saw once when I was two years old. We four were the
family, and look, until yesterday we were all living, our years being
from 63 to 70—all five of us born in just six and one half years,
imagine! My mother was a reckless woman determined to have her
family all at once, as she said; all our lives we children knew one
thing for a certainty—that our mother wanted us, and brought us
into the world against all kinds of worldly and sophisticated influ-

ences and advice. And now her children are beginning to go home to her . . .

Gertrude angel I have cried so much about Lily I would have said I had no tears left; yet there is something in his death that comes nearer to me than any other I ever knew except my niece Mary Alice who died when she was six, this last 19th of July, thirty six years ago, and this year the first time I did not remember her anniversary; but we have been spoiled to living! I do not know how to reconcile myself with the death of one of my own . . .

There is something I want so badly to say, but I am not saying it at all, and you must forgive this wandering strange letter. Last night sitting here, I had a frightful fury of suffering, it was all I could do to hold myself from tearing my hair and howling like a beast; I did finally get enough control to allow myself to cry aloud—I felt safe in my empty house in the middle of a twenty acre wood and meadow, nobody could hear, nobody would come.

I talked to my sister Gay this afternoon, you know how wonderfully calm and composed she can be, and how deeply and fearfully she feels everything; and I said, "Oh, it seems so strange to be without him!" And my sister said, "Honey, you know me—I believe we've still got him." Isn't that superb and lovely? And I asked her why she couldn't just take a plane and come up and sit around with me until she got bored—she gets bored pretty easily, more especially with her family, much as she loves us, all of us—and she said, No, "I'll come up next spring, or if I don't, I'll send my ghost—that is all you lack there, no doubt."

Sunday about noon, 25 September

No it is now the 29th of September, Thursday. I had just begun to take up this letter again when I was called to the telephone, and though I cannot now remember what it was, it was enough to distract me, send me onto something else. In the meantime, I had got a call from New York to tell me of the death of my old friend and publisher of twenty five years (last spring was the anniversary of them planning to publish my first little book.) He was Donald Brace of the firm of Harcourt Brace . . . it is so very strange that these three bonds, each so strong in its own way, yet in no way comparable except that each loss has touched my life on the quick, and will make such changes in it as I can't even imagine, should happen exactly from the 20th of July to the 21st of September this fateful year. I am sorry darling, but my shock is beginning to benumb me, I can't work, or write letters; yet don't sleep, don't want to see any one just for the present; and yet wander about idly lost and wretched when I am alone . . . Paul came straight back from the funeral, and he said it was *wonderful,* grand, beautiful, he had been so afraid of it he was tempted to run away; but now his father's whole life is shaped and ended so harmoniously by this death and this farewell: so then, we spent the week-end planting tulips and pruning the roses, and pulling weeds and getting flower-pots ready for more bulbs: I cooked and we ate well, and listened to music, and gathered twigs and driftwood and made fires, and sat in the evenings over our whiskey and talked and remembered; and the edges of the wound began to draw together and to heal a little, and we will never forget this time.

. . . It is now about 1 o'clock afternoon, 4th October, and I have always left this unfinished letter in the machine, have written no others nor anything at all, no matter how urgent or important it might be. I have been quite passive, indifferent, to any practical or worldly affairs, childlishly clinging to little human things and small daily pleasures. On Sunday my dear old friends Cleanth and Tinkum (Edith) Brooks and John Palmer came over from near New Haven, and I did a big old fashioned mid-day Sunday dinner for them: pork roast—half a fresh ham—with sweet potato puree, hot home-rolls and currant jelly and plenty of gravy and little golden squash very delicately cooked with sweet butter, and baskets of fruits with five different cheeses, and this was the first real dinner I have given to friends since I came back from Europe. Alas we did not have the stout burgundy, the only wine that can stand up to such a combination of food, but cocktails before, beer with, and whiskey afterwards, before the big fire in the large many-windowed room that lets the whole lively landscape in; actually it is windowed on all four sides, but the open outlook is to the north east, and east to southerly, which would be thought a very bad arrangement in our country, where southern exposure is considered the only possible one. But here, it works; the house is on a hill with famous scenery on all sides, and no matter where we see the sun, it is welcome. Well, we were very warm and gay, a re-union; and I am going over to them for the next week-end. They are on the Yale faculty—John Palmer edits the *Yale Review,* Brooks is

something important on the Faculty of English—I can never remember titles—and the Brookses, being Louisiana born, have
bought themselves a 300-year-old Connecticut house, and it is a
marvel of beauty and comfort. Palmer is native of Tennessee. I
don't suppose it is really odd that nearly all my best friends in the
east are all southern by origin. We just gravitate towards our own,
and I think it is a good instinct we should never deny or frustrate.

Then, yesterday, my darling Anne and her husband and first
little boy, David, who is now very nearly three and one half years
old, drove over and took me to the Danbury Fair, and it was merely
wonderful. . . . They gave me a beautiful present—a gyroscope,
which even now, an hour ago, while the bread was baking, I sat and
spun and watched with great pleasure: and I thought most of Lily,
who never lost her delicate taste for just daily life, who went in the
kitchen and cooked something pretty for her darlings almost at her
last day. And oh, how keenly your words about her struck me as
truth almost beyond words—how all the time, "a very strong un-
dertow was pulling her out of life." I feel that it was exactly her own
marvelous prescience that warned her that the time was near—and
that she went of her own will and pleasure to the hospital, (and how
beautifully I see her every moment to the end, through your eyes,
but my own memory too) and that she took her death out of the
house purposely, just as my brother did. He insisted on being taken
to the hospital at a certain point, though no one believed that death
was nearer than it had been on many times before: and both of them
died when no one of the family was present. Death is loneliness in
its purest form, and they met it alone; oh admirable and heartbreak-
ing!

. . . . I loved your sweet telegram, and I love you. Gay tells
me your suit is on hand this minute, and I hope with all my heart
that you win a good round sum, enough to keep you in that state
of elegance which is your divine right. I'll never forget my friend
George Platt Lynes' stare of astonishment at first sight of you—at
our party, remember, in New York—and his remark: "She looks
like the Empress of Austria!" He meant Elizabeth, the arch-type
Empress; judging by her photographs, I told George I thought you
were more beautiful than she: and he said, "Well, its all I can think
of for a comparison!"

Tell me how you are. After all, you were badly crippled in an accident, and you hardly mention it, and you never complain of anything. Complain to me a little if you like—or no—if you had wished, you would have, long ago. I love your sense of grandeur and nobility of feeling, my love, I am glad you are exactly what you are, and please *do* outlive me, because when you leave the world you will take with you the virtues and graces that always were rare in the world but are now nearly disappearing. Or does it just seem, as one grows older, that the hoodlums and the hooligans are really winning the day? When I was young I fought them, bitterly; and I cannot see where I fought. They have over-run the field! Just the same, I know who and what I am, and I know you, too, and I do not really believe that your sort of human being is going to vanish . . . or let me vanish first, and never know.

Angel, it is just two weeks since I started this letter . . . such a time it has been. Bless you,

Katherine Anne

To SEYMOUR LAWRENCE   Roxbury Road
                         Southbury, Connecticut
                         29 October, 1955

Dear Mr. Lawrence:

. . . . About my wish to make a change in publishers, and your very tentative offers in that direction, I must say this, that my publishers object very seriously to my going, it is a habit with them to think of me as a permanent property of HBCO, and while they have made some offers of change and progress in my affairs, still not enough for me, because too many old remnants of habit and ways of thinking still cling; and at this point, even if they did everything I wanted and more, I still have no sense of renewal or promise of action; there comes a time when change is necessary.

I have talked with the President and the Vice-President to-gether, and they gave me a sketchy verbal report on my advances there: they will not dream of giving up a single published title, that is final. There are four unfulfilled contracts, the novel, my journals, I think a book of stories and another miscellany on the order of

The Days Before . . . The sum I owe on these is something over five thousand dollars. I have asked them to mail me the exact figures, but this is near enough to reckon on. What I must have in addition: $2,500 in cash on signing of contract, and $400 a month for 12 months beginning on the first of the month following the signing of the contract.

My royalty runs 15% from the first copy sold straight through. 10% to the publisher of moving picture rights, etc., the usual foreign and translation and reprint rights, standard contract approved by the Authors League; and one immense clause that I thought up for myself, and I believe that I am the first author in this country at least, to have won this most important point—*no book you publish of mine shall be allowed to go out of print during my lifetime.* This has been the secret of my survival, for HBCO has never advertised me to any extent worth mentioning, or ever departed from their belief that I am a writer's writer who cannot expect to have sales. I believe I may have had the best most friendly press of any writer in this country, though, and by insisting that my books be kept in print and available, little by little I have accumulated readers . . . So this is one clause that must go in any contract I make anywhere.

Now sincerely I wish to make a change, but not unless I go to something better than I am leaving. There are points that I have omitted which you may bring up or not as you please: what I have mentioned are *my* points, the things I must have, and any discussion we have in future must be based on the fact that they are unchangeable, and a minimum. We must have everything clear as day, and perfectly understood, by everybody concerned.

There is one thing: if you decide to take over my contracts, (unfulfilled) from Harcourt, at least two of those projected books were planned so long ago, they have grown out of date, in a way, and you may want to talk about other plans and projects I have in mind. There is always the huge history of Cotton Mather, of which I have eleven chapters, three of which have been published in *Hound and Horn,* years ago, and two chapters later in *Accent,* and are throwing around somewhere; even if we don't make an agreement about publishing books, maybe the *Atlantic* monthly would be interested in my three main chapters on the witchcraft scandal, in which I really do feel I found something rather generally overlooked in the histories of that time. (But this is an aside.) I want to finish the Mather book, the novel, a book of occasional writings, and a collection of stories, long and short. That is for the present all I have in mind, and it could very well turn out to be ALL. So let's not go further until this is cleared up, providing we ever start out at all!

This is as near as I can come at the moment to giving you a clear look at the situation. I think what I dread most is a dreary bargaining, and I beg of you, all concerned, to consider everything well, and decide, and let me know, one way or another, so I may feel settled and get down to steady work.

I'll be happy to hear from you about this.

Sincerely yours
Katherine Anne Porter

To SEYMOUR LAWRENCE   [Southbury, Connecticut]
29 December, 1955

Dear Seymour—

Just this afternoon, 5 o'clock, the mysterious express package was brought to me, after due notices and all, and how could I on my Connecticut Hillside entirely surrounded by nuthatches, snow-birds and squirrels, even dream of a Magnum of Bollinger Brut 1947? It was the most heavenly surprise of my entire Christmas-time for I could not imagine what it could be, (aside from something from a Vintner!) nor who could have sent it. And the noble presence of it will be quite enough to content me for some time to come—I shan't really want to drink it until some special and beautiful occasion.

Please thank everybody concerned—Please let me know all your names!—and let me praise you for knowing that nothing could have given me more delight and gayety than this delicious gift!

Blessed New Year to all of you

Katherine Anne

TO JAMES F. POWERS   Roxbury Road
                              Southbury, Connecticut
                              Christmas 1955

Dear Jim:

. . . . If I am to tell you simply how marvellous I think these stories are, [*The Presence of Grace*] it has to be ink, and I hope its not unreadable—The grain of your mind and the set of your temperament have a long time ago declared themselves—You have a thumb print, as clear and unmistakable as Mozart's, let's say—I believe I could pick a sentence by you out of a grab-bage! Easy and firm, tough and finegrained. . . .

And please tell me about my Katherine Anne namesake, and her birthdate, and how old she is and what do her parents think of her now, and she of them? . . . .

I have this house for 2 years—Have also left HBCO and gone to Atlantic Press—Little Brown—off with the raggle-taggle Beacon Street gypsies O! Finishing my novel at last, you'll be glad to hear! . . . .

With my admiration and love and greater hopes than ever for you!

Katherine Anne

TO JAMES F. POWERS   Roxbury Road
                              Southbury, Connecticut
                              7 January, 1956

Dear Jim:

Our Katherine Anne is beautiful, and my nephew Paul, here for New Year, remarked that she seemed to have my coloring when I was starting out—black hair, grey eyes, white skin; Irish, in fact. She's prettier than I was, most certainly, but still, I believe our coloring was the same. I hope she is as intelligent as she looks, and I still would like to know the exact day, month and year of her birth. . . .

For a year I was in University of Michigan, until July 1954. September 1954, off to Belgium, University of Liège, Fulbright lecturer. I had been assured that I should have one lecture a week, and all the time in the world to write. Of course, there would be an occasional invitation to lecture before various Belgo-American organizations, or European Universities, but only a very few, and acceptance was not compulsory: I was free to refuse whatever did not appeal to me . . . So I was set down in a horrible dull suburban flat where I froze among furniture that looked like the Belgian version of Sears Roebuck 1905, with the most primitive housekeeping devices, a five dollar taxicab drive away from the center of Liège and the University. My lecture was on Thursday afternoon. The outside invitations began at once, and became a landslide: Not only half a dozen Belgo-American clubs in as many cities, and the P.E.N. clubs and Women's Cultural thing-amajigs, but four Embassies, besides the universities of Madrid, Copenhagen, Stockholm, Paris, the Sorbonne—series of three—Rome—five days—Brussels, three times, besides Luxembourg, Utrecht—five days—Antwerp, Rennes, Grenoble, Lille, and that is all I remember. Between each lecture I was supposed to beat my way back by plane across Europe to make that Thursday four o'clock lecture at Liège. Well, needless to say, after a short course of climbing railway stairs, catching planes on windy fields, carrying my luggage, eating and sleeping when I could, and being exposed day after day to hundreds and hundreds of people all fresh as tigers, I blew up. I resigned. I spent some time in a Brussels hospital, the most delightful place I remember to have seen in all Europe, this time. The Foundation was charming, sent me home by way of Cannes on the *Andrea Doria,* saw me off with kisses and flowers as if I had covered myself with laurel, and happily I had been able to save enough from my 11,600 dollar wages at Michigan to afford a real old-fashioned break-down and rest cure . . . and with what was left, I got up and a friend helped me find this house and I moved in on my last dollar and last ounce of resolution, took it for two years and a possible three; broke free of Harcourt Brace after all these years (Donald Brace died last September, and there was no one left I knew there, no reason to stay) and though they were not willing to do anything for me, they were also very unwilling to let me go; it took all kinds of trouble, but I got away. And am settled very profitably and happily with Atlantic

Monthly Press—Little Brown, on an adequate regularly paid income, advance on royalties of course: and with nothing on this earth to do but deliver that novel next April fifteenth, which if I live and I do expect to, you may consider as done. So much for that . . . I hope this hasn't bored you, but all these years you have known nothing about what was happening to me, and now you DO know, and whenever you want to know anything else, ask me, for I am the only living human who can give you the straight of it . . . I not only know what is happening, but I've got all the papers to prove it! One thing, I did meet some delightful new people, I was beautifully treated everywhere, and if I had been based in Brussels I believe I could have stood the gaff. But I wasn't, and it was all very wasteful. Just the same, I took a helicopter out of Liège on December 21st last Christmas, to Brussels; took a plane to London, read "The Circus" on BBC. Took off to Rome by air, spent five days there, seeing friends and sights, (and returned to the fold for midnight Mass at *Ara Coeli*) then to Paris for New Year, my first and as it turned out, last escapade, the only time off I took. In Paris I went down with influenza, and by January I was invalid, in bed, then to hospital, and so by easy stages back to New York, everything lost except, so I can only hope, honor.

What I want to say to you is this: please if you have not already, begin sending your stories to Russell Lynes, on *Harper's Magazine*—managing editor. Say I advised you to. I shall write to him, if you don't mind. It is not a favor nor an obligation you will take on. We are here to believe in and help each other, and I have had wonderful help, and was glad of it, and remember it not with a sense of burden but of happiness that I had friends. I take any help I can get from anywhere, and so please do you do the same . . . Send something to Cyrilly Abels, *Mademoiselle Magazine,* 575 Madison Avenue, New York 22. I will write to her or talk over the telephone as we do now and then. She is managing editor. I should think Carmel Show on *Harper's Bazaar* would like your stories. I can't speak there, though, as we fell out a good while ago when she accepted "The Leaning Tower" and then tried to have its vitals cut out before printing. I took it back, and though she has asked me for stories since, I haven't sent anything and shan't . . . but try her—you know these magazines watch the little magazines and are apt to take what they take! This is what the little magazines have done! Edward Weeks, editor of *Atlantic Monthly* is very friendly to me—they celebrated my coming to Little Brown and Atlantic by sending me a magnum of Champagne, Bollinger Brut 1947, which I am still hoarding for some gay occasion; I'm sure he knows you, and they pay about the same as *Harper's*, but I think not as much as *Mademoiselle* . . . Have you tried the *New Yorker?* I have for twenty odd years now made what turns out to be a career of refusing to send them a story, because during Ross's time they wanted everything re-written so it would all look as if it were written by Ross . . . This policy seems to have been changed, but it is too late for me to change, I think, and there is no need, really—I have done nicely without them, and they me, though I could paper a room by now with their letters asking me to send them a story. Well, all the young ones, and some of the best, are sending things there now, and the pay I'm told is splendid, and "Blue Island" could have gone there, if I am any judge . . .

You know what I am trying to say: it is time for you to make a little money with your writing. You have grown into your style, your point of view, I think you are safe from writing anything but what you wish to write, (as nearly as any of us can) and though we are all corruptible, I think perhaps you are not in much danger now. I suppose I should wait to give all this advice until I KNOW what you have actually been doing, but—well, have you ever thought of Princess Caetani's *Botteghe Oscure,* 32 via Botteghe Oscure, Rome, Italy—remember that place? She pays well, but wants to print first, remember . . . I think you are a wonderful short story writer, and I want you to get into circulation . . . The time is simply here, and with your book coming out and all. Please let me know what you think about all this . . . I am going to stop more or less abruptly and go to work again. If you have occasional writings, essays, criticism, articles, all these editors are interested in that sort of thing too.

A happy New Year to you and Betty and Katherine Anne and the three little ones I don't know yet,

Yours,
Katherine Anne

Are you teaching? Where, if—What you say about Allen's newest progress in his Career as Convert does not surprise me! But then, almost nothing does!

K.A.

To Eudora Welty   Roxbury Road
                                       Southbury, Connecticut
                                       20 February, 1956

Eudora darling:

Your *Place in Fiction* brought me the pure pleasure I always
have in reading anything you publish, and also something wonderfully timely to read, that is, something good and clear and true
about your discoveries in the art of novel-writing, your considered
point of view as to its practise: and all so vivid and *gay,* so beautifully illustrated—the little night-lamp, Eliza and the forty hounds
of confusion—how you do clean up on *that* picture! the examples
you give from other writers of what you mean, all all delights me,
and doubly because it came just when I was in the middle of an
attempt to explain, in a few well-chosen words, the sources in my
life of "Noon Wine." I promised this to Robert Penn Warren for
a collection of some sort he is getting together, and my God, I can
compare the process only to tapping my own spinal fluid, so nearly
does it come to the quick of memory, that is, numberless memories
all fused together, sometimes no more tangible than dust-particles
floating in a sunbeam; but the real difficulty is explaining how, by
the organic process of creation, the scattered and seemingly random events remembered through many years become fiction, that
is—not a lie, really as I think you call it—but symbolic truth. I can
only hope I am being a little less dull and more explicit in the piece
I am writing. Place as a brimming frame: place as sense of form; as
equilibrium—I am enchanted with the way your mind works it all
out. I like your little side- blow at some of the new novels: confes-
sions, rather than communications. I used to call them "case-histo-
ries" and there are now several little paper bound periodicals
devoted entirely to this dreary school of couch-mutterers.

Bless you for writing it in the first place, and bless you for
sending it. I hope sometime you will make a collection of these
pieces: next to the *Odyssey,* perhaps it is about my favorite reading
matter now—but there is so little of it, these lovely sparks flying off
between the hammer and the anvil of a good writer's main work
. . . I hope you'll feel like doing a lot of them. . . .

I think our pieces about Circe so near together a strange coincidence—after thinking about it for some 15 years I finally got to it in March 1954 in Ann Arbor.

> With my love
> *Katherine Anne*

To Seymour Lawrence   Roxbury Road
                                          Southbury, Connecticut
                                          5 April, 1956

Dear Seymour:

I am in a low frame of mind because I have just been called a "thoroughly vile woman" by a man who signs himself Marc T. Greene, American Foreign Correspondent—perfect stranger to me, from Thomaston Maine. I give you these particulars because by now no doubt he has cancelled his subscription if he had one to the *Atlantic*.

He took frenzied offense to only one phrase, really, (I shall leave you to guess which one. It *is* offensive, spoken by an offensive character, and I meant it to be so.) Then says: "This magazine once stood for the culture, dignity and excellence in letters of New England in its full flower. Under the present editorial direction it has sunk a long way from this eminence"—but, in effect he never expected you to fall so low as to publish anything by "a woman who is so thoroughly vile as to write anything like" the phrase he objects to, and he is not only startled, he is shocked.

The handwriting looks like that of an old man, and I could easily believe he is remembering the dear dead days when dear good William Dean Howells advised dear good blessed Mark Twain to "take that swearing out" when either Tom Sawyer or Huck Finn said "damn?" or was it the phrase "they comb you all to hell?" Well, anyway, some very great writers have got along nicely with not a bawdy scene or crooked word, and others as good have not. And I have too often been revolted by the nastiness of certain writers—Norman Mailer comes to mind first, but there are plenty others; but not because they see and write about the baseness and cheapness of life, but because *they know nothing else,* or will not admit the truth of anything higher. I write of the base aspects of human character out of a loathing of it, really—yet it is there, all mixed in with the good and the desirable: I have some very good people on my boat as you'll see, and some utterly wicked ones, but mostly a mixture of frailty and virtues of one kind or another: and I think I shall have just to go on the way I'm going, and take a chance on shocking certain people—who I believe do go on think-ing of literature as one thing and life as quite another, and I have got the two so identified in my mind, I wouldn't know how to begin trying to separate them. Well, let me remember that a Catholic reviewer once called "That Tree"—I think it was—"obscene" and added that obscenity was very unbecoming to a woman. I think so too—in fact, I think it is very unbecoming to anybody, but it exists, and I'm dealing with a boatload of mixed characters who think they are only going to Europe, but they are really going towards the Judgement Day. I called the two installments in the *Atlantic* "Ship of Fools" because that was my original title and it is based on a medieval morality "Narrenschiffe" literally ship of fools; a parable of course of the voyage from this world to the next. Well, I'm sorry if the *Atlantic* loses friends and subscribers, but it is done now!

I am working steadily along and will mail you another batch next Monday morning.

All my best wishes.

Yours
Katherine Anne

TO SEYMOUR LAWRENCE   Roxbury Road
Southbury, Connecticut
Sunday, April 29, 1956

Dear Seymour:

You have somewhere among the papers connected with this novel an outline of the latter part, taken up from the point I had then reached, which I made by request for somebody who was considering it for the moving pictures. After reading the outline, he changed his mind. Please read that again, for I have not changed from my original plan, and I doubt I could explain it much more clearly today. I am sorry somebody there seems to be worried about the plot. There is no plot: there is only a theme which is illustrated from every point I am able to command, over and over and over, in a series of sub-plots or incidents which keep the characters in movement and the theme developing as we go. I am sending you an "author's apology"—this in the old sense of this word apologia pro vita sua which I wrote when I began and in less than three months of enchanted work and freedom, I wrote the first 175 pages of this book; expected to have it finished in another three or four months. Was interrupted by some unmanageable personal catastrophe—my life then was terribly at the mercy of my domestic situation which caused catastrophe—and so I was interrupted for a year, then seized a brief breathing spell from work I did to make a living—teaching, reading, writers' conferences, lecturing in Universities—the same old rigmarole of the writer of my sort, doing my writing on the margin of my time and energies, when every other thing expected of me had been performed. So finally I had to break off, in despair, at the 229th page, and until now, fourteen years later, I have never been able to go on with this novel. But in essentials it was finished then, for I am simply doing a very little re-touching as I go, and putting in the transitions and connective tissues between long finished passages written then. As you notice, I said then I was not going to bring this novel up to date, and I still do not intend to: the scene of this story is *then* and *there,* (as well as here and now,) in the sense that people are still as wasteful self-centered, unloving, and illusioned as always (yet with their virtues, their strengths, their hopes!) and though on one level this is a parable of political action—no party or system is named. And though it is a parable of the ship of this world on its voyage to eternity, it is also literally a ship with a name and destination which sailed from Vera Cruz in August 1931 for Bremerhavn on a 27 day voyage. I wish you could find some one there to read it and describe it from his point of view, let me see it and I will try to help with suggestions. I am unable to do the page you ask for. I have taken this day to answer letters and to refuse requests to do this and that and to refuse invitations, but the real worry has been about this page for the catalogue.

Please keep this Author's Apology and return to me after

you have finished with it, if it is at all useful to you, as it is my only copy.

It delights me that the readers there have curiosity, I do not break off purposely to excite it, I just work along until I have just time to do the pen-corrections and make the Monday morning mail so you will have fresh ms. on Wednesday.

About corrections: Page 20 line 8 from the bottom. (About Denny's claim on the lower berth:)

The lines read: "There were two strange suitcases and a battered leather bag open on Denny's berth, the lower. At least he had been promised the lower berth, and he was going to have it."

For the sake of clarification, change to:

"There were two strange suitcases and a battered leather bag on Denny's berth, the lower. His ticket called for the lower, and he was going to have it; no use starting out letting himself get gypped."

I hope that will settle that!

Page 78, line 26: "Indians not got enough to eat" is a Jewish turn of phrase. I am very familiar with this argot, and I wish this distortion to stand. It shouldn't sound right, its all wrong and meant to be.

Page 94, line 21, Should be "Any sort of man so long as he was young" which is another idiomatic phrase. Let it stand.

At nine this morning I had a long distance call from Mr. Warburg, who wants to come to see me next Sunday morning. He is coming by train to Bethel, then I have to send a taxi from Southbury to pick him up and return him to his train, and as the nearest restaurant is about nine miles away, I shall have to make lunch; and in the meantime I shall have to do a little house cleaning and shopping, and oh God, if Mr. Warburg could dream of what trouble he is bringing me, he wouldn't, I know. I see no earthly reason for a personal interview . . . but don't give a hint to him—as if you would! if you see him. At any other time in the world I should be delighted to see him. . . .

Thank you for your letter.

Yours
Katherine Anne

To Seymour Lawrence   Roxbury Road
                        Southbury, Connecticut
                        2 May, 1956

Dear Seymour:

Your text for the catalogue does boldly this: it praises my work as I should never dare to do, even if I were vain enough, which I am not. It would be absurd to deny that I believe what I write is worth writing or I should never take the trouble: but only I can know how far short it falls of my aims and hopes. So it is better to let some one else do the judging, and especially, the advertising. Thank you!

You will see that my changes are few but decided. The word *brute* humanity to describe the people in the steerage. A good artist is down there, a carver of little wooden animals. He is coming up in the next installment. A truly wildly noble, disinterested act of heroism and suicidal charity is performed by a Basque in the steerage—the only act of the kind in the whole book.

At the risk of being called a horrid name like Feminist, I object, always have, to being called a *woman* writer; men say this I am sure without really knowing they are making a faintly derogatory discrimination: they do after all set the standards, nobody can deny that, and to say I am considered the most distinguished *woman* writer is to say I am not judged by the great standard. If I am distinguished, please allow me my level of distinction in the first-rank company. I am not ashamed to be in the company of Emily Brontë, George Eliot, Virginia Woolf, but they certainly belong in the company of Flaubert and Turgenev and Henry James and—make your own favorite list. I consider *Wuthering Heights* the purest act of genius in the world of the novel; nobody male or female has ever beat Emily Brontë at that! So it is not contempt of my kind, nor of their level of gifts, but just simply that I must be judged as an artist, and not a woman artist. How does it sound to say, T.S. Eliot is one of the most distinguished men poets, etc? If you really believe I belong in the first rank, then don't please put me by implication at the head of the second.

Enough of this trite topic.

Your copy is wonderfully accurate in its description. There is one point, but maybe its too late to put it in: one thread of the multiple-ply theme is the blindness of people to what is going on around them: we were on the edge of world-catastrophe, I felt the very earth of Europe shake under my feet when I stepped ashore, but then I had been a little prepared to disaster through my political experience in Mexico—I already knew about Mussolini, and a little but not enough about Hitler. And on this ship and everywhere in Europe it was appalling to see how people just resolutely refused to look about them or to think about anything: and of course, most of them were incapable. It is this I try to bring out without saying the words, in all the episodes of personal unkindness and even cruelty, the stubborn prejudices, the religious opinions, the reciprocal and destructive hatred between Jew and Christian, between one Christian sect and another, the political and economic cross currents—All this. It is an enormous order, and though it has been sixteen years since I began writing it, in all that time, with this period included, I will have managed to get in less than a full year's work on it altogether, due to pressure of teaching, editing, doing all sorts [of] distracting and exhausting work in order to make a living. It is practically a one-draft work. But I am not offering an apology for anything. I doubt I could have done better if I had all the time in the world. I would only have finished it many years ago, which I suppose doesn't matter at all.

Well, I should be copying away at that novel instead of talking about it!

Thank you for your letter. All my thanks and good wishes for your kindnesses and especially this fearfully difficult business of writing the catalogue note. You did wonderfully.

Yours
Katherine Anne

To John Malcolm
Brinnin
Roxbury Road
Southbury, Connecticut
2 May, 1956

Dear John:

I *am* a Franciscan, did you not know? For years I belonged
formally to the Third Order, which is the invisible member of the
three orders of St. Francis; that is we live in the world and take no
vows, but try to keep a Franciscan view of things. But now of course
I am a mere backslider, as the Methodists say, and so far gone in
unFranciscan wickedness, I find all those literary converts such a
crashing bore—beginning with Evelyn Waugh, to Graham Green
to Caroline Gordon to my dear Edith (Dr. Dame) Sitwell, with all
between, and their name sho nuff is Legion by now—I would have
to stay out of the church just to keep out of bad company!

But as to the sweet and blessed birds—did I tell you how the
little hellions fought each other over the seeds—and suet, though
there were pounds of it every day, and squared up to each other
like boxers, throwing their one and one half ounce weights around
in perfect recklessness? Well, as I say, the sweet little birds make
it easy to remember St. Francis again, and even the squirrels are his
creatures, though I did have to stop feeding them and shoo them
off my tulip beds. I didn't exactly stop feeding them, I began
distributing heads of chopped lettuce a good distance away from
the tulips and they took the hint. There is enough wild greenery
now for them, and the swallows who built a nest under the eaves
of the front porch last year are already back and have built another,
throwing out the debris of the old one on the floor. I am hopelessly
sentimental about swallows: when I began to renovate South Hill,
we had to hold the work up until a swallow in the eaves of the
summer kitchen could lay her eggs, hatch her young and teach them
to fly. But I said to the carpenters, "We will not start by disgracing
this house," and do you know, those charming fellows agreed with
me, one of them said, "Oh, we weren't going to disturb her!"

I know perfectly what I am doing—I am gossiping with you
when I ought to be on that Novel; and I am deliberately holding
off on the birthday visit because that gives me an excuse to write
more . . . Now then, I think 16th of May will be lovely. I meant

to have a party with champagne on the 15th, but two friends I wanted are getting off to Italy, another is on a lecture tour, another, so far as I could make out from his recent postcard is in Persia, why, I do not know, and you cannot get here till the day after: and of my projected guest list, that leaves two. So I am calling it off. I have a magnum and a jeroboam of Bollinger 1947 champagne, which I am hanging onto like grim mad for a suitably grand occasion: I'd open the magnum, but I doubt we could drink a quart of champagne apiece, even in a long evening. I'd hate to try it, frankly, much as I love the dear stuff. In fact, because I do love it I don't want to abuse it. So if you like it, I'll get a reasonable sized bottle for our little evening. But your offer to bring a steak from the Pride of Texas halts me, for that takes a good dry Burgundy, big and booty! And I have all kinds of Bourbon and a collection of liqueurs and aperitifs and gin; I think if you bring the steak that is more than enough.

I'll get one wine. If the weather is right, we'll broil the steak outside on my little but nice charcoal grille, and we'll have fresh asparagus and if we hold out long enough, I'll make crêpes Suzette, or tell me if you prefer cherries jubilee. I've got the real makings for either.

I don't know how far you are away, but should we have dinner very early, like half past six; when should you be going back? I'd hate you to come for a little pleasant visit and be tired and sad the next day. That's no good at all. So let's be *sage* and you tell me what hours you will need to keep. But I'll be expecting you to get here about 5/—afternoon, of course, not a.m. (Remember my Dylan story?)

Wish me luck. I am sending bales of novel every week to Seymour, who is merely an angel of consideration and helpfulness and courtesy and continual interest in this job, and he does help to keep me going when sometimes I should like—I like to think!—[to] lie down and die of sheer fatigue . . . It is never true, of course. It is just my extravagant way of saying I'd like a day off sometime from being a writer—even those days and even years I didn't write a word, were not holidays from writing, after all. You know what I feel I would like? I wish I could make a little money and have some things I want, and give parties for my friends, and have a twenty-two carat emerald ring—emerald my birthstone—and all my clothes made by Fontana and that Irish Romantic what is her name? Connolly? Sybil! and be free to get up and take a plane to any part of the world on two-hours notice. If I could do all this, I could afford to hire a housekeeper, so I expect that is what I would do—hire a housekeeper and sit down and get out that book of long stories I have in mind.

Now I am day-dreaming, so goodbye until the 16th of May, when I shall have with good luck begun another year in this long life of mine!

> With my love
> *Katherine Anne*

To Daniel Curley
Roxbury Road
Southbury, Connecticut
25 June, 1956

Dear Mr. Curley:

. . . . Have you got enough stories together to make a book. . . . There are a lot of publishers around who publish them now; as for me, I am all for the inexpensive big-edition paper-backs. What I want is readers—don't you? If you will tell me what you are doing in this way, I'd be glad to suggest names of those likely to publish your work . . . I don't know that I could do anything, but I can try, and would like to. And don't feel obliged to me any more than just in the way of human courtesy, because we are here to help each other, and I have had so much and so generously given, I was made to feel it was their pleasure; and now I believe this, for it is a happiness to me to be able to do any smallest or greatest thing I am able for any one whose work I admire and believe in.

What occasioned my card is this: I had put up your name as my candidate for a Grant—annual affair—from the National Institute of Arts and Letters, and the Secretary wrote back that she did not know your work, and I want lists of your stories and where they appeared so I can refer the Committee to them. This is the longest kind of gamble, and yet sooner or later you will have it, I am certain of that. Maybe I am being premature, because certainly after you publish a book it will be easier . . . And I would not have let you know what I was up to, in fact I should have asked Kerker to keep it quiet, for there is no good in making scenes and then having plans fall through! I didn't know he would pass it on to you. It doesn't really matter, does it? It is sometimes a little like a Guggenheim—some of the best writers have to be put up again and again; happily, committees change, and the judgement of one year will be reversed by the next!. . . .

Thank you for your good friendly letter.

Yours
Katherine Anne Porter

To Glenway Wescott   Roxbury Road
                         Southbury, Connecticut
                         Saturday afternoon 7th July,
                         1956

Dear Glenway:

Your letter was left in the postbox when mine was picked up for the mails, so they have crossed as usual, but yours has some new things I should like to answer somewhat. I have been in a frightful trough now for weeks—one day following another in the dying hope that I am going to find courage really to grapple this long last dark passage to the end of this devilish book.

Next day, morning. I am at such a point in the matter I can hardly drive myself to this typewriter even to write the most necessary letters; even to write letters I WANT to write. I am horrified at the passing of time, at the responsibility of my promise to my new publishers, at the deadline I have already missed, and what remains of the novel to be written—the stacks of notes and the outline, I mean—look to me just like so much waste paper! Yet it is not that I have forgot what I meant to say—I know it all too well! . . . and I have had these cavings-in of the psyche before, and always, always recovered; so I have had hopes this time too: and indeed, have not lost it altogether yet. This state is always accompanied by a physical lassitude, perpetual weariness, a wish to stay in bed and read and sleep—nothing more. I lose interest in food, and wish only to be unconscious, oblivious—yet if I said I wish to die, it would not be true. I wish to live—yet I have a strong tide against it apparently that runs very far out to sea; I'm sure that twenty analysts and psychiatrists could give twenty perfectly plain, logical explanations of my state, none of them in the least creditable to me! For myself, it is mysterious, for I can give reasons too, but there is something beyond, that analysing neither explains, changes, or helps. I still have nervous choking and vomiting fits—not nausea at all, just pure contraction.

Well, I find I have quite warmed up to this dull subject, and it is not what I started out to say.

No, Olivet 1940 wasn't my first conference: Olivet 1936 it was, during my first visit back to the U.S. that early spring; in the summer the Tates mentioned me to Joe Brewer who invited me, and I went in a picnic sort of mood, never dreaming it was the beginning of years and years of that sort of thing. Brewster Ghiselin has invited me twice to Utah, but I have not been able to get there. And to think you were there *now,* you might say, and reading my stories and talking about me, keeping me alive and real to all those people; and I should so like to hear you read those parts of "Noon Wine" you read to them. I am not sure what the half-page of my note-book in Ghiselin's *Creative Process* is, unless it is taken from a longer passage published by Jay Laughlin in *New Directions,* I think 1940: can't remember quite. And as for my letters you mention, darling, I can't remember either of them, nor what I wrote, nor on what occasion, but am still able to say, no matter what it was, I meant it! But it would be interesting to know and sometimes you must let me see some of my letters to you. I have all yours, and we have covered a good deal of ground in our colloquies. . . .

Bless you. With my love.

Katherine Anne

To James F. Powers   Roxbury Road
                       Southbury, Connecticut
                       20th July, 1956

Dear Jim:

. . . . Do you know, I learned a good while ago that utter solitude, trying as it can sometimes be, is entirely preferable to dull company, or the wrong kind of company. And I haven't a TV because I know how awful most of it is; nor radio, because all it ever offered was music and the news. I don't care anything about the news, and have deliberately freed myself of it: I don't even read a newspaper. And for music I have my collection of records I began in Paris just twenty four years ago. This stripping away of what now seem to me non-essentials has probably something to do with age; I didn't miss much, as I look back; missed nothing that I really wanted. Saw and heard an awful lot of all sorts of things—can't account at all for the fantastic variety and unbelievable *levels* on which my life carried itself out; and don't really feel the need to. Only, for several years past, I have suddenly felt, while reading, listening to new music, looking at a picture, examining a fashion magazine, or even just talking to some one, that I have been there before, I've *had* this already, really no good going over *that* again! Ah fatal sign of long-lost youth no doubt . . . and high time, *too*. But I will tell you something and you can remember it later: the old things go to make room and give you time for the new things that happen to you, you clear out the worn things to give space to the new clutter, you have no sense of having lost anything because it was ready to go, finished; and you are finished with it. And to think, nobody told me this—I had to find it out for myself. And people go on being so uninstructed about this important thing. Not long ago, a youngish doctor—about forty—when he found out what I was up to, the amount of work I was doing and planned to do, and how I had never dreamed of ceding anything to age and infirmity, said to me very sweetly, "But Mrs. Porter, as one grows older, one must learn a little resignation!" And I asked him honestly, "Resignation to *what?* I haven't got anything to be resigned to!"

. . . . I'd love to talk shop with you, especially about the Novel as an Instrument of Torture, and how I wish you would write a piece about that, out of your heart's blood as it would have to be, and print it somewhere. It would find readers.

You know, I never had anything against short story writers writing novels, if they wanted to or felt they could, or should. My whole argument was against a short story writer being compelled to write novels when he didn't know how, or wasn't ready. If you really do find you are a novel writer, I shall be delighted. You are already a short story writer, if you never write another your place is made. My stand is childishly simple—we should all write what we can or like to write, in any form we are able to write. I can't re-write much on my novel: I just polish it up a little while I am making the three copies for the publisher from my first draft—the last quarter is still just in notes with long crucial passages fully written, I am making pontoons from one island to another; I don't think my style or method has changed much—but some day I will tell you what is new and what is old—if you can bear it!—and ask you if you see differences, or where the parts have been joined together. I feel that I just fall into that mood, that way of thinking, in which I began it: and I have passages actually copied literally from my diary of the voyage, together with new stuff written only last week . . . I don't know what this proves, if anything. It is only a fact.

I did so enjoy Auden's lecture, which came this morning. My three favorite poets (living) are John Crowe Ransom, Auden and Robert Graves—Ransom first by far, the other two about even. I know of no gifted human being of whose morals, manners, whole way and conduct of life, I disapprove of more entirely than I do Auden's—I think he is perfectly awful. And how I love his poetry, and his choice of other peoples' poetry, and all the workings of that crooked, powerful, opinionated mind. I have known him off and on, here and there, for years. He once spent a week-end with Albert Erskine and me in Baton Rouge, with that appalling Chester Kallmann, then a raw evil boy. He was charming to have around the house, sock feet and all. I don't think he cares for me, work or anything else, and I don't in the least mind. Yet he should trust me, on his own grounds, for I passed his four test questions, not knowing his answer; and yet do not consider myself a critic at all. Well, my test of a writer is when he interests me so much I'll read anything he prints! Auden is one of a half dozen who pass that test without trying. . . .

Don't have a literary agent . . . You can do everything by yourself and no doubt better than any one could have done it for you . . . I have none and never had; I think it much better to make your friendly arrangements with each editor on each story: they feel nearer to you and get a personal interest in what you are doing. Agents seem somehow to me not quite human . . . I have one for moving pictures etc . . . and much good he has done me!

Best to you and all in the house.

Yours
Katherine Anne

U. of Michigan, faculty and students were wonderful to me—One of the hardest worked years I ever spent, but I wouldn't have missed it. I made *all* my students read your stories—They were best sellers there! One thing—generally the young men students like them better than the young girl students. I wondered why, but neither could explain.

K.A.

To Mr. Daniel Curley   Roxbury Road
                            Southbury, Connecticut
                            18 August, 1956

Dear Mr. Curley:

. . . . It is somehow consoling and pleasant to know we all have about the same experiences in writing: over and over I have thought I could surely never write another line, and once or twice it was just the beginning of something new. I do a lot of brooding away from the typewriter, and then go and put it down in a great burst of speed. But it is the most wonderful thing of all that as you work, you do warm up some centers of energy and imagination and find yourself doing something you hadn't proposed and much better than anything you had planned.

I like to think the humility of those rejected authors is a little better than the confessing Communists: what they need in youth and early training is to have some sort of standard to aim for, and this most of them have not had: I am simply horrified at the slackness and third-rateness of courses in literature in even the best Universities, the what-ever-you-like-is-good kind of laissez-faire of too many teachers. It is a fact that most of them don't care for literature, or can't find out what it really is. And these earnest writers run into somebody who seems to have standards and to know what he is talking about, and their gratitude is pitiable! No, they shouldn't *have* to be so grateful, but maybe they never had anybody take their efforts seriously, and it bowls them over. I never had but two rejections, and the reasons given were so trivial that I had to believe one of two things: the editors did not know what they were talking about: or, they were trying to conceal their real opinion and spare my feelings. This was twenty-odd years ago, and time has confirmed that my first judgement was the correct one.

Well, back to work: and I do hope you are right, and that your teaching and editing will leave you still some margin for writing. Serious American writers are I think handicapped by the fact that once they have published one or two things, people swarm from all directions offering them jobs and well paid ones, to do anything but writing. So the need to make a living pulls us off the track. What we all need I think is our equivalent of Virginia Woolf's *Five Hundred Pounds A Year:* I don't think garrets and cellars or perpetual anxiety about money is any better for artists than it is for anybody else. Many have survived and done nobly, but that is no proof that the condition is good.

I have a review of Ezra Pound's *Letters* in my *Days Before.* His boldness was so delightful and I think he was astonishingly right about so many things; but to very few of us in this world is granted the blessed gift of being unable to imagine ourselves wrong about anything! For me, his company in this world in my time has been invaluable, I wouldn't take anything for having found him for myself when I was starting out all those years ago, and it used to please me when some of my youngest students took to him gladly as a contemporary.

I hope Seymour does something definite very soon about your stories.

Sincerely yours,
Katherine Anne

To SEYMOUR LAWRENCE   Roxbury Road, etc.
Sunday afternoon, 19 August,
1956

Dear Seymour:

This is a lamentable performance for a week, but it was a very sharp corner and I had some trouble turning it. I don't mean either to complain or apologize. I am finding that after all these years, sometimes I cannot myself believe in what was going on in those years—the states of mind, as you say, the Hitler mentality which was of course a natural state of mind in Germany, he was only what other gangsters used to call, *the popular* German "mouthpiece"; but in other nations as well; and I am afraid of exaggerating. And I have to remind myself that, in the light of what all of us know really happened afterward, I CANNOT exaggerate.

Never mind, or try not to: I will send you what I have got for the week every Monday Morning until death do us part, special delivery: and one day there will be a book.

I was pleased of course to think that the Readers' Subscription would like to have *Ship of Fools.* But I would like to be very sure first that my old friend Harry Scherman on Book-of-the-Month has had the refusal of it. Please let him see what you have of the mss, including this installment, and give him every chance on earth to take it. After all, it WAS the Book-of-the-Month that gathered the jury which voted me one of the best neglected writers in America, in 1937? and gave me Two Thousand Five Hundred Dollars folding money for being this, and I have never yet been able to imagine what I should have done at that time if they had not rushed to the rescue in this way. I hope to make some money on this book, so that I shan't have to worry about how I am to live, or to live in debt as I am doing now, but can be free just to know what I can depend upon and spend my time at my work . . . I don't believe that is an unreasonable hope, do you?

Thank you for your good letter about the other batch, and they will keep coming on!

Yours
Katherine Anne

514

To William Faulkner   Roxbury Road
                          Southbury, Connecticut
                          26 September, 1956

Mr. William Faulkner
Care Miss Jean Ennis:

Dear Mr. Faulkner:

I shall not make this the occasion for a fan letter. I believe you should not have lent your great name and prestige to this purely expedient political device of a Presidential election campaign. This with no hint of adverse criticism of President Eisenhower, who is a man of good faith, but who cannot in this noise and confusion, look closely into every scheme presented to him by his advisers.

I believe this is a completely artificial issue manufactured out of campaign smoke and cinders; there is no clause in this plan that the Democrats have not believed in for years and have worked hard and practically to bring about International peace and understanding by every means within their power; and have been consistently and bitterly opposed by the Republicans at every step. IF it could happen that the Republicans might actually try to carry out this plan if they stay in power, I can go along cheerfully with them without changing my vote or a single idea—it is only what the Democrats have [been] trying to do for years! I am voting for Adlai Stevenson.

                          Sincerely yours,
                          Katherine Anne Porter

To Edith Sitwell   [undated, circa Autumn 1956]
[fragment]

. . . . Please tell your brother for me how I have read again the four books of his memoirs which I read one at a time as they appeared. They belong with our small fortune in autobiographical writings, few but precious, W.B. Yeats, Henry James—André Gide—*such* different geniuses, with experiences so different too, they might have taken place on different planets—Yet they all lived, or live, writing within my lifetime, and the views they are able to give me of their worlds and their experiences most certainly have helped me to form also a much clearer view of my own—

Silence, distance, time, mean nothing to me in that climate without seasons which is my affectionate admiration for you and your incomparable poetry!! So, belated as it might seem, I only write a letter of what I think and feel always—

Yours
Katherine Anne Porter

TO GLENWAY WESCOTT   Roxbury Road
Southbury, Connecticut
1 January, 1957

Dear Glenway:

Thank you for sending me the collection of George's ballet photographs. It is a pity he couldn't have seen it, and read all those delightful things his friends wrote about him. I couldn't quite make out who did the choosing, or got it up, but you wrote about him beautifully and justly, again; and though I am pleased with these photographs, as far as they go, it seems very limited—I remember dozens I should so love to see again; and I was never able to understand what obstacle stood in the way of George's getting out a book of his own, or even two—all ballet, and all portraits, for example. But this touched me in some very deep springs of memory and feeling: I never have shed any tears for George, his fate was so hard, and the homeless wretchedness of his last months were too tragic to cry about; but I felt like weeping at sight of that strange photograph by Beaton, one I know so well, with exactly the look that I have seen so often on his face.

We had an odd kind of friendship, but it was a real one, and it lasted our time. You do know I am not one who is given to feeling slighted or neglected: yet I do think it was rather pointed (or perhaps blunt?) on the part of whoever had the decisive word in this collection, not to have let me write a few little words about him, too. Even if his photographs of me are not among his most successful, still he did make a few very fine ones of me, and it distresses me to see them disappear. But none of this really troubles me; what I grieve for is the death of a friend, and there is just a blank space in air where he was, and will always be. It does not take death to teach me that every human being we love is utterly irreplaceable, I always knew that; I am only dismayed by the finality of the separation.

I am saying what I am trying to say very badly. It is too painful to think about. My head is curiously benumbed anyway, from another round of miracle drugs—this time a sudden flare-up of a very nasty intestinal flu which I picked up on that tour. I almost cancelled the last three engagements, but decided not to when a doctor gave me something that kept me going. But about ten days ago—21st Dec., I woke up at half past three in the morning in most wretched pains and convulsive vomiting and a fever going up fast. At about ten I called the hospital and asked for a doctor; they got me one, I described my symptoms and he sent an ambulance—a bright fire-engine red one, all over gilded lettering and trimming, which turns out to be the pet, pride and community project of Southbury; kept up by public subscription and run by volunteers. (I sent them $25.00 for my ride!) The volunteers were wearing bright red coats, and insisted on carrying me out bodily though I was still able to walk, or nearly; and we tore through the wintry countryside with our siren moaning low and scaring everybody off the road. Well of course, just going to bed and being stuck with needles eight or ten times a day, intravenous feedings of some kind, and getting tapped for blood tests three or four times, was an anticlimax. But whatever they did—with the help of X-rays—it all worked and they got me up on my feet in six days with ne'er a symptom, and I haven't had any since except a slightly watery nose and a mind that doesn't like to sit down to a straight line of thinking about anything . . . I am back writing somewhat on that novel, but in my sleep, you might say—I got home four days ago (I forgot to say the gall bladder was kicking up again, and they talked a little about an emergency operation, but that passed over, thank God). I am on a nearly no-fat diet, which I find not dull, but difficult—WHAT is there to eat that has no fat in it? I am so happy at feeling well again I will cheerfully follow any rule the Doctor makes. By the way he is a *young* doctor, really young, in his twenties still, and he belongs to the latest school

of thought which has swung around nearly full circle, and he prac-
tises real materia medica and lets your psyche strictly alone, and
does not in the least believe that it was anxiety that caused my gall
bladder to kick up, but too much fat in my diet—a great relief to
me, for I do hate people scratting around in my subconscious
mind—I feel that that is one spot that really belongs to me, and
anything that is stored away there I want reserved for my own use.
Strangers just mess the place up—they don't know where things
belong or what goes with what. Well, bless this young non-pareil,
he just doctored the ailing physical organism with strictly material
substances, and the results were gratifying no end . . . He says if
I will just be reasonably careful of my food I need not have this
trouble, and gave me a kind of list to go by; why didn't the doctors
tell me this last year, or any number years before that? Sometimes
I am tempted to fall down and adore Common Sense above all
things in the universe. It *works* so nicely.

Well, my dear, I am going to spend this day writing notes to
friends—as good a start for the New Year as any. I got so many
cards and messages it was like a big warm cloak to my spirits; and
I didn't even get all my cards out—I had just got to the letter G
in the address book when I was stricken. But I mean to finish out
with little notes, because this is the sacred, the portentous time of
year when we remember each other specially and say those things
we might be too shy to say any other time, such as: I love you
dearly, my good friend Glenway, and am awfully glad you're here,
and I wish I could see you oftener, for I enjoy your company
immensely. Happy New Year!

Yours
Katherine Anne

Oh I did want to say, don't you feel badly if I don't get that medal.
I shan't. I don't really expect it. God knows I'm not in very good
company, if I can't win over that field, I should say I never shall over
any, so let's forget that question for good, once this election is over!
And I was so entertained with your account of the arguments at the
meeting—

To Marianne Moore   Roxbury Road
                          Southbury, Connecticut
                          1 January 1957

Dear Marianne:

Bless you for sending me "Like a Bulwark" for you know I am one of your most attentive and loving readers; it has been wonderful seeing "Tom Fool at Jamaica" and "Then the Ermine" *(that* with a special kind of personal feeling) "Rosemary"—and then reading for the first glorious time "Style" and "Logic and the 'Magic Flute'—" Oh what fine spare athletic noble poetry it is—some of your very best things are here; you are a better poet than you were, even.

I've had great joy of your poetry always—I have every book you ever published, and this one is going up here on the poetry shelves on my work porch with all your others.

> *blessed is the author*
> *who favors what the supercilious do not favor—*
> *who will not comply. Blessed, the unaccommodating*
> *man.*

Amen. Except I have ruined the effect on the page by not gauging my spacing properly. Sorry.

I spent Christmas week in the Waterbury hospital getting rid of a very nasty flu-germ I picked up on my reading tour—it flared up rather suddenly again and I had a fine ride in a fire-engine red ambulance with gilded trimmings. But miracle drugs again performed miracles, I caught up on my sleep, and now am in fine health but a little scattered in my psyche. How heavenly of you to give all the words of "Sentir avec Ardeur": and now I shall take its advice about les longs propos—It is always good to see you, dear Marianne, but specially nice to see you here, and I hope you will come again soon—Monroe will bring you.

My struggle with the typewriter is always an unequal one but today total defeat!

                          Love
                          Katherine Anne

To James F. Powers   Roxbury Road
Southbury, Connecticut
5 January, 1957

Dear Jim:

Your graceful white dove with the green satin olive branch in its beak at once took its proper place suspended from the ceiling beam over the fireplace, at just the right height so one could touch it now and then to see it fly; it is now put away in blue tissue paper and a good strong pasteboard box for next year, and the next, along with Eudora's big gilded star—last Christmas—and a little jewelled Christmas tree made by a friend, and my nephew Paul's decorated eggs—he blows a shell empty and then decorates according to the season, I have them for Easter, Christmas, my birthday, and so on—he is making me a collection. There is one with a very nicely done miniature portrait of me on it: and a set of little candles in brass holders with red hearts in gilded wreaths all over them: Malcolm Brinnin—I haven't had the heart to light them, though. Maybe next Christmas! But your beautiful white bird flew above all of it and the cards and the messages. My Swedish nephew-in-law admired it too, and knew something about it to tell me: that it is carved out of a single piece of wood. I *might* have found this out for myself after a while, but I hadn't until then . . . I had to be very hard-hearted with my niece's two little boys, aged four and a half and two years, who could hardly be restrained from standing on a tall kitchen stool and hauling it down and tearing it apart. But I won—its still intact. . . .

What really got me to this typewriter was your "Footnote to 'Footnotes' " for Leslie Fiedler. I had read his piece on the rather random assortment of fiction he had chosen, apparently, and much resented his patronizing airs and the sheer dishonesty of his side-stepping into irrelevancies to avoid reviewing you justly. But let me tell you, I do not share your expressed respect for Fiedler or any of his works: I detest and despise him as man and as writer more than anybody I know or have known for years. I think he has a mind of the most total crookedness I know, and a nature entirely incapable of generosity and therefore incapable of any clear judgement in literature or anything else. I first noticed him by way of that really disgraceful bid for notoriety, what I call the Raft piece, you must have seen it—and again, his defense of the Rosenbergs—these two are quite enough, but he compounds his infamy every now and then. Alas, I am stymied, for I had just got my sleeves rolled up and the notes taken, meaning to skin him so far as I am able, about the Raft piece, when he includes my *The Days Before* in another one of his grab-bag reviews, and tried to brush me off even rather more than he did you. He remarked that my notions on Whitman and James were "standard." If he knew anything about writing in America for the past thirty years, and had noticed the date line on my *Partisan Review* piece, he would have known that when I expressed these notions, they were by no means standard. I was glad of your letter to him, and I praise your restraint and decent manners, though they will no doubt both be wasted on him. Yet I am glad you have them and use them, and I believe quite certainly that you will outlive him nicely, and that is the main thing!

Well, anyway, I never did finish my piece about him, because I knew well enough it would be set down to pique and female fury at having been dismissed with a derogatory phrase; and I saw no point in getting into any kind of hassle with some one whom I do really consider a very inferior and mischievous sort. So I did nothing, but I am so pleased that you did; and if you really like his fiction, and I am bound to believe you do because you have said so, and why would you say so if you do not mean it? I am sorry merely because I find it as poor and shabby-souled as all the rest of his stuff.

Your defense of the *New Yorker* as a good place to publish fiction is also timely. This is a mere hang-over from the days of Harold Ross, when his aim was to have everything read as if it were written by a syndicate: he did tamper, and he did throw off by it writers like me, and a good many of us, who wished to write our own stories instead of signing something re-written by somebody else. It still seems a reasonable point of view to me, and I have put up quite a fight with more than one editor, and have at least won my own personal battle, and hoped I was winning something for some one else, too. But with Rosses death, that is changed altogether: and though I refused for twenty years to send anything, I should like to have something to send now, and maybe shall someday. They still invite and I am beginning to make vague promises.

So poor stupid Fiedler in his eagerness to be malicious, really is bogged down in a very deep ditch of the past; and I'm all for leaving him right there.

I should at this moment be scratting through all the tangled records trying to find out how much income tax I owe—I always finally turn it over to a CPA but there is still preliminary work that I must do—and of course, I should be writing on that novel—but as you see, this does not stop me from writing you a long letter— don't be discouraged, it doesn't call for an instant answer, if at all. This time of year I nearly go under with the accumulated fatigues and distractions, but so far, I survive: and I wish you not only survival but survival with triumph, and the appreciation that you should have. Don't let anybody tell you that glory is not glorious and an honorable aim for an honorable artist or any other honest man of gifts and feelings. This is my roundabout way of wishing you a very good New Year, and many of them, and to say that I HOPE you get the Guggenheim and that I think you never published a poor story or anything near it: I have my favorites, and several I judge to be better than the others, but that is only the natural thing; you really do keep a high level; and I wish you a stouter heart against those editors who don't know your best from your next-best; don't let them kill you little by little—not even one cell at a time. They should not have that hold over you; please believe first in yourself and then in your friends who love and admire and believe in your work.

Yours
Katherine Anne

To Glenway Wescott   Roxbury Road
Southbury, Connecticut
9th January, 1957

Glenway my dear

No, No—those jays are the Furies, never trust them, never be deceived by them! Superstition or not, and who cares? surely not us—in these very days that the blue jays are raiding Stone-blossom (someday I am going to get that lovely name written *right!*) and raids are all they know, I have had a plague of them! Last year, I began feeding the small birds and the squirrels after the winter had really set in; and the winter last year was much colder than this winter until now. So the blue jays had evidently migrated; I did not see any until just before spring, and then only a few. My heart sank at the sight of them, even one blue jay is too many, and three then looked like a plague; but this year, I began early, and the jays simply stayed on. Little by little they have over-run everything, the bird feeding station where they grab all the suet and all the sunflower seeds, and now they have discovered the squirrel feeding ground and eat all the peanuts! The squirrels have put up a fairly good fight, but alas, they can't fly and they haven't sharp beaks and claws. Given their disadvantages, they have a wonderful strategy of simply whirling in circles and leaping on the spot, they cannot quite be chased away but they don't get much to eat either. I am sitting here at the southwest window—a corner window that faces east-south-west all at once, and the squirrel feeding ground is exactly before my eyes between the three large maples on the edge of the drive-way circle. I seem to have no guests and this well warmed room full of light and a good solid table seemed going to waste. So I have come in here to work instead of heating that glass-porch by electricity, so very wasteful, after all. But I see always that predatory kind of bird thieving and raiding and gluttonizing everything in sight, and I am afraid my real desire to get a twenty-two rifle and simply wipe them out, a murderous impulse, after all, is getting into my novel! Last year, when the little sweet birds I want to feed and save were all gathering in great flights at the seed table, I looked up one day and saw the hawks hovering in pairs above the meadow and little woods to the north, and it came over me with dismay that I had simply drawn the little birds together to make easier hunting for the hawks! But the little birds were skilled and quick, and we know they can make common cause and chase a hawk away—we have seen that together, right at Mulhocaway. And in some way, I cannot hate a hawk—it is a noble kind of bird who has to hunt for living food in order to live, his risks and his privations are great. But the jay! There is no excuse for his existence, and there should be a bounty on every ugly hammer-head of them!

No, dear Glenway, they are the Furies, and I should know them when I see or hear them—

But just the same, the little birds and the squirrels manage to salvage something, and the chipmunks too; and of course, the moles, who will cut the stems of my tulips through next spring when they are just at their best bloom. Well, I have not thought of any effective thing to do about Jays, but I already have a strong poison to administer to moles as soon as the snows melt and I can see their ridges in the ground.

Further gardening notes: William Maxwell had that famous garden in Mentor, Ohio, send me a yellow damask rose called Golden Wings. I had lunch with him and Frank O'Connor way last spring in New York, and we talked about roses, among other things and he said he would like to send me this one. It came early last fall and was planted richly and thoroughly on a point of the flower bed to the southeast and west where it will get sun yet be sheltered from the north. I planted a hundred tulips; and I have two great French lilies that grow stems four feet tall and bloom in clusters of eight and ten; and hundreds of irises and peonies were already here: and I set pots of white narcissus which are now in full bloom: and a friend gave me a pot of lilies of the valley and they are in full bloom too, downstairs, along with three flowering azalea trees, very shapely and blooming like a basket of flowers instead of trees . . . white and pink and pale red . . . So I must send away and get two Amaryllis, and here they are in the window near me, making a great effort to put forth: there are disadvantages to living in the country, even under such nearly ideal conditions as, in our very different ways, we both have; but I do live better where I see things growing, and I love the clean pure air and the silence; I suffer sometimes from the loneliness of separation from my few but beloved friends; and I find it sometimes a question how to keep my time and energy defended from certain kinds of people who try to attach their empty and unattractive lives to mine in one way or another—people I am surprised to find on the same planet with me, much less in the same house. They are sometimes as rapacious and hard to fight off as bluejays—but I have developed a severity of rejection I did not know I was capable of. And then too we are all brought up on the Christian and noble idea that we have no right to deny our lives and substance to any one that seems to need either or both. Never was a fonder delusion, or more wasteful and reckless. Because each one of us with some gift, or margin of plenty of any sort, can pour the contents of twenty lives down as many bottomless pits of need, destroying ourselves without trace. Yet, I reasoned once, that I have had help, a good deal, too, and it *was* help, and I used all of it, in the end; and those who helped me were taking a long chance—they could easily have been feeding the bottomless pit!

Well, where am I going? All this from your charming three cards saying the jays had come, reminding you of my reading "Noon Wine" with the Furies chattering and shrieking and squawking in the summer trees; I remember it very well . . . But I did not in the least imagine that you remembered in such wonderful symbolic terms . . . I am afraid I just thought, "damn those birds!" and kept going . . .

I am getting back a little sense of life very slowly; being faithful to doctor's orders and—is this a sinister sign, I wonder?—not missing any of the forbidden things at all, being very content with my limited, childish diet, it all tastes very fresh and pure and besides, I know now what causes my dreadful pains, and am happy to do or leave undone anything that will help me avoid them.

The best news I could have had for this year is that you are really not only writing, but beginning again to publish. This not only because it will be a life-giving thing for you, but will bring me I hope a fine batch of my favorite reading matter. It is in that diet that I suffer a prolonged famine.

Next morning: There is another heavy snow—my dear Hottentot couldn't get here, and yesterday the oil truck that refuels the 500 gallon tank under the house, and accounts for summer weather in it, stalled on the stony brow of that hill and though I watched them from the window and prayed fervently for them, they backed down slowly and went away. I looked at the tank meter—it is a little less than half full. I don't intend to give it another thought, or pray about it either.

—I find it hard to end this letter, because there is something else I want to say, but I am too tired this morning, after a good sleep, to try to put down anything sensibly. I must write to Monroe too—how could I have dreamed he had advised Lincoln against asking me for a word about George because I was busy on a piece of work? What a friend he is, and how true it is I have no business even writing letters until I get that novel off. But if you could see my mail! If I have ten letters, two will be from friends, three are trying to sell me something, and the other seven are divided between two kinds—requests for contributions to this and that cause, and requests for just almost anything—mostly asking for 500 well chosen words about how I happened to be a writer and how do I do it, as the asker is writing a piece about me—a term paper or a thesis or just an essay—and knows nothing about me or my work, so will I please write it for him? Or would I just fill out this questionnaire as the asker is making a survey of artists and "creative" writers and trying to find out what they are really up to. Or somebody needs a Guggenheim or a Fulbright (these two I gladly got into action for—good men both of them) or a young man—the umpteenth—is doing a TV or Movie version of "Noon Wine" and wants me to help him with it. Or maybe it is just my sweet Cousin Gertrude and her life-work on Hamlet, who wants me to recommend a publisher. I shall, cheerfully—but darling, if I did only just the things every day that perfect strangers ask me as a matter of course—they even call me long distance in the middle of the afternoon when I am lying down for an hour—I should be busy eight hours a day and never get one thing of my own done. I hardly do anyway, for these things burden and distract me so. And now darling, I *shall* say goodbye for the moment—that tone of complaint and objection that your brother—and a whole society—pronounce so unattractive, is getting into my sentences, and that's no place for it!

More later when I am perhaps not more clear in the head, but less crowded—I cannot see my way out of this mountain of paper!

With my love
Katherine Anne

To Monroe Wheeler   Roxbury Road
                          Southbury, Connecticut
                          11 January, 1957

Monroe darling:

This morning the thermometer on the north porch stood at exactly 10 above zero, the whole region seems to be three feet at least in snow, but the sun is shining brilliantly. And yesterday, the day for Lila to come, she called and said she was afraid to drive. I said that was quite all right. To come whenever she was able. This morning early I looked out and there was Lila slogging up that hill, her car parked below. She has made the bed, cleaned the kitchen, scrubbed the bathroom, and has brought in fire wood—filled the big basket, laid the fire for tomorrow morning—even alone, one develops little rituals and ceremonies of common life, and I have a Coffee Fire every morning, besides other little reassuring stations of the day as it goes on—scrubbed the bathroom, and is now having lamb stew and a can of beer before taking off—only half time but enough. God knows what I would do without her; and I tell you this because you know that household help is really the most important thing in daily life. It is a true slavery at best, household work, and how any one can consent to do it even for good pay is a mystery to me—but the lack of that help has nearly ruined my life more than once . . . So I am fostering this godsend, and long may she wave.

I am being careful and eating tapioca pudding—I hadn't thought of it until your letter, but I made apple sauce and tapioca and it is delicious. I do exactly as the doctor said, and though I am being a little slow getting back my grasshopper style of moving, I still do feel better, and I have never once wavered slightly in my belief that it is all worth doing! Way back in 1938 or 39 when I was living in Baton Rouge, a dreadful popular song broke out like a pox on the radio: "I loooooove LIFE, I wanna live" and I thought then how odd it was that a sentiment so revoltingly expressed was still one with which I could not on any grounds disagree. I feel more at ease with such statements when Jean Cocteau makes them. I have been reading his *Journals* (in translation, the first time I have read him in translation since *Cock and Harlequin*, in 1921 or 2: my first sight of him, and he has been my delight and instruction ever since.) It seems so odd that I should never have seen him, even by accident, at a distance, living all those years in Paris. Yet it is perhaps just as well. I liked the things he did when he was the legendary *Enfant Terrible* of all the arts, and by rumor at least in his private life as well. It all seemed exquisitely and satisfactorily none of my business, I had only to enjoy the delightful things he put forth in so many directions. When I did see him, in 1952 in Paris at the performance of *Oedipe* looking very elegant in his own idea of black tie, intoning the poetry while Stravinsky conducted his own music, it was enchanting. But by then obviously it had become a tradition for Paris audiences to whistle and jeer at Cocteau, so this audience worked up a slovenly little imitation of a riot at one point. The performance stopped. Cocteau rose to his feet and said, "If you have no respect for me and my work, at least respect Stravinsky who is a great composer!" The audience was quiet. He sat down again, and smoothed out the pages he was reading from, in perfect stillness and silence, but his face looked as if he might shed tears. It was the most touching and deep look of patience and grief I have ever seen on a face that apparently had not tightened a muscle. Then Stravinsky lifted his hand and the music started again. After that, the people behaved themselves, though, if I know Parisians at all, not from any sense of shame. It was still the lovely stuff I remembered from it seems now centuries ago, but when now and then I hear again, or see or read again, something that seemed new and glorious to us then, thirty, thirtyfive, forty years ago, it gives me a feeling of great good luck to have been young in a time when I could love and admire my contemporaries and those just a decade or so ahead of me, without having to apologize and try to make reparation to myself now that I am older.

Well, darling! All this probably because I was reading Jean Cocteau's *Journals* last night, and then this morning comes a list of distinguished foreign candidates for honorary membership in the National Institute, etc., Benjamin Britten, Jean Cocteau—(I didn't look any further, but put my big X mark YES next to his name, for not only is he my favorite foreigner but he was put up by three of my favorite persons, Glenway, Marianne, Padraic, in that order) and then I went on to see who else: I was shocked to see Isak Dinesen in that company—I know nothing of Nervi—for I read her painstakingly after all the huzza and hullabaloo, and think her not even a good shilling shocker—her stories the most contrived and empty, with the most invented meaningless endings; a tiresome kind of "literary" effort that showed the stitches at every seam. I think Louise Bogan is a wonderful poet, but not much of a critic, or certainly not of prose: and how she could name Dinesen in the same line with Virginia Woolf and Colette is beyond me entirely . . .

I am in deep deep snow, the thermometer on the north porch says 10 above Zero Fahrenheit, and Lila says nonsense, it is 16 *below zero* in front of the filling station where she stopped on her way here. (Darling, I am repeating myself about the weather, as I glance back to see what ground I have covered—I take it for a sign that this should end.) Truth is, sitting as I do at a wide window facing east south and west, I see nothing but weather in one of its more acute forms—no wonder it creeps back into the page now and again. I want you to come to see me, and Glenway and Marianne, but you can't get up this driveway now except by walking. The poor milkman, the refuse removal gent, and anybody else, has to leave his machinery at the foot of the hill, and slog up like pilgrims. So we must wait a while.

I shall—having invited the invitation—try to pull myself together and send Lincoln something about George for the book, it would really be a lapse on my part not to do this. I had of course no faintest notion that you were involved in it at that stage. Now I am told that the Institute of International Education is getting out a report on the October Arts Conference, and they say "the report is now in the hands of the Museum of Modern Art which is assisting us with the layout and design." You, they mean? Well, I am in that. They invited me to speak at the Conference and I couldn't of course, so they sent me an agenda to make marginal notes on, which I did, and Mrs. Barbara Walton of Policy Planning staff reports that "we found your remarks so stimulating that we would like to include them in the final report," and so I consented gladly, and have let them go without one word of editing. They edited a sentence, and I don't care.

Well, my blessed angel, goodbye for the present, or I'll just go on the rest of the day with this. I miss you fearfully, but that cannot be news any more, and I hope you are well and merry, and are getting nicely into a fine new year.

Your devoted
Katherine Anne

To James F. Powers   Roxbury Road
Southbury, Connecticut
14 January, 1957

Dear Jim:

. . . . I must tell you I do not know what you mean when you say you have not the right kind of mind? What could be more right for you than the mind you have? And please, that is not a question screaming for an answer: I do not intend to involve you in a long criss-cross of self-analysis: truth is, I take you cheerfully as you are, I have enjoyed your stories from the first time I saw one, and I am all inclined to go along with you, with great warmth of sympathy, and let's see where you wind up. Only God knows, it is perhaps not even our business to inquire. Ours just to do what we can.

My fault has always been—if it is a fault, and it could very well be, I am not sure—the desire, the pride, of excellence. I couldn't bear to do less than my best, and I never showed my first bad drafts to any one—I destroy my notes as I go, and no editor sees anything of mine until I have brought it to the point where I intend it to stay; and I will take the responsibility for it. But never think I am trying to claim a special courage, or virtue of any kind; this was not only the easiest way for me, it was the only possible one. I am now talking strictly about stories: I am collecting slowly a book of occasional writing again, something I love to do, and putting back all the things I left out when they were printed in magazines, because the editor wanted just so many words.

It is a commonplace of a joke—it is not a joke at all, they mean it bitterly—among editors and publishers that it would be a nice business if it were not for the authors. This goes double the other way about, I think; and I am not joking, either. . . .

Yours
Katherine Anne

To Seymour Lawrence Southborough, Massachusetts
          Monday afternoon,
          March 25, Lady-Day 1957

Dear Seymour:

I have only two questions to ask about the technic of rescue at sea by lifeboat, but each one has subheads. So I shall start with a short outline of the time, place, and situation: then to the questions—

Mid-voyage between Vera Cruz, Mexico, to Santa Cruz de Tenerife, early evening, early September but still warm weather, clear sky, and a rather stuffy second-rate North German Lloyd boat, on her way back to home port, Bremerhavn, from a long voyage to South America, a dozen ports and round by way of Galveston, Houston, Tampico, Vera Cruz and Merida, Mexico is rolling along at about 12 knots an hour, and the waters are illuminated in a limited radius by the fully lighted ship. From Santa Cruz she will stop at Vigo, Gijon, pass Brest, Le Havre, stand out at Boulogne for the disembarkation of some of her passengers, by tender. Same at Southhampton. Then on up the river Weser to Bremerhavn. Only two classes: First class, so-called (equal to about third on a good boat) and third, or steerage. About 45 first class passengers, and a frightfully overcrowded steerage. Uncovered decks, of course. This is only to set the scene, and the kind of boat. The Crew and officers ran it with perfectly good discipline and efficiency. But it was a fearfully crowded, dull little tub. The voyage, that part of it the book tells of, from Vera Cruz to Bremerhavn, took 27 days.

Two villainous children, on this pleasant evening, throw overboard a fat white bull dog whom they catch out roaming by himself, a little seasick as usual. He is the darling of a fat elderly couple. A Basque peasant in the steerage, leaning over the rail and looking at the water, sees the dog hit the waves, sink and come up again at once, and leaps without hesitation overboard to save him. Other people at the rails of both decks also see this, and set up screams and shouts; sailors on duty take one look and scurry to give the alarm.

My nephew Paul helped me on the next step. He called up a North German Lloyd official in New York and asked about signals, etc. Here are my notes from his conversation over the telephone: "Each individual Captain is free to make his own rules, his own orders, in an emergency, and anything he does is right—that is, is obeyed without question. He can also make his own system of signals. On North German Lloyd ships the signal for *Man Overboard, Fire, Abandon Ship,* are all the same. Customary order of alarm is, first, ship's bells in as loud a clamor as possible; then the horns sound more than four times in rapid succession. Captain, officers, give order through the loudspeaker, or state the nature of the emergency. Sailors take charge of passengers and life boats in case of *fire* or *abandon ship."* In this case, *Man Overboard.* Loud speaker shouts it over and over, it roars through the passageways to the remotest corners of the ship, with the steerage passengers being warned on their deck in a very funny Spanish accent. Also I have been told by a traveller who witnessed such a rescue at sea, that life-belts hit the water literally within a few seconds of the alarm, a lifeboat was down almost at the same time—all really a matter of seconds, not minutes—and the ship began a slow circling round the place of rescue, with searchlights moving slowly over the boat and the life-rings and the two creatures in the water.

Did he get it straight? It was a small passenger and—not a freighter, of course, but a heavy cargo vessel—passengers were incidental to the stuff they brought back in the hold.

(This is a landlubber's book, I am not going to pretend to any knowledge of the sea and its ways, nor try to use a sea-going vocabulary. This is the story of a lot of people on a boat going somewhere. I just don't want to make any *gaffes* about what might happen in such an emergency. So for the questions.)

1. Note. The rescue is to be complete in the sense that both man and dog are picked up and deposited safely back on the ship: except that the dog is in fairly good shape, but the man is drowned, dies in the life boat and does not respond to any efforts at resuscitation.

Question: How exactly do the sailors proceed to lift people—or dogs—from the sea into a life-boat? How would the man and the dog be delivered to the deck? The man is a steerage passenger—would he be put back in the steerage or brought to the upper deck for treatment? There was no sick-bay for passengers on this ship—only a small one for the crew. The ship's doctor, a sailor skilled in manipulating drowned men, and a priest who is passenger are waiting to look after him—where would he be taken for treatment?

And the dog—I have in mind a scene, somewhat ironical, where the woman who owns the dog and her husband—they are fat too, poor things—are weeping and embracing each other while they watch the rescue from the main deck—there are only three decks, or two and a half—the steerage, the Main, and the boat . . . The dog, very waterlogged, is too wobbly to walk, he is carried by a sailor and handed to them. The woman takes him in her arms like a mother, and slowly sinks to her knees saying a prayer of gratitude.

I am sure this is not an improbable incident, but I want it to happen in a way that no body can say—No, that doesn't happen on a ship! The man and the dog are in the same life-boat. Exactly how and where are they deposited on deck? Is it from the life boat over the deck rail, or how and where? Some one suggested that a sailor brought the dog up a ladder—the Pilot's ladder, or something like it . . . It sounds unlikely. But do give me expert, first hand information not just by an eye-witness of a rescue, but some experienced sailor who can make it all perfectly clear to me.

I believe this is all. But when I remember the six-months-long argument between sailors of all branches of service and all ages, from those who sailed clipper ships and spent their leisure making model ships in bottles, to those in submarines in World War II, about the difference between "under weigh" and "under way" (I used under weigh, in the sense of weighing the anchor preparing to sail, but many did not understand this, or think it correct if they did understand it—) and the small but acute flurry caused in the *Atlantic Monthly* by my slip about the philacteries—We really cannot exaggerate the importance of getting these details straight.

This incident is crucial, too—the very turning point of the book.

Well, I shall get on with some other part while waiting for this. But I like better writing straight on—Thank you

Yours
Katherine Anne

P.S. Personal. Your Big and Booty Burgundy, which did hold its own so well with those beefsteaks, is still here, what we left of it, and I had it put in the ice-box so it wouldn't turn to vinegar, and some day soon I shall finish it off. It was so very good and enlivening . . . When I said, in my all-out way, that I don't like this world—why, I don't, that is true, in any mood, any time of day. But I do like and treasure and hold on to a number of persons in it. What has discouraged me is simply the fact that from Mussolini and on—Franco, Hitler, Tito, Peron, Batista, Trujillo, in a rapidly descending scale to Nasser, our government has without fail backed and supported, in completely criminal collusion, every foul and stinking political dictator in turn as they rise, with the hypocritical excuse that these are all "anti-Communist." It would be wonderful if they were, but they are only thugs with no beliefs at all! What scares the boots off me is simply this—am I to take our State Department—and all the rest of the government, for a lot of scoundrels, or dupes? For some reason, after all these horrible years of our sinking lower and lower into moral degradation, greed, and the abuse of power, the very last little straw that broke not only my back but my heart, was that announcement from the State Department that they could not take any effective action about Nasser's coming back into the Gaza Strip, *because they did not know and could not find out, just what Nasser had in mind, or intended to do.*

They themselves apparently have nothing in mind, and intend to do nothing—nothing to threaten their getting concession for all that oil.

If you give this letter to some sea-going man to read—will save trouble if you do—Please cut off this part?

K.A.

TO SEYMOUR LAWRENCE   Roxbury Road
                        Southbury, Connecticut
                        3 April 1957

Dear Seymour:

. . . . Book is Divided into Three Parts—no Chapters, only Three line breaks to indicate passages of time, change of scene or characters, or both.

Part 1: Embarkation. Page 1
"Quand partons-nous vers le bonheur?"
(Baudelaire.)

Part 2: High Sea. Page 58
"Kein Haus, Keine Heimat . . ." (Brahms)

Part 3: The Harbors: (don't know page yet.)
"For here have we no continuing city . . ."
(St. Paul)

I simply had not thought of chapters, numbered—and certainly, there couldn't be any headings, or titles. I have thought of the book from the beginning as being in three parts, and their mottoes describe the movement of the book, from uncertainty—"When shall we sail towards happiness?" (You remember Baudelaire's poem, with the little ships talking among themselves about their voyages, and asking this question?) To homelessness: "No House, no homeland . . ." to the ports that seem strange as the travellers approach them—"For here have we no continuing city."

I am sending a Table of Contents which obviously I omitted—I can't find it in my copy . . . It goes—well, I don't really quite know where, but I should think somewhat like this.

Title: Ship of Fools,

A Novel
by Katherine Anne Porter

Next Page: Note on source of Title, etc.

Next Page: dedication to Barbara, with 1957 instead
of 6

Next: Cast of Characters, and list of Cabin mates.

Next: (or is it? should it come earlier?)

Table of Contents . . .

You will be much safer to estimate around 170.000 words . . .

I stopped this letter and began running through the first part of the novel, and I find it can be divided quite logically into five chapters of varying lengths . . . But the question is, why should we? Do you not think the reader can be brought up to the point where a pause or change is indicated, by a simple three-line break? I didn't want it cut up into chapters, I want it to roll along in the rhythms of the ship, of the sea, of the people walking around and around the decks, from top to bottom of the ship, in and out of cabins, and all that. I did not work this out as a plan, the story took that form and I did not realize myself this effect of constant movement in earth and sea and sky and on board, the changes of weather, and in the feelings and words of people and in the episodes—all constantly changing and folding in upon each other and falling away again—It is the way it should be, and I feel that to break it up in chapters is to lose some internal harmony that I have felt so naturally I did not even have to think about it . . . I am only trying to tell the story, and the form already exists in it . . . I know what numbers of critics think about this kind of thing, but I cannot take time to explain to critics that I am perfectly conscious of what I am doing and am not getting in a word for the "unconscious" artist . . . (if there is such an animal and I doubt it.) I can't be bothered with critics, and though I should like to make the reading easier for the reader, I don't know how, because I don't know which reader would like it easier. So try to leave out the chapter divisions . . . I think it will be charming if Mr. Kepes—you seem to think I have forgotten that memorable cover he did for last March a year for my passages from *Ship of Fools,* but I haven't!—can somehow work in the ship's voyage from Vera Cruz to Bremerhavn—In his Style, but still making it recognizable to any one who ever sailed that route!— Must stop. . . .

> Yours
> *Katherine Anne*

To SEYMOUR LAWRENCE   Roxbury Road
Southbury, Connecticut
11 April, 1957

Dear Seymour:

. . . . You know, when I begin a story I always lean down and touch the palm of my hand to the earth—that is, I begin with an incident, a situation, a place, certain persons, something in the most factual, verifiable sense *real;* and often I do not change a name, or a location, or the time of year in which something occurred that took root in my mind and became fiction; so, I have not changed the name of the real ship on which I sailed from Vera Cruz on August 22, 1931. The *Werra,* owners Nord Deutscher Lloyd . . . I can't imagine anybody minding, not even the public relations agents of the company, but if you think best, we can change the names—it must be a German boat and German company, but I can surely invent something! If you think this is worth looking after— and it WAS the first thing that caught the eye of our expert ad- viser—let me know. By now anyway at all, the old *Werra* is in one sense a painted ship upon a painted ocean, and in another, the ship of this world on her way to eternity, and in another, a ship of no company or country at all, but a new ship and company I have made out of the timbers and passengers of a real voyage—I feel this is a real voyage too, but not the one I made in that year, but the voyage I have been making all my life. . . .

Yours,
Katherine Anne

To Seymour Lawrence   Roxbury Road
Southbury, Connecticut
Palm Sunday, 14th April, 1957

Dear Seymour:

     . . . . I have heard the younger ones—and I heard the ones of my own time, too, and the ones of times before me, take turns about telling what is wrong with Flaubert and with his novel; and, reading their books, and trying to write my own, I keep on feeling that I prefer, if I must be wrong, to be wrong with Flaubert (and Henry James, and Emily Brontë and a list of the great Wrong 'Uns). Such wrongness is good enough for me, and the rightness of their detrac- tors is not right enough by half . . .

     Well, I was just going back cheerfully and touching base with this new and fine translation [by Francis Steegmuller] of *Madame Bovary,* and finding myself simply unable to read a line of several new highly-promising, they say, novels—when along come O'Faolain, and here I have been, reading him one evening and Flaubert the next and God knows two men couldn't be more unlike except for the one great likeness: they are first rate artists, and they don't get in each other's way at all.

It is such a restful kind of thing to be able to let all holds go and just trust a writer to tell you the story in his own way to the end.

My favorite stories are here, from the first one I ever read, "The Born Genius," when it was published quite years ago in a little book by I think Schumann, (who published a magazine called *Signatures* then) and he published "Noon Wine" in that series too. Then I remember "Midsummer Night Madness," "The Man Who Invented Sin," "Childybawn," "The End of the Record"—oh all such jewels, and what makes him think he has changed? They are all by the same man, only at different ages and in different situations, and even as he whittles his style and gets at once easier and more disciplined, and can say, as he goes on, more with fewer words—why, it isn't change, but only the further stages and developements of the same gift he began with. And I wish he could have left Hemingway out of it. I don't mean that Hemingway isn't admirable, and he has done things his own way that no one else could do at all. I have watched for years in distress the struggles of that centerless, mindless, uncreated man to present an image of himself to the world that will hide, perhaps even from himself, the cureless fear and the despair that comes of fear—fear of his own human instinct, of his own thoughts, of the feelings of others, of language itself . . . His true genius is for simple, complete misunderstanding of himself and of others, of all human motives.

I'm not going on with this. Mr. O'Faolain's tastes in writers is his own affair and he only knows the secret of it. What I want to say is this, I'd love to have him write something in his book for me, and I'll do the same for him merrily. I've loved his stories for a great while now, and how did I miss "Sinners"? And "Lord and Master"? And the great (all of them are great,) "Lovers of the Lake"? About this last one I am uneasy. It sounds so familiar, I read knowing what was coming next, yet I do not remember reading it before. And I talked years ago with an Irish girl who had made that pilgrimage, it would be about thirty five years ago by now, and again with Denis

Devlin in Washington, when he was reading his poem "Lough Derg" to some of us there, his friends; so I am in the state of one who not only believes she has read this story, a long time ago, but was actually one of the pilgrims there, one time or another—which is very simply not true. I never was there, except in these three vivid imaginations. I love the story. . . .

Yours
Katherine Anne

To Donald Elder   Roxbury Road
Southbury, Connecticut
29 May, 1957

Donald Darling:

. . . . Let your folly go. I don't know what is wrong with either of us in this love business. Both constitutionally incapable of picking anything not meant for disaster sooner or later—usually sooner. And I don't want to hear one word from anybody about how it is because we don't WANT anything better. We don't usually make such mistakes in friendship, do we? I rather pride myself that I have some quite superior friends, who are good for our lifetime . . . Yet there was one man who loved me and still does, and about every four or five years he calls me by telephone and we exchange letters—yet that love was founded on a wrong to some one else, and a real treachery on his part all around! Yet he says in his latest letter: (after recalling the day and place and year of our meeting and how he felt about me on sight) "You still are very close to me, or with me, or inside me—how does one say it now? My once and for a life-time love . . ."

And he has not forgotten one of the things we heard and saw together as we flew around at least three feet off the ground in the gay summer weather . . . It didn't last, in one way, and in another, as you see, it does not end . . .

But what I wonder at is why no one—not just a lover or a husband, or relative, but a friend maybe, cannot share a life with me—or is it I cannot share with any one? Oh, let's not ask, for I've asked many times and I don't hear an answer that satisfies either my mind or my heart. So darling, I send you my love again, and wish you may find a way to live better than you are doing, that is, more to your own wish; and above all—how inevitable—what I really want for you is that you write a splendid book all your own that pleases you!

Yours
Katherine Anne

To Glenway Wescott   Roxbury Road
                        Southbury, Connecticut
                        29th June, 1957

Dearest Glenway:

I haven't called or written because my third deadline has passed and the novel is not finished, and I have stopped to see if I could not refresh myself by writing a 30th anniversary piece about the Sacco-Vanzetti† scandal. I was there for the last few days, picketed, was jailed and bailed out with many others, spent my spare time in the office copying Sacco and Vanzetti's letters, went to mass meetings in the evenings where people of all sorts from, as the saying is, every walk of life, made stormy speeches and the Italian working men shook their fists and shouted in rage with the tears running down their faces. I went to the Charlestown Prison with quite thousands of others, and stood watching the light in the tower which would flicker on and off at the time of the executions. Police on horseback with pistols and clubs and hand grenades and tear gas bombs were galloping about, charging any one who stepped beyond an invisible line in the square; and at midnight the thing was done, and from that day to this I have never been able to write about it. I kept notes at the time, and am doing something from those. There were quite dozens of writers there, and I think a mountain of really awful bathos, in prose and poetry, has been written about it—I do hate like the devil to add to it. Yet I do want

---

†*She published this memoir,* The Never-Ending Wrong, *for the 50th anniversary in 1977.*

to write it out, just as simply as I can: up to the solemn tragedy in the prison with the dimly lighted masses in the square, the blurred faces turned up to the tower—and the farce of our trial next morning, when our lawyers connived with the judge to get rid of us quickly; we were fined five dollars each for "loitering and obstructing traffic," and no sooner was I, for one, out on the sidewalk again, than an officious committee member of my special group (Communist, by the way, though I didn't know that until I was in Boston, and didn't care much then) pressed a railway ticket to New York in my hand, added ten dollars cash, said, "Now you just go straight to the station and take the next train." I did, and found a large party of others being banished from the scene of the crime. . . .

> With my love
> *Katherine Anne*

To Norman Pearson   Roxbury Road
                        Southbury, Connecticut
                        30th December, 1957

Dear Mr. Pearson:

I had no notion whatever who it might be who had sold my letters, yet my dear Bob's [McAlmon] name came as a painful shock, not because he sold them, but because he was at such extremity of need and I did not know it. Even if I had not been able to help him myself, more than likely not, still I might have found some one who could before he was so reduced . . . We were good and gentle friends for many years, a funny kind of hit-or-miss catch-as-catch-can association, just seeing each other now and then, in New York, Paris, Berlin, where ever I happened to be; and now, remembering, it seems to me that I never did see Bob really sober, and our meetings were the occasion for some wild binges—wild even by Bob's standards—to me they were quite delirious. If it hadn't been for him repairing all sorts of gaps in my education, I should never have got such prismatic views of the seamiest side of the European underworld—well, with most of the seams rather gilded, perhaps, but seamy! Someday I should like to tell you some of the strange places we went and the very odd people we saw there; and in some places, I found that I, just merely a natural woman with no curious leanings of any kind, was the oddity in that society! On the last really spectacular round we made together, which lasted, with short intervals for sleep and baths and change of wear, for just three nights and two days!—we were thrown out of so many places towards morning I have lost count, because at a certain point Bob would sing his Chinese Opera, which he meant to sound like a free-for-all catfight, and it did, and was peculiarly irritating to bartenders.

After I left Europe we went on writing to each other, I have some lovely letters from him; and I cannot now even remember the year, I hope you can tell me, when I had a letter from him saying he was in California; and a second letter told me he was not well, and he asked me to come out and share a house with him, and of course, I could not do such a thing, not for any conventional reason, but because I had no money, and it would have been fatal to pull my whole life up by the roots and go out to nurse him, for I knew that was what he needed even if he didn't know it—and after that, I never heard from him again, though I always expected to—and then some one just happened by to see me, and casually remarked that Bob was dead, and it had happened months before, and not a soul near him had written to me about it. So I wondered if he had died feeling bitterly towards me, or disappointed when really we had been such faithful cronies, he didn't treat me as he did so many others, and even in his book *Being Geniuses Together,* he spoke of me with such tact and reserve I told him I was sorry he couldn't tell the real merry tale of our hoopla in the dens of vice in the capitals of Europe. And he said, "YOU tell it sometime." And so maybe, sometime I shall. . . .

Letters! It is a great question. I would give almost anything to be able to collect such of mine as still exist—I have written thousands and received thousands, and I keep them nearly all. But I wonder if I would be willing to exchange the letters I have got for the letters I sent. Probably not. But I have often thought of offering to copy and send back any that friends might send me. But if they asked me to return theirs, my God! it would mean days and maybe weeks of rummaging in containers just to find the letters, except for perhaps a hundred very valuable ones from famous people now dead, mostly, they are all mixed helter-skelter, and I don't doubt mine are in the same muddle where ever they are. About ten years ago a friend advised me to keep copies of letters, which had always seemed to me rather a calculating thing to do. But as he said, it helps one remember what one wrote to who, which is important. And now I do keep copies of every typewritten letter, including this one, and some times even those written by hand, because I had not known that I have no power over the disposition of my letters—two different executors of literary remains in the past few years have informed me that they have impounded my letters for fifty years along with the other estate, and this without making copies for me, or photostats, and I got the same disagreeable shock as when my publishers, making contracts with producers etc, describe themselves as OWNERS of my books. Everybody except the writer seems to own what he writes, even to his personal letters! . . . .

Yours,
Katherine Anne Porter

To Mr. Fred. Warburg   Roxbury Road
                          Southbury, Conn.
                          8th January, 1958

Dear Mr. Warburg:

The reason given by the editors of *Encounter* for refusing my poem, "After a Long Journey" is so comically disingenuous, not to say devious, I almost despair of attempting in any way to deal with it. Yet . . .

The poem was first published by a "large glossy magazine" called *Mademoiselle:* one of its editors is a dear friend of mine, Miss Cyrilly Abels. She, and the other editors of the magazine also published the earliest work of James Purdy, Dylan Thomas' *Under Milk Wood,* stories by Eudora Welty, Robert Penn Warren, others of such standing, and they rather eagerly try to intercept works of this kind on their way to literary quarterlies. I could easily have published my poem in any one of a half a dozen literary quarterlies here. I have done it for years and continued to do so long after I

543

was in some request from magazines of wider circulation and higher space rates: and long before either Mr. Spender or Mr. Kristol had published a line anywhere.

I was really one of those who fought that war to a finish in this country, and considered it won at least in part when magazines which could afford to pay well would be happy to publish the same kind of thing as the magazines which could not afford to pay. These *Encounter* editors, with their talent for occupying fairly safe jobs, their really remarkable sense of career and self-promotion, their real genius for pushing themselves into any situation where they may exercise some power over the writings of others, should I think be asked to understand at this moment that I should be allowed to get what money I can for my work: I have been and am the least commercial and least suggestible of writers, as they should know without being told. My poem was written as all my other work was written, to my own order: once it was finished I admit without reservations that I sent it to an editor who would send me a good check for it: I have no exemptions from the ordinary human financial responsibilities, and I have no other commodity for sale.

It is not surprising that Mr. Spender does not know of the present publishing conditions in this country, but Mr. Kristol *should* know. It rather chills my blood that a magazine published under your aegis, no doubt having a positive influence in the literary world, should be edited by people who judge a piece of work by where it was published instead of accepting or rejecting it in the light of their own editorial judgement . . .

No, in spite of my contempt and indignation, I know this is a matter for ridicule rather than any serious response, even though this is a serious question. It is quite simply the most imbecile statement I ever received or heard of from any editor. I have had very few rejections in a long life of writing, and I have always preferred the honesty and directness of editors who said (1) "I don't like this," or (2) "This is not suitable for us." Perhaps you may suggest very tactfully to your editors that this is a good style to adopt, inoffensive to any sensible author and an effective disguise for their own dubious motives and astounding snobbery. I write exactly as I do write, and in no other way: I wish to be published and read, and though certainly I have my preferences for certain kinds of magazines, if the editor printed my writings on a six-foot bill and pasted it on a wall board on a vacant lot, I shouldn't mind—the work would be no different than if it appeared in—let's say *Encounter?*

Well—I am sorry to have given you this trouble, and yet not for anything would I have missed this priceless example of fatuity—it makes a lovely story! Thank you for sending it on.

I mailed a letter to you yesterday about such business as we had on hand then, and there is nothing to add now, except to thank you for trying to place my poem, and to say that I did hope to sell it and make a little money. I need it.

Sincerely yours,
Katherine Anne Porter

TO JAMES F. POWERS

Roxbury Road
Southbury, Connecticut
2 February, 1958

Dear Jim:

. . . . I wondered where you had gone, I was sure somewhere far away; you had been uneasy about your childrens' educations here; I think an education can be got here but it takes a lot of finding! I feel that the only hope is the good private school; but there seems to be a kind of opposition on foot to such schools as still teach languages, humanities, classics, now and again I see an attack in the newspapers or magazines accusing them of obsolete views, unrealistic attitudes, impracticality, and above all, snobbery. The real resentment appears to be against giving a child the kind of education which might elevate his mind and character above the lowest of his fellow citizens. I have never seen or heard of anywhere in history such a powerful and determined movement of pure guttersnippery to rule on its own terms; the old servile "I'm as good as you are," has changed to "You're no better than I am." The dirty servant who once dared only to spit in his master's soup now can safely spit in his face. That is I am afraid what has come finally of the high-minded notions of our good Founding Fathers—and they were remarkably fine men with some great and noble ideas, and I am glad they're dead and gone and can never know what their efforts to form a good society came to! Yeats really said it very clearly as he said so many things in the truth of his poetry: "The best lack all conviction, and the worst Are filled with passionate intensity . . ." That's from memory, I hope its right.

The best have simply betrayed themselves on the side of their humane beliefs and are rather in the fix of that Arab who let the camel get his nose through the tentflap . . . I think you are right to try to give your children a real education in the old style. I believe they will be happier for having a store of the world's wonder in their heads, no matter what else happens to them. . . .

Katherine Anne

To Cyrilly Abels   Roxbury Road
                                    Southbury, Connecticut
                                    20th February, 1958

Cyrilly darling:

That notion of offering you a large swatch of That Novel occurred to me so suddenly, and I promised so hastily to send it at once, I haven't been able to pick out the passages that go consecutively on one theme: there is a line of events for almost every character, they are all internetted and act upon each other, one thing leads to another inevitably but so intricately, maybe when you read this, if you are able to read such a mss! (I'm sorry, but I can do no better at this moment), you will understand realistically what you have always understood sympathetically, why this book has taken so hellish long to write. It has about everything in it, and I feel it all belongs there. It is a long exposition of the disastrous things people do to each other out of ignorance, prejudice, presumptuousness, self-love and self-hate, with religion, or politics, or race, or social distinctions, or even just nationality or a difference in customs—later on, my Swede Arne Hansen (who thinks he is a radical but who really just hates about everybody) remarks on the causes of war: for example, in France all the bottles have shoulders—in Germany, all the bottles taper—that's all the difference they need to go to war! millions of men have laid down their lives for something just as unimportant as that!—and—this is the other side of the question, out of inertia, moral apathy, timidity, indifference, and even a subconscious criminal collusion, people allow others to do every kind of wrong, and even, if the wrongdoers are successful, finally rather approve of them, perhaps envy them a little. You will see all of this at work somewhere, everywhere, in this long passage I am sending you, and I hope you may choose the most possible one. . . .

> With my love
> *Katherine Anne*

To Edward Schwartz   Route 1, Box 52
Roxbury Road
Southbury, Connecticut
Wednesday, March 26, 1958

Dear Mr. Schwartz:

. . . . I love especially your analysis of "The Grave" which almost nobody has noticed and it is of immense importance in that cycle . . . as I needn't tell you. And your analysis of Miranda's vision of Adam's death by arrows in the wood is marvelously certain and pure. Should I remind you that a wood—the dark Forest, is most certainly an ancient almost universal symbol of lostness, of fear of the unknown, of the terrible uncertainty of human future, taking one step forward into darkness and strangeness? Remember Dante's Midway in this mortal life, when he found himself at the edge, wasn't it, of a deep wood? Miranda's dream takes in something of the Adonis legend too—he was transfixed by arrows to a tree in a wood, remember? One of the origins of the Crucifixion legend. Of course we know that nothing is new, everything is netted together, all symbols are universal and have basically the same meanings. Even the ancient Jews, apparently coming late as they did with a really new religion, bent on destroying all that went before, still wandered forty years in a wilderness, and had most of the human adventures, even if they gave them different interpretations, and all their yearly cycle of feasts new names. And that brings me to Freud, and your use of his theories in one passage of "Pale Horse Pale Rider." Page 18 your copy, from line 5 from bottom: about illness as escape, "her opportunity to assume the active role of the male," and the note about the sailing away into the jungle (Freudian point of view) "a wish for the male role." To me this is so wrong it is shocking, and yet it is almost impossible for any woman to convince any man that this is false.

In the first place, there are so many women, and we have all heard them, who wish loudly they had been born men, simply because they have been taught that men have more freedom, in every direction. What they really want, I think, is not a change of sex, but a change of the limited conditions of their lives which have been imposed because of their sexual functions. They do not seem to realize that men are not free either, and exactly on the grounds of their sexual functions. The uneasy sexual vanity that makes a man resent a woman who is his equal mentally or in any other way; his terrible organic need to be pre-potent in bed; his fear of impotence, especially as he grows older; his awful anxiety to prove and prove again and keep on proving the superiority of his sex over the other: his will to be God, in a word, whom he has created in his own image; and above all, the heavy responsibility of wielding all that power and authority he has taken upon himself—O poor man, I for one woman, would not change places with him, nor swap my troubles for his. The fact is, a horrid truth, there are more men now trying to be women than there are women trying to be men! But I reject for such unfortunates the term "effeminate." There is nothing in the faintest degree feminine or womanly about them. They are incomplete, sometimes mutilated men, and they can never be anything else, and women are right to resent this insult aimed at the very core of their existence, their sexual life as women; to refuse that term to describe a perverted man. Alas, women have enough mutilées and perverts of their own, without taking on the men's share, too. No, you simply have to keep and claim them, you can't put them off on us!

Now then, you must remember, so far as Freud himself is concerned, and no doubt at all he must be held responsible for most dreadful and dangerous misconceptions about human motives and instincts, besides a lamentable mis-reading of symbols— he was a Jew, (not religiously, just traditionally and psychically) that is to say, an Oriental; and the condition of women in the western world has been lowered abysmally since the Jewish heresy, Christianity, slowly inundated the west, bringing its terrible tide of Oriental custom and superstition. Well, just the same, what men find it hard to believe is that a strong woman is not necessarily imitating a male, or wishing to play the role of one. Strength—of body or mind or character or talent—is not a matter of sex. A woman who knows how to be a woman not only needs and must have an active force of character and mind, but she has invariably, I have never known it to fail, an intense self-respect, precisely for *herself,* her attributes and functions as a female, and I never knew a woman worth her self who really wanted to be a man. What she wants is the right *really* to be a woman, and not a kind of image doing and saying what she is expected to say by a man who is only afraid of one thing from her—that one day she will forget and tell him the truth!

As a woman, I have a sexual pride quite the equal of any man's I ever knew. Men are continually accusing women of trying to castrate them by insulting their maleness, treating it with disrespect, trying to diminish their confidence in their own manhood. I am sure this is true, it is a kind of revenge some women take on some men for whatever reasons they may have. But do you forget that all boys start this kind of thing with all girls very early, and they keep it up very late? I know that when a woman loves a man, she builds him up and supports him and helps him in every possible way to live . . . I never knew a man who loved a woman enough for this. He cannot help it, it is his deepest instinct to destroy, quite often subtly, insidiously, but constantly and endlessly, her very center of being, her confidence in herself as woman. Its a great mystery, but there it is. I don't quarrel with it, I just see it and know it is there and try to deal with it, to come to terms with it, and of course as I grow older and men lose their interest in me as a woman, they also lose a great deal of their antagonism to me, and I find I can speak more freely and openly and they don't fly into a rage. They are apt to say, "Oh, you are just talking like a woman!" And I say, "What do you expect me to talk like?" and one very gallant old friend said, "Like an arch-angel, of course!" So, I give it up at that point while tempers are still good. When I think well and am intelligent, the critics say I have a man's mind. When I am silly or not at my best, they admit indulgently that I am very feminine. . . .

I sincerely love your essay† and think it a splendid piece of work. Not for one instant do I expect you to agree with me, or change your point of view to harmonize with mine. I wish only to say what I think and feel on that particular point, where your interpretation is quite convincing if one accepts the premise: I don't, but that is because I know something about women, a fairly representative lot of them—and a great deal about myself, and I know something that Dr. Freud never dreamed of: (I can't think why!) that not all little girls when seeing little boys without clothes on for the first time, wonder what is the matter with *themselves* as girls. It is a matter of record that little girls have been known to ask, at sight of a baby boy having his diaper changed, "Oh, *what* happened to him? Will he get well?" And the grown-ups had to take great pains to assure her that he was perfectly all right, just exactly like little boys should be. I should know, because that was Miranda at the age of about four, and that is a favorite family story. And don't tell me I am unique or odd in any way about this, because I happen to know quite well that I am not.

Bless you again, and now I must get on with my packing and scratting among papers. At Weslyean College, I am going to read "He," "Rope," and "The Circus," in that order, and tell a little about each as I go.

With my thanks and sincere good wishes, yours

Katherine Anne Porter

---

†*Katherine Anne Porter noted:* " 'The Fictions of Memory'—*wonderful title.* " *Published in* Southwest Review, *vol. 45, Summer 1960, pp. 204–15.*

TO SENATOR JOHN
FITZGERALD KENNEDY

[June 17, 1958]
After September 1, 1958:
Department of English, 580
Cabell Hall
University of Virginia
Charlottesville, Virginia

Dear Senator Kennedy:

That was a charming day altogether at Smith College,† and besides the pleasure of meeting you at the Commencement luncheon at the President's home, I specially enjoyed your address to the graduating class of '58, and so, very apparently, did they.

Please let me say that, aside from my personal good wishes, I wish you well heartily in your public life, and am greatly in sympathy with your aims and ideas as I have been able to follow them in the press. I found a long time ago that one need not always know who a man's friends are, but a good look at his enemies helps much in forming a notion of his character and motives.

But that cannot be news to you.

Sincerely yours,
Katherine Anne Porter

†*In June 1958 Katherine Anne Porter was awarded an honorary degree, Doctor of Letters, with the white and gold Smith hood. Others honored with her included Janet Flanner, Barbara McClintock, Nadia Boulanger, and Mary Parsons.*

SECTION 10

University of Virginia, Washington and Lee University

September 1958 to July 1959

Yes, you are right, ladies especially ladies trying to write! have a hard time. But I have observed that the gentlemen so engaged also have their peculiar troubles. . . . But we do have a narrow margin of territory of common humanity on which to meet now and then.

Katherine Anne Porter to Robert Penn Warren
May 6, 1959

PAST JEFFERSON'S SERPENTINE BRICK WALL KATHERINE ANNE *Porter walks to her lectures at the University of Virginia, where she is writer-in-residence following Faulkner, "bathed in the glow of Jefferson's spirit." Sundays she goes to her favorite game, Polo. She still gets in some good use of her yard-wide cartwheel black hat she had got to go up to Smith College, "my feeling being that though its nice to be a D. Litt. it isn't nice to look like one." On tour she sees four Benedictine nuns in the audience and almost changes her program, for she is about to read a low-comedy seduction scene on deck from* Ship of Fools. *But she goes ahead and they laugh at all the right places. Of a dinner party at the president's house in Lexington where she teaches at Washington and Lee University, she says "I love this elegance and dignity with such gayety and life. Everybody is witty and good mannered at once, with the light touch."*

To James F. Powers   Department of English
                                  530 Cabell Hall
                                  University of Virginia
                                  Charlottesville, Virginia
                                  14th September, 1958

Dear Jim:

What is there about my letters that make them hard to answer? You are not the first one to tell me this. It makes me very uneasy, as if I burden the mind of some one I meant only to divert a little or gossip with, or keep in touch with . . . I write at top speed with no effort, if I didn't I'd never get time to write letters at all. . . .

I love memoirs better than any kind of reading except somebody else's most private letters, after they are safely dead of course. I am saving all mine and every body's just because it will make such lively reading matter for those to come after us. Please save my letters—I have every one of yours, I hope you won't be alarmed to hear. I have done one autobiographical piece, called "St. Augustine and the Bull Fight," and mean to do more. All my letters, yours too, are autobiography in a very pure sense. . . .

                                  Yours,
                                  Katherine Anne

To Cyrilly Abels   Department of English
                                  530 Cabell Hall
                                  University of Virginia
                                  Charlottesville, Virginia
                                  20 September, Monday 1958

Cyrilly darling:

. . . . Yesterday I went to the Polo game, my favorite of all games to watch—there isn't anything for me to compare with it for elegance and excitement and skill and the ancient wonderful sight of men and horses playing a game together, because the horses know as much about it as the men and are just as skillful and elegant! I had never thought of it before, but I wonder how many Universities in this country has its own polo team? There is to be a whole series of Sundays of course, so I know what I shall be doing on Polo Sunday afternoons from now on . . . Dr. Stovall, chairman of my department, and his wife, took me yesterday to the game. They are from Texas, both of them born within twenty miles of where I was born, he is about my age, and we remember nearly exactly the same things. It is delightful. . . .

We are still wearing summer clothes here and I am getting in some good use of my beautiful yard wide cartwheel black hat I got last spring to go up to Smith College, my feeling being that though its nice to be a D.Litt. it *isn't* nice to look like one. I wore it to my cocktail party here, and am going to speak at a lunch at Longwood College soon and wear it again—probably for the last time this season. Did Arthur tell you about my hat binge? I have boxes of them now, all just a little wild, though I think the black ostrich plume fright-wig is the most advanced, I haven't worn it yet. . . .

Katherine Anne

To Ann Heintze   Department of English
                                 530 Cabell Hall
                                 University of Virginia
                                 Charlottesville, Virginia
                                 29th October, 1958

Ann darling:

Got back last Saturday night from my wild escapade across Texas and Oklahoma; left Tuesday morning from local airfield, changed at Washington; changed at Dallas; arrived in Austin same evening after nearly thirteen hours travel time so far as I can make out, having turned my watch back and forth at every stop to match the clock in the lobby. I was met there by old friends who took me to see the beautiful capitol at once, because when I was about six years old my grandmother took me there—(I had just been vaccinated, I remember, and was miserable) and took me up in the old water-propelled elevator to the fourth balcony. It was the first grand beautiful thing I had ever seen, and I never forgot it. And I was happy to see that it really is grand and noble and beautiful and that Palladio did this country a good turn by setting a fashion in architecture that will never be ugly or stupid—it just has the innate grandeur of height overhead and light and dignity . . . His rotunda has never been beaten for grace, and I nearly shed tears for joy and I said, "Well, it wasn't a bad start for a child's first sight of the world, was it?" The people there love it and wouldn't let it be harmed or neglected for anything. It is the first building of any consequence built in Texas after it became a sovereign state.

Well, it was a home-coming! The great hall was packed, with people standing in masses at the back: they opened four audition rooms with loudspeakers for the overflow, and they were all over-flowed, too! And darling, in the morning before the evening, I had telephone calls from women who had been little girls with me in Kyle and some who even knew the farm near Buda—which is the place I remember best—and called me by a little name I had forgotten, and they were all elderly-and-worse widows, who had prospered nicely, and they all remembered me, and each one told me a story about me and them together which I had forgotten, and they are just legends, I feel sure. And I just thought, why, I'm going to take Aunt Cat Porter's place here if I don't look out. Well, four of them showed up for the performance, nice old gals prettily dressed and so sobered down and grandmotherly, and we all kissed and the names were so familiar, and not a face I could see one familiar feature in. So we all swore we hadn't changed a bit, lying gallantly as southern ladies are supposed to in these matters, and gazed rather wistfully and seekingly over the abyss of time gaping between us—but no, all we could see was a far away raggle-taggle lot of little girls—and I don't remember them as being so friendly to me *then,* though now they swear they loved me and never forgot me— insubstantial as motes dancing in a sunbeam, vanished, gone forever. So we said goodbye, and they moved away in a little group, and the crowd closed in and shut them off. I didn't think until afterward, when I had signed at least a hundred books brought me by my audience, that not one of them had brought one for me to write in! . . . .

With my same devoted love

(Aunt) Katherine Anne

559

"Callie" for short! Oh, how *funny* that did sound after all these years—

To Edith Sitwell   7 January, 1959
until January 31 next:
Department of English
University of Virginia
Charlottesville, Virginia

My dear Edith:

. . . . Your anthology is a continued treasure; you have done two things; given us a fine plenty of the long, large, ample things; and then such marvels of lyrics and light gay songs, and some poems by my beloved Samuel Daniel and Michael Drayton that I did not know. Oh more than that, a storehouse and something to take to Heaven with me if ever I get there; or maybe to bootleg into Hell to soften the penalty of having to read the Beat Generation. I am grateful to you, and feel now that I did not say half enough in praise of it.

But I lead an odd sort of life; after I saw you that time in what *They* called a garden apartment, as if I didn't know a cellar when I saw one! I moved lock stock and barrel to a pleasant small house on a hillside in Roxbury Road, near Southbury, Connecticut. And there I bided for three years, finishing up that novel. The first title for it, to which I have returned, is *Ship of Fools,* from *Narrenschiff* from *Stultitia Navis* (and you have to see to believe how it degenerates from language to language) and I suppose it will be out early this year. . . .

Love to Osbert, and to you!
Katherine Anne

TO ANN HEINTZE   Department of English
                               Washington and Lee University
                               Lexington, Virginia
                               16 February, 1959

Ann darling:

 Maybe you saw the announcement this morning, but if not, the Ford grant-in-aid went through, I got one! not quite as much as I had been led to expect, but a good though odd sort of sum—$13000 for the two years, about half of what I could make if I put my mind on it, at writing *and* reading engagements, but this will be as much or more, really, because I can settle in somewhere and control my expenses, which is more than I can do now! The expense of travel and wardrobe for this work is disastrous. I am supposed to cancel every engagement of the sort and do NOTHING but write. Can you imagine such a delirious dream of joy? I shall be on "Camera Three" next Sunday morning at 11:30 and shall go to California in May for the two lectures on Mark Twain at the University of California, Los Angeles, in May—(14th and 15th) but that I suppose ends it. I don't know yet where I shall settle in, it doesn't matter much where just so I get out of circulation and stay there. And get a scale of living suitable to my tidy little fortune—exactly 1,625 dollars every quarter for two years—so that I shan't have to worry about money; that alone will give me a new life. And there is nobody I have to help or give it to, because almost everybody I know is now doing much better than I do; so I can live and work with an easy mind . . . the first time in my whole life, imagine. High time, you'd say! . . . .

          Love again, angel
          Aunt Kat.

To EDWARD G. SCHWARTZ   Department of English
Washington and Lee University
Lexington, Virginia
19 March, 1959

Dear Edward:

. . . . One point in his [Daniel Curley's] view of my ways of working. He will not believe me when I say I do not really know how or why I did any given thing. I would think as a writer himself he would know that some things come from very deep down in the consciousness, whatever that may be, or wherever it resides, and that we tap it no doubt intentionally, but we cannot always foresee what will be brought up. The God's truth that I cannot make anybody believe is that I only know exactly WHAT I want to tell, and the way of telling it shapes itself slowly and broodingly as if it had a life of its own, and all the things he sees in it are there, and they are made out of my own life, yet it would be utterly false to say that I deliberately set out to do what I did finally effect, or that I was choosing my symbols and watching the form and style. Not at all; it was written in one single sitting in a great burst of emotional recollection yet with my mind working soberly as a carpenter at his bench, choosing the right pieces and cutting them to shape and scale—this is not duality, not really, but we have many faculties material and immaterial and they work together harmoniously sometimes . . .

I don't know what else to say. I am hardly ever able to answer any criticism, whether hostile, cold; or warmly friendly and reassuring like Daniel's because no matter what any of them say, what theories they advance, the thing that happens to me when I am writing, really sunk in it and freed of all doubts and fears of interruptions and distractions, is not at all like anything they say. It is not a tranced state but a condition in which my forces such as they are work with speed and sureness and it is frightfully hard work and a joy as nearly pure as I expect to have on this earth. . . .

Yours
Katherine Anne Porter

TO GLENWAY WESCOTT   Col' Alto
                          Lexington, Virginia
                          3 April, 1959

Glenway darling:

Your "Best of All Possible Worlds" is in your very best vein; I read it fast and then went back and read it slow, and wanted more. I shall be happy to hear you say it, and happy to see you.

Here the work is not half so much as Charlottesville, and I have cancelled all outside dates except California in May and the Air Force Library at the Air Force Base near Montgomery Alabama. I saw Charles again on my visit there—was it January?—and we kissed in kindness, like Christopher Smart's cat when he met another. He never saw me young, so it doesn't matter. But I did see him in his golden glory, and he had not changed when I saw him again for the first time after we parted—five years. But that was nearly ten years ago, and that fatal ten years between thirty five and forty five that is neither youth nor age, the beauty of youth declined and the beauty of age not yet arrived. I can't tell you how sad it made me, I who never bewept my own youth because I really never knew I had any, nor what it might have been; and escaped from it as from some sort of trap or cheat, and never regretted what I had never valued. But I did love his beauty and goldness and savory sweet-smelling firm body with its light down of golden fur like an infant lion . . . His health and hardness and sweetness and his endless pleasure in me and my presence and all we did and had and knew together . . . Entirely too many men have said they loved me, but this one *did*.

And does. By now, both of us know very well what we had, and that it happens once in a long life time if one is very lucky, and to most of the human race it never happens at all because they have not been able to imagine love. . . .

                          Love,
                          Katherine Anne

To Robert Penn Warren   Department of English
                          Washington and Lee University
                          Lexington, Virginia
                          6 May, 1959

Dear Red:

. . . . The semester ends here at the end of May, and I had
lovely plans. First, I had been invited to give the Ewing Lectures
at the University of California in Los Angeles, (a plum, pick your
own subject, and a $2500 fee! two lectures one afternoon, one
evening, with a day between) and I chose Mark Twain; and everything including the round trip flight had been arranged; So, I flew
off to Montgomery Alabama on the 23rd of May to speak at a
banquet of the Air Force University Library at the field there, and
on the plane with air conditioning down the back of my neck all
the way—I lost my voice completely and it has come back only a
little, a kind of apologetic croak, and I have had to cancel my
wonderful paying job.

. . . . Now I am going to pick up my Ford grant right away,
and go somewhere as retired as Roxbury Road, and get to work
again . . . High time! Looking back on my life, Roxbury Road was
the nearest I ever came to having my life arranged just the way I
wanted and needed it, it was the best time I ever had . . . Maybe
you'll think I haven't had a very good time, and you will be right—I
haven't. But I always did know what I wanted and what was good
for me—my trouble was a failure of practical execution—I never
could fight the opposition hard enough, either. Silence and solitude, maybe now I shall really have them—distance and space, air
to breathe and room to turn in; surely they will come for a little
while. A little while would be all I needed. I have so much I want
to do, and maybe now I shall be free for it. . . .

Yes, you are right, ladies especially ladies trying to write! have
a hard time. But I have observed that the gentlemen so engaged
also have their peculiar troubles. I'm not sure that I would swop my
kind of troubles for theirs. Oh yes I am too, sure. I wouldn't for
anything, because I sort of understand mine and theirs are very
mysterious to me. But we do have a narrow margin of territory of
common humanity on which to meet now and then, and I don't feel
an utter stranger in this world, though women do seem, historically

even, to be an alien race; somehow not quite human. I can't think why, but I haven't even been able to discuss it with a man, so I have only my own feelings and observations to go by. . . .

Meantime, I do not know where I shall be, I cannot make up my mind but I will let you know. I live here in the most charming atmosphere of friendly goodness, I love this little place, I would like to stay here; but it is impossible as social life goes at top speed day in day out, and it is simply beyond their lovely Virginia Imaginations how any one could be so barbarous as to say No, or to have a previous engagement with nothing but a job of writing! That can always be done tomorrow! So I must get out, and quickly. I may just go no further than Washington, I may just go somewhere I've never been. But I am brought to such a pause by this sudden change in my whole life brought about by this failure of my vocal cords, I can't make any plan except the general one that I must get to a safe quiet place with my unfinished mss. and hereafter take nobody's advice but my own—

Love to my Rosanna, to Gabriel, to Eleanor, to you, to the house, love and love again.

Yours
Katherine Anne

To Paul Porter   [Jefferson Hotel
                        1200 Sixteenth Street
                        Washington 6, D.C.]
                        Sunday 19 July, 1959

Paul darling,

. . . . That Galina Ulanova is the most magical creature I ever saw dance—greater than Pavlova because she has indwelling light! Its strange and mysterious but nothing more a simple *fact* than that certain persons have a spiritual overtone that adds wonder to all they do, and that ballerina has it!

Love—
Aunt Katherine Anne

SECTION II

Washington, Pigeon Cove
October 1959 to October 1962

I always knew one thing, that life is made bearable and possible and liveable by the relations of one human being to another, the individual love and gentleness between persons, or in any case, the unbreakable bond that grows and fastens lives together in all sorts of mysterious ways.

Katherine Anne Porter to Barbara Wescott
May 3, 1962

IN THE SPRING OF 1960, KATHERINE ANNE PORTER GOES TO Mexico *on a tour of duty for the State Department. "The Fig Tree" is published in June, and "Holiday" in December. It is at Pigeon Cove, Massachusetts, breathing the sea air she loves, that she finishes the novel— but she is not in the least willing to let it go. She says of the book she has been working on for several decades, "Trouble is, as I copy or edit, I write in new passages just to amuse myself, so I'll have something fresh to read when I'm correcting the mss." With the Warrens, during a blizzard the following winter, "We went out, Rosanna, Gabriel, Eleanor and I, and went sliding down a long beautiful ski-run in those large saucers." In the spring, after the party to celebrate the publication of* Ship of Fools, *she escapes to Taormina.*

To Sylvia Beach   3112 "Q" Street, N.W.
                         Washington 7, D.C.
                         19th October 1959

Dearest Sylvia:

Heavens how homesick all this is making me—the Catalogue of your "Twenties" show, then your lovely clear sweet book; and its Paris, Paris where I should most like to be—only of course, the Paris that was *then,* not now. I have been too long away I should be afraid of being a stranger where I once for a good number of years had the perfect illusion of being at home—*chez moi* in the happiest sense of the phrase. Well, it is still all there just where I left it!

Do you remember one day you had just come in to see me in my cellar in New York (THEY called it the garden apartment, but I knew better) and Alphonse Daudet's daughter had just dropped in on me from Canada, I who didn't even know he had daughter, and took my last ten dollars and told me that Reine de Roussy de Sales had sent her to me, God knows why. And you insisted on lending me ten dollars at once, saying "Only poor people can do these things for each other!" And here enfin is that money though by now it should be doubled with interest. And bless you and thank you again, my dearly remembered Sylvia. I think of Adrienne† so often, and just now, unpacking books here in this house where I shall be for the next three years at least, I was looking again at that treasured complete file of *Le Navire d'Argent* which she gave me; what wonderful things are in it, what a genius she had for recognizing genius . . . and at her own high level. I thought she had great beauty and—I am disappointed that there seem to be no good pictures of her.

My address is above. I hope we see each‡ other again, either here or there.

                         Love
                         Katherine Anne

†See *"A Letter to Sylvia Beach"* (on the death of Adrienne Monnier), Collected Essays, pp. 107–08.
‡KAP noted on October 28, 1974, "We never did see each other again—"

To James F. Powers   3112 Que Street, N.W.
                                  Washington 7, D.C.
                                  22 October, 1959

Dear Jim:

      . . . . I know about the death of a friend—of friends. I have
come to a time when death is a most familiar presence, it strikes
here and there among the few and dear friends I had expected
somehow to end my days with in joy. And then, in a few short
months, my only brother—Paul in "THE GRAVE"—my favorite
cousin, Lily Cahill the actress, my twentyfive years publisher and
friend, Donald Brace, and George Platt Lynes the friend and Photographer who made all my photographs for twenty years; and
then, so many of those pleasant or interesting or touching persons
I met here and there, and liked and remembered and expected to
see again, and I pick up the paper and see a name; or some one says,
Why he (she) is dead, hadn't you heard? until all time and space
in my life is full of holes, empty spots where these persons had been.
It is very strange, I had not been able to imagine this kind of
loneliness. It has always been impossible to see much of my
friends—they are all so scattered, but I knew they were in the
world, where they were, what doing . . .

> "A cry of Absence, Absence, in the heart,
> And in the wood the furious winter blowing."

      It is terrible to think of your losing two chapters of the novel,
there is a loss just next to death itself . . . I wrote the first two pages
of a story once, and lost or misplaced them; after outrageous search
and despair, I tried to remember them and write them again, but
I could never finish the story, have not to this day. But years later
in moving my papers, I find the first draft, compared it with the
other, and they were except for a word or two, exactly alike . . .
But I wrote the first "Cracked Looking Glass" in Mexico, and
Dorothy Day asked to read it, took it away and when, after ten days
or so, I asked her to give it back—I had no copy—she said coolly
and with malice that she had lost it. She was not then the saint and
ministering angel she became after she was converted to the Catholic faith. Oh these converts, they are always more Catholic than the

Pope . . . Well, let's not get off on that subject. So, as to the "Cracked Looking Glass," I wrote it again in Berlin, just after leaving Mexico, and it is the same story, but told in quite a different tone from the first. So you will write your chapters again, but yes, it is a heart-shaking job of work, all right! But be sure they are really lost, not just packed away with something else unrelated, as my belongings so often are. I wish you may find them even yet, though it is too likely that you know they are lost, really. . . .

I love pungent or appealing minor characters. Mine in *Ship of Fools* is a seasick bull dog who never makes a sound but twice—once a growl, once a howl . . . I am foolishly fond of him. . . .

In the University of Texas, did I tell you this? they are building a new Library and have named it for me. Not everybody gets to walk around in his own monument, does he? If I live! I will be seventy years old my next birthday, and the very sound of the number is absurd. My "public" age is four years off, and it was by a typographical error a good while ago, not my fault at first, it became my fault as time went on and I did not correct it. My first impulse was to do so, but people near me advised me against it—what business, said they, is it of the reader how old you are? And I, who had always been above that kind of vanity, or so I thought, listened to the siren voices of this world and let the mistake stand . . . I even compounded the error by putting it on my passports. Don't tell on me, please! I feel silly enough already . . . But next year I aim to give a birthday party for myself, and celebrate my unexpected great age—for when one has died once, one cannot do it again—and I have been living out of turn, you might say, since the Great Plague of 1918, when I was given up for dead. I have seen my own obituary notice, set up and ready to go, with only the day and hour omitted: and have seen the telegrams between my father and sister arranging my funeral . . . There remains only, as I said, for me to walk around in my monument, and I shall be quite ready to go. If I still owe God a death, may I at the risk of blasphemy say, Maybe He owes me an easy one, as I have already suffered the agonies of it, surely no one is required to do that twice? . . . .

Yours
Katherine Anne

To Stephen Spender   3112 Q Street, N.W.
                            Washington 7, D.C.
                            28 November 1959

Dear Mr. Spender:

Your cable came yesterday asking me to apply extra pages to my "A Wreath For the Gamekeeper." (By the way, Marvin Perry did not think he had time to send me proofs. I notice the set of proofs you send me is called "Lady Chatterley in America." Is this your title or Dr. Perry's? In either or both cases, I object. I choose my titles very carefully and I want them to be used. I have had this trouble before. I once wrote a piece about Gertrude Stein which I called "The Wooden Umbrella: a Self-Portrait." And began it with a quotation in small print of a passage from Miss Stein's journals describing Miss Hennessy's wooden umbrella. Unless the reader read that paragraph attentively, he would probably not grasp the meaning of the last paragraph of the article without the title to guide his attention. So my busy editor changed the title to "Gertrude Stein: A Self-Portrait." It is this kind of thing that has done a good deal to discourage me from publishing in magazines.)

Well, the title is "A Wreath For the Game Keeper," it being my hope that I am helping to inter this sadly over-wrought question, so leave it, please. And I cannot use these proofs because I have done a good deal of revision on the grounds of my first notes, and have offered you that revision, and am sending on in a few days the copy I wish you to use, if you use any at all. Also, Marvin Perry called me and asked me to agree with him that he should have the right to publish it before any one else, anywhere, and I did and do agree, as he suggested the article in the first place, after hearing me talk to a class on the subject. He said he was going to send you a cable or a letter, I forget which, making his attitude clear, and I asked him to be sure to tell you that I intended to respect his wishes in the matter. He has only American first serial rights, I can dispose of the others anywhere I like, but I prefer to stand by my original agreement with Dr. Perry. I do hope you understand and will not rush the matter even if I should get the mss, to you in time for immediate publication. It is only a matter of typing a final copy, three or four more pages . . . Please also do remember that I cannot

have any editing or cutting or revision of any kind at all—it must
be published as I wrote it, and if possible I should like proofs to look
over once more. I shall in these circumstances be happy for you to
bring it out in England; Dr. Perry seems to think it is going to
explode a hornet's nest here, and it may. I really don't know, and
don't care either.

Sincerely yours
Katherine Anne Porter

To Glenway Wescott   3112 Que Street, N.W.
Washington 7, D.C.
Sunday morning,
6 March, 1960

Glenway darling:

I had such an impulse to speak to you this morning I went to
call you by telephone, and found your name and all completely
wiped out along with a whole page of W's where I had spilt wine
on it. I suppose you are not in Stone-blossom any more, but "Wish
way *are* you," as Alphonse Daudet's daughter, a minute, decrepit
wretch, asked on a postcard after I left 17th Street. How Daudet's
daughter, who lives in Canada, got sicked on to my trail by Reine
de Roussy de Sales is another story and not at all what I mean to
write you about!

Its just that I want to say how lovely besides handsome and
good and superb your piece about Isak Dinesen was—is—and to
say again what strikes me again, every time I read one of your
appreciations of writers you care for, how truly generous and self-
less you are in your praise. Yet not fulsome—it convinces me, even
if I do not always share entirely your estimate of a given writer, still
I feel that you have simply (simply!) discovered qualities that I have
missed, or explored more sympathetically and more deeply. I admit
I am more attracted by the Baroness, the Personage, than I am by
the artist, but that is no matter, I hope. She has very choice readers
and admirers, a reputation like hers is not gained just on a stunning
personality or careful publicity. I must content myself with the

feelings and judgements of my friends—you especially my dear, a touchstone for recondite merit! If it is there, you'll find it and give it your scrupulous attention and gentle criticism . . . Just the same, I should have liked to be present when you and Marianne and Isak Dinesen were together . . . I hope this piece of yours will go into that book of your writings I am waiting for so hopefully . . .

Hopefully! I thought it was so touching, so formidably Northern, the terrible unthawing iceberg of the Norse character, her admonishment for us to work a little every day . . . without faith, without hope . . . and all at once we would find it finished! I lent my copy to the young man who lives in the basement, so cannot write it exactly. Her words were beautiful and painful, for I cannot live without either, much less work without them; and when I am really working, I am calm but elated, and happy—really happy, the only true happiness I have ever known; it is *joy* in the pure sense of that word. It is rare but it happens and it keeps me living when I suppose there is no particularly visible reason for it. So her utter, total courage, the spareness of her afflicted little body, the gauntness of her wit, even her one oyster and three grapes and a sip of champagne, all at once nearly moves me to tears, and altogether to an exultation of the spirit—you have made me see her and love her, *for herself alone,* her work aside: I love the Being which made the work possible. With that will, she could have done anything!

I am sending this in care of Russell, imagine, because I have somehow lost your whereabouts. "Wish way . . . ?"

With my same love
Katherine Anne

To Eleanor Clark   3112 Q Street, N.W.
Warren   Washington, D.C.
                          24 July, 1960

Eleanor darling,

How could I have gone so wrong on the birthdates? Here is what I have had in mind all this time, apparently: that your birthday is the 6th of July, and how did I get the notion that either Gabriel or Rosanna's birthday was the day after yours? Oh I had doubts, and I should have asked, for I KNOW that Rosanna's sign is Leo, and her birthstone is a ruby, and that sign doesn't come in until the 21st of July a little more or less—it varies a day nearly every year, one way or another—and that you and Gabriel are in the same sign, Cancer, and I forget what your birthstone is. Red's is Aries, the diamond, mine is Taurus, the emerald, Ann's is Gemini, the pearl, Rosanna is a ruby—now there are amethysts, sapphires, topazes, opals, all sorts of beautiful things to be distributed fairly, but I don't know where they belong.

Let me get this list straight for once. Here are the July birthdays in my life.

	Eleanor	July 6
	Gabriel	July 19
	Rosanna	July 27
Others:		
	My Mother:	July 22
	My Sister:	July 25
	My nephew Paul:	July 29

Do you not think that that is quite a den of Leos for a Taurus to try to live in? Even my god daughter!

Could you, do you think, correct that little engraving that says 7 July? Is there room enough to put a little 2 on the left hand side? I can't tell you how your description of Rosanna with her tea set, and Gabriel with his fiddle, delighted me, and does delight me. I love the way you can express your love and joy in the children, catching those moments of enchantment which are, after all, all we can remember later on. If that [is] sap, I say, more and better sap is what we need, that life-giving stuff that keeps our feelings fresh! I have little letters from you about first Rosanna, then Gabriel and Rosanna together, from their beginnings and I wish to give them to the children later; no children could ever have been written about by a mother with such poetry of love. . . .

Bless all of you, I love you separately and en masse!

Katherine Anne

To Paul Porter   3112 Q Street, N.W.
                                  Washington 7, D.C.
                                  Friday, 5th August, 1960

Paul darling:

    . . . . I am glad he [S.F. Johnson] quoted that passage of mine
which does give H. [Hardy] a little due of praise—he had some
noble qualities and they keep getting into his works in spite of that
blunderbuss style, and it is really for that nobility of feeling that I
can't give him up. I know this is out of style, goodness is supposed
to be very dull, if not deeply suspect; but it isn't to me, and that is
all I can say about it, at this moment. . . .

                                  Love again as always
                                  Aunt Katherine Anne

To Monroe Wheeler   3112 Q Street, N.W.
                                  Washington, 7, D.C.
                                  27 December, Imagine! 1960
                                  4 days to go and here we go
                                  again!

Monroe darling:

    . . . . Bless you, I love you dearly and have for so long now
it might just as well be called always. Strangely invariable, change-
less, in this shifting world—do you remember I used to sign myself
sometimes "with my same old monotonous love"—? But I was only
half-serious, for to me no love could ever get monotonous, but
then, I always tried to make some leeway in my mind for what the
other person, the loved one—had in mind or feeling. . . .
    You do know that I have published two stories and am going
into my third; Once I said, quite years ago, that I never had to
have another idea in my life, all I had to do was to write the forty
or fifty odd stories I had in mind or notes. It must have sounded
like pure boasting, but I didn't think of that—it wasn't boasting,
it was just mere statement of what Eudora calls "daylight fact."

And from now on, with time off to write a few stray pieces about things that interest me outside of fiction, I expect for the rest of my life to be engaged in just that occupation. From now on, any story you may see of mine you may take for granted has been in notes for anywhere from twenty five to forty years. It took me five and one-half hours to write "Flowering Judas," but after ten years cogitation. "Holiday" is based on something that happened to me when I was twenty. At thirty I started trying to write it. At intervals for the next ten years I made three drafts, all rejected by me. Last spring in turning over my papers, I found it and started working on it again. I realized then that except for the very crux of the matter, *I had done the story in the first draft.* So I used that and threaded in as I went along the things I was unable to say so long ago, and got it said somehow without disturbing the shape or tone or pace or direction of the original story. Forty years to write a short story darling! But then, you know so well that anything you do is worth a lifetime or nothing! But I am grown very careful about saying anything like this to my students and young writers. It scares the britches off the serious ones, and rouses a mean scoffery in the lightweights. Let 'em find out for themselves, I say—The real ones will, and the others don't matter. . . .

> Love again and always
> *Katherine Anne*

To Seymour Lawrence   3112 Q Street, N.W.
Washington, D.C.
December 28, 1960

Dear Seymour:

. . . . First off, the snapshot of the children is enchanting, I show it to every one who comes. My Macy-child is an enchantress born, pure Circe, and you know what I think about Circe—I don't in the least share the stupid popular notion. She has the smile of a fascinating person, she will never be anything but beautiful as long as she lives. Nicholas is a charmer in his own way, but the contrast in their features and expressions is awesome; Macy so easily at home in her world, so sure of her place and so happy in it, and Nicholas still perfectly astounded at the unheard-of Crazy-place he has tumbled into, somehow—he doesn't quite yet get the hang of it, but he will! Oh that darling solemn amazed face, aren't you delighted to have him? Could he have been better in any way? I can't think so. When I look at these two little pilgrims just setting out, I feel what it is to be old, to realize all the time to come in this world that I shall not know, but these children will take part in the next two or three or four generations of it; I remember when I was three and a little older, my grandmother and people of her time used to look at me gently and wonderingly and say: "This child will see a world very different from ours." Or: "To think she will see a world we can't even imagine!" And they were right. I think the difference between them and me however was mostly that they seemed to regret they would not know the life on earth to come, and I am very glad indeed that I shall not. I have seen enough and too much already . . . But Macy and Nicholas will find everything new, it will be *their* time, they will be as eager as I was when I started out. You remember what it was like? Or are you and Merloyd too young yet to remember your childhood? Or maybe you just won't have time for it in the next fifteen years, watching childhood in full tilt!

And coping with it courageously, I don't doubt.

Now then, Seymour, I have had so many letters and notes about "Holiday" of course mostly from friends, but still, tens of dozens of Christmas cards and nearly every one praising the story—over and over they make me a little uneasy by saying in effect it is the best thing I ever did . . . I hope not, somehow,—or anyway, not the best thing I shall ever do . . . And my God, the efforts of that idiot typesetter to ruin it didn't quite come off: I was so outraged by "hysterical" instead of "mystical" I didn't mention two other beastly things: one, a phrase about the German peasants, landloving, who "struck their mattocks" into the earth. The idiot set it up as "stuck," turning a word of some force and dignity into something trivial and ignoble. Further, the Idiot—I think he deserves a capital letter by now! mangled a whole important passage about the fireflies in the orchard. My corrected proof reads the way I wrote it and wanted it to appear: "When I went through the orchard the trees were all abloom with fireflies." The reference to the fireflies, the sole, single reason for describing the scene at all, was *left out!* the Idiot just jumped the line and went on blindly in his ape-like way! Dear Seymour, need we be so utterly at the mercy of this kind of creature? haven't you got any way at all to find out who does such things? Do you have to keep him on and pay him for such tricks?

Well, I know you have nothing much to do with the magazine, and I'm glad of it! Do you know, of course I hadn't noticed it, but a friend did, that in spite of my three sections of the novel appearing, my name has never been mentioned as a contributor in the advertisements? I think this is not very important, but it does rather go along with the rest.

Just the same, my dear, the *Atlantic* people shouldn't think I am too difficult—tell them to read about Dr. Seuss in the *New Yorker* if they want to see what a really difficult customer can be! I am sorry to trouble you who are my good friend and counselor and defender, but I am sick to death of the mean little people who swarm over everything decent and worth doing in this world and louse it up with their dirty cynical carelessness, I cannot hate and despise them enough and I shall fight them until I die. They have stood between me and what I am trying to do well ever since I published my first line, and if I can do no more in self-defense than to remind them now and then of what they really are and how they look to a human being, why, then, I shall do that! And I wish I believed in a Hell—it would be so pleasant to think of them stewing there eternally.

It is incredible the amount of disturbance and uneasiness and suffering this business has caused me, it makes me afraid to try to publish another story. And yet, I have published a good many and never had such a disastrous experience as this . . . I am going on of course, and I am going to stop thinking about this but it has ruined Christmas for me, and made me unable to work at anything. Seymour darling, the god-damned book will be ready soon, but we MUST make certain that nobody is allowed to touch it, not one word must be changed or tampered with by ANYBODY but me, and nobody's advice must be taken but yours—I am firmly determined that if anything goes wrong this time, we shall know exactly where to place the responsibility; in book galleys the typesetter's sign or initials appears on every galley, we shall be able to identify any one who muddles a line or changes a word. Please let us see to this. I had rather destroy the whole novel and forget it, than to have it made absurd by the imbecility of some typesetter. Shouldn't there be some sort of literacy test for people of that kind?

Oh yes, I can see my way through the thing now, you are right, this should be Our Year, and it shall be. Bless you for everything, give my love to my special darling and to all who will have it, and I will write again when I am a little less upset.

Faithfully yours and happy New Year to you! As if you needed such a wish. Macy and Nicholas will look after the New Year for you and Merloyd.

Katherine Anne

Heaven help us! The roses! They are standing here looking at me, tall and a real red velvet color, like the hangings on the Blessed Virgin's bed in medieval Flemish paintings. They have a delicate perfume and their name is Happiness. Thank you.

TO CYRILLY ABELS   3112 Q Street, N.W.
                               Washington, 7, D.C.
                               December 31, 1960

Cyrilly darling:

. . . . About some things I wish we could simply talk, for your letter after reading "Holiday" (about your sister, and all the strangeness of that life) simply overwhelmed me, for all sorts of reasons. One of them is this, that again and again I am astounded at how very little I do know of the intimate lives of my dearest friends,† persons who seem and are so very close to my heart. It comes out in all kinds of ways. Once years ago an FBI man called on me to ask me about a friend of mine suspected of Communism (it was during one of those flurries) and now, would you believe it? I had known this friend for years, we had spent our leisure time together just talking about everything, one might have said; and we

---

†*Cf. KAP's letter to Donald Elder, June 14, 1942: ". . . it is surprising to find how little one does know about the actual life of one's friends."*

wrote long letters to each other for years; and I should have said we pretty well knew everything worth knowing about each other. I was floored when this agent looked upon her as a seriously subversive and conspiratorial character. I was happy to tell him the entire truth, that I had never dreamed of such a thing, that so far as I had ever known she had no politics at all, Right, Left or Center. He looked dissatisfied but went away. And quite years later I learned that she was a Communist, and had been all along, and had got a good government job and was busy gnawing away in the woodwork; can you imagine? . . . .

Love
Katherine Anne

TO SEYMOUR LAWRENCE 3112 Q Street, N.W.
Washington, 7, D.C.
20 January, 1961

Dear Seymour:

It seems Carson McCullers didn't get here, and I know that Tennessee didn't. He telegraphed saying he was in doctor's care in Florida I forget where, and can't make it either. So after the flurry it did look as if life might settle down. I didn't go to the Lippmann's tea party yesterday, but had to explain to three different persons by telephone all afternoon about it. There was a blinding snowstorm yesterday, today it is 20 degrees above zero and brilliant sun. I didn't go to pick up my tickets and write my name in the guestbook for President and Mrs. Kennedy. And today I decided I would not get stuck in that grandstand for the Parade, and of course, never thought of going to the ball, as I would have only one ticket. Well, it is now a little after 10 morning, at 20 minutes after eleven President Elect goes to the White House to pick up the President, they go together to the Capital to swear in the new one; this I mean to watch by television. SO—about fifteen minutes ago Allen Tate called and after some little discussion of ways and means, my part in this has been arranged thus: The Richard Eberharts are giving dinner for Allen and Isabella, Robert and Elizabeth Lowell, me, themselves and a blind date for me—I haven't any notion who my squire will be, but was assured he was presentable and hetero-sexual—"not like Tennessee," said Allen, merrily. Well, they were none of them able yet to get taxis to take them to the grandstand, we still don't quite know how I am to get to the dinner—it is only around the corner and up the street a ways as everybody in George-town is—as I cannot walk in a trailing black lace evening gown and green satin slippers, indeed, who would want me to?—there surely won't be taxis, the Eberhart's can't call for me because they'll be up to the eyebrows in dinner-giving; I shall probably have to ask the young man in the basement to drive me there, though he hates driving in snow. And so on . . . I simply don't need or want ANY of this, and I have done my best to keep out of it, but the pull and hail from all sides is simply frightful. There is something in me that just instinctively resists mass movements and popular landslides of all kinds, but try saying No!—a word nobody can hear, apparently. Did you ever try to resign from some organization that had elected you without asking you first? Try it sometime. You'll see better what I mean.

(Later, about 2 o'clock.) I watched the swearing in ceremony. The meeting of the Presidents and Vice-Presidents and all persons around them, wearing top hats again for a pleasant change, and the ladies, God bless them, looking very well, at the White [House] before the drive to the Capital, was very touching.

There was dignity and grace in everybody's manner, and ex-citement too and I felt most of all the moments when the Kennedys walked together through the main door of the White House, for the first time in their new life, and later, when President and Mrs. Eisenhower came out that door together for the last time. But when we got to the inaugural scene, there were delays, hitches, The Elect stood ready to go on, got tired of waiting, turned around and disappeared and came back later. Four senile longwinded old reli-gious prayed in turn; either the archbishop of Boston or a Cardinal from there went on and on in a loud drone instructing God as to his attitude towards this new administration, and the lectern caught on fire and smoked all around him, and secret service men swarmed about trying to catch his eye and stop him, but on he went, and it looked like a good blaze before he finally said Amen. It was an electric heater under the lectern. Every time anything was done to further the taking of the oaths, we were interrupted further for prayer by a preacher of the Christian church, Austin, Texas, a Greek Orthodox priest, and a very reformed Jewish rabbi—he wore no skull cap—and somewhere along as a sop to the downtrodden colored minority, poor old Marian Anderson sang the "Star Spangled Banner," all of it, in a cracked doleful voice off key in the high notes. Very well, let's see what the Methodists and the Hardshell Baptists and the Seventh Day Adventists and the Mormons and Jehovah's Witnesses, to say nothing of the Armenians, the Syrians, the Turks, the Ukranians, the Poles, the Polynesians and the Eskimos are going to say to such favoritism of these few, and a pretty damn dull unattractive few they were, too! and of course, like all of us, I clean forgot The American Indian! To say nothing of Robert Frost.

The camera played out and over all the faces that were of interest for the occasion, and they were studies of fatigue and boredom and anxiety and a patient hardy endurance of the utter misery of these moments, or hours, rather, and I admired them all, and had great human tender sympathy for them—they every one behaved like heroes . . . I swear I am sure it takes more courage, or anyway courage of a more lasting sort, to sit through things like this than it does to lead a squad of flame throwers in battle.

The new President made a good straight energetic speech, with a good deal of wit and turns of phrase that really stuck in the mind. I like him immensely, his positive force of character and confidence in the effectiveness of action taken for the right reasons . . . Well, we'll see. It is lovely to feel hopeful, if only for a day!

I don't know why I am writing all this, you must have seen the television yourself, and have your own impressions.

I am going to try to disappear, hope I will be ready for you when you arrive, I do believe this may be the finish, and may be I am going to survive and live to see the *Ship of Fools* set out on its voyage.

Yours
Katherine Anne

By the way I think for the first inauguration in the past 70 years there were no American Indian Chiefs in war bonnets to be seen! What are we to think of this?

To Seymour Lawrence   Rockport, Mass.
[postcard]   22 June 1961

Dear Seymour,

I'm getting a little superstitious about mentioning *The Subject* but I believe the good ship is coming to port about on the date expected. Trouble is, as I copy or edit, I write in new passages just to amuse myself, so I'll have something fresh to read when I'm correcting the mss. I am staying on to the 30th—I hope thats all right? I feel well and wonderfully cheerful. Love to Merloyd and you.

Katherine Anne

To Mrs. Robert Penn   25 June, 1961
Warren [postcard]

Dear Eleanor:

. . . . I love this place [Yankee Clipper Inn, Pigeon Cove] and mean to come back when I can. I live like a discalced Carmelite and *love* it, thrive on it—work on it like a good busy carpenter, with the shavings and chips falling everywhere. I hope you are all well, happy, working.

To Jordon Pecile   3112 Q Street, N.W.
     Washington, 7, D.C.
     3 July, 1961

Dear Giordano:

No alas, not even with a magnifying glass was I able to find you on that most impressive portrait of the USS *Forrestal.* But I do know more or less where you are, or were, the last letter I got—in the Aegean sea, lucky dog . . . I have so much to write I don't know where to begin. Well, first, Ernest Hemingway committed suicide yesterday with a double-barrelled shotgun in the front hall of his own house, at 7:30 more or less, in the morning, and it has been more or less announced as an accident while he was cleaning the gun.

I think this kind of nonsense would bring Ernest right up out of his grave. Imagine!

1: The first thing you do when you clean a gun is to unload it. The cartridge-chambers must be cleaned too. Nobody but an idiot would try to clean a loaded gun.

2: You can't shoot yourself with a rifle or a shotgun accidentally. You can be careless and shoot somebody else accidentally, but not yourself. The gun is too long, and you have to pull the trigger with your toe, or cock it and give it a good sharp bump on the ground or floor to blow your head off. This is chancy, it mightn't go off even so. Ernest Hemingway undoubtedly knew about guns and what they are good for.

3: What would you think of a man who got up at 7 A.M. or earlier, and in his pajamas and dressing gown took a loaded shotgun into his front hall of all places to clean it? Hemingway had his sillier moments as who doesn't? but they didn't take that form, I feel pretty certain. YET: his father killed himself after a long time of bad health. Hemingway had a very violent life, all of it intentional, he had two bad headwounds, and he hasn't been sane I daresay since the African plane crashes. His poor wife was asleep upstairs when he shot himself and heard it dimly in her sleep and said, it sounded as if he had pulled out a bureau drawer and dropped it . . . the kind of blundering around my poor father did after his mild stroke which led to his death a few months later. And he did this, and let her walk into it—going down stairs and finding his body there. A horrible cruel trick—he must have been crazy. Not a word so far as anybody knows now. He should have left her a note . . .

4: Still I think he must have depended on people knowing that of course he had shot himself—he woke up, or maybe hadn't slept, and knew that he couldn't take it another minute, and just got up and did the first thing that occurred to him, and don't I know how he felt? But he bungled things a little as he always did, leaving the margins a little scumbled, that was his style, and if his widow wants to say that she was married to the kind of natural idiot who, after half a lifetime as sportsman, big game hunter, dead-shot and self-made hero, didn't know how to clean a gun without shooting himself, why, let her. It may be for her better than admitting that at the last he didn't give a damn about her any more than he did about anything or anybody else, except himself, or rather his view of himself, and he just got up and left her with all the rest of the rubbish.

Well, its done and finished and this man, such a bore of a man really and such an incomplete artist, and so pitiable and so ill-conducted—I can hardly think of another man of his world fame who to me was so completely uninteresting and insignificant—has quite literally taken a whole era into the past with him. He really represented a period and a place and a point of view, and he did great harm in the sense that he confirmed mean little minds and limited intelligences in a kind of Hollywood notion of the deadpan hero—actually his code was not much above that of the Hollywood cowboy deadpan hero, and as for his famous too-much quoted phrase about "grace under pressure"—well, somebody had said that a long time ago, I cannot now remember who but it wasn't Hemingway's; he just had T.S. Eliot's habit of quoting without quotation marks. They were writing for one of the most illiterate publics this world ever saw in modern times at least—that noisy little Twenties crowd; they didn't ever expect any one to catch up to them. Or as I ventured in Eliot's case, he believed everybody had read the same books he had, and would recognize his sources. He made a reputation, actually! on Thoreau's famous opening line—or on the first page, anyway, of Walden "Most men lead lives of quiet desperation." (At the risk of being called a feminist, I would say, that goes for women, too doubled in spades. But I'm sure Thoreau meant, the human race.) I have always thought Hemingway's life was sad, and I suppose given his temperament and situation, sick, and no longer young (he aged very suddenly and prematurely, he looked and talked like an old man when he was barely fifty, and that is the high point in living to a normally maturing, aging person.) I suppose suicide was bound to be his way out. I only wish he had made a cleaner, franker job of it, but I do not know whether he was sane or not. Its a shock just the same—a very pathetic end, and to think of such despair and such loneliness! . . . .

Goodbye my dear Giordano with my same faithful friendly love, yours

Katherine Anne

To Ann Heintze   The Quarterdeck,
Yankee Clipper Inn
Pigeon Cove, etc.
Sunday morning,
27 August, 1961

Ann darling:

    . . . . Tell David and Donald I went sailing yesterday, in a high wind and lots of waves, and helped to sail a catboat, and it was such fun I wished they were along too. There is a whole club of seventeen catboats out there right now, stringing out to gather at the starting point, and pretty soon the gun will be fired and they'll all come racing back and it simply makes your mind dance with joy, it is so beautiful. . . .

    Whoops, here comes breakfast, my lumly coffee and cornflakes and cream and milk and buttered toast and strawberry jam and orange juice!!!! Where shall I begin with all this deliciousness? Right in the middle. They bring it on a big tray and set it on my luggage rack near the long open window—I have a glass wall, with long panel windows on each side—where the wind blows over me and the smell of the coffee and the sea smell—which is really seaweed when the tide is way out in the mornings, and my blissful well being—I haven't a pain or trouble in the world, darling, and I thought you'd be glad to know! it can't last, but its here now— well, this sentence has about got away from me, but I'm only trying to say, I can't imagine anything I could like better than this. Of course, the real reason is, the novel's finished. Without that, as you know, *nothing* was any good!. . . .

Love again, angel
Aunt Kat

To President John F. [3112 Q Street, N.W.
Kennedy Washington 7, D.C.]
 October 28, 1961

My dear Mr. President:

It was delightful to be given the opportunity to write in your guest artists' Album, to express simply and sincerely my happiness in seeing your Inauguration day arrive and the further pleasure of taking part in it by the invitation of you and Mrs. Kennedy.

I appreciate deeply your request for suggestions in the collaboration between government and the arts; it is a new thing, a real and exciting experiment in our country, and I dearly hope to be somehow useful in it. With my continuing thanks and regards to you and Mrs. Kennedy.

Very respectfully,
Katherine Anne Porter

To John Malcolm 3112 Q Street, N.W.
Brinnin Washington, 7, D.C.
 4 November, 1961

Dear Malcolm:

. . . . Well, my short but pretty dream of living in the glass-walled house over the cove just beyond Folly Cove is past, but I say there are other coves and other houses, and I shall find one over the water with a little inner cove of its own where I can harbor my fleet of catboats: they are already named, *The Dreadnaught, The Resolute, The Challenge,* and their dingies are named *El Listo, El Vivo,* and *El Bravo.* The Lively, The Ready, and The Brave—These were the names of the tugs that used to haul the train by ferry when we went from Texas to New Orleans. Did you ever see anything like that? The whole train ran onto tracks on an immense ferry like a wharf, and these busy little tugs grabbed on and dragged this monstrous object clear across the river, fitting the tracks to the tracks on the other side, and the trains just rolled onto them and away we went once more. Why did I remember their names, I wonder? It was an all-night trip from San Antonio and I used to wake up in the morning with all the commotion and look out either side of the car and see the little tugs that somehow reminded me of fighting bulldogs, gripping and struggling; and I could not see how such little fellows did such a huge job. . . .

Your friend
Katherine Anne

To Barbara Wescott   3112 Q Street, N.W.
Washington, 7, D.C.
3 May, 1962

Barbara darling:

    . . . . The reviewers have been calling me skeptical and pessimistic, poor misguided men. My trouble—and yours with me, and other friends who have borne with me—is that I am wildly believing and optimistic to simple idiocy. My belief is, there is nothing I cannot bring to pass by simply making a far-sighted plan and seeing it through, step by step. This has been known to work with so many people it cannot be called altogether sancta simplicitas. But me, the flaw is I plan without regard to the plans of the world around me, if not the entire planetary system, I make no provision for that margin of human error, mine and everybody else's, and so I wind up at this time of life with about a half-million dollars I can't get my hands on, my ideal house hovering on the edge of reality with only 57,000 dollars to go, and an emerald ring that will bring joy to your eyes, it is as beautiful a ring as ever I saw; and all this looks pretty mad from exactly where we stand now, and yet, they seem rather simple and basic desires—(Do you remember that *New Yorker* joke about the woman so improvident she hadn't even got her basic mink yet?) at least, nothing a woman shouldn't be allowed to have after fifty-odd years of wanting them! I know that's no guarantee—this earth is made up layer upon layer of the dust of those who went to their graves unsatisfied, unfulfilled of everything. After all, these material pretties were not the main thing with me, if they had been I believe I might have got them long ago: but they will be a kind of dessert, something nice—I don't care for desserts, let's say brandy and coffee, at the end of what has been, after all, a long, strenuous but exciting party! . . . .

So, angel, its done now, the line is crossed, I'm going to have that house, the very best house for me I ever saw, and you and Lloyd are right, it is a good buy . . . I have never seen anything at all to compare with it even at a greater price . . . But above all, I love the space and variety of its plan, that little brook, all that lovely land to plant things on, and that swimming pool, pure *lagniappe, that* I never dreamed of, but I shall love having it.

Imagine, they keep telling me—(THEY are of course, those Little Brown people you were looking for at the party, remember? I forget who said, more or less, that the Little, Brown people were doing this charade, and you asked, "What little brown people? I don't see any," which for me is the delightful mot of the evening. I don't dare pass it on, but its beautiful.) Well, they keep telling me that I have been since the second week the No. 1 best seller from coast to coast in everywhich way, and it does seem so odd that I have to borrow from my best friend and negotiate with lawyers who will negotiate for me, I hope, with a bank, and all this hoopla to get a house to live in, at my time of life. I wonder why some of the reviewers think I take a gloomy view of the state of this world . . . I always knew one thing, that life is made bearable and possible and liveable by the relations of one human being to another, the individual love and gentleness between persons, or in any case, the unbreakable bond that grows and fastens lives together in all sorts of mysterious ways; nothing else seems to work at all except by some impersonal force that seems to me evil in essence; but I don't insist. I know what I have learned, and am pretty sure of my feelings, which are fairly steadfast . . .

Katherine Anne

To Barbara Wescott 3112 Q Street, N.W.
Washington, 7, D.C.
19 May, 1962

Barbara darling,

I have really had one hell of a slam-bang setback about that house business; this morning bright and early by special delivery came letters from the natural guardians and mentors of the female sex, especially about money, two lawyers and a publisher, and they pointed out to me unmistakably that I cannot afford the lovely place, and indeed, I gather, what with the revenooers and all and our troubled times, not anything else, either. So what the hell? I now possess a twenty-one carat emerald ring, full of "silks" as they say in the trade, that is, flawed, but a fine deep color, entirely surrounded by twenty four pretty good looking diamonds adding up to about two carats, and this, obviously, is about all I can expect for the next two years . . . Well, darling, I didn't expect even this, this time a year ago, or ever, so I growl not, as the Schubert song so sweetly says. (*Ich grolle nicht,* in case you haven't got it in mind at the moment.)

Well, take back your beautiful loan, its all over; I am simply going to forget about a house until I can accumulate "a little sumpen," as poor people used to say in Texas, and I am in the mood that this kind of thing awlays brings me—a kind of hilarious don't-give-a-damn mood that I suppose carried me over safely from one human disappointment to another. Barbara, I wouldn't for the world let you think I regard you as an angel, but I must simply say that on any occasional crisis, you invariably act like one. I don't know how you do it, and its none of my business, but it raises my spirits and gives me faith in all sorts of human adventures. And I never stopped being surprised at myself, the way I can see a house I like and would like to have, and then simply do it over perfectly and move in and live there happily for the rest of my life, and all in fifteen minutes! I noticed this in myself many years ago. Its next best—and you do know what we both think of the next best!—thing to really living in it. Dear me, I had even bought a little third-hand jalopy and was driving again. (mind's eye only, darling, a small added fillip to the dream.)

Now then, I am flying *Air France* on June 3rd to Paris with Ann; I invited her and got her hopes up to fever degree, and so now we are going; but first to Paris for eight days and then to Rome for eight days and on to Sicily—Taormina, NOT Capri, and so back to New York *Alitalia,* and if that little interlude doesn't knock the soreness out of my mind, nothing will. After that I have really no plans except to find a quiet spot where I can sit down not too expensively and finish my Cotton Mather book which I began researching for in 1928 and started writing in 1929. I still want to write it. I have eleven chapters—(I wrote *pages,* can you imagine?) of a 20-chapter book, I may be able to condense and cut down but I'll have to wait and see. . . .

This is the last you'll hear from me about money, you might be glad to hear. But what use is there with my unsettled life, to make any plans? I'll write where ever I am, and go to Hollywood when the time comes, and come back again when the stint is ended. I don't know where I'll come back to, and I am not going to think about it. In a rather specific way I do seem to have here no continuing city, except in my head, in my heart. I live where my friends are, in my thoughts and my love and surely that is enough! . . . .

> Love as always
> *Katherine Anne*

TO GLENWAY WESCOTT San Domenico Palace Hotel
Taormina (Sicilia)
18 June, 1962

Glenway darling,

Your letter came this morning while I was sitting in monastic ease at my austere breakfast of a delicious roll, curls of sweet Irish butter, café au lait, and strawberry jam; looking on a landscape of unscalable peaks with terraces and a cross at the top—terraces of lemon groves, bougainvillea, yews, cypresses, pomegranates in flower, fig trees in green fruit. . . .

I haven't had my bath yet even, and it is nearly ten o'clock.

This is the last week of our beautiful holiday. Yesterday, we left Rome by Alitalia at 4.15 arrived at Catania Airport 15 to 6, drove 60 miles through Catania, Paestum and other small villages whose name I didn't catch, all the way a clamor of church bells, bursting rockets and all sorts of fireworks, processions of guilds of various kinds carrying banners; and in each procession a statue of St. Anthony of Padua being carried aloft, with lilies at his feet and a child in his arms—little orphans in procession with solemn Antonian nuns and monks marched orderly sweetly dressed, with a gang of 10 year old girls among them wearing their first Communion dress. But I shall remember when everything else is gone, a procession of about twenty babies, between 2 1/2 and 3, marching 2 and 2 with a nun at head and foot, *singing in Latin* a lovely hymn, with tiny tender *true* voices, really singing in a trained, serious fashion. I shed tears, darling. It was too much for me!

I was told that all these hundreds of children, boys and girls from 2 1/2 to 12 or 13, were *orphans,* cared for by nuns and monks, and of course, St. Anthony is the patron of children, animals, and lost things and lost people, and here—perhaps other places too, but I never saw it—this is the feast of the Orphans and the friendless in honor of St. Anthony. . . .

Same devoted love—
Katherine Anne

To Gay Holloway [3112 Q Street, N.W.
Washington 7, D.C.]
1 October, 1962

Sister darling:

Here is another check, and I suppose the last one to be sent directly from me to you, as I want to make certain it reaches you anyhow by the fifth of every month, and I shall be in Europe for a good while. So Little, Brown and Co will have their bank send the money to your bank in Houston, and there we'll be, all cosy.

As always, when I spoke to my bank, they seemed to think there must be some legal thing about transferring a $3600 per year gift to anybody; but my CPA tells me *no.* It is a gift outright, and you don't have to pay income tax on it, but, hooray! neither do I. You just enjoy it as far as it goes, and I'll just forget the whole thing. The bank can look after our grandiose financial affairs.

Thousands of things to do, angel, and half a dozen trips out of town to speak or read. . . .

Love as always
Sis K.A.

SECTION 12

Rome, Paris, Washington
November 1962 to
November 1963

Being a writer of fiction, it is fearfully important for me to know always as nearly as I can find out, just what really happened! *Otherwise how could I let it work in my imagination until it turns into fiction . . . ?*

Katherine Anne Porter to Barbara Wescott
December 22, 1962

THE *LEONARDO DA VINCI* RUNS AROUND ALL STORMS AT SEA. *In Rome Katherine Anne Porter almost takes a whole floor in the Palazzo Fiorentini from a certain marchesa, but her lawyer says, "You have to look out for these Milanese Nobilities." In Florence, "I was so enchanted with the Duomo . . . and above all else, Giotto's Tower with the great bell in it that simply wrung my heart and soul with something near an ecstasy." Pope John XXIII dies while she is in Venice, at nearly eight in the evening, on June 3, 1963. "The great bells have rung and clamored, but there is a lightness in the air . . . and the whole place seems gay again. Isn't that a lovely way to take death—and life too?" She warns Flannery O'Connor that she, too, would be "teamed with any number of unlikely running mates. . . . And now I have graduated into the society of Flaubert, Melville, Stendhal, Henry James, and even Tolstoy. Fast company, I call it, and it does me no earthly good, and it is the device of lazy-minded third-rate reviewers who can't read." Katherine Anne Porter returns to the United States. She goes to the Capitol, to the lying-in-state of the assassinated President.*

To Glenway Wescott   American Express
[postcard]   38 Piazza di Spagna
                            Rome, Italy
                            30 November, 1962

Dear Glenway:

For long, my theory has been that sloppiness, carelessness, stupidity cause more muddle than downright malice—in effect, they often add up to malice! Example: the current nomination sheet. The howler in the 5th line of my citation for Flannery, the word, as I remember, was *severity*. Is there any known way of getting this tacky little gaffe corrected? I am quite simply disgusted. And after all these years, they have not noticed how I sign my name. It is *not* Katharine as on the envelope, and even less Katherine <u>A</u>. as it appears on the citation . . . I am writing a note to Flannery and to Eudora—but I know that such idiocy cannot really be dealt with or corrected or cured . . . I can only tell them what I really wrote, and leave the rest to their knowledge of what I think and feel about them—

                            Love as ever—
                            Katherine Anne

To Barbara Wescott   Hotel Eden
                            49 Via Ludovisi
                            Rome, Italy
                            22 December, 1962

Barbara darling:

. . . . Yes, I am really living it up, rumors are right for once, though not in the Palazzo Fiorentini which I had seriously in mind. Almost automatically I looked about for an apartment, meaning to take it for a year, saw half a dozen with a brash go-gettum young Sicilian, all beautiful, any one of which would have done nicely, but I fell in love with this great floor in a 15th century palace in the old Florentine section of town, renovated but not ruined, with twenty foot ceilings, and the whole interior a 15th century Florentine day-dream of gold leaf everywhere it would stick on ceiling, fifteen-foot looking glasses, and furniture. It was a pure riot of gold, silver and brocade curtains, draperies, even the beds looked as if they wore head dresses and trains of brocade and gold cloth. The closets were full of silk and linen sheets, and so on. Great shelves of Venetian glassware, vermeil table ware, marvelous porcelain, and oddments like a five-gallon pure silver soup tureen that looked a good deal like an enlarged version of that famous salt-cellar by—oh, what is his name? We've known it all our lives—the one who wrote a highly fictitious version of his countless escapades with easy ladies—still the name does not come. My mind has been behaving like this ever since I turned it out to grass for a while.* Well, let me get on with this story, which contains only plain facts and some not so plain. Slender silver wine pitchers two feet tall. Marble, marble, everywhere. Even the two fine baths, not counting the servants apartment, were all marble and handmade tiles and glass, and the kitchen was a miracle of how many ovens and washing machines and ice boxes and deep freezers and whatever other electrical housekeeping machinery there is—that could be concealed in a fancy glass and tile wall! I just say of these labor saving devices it would be a full time job for one person to operate them. Well, needless to say, I have never lived in a palace, and I thought this was as good a time as any to give it a try. I was delighted as a child at a Christmas tree, and though it was expensive, I hastily re-organized my budget to accommodate my new palace life, wrote at once to some one—could it have been Glenway? telling my fine news, the agent went to get up the lease and we went back the next day, I think it was, in the evening, to see the owner and sign the lease. By now I had an interpreter from the hotel, as my Sicilian knew just enough English to say that he did not speak it, and neither did the owner, a certain Marchesa Venaro. She showed up under the great entrance in her pram-sized car, a good looking blonde woman in early middle life, very healthy and full of zing, with a lovely smiling face, huge grey eyes, wearing good looking country clothes. She turned out to have the flat just above the one I was until

*3 hours later! aha! Cellini!

then regarding as mine, but spends most of her time out of town somewhere.

Well . . . The brocades and gold cloth were stripped from the beds, with plain white counterpanes in their place. Gone were the silver, gold, porcelain, silk and linen, and the gold leaf chairs and canapés were covered with a plain dull red stuff, and indeed after a good look around, I asked one question: "Is this really the same place I saw yesterday?" As La Marchesa talked, and my interpreter asked her some searching questions, her manner changed—she showed the high spirits, bad temper and senseless excitement of a badly trained horse, and that good looking face was tough as a boot. What she wanted and would have, besides all that rent, was a deposit of two thousand dollars against possible wear and tear or damage or loss, two months rent in advance, (the first two months, not one now and the other for the last month) and I would have to supply my own linen. A whole battery of kitchen things like electric mixers, grinders, beaters, skillets—everything movable, nearly, was gone too. She must have had a squad of people working in there to have got so much done in that little time. When she showed me the servants' quarters again, two bedrooms, living room and bath, the mattresses even were gone. She seemed entirely unconscious of my total silence; I was letting the agent, the interpreter and La Marchesa do the talking, but my mind had been severely made up for a good while. "Of course, you will need two servants at least," she said, and the interpreter handed this remark on to me with a hasty addition of his own—"Don't you sign anything until you've seen a lawyer," running the sentence together until it sounded like one word. I said "Don't worry, I'm not going to sign anything. Tell the lady we will let her know tomorrow."

There was a final kind of flurry, the agent, who had got out his lease paper, put it back, we said rather hasty good evenings, and left. Out of sheer curiosity, I asked for the lease, and took it the next day to an old Italian hand in Foreign Service, used to be lawyer for the American Embassy, now practising with a younger Italian partner. My lawyer was from somewhere in the Middle West and he speaks Italian just the same way he speaks English—like somebody from Squeedunk, Ioway. And an old sweetheart he turned out to be. His Italian partner said, "You have to look out for these Milanese Nobilities, in the first place. Second, these leases are sometimes so complicated even an Italian lawyer can't make anything of them." And he said—bless him, "You just be glad you're out [of] *that*" (he graduated from Harvard law school.) I feel sure that most of the time, first impressions, whatever they may be, work both ways. And I can hardly remember when I got such a downright scunner on anybody as I did our thug Marchesa; I couldn't think of anybody I would care less to have in any affair of mine, at any distance, than she, and here she was going to be, part of the household just the next floor up and over my head, and she not liking me, either!

So. That has ended for the present, maybe for ever, my little project to live in a palace. And I tell it in detail because it is such a pleasure to me to set trivial facts straight before they swell into pure fantasy and take off into the Cloud Cuckoo Land of Legend. Being a writer of fiction, it is fearfully important for me to know always as nearly as I can find out, *just what really happened!* Otherwise how could I let it work in my imagination until it turned into fiction, like grapejuice into wine, let's say, or milk to clabber, maybe, or God help us, wine into vinegar, though that is the *best* vinegar, and I like clabber and sour cream and cottage cheese and so on, and how did I ever got tangled up with this series of comparisons of the way the imagination works? Its not like any of that at all. If I really knew I'd be happy to tell, but I don't. I just know its quite different from facts and yet made out of the same stuff with something added.

Oh, I must tell you this: When the young Italian law partner came in, and heard my name he asked if I were the writer. I said yes, naturally, and he said, "I read your *Ship of Fools* last spring. My mother was in New York when it came out and brought me a copy." And he praised it very nicely, while I glowed and glimmered, as you might know. Then he gave me a puzzled look, and asked quite seriously, "Did you *really* write that book?" At this, all three of us laughed, and the Italian said to his American partner, "Such a tender looking lady, and such a tough book!" I shouldn't go bragging like this, but I admit it made my day, and I forgot all about the Fiorentini fizzle. . . .

Day before yesterday between four thirty and five, when the clear twilight was coming on, I climbed those steep marble stairs in the tall house at the right hand side of the Spanish Steps if you remember, to visit the room where Keats died. I thought as I climbed what a thing for a man dying of tuberculosis to be doing! There is a beautiful long room, the entire floor apparently except for Keats' room and the old ceilings are there, but everything else changed. The room is so very little, so narrow, with a marble fireplace on the inner wall, and a great window looking out over the steps and up to the great church, and the houses across the way, it can hardly have changed at all. I looked at that scene, the very last he ever looked at, and I can't tell you how nearly his presence took *shape* there in that place; I never felt such a living sympathy with a dead person before, except with Alexander—the Adam of my World War I story, and my little six-year-old niece who died a few months after him. It was all very touching and gentle, unexpected too, for I had no special interest when I went in, only a perhaps easy kind of piety, a memorial visit. And I found myself wondering with a kind of anguish if that narrow little space beside the fireplace against the end wall was where he had his bed, for there was no place anywhere else but beside the window, and he died in February and we know he was cold in that room; and Severn's letter telling how glad Keats was when he knew that death had really touched him, this time he would be set free. My dear, a spirit lives there of love and remembrance; all those letters and little keepsakes and treasured small portraits and the humble little objects—he had almost no possessions, but he did love and was loved again; and the heart-breaking faithfulness of Severn's care for him to the last breath—all of it broke up some ice-floe or terrible hardening and numbness of my heart which has been forming a defensive shell almost without my knowing it; I came out and it was early dark, five o'clock, and the lights were on and the whole Piazza glittered with Christmas lights and shop windows full of holiday things. I walked back to the hotel, up that hill, slowly and happily with my entire being warmed and softened, a kind of gratitude of tears that the roots of my feelings and my beliefs that I have lived by were not dead, but just somehow beaten unconscious for a while by the savage forces that were nearly too much for me. The presence of that bravery and that genius and that love flourishing in the narrow room in the very face of a hard life and a long death, has touched and changed me, turned me back into my own path, has restored me to my own life: I was suffering more than I knew, as if I had lost everything and yet could not name it or tell when it began to go. Bless you, my angel, be patient to read this. I am strangely and wonderfully happy!

Have a splendid New Year. With my love to you both.

KA

To Donald Elder   Hotel Eden
                                   49 Via Ludovisi
                                   Rome, Italy
                                   17 March, 1963

Happy Birthday to yo-o-o-o-o-o-o-o!

Dear Donald:

By the time this letter reaches you, Aries will have moved into place, if I've read the calendar properly, and I hope the scrap of paper in it will help a little to change the luck—you know, I promised it you when we saw each other last November just before I sailed. I feel I *owe* it to you, in the happiest sort of way, positively lightheaded, maybe, because of course, I am paying back after all these years that time you tapped a source and out sprang $1500 to help me get to Reno and scrape off the albatross I had somehow got round my neck: I could never have done it without you, and I never forgot; even though I did have a few windfalls afterwards, I always had so many people right at my elbow waiting to snap up every dollar as it came, and that as if by *right,* mind you. I have never had a dollar repaid to me in my life, and I never expect to have; and I have a sort of pride in being able to say I have repaid everything, loans, even some gifts; or never was given a grant or fellowship that I hadn't already earned, or so they said . . . But THIS little deal is just something else, and it delights me . . . You got it from a publisher for me, just tossing your power around where it would do the most good, and *saved* my *reason,* if not my *life*—no, no the other way around! That was the rockbottom of my despair, disillusionment, that period finished off something in my life that never came again . . . And there you were, just saving the whole awfulness of the business with $1500. . . .

So this is a joyful, Robin Hood's barn way of straightening out a debt: I owe it to you somehow more than I do to those rolling-in-money publishers, and they're still rolling. This wouldn't pay their liquor bill. And it doesn't hurt me, either. I've got an income for life . . . not huge but enough. I just won a $1000 prize from Texas Institute of Literature and got $590-odd dollars royalty off some recordings made ten years ago—the Caedmon and the CBS have never tried to sell them, but apparently they haven't been able to avoid it since *Ship of Fools* came out—and I am sending this, because it is all so damned tidy, isn't it? Darling, may it do you good, it makes me happy to send it, I wish I knew the address of the hospital and I'd send it there. But maybe you'll be out, or have somebody to bring your mail. Please get well—let me know what they find wrong with you. And get well. Bless you, my dear good old-time friend, can you believe how long we have known and really *liked* each other? Love again as before and always

Katherine Anne

To GLENWAY WESCOTT   Hotel Eden
Via Ludovisi
Rome, Italy
2 April, 1963

Glenway my dear:

. . . . *Current Biography* starts out by publishing my full name, I think for the first time, and I wonder who told them. In any case they leave out the one that I think is interesting, and I will write it all out now for you with the omitted one restored in parenthesis: Katherine Anne Maria Veronica (Callista) Russell Porter. Katherine Anne for my maternal Grandmother, Maria Veronica confirmation name, Callista Russell for a girlhood friend of my mother; and they can always take time to look up such irrelevant stuff, and then get important things all wrong. It is discouraging. . . .

Proceedings, Second Series, Number Thirteen of the AAAL

and NIAL came yesterday and it seems to have been a brilliant year, from our point of view, and a few things I should have liked attending, such as Marianne's Birthday party, and I should have been happy to hear you and Eudora present medals, and all. . . .

I have read the report with pleasure—what a party. I should be so happy to see you and Monroe and Eudora and Marianne all at once, but I have no real hopes that this can ever happen.

The only false note was having Dos Passos speak the Eulogy for Faulkner . . . poor old Dos who has been lacking in almost every faculty required to make even a second rate writing man, has somehow done it with a kind of gobbish, shapeless emotionalism, I think I never saw anybody who so completely misses the point of everything simply because he has not got the necessary pores in his skin nor the brains in his head! to take in what he needs to absorb . . . Enough of this. There was a line of them from all directions and all sorts—Witter Bynner, Richard Aldington, Stephen Saint-Vincent Benet, John Dos Passos, Malcolm Cowley—make your own list . . . Oh how I *love* Admiral Samuel Eliot Morison and his good solid clear mind, and how grateful I am for his histories, that I treasure and turn to when such as those in the upper list nearly discourage me from living! (and very much in your own ear, I want to tell you something that happened at the Nobel Prize Winners Dinner at the White House. I did tell you how I met James Baldwin again after ten years, and we talked and he beamed, he was enormously shining-eyed and excited already—this was early in the evening—and as we all know he lives at pretty high tension, anyway. Well, did I tell you that later in the evening as we were standing in the long corridor waiting for the President and Mrs. Kennedy to pass on their way to the stairs, James Baldwin came leaping back, seized both my hands, put his face very close to mine and shouted, "I LOVE YOU!" and leaped away, leaving me a little surprised to say the least . . . That is all about that. But a few days later I met some one else who had been to that party, and he told me that James Baldwin had discovered Admiral Morison, and simply haunted him for the rest of the evening . . . couldn't be shaken off. And the Admiral later asked this man telling me the story, asked in great annoyance, "Who WAS that ugly little dinge who pestered me all night?"

I was thinking what would be said and thought and written

about a Southerner who should so far forget himself as to make such a remark? But from this justly famous member of a fine old New England Abolitionist family, it was not only well received, but with hilarious enjoyment!

It is when hearing things like this that I feel I am a member of a down-trodden minority, a rapidly disappearing species. It makes me feel lonely.)

Glenway there seem to be dozens of other things I wished to say, to answer your wonderful letter, but my mind doesn't stay fixed, there are too many layers of attention being constantly harassed, and with things not very entertaining to write about. I am sending with this the first number of a magazine ever dedicated to me, my sweet La Salle College who gave me the D.Litt too, last summer. There was some over flow into the following number, with a lovely piece by Caroline Gordon. They only sent me one copy and it has mysteriously disappeared. I shall send for more, and send it on to you. Heilmann's piece is very good, I think, (I knew him in the Louisiana *Southern Review* times) but I am always surprised that people cannot understand range and change and variety and contradiction and tragic feeling and a saving dash of frivolity and the deep sense of comedy, the salt of life that makes our daily bread bearable. But he is a good serious man and did well, I think.

And now I must stop this letter that I have been 10 days trying to get written . . . With my love and devoted attention, quand même—I will let you know when I get away on my holiday, taking four pieces of work and my typewriter with me! No good trying here.

Yours
Katherine Anne

TO JAMES F. POWERS

Hotel Eden
49 Via Ludovisi
Rome, Italy
Easter Tuesday, 16 April, 1963

Dear Jim:

. . . . It is dismaying to hear that *Morte d'Urban* is not selling well. I thought it must be, or would be going up when the award was announced; it had some very intelligent friendly reviews, as well as some sour ones that don't really do a writer any harm! And I have seen a continual casual passing reference to it in so many columns and news letters and all, the sort of thing that does a book more good I think than any amount of set-reviews; so I was at ease in my mind, and enjoying your success; for to have written a first rate book and then to have it praised and rewarded a little, and to have the admiration and confidence of your fellow writers that you can trust, IS success by my standards, the only kind I respect, the only kind I wanted; and I had it, for years, and was happy in it; I never expected anything more. But when, at that party given at 21 by my publishers, a purely commercial circus, full of reviewers and reporters and editors, some idiot I had met years before, and hadn't seen or thought of since, (I never did remember his name) rushed up and grabbed my hand, and shouted, "My GOD, Katherine Anne, isn't it like being brought back from the dead?" I knew I had wandered onto another planet, and a forever strange one. I am happy to be able to tell you that I collected my wits and said merrily, merrily! "Why, nobody told me you'd been dead!" I didn't see him any more, but it gave me an unpleasant jolt—I had rather forgot that people like that exist and in great mobs and they are noisy and they are everywhere—everywhere except where I live, and I have no business in that company. . . .

In the twenty years between the time I started that novel and finished it, I have done my best to figure up the time I really spent on it, and it runs like this: August 1921 N.Y. Two months—Began. Reno Nevada and Colorado, three months, summer 1942. Ten years without touching it or even looking at it. Accumulating notes and thinking about it now and then. I didn't want to write this novel, remember please. I had intended it to be the fourth of my group of short Novels, "Pale Horse, Pale Rider," "Old Mortality," and "Noon Wine." It wouldn't compress properly, so I rather lost interest in it. I had been so brutally nagged by publishers and others to write a novel I got in a state of catatonic resistance. I was a short story writer and by God they were going to acknowledge this or else!

Ho hum! Are you asleep? I couldn't blame you.

So then, I worked about two and a half months in a cellar apartment in 17th Street in New York 1952–54, went to University of Michigan, then to Liège Belgium, and so nothing more until I got to a country house in Connecticut summer of 1955, where I settled down for three years—one of the happy times of my life—in a country hermit existence, growing flowers, listening to music, reading, idling as I love to do, and nearly every day working a few hours on my novel, which suddenly pulled itself together and began to march. Let's say I spent a year of the three there on the novel. I don't believe it, but still, it makes a nice even number.

More interruptions—University of Virginia, Washington and Lee, move to Washington, D.C. a disaster; and then my publishers and I made up our minds together and I went up to Cape Ann and sat in an inn and finished that hellish book. It was five months altogether, and so that adds up: to a fraction over two years in all—I believe considered a normal amount of time to put in on a book—that is, normal by the standards of newspaper reviewers and publishers, who don't write them, and apparently have never found out how they ARE written. Anyway, this is how I remember it, and I can do no more. . . .

Back to the beginning! I hope *Morte d'Urban* SELLS!

Bless you. Yours
Katherine Anne

To EDWARD DONAHOE   19 Avenue du Général LeClerc
                       Villa Adrienne
                       Paris XIV, France
                       July 14, 1963

Dear Edward:

     .... What I really want to write to you about is this: for years and years I had in mind a collection of short stories very personal to my own tastes, just certain stories that impressed me and have stayed by me through the years, for their own reasons; of course as time goes, the list changes a little, I add and subtract, but at last, my Boston publishers have nailed me down and I have got up my final list and sent it in and am beginning my long preface. And I want to ask you—a little belatedly, but then I was never sure until just now that I really would ever do that anthology! for your "Head By Scopas," which has been on the list from the beginning! It is strange how many persons I meet here and there, through the decades really, who remember that story! Maybe you are tired of it—For ten years at least I was known as the author of "Flowering Judas," and nobody would pay any attention to anything else of mine. It used to discourage me a little. One time Padraic Colum was reading his poems to an audience, and I asked him for "An Old Woman On The Roads," one of my favorites, and apparently, everybody else's, for he gave me a look that was as nearly bitter as that angelic countenance could raise, and said in a murmurous voice, *"I wish I had never written that poem!"*

     Well, just the same, I am glad I wrote "Flowering Judas," and I am glad Padraic wrote "The Old Woman," and a lot of people as well as myself are glad you wrote "Head by Scopas." I have met here in Paris lately two young men in Foreign Service, one from Texas, one from Oklahoma, who asked me about you; they brought up your name first, for I had no notion who they were—you know how it is apt to be at these large afternoon parties; and I am notably a Babe in the Woods—in such things; sometimes don't know exactly where I am, much less who I am talking to. But there you were, your story being remembered and loved and talked about here in Paris at this time, and it having been published so long ago—wasn't it in *Southern Review* in Baton Rouge? It should have been but I can't remember exactly. So when my editor, Seymour Lawrence, saw my list, he was pleased and wrote: "I was very interested to find one or two 1st favorites of mine such as 'HEAD BY SCOPAS,' and it brought back to me the memories of Donahoe as told me by an Oklahoma classmate of mine one evening during our undergraduate days. Amazing to see the name here!"

Well, the next thing will be of course letters to your publisher asking permission and offering a fee, that is out of our hands; but I hope you will be pleased to be in my book, which is going to be a company of my friends—my idea of a friend in an anthology being some one who has written a story I love, which appealed to me for reasons particular to myself and nobody else! So I CANNOT leave out your story, unless you forbid me to have it—which I shall not for one moment believe unless you write me! . . . .

Love as ever, please write to me—

Katherine Anne

To Robert Penn Warren Villa Adrienne
19 Avenue du Général LeClerc
Paris XIV, France
22 July, 1963

Dear Red:

A funny thing happened on my scamper across country, across ocean, across some more country, from Washington to New York to Rome to Naples to Florence to Venice to Paris—now nearly nine months of freedom (limited) and recovery (slow) from the appalling consequences of having at last broken down and, against my better judgment, finished *that book.* No, I can't be sorry I finished it: I'm just sorry it brought so many curious forms of life out of the rocks and wood work; and I was just too tired and bedevilled to cope. But the funny thing that happened—there were several, but you know about this one—is, that somewhere along the road, I think Florence, among the packet of mail I get sent on from time to time, there came two letters: one, from the committee of four from *Partisan Review,* asking me to send $250.00 towards getting up a fund to tide over the *Review* until it can make it safely to the shelter of some University: the second was a slight nudge from Mr. Trilling saying they had not received my check or any answer. You know, don't you? from experience, how suddenly your daily mail is crowded with requests for contributions from every possible or imaginable source; I have never been granted a fellowship or even got a little prize for something or other, that I didn't have letters asking for sums that were four or five times more than the money I had received. So this was no surprise, except for this: I have not seen a copy of the *Partisan Review* for at least ten years or more: They have not shown any faintest interest in my work for even a longer time, I should say. I have never really been sympathetic to their literary politics and I cannot learn to trust the judgment in any matter of any one who was ever a Trotskyist; and after observing their strategic shifts and changes through the years, I gave up reading them.

Now I saw that you were one of the four signers of the original request: and this shook me a little. I felt a little that I should contribute to a review you believed to be worth saving. And yet . . . the *Partisan Review,* all of its editors and most of its contributors, and I, have got along so nicely without each other all these years, I have a certain uneasiness about changing the situation or the relationship at this late day, and for no reason that I am able to see EXCEPT that you, my old valued friend and most-loved and admired poet and critic, are associated with it. You see how remote it is from me: I did not know this was true, and I have no idea how it came about. But just the same, I am glad that these letters reached me at least a month late, perhaps more: I haven't them by me now, I make up occasional packets of letters and send them back to storage! and at a time when I was pretty well sunk in some other peoples' needs and troubles, or I might just have weakened and sent it! But, in the next mail, came a copy of the review of my book that P.R. had published. It had been torn out and mailed with apologies from some one, one of my kind friends who misguidedly tried to protect me from such *curare* arrows as appeared in *Commentary.* This is touching and all, but it makes me furious . . . I wanted to see everything, it has been simply fascinating to see how enraged reviewers got and each one for his particular sore spot; and God they were a sore-spotted crowd, mostly. But where the poor little

Commentary man just frothed and spewed, the other one—I never heard of either and can't remember their names—the PR hatchetman, did a mean, cold nasty job of belittlement; it was odd to see Mary McCarthy's remarks about the deliberate attempts to destroy another book she had in mind, so perfectly illustrated here in this piece. But you should have seen the English reviewers! I had three lovely ones, and the rest just went blind, and their stuff was more like plain assault and battery than reviewing. Well, darling, you know how wonderfully I have been treated all my writing life by the press and by the best critics in my country: I was just rotten spoiled and didn't realize it . . . I was just happily reposing in this confidence of my friends. And I wouldn't take anything for my beautiful, long-lasting reputation, which I would never have had if I had not been lucky in my gifted friends who really read me and knew what I was trying to do . . . That, nothing can take away from me. And this sudden onslaught from a real lynching mob, out for my blood, was—Red this is disgraceful—entirely exhilarating! I have been gleefully entertained watching these perfect strangers make total fools of themselves, because not one of them has ever hit anywhere near what that book is "about." (Do you remember in Forster's remark that a certain book was about a certain thing in the same way that Moby Dick is a book about a whale?) Even those who praised it didn't put their finger on the point. And it seems to me so clear I would be ashamed to explain it any further . . . But I did finally write to one of the English publishers who really apologized for the low state of British reviewing, and I said, It just comes to this, that people who can't read shouldn't be given books to review . . .

But at any rate, there was only one truly frightful thing said about my work, which was certainly as false as anything ever said, but it came from one from whom I least expected such treachery: Robert Lowell—its true I have known him since he was nineteen, but then, I have known Edmund Wilson since 1922, and I can't call Robert *Cal* nor Edmund *Bunny.* I just don't know them well enough. And I could never call you anything but *Red*—and can you ever hear me calling Tinkum Edith? but anyway, what possessed poor Robert Lowell to say I was a sort of Mrs. Wharton? Suppose I should call him a sort of W.B. Yeats? It would be a damn sight more flattering, but no nearer the facts in the case!

Well, what a dance around Robin Hood's barn just because I decided to let the PR struggle along without me, as it always has, and look how nicely we have both done! It is true, Red, I have made a lot of money on that book, just a small fraction less than a million up to last December 2nd, and there is more to come from all directions and all sorts of publications—as my publishers tell me, a whole field not touched yet. Of course I cannot have the money; but I have got a perfectly good income, which was settled on before the book was published; they wanted me to take much more, but I refused, because I didn't have the faith in the financial side that they had. But it is not so bad. . . .

> With my same love
> *Katherine Anne*

To James Stern   Villa Adrienne etcetera
                            Paris XIV
                            16 August, 1963

Dear Jimmie:

   . . . . The mystery to me is, why one human being can bear his life to its natural end, and yet his fate may be no less terrible and incurable than that of his friend who will despair and make an end to himself. We blame bad marriages and so on, but no one needs to go on with a bad marriage. There is in *Under The Volcano* expressed a most horrible hatred of women, but many many men hate women even worse than he did, and many women hate men, and yet they manage to live rather cheerfully, all things considered. No, it *cannot* be what actually happens to any one, it is a matter of resistance, of a fibre that can take any strain, that accounts for survival. I used to think I would die of my troubles, and more than once I meditated suicide. But every time I was seriously threatened, I resisted instinctively, even against my will as it sometimes seemed; but I know now that only accident or the natural wearing away of vitality will put me down . . . So my mind is all made up, and I intend to make the best of what is left of this quite gruesome (in spots) world.

I'm delighted you agree with my views in the interview [in *The Paris Review*]. That was a most remarkably intelligent and beautiful young personage who made that interview—we had two long sessions, millions of words, two consecutive summers, 1960–1961, and meantime she had left off journalism and got married to some high-up cabinet minister in Pakistan, a Mohammedan, and had gone to live in that intransigent and untidy country, and already has two little boys, and I am godmother to the second, a swarthy black-eyed little Christian, as I take him to be: I think the godmother relation is a Catholic custom? Anyway, his name is Dan-i-yal, and he is cute as a button. And Barbara [Thompson] seems to be thriving. She is immensely beautiful and there are young men stashed around in American Embassies in four countries, to say nothing of South African Cultural Attachés and sundry naval officers and all, who cherish her memory; and when, according to her marriage contract, she returns for three months of every year to her native land, (and also at each birth of her children) she has a kind of triumphal procession, being entertained by her former suitors. In Rome last February it was wonderful to see her, as pregnant as a woman can get, I'd say, at cocktail and dinner parties, and out to lunch, all arranged by her Rome beau. She had been through the Paris and London ones, and was on her triumphal way to New York . . . The most modest, gently reserved, properly behaved, moral young woman you'll ever see, she just has that fatal charm which she exudes as naturally as breathing. She does not try, she demands nothing, and she *gives* nothing except that exhilarating sense of joy and well-being that she rouses in men and makes them happy just to sit in the same room with her . . . Its a rare gift and one not had for the asking and nothing one can "use." I gave Dan-i-yal, who wasn't born yet, one of those lovely Italian silk blankets; houses are cold in Pakistan, Barbara told me. Well, that is a long rigamarole about the interview, but I do think she did a good job. There are a few little errors in names, etc. but not serious. I find the *Paris Review* crowd even goofier and with worse manners than *Encounter.* But that is their business. I have got along nicely all these years without them and can go on nicely to the end. . . .

About "Charles Congreve Esquire." My editor sent me a bale of photostats and among them "The Woman Who was Loved," and it is just as good as ever it was, and it has a center and a meaning that I would like to write a little about, and so, if you don't mind, I'll just settle for this, because it is fine and also it "goes with" other choices—I find a line of continuity in my choices, there is something I look for in each one, and they all relate to a central esthetic and moral article of faith in my own mind; I must think this out and say it as clearly as I can: it is not that I have all these years been choosing stories that agreed with my point of view; but that unconsciously my choice has been guided by *some profound element in my own character, which also formed my own work and life.* Well, that's enough for now. I'll try to say it better in the preface. . . .

Love
Katherine Anne

To MONROE WHEELER   Villa Adrienne
19 Avenue du Général LeClerc
Paris XIV, France
September 3, 1963

Monroe darling:

     . . . . The real news, the heart of the day is of course that Braque is dead, and do you know, he lived just around the corner from where I am, no. 6 rue Douanier, and today until 4 o'clock people will be received to bring flowers and sign the memorial book; I am going to sign, and take a bouquet of little clear-red roses. He will be taken away tonight and buried in a Marine cemetery near his country place, Varengeville-sur-Mer. From the earliest times of their careers, I loved best Klee, Modigliani, Juan Gris—Braque dawned on me more slowly, and you remember when I first saw those miraculous great windows opening into gardens of Bonnard; these were and are my loves, one can no more account for tastes and feelings in painting or music or poetry than one can for any other kind of love . . . But I can't tell you how touched I am, how strangely joyful to tears I am to know that the great wonderful old master, one of the glories of his time, is safe and resting after his long suffering; but in the most mysterious way I feel his presence; knowing he was there has left a special radiance in this rather dull work-a-day neighborhood; I cannot regret the death of one so old and who had so grandly accomplished his life; but if I had known he was so near I should have taken flowers to his door before this. I would have just left them for him, you know I would never have asked to see him. . . .

I'm so happy about Glenway's *Farewell to Wisconsin* [sic] coming out in paper back: I've sent a few lines to go on the jacket†
. . . Now I hope they'll bring out the others—I want to see *Apartment in Athens* and *The Pilgrim Hawk* and the first two: *Apple* and *Grandmothers*—ALL in paperback with a million readers. . . .

Bye darling, for the moment. You sound so well and merry!

Katherine Anne

---

†*The few lines for the jacket of* Good-Bye Wisconsin:

"*These stories by Glenway Wescott may be read with pleasure, and reread, for every reading brings out new shades of meaning and richness of feeling. The plain but dense style, full of warmth and reservations, can be misleading: it makes things seem simple. Better look again. You are reading the stories of one of the best-endowed writers this country has ever produced. All his work shows a rare balance of power between his intelligence, which plays like a high-powered searchlight over his emotions, which are deep and violent; his view of life, which is innately tragic—yet he has a genius for friendship; and his social sense, which is acutely developed and active. These good and dangerous gifts take scrupulous handling or they can run away with a life. Genius has won the day, as it sometimes does, and his powers have been put to scrupulous good use. His love stories are about persons who really love each other, no matter how unfortunately; his really unfortunate persons are those who cannot love, but you believe in all of them, their happiness or their disasters. His horror stories are really horrifying because he does know exactly the nature of what he is telling. His people are humble, mostly, sometimes sadly defeated by their circumstances, for one deplorable weakness or another, but they are not moral imbeciles or subhuman waterheads, as too often the presently acceptable hero seems to be. If they are monsters, Mr. Wescott sees them clearly, and we see them clearly too; he does not try to trap us into the sentimental sympathy, which is criminal collusion.*"

To Ann Heintze

Villa Adrienne
19 Avenue du Général LeClerc
Paris XIV, France
23 September, 1963

Ann darling:

. . . . In getting up my anthology, I have gone back years and years, gathering up stories I have remembered and loved, things you don't see in the anthologies, people just go on reprinting the same things; this is a fairly unfamiliar collection; and I wrote to an old friend to ask permission to re-print his story, "Head By Scopas" which appeared it must be thirty years ago in a little magazine. He has been in a rest-home in Mexico, had a complete break-up many years ago, thought this story was forgotten, and it has been terrible and touching and sweet to see what an effect my finding him has had on his spirits. He writes me constantly, sometimes two letters a day, and says the same thing over and over and over, with just the smallest variation or addition or omission, apparently quite hopelessly gone in his mind, and yet what gentleness and affection and charm he has, just as always; and he makes plans for us to meet, and we'll see each other in Paris, or London—he once knew everybody in the "smart" international crowd that I used to run from and remembers his life eagerly and somehow dreams that next spring—always next spring—he will be travelling and seeing his friends; And he says I have worked a miracle in him and he is going to write again! Oh, it is heart breaking, and he was such a delightful, dear, talented sort of person, we all loved him; and I try to tell him he is by no means forgotten, nor his story, and that is true. Right here in Paris at a lunch party I mentioned him to two young men from Texas and Okalhoma—his part of the country—and they knew all about him, and remembered his famous story, and wondered if he had any unpublished ones. I told him that and he was lyrical with joy . . . Oh, imagine such a fate? So I write to him all the time, and just as if he were perfectly well and sane; he is in a very nice place and cared for by very good people, but—

. . . . Bye bye love, and love to my sweet sister, and to all the boys!

Little Sis, Aunt Kat, as you like!

To James F. Powers   Villa Adrienne
Avenue du Général LeClerc
Paris XIV, France
11 October, 1963

Dear Jim:

. . . . I send you a letter to St. Cloud and you answer it fairly soon from Greystones, Ireland. I have tottered on the brink a dozen times of just taking a plane and landing in Ireland and seeing the place with friends, but I never have and maybe never will. It seems strange for I have a mysterious love of—not the place itself, how could I? I never saw it—but its legend and history and poetry and the way the Irish write English! That is probably what I really love about Ireland! I wish you might live there and be happy, but then, you might wish for me the same thing, Ireland or anywhere else . . . I couldn't be more utterly homeless and dispossessed if I had been thrown out on my ear and my household gear confiscated. For I do not own a foot of land or a roof anywhere, either, and in the very depths of my heart I probably don't want to, for there is nothing stopping me now except a perfect disinclination to choose a place where I can bear to stay for any time at all . . . Your mood, and Betty's, is so like my own it gives me a slight cold chill—are we the only ones in this state of mind? I think not. And it is a terrible state of mind to be in—to be estranged from one's own country without being able to adopt another. My fix is precisely this: I have a real dread of going back to the USA, and yet I cannot face the idea of spending the rest of my life in a country where, no matter what, I shall always be regarded as a foreigner, and as you know, a hated one at that. Hatred of America and Americans for Europe— as well as England and all, has supplanted all other ancient ha- treds—of Jews, of Asiatics, of Africans, even of other Europeans! until I feel that this united hatred may serve after all these two thousand odd years to bring Europeans together, to cause them to make alliances among themselves against their common enemy. And the negroes are beginning to pile in on them too, from all parts of the world, which will help relieve our tensions, and give the Europeans something new to think about! But at any rate, I do know very well, who I am, and where I am, and what I am doing, and no matter what my life is, that is what I must accept and make what I can of it . . . So I am going back, and try once more. . . .

It is just true that nothing in this world matters one single damn except to get your work done. But sometimes the obstacles are just too many and too great, and my own experience is that nothing in this world sets you free like a sum of money put at your disposal to use for your own purposes. This is the reason I am in touch with every foundation and have candidates everywhere, every year, because I know what it is to be so poor. I suffered for years literally from hunger and cold and every medical neglect, and it does not do any good. My only excuse is that I did not know how to make a living and learn to be an artist too; and in that time there were not all these foundations with money to invest in one's future, or recognize one's past achievement . . . I don't regret anything and I never felt sorry for myself and there was never any need to pity me for anything. But I try to help where I can, because such privations slow you down, sap your vitality, lessen the amount of work you can do. By the time I got to where I could live even decently, I was so exhausted it is a miracle that I ever did anything. . . .

With my same admiration, and affectionate remembrance

Katherine Anne

To FLANNERY O'CONNOR   Last word from Villa Adrienne
Pavillon Poussin
19 Avenue du Général LeClerc
Paris XIV, La France
20 October 1963

Dear Flannery:

. . . . Here is that news cutting I mentioned, and I see you are on the same page at least with Mary McCarthy, "whose place in contemporary American letters is so very particular one can only compare her (reputation) to that of Madame Nathalie Sarraute with us." There is such a thing as fractured English too. Well, anyway, its a pretty good review of your now celebrated *Brave Men Do Not*

Run In The Streets, meaning I am sure, that they are Hard to Find, or Do Not Grow On Bushes. This Kanters is the man who keeps writing about the "Jewish Renascence" in American literature, and seems to think the American short story began with Dorothy Parker, but just the same, he nearly knows what he is reading in your stories, he is limited but good as far as he goes: but a man who thinks of Sarraute and Parker, McCarthy and O'Connor in the same review is not to be trusted in the long run; and a nice long run you're going to have, that's certain. And you will for some time find yourself teamed with any number of unlikely running mates—I was for years upon years compared with Katherine Mansfield. My own view was, and is, that we were both women, both named Katherine, and both wrote short stories, and there the resemblance ends. Then it was Willa Cather. Then it was Hemingway and even Faulkner, now and then. And now I have graduated into the society of Flaubert, Melville, Stendhal, Henry James, and even Tolstoy. Fast company, I call it, and it does me no earthly good, and it is the device of lazy-minded third-rate reviewers who can't read . . . They have heard these names or perhaps know certain persons who have read them, but I daresay that is all. . . .

André Malraux has at last found out what he believes in—house-work and plenty of it for everybody! And what a lovely job he is making of Paris! I never saw this city before, really, though I lived here for five years. The Opera, Place Vendôme, the Louvre, the Palace, the Madeleine—all all, are glowing and shimmering in rose and pale ochre and beige and streaked near-white and blue-grey stone and marble, and everything that was gold before is gold again and I hope you will rush here to take a look before the soot and grime begin to cover it once more. I just walk about looking and loving this place! No interest whatever in the literary or social life, no theatre or moving pictures, no music even, just this city, and my favorite places to walk in it—The Invalides, the Observatoire, the Tuileries, the Luxembourg—all around the neighborhood of Notre Dame, the whole length of the Faubourg St-Honoré (for clothes) and a congeries of little old narrow dark streets on the Left Bank where I used to live, for the crowded little antique shops, curiosity shops rather, and the curiously ingrown life that goes on there, as if it were another city—and maybe it is. But I don't work well, I have disappointed myself, and can't be happy here or anywhere until I get settled and dug into my own real life job again . . . Its a life sentence, all right, as you have known all along, but I cannot imagine life without it.

I hope I shall see you again sometime soon; I hope you are doing well and also doing whatever you want! This picture of you is better than the other, but it isn't flattering, either. I like best your self-portrait, and if you have a photograph of it, I wish you would give me one! I'll swap, if you like. I haven't got a hand-painted one, but I have one that looks somewhat like me, for the present, and will be glad to send it when I am back in the country. (I remember well Marianne Moore's warning against sending unsolicited photographs, I do it in hell's despite, of course.)

> Hasta luego! with affections
> *Katherine Anne*

Postscript:
There has been a marvelous joyous carnival of mourning for Edith Piaf and Jean Cocteau, and it was *real*! They died as they had lived, with style and grace and their proper eccentricity; and Paris loves anybody who can live anarchically and be delightful entertainment at the same time. So do I. I loved them both, and I shed my few difficult tears for them, and I miss them—especially Cocteau, who was exactly of my generation.

> *KA*

TO ROBERT PENN WARREN, ESQUIRE [postcard]
The Jefferson Hotel
1200 Sixteenth Street, N.W.
Washington 6, D.C.
Sunday, 24 November, 1963

Dear Red:

. . . . Going now to Capital to the lying-in-state—What is this—Vietnam or a banana Republic?

> Love—
> *Katherine Anne*

Epilogue
From a Godmother

To Rosanna Warren   3601 49th Street, N.W.
                      Washington D.C. 20016
                      Columbus Day, 1964

Rosanna my delightful Godchild!

    This is not merely Columbus Day in Spring Valley, Washington D.C.—it is Robert-Eleanor-Rosanna-Gabriel Penn Warren-and-Joey-Day in Romantic 49th Street, National Capital.
    14 October, same year: And a fine day it was, most beautiful soft weather and just right for transplanting violets and digging ferns to put in pots in the glass gallery, and answer the telephone and the doorbell, and so on with all the daily things of life. BUT all the time, I was reading *The Joey Story,* and Rosanna, you make it all so real I was positively worn out at the end, trying to house break Joey: it did look as if he would never learn. And I remembered in my youth a row of them: a beagle named Bozo: a great Dane named Hector: a Dalmation named, of course, Spotty: and a nice flop-eared, oldfashioned pure Hound Dog named Ketchem—we had a home-made, household humorist apparently who named the dogs—and ALL of them in turn had to be taught to use the bath room outside . . . after we grew up, my brother took to Walker hounds, my older sister to Scotch collies, my favorite cousin to Boston Bulls, and I? I took to cats. In fact, I started with cats. I love and adore cats and they are the easiest creatures to housebreak in the world. I have a little diary somewhere with the name of every cat I ever had in my life: they have short lives and are given to disastrous accidents, but I love them and they love me, for they are most devoted creatures once they give their hearts. And that is something wonderful in any kind of being, humans especially!
    Your dedication with the heap of love illustrated is most charming and funny . . . Do some more drawings, too! And Rosanna, I want to ask you to do something for me. Your Mommy and Poppy don't seem to notice that I have no pictures of *any* of you, and as your Godmother—one of them—I feel it would be lovely to have a copy of the photograph of you and Gabriel and Joey and Aslan just as it appears on your book, but signed at least by you and Gabriel, with date, and all . . . I'd

627

frame it and keep it in my workroom, which is where I spend most of my time . . .

I tried to persuade a copy of your Mommy with you and Gabriel and Joey and Aslan, as it appeared on HER book, but nothing happened. So do my dear one use your influence to find me these pictures, which would make me very happy.

Some day I want to hear you play and sing again that first little song you composed, which I do not forget, and I hope you haven't either.

Another thing, can you tell me exactly what size dress you wear, for I have seen something I like and believe you would too . . . Please let me know, how tall, and how big around!

Now I'll ask you the silly question I get from people who come up to me and say: "What is it like to be famous?" And I say, truthfully, "It's *awful.*"

With my love and thanks for your book

Katherine Anne

To Katherine Anne   3601 49th Street, N.W.
Powers   Washington, D.C.
                           15 December 1966

My dear God Daughter Katherine Anne:

When I first thought of giving you a little present—the occasion I thought was the beginning of your Freshman year at Smith. This I thought I heard from your father, when we met for the first time after all these years in Smyrna Tennessee, both of us friends with the dear Cheneys, and we had a delightful short—too short—evening with our friends, and a delightful glimpse of each other: So I went out and found a baroque pearl necklace in one place, and a bubbly-looking emerald quartz clasp in another, and had my special jeweller—whose job for me is setting watches in repair every two years—put them together, and I had a happy fantasy about it looking just like you—it belongs around a young throat, and it is on its way to you this day, or tomorrow at least. A young man from the University has offered to get it safely into the mails for me. This because I had thought I must be sending it to Smith; but Seymour Lawrence, my friend and publisher, said, NO, not at all. You had done your freshman year *last* year, and this year you were back in Ireland . . . So much for keeping up with the news.

Now, here is the trick. Your necklace is being sent registered and insured, sealed like Fort Knox, all expense paid so far as we are able. Here is where the pestiferous international Customs thing comes in. I sent it marked as an "unsolicited gift" which heaven knows it is, and that may mean no duty on the object. We tried—a whole committee of us, to run down reliable information on the subject, and there seemed to be one answer: there may be duty to be paid on this object, or not, as the case may be: but if there is duty to be paid, it must be paid at the Irish customs port, and not here. How really frustrating. Just the same, your necklace is going to reach you for Christmas if the Postal System does not collapse altogether; but YOU or your father will have to pay the duty—if any—and the whole point of this ragged tale is, that you must let me know *at once* what the sum is, so I can return it to you *at once.* This is the sort of thing one trips into when dealing with frontiers. I am sorry, but it need not be too bad. Just let me know. The clasp is a kind of pendant: you will see that the clasp goes on the right side and the bauble on the left: the little slot is there safely to close it up. It is all a little baroque, that is, off-shape or what I believe is now called "free form" and I hope it is becoming to you, and I wish you a joyous Christmas.

How long will you be in Ireland this time? It has been my hope to come there, all these years, and I haven't made it yet. Frank O'Connor and Padraic Colum both promised me dearly to show me the country, I wouldn't be just another stranger stumbling around, but its too late for Frank now, and even for Padraic, I'm afraid, and yes, even for me! I have been now for more than three years trying to keep my chin above ground, and though so far I have won the battles, the war is not finished . . .

Bless you. I wish you had been nearer to me, or that we could have had more news from each other, but just the same, you have been in my thoughts and my hopes, and will be . . .

With my love
Godmother Katherine Anne

INDEX

Wheeler, Monroe, 75, 105, 106, 108,
132, 164, 198, 236, 257,
320–21, 322, 336, 485, 608
letters to, 98, 99, 110, 120, 138, 145,
152, 294, 303, 311, 322, 328,
355, 359, 363, 373, 455, 526,
578, 618
"Where the Sun Died" (Selman), 238
White Goddess, The (Graves), 362
White Mule (William Carlos Williams),
167
Whitman, Walt, 521
Wilde, Oscar, 401
Wilder, Billy, 311, 312, 460
Wilder, Thornton, 410
Wiley (Wylie) family, 68–69, 91
Williams, Bert, 405
Williams, Tennessee, 583, 584
Williams, William Carlos, 167, 295
Willis, Florence, 356–57
Willison, George, 310, 319, 321, 409
Willison, Toni, 310, 321
Willkie, Wendell, 258
Wilson, Edmund, 15, 23, 37, 295,
328–29, 615
Winkler, Margaret, 364
Winslow, Marcella, 315
Winters, Janet, 37
Winters, Joanna, 37
Winters, Yvor, 22
"Woman Who Was Loved, The"
(Stern), 617–18
Woodburn, John, 238

Woolf, Virginia, 207, 210, 466–67,
513, 528
World War II, 132, 134, 182–83,
197–98, 200–01, 214–15, 264,
271, 285, 389, 391
fall of Paris, 178–79, 182, 183
on the home front, 215–16,
229–30
Victory in Japan Day, 309
"Wreath for the Gamekeeper, A,"
574–75
Wuthering Heights (Brontë), 365,
503
Wyler, Margaret Tallichet, 309, 337,
338
Wyler, William, 337–38

Yaddo, 219, 267, 287, 288, 348, 368,
369, 372, 415
Yale Review, 489
Yale University, 489–90
Yeats, W. B., 206–07, 245, 418, 464,
477, 515
Young, Marguerite, 308n., 309

Zabel, Morton Dauwen, 192, 234, 301,
359, 372
letter to, 467
Zanuck, Daryl, 267
Zéro de conduite, 349
Zuleika Dobson (Beerbohm), 145